THE COLLAPSE
OF COMMUNISM

Revised and Updated

THE
COLLAPSE
OF
COMMUNISM

REVISED AND UPDATED

Edited by Bernard Gwertzman
and Michael T. Kaufman

TIMES 𝕿 BOOKS

RANDOM HOUSE

Library of Congress Cataloging-in-Publication Data

The Collapse of communism / edited by Bernard Gwertzman and Michael T. Kaufman. — Rev. and updated.
    p.   cm.
  Includes index.
  ISBN 0-8129-1941-6 (pbk.)
    1. Communism—1945–   2. Communist countries—Economic conditions.
I. Gwertzman, Bernard M.   II. Kaufman, Michael T.
HX44.C6415   1991
335.43'09'048—dc20   91-50183

Manufactured in the United States of America

9 8 7 6 5 4 3 2

Revised Edition

CONTENTS

INTRODUCTION
Bernard Gwertzman

Whatever his aspirations when he became the Soviet leader in 1985, Mikhail S. Gorbachev could not have foreseen that he would be remembered as the man who presided over not only the loss of Moscow's dominion over East Europe but the collapse of Communism in the Soviet Union as well. Opposition to the once-omniscient Communist Party grew in strength throughout the former bloc, leading to the fall of leader after leader in 1989–90–91, and then exploded within the Soviet Union in the late summer of 1991 after a junta of Gorbachev's former top aides failed in an attempt to reverse his policies of reform through a crude coup.

As these words are written, it is not possible to predict the ultimate results of these developments, whether the Soviet Union will survive as a centralized state or will become some kind of loose federation of highly nationalized sovereign states led by a dominant Russian Republic under Boris N. Yeltsin. What can be documented is that by the autumn of 1991, there was no longer a Soviet alliance and Communism as a political force was virtually unrecognizable outside of Cuba and Asia. Even Albania, once thought immune to change, opened its borders and invited free elections for the first time, leading to the formation of a non-Communist government. And in Yugoslavia, not a member of the bloc, Communists were toppled as that country struggled with secessionist movements in Slovenia and Croatia, which produced considerable bloodshed.

The Communist Party remained in power nowhere in Europe. The failed coup against Gorbachev that began on August 18 and lasted only three days produced a revolutionary wave in the Soviet Union which led to Gorbachev's resignation as party leader and the suspension of party activities around the country. Republic after republic sought to emulate the Baltic states of Estonia, Latvia and Lithuania and announce their independence even as Gorbachev sought to keep some kind of unity in this former superpower.

Already in 1991, reflecting the unpopularity of the Soviet Union in its former bloc, the Warsaw Pact had been dissolved. Soviet troops began pulling back in disgrace from Czechoslovakia, Hungary, Poland and Germany. The remaining garrison in what formerly was East Germany was subsidized by the Bonn government as part of the price for Soviet acquiescence in 1990 to the unification of the two Germanys.

However, whatever jubilation there had been in 1989 over the sudden collapse of Communism gave way to a more sober analysis of the problems ahead. "As the euphoria generated by the removal of the Communist yoke subsides, the harsh realities of starting anew have set in," said a report issued by Freedom House and the American Jewish Committee. "Economic shocks, political uncertainty and the revival of old ethnic and nationalistic tensions threaten to overwhelm the fragile democracies before they can become institutionalized." There was a "morning after" realization that simply getting rid of the old bogeymen would not in itself ensure a smooth transition to the future. As Serge Schmemann pointed out in the fall of 1990 (see page 493), disillusion was everywhere. A group of Czechoslovak students, most of whom had participated in the street demonstrations in November 1989 which brought down the Communist government, issued a statement urging that the anniversary not be marked because "we don't want former Communist officials coming out cheering and laughing in our faces."

The staff of *The New York Times* has paid close attention to the situation in the Soviet Union and its former bloc during these turbulent years. In 1989, the main focus in the first edition of this book was on the utter breakdown of Communism in Eastern Europe. In 1991, as this second edition of this book demonstrates, the focus was threefold: on the obvious problems faced in forming a new society in Eastern Europe; on the growing disarray in the Soviet Union; and lastly, on the historic developments in Germany, where the move to unification proceeded more quickly and in more dramatic fashion than anyone had envisaged in November 1989 when the Berlin Wall was opened, ending the division of the city, and with it the cold war.

Through it all, the central figure was Gorbachev, whose behavior continued to astound the West and to anger both traditionalists in the Soviet leadership, who found it hard to accept the sudden shifts in the geopolitical map and the loss of control at home, and his former liberal allies, who felt he had betrayed his former ideals by his compromises with the hard-liners. In 1990 and 1991, Gorbachev threw his support behind President Bush's military moves in the Persian Gulf, making it possible for the United Nations Security Council to act with unanimity on a crisis situation for the first time. This won him praise from the White House and disdain from the Soviet military, which seemed to regret not being able to help out the U.S.S.R.'s long-time ally in Baghdad.

Inside the Soviet Union, Mr. Gorbachev increasingly displayed Hamlet-like indecision, which precipitated the failed coup. Faced with the secession movement in Lithuania, which if allowed to succeed could lead to several other republics quickly following suit, Gorbachev was at first defiant, sending his military into action and ordering a partial economic embargo. But he could not sustain a full-scale crackdown and in the end opted for negotiations. These negotiations produced a new treaty between the Kremlin and the republics, a treaty that in fact probably precipitated the coup, since it was to have been signed on August 20. Georgia also opted for independence, and after the coup failed, Latvia and Estonia also signaled independence, as did Moldavia, once part of Rumania, and Azerbaijan, Armenia, and Tadjikistan. Other republics also announced their independence, but it was uncertain whether these small states could sustain it even if they received it.

What was remarkable was the decided drop in Gorbachev's popularity in 1990 and 1991. Despite repeated promises to do so, Gorbachev failed to come up with an economic plan that could either improve the life of the Soviet people or at least point the way dramatically in a new direction. In December 1990, one of Gorbachev's closest colleagues, Eduard A. Shevardnadze, resigned without warning from his post as foreign minister, claiming that a new dictatorship might emerge if the reactionaries took over. His warning proved eerily prescient nine months later.

On Germany, Gorbachev contributed to the demise of East Germany by his failure to support the old Communist Erich Honecker in the fall of 1989 and by ruling out the use of force to put down the street demonstrations that led to the regime's collapse. But neither he, nor the succession of East Germans who replaced Honecker, nor Western leaders could have predicted the speed with which the idea of unity took over the people of East Germany. As the reporting by *Times* correspondents shows, Gorbachev in the end did little to delay unification. After briefly holding out for a neutral Germany, he agreed to the united Germany being part of NATO. His hope, of course, was for large-scale economic aid from the West, which was slow in coming because of the disappointing management of the Soviet economy and the questions raised about Moscow's creditworthiness.

It was Gorbachev, of course, who was most deeply responsible for the cataclysmic changes that shook Eastern Europe in 1989. Although he had earlier promised not to interfere in Eastern Europe, few in the East or West expected him to live up to his word and be so indifferent to the swirl around him.

At every turn, he either did nothing or actually appeared to support those in Eastern Europe seeking more freedom and an end to Communist domination. He ordered Soviet troops out of Afghanistan, urged the Vietnamese to depart from Cambodia, and the Cubans from Angola, and he had seemed to lend his personal prestige to the ouster of such veteran Eastern European leaders as Honecker in East Germany, Milos Jakos in Czechoslovakia, Todor Zhivkov in Bulgaria, and Nicolae Ceausescu in Rumania. He had tolerated, if not encouraged, the opening of the Berlin Wall, Solidarity taking over the government in Poland, and the Hungarian Communists setting elections, which meant their own suicide. Gorbachev was also perceived by Chinese students during his trip to Beijing in China in May 1989 to be backing the student revolt that was ruthlessly put down with force in June by the leadership.

The domino effect that President Eisenhower had once feared might topple nations one after another toward Communism has clearly worked in the opposite direction. As much as the changes themselves, it was the swiftness of the process that stunned the world. After all, there had been something comfortable about the cold war. Statesmen, journalists, novelists had become accustomed to the stability of the division of Europe. In truth, of course, the separation was less than total. The Iron Curtain had long ago showed signs of serious corrosion. In today's era of modern communications and technology, it had become increasingly difficult for the Communist leaders to immunize their peoples from contact with the outside world.

In fact, Communist leaders had found themselves inept at taking advantage of the possibilities of the new high-tech era. And at a time of astonishing prosperity in the West, the Eastern bloc simply fell into an economic and moral slump to which there seemed no end in sight. It was this pressure for change from the outside, combined with the disintegration on the inside that led to the rapidity of the collapse in the past two years. The toughness of the Soviet bloc turned out to be very brittle indeed.

What follows is a summary of the background to the events country-by-country in Eastern Europe.

Poland

It was appropriate that the upheavals of 1989 began with Poland—the first nation to be compelled by the victorious Soviet Union to accept Communist domination at the end of World War II. The Poles were always the most rebellious in the bloc, and from time to time were led by nationalist Communist leaders, such as Wladyslaw Gomulka, who in 1956 sought to limit Moscow's direct control. But the Communists were always tainted, in the eyes of Poles, both because of the Communists' allegiance to Moscow and because of the hostility of the Catholic Church.

The rise of the trade union movement Solidarity in 1980 marked a new chapter in Poland, and in the bloc. It demonstrated that an opposition group could be formed that could challenge the Communists for leadership. The martial law crackdown in 1981 only thrust Poland into a worsening economic situation. A series of strikes in 1988 finally forced the regime of President Jaruzelski to hold roundtable talks with Solidarity to seek that group's help. That in turn led to a fateful agreement to hold free elections in Poland in June 1989.

The results of those elections—the first open ones in East Europe since the Communist takeover—shocked even Solidarity supporters. Instead of simply winning enough seats to play a role in the new government, the Solidarity candidates did so well that the Communists were eventually forced to ask Solidarity in August to lead a coalition government under prime minister Tadeusz Mazowiecki. The significance was not lost on the rest of the bloc—this was the first time that Communists had relinquished power peacefully.

Hungary

In the immediate aftermath of World War II, Hungary was not immediately forced by the Red Army to become a Communist state. The Hungarians, in fact, had had an earlier brief Communist rule following World War I, under Bela Kun, which was not a happy period for most Hungarians. But after the conservative Smallholder Party won 60 percent of the first election in November 1945, and the Communists only 17 percent, the Soviet authorities gradually began to force the country to adapt to their demands so that by 1949, Hungary was considered a Soviet satellite.

The tumultous days of the 1956 revolution under Imre Nagy showed the country's antipathy toward Communism and toward the Soviet Union. Nevertheless, Janos Kadar, who took over after Nagy's failed revolt, eventually won respect inside Hungary and began to open up his country to a more liberal internal system, known as "goulash Communism." For many years in the 1960's and 1970's, Kadar was probably one of the most popular of the world's Communist leaders. But an economic crisis in the 1980's and a sense of no confidence in the aging Kadar began to sweep the country. By 1987, demands for change were everywhere. In May 1988, Kadar was ousted from power and replaced by Karoly Grosz. By 1989, the splits within the ruling Communist Party—known officially as the Hungarian Socialist Workers' Party—became pronounced.

In June, Grosz was replaced as leader by a four-man group of Grosz, Imre Fozsgay, Rezso Nyers, and Prime Minister Miklos Nemeth. In October, at a party congress, the ruling party changed its name to the Hungarian Socialist Party and voted to adopt more liberal reforms. Pozsgay was its presidential candidate for multiparty elections to be held in 1990. But the effort of the Communists to stay in power failed. By the spring of 1990, Jozsef Antall, the leader of the Hungarian Democratic Forum, a centrist democratic party, became prime minister, and Hungary took the lead in ending the military part of the Warsaw Pact.

If the changes in Poland and Hungary were carefully plotted and resulted, to a great extent, in public balloting, the upheavals that were to dominate the news in the latter part of 1989 came unexpectedly and from the streets.

East Germany

In the aftermath of World War II, the division of Germany between East and West became the symbol of the cold war that was to dominate international relations for the next 45 years. After three years of trying to negotiate some way of uniting the occupation zones, the four powers in effect by 1949 acknowledged their failure. The West created what became the Federal Republic of Germany, and the Soviet Union, the German Democratic Republic. The former capital, Berlin, was also divided into zones. The eastern part of the city became the capital of the G.D.R. Bonn became the capital of West Germany, and West

Berlin remained an outpost in the midst of East Germany—a symbol of Western determination to keep the city open despite a land and rail blockade in 1948.

In 1961, in the midst of a crisis in East-West relations, thousands of East Germans poured into the West through West Berlin. Nikita S. Khrushchev, the Soviet leader, ordered the East Germans to put up a wall to lock in the East German people. A succession of East-West accords in the 1970's seemed to make formal the division of Germany. The reunification of Germany, once the leading East-West issue, faded into memory, to be revived in 1989.

The first inkling of change in 1989 took place in August. East Germans had been permitted for some time to travel freely to other Communist states, but no farther. But because Hungary had taken down its barbed wire border with Austria, East German tourists in Hungary were able to flee to the West by in effect going out the back door. Word spread quickly, and by early November some 120,000 East Germans, many of them highly skilled workers, had left via Hungary.

The exodus was a deep embarrassment to longtime leader Erich Honecker, who had opposed the liberal policies of Gorbachev. Suddenly, in this most repressive of countries, voices of opposition were heard. The Evangelical Church played an important role in providing sanctuary for dissidents. Groups such as the New Forum began to take on the coloration of a formal opposition, even though they were not really political parties.

The East Germans had developed a reputation for suppression of dissent. And because of the importance of East Germany to Soviet security, and the presence of 300,000 Soviet troops there, it was long supposed that Moscow would countenance no dramatic change. But by early October, with the arrival of Gorbachev for ceremonies marking the fortieth anniversary of the G.D.R., thousands of people—many of them students—took to the streets of Berlin, Leipzig and Dresden. The East German leadership had earlier praised the Chinese for their decisive action in Tiananmen Square, but it backed away from using the same kind of force itself, apparently after finding out that the Soviet forces would not help them.

Having disavowed force, the East German leaders seemed to panic. They saw no way of stopping the exodus but to institute changes quickly. The leadership persuaded Honecker to step down, starting a succession of changes. Egon Krenz, who had been his protégé, was

Honecker's initial replacement. In his six weeks in office, Krenz went beyond what anyone imagined likely, when the East Germans suddenly announced on November 9 the opening of the Berlin Wall. That historic move was followed by decrees abolishing the monopoly of power guaranteed to the Communists, and new freedom for the press.

Bulgaria

A Soviet satellite since the last days of World War II, Bulgaria had one of the least imaginative Communist regimes in Europe. For 35 years, Todor Zhivkov was a virtual dictator. There was little inkling abroad or even in Bulgaria that his rule would come to an abrupt end in 1989. The first sign of trouble for him erupted in October during an East-West meeting on environmental affairs, when a group called Eco-Glasnost was allowed to solicit signatures on a petition on ecological issues and organize a march. Some 5,000 people took part. Rallies were held in the Southern Park in Sofia, where different points of view were permitted to be heard.

For reasons still not clear, on November 10, the Communist Party Central Committee held a meeting, and it was there that Zhivkov was told that he had "resigned" as leader. It was a political coup, which was believed to have been spurred by resentment within the party at Zhivkov's dictatorial habits. Petar Mladenov, who had been foreign minister for eighteen years, was chosen to replace him. Mladenov had no real experience in domestic affairs, but had the backing of the country's army and party apparatus.

But the effort by the Bulgarian Communists to remain in power, even on a reform basis, foundered by the end of 1990, and into early 1991, as a coalition took command away from the Communists.

Czechoslovakia

After World War II, Czechoslovakia was permitted the freest multiparty democracy in Eastern Europe. In part, it was because there was a genuine sympathy for the Communists among the electorate. But by 1948, support for the Communist Party was eroding, as tensions grew in Europe. Non-Communists in the government resigned to force new elections, which they thought they could win. But instead, the Communists organized a coup d'état in February 1948, and seized power through the unions and police. The "fall" of Czechoslovakia to the Communists and the death of the popular foreign minister Jan Masaryk in March (he either jumped or was pushed from a window) led President Truman to conclude that it was crucial for the West to rearm or face a new war. The cold war was launched.

In the mid-1960's, a cultural awakening occurred in Czechoslovakia, which had been one of the most repressive of the Communist regimes. In late 1967, demonstrations by students, moves to more equality among the Slovaks, and a continuing economic stagnation led the party to replace Antonin Novotny with Alexander Dubcek. The developments in Prague in 1968 presaged what happened in 1989, but in 1968, there was one major difference. The Soviet Union under Leonid I. Brezhnev was frightened by the liberal changes taking place and in August forced the other Warsaw Pact states, except Rumania, to join it in invading Czechoslovakia and in crushing the new freedoms.

Although the Czechoslovak regime was regarded as one of the most repressive, the dissidents never gave up. Led by Vaclav Havel, the playwright, dissidents under the banner of Charter 77 staged frequent protests. Havel and other dissidents were frequently arrested. Demonstrations continued in early 1989, but no one predicted what would happen in November.

On November 17, some 3,000 students had demonstrated for free elections along Narodni Street, near Wenceslas Square in Prague. On the orders of local party leaders, riot police used batons to beat up demonstrators. Many of the students were badly injured. The combination of the bloodletting and the example of the changes brought by demonstrations in East Germany a week earlier inspired students to organize continuous massive demonstrations—there were as many as 500,000 people a day. This culminated in the resignation of the Communist Party leadership on November 24. As in East Germany, a succession of political changes occurred. Karel Urbanek, the head of the Czech party, took over as the new party leader, but he in turn was replaced on December 21 by former prime minister Ladislav Adamec. Eventually, in developments symbolizing the changed political situation. Havel became president and Dubcek head of the Parliament.

Rumania

The Rumanians came out of World War II at a certain advantage, since they had switched sides in the middle and thrown their support to the Russians after earlier fighting for the Nazis. But the Russians nevertheless imposed a Communist regime on the country, which had probably the weakest Communist Party in the region. The few Communists in Rumania were by and large non-Rumanian, and this caused them to be seen as largely alien. Moscow settled on Gheorge Gheorgiu-Dej, who was Rumanian, and Gheorgiu-Dej surprisingly took an independent tack in the early 1960s, emboldened by the withdrawal of Soviet troops in 1958. He sought to reduce the Soviet control in his country.

That more independent course was advanced by his successor Nicolae Ceausescu, who after taking over in 1965 became a maverick in the Communist world. He declined to join in the invasion of Czechoslovakia, curried favor with China when it was at odds with Russia, did not break ties with Israel after the 1967 war, and set out on an ambitious industrialization policy that eventually failed. But this dynamic leader, who was feted in Western capitals throughout the 1970's, became increasingly ruthless and dictatorial in the 1980's. He relied on nepotism. His wife, Elena, was made second in command, and his sons, brothers and in-laws played key roles in running the country.

The winds of change finally reached Rumania just before Christmas 1989. Security police killed hundreds of demonstrators in Timosoara who were initially seeking to protect a Hungarian clergyman from deportation. That led to more brutal measures by the security police and open defiance of Ceausescu in Bucharest. The Ceausescus surprisingly fled but were captured by army units that had gone over to the popular revolt. The Ceausescus were executed, the only change in power in 1989 brought about by such means. There was no solid institution to replace Ceausescu. Many former party members, forced out of office by Ceausescu earlier, returned under army auspices to take part in the Front of National Salvation and the Council of the Front, which is headed by President Ion Iliescu and Prime Minister Petre Roman. Iliescu in fact won the first multiparty elections in April, but because he and many in his Front are former Communists, the road to full democracy has been a stormy one.

Albania

Of all the states in Europe, none has been more backward than Albania. After some 450 years under Turkish rule, the Albanians declared their independence in 1912, and the country was ruled in the years preceding World War II by King Zog I until Albania was invaded and occupied by Italy in 1939. A Communist underground headed by General Enver Hoxha took control in the waning years of the war but never carried out promises for free elections. The party took over complete control and seemed immune from the winds of change that swept through Eastern Europe in the post-Stalin era and again in the 1980's. But after Hoxha's death in 1985, change began to occur.

Ramiz Alia, who took over Hoxha's leadership jobs, found himself facing demonstrations in 1990 and general discontent, opened his doors to the West, permitted dissidents to leave, held elections, won in the first instance by Communists, and allowed a non-Communist government to be set up in 1991 to lead the country.

Many of the developments that occurred in these countries, as well as in the Soviet Union, Afghanistan and China form the subject of this book. This is how the correspondents of *The New York Times* saw the momentous events of 1989, 1990, and 1991.

WINTER 1988-89

As the year opened, it was already evident that as an ideology and as a formula for totalitarian rule Communism was in retreat, if not yet in outright decay. In a number of countries where Communism had been imposed, old orthodoxy was being challenged by deviant strains. In the name of reform, people who still called themselves Communist were countenancing, even advocating, private ownership and private enterprise. In Hungary, bonds were being traded on a stock market. In Poland, the once tightly censored official media was revealing more and more as it was forced to compete for credibility and readers with a vast network of independent clandestine publishers. In China, officials were advocating freer markets to encourage modernity, and in Moscow, Mikhail Gorbachev, the chief apostle of Communist reformation, was spearheading a move to introduce limited representative government on a western parliamentary model that not so long ago was reviled as bourgeois democracy. Amid such developments, what did it mean to be a Communist? Were there still basic tenets of belief that applied everywhere? Were Communists still supposed to believe in the teachings of Marx and Lenin if not the practice of Stalin and Mao? Did they still cling to the idea that Communism was inevitably destined to overwhelm and supersede capitalism? To find out, correspondents of The New York Times interviewed Communists from many countries, asking them such questions as who they considered to be their leaders and how specifically their views and hopes had changed. On the basis of these responses The Times published a series in January under the rubric "Communism Now: What Is It?" This is how it began.

In Hope and Dismay, Lenin's Heirs Speak
By Serge Schmemann

In the Communist world, the underground joke is often the best index of conditions. "What is Communism?" asks one that has recently been making the rounds.

3

"Communism," goes the reply, "is the longest and most painful route from capitalism to capitalism."

That joke, heard in Moscow, would be immediately understood in Beijing, Budapest or any other Communist-ruled capital where a battered economy, systematic repression and chronic corruption are prompting fundamental and wrenching reappraisal.

The process of reform, personified now by Mikhail S. Gorbachev, the Soviet leader, evokes both hope and dismay: hope that at last the millions who have lived through the tyrannies and chronic shortages endemic to Communist states could find some relief; dismay that so much of the terrible sacrifice, struggle and deprivation they have endured for so long must now be acknowledged to have been in vain, that the secular faith that once promised so much now stands revealed to its own adherents as a failure.

Nascent stock exchanges have opened in Shanghai and Budapest. State-owned companies in the Communist East are eagerly canvassing for joint ventures with capitalist behemoths from the West to gain access to post-industrial technology that has passed them by. The movement's once sacred history has been reopened to increasingly bold and brutal scrutiny. In this upheaval, what does it mean any more to be a Communist?

What remains of the old zeal and idealism, the sense of historical inevitability, of an inspired vanguard leading the masses to utopia? What, if anything, remains of the old faith?

To get a sense of how Communists now see themselves and their movement in a rapidly changing world, 26 correspondents of *The New York Times* had extensive interviews with 50 Communists from 23 countries. The aim was to hear the voices of individual Communists—leaders, intellectuals, ordinary party members, including some in countries where the Communists are out of power and still regard themselves as revolutionaries—to hear their reflections on the newly acknowledged moral and political failures that have beset their cause and to learn how they gauge its prospects.

In the broad diversity of their answers, in the degree of their faith or doubt, these Communists gave a human face to the plight of a formerly monolithic faith that once spread fear and hope throughout the world—a faith that now, according to the best available estimate, by the Hoover Institution at Stanford University, has 88.6 million adherents worldwide, 4.5 million of them living in non-Communist countries.

The sense of lost idealism common among old revolutionaries was expressed by Tran Bach Dang, a Vietnamese Communist who has spent most of his life hiding and fighting. "In the past, when fighting with the enemy, I enjoyed life more than now," he said. "For now we have to take responsibility for the fate of the entire society. The problems of peace are more complex than those of war."

More bluntly, a high-ranking Yugoslav official, Matjaz Kmecl, replied when asked what made him proud to be a Communist: "At the moment, nothing."

Even before the rise of Mr. Gorbachev in Moscow, China had renounced most of the Maoist creed that had defined its revolution. Hungary and Yugoslavia had experimented with new forms of economic management. But it was when the new Soviet leader raised the three banners of glasnost, perestroika and new thinking over the red ramparts of the Kremlin, the symbolic heart of the Communist universe, that the secular religion of Marx and Lenin was shaken to its core.

To the West, Mr. Gorbachev may seem merely pragmatic in admitting the profound "mistakes" of virtually all his predecessors since Lenin, in abandoning the dream of Communism in our lifetime, in acknowledging the legitimacy of other social systems, in withdrawing troops from Afghanistan or in seeking to inject competition, democratic debate and diversity into his society.

Yet in the process, he has also called into question the last surviving precepts of the faith he claims to defend—democratic centralism, class struggle, world revolution, party discipline and, finally, even the dominant role of the party itself. Saints have been toppled and heretics have been rehabilitated by the millions, usually posthumously.

"All happy families are alike, but an unhappy family is unhappy after its own fashion," wrote Leo Tolstoy. So too among the Communists in nations where the party won power in revolution, whether the Soviet Union, China or Vietnam: if the romantic early stages were filled with similar slogans, cameraderie and hope, the later hardships have been varied and the responses different.

Among Russians, the prevailing debate is predictably over Mr. Gorbachev. There are intellectuals like Erik M. Ametistov, a 54-year-old lawyer, who unabashedly described himself "a fervent supporter of Gorbachev" and as an equally fervent opponent of any vestiges of Stalinism. "I cannot accept that I share ideals with thousands who are guilty of mass repressions during the Stalin era," he declared with feeling.

Yet the excited praise for the "new thinking" clashes with the voice of a Nina A. Andreyeva, the Old Guard loyalist whose letter to the press last spring became the manifesto of conservative resistance to Mr. Gorbachev.

In her first interview with a Western reporter, Mrs. Andreyeva agreed with great reluctance that "mistakes" had been made under Stalin. But she said the assault on his rule marked the start of a total dismantling of the uncomplicated faith on which she was reared: "Next Lenin's teachings will be criticized, then they'll put into doubt socialism itself—which was built and defended in battle."

In China, from the perspective of a writer in his late 60's, Huang Gang expressed a similar regret that basic tenets and ideals are being eroded in the rush to modernize and Westernize. Increasingly, he said, the young are straying from "correct" understandings of socialism, and those like himself who rigorously protected the orthodox views are being pushed aside.

Mr. Huang, too, acknowledged "mistakes"—the universal Communist euphemism for the atrocities committed in the name of building a new world. In China, the epic "mistake" was the Cultural Revolution, under which party zealots were set loose to hound all who fell short of their radical standards. But it was party members, Mr. Huang insisted, who had righted the wrongs.

Those same "mistakes," however, profoundly shook the faith of Li Shuxian, a 53-year-old professor who is the wife of China's most prominent dissident, Fang Lizhi, an astrophysicist. She spoke poignantly of her loss of faith, which she said was common in the Chinese intelligentsia: "We had thought the party was so pure and clean, and maybe the top leaders simply didn't know what was happening in the country. But then in the Cultural Revolution everything came out."

The religious metaphors came up again and again. In its claim to be a comprehensive guide not only to economics and politics but also to morality, social organization and behavior—in its promise of a New Man—Marxism has become a caricature of the religion that its founder had declared an opiate.

In Vietnam, as in the Soviet Union, China and some other Communist lands, the death of a charismatic revolutionary leader marked the end of the romantic struggle, when crusaders for the faith could justify violence in the name of a grand future, and ushered in the gray realities of a flawed system.

In every land where Communists attained power, idealism and enthusiasm gave way to careerism and cynicism. Industrial powers

6

watched their exports shrink as quality and innovation were throttled by vast central bureaucracies. Food supplies dwindled in inverse proportion to land collectivization.

Nations with great cultures found their writers and thinkers suppressed, jailed or exiled. Elemental rights and freedoms—travel, communication, information, religion—were denied in the name of the worker and a brave new world. And old truths were challenged as old alliances crumbled—the Chinese split with Russians, the Cubans split with both, and eventually Vietnam even stopped its summary and ritual rejection of American overtures.

As recently as 1960, Nikita S. Khrushchev could thump his shoe in the belief that the Soviet Union would overtake the West. But there was none of that bravado in the interviews of 1988–89. Many of the Communists seem defensive or ashamed of their party's history, or, in Mrs. Andreyeva's case, nostalgic for the old iron fist.

She spoke with dark suspicion of intellectuals—most of those she named were prominent Jews—and of the West. Yet in her nostalgia for a simpler past and an unquestioned order, in her invocation of the sacrifice of her precedessors and her faith in Lenin, she seemed to speak for many in her generation.

That reluctance to relinquish the faith is taking a different form in different lands. For people who live in China, the revolution is the antithesis of the corruption of the Nationalists and the backwardness of the past; for the Vietnamese, the memory of the struggle is still fresh.

In the Soviet Union, where it all began, there is no democratic tradition to fall back on, and too much blood has been spilled to abandon the cause. However discredited the ideology, Marxism remains the sole source of legitimacy for the state, and it is unthinkable for a party member not to invoke Lenin or Communism either in seeking or resisting change.

Mr. Gorbachev, for example, declared his perestroika and glasnost the only path to Lenin's true intent. Yet as glasnost rummages ever deeper in the Stalinist hell, it seems inevitable—as Mrs. Andreyeva feared—that some tarnish will begin to show on Lenin's halo.

And if Lenin is not secure, no demigod is. If Mao shared Lenin's revolutionary aura, he also shared Stalin's brutality. If the gods are falling, it is hard to see what remains of the old faith. Already the deadline for achieving utopia has been pushed far beyond the horizon, the once-damned West is revealed to be a viable model, global revolution is no longer certain or necessary, and glasnost is playing havoc with virtually every sacred myth.

On the economic front, Mr. Gorbachev has challenged presumptions on which generations of Soviet youths had been raised. State monopoly has been stripped of its sanctity and capitalism of its pointed tail. Long-scorned notions like flexible pricing, free trade, labor and capital markets, joint ventures, even competition were set loose on the land.

Private entrepreneurs, so recently caricatured as fat capitalists with silk top hats or as sleazy black-marketeers, were given respectability, though to maintain a proper Marxist facade their restaurants and services had to be called "cooperatives." Even that most fundamental bedrock of the Soviet social contract, cradle-to-grave security, came under threat in vague discussions of layoffs.

None of the Communists claimed a monopoly on truth or even social justice. At most, they viewed their party membership as a shared responsibility for vague humanitarian and social principles. To paraphrase Dwight D. Eisenhower, what matters is that you profess belief in Marx, and it doesn't matter what Marx you believe in.

Roy A. Medvedev, a Marxist historian who stood in the ranks of dissidents until Mr. Gorbachev came to power and is now much in demand in Moscow as a social and political critic, reported that members of the party who support the "new thinking" no longer like to speak of themselves as Communists.

"When I say I'm an adherent of socialism, it's clear that I'm a man who wants to build a humane society," he said. "But to be a Communist means to be a member of a party that lost considerable prestige, to be subject to its discipline.

"I think the time will come when nobody talks of 'Marxism-Leninism' anymore. Our system will be called something else, something like 'developed socialism.' " . . .

Mr. Gorbachev himself came from the generation of the "thaw," men and women who joined the party in the period of heady optimism that came with Mr. Khrushchev's condemnation of Stalin's crimes.

And now Mr. Gorbachev's own "thaw"—and the warming that has followed it in other Communist lands—is certain to profoundly affect those who now join or remain in the party. . . .

Other voices presented in the series belonged to people like Enrique Lister, an 81-year-old Spanish general, a veteran of the Civil War who had outlived Franco and who while insisting that Marxism was a proven science claimed, "We have a long way to go yet; Communist society is yet to come." The manager of a Polish pencil company bragged about how much money he earns but complained that despite his windfall profits he could not buy his son the Yamaha motorbike that the teenager yearned for, and as a result the boy had misgivings about the system. A Sicilian editor who wears a ring made from the metal of a U.S. plane downed by the Vietnamese told of his disillusionment when the Italian party sought an alliance with Christian Democrats. Italy, he realized, is no longer "a country of poor folk with nothing to lose but their chains," but rather one in which people "now have automobiles and houses."

From the third world came opinions of men like Gustavo Espinoza Montesinos of Peru, who defended the Soviet invasion of Czechoslovakia. There was also the anger of Safdar Hashmi, an Indian theater director, who deplored the then planned though not yet carried out Soviet withdrawal from Afghanistan. "We have defended the presence there of Soviet troops," he said. "Now you have the Soviets saying they have no business to be there. So what happens to the class struggle? Do you abandon Nicaragua and Ethiopia too? What will happen to them?" Soon after he offered his views, he was beaten to death by a gang after refusing to stop production of a political street play.

There was the testimony of the Nicaraguan Bayardo Arce, who said he read Henry Kissinger but could not get through Karl Marx. There was the Chilean architect who recalled wistfully that he had "entered adolescence together with a woman who was begining to mature and who was called the Cuban revolution." And finally, there was Mzala, a 32-year-old South African living in London for whom Communism essentially meant an ideology that he thought bound him in communion with comrades around the world but which also most alarmed his enemies, the architects and technicians of apartheid. "I think we are driven to our quest for Marxist theory by the South African Government itself because, from the time we became politically conscious in South Africa, the Government has been, and continues to be, at pains to show that, more than any other political entity, it opposes and it is afraid of the Communist Party."

•   •   •

The year's first dramatic reflection of Communism's attrition came when Moscow ordered the withdrawal of all Soviet troops from Af-

*ghanistan. For nine years the Soviets had fought there to bolster succes-
sive Marxist regimes. During that span thousands of Soviet soldiers
had been killed, more than 100,000 were wounded, and still others
were captured in battles with sharpshooting Muslim warriors. In April
of the previous year, the Soviet Union had agreed in Geneva to withdraw its forces by February 15, 1989. Such a pullback would mark the
first time since the Second World War that Soviet Union was relinquishing territory it had sought to dominate.*

Getting Out with Honor
By Bill Keller

MOSCOW, Feb. 2—As the last Soviet troops muster in Kabul for their
convoy home from Afghanistan, the Kremlin has already turned its
attention to a desperate salvage operation aimed at snatching as much
honor as possible from the jaws of retreat.

With the hope of a last-ditch political settlement all but dissolved,
and the search for any long-term lessons postponed to the future,
Soviet officials have focused their diplomatic and military efforts on
a set of more immediate goals.

"The main object of all this activity," a Western diplomat said,
answering the question of what Moscow wants, "is to prevent the
Soviet Union from being humiliated."

What Moscow seems to want, first, is to get out without further
indignities avoiding heavy casualties as the final Soviet convoy moves
north in the next few days.

To this end, the military has bombarded guerrilla strongholds along
the main highway from Kabul to the Soviet Union, and Soviet diplomats have warned the opposition to hold its fire or risk reprisals.

Second, the Soviets want to demonstrate to their own people—and
to clients elsewhere who may see the withdrawal as a betrayal of
Communist solidarity—that they are doing all they can to prevent
their clients from being quickly submerged in a bloodbath.

This means the diplomatic overtures aimed at forming a coalition
government will continue, and perhaps intensify, after the troops have
gone. Some diplomats say they believe it will also mean continued
bombing runs from Soviet territory to help the Afghan Army, although this would draw protests from the West. The Soviet commander in Afghanistan has said this will not be done, but some
diplomats believe that will depend on how the tide turns after the
withdrawal.

10

Soviet officials seem to believe that the Afghan Government of President Najibullah will show greater staying power after the withdrawal than most Western diplomats expect, holding Kabul and perhaps some other major cities.

"I think the Soviets hope they can hold on to Kabul for at least six months while the negotiations continue," a Western diplomat said.

Third, the Soviets hope to salvage enough influence in the region to assure peaceful relations with their southern neighbor, whoever is in power, and to prevent Afghanistan from falling under the thrall of other powers, especially Pakistan. . . .

And fourth, Kremlin leaders are preparing to extract the remaining political benefits of the retreat, both at home and abroad.

At home, this means using the Afghanistan failure as an additional justification for cutting the military budget and diverting resources to shore up the fragile civilian economy.

Abroad, it means aggressively pursuing new opportunities for better relations with China and the Arab world, where the Afghan conflict has been a major diplomatic obstruction. Foreign Minister Eduard A. Shevardnadze was in Beijing today, laying plans for a Soviet-Chinese summit meeting that would have been impossible while Soviet troops were fighting in Afghanistan.

The mood in Moscow in the closing days of this nine-year misadventure is neither celebration nor defeat, but fatigue.

The Soviet public, having long since breathed its relief over the withdrawal and disinclined to dwell on the possible collapse of the Afghan regime, now seems eager to put the whole affair behind them.

"We are leaving as we arrived: neither victorious nor vanquished," Vladimir Bavin, who served with the Soviet Army in Afghanistan from 1984 to 1986, said in an interview this week at a club for war veterans. "So I don't think there will be a national holiday on February 15." That is the day the Soviet withdrawal is to be completed under the Geneva accords signed last April. . . .

Soviet officials have already set forth in general terms what they consider to be the broad lessons of Afghanistan.

Mr. Shevardnadze has cited the decision to send troops as evidence of the need for wider and more public discussion of foreign policy decisions, including involvement of the Soviet Parliament, which is supposed to be given new powers this year.

Mikhail S. Gorbachev, the Soviet leader, certainly had Afghanistan in mind when he told the United Nations General Assembly in December that the major powers should "totally rule out any outward-directed use of force," or even the threat of force, as an instrument of foreign policy.

By citing the cost of the war in Afghanistan as one culprit in a staggering Soviet budget deficit, Mr. Gorbachev has also made clear that he intends to use the war in pressing his case for cuts in the military budget.

"I think we will learn from Afghanistan the lesson you learned in Vietnam—that military force is a limited instrument of foreign policy," a Soviet journalist said today. "Given the state our economy is in right now, that happens to be a very timely lesson."

Pravda wrote on Wednesday that "it still remains for politicians and military historians" to explain what went wrong. It added, "Probably everything will be told, without secrets or evasions, even about what the leaders of the party and country have called 'sins.' "

A day later the Soviet press offered a new and thorough reckoning of old Soviet "sins."

Major Soviet Paper Says 20 Million Died as Victims of Stalin
By Bill Keller

MOSCOW, Feb. 3—A Soviet weekly newspaper today published the most detailed accounting of Stalin's victims yet presented to a mass audience here, indicating that about 20 million died in labor camps, forced collectivization, famine and executions.

The estimates, by the historian Roy Medvedev, were printed in the weekly tabloid *Argumenti i Fakti*, which has a circulation of more than 20 million.

The estimated number of deaths is about equal to the number of Soviet soldiers and civilians believed killed in World War II.

Mr. Medvedev's grim arithmetic was reported in a less detailed version last November in *Moscow News*, a limited-circulation weekly, which sells about 200,000 copies in Russian, but today's article marked the first time the numbers have been disclosed to a nationwide audience.

In all, Mr. Medvedev calculated about 40 million victims of Stalin's repressions, including those arrested, driven from their land or black-listed.

Although the bookkeeping of Stalin's terror is an inexact and contentious science, Mr. Medvedev's estimates are generally in line with Western calculations that have long been disparaged by more official Soviet historians.

"It's important that they published it, although the numbers themselves are horrible," Mr. Medvedev said in an interview tonight. "Those numbers include my father."

Mr. Medvedev, a dissident Marxist who has recently been rescued from official obscurity and honored as a leading authority on dark corners of Soviet history, said the weekly newspaper solicited the article and presumably showed the contents to officials before publishing it.

Mr. Medvedev said he had no special access to official archives, but relied on his own compilations of material over the years and recent publications in the Soviet press.

Under a headline proclaiming "The Number of Victims of Stalinism Is About 40 Million People," in a terse, question-and-answer format, Mr. Medvedev cited the human cost of Stalin's leadership year by year, leaving it to the reader to complete the arithmetic.

Mr. Medvedev's accounting included these victims:

- One million imprisoned or exiled from 1927 to 1929, falsely accused of being saboteurs or members of opposition parties.
- Nine million to 11 million of the more prosperous peasants driven from their lands and another 2 million to 3 million arrested or exiled in the early 1930's campaign of forced farm collectivization. Many of these were believed to have been killed.
- Six million to 7 million killed in the punitive famine inflicted on peasants in 1932 and 1933.
- One million exiled from Moscow and Leningrad in 1935 for belonging to families of former nobility, merchants, capitalists and officials.
- About 1 million executed in the "great terror" of 1937–38, and another 4 million to 6 million sent to forced labor camps from which most, including Mr. Medvedev's father, did not return.
- Two million to 3 million sent to camps for violating absurdly strict labor laws imposed in 1940.
- At least 10 million to 12 million "repressed" in World War II, including millions of Soviet-Germans and other ethnic minorities forcibly relocated.
- More than 1 million arrested on political grounds from 1946 to Stalin's death in 1953.

The Soviet press has left little unsaid about Stalin's shortcomings, probing into sacred myths like his conduct of World War II, likening him to Hitler, dissecting his cruelties period by period. But official historians have shied away from putting a number to it all.

Mr. Medvedev acknowledged in *Argumenti i Fakti*, and repeated tonight, that many periods of repression will never be fully measured because records have been lost or never existed.

Meanwhile, as the withdrawal of troops continued, the Soviets virtually trumpeted their retreat.

Soviets Delighted to Survive
By Bill Keller

TERMEZ, U.S.S.R., Feb. 6—The Soviet Union marked the final stage of its withdrawal from Afghanistan with a show for the press today in this dusty border city.

Nine years and 41 days after troops parachuted into Afghanistan to support the Soviet-sponsored Government in Kabul, a token paratroop regiment rumbled back across a railroad bridge over the Amu Darya River, to be greeted by an anxious group of parents and fiancees, assorted minor dignitaries, 200 reporters from all over the world, and an all-girl, all-drum band from a Termez school.

The ceremony was more weary than festive, and just a bit premature.

Army officers here said this morning that as many as 20,000 Soviet soldiers were still in Afghanistan, awaiting airlift to Soviet territory or gathered in convoys converging on Termez or the western border crossing at Kushka.

But the authorities said the last soldiers had left Kabul and its environs, including the airport that had been a virtual Soviet military base. . . .

The display in Termez today was intended to show the world that the Soviet Union is abiding by its commitment to vacate Afghanistan before February 15, and to show the home audience that the Kremlin was not going to let its soldiers slink home as if no one cared.

The authorities flew in more than 100 foreign journalists from Moscow, and 45 more were allowed to ride in with the paratroopers from north of Mazar-i-Sharif.

Today's show took place at a dirt parade ground overlooking a railroad bridge named Friendship, which connects Termez with the Afghan town of Heiratan.

People in Termez, many wearing the quilted, multicolored robes traditional in Uzbekistan, came to feast on meat pies and kebab and to browse at tents selling chocolate bars, soap, toothpaste and other scarce items.

At about 11:30, the paratroopers climbed atop armored personel carriers and roared across the bridge from Heiratan, where they had spent the night bathing and watching a variety show.

Stepping up to a reviewing stand decorated with flags and a large, decidedly Asian-looking visage of Lenin, Lieut. Col. Aleksandr I. Skachkov, a regiment commander, announced to the local authorities that "the battalion, having fulfilled its international duty, has come home."

A military band played the Soviet national anthem, followed by a girl from the Termez school who recited a patriotic poem in high-pitched fervor.

One thing that did not seem staged was the joy of the 300 weary paratroopers chosen to symbolize the war's end for the world's cameras. They waved and grinned in happy exhaustion.

The soldiers said the convoy home was slowed by slick roads in the Salang Tunnel and mountain passes. An avalanche reportedly swept several vehicles into a ravine, killing three men. But they said they encountered no attacks from guerrillas.

Girls from Termez passed through the ranks on the parade ground with carnations, cigarettes and blank telegram forms for word to loved ones far away.

"I'm back home, I'm alive and well," Pavel Nochikov scrawled to his mother in the Komi region.

Reporters were given only half an hour to mingle with the troops before the men boarded their vehicles. In that time, traces of bitterness were evident along with relief.

Asked what he felt he and his comrades had accomplished in Afghanistan, one private paused a long time, shrugged, and said, "We survived."

Some waiting relatives were similarly candid. "They say it's a mistake, but when so many people die for a mistake, it's terrible," said Nina Peshkova, 27 years old, an officer's wife from Siberia who came for her husband's homecoming. She added: "I think the regime of

Najibullah has hardly any support. The people should decide for themselves."

Maria G. Sabriva, a tiny woman from the Termez region, found her grandson among the arriving soldiers and was quickly surrounded by reporters eager to record the moment. "At least he was healthy," Mrs. Sabriva said of her grandson, who had written her that he was in Mongolia so she would not worry.

More than 600,000 men have served in Afghanistan since the war began, and more than 13,000—by the last official count, not updated since May—have died there.

Meanwhile, in Warsaw, another group of people who had been struggling against Communist domination for about as long as the Afghan Mujahaddin were also making sudden gains. The Solidarity free trade union movement had been born when workers in Gdansk set off a wave of strikes that linked demands for better pay to calls for political liberty and civil rights. The movement was at first legalized, but then in 1981 General Wojciech Jaruzelski declared martial law and most of the union leaders were arrested. But enough escaped to build a nationwide conspiracy in which ordinary people increasingly acted like free men and women, meeting in churches, ignoring censorship and paying more attention to the leadership of Lech Walesa, the electrician who founded the union, than to the general who headed the party. For several years the Communists contended that Solidarity had had its day and was a spent force. But finally, as the country's economy worsened, they were forced to reckon with ideas they could not squelch and men they could not subdue.

Warsaw Opens Parley with Solidarity
By John Tagliabue

WARSAW, Feb. 6—The Government and the banned labor union Solidarity began discussions today on broad political and economic change in Poland. The Government offered to reinstate the union and give it a share of parliamentary power through "nonconfrontational elections" in exchange for Solidarity support of Government economic programs.

The Interior Minister, Gen. Czeslaw Kiszczak, said in a keynote address that such elections could lead to the formation of a broad coalition government to prevent Poland from degenerating into "the sick man of Europe."

One key issue facing Solidarity will be whether to accept what would in effect be rigged elections that the Government has suggested in the past would assure the union 30 percent to 40 percent of the seats in Parliament. That would not represent a dramatic shift in power, but would open the door to greater influence for the union and its poltical allies and create a base for further future change.

General Kiszczak, who headed the Government delegation, said an overhaul of Poland's political system was needed for economic and social change. But he said the restoration of Solidarity should rule out a return to the "anarchy and destruction" that marked its legal existence in 1980–81.

Speaking for Solidarity, the banned union's leader, Lech Walesa, called for a gradual dismantling of Poland's one-party state, asserting that such a process should commence with "the reinstatement of trade union pluralism, the reinstatement of Solidarity."

As part of an agreement to end a wave of strikes in August, the Government of Gen. Wojciech Jaruzelski promised to include Solidarity in discussions on Poland's problems, including a $38.9 billion debt and chronic consumer shortages. The Government banned Solidarity after martial law was declared in December 1981.

Fifty-seven delegates from the Government, the opposition and the Roman Catholic Church gathered for the round-table talks at the Governor's Palace

General Kiszczak proposed these three measures as a new "social accord":

- An increase in the opposition's representation in the Parliament, through what he called "nonconfrontational elections."
- A program of economic recovery, whose aim above all would be to stifle inflation, restructure industry and resolve Poland's pressing foreign debt.
- Resolution of the problem of trade union pluralism, through the legalization of Solidarity.

The delegates are expected to continue discussions in small groups this week before convening again in full session.

In their opening addresses, which were televised nationally this evening, both sides appeared to be staking maximalist positions, reflecting the Government's desire to retain the last word on political change, and Solidarity's wish to claim an area of independent activity within Polish society.

In his address, Mr. Walesa asserted that a "new law on associations should create real freedom of association for everyone."

"This must not depend on arbitrary decisions of administrative authorities," he added.

"In this way union and social pluralism will create an area of freedom that Poles need as much as they need air," he said.

Mr. Walesa also blamed the Communists for Poland's situation.

"We know it—the country is ruined," he said, "but it wasn't some elves who ruined it, but a system of exercising authority that detaches citizens from their rights and wastes the fruits of their labor."

Among the conclusions the Government has drawn from experience, General Kiszczak said, was that, "renewal requires social peace, the consideration and responsibility of all the partners, and the expansion of the social base of reforms and ruling."

But he added, "No national problem will be solved by denying the historical achievements and undermining the socialist shape of Poland."

As rivals talked in Poland, in Afghanistan the invaders departed.

Last Soviet Soldiers Leave Afghanistan After 9 Years, 15,000 Dead and Great Cost
By Bill Keller

MOSCOW, Feb. 15—The last Soviet soldier came home from Afghanistan this morning, the Soviet Union announced, leaving behind a war that had become a domestic burden and an international embarrassment for Moscow.

The final Soviet departure came on the day set as a deadline by the Geneva accords last April. It left two heavily armed adversaries, the Kremlin-backed Government of President Najibullah and a fractious but powerful array of Muslim insurgents, backed by the United States and Pakistan, to conclude their civil war on their own.

Lieut. Gen. Boris V. Gromov, the commander of the Soviet forces in Afghanistan, walked across the steel Friendship Bridge to the border city of Termez, in Uzbekistan, at 11:55 A.M. local time (1:55 A.M., Eastern time), 9 years and 50 days after Soviet troops intervened to support a coup by a Marxist ally.

"There is not a single Soviet soldier or officer left behind me," General Gromov told a Soviet television reporter waiting on the bridge. "Our nine-year stay ends with this."

Today's final departure is the end of a steady process of withdrawal since last spring, when Moscow says, there were 100,300 Soviet troops in Afghanistan. At the height of the Soviet commitment, according to Western intelligence estimates, there were 115,000 troops deployed.

This morning, as the last armored troop carriers rumbled home across the border, a Soviet newspaper carried the first report of atrocities committed in the war by the nation's military forces.

The weekly *Literaturnaya Gazeta* described the killing of a carload of Afghan civilians, including women and children, and the order by a commander to cover it up.

The article was a foretaste of recriminations expected in the months ahead.

The war cost the Soviet Union roughly 15,000 lives and undisclosed billions of rubles. It scarred a generation of young people and undermined the cherished image of an invincible Soviet army. Moscow's involvement in Afghanistan was often compared to the American experience in the Vietnam War, in which more than 58,000 Americans died.

The Soviet intervention, which received international condemnation, cast a pall over relations with China, the Muslim world and the West. It led to an American trade embargo and a Western boycott of the 1980 Olympic Games in Moscow.

"The day that millions of Soviet people have waited for has come," General Gromov said to an army rally in Termez, Reuters reported. "In spite of our sacrifices and losses, we have totally fulfilled our internationalist duty."

The official press agency Tass said the Defense Ministry presented all of the returning soldiers with wristwatches. . . .

At home, the Soviet Government now faces a period of reckoning with the roots and consequences of the war.

In Pravda, the authoritative Communist Party newspaper, a commentator insisted today that the intervention was carried out with the best intentions—including maintaining the security of the Soviet Union's southern border. But he said that the war was characterized by the mistakes and misjudgments of previous leaders.

"One can question the Brezhnev leadership's assessment of the military threat," the commentary said. "One can say that in the future such vital issues as the use of troops must not be decided in secrecy, without the approval of the country's Parliament." Other commentators, who have been constrained while Soviet soldiers were still fighting on Afghan territory, can now be expected to question more pointedly how the Soviet Union got into Afghanistan, what it did there, why it stayed so long and what lessons it has learned. . . .

And days after the Afghan pullout, there was news from Warsaw of another breakthrough, a seeming concession by the Communists to allow Solidarity a share of political power.

Solidarity May Win 40 Percent of Parliament
By John Tagliabue

WARSAW, Feb. 19—Two weeks after the start of talks between the Government and the outlawed opposition, both sides say they have reached "fundamental accord" on allowing the Solidarity-led opposition to control as many as two-fifths of the seats in Parliament through pre-arranged elections.

As outlined by a senior party official, the accord would allow Poland's Solidarity-based opposition roughly 40 percent of the seats in Parliament under an agreement by which the sides would divide electoral districts beforehand, then refrain from running candidates in each other's districts or "sabotaging" their campaigns.

In exchange, the officials said, Solidarity is being asked to provide popular support for unpopular Government economic policies. . . .

Both sides stressed that the accord could unravel before a final agreement is reached . . . but it appeared to represent major concessions by both sides. The Communist Party has never permitted more than token opposition in the largely rubber-stamp Parliament, and Solidarity has boycotted all Polish elections, denouncing them as hoaxes designed to cement party control. . . .

The impetus behind the political bargaining, which includes the Government, the party, Solidarity and the Church, as well as Communist-backed labor unions and other organizations, is a looming economic crisis that representatives of Government and Solidarity fear could provoke new outbursts of industrial strife.

But the proposals also reflected the broad political liberalization in several countries of East Europe, including Hungary and Yugoslavia. Both countries, in addition to Poland, are testing the waters of multiparty government.

A senior Church official said "free elections are impossible." But he and Solidarity strategists appeared to suggest that an infusion of opposition politicians into Parliament would favorably influence the development of democratic institutions and augment pressure on the Communist party for further change. . . .

It was hardly yet a contagion of freedom, but before winter loosened its grip there were remarkable stirrings along the Baltic, most notably among the Lithuanians. They were now Soviet citizens and their land was a Soviet Republic. But as with the Poles, to whom they once were linked in monarchial union, they were many among them openly yearning and striving to stand alone.

Lithuania Nationalists: A Fine and Fragile Line
By Bill Keller

VILNIUS, U.S.S.R., March 9—Ignoring damp snowflakes, Lithuanians by the thousands filed into the sylvan amphitheater of a Vilnius park the other day for an election rally.

They cheered the candidates of the popular movement called Sajudis, whistled their collective disdain for the Communist Party, listened stoically as their leaders appealed for calm in the face of official resistance, and then lifted perhaps 15,000 voices in the Sajudis oath: "Our goal is a free Lithuania!"

A few weeks ago these were words of nostalgia and bravado. But in the heat of an uninhibited Soviet election campaign, the notion of "free Lithuania"—free, that is, of the Soviet Union—has become a live and explosive issue.

In February, Sajudis, now a commanding political presence in this republic of 3.7 million people, took a daring step by announcing that its ultimate goal is to restore "an independent and neutral Lithuanian state in a demilitarized zone," like the nation that existed here between the two world wars, until the Soviet Union annexed the Baltic states in 1940.

The group had earlier called for a form of home rule, but stopped short of endorsing independence. But with the new declaration, including the statement that Lithuania had been "occupied" by the Red Army against its will, Sajudis portrayed itself as a lineal descendant of the partisans who waged armed resistance against Soviet power until 1953.

The declaration made Sajudis the first of the Baltic Popular Fronts to explicitly chart a separatist course, although similar groups in Estonia and Latvia include factions that favor full independence.

The group's leaders say their declaration was a statement of principle, not a short-term program. But some Sajudis members who are running for office in the election on March 26 are quite prepared to push for secession almost immediately.

The Lithuanian Communist Party leader, Algirdas Brazauskas, who had been nervously tolerant of the nationalist group, was called to Moscow for consultations last month, and returned with a new, firm set to his square jaw.

The party promptly announced new limits on Sajudis's independent press, purged several party and government officials considered sympathetic to the movement, and warned of a possible state of emergency if the separatist calls did not subside.

"We have told Sajudis that together we can approach that red line, but we, the official leadership, cannot cross it," Mr. Brazauskas said in an interview, adding that he "cannot imagine the consequences" if Sajudis pushes for secession.

"On the other side of the line, we can no longer remain friends or support their ideas," he said. "You can criticize us, you can mistrust us—whatever. But we won't cross that line."

What makes the debate especially pointed is the prospect that, thanks to the Soviet Union's first competitive elections, Sajudis is likely soon to acquire real power in the Lithuanian government.

The organization is backing candidates for 39 of Lithuania's 42 seats in a new national congress to be elected on March 26, and even party officials concede that the movement stands a good chance of winning most of them. The Popular Fronts in Latvia and Estonia are also backing candidates, but have not organized such complete slates. . . .

More important, Sajudis expects to win control of the republic's legislature in the next round of local elections. Already, Sajudis has gone up against the party in three special elections to fill vacant seats in the Lithuanian legislature and won all of them handily.

Alarmed that Sajudis members might use a majority in the legislature to formally declare Lithuanian independence, the Communist Party is now pressing to have the local legislative elections postponed from next fall until at least the following spring.

Both Sajudis and the Communist Party are divided about how to continue their troubled relationship.

Vytautas Landsbergis, the president of the independent movement, has tried to steer his group away from outright confrontation with the party. He and other Sajudis leaders say that if Lithuania is allowed to develop its own experimental economy—to shut down polluting heavy industries, develop private factories and farming, engage in free trade with the West, and create its own monetary system, then Lithuania can remain part of a Soviet federation, at least for now.

Separatist talk, the Sajudis moderates argue, simply provokes Moscow's anger, and in any case the republic will need perhaps 10 years of economic development before it is ready to stand on its own.

"The prevailing view, which I suppose you could call utopian, is that Lithuania should help the Soviet Union by providing an intelligent economic model," Mr. Landsbergis said. "The other view, which is the radical view, is to jump out of a sinking boat."

Keeping these two factions together in Sajudis "is my biggest problem," he added.

Others on the group's executive council, like Arvydas Juozaitis, a 32-year-old political scientist, say that Sajudis has taken the first logical step toward secession by proclaiming Lithuania an occupied country. Economic independence is another step on that road, he said.

"We know very well what it actually means to introduce private enterprise and a free economic zone in Lithuania," Mr. Juozaitis said. "In fact, it will be a decisive step toward seceding from the Soviet Union."

Even if Moscow gives Lithuania economic free range, the Kremlin is unlikely to tolerate another Sajudis demand—that the republic be removed from Soviet military jurisdiction.

Mr. Brazauskas, a former industrial planner regarded by Sajudis as a reasonable but indecisive moderate, has supported greater sovereignty for Lithuania within the framework of the Soviet Union. He argues that disengaging Lithuania economically is wildly impractical and that demilitarization is politically unthinkable.

The republic party leader made several concessions, including restoration of the old Lithuanian flag and a tough new language law that will require officials to speak basic Lithuanian within two years, and has promised that the republic will have vastly greater economic power next year.

"Compared with the other republics we have gone very far," he said. "Everyone wants to forget this and look ahead to see what is going to happen next."

The party leader warned that "extremist slogans" arouse the resentment of the Soviet Union's Russian-speaking majority and could undermine Mikhail S. Gorbachev, the nation's leader.

"Without a doubt, such demarches can influence society's opinion of Gorbachev's authority," he said.

Mr. Brazauskas seems to be under heavy pressure from Moscow, where some Kremlin leaders are alarmed at how quickly Lithuania is increasing its demands, and worried by signs that the nationalist sentiment is spreading to two much larger republics, the Ukraine and Byelorussia.

Last month, the Government banned Sajudis's weekly television show, a live call-in program that has provided some of the most astonishing moments in Soviet television. On one of last programs, on February 1, Julius Juzeliunas, a composer, praised the Lithuanian partisans who haunted the woods of the republic until 1953 picking off Soviet soldiers.

"This is the state television network, not a private company," Mr. Brazauskas said, defending the decision to cancel the program. He said the issue would be reconsidered after the elections.

Most Sajudis leaders are sympathetic to Mr. Brazauskas' predicament and see the need for conciliation.

"He's under a lot of pressure," said Romualdas Ozolas, editor of the main Sajudis newspaper. "I wouldn't want to be in his place."

Earlier this month, Sajudis candidates withdrew from the election districts where Mr. Brazauskas and the No. 2 two republic party leader are running, fearful that if the moderates were beaten, Moscow would replace them with hard-liners.

The people who make the movement's decisions are no scraggly band of dissidents, but solid civic leaders. The 35-member executive council that meets each Tuesday to map strategy includes prominent economists, lawyers, cultural figures and scholars, and a priest, indicating the tacit support of the Roman Catholic Church, which is still a power in this heavily Catholic republic.

Perhaps most surprising, 14 of the 35 Sajudis council members are also Communist Party members.

Lithuania was the last of the three Baltic states to form its independent political movement. Sajudis was organized in October after creation of the Popular Fronts in Estonia and Latvia.

But Sajudis has moved ahead of neighboring groups by making full use of the new election law.

Adolfas Uza, a journalist for the Lithuanian state press agency and a Sajudis spokesman, said the movement may have grown faster because Lithuania is less Russified than the other republics—80 percent of the people are ethnic Lithuanians, while the indigenous population is less than two-thirds in Estonia and about half in Latvia.

"We have to take the step first because we have the better demographic situation," Mr. Uza said. "Estonia and Latvia look to us with great hope. The further we go toward independence, the easier it will be for them."

Democracy—or at least a half measure called "democratization"—was also churning debate and hopes in the Soviet Union. As spring came, citizens there were preparing for the first time in their lives to vote clearly and unmistakably for the candidate they preferred and against those they disdained.

In Moscow's TV Political Debates, the Unspeakable Is Now Routine
By Bill Keller

MOSCOW, March 21—"Do you believe in God?" the moderator asked the candidates in one of Moscow's first televised campaign debates.

"I do not believe in God," replied Boris N. Yeltsin, the city's former Communist Party leader, smiling a wan smile at an audience estimated in the millions.

"I am an atheist," concurred his adversary, Yevgeny A. Brakov, an auto-factory director, who was visibly ill at ease.

It was the politically correct answer for two career members of the Communist Party, but not necessarily a vote-getter in a nation of many devout believers, and certainly not a question that party luminaries are accustomed to being asked on live television.

Since the beginning of March, the popular nightly program "Good Evening, Moscow" has been been subjecting candidates to questions submitted by viewers in preparation for the Soviet Union's first competitive national elections this coming Sunday.

The elections are to choose 1,500 territorial representatives to a new national Congress of People's Deputies, largely in contested races. Together with 750 deputies named directly by the Communist Party and other official organizations, they will set general policy and select a standing legislature and president from their ranks.

For voters accustomed to unopposed candidates with look-alike platforms, the uncensored programs have represented a crash course in the new Soviet approach to political pluralism.

The program has also caused one political tempest, when supporters of Mr. Yeltsin charged that hostile questions were planted on the show to embarrass their candidate.

The questions, phoned in beforehand by viewers and selected by Andrei G. Skryabin, the moderator of the debates, range from the brazenly personal—"How big is your apartment?"—to the politically provocative. Candidates can count on blunt questions about legalizing opposition political parties, abolishing the draft, banning nuclear power or slashing the space program.

"Not long ago, if somebody had come on my show and said one-tenth of the things that are said in these debates, at the very least I would be out of a job," said Mr. Skryabin, a fast-talking former science reporter.

Viewers frequently demand to know what magazines the candidates read, a favorite barometer of political inclinations.

Candidates in all 27 Moscow election districts have agreed to submit to the televised encounters, which, like American presidential debates, are really side-by-side interviews more than classic debates.

One Moscow candidate who escaped the televised cross-examination was Lev N. Zaikov, Mr. Yeltsin's successor as chief of the Moscow Communist Party organization. Along with Mikhail S. Gorbachev, the Soviet leader, and most other top party officials, Mr. Zaikov was named to the new congress as part of the party's slate, without opposition or a vote by the public.

Mr. Skryabin said the debates are without precedent and, as far as he knows, unique to Moscow. And in a campaign with no paid commercials and spotty Soviet press coverage, many believe that they could prove decisive.

If Ilya I. Zaslavsky, a 29-year-old campaigner from an unofficial association for the disabled, wins Sunday in his campaign to represent the Oktyabrsky region of Moscow, it may well be because he quietly dominated the televised debate against his better-known opponent, a popular television journalist named Aleksandr N. Krutov.

Mr. Zaslavsky, whose legs are withered as a result of a contaminated polio vaccination he received as a child, outlined a detailed program to improve health care, stiffen environmental protection and assist those on fixed incomes. Mr. Krutov lost points by making patronizing comments about the disabled and by declining to disavow an endorsement from the extreme Russian nationalist group Pamyat.

Valery M. Savitsky, a lawyer and highly regarded civil rights specialist, appearently damaged his campaign against a prominent economist when he bobbled a question about his ex-wife, the daughter of a top Soviet official.

"He hesitated and mumbled," as if apologizing for his marriage, Mr. Skryabin said. "It was not the way a man behaves toward his wife. It was an unquestionable defeat."

Mr. Skryabin said there are no reliable studies of how many people are watching the debates, but since about 30 million people can pick up the broadcasts, and since "Good Evening, Moscow" is one of the most popular programs on local television, it is likely that millions have tuned in.

The format of the program is simple: each candidate has six minutes to describe his platform, and then they take turns giving one-minute answers to the questions Mr. Skryabin has picked. The host sorts the hundreds of questions phoned in each day by viewers, selecting those that seem to reflect wide interest, and those that are the most pointed.

"I immediately discard questions like 'My dear Comrade Brakov! We greet you, we love you, you are our friend and brother,'" he said. "Next, I throw out questions of a personal nature: 'help us fix our roof.'"

The candidates are given the questions shortly before the program so they will not be caught totally by surprise. A few days after the Yeltsin debate, in which the former Moscow party chief fielded a number of unfriendly queries about his conflicts with party leaders, a commentator for the Novosti news-feature agency, a Yeltsin supporter, charged that he had tried to track down the authors of the questions and found that most did not exist.

Mr. Yeltsin and his backers alleged that this was part of an organized campaign to discredit the candidate.

Mr. Skryabin said producers of the show did their own investigation and located all but one of the questioners. It is true that Mr. Yeltsin drew the more aggressive questions, he said, but that was because he is controversial.

Mr. Skryabin said he could recall only once when his superiors at central television complained about the debates. The question about God, they told him, was out of bounds.

"Maybe it was a mistake to ask that question," he mused later. "It does not relate to their qualifications for public office. But what the devil, they didn't have to answer it."

After the campaign came the vote.

Soviets Savor Vote in Freest Election Since '17 Revolution

By Bill Keller

MOSCOW, March 26—Soviet voters today relished their freest elections in more than 70 years, choosing a new national Congress of Deputies that is to replace a legislature wholly subservient to the Communist Party.

In the race that some regarded as a plebiscite on the establishment, Boris N. Yeltsin, the deposed Moscow Communist Party leader, appeared headed for a victory over a candidate backed by the Moscow party machine.

Mr. Yeltsin, campaigning against party privileges and for greater political pluralism, seemed to have overwhelming support over Yevgeny A. Brakov, the director of the Zil limousine factory, in a contest to represent the city in the congress.

An informal sampling by Western news organizations of more than 2,300 voters at polling places around the city found that more than 90 percent had supported Mr. Yeltsin's comeback. The first official tallies from scattered polling places also pointed to a Yeltsin landslide.

Today's voting was the first nationwide, competitive election since the autumn of 1917, when Lenin's Bolshevik party was outpolled by the Socialist Revolutionaries. The following July, Lenin ousted the rival party from the Government and began the one-party state that exists to this day.

The new congress and the standing legislature it must appoint within two months are certain to be dominated by the Communist Party on all major policy questions. But voters appeared likely to elect enough independent-minded deputies to make open clashes of ideas highly likely.

Soviet citizens seemed to revel in their first opportunity to vote for candidates like Mr. Yeltsin, who promised to accelerate the pace of change and railed against the bureaucrats and power brokers.

One woman may have embodied the national mood when, asked by a Soviet television crew how she had voted, she replied firmly, "Against what we have now."

Mikhail S. Gorbachev, the Soviet leader, while declining to say how he had voted, cautioned against the impatience evident among Mr. Yeltsin's army of supporters.

"We must not commit stupidities, attempt great leaps forward, or overreach ourselves because we could put the people's future at risk,"

28

Mr. Gorbachev said after casting his ballot at the headquarters of the Association of Soviet Chemists. . . .

Mr. Gorbachev, who is expected to be named to an enhanced position of President when the new congress convenes, was also asked how he felt about the widespread discussion of a multiparty system that has arisen during the campaign.

The Soviet leader, who not long ago dismissed the idea as "rubbish," today seemed to soften his longstanding opposition to the prospect of genuine political competition. He repeated his contention that creating more parties "is not a solution," but he stopped short of condemning the idea. . . .

Mr. Yeltsin, considered a popular figure but a temperamental administrator, resigned from the ruling Politburo in 1987, complaining of obstruction by Yegor K. Ligachev, then the party ideologist.

He was drummed out of his Moscow party leadership after a ritual denunciation by his comrades but allowed to keep a high-ranking post in the Construction Ministry, which he must forfeit when he assumes his legislative post.

His campaign to win the congressional seat in what is known officially as National District No. 1 became a vehicle for a multitude of public discontents.

Among intellectuals, many had misgivings about Mr. Yeltsin's maverick qualities, his upbringing as a Communist Party apparatchik, and his suspiciousness on such issues as private business. But in these circles, his candidacy represented the seed of an opposition that would goad the party leadership toward wider civil rights and pluralism.

"Perhaps he does not represent the democratic ideal, but he represents the hope for change," said Viktoriya O. Chalikova, a sociologist interviewed after voting for Mr. Yeltsin at a polling station in south Moscow. . . .

"I hope this is all for real," said Boris Mamedov, a court clerk, at his voting place in south Moscow. "We've never had anything like it before— discussions, debates, fighting. Before people dropped a piece of paper in a slot. You couldn't describe it as a choice." Aleksandr A. Sokolov, an artist interviewed after voting in the city center, added: "The real test of this election is whether the people we elect stick to their principles and ideals. If not, this will turn out to be just like all the elections in the past."

The voters, having been given the right of choice and discretion, apparently used it.

Soviet Voters Deal Humiliating Blow to Party Officials

By Bill Keller

MOSCOW, March 27—The Soviet electorate has dealt a mortifying rebuke to the high and mighty in elections for a new national congress, including stunning upsets of a Politburo member and several other senior Communist Party officials who ran without opposition.

Results piling up today from the freest nationwide elections since 1917 showed that the mayor and the second-ranking Communist official of Moscow, the Communist Party leader in Leningrad, the commander of the Northern Fleet, the President and Premier of Lithuania, the Estonian K.G.B. chief, the commander of Soviet troops in East Germany and other prominent officials were defeated by candidates promising more rapid change.

The elections on Sunday, for the new and theoretically powerful Congress of People's Deputies, swept in a substantial minority of independent candidates, planting the seeds of the first national opposition since the time of Lenin. . . .

The more independent candidates have, almost without exception, pledged their loyalty to Mr. Gorbachev and his program of political and economic change.

The Soviet leader may thus use his new parliament—which he is expected to head from the newly enhanced post of President—to push his program faster than hard-liners the party would like.

But Mr. Gorbachev may also find that a free-thinking legislature will make his life more difficult, with some nationalist deputies threatening to bolt from the Soviet Union and reformers impatient for more radical change than even he wants.

The best known of the victorious candidates in Sunday's elections, Mr. Yeltsin, fell from Mr. Gorbachev's favor because he became impatient with change, and Mr. Gorbachev on election day pointedly warned against "great leaps."

The campaign over, Mr. Gorbachev went on the first of what were to be several foreign visits, a voyage to Cuba. As elsewhere he was widely seen an apostle for liberalized Communism, something that Fidel Castro, his host, found reproachful.

Gorbachev-Castro Face-off: A Clash of Style and Policies

By Bill Keller

HAVANA, April 1—The guest is Mikhail S. Gorbachev, the smooth salesman of new Communist pragmatism, who preaches economic experimentation, social liberalization and peaceful coexistence.

The host is Fidel Castro, the khaki-clad revolutionary ideologue, who has said of Mr. Gorbachev's new doctrine: "Perestroika is another man's wife. I don't want to get involved."

Their meeting, which is to begin Sunday with a carefully staged welcome by half a million Cubans in the streets of Havana, will be Mr. Gorbachev's diplomatic debut in America's tropical backyard.

The Soviet leader's task will be to see if Cuba—long an outpost of Leninist orthodoxy and an agent of international revolution—can be made a partner in spreading the Gorbachev image of Communism in Latin America.

According to Soviet officials, Mr. Gorbachev would like to encourage domestic changes in Cuba that would ease the burden of bankrolling Mr. Castro's vision of Communism.

By American estimates, Moscow pays $6 billion to $8 billion a year to arm Mr. Castro's military and to prop up Cuba's economy, mostly by buying sugar at inflated prices and selling Soviet oil at a discount. . . .

Gorbachev Begins His Visit to Cuba with Castro's Hug

By Bill Keller

HAVANA, April 2—Mikhail S. Gorbachev arrived in Cuba tonight to an effusive welcome from one of his prickliest allies, Fidel Castro.

On his first diplomatic venture to Latin America, the Soviet leader was greeted with a bear hug and kisses by Mr. Castro, who depends heavily on Soviet subsidies but has little use for Mr. Gorbachev's more flexible brand of Communism.

Mr. Castro turned out much of Havana for the occasion and turned on the charm, clearly hoping to dispel any impression of friction.

Mr. Gorbachev's mission is apparently to reassure the Cuban leader of continued friendship while enlisting his support for economic restructuring and detente diplomacy. . . .

For many Cubans, the visit and speeches will be their first detailed exposure to the Soviet leader.

Mr. Gorbachev's speeches and programs are reported selectively here in the Government-controlled press. Spanish-language Soviet publications are difficult to come by, and many residents profess only scant knowledge of the competitive elections, the freer debate and the market-oriented economic experiments under way in the Soviet Union.

"It is not permitted," said one worshiper this morning at Corpus Christi Roman Catholic Church in the Miromar neighborhood of Havana. "Nothing is permitted here."

As the ten o'clock Mass ended, several parishioners stood by the pews of the church, and after assuring themselves that visiting American reporters were not state security policemen, they spoke excitedly of their hopes that Mr. Gorbachev's visit would inspire a political liberalization, including greater religious freedom.

Parishioners said they had gotten most of their news about Mr. Gorbachev from Radio Marti, the United States Government station that Mr. Castro regards as a vehicle of imperialist propaganda.

"Cuba needs perestroika and glasnost," said one woman, who asked that her name not be used because "you will leave, but we have to stay."

"God has put Gorbachev in the world, and we are grateful," she added.

Silvia Valdez, a teacher of Spanish literature, hailed Mr. Gorbachev as "a man who understands that his country has problems, and he is doing things to change it."

"We hope he will bring about a change in Cuba, to make it more democratic," she said. . . .

Sitting with friends on the crowded beach at the city's eastern edge, Armando Ramos, a young warehouse worker, said: "I understand very well Mr. Gorbachev's reforms. But I also understand the process here. In the future I think we will probably have the same process here as they have in the Soviet Union. But not now. We're not at the same stage of development. We have a long way to go." . . .

Gorbachev Signs Treaty with Cuba
By Bill Keller

HAVANA, April 4—Mikhail S. Gorbachev called today for an end to all outside military aid to Latin America, and signed a friendship treaty with Cuba condemning the use of force as an instrument of foreign policy.

In a speech to the Cuban National Assembly that had been billed as the high point of his first visit to the region, Mr. Gorbachev presented no specific new initiatives, confounding speculation that he would outline a peace plan for Central America or would cancel Cuba's huge debt.

The Soviet leader was upstaged by his host, Fidel Castro, who turned his introductory remarks into a blistering anti-American diatribe that seemed to raise serious doubt about whether the two Communist leaders had come to a meeting of the minds. Mr. Castro spoke for 45 minutes, almost as long as Mr. Gorbachev.

While praising Mr. Gorbachev as a peacemaker and reformer, Mr. Castro left little doubt that he did not intend to follow Mr. Gorbachev's conciliatory approach to the United States or his formula for internal economic and political change. . . .

In Warsaw the round-table talks between Communists and those who had challenged them under the banner of Solidarity were proving remarkably fruitful. Government officials and people they had imprisoned were exchanging handshakes and were making progress on a plan for free elections that went beyond anything ever put forth in any Communist country.

Poland Sets Free Vote in June, First Since '45; Solidarity Reinstated
By John Tagliabue

WARSAW, April 5—The leaders of Solidarity signed accords with the Government today restoring the banned union's legal status and providing for the first free and open elections in this country since World War II.

If carried out, the accords could markedly change the political system in this country, one of the first to be put under Soviet domination after the war. The political structure in Poland was more or less followed in the other countries that one by one were attached to the Soviet bloc in the late 1940's.

Poland was the first Soviet-dominated satellite to achieve a measure of independence in 1956, and it now appears that Poles, driven by economic disaster, have taken advantage of the changes wrought in the Soviet Union by Mikhail S. Gorbachev to forge new agreements that go well beyond anything current in the bloc.

These will be the most immediate effects of the accords:

- Restoration of Solidarity, the trade union that was formed in 1980 and then crushed after martial law was imposed in December 1981. The farmers union, Rural Solidarity, and the Independent Student Association, will also be restored to legal status.

- Elections in June for a two-house parliament, in which 35 percent of the 460 seats in the newly structured lower house will be allocated to delegates of the Solidarity-based opposition. The Communists will have another 38 percent, and parties formerly aligned with the Communists the rest.

- Restoration of Poland's upper house of Parliament, which was disbanded after World War II. It will have 100 members, who will be chosen in free and open elections. The upper house will be able to veto legislation of the lower house.

- Establishment of the post of president of the republic; the holder will be elected by the two houses of Parliament for a six-year term. The President will have broad powers to dissolve Parliament, and to veto laws passed by the lower house. The lower house can overturn vetoes by a two-thirds vote.

- Broad changes in the running of the economy, including the installment of a wage indexing plan, by which workers and retired people will receive compensation to 80 percent of any increase in the cost of living.

The announcement of the accords was broadcast on national television, a measure of the change already wrought since the Government began serious talks with Solidarity last August, after years of repression that culminated last year in two serious waves of labor unrest.

The current Sejm, or Parliament, is expected to meet on Friday to make the agreements into law.

Today's developments came at a formal closing session of the round-table talks, which began eight weeks ago. The ceremony today involved the Interior Minister, Gen. Czeslaw Kiszczak, and Lech Walesa, the Nobel Peace laureate and leader of Solidarity.

Mr. Walesa endorsed the accords in a 10-minute speech after General Kiszczak addressed the round table.

For Mr. Walesa it was an almost dizzying moment of triumph: The union leader congratulating the Communist official who, together with Gen. Wojciech Jaruzelski, was one of the people who engineered the imposition of martial law on December 13, 1981, and ordered the imprisonment of nearly all the union leaders, Mr. Walesa included.

The most ambitious gains, after the union's legalization, appeared to have come in the political agreement. It announced that the authorities would cede 35 percent of the 460 seats of the lower house of Parliament, leaving the Communist Party with only 38 percent, a minority for the first time since 1944. The remainder of the seats will fall to small parties that until now have been faithful allies of the Communists in a ruling coalition.

Perhaps the most startling concession, however, was the Government's agreement to restore Poland's upper house of Parliament with free and open elections. The upper house was abolished in 1946 in a rigged referendum, although some of the elections that year were free. The Government also agreed to create the office of president, who will be elected by a joint session of both houses. It is generally accepted that General Jaruzelski will be chosen the first president, for a six-year term, with the possibility of one more term. . . .

The Government also agreed to make the state-controlled press available to Solidarity by allowing the union a half hour of air time weekly on television and one hour weekly of radio time. In addition the union will be allowed its own daily national newspaper and regional weekly papers. Government censorship is to be eased, though not abolished.

The agreements require the Government to make broad changes to assure the independence of judges and the courts, to assure that Poles can freely form associations and clubs, though not political parties, and to bring about an overhaul of the economy. . . .

Mr. Walesa, a 45-year-old shipyard electrician who in August 1980 founded Solidarity, said: "I have to emphasize that for the first time we have talked to each other using the force of arguments, and not arguments of force. It bids well for the future, I believe, that the round-table discussions can become the beginning of the road for democracy and a free Poland."

"Either we'll be able to build Poland as a nation in a peaceful way, independent, sovereign and safe, with equal alliances," he said, "or we'll sink in the chaos of demagogy, which could result in civil war in which there will be no victors."

General Kiszczak seemed to be playing down the notion that the Government had surrendered substantial ground. "There's only one victor, the nation, our fatherland," he said.

Walesa Isn't Among Candidates Solidarity Lists for June Elections

By John Tagliabue

WARSAW, April 13—Solidarity spokesmen said today that several of the union's most prominent national advisers would lead its slate in open elections for Parliament.

The slate is to include Adam Michnik, an influential theoretician of Solidarity; Jacek Kuron, a former Communist and leading dissident whom Mr. Michnik has often described as his mentor, and Ryszard Bugaj, one of the union's leading economic strategists.

At a news conference in Gdansk, Lech Walesa, the Nobel Peace Prize winner and founder of the union, said that despite "strong pressure" for him to run, he did not intend to be a candidate for office in the coming elections, which essentially pit the ruling Communists against the Solidarity-based opposition.

Instead, Mr. Walesa told reporters of his intention to run in 1995 for President of Poland, an office that is to be restored under the accords last week between the authorities and Solidarity. . . .

For those Poles who had been waging an anti-totalitarian struggle, it was a time of both jubilation and confusion. They had battled and sacrificed for the idea of democracy, but few had ever experienced it in practice. They had been excellent dissidents, which meant standing up, telling the truth and if necessary, going to jail. Now, however, what was needed were politicians, not dissidents, and politics has to do largely with compromise. In the transformation an underground paper that had defied censorship was turned into a legal journal that accepted restrictions, and men who had been sent to prison were campaigning to to enter a parliament that seemed destined to be dominated by the same men who had imprisoned them.

For Paper, Jungle (and Censor) Await

By John Tagliabue

WARSAW, April 21—This month, the most influential source of un-censored information in Poland was laid to rest. Next month it will be reborn as the first independently published daily newspaper in the East bloc.

The new national daily, which will be the election campaign publication of Poland's newly legalized Solidarity trade union, will be under Government censorship as it prepares voters for democratic elections in June. The paper, which has no name, will probably be called simply *Gazeta*.

The weekly it is replacing is *Tygodnik Mazowsze*, or Weekly of Mazowia, in central Poland. The weekly was founded in 1982 and became one of hundreds of underground publications, from a children's magazine to scholarly quarterlies, that shielded the flame of Solidarity.

Despite raids and arrests, *Tygodnik Mazowsze* became an institution, with an average printing that opposition sources said was around 15,000 copies. But the new paper, unlike the old one, will be subject to censorship, a condition demanded by Government negotiators at the recent round-table talks with Solidarity that produced the legalization of the union and an agreemnent on sweeping political and economic change in Poland.

"How do we justify it?" asked Helena Luczywo, a principal editor of *Tygodnik Mazowsze*, who will be responsible for running the new paper. "It will be a daily paper with much bigger circulation, much bigger access. We could stay underground. I do think others might stay underground. But it's an opportunity, because 500,000 copies can be published daily and sold legally in the kiosks."

Adam Michnik, one of the opposition movement's most influential intellectuals, will be editor in chief and bear final responsibility. But Mrs. Luczywo, who began her career in opposition journalism in 1977 at Robotnik, an underground publication, will head day-to-day operations.

"It is impossible to have a daily newspaper in Poland without censorship," said Mrs. Luczywo, who gained familiarity with American newspapers while at Radcliffe in 1986.

"But here I will be pragmatic," she added, sipping tea in her apartment, which is also the site of editorial meetings. "In a sense this is what we did at the round-table talks. You give up something to get something. It's a calculation."

Mrs. Luczywo said the first edition, scheduled to appear in early May, will have eight pages in tabloid format, which may be supplemented later by an advertising insert. The layout, she said, was developed with the help of French designers on loan from the Parisian daily *Liberation.*

"The main problem," she said, "will be the reliability of information. We think a staff of around 50 people will be enough, and there is a small Solidarity news agency. But there is not a good tradition of reliable information." . . .

Seasoned underground reporters like Mrs. Luczywo recall that *Tygodnik Mazowsze*, over its 290 issues, changed format several times according to supplies, missing a week or even two and at times even appearing on green paper once.

Technologically, too, Mrs. Luczywo acknowledged, legalization will be a setback. In recent years the underground weekly has been published on personal computers with laser printers. But the printing house assigned to the above-ground weekly, which it will share with the Communist Party's own daily, *Trybuna Ludu*, has no such sophisticated equipment. . . .

Slogans Ready, Solidarity Takes Stab at the Hustings

By John Tagliabue

CRACOW, Poland, May 7—In a concrete schoolyard in the Nowa Huta district of Cracow, Mieczyslaw Gil's jabbing hand seemed to be poking a hole in a wall of popular doubt about Poland's coming elections.

Three years ago, Mr. Gil sat in prison, serving a four-year term handed down by a military court for his role in setting up Solidarity in 1980 as the East bloc's first free trade union.

Roughly a year ago, fleeing the police and finding shelter in colleagues' apartments and church cellars, Mr. Gil steered the strikes that crippled Nowa Huta's enormous steel mill, ultimately pressuring the Government to recognize Solidarity and introduce sweeping political and economic changes.

Today the burly 45-year-old steel worker is Soldarity candidate in cantankerous Nowa Huta, a Solidarity stronghold, struggling to convince workers that acceptance of elections that are not entirely free—

though the freest Poland has known since World War II—was the politically correct answer to the Government's offer to restore Solidarity.

"These are not yet entirely free elections," Mr. Gil shouted to several hundred Solidarity stalwarts. "In '81 they first legalized us, then crushed us. There will be more seasonal gestures, and we fear that the same thing can happen again. So we are creating democratic institutions to make it less likely."

Glancing over at Edward Nowak, a lanky 39-year-old steelman and Solidarity veteran who shared the platform, Mr. Gil said, "When we sat in the same cell in jail, we never thought we'd be candidates together."

Most of the crowd of several hundred Solidarity supporters would have shared Mr. Gil's incredulity, for in the last few weeks, as the campaign warms up for the elections next month, the unheard of has become the routine. . . .

In at least three areas of Poland, Solidarity has accused the police of tearing down Solidarity campaign posters, and last week Solidarity's national spokesman, Janusz Onyszkiewicz, said the union was dissatisfied with the party's observance of agreements on the number of seats the opposition can contest.

But in Cracow and neighboring towns, large white posters urge: "Vote for Solidarity: Elections '89." Newsstands in Cracow, including those in the principal hotels, sell copies of a local Solidarity weekly, *Glos Wyborczy Solidarnosci*, or Solidarity's Election Voice, whose first issue printed the schedule of Solidarity radio programs.

Poles have already grown used to seeing Solidarity leaders in televised debates, though the union's leaders say coverage by the state television can still be manipulative. Last week, when the union strategist, Adam Michnik, debated the campaign in Gdansk, television broadcast only snippets of remarks highly flattering to the Polish leader, Gen. Wojciech Jaruzelski.

An editorial in the Cracow paper's first issue—published over a cartoon of Karl Marx begging on a streetcorner, hat in outstretched hand—said, "Poland Returns to Europe." . . . Over tripe soup and a pork schnitzel, Mr. Gil reflected on the campaign. "Most difficult to answer are the basic questions involving trust and doubt," he said. "They still don't really believe in it."

"But slowly, slowly a mood is building," he went on. "People are becoming aware of enormous changes."

At the rally Saturday in Nowa Huta, Mr. Nowak got the most

applause when he summed up his view of Communist Poland since the war.

"For forty years we've been driving in one car," he said. "They're trying to paint it, to fix it, repair it. We have to change to another car."

SPRING 1989

Something was stirring in China. On April 15, Hu Yaobang, the maverick who had sought to steer China away from Communist orthodoxy, died at the age of 73. He had reportedly suffered a heart attack at a politburo meeting a week earlier. He had been on the Long March in 1934 and 1935 and he lived through the Cultural Revolution, when his head was shaved and he was sent to the countryside to tend livestock. But then after Mao died in 1977, he and his mentor Deng Xiaoping mounted a slow but steady return to power. Then in 1987 he was again forced out of the innermost circles of leadership after a siege of student demonstrations. More than any of the Chinese oligarchs, he had captured the hearts of young people, and within days of his death, students at Beijing University sneaked off at night to hang up illegal posters that expressed sadness and guilt. In the middle of April, Nicholas D. Kristoff wrote in The Times that "The common theme in the posters was that the wrong leader had died." Among the messages he noted in the poster campaign were "Xiaoping is still healthy at the age of 84. Yaobang, only 73 years old, has died first," and, "When you were deprived of your post, why didn't we stand up? We feel guilty. Our conscience bleeds." In the last two weeks of April the students became bolder with each passing day, moving out from the campuses onto the streets. Their marches grew steadily in size, surging ever closer to the seat of political power.

Urging Chinese Democracy, 100,000 Surge Past Police

By Nicholas D. Kristof

BEIJING, May 4—A defiant and enthusiastic crowd of more than 100,000 workers and students forced its way through police cordons in the capital today to demand more democracy, and smaller demonstrations were held in many other cities around China.

41

The occasion for the marches today was the 70th anniversary of famous nationalist demonstrations in Beijing that led to the May 4 Movement, which led a generation of Chinese intellectuals to seek a major re-examination of Chinese society. The movement also foreshadowed the rise of the Communist Party.

By far the largest demonstration outside Beijing was in Shanghai, China's largest city, where the crowd suddenly swelled tonight to perhaps 20,000 or more, said a Western resident of the city who witnessed the march.

The flurry of demonstrations was among the largest in Communist China's history, and in Beijing the protest appeared to draw record numbers of workers.

While the nucleus of the crowd was still students, they were easily outnumbered by the young workers who came to express dissatisfaction with the inflation, corruption and other frustrations that most bother them. Inflation is running at a rate of about 27 percent a year.

"I hope student demonstrations will make the Government do something about inflation," said Yuan Jun, an iron worker who came from out of town to join in the demonstration. "But even if the students don't bring up the inflation problem, I'll still support them. They demand press freedom, which is something we need, too. Now we have no freedom at all."

Worker participation in the recent unrest has been one of the Government's greatest fears, but today the workers still seemed to be coalescing around the students rather than forming their own organizations. This is likely to give the Government some reprieve, particularly as most of the students seem to be planning to end their class boycott and focus their attention once more on their books.

Wuer Kaixi, a student leader, told the crowd that the students reserved the right to hold further demonstrations, but for now there was no clear issue that seemed likely to send large numbers of them into the streets.

Their protests began as mourning for Hu Yaobang, the dismissed Communist Party leader who died April 15, and then drew inspiration in the approach to today's anniversary of the founding of the May 4 Movement.

Important anniversaries often carry more political significance and resonance in China than they would in the West. Because the original May 4 protesters—numbering only 3,000—have been sanctified by history, both the Government and the students have been jostling to gain the legitimacy that comes with being seen as the rightful inheritors of the May 4 legacy.

The Communist Party held its own parades and festivals today to commemmorate the anniversary, but they paled beside the outpouring for the students' illegal march.

In the northeastern city of Changchun, 8,000 to 10,000 student demonstrators gathered at the provincial headquarters this afternoon, while in the port city of Dalian more than 2,000 students from several universities marched for democracy, a Western diplomat said tonight.

In addition, the diplomat said, student demonstrators in the northeastern cities of Shenyang and Harbin were locked into their campuses and not allowed to march onto the streets.

Other small demonstrations also occurred today in the cities of Changsha, Nanjing, Wuhan and Xian, reports reaching Beijing said.

The protests today were a display of support for the students and their demands—particularly freedom of the press, which has become an increasingly important issue in the last few weeks. But the march in Beijing lacked the drama and fervor of the protest a week ago, which is already being viewed as a historic occasion by students and intellectuals in China.

On that occasion, a crackdown seemed imminent, and army troops had been called in to stop the students. Some thought that the demonstration would fizzle completely, and yet more than 150,000 protesters, applauded by hundreds of thousands of cheering onlookers, swept through the city like a liberating army, forcing the Government to back away from the repression that had apparently been planned.

Perhaps it was only a sign of how much has changed in the last two weeks that today a crowd of more than 100,000 could roll through police lines to take over Tiananmen Square, the political focal point of the nation, without anyone registering much surprise.

"The Government can't crack down on us," said a worker in a radio factory who took part in today's march, "because 90 percent of the population supports the students."

Several hundred journalists for official publications gathered today in front of the official New China News Agency to protest false and biased reporting and to call for the reinstatement of Qin Benli, the editor of a Shanghai newspaper and one of the boldest journalists in the country. Mr. Qin was dismissed last week after insisting on publishing comments that supported student demonstrators.

Students were delighted to receive support from the journalists, and as they marched by they shouted, "Long live journalists with a conscience!"

The journalists shouted back: "We support you! Long live the students!"

The audacity of the students was spreading. In early May, more and more workers were joining in the marches and journalists were also finding their voices.

China Newspapers Try New Openness
By Sheryl WuDunn

BEIJING, May 5—After studiously ignoring pro-democracy protests for the last two weeks, China's official newspapers seemed today to display a new openness in their reports of a mass demonstration held here on Thursday.

Photographs of streets filled with students waving banners as far as the eye could see ran on the front pages of most newspapers. The newspapers also reported details of demonstrations not only in the capital but in many other cities. Some of those demonstrations had not previously been reported.

The largest demonstration was in Beijing, where 100,000 people gathered in the central square to call for greater democracy and an end to corruption.

China Youth News reported demonstrations in at least 11 cities outside Beijing, and reported that in Shanghai, Xian and Wuhan, more than 10,000 students took part. The other cities were Changsha, Hangzhou, Nanjing, Taiyuan, Chengdu, Chongqing, Lanzhou, and Xining.

More accurate reporting has been one of the demonstrators' principal demands, and today's articles and photos seemed to be a move to satisfy the demand. While the articles were not as comprehensive as the students would have liked, the surprise was that they appeared at all.

The articles noted that the demonstrations were called on the occasion of the 70th anniversary of the nationalist demonstrations that led to the May 4 Movement. The movement called for China's political and cultural modernization and led to the birth of the Chinese Communist Party. To some extent, the articles tried to portray the demonstrators as patriotic citizens commemorating a historic occasion.

But the articles also referred explicitly to the demands of the student demonstrators who blanketed Tiananmen Square for an afternoon of speeches, chanting and singing.

"Several hundred thousand spectators watched the students marching along the streets, and many of them donated cold drinks and food," read part of an article from the official People's Daily. "As long as there is corruption, this country will never be stable," the article quoted a banner as saying.

Such articles were unusual only given the Government's previous determination to avoid references to the demonstrations. It is not clear if today's articles and photos in the official press mark a permanent step toward openness that will let Chinese people learn about events as they happen.

Today's newspapers also quoted the Communist Party General Secretary, Zhao Ziyang, as saying that corruption occurs partly because there is a "lack of openness in the system of work." That seemed to be another call for more openness in Chinese society, one of the major student demands.

University students said today that they had no immediate plans for further demonstrations.

From the outset, the students in China, like the Polish workers in Solidarity, had stressed nonviolence, but in Beijing the demonstrators were evolving their own specific form of petition and protest.

A Chinese Lesson in Polite Protest
By Nicholas D. Kristof

BEIJING, May 6—For anyone tempted to think that rebellious Chinese students must be fighting for capitalism and multi-party democracy, a banner fluttering over People's University marchers on Thursday was a rude shock. It read, "We firmly support the correct leadership of the Communist Party."

If South Korean university students are at the militant extreme, totally rejecting the Government and battering lines of police with firebombs and wooden staves, then Chinese demonstrators are at the peaceful extreme.

They sometimes go out of their way to say nice things about the Communist Party, even when it is clear they do not believe them, and they overwhelm the police as much with courtesy as with force.

45

When approaching lines of the police, the students try to ingratiate themselves by chanting, "The people love the people's police; the people's police love the people." After some hard pushing, but never any blows, the police usually give way to the students.

That is when the demonstrators pause to bellow, "Thank you, police." A few students are even assigned to pick up any shoes lost in the shoving and return them to their owners, be they police or protesters.

Such tactics, which resemble those employed in the Philippine uprising rather than those in South Korea, have been enormously successful so far. It has been difficult for the Communist Party to crack down on those who politely call on the party to uphold its own ideals of honesty and democracy. And the students' charm has won grins and support from many ordinary workers.

Student comments in favor of Communist rule are perhaps more difficult to decipher, but interviews with dozens of students in the last two weeks suggest that they are partly tactical and partly sincere. Early last week, when the Government seemed about to proclaim a crackdown against students who it said wanted to overthrow the socialist system and Communist rule, many student leaders seemed to feel that their best defense was to deny the charges and wage their struggle for more democracy in the guise of a devoted attempt to cleanse the party of its faults.

The fiercest slogans—like "Overthrow the dictatorship!"—were mostly replaced by slogans like "Down with graft!" Students also began to wave pro-Communist banners, rather like amulets intended to ward off the police.

Yet the slogans are not only a form of protection, for many students genuinely believe in Communist Party rule. Or, perhaps more accurately, they genuinely believe that there is no alternative any time soon to Communist Party rule.

"In an ideal world, a multi-party system would be better," said Xia A. P., a graduate student in politics who has taken part in the demonstrations. "But it's not feasible now. We want what is practical."

"It would be difficult for the Communist Party to move forward without a push," Mr. Xia added. "The aim of the student movement is to give the Communist Party an outside push so that it can reform itself."

Several of the student movement's leaders have said that they would consider joining the Communist Party at some point in their careers. Even Wang Dan, the Beijing University student leader who is regarded as among the most aggressive in the movement, scarcely paused when he was asked if he supported the leading role of the Communist Party in China.

"You can say I support correct leadership by the Communist Party," Mr. Wang said, putting emphasis on the word "correct." He seemed to mean that he was willing to tolerate the leading role of the party, so long as it was upright and permitted greater democracy.

When a group of students at Qinghua University was asked if they opposed the Communist Party, they mustered as much indignation as possible.

"The reason we demonstrate is that we still have some faith in the Communist Party," one said.

Another added: "We're not against the Government, just against the way it is run. It's a question of the party atmosphere, of corruption and of the bureaucracy."

Then the students looked a bit uneasy, as if they might be giving a foreign reporter the wrong idea about their goals. One ventured: "Remember, though, we can't always say what we think."

In private, students express almost no interest in socialism or communism as an ideology, and say instead that they favor whatever will make China strong and rich. But in the absence of any realistic alternative, and to avoid being labeled as counterrevolutionaries, they are willing to say they support the Communist Party.

Even this degree of consensus seems to break down when students contemplate the economy. When they are asked if they favor capitalism or socialism, the overwhelming majority of students reply that they do not know.

"I haven't thought about that," said Xiong Wei, a 22-year-old electrical engineer and student leader.

As the protests mounted, the old men who ruled China intensified their deliberations on whether to try to accommodate the demands, co-opt, divert, or crush those who were raising them. As an atmosphere of crisis thickened, the advocates of gentler approaches clashed with those who argued for harsh responses.

·

China Party Chief Appears to Gain in Power Struggle

By Nicholas D. Kristof

BEIJING, May 13—An unannounced Politburo meeting has endorsed the moderate line of the Communist Party leader, Zhao Ziyang, toward student demonstrators, including more discussions with the students and limited steps toward greater democracy, Chinese with high party connections say.

The situation remains extremely unsettled, as the debate over recent student demonstrations continues to reverberate through the leadership and exacerbate the power struggle here. However, three Chinese familiar with the Politburo proceedings say that the result of a tense meeting held on Wednesday and Thursday in the capital was to strengthen Mr. Zhao's faction, favoring more rapid economic and political change over one preferring a more cautious path.

The result, at least for now, is a reversal in the fortunes of Mr. Zhao, whose influence had slipped greatly over the last year and reached its nadir at the beginning of the student protests last month. Many of the students had worried that their demonstrations might lead to his dismissal.

The eventual outcome of the party's internal conflicts remains uncertain, however, and officials say that further student demonstrations might affect the competition and possibly hurt Mr. Zhao. Today, students continued their protests by taking a new tactic and going on a hunger strike to back their demands for more democracy and a meaningful dialogue with the nation's leaders.

More than 20,000 spectators watched in Beijing's Tiananmen Square as more than 1,000 university students staged the strike in the middle of the square. Some students said they would remain until Mikhail S. Gorbachev, the Soviet leader, arrives on Monday for the first Chinese-Soviet summit meeting in 30 years. . . .

And indeed, Mr. Gorbachev was once again being cast in the role of a catalyst. The apostle of economic modernization and some greater though still limited freedom of expression was being hailed in China as a man pointing the way out of a fossilized system just as he had been welcomed on earlier trips abroad to such places as Hungary and Czechoslovakia.

China's Hero of Democracy: Gorbachev
By Nicholas D. Kristof

BEIJING, May 13—When Mikhail S. Gorbachev arrives on Monday for four days of talks designed to restore normal relations between China and the Soviet Union, he will be cast in the unusual role of champion of democracy.

It is the role that American Presidents like to fill, but there is much more anticipation in China's democratic movement today than there was on the eve of President Bush's visit in February. Almost everybody seems to think that the Soviet leader's visit will do more for democracy in China than Mr. Bush's trip did, and some believe that the Soviet Union will do more than the United States to inspire political liberalization in China.

"China used to be afraid of influence from the West," said Yan Jiaqi, a prominent political scientist and supporter of greater democracy. "Now we are afraid of influence from the Soviet Union.

"If we want to keep out Western influence, we can say we're against 'bourgeois liberalization,' or against 'total Westernization,' " Mr. Yan added. "But we can't use that pretext against Soviet influence. Nobody, not even Deng Xiaoping, can resist the Soviet influence, because there is no ideological concept to resist it."

The perception of Mr. Gorbachev as an evangelist for democracy might surprise some political dissidents in the Soviet Union, and it has little to do with the real purposes of his talks with Chinese leaders from Monday through Thursday. The agenda of the summit includes trade, economic cooperation and the Cambodian conflict, not democracy and human rights.

Nonetheless, the enthusiasm for Mr. Gorbachev is a tribute to the extent to which he has opened up the political system in the Soviet Union. It is a commonplace, here as well as abroad, that China has gone further than the Soviet Union in economic liberalization but that the Soviet Union has done much more in political liberalization.

The result is not quite Soviet fever, for most intellectuals here seem much more interested in visiting New York than Leningrad. Many seem to regard the Soviet restructuring less as a model to be meticulously examined than as a key debating point to push for change in China.

The support for Mr. Gorbachev is a deep embarrassment for the man who otherwise might well regard the summit as a personal triumph: Deng Xiaoping. Mr.Gorbachev is coming to Beijing mostly on Mr. Deng's terms, having withdrawn troops from Afghanistan, reduced Soviet forces on the Chinese border and brought pressure on Vietnam to end its occupation of Cambodia. Moreover, this may be one of Mr. Deng's last major acts, for the capital is full of rumors of his impending retirement.

Mr. Deng, however, has been humiliated by the recent student demonstrations, and by the successful defiance of his order last month that they be suppressed. After having made his career as a daring reformer, Mr. Deng is suddenly made to look like a stodgy old man outshined by the strong young socialist dynamo from Moscow.

The contrasts have been evident even in the Chinese press. The *China Youth News* published a long account in which a Soviet citizen was quoted as saying that before Mr. Gorbachev "our country was run by old and sickly people who need help to walk, who lack the breath to speak, whose minds are stiff and muddled." In a country where criticisms are always made indirectly, this appeared to be a comment on Mr. Deng and a call for "a young and strong leader," as the article described Mr. Gorbachev.

The differences are also evident on China's campuses, where the talk is often bitterly critical of Mr. Deng these days. At Beijing University, the most important institution in the country, thousands of students have signed an open letter inviting Mr. Gorbachev to speak at the school. The authorities have said that Mr. Gorbachev's schedule is full, but the gesture was an indication that many students who dislike their own leader regard Mr. Gorbachev as a hero. . . .

The arrival of Mr. Gorbachev in Peking, on a visit that had been scheduled long before, would have been historic even without the growing uproar in the streets. The Soviet leader had come to signal an end to the split between the world's two most powerful Communist states. But the noises and shouts raised by ordinary people were clearly being heard in the chambers where the leaders meeting.

Gorbachev Meets Deng in Beijing; Protest Goes On
By Nicholas D. Kristof

BEIJING, Tuesday, May 16—Deng Xiaoping and Mikhail S. Gorbachev shook hands today to signal the formal end of three decades of hostility between China and the Soviet Union.

The two leaders then met for two and a half hours. Afterward, Mr. Deng was the host at a banquet for the Soviet President.

The 84-year-old Mr. Deng, whose frailty and stumbling speech contrasted with the strength and vigor of the 58-year-old Mr. Gorbachev, said as they met that several years ago he had noted a new mood in the Soviet Union and had hoped for the summit meeting. Mr. Deng added that he believed the new Soviet outlook held the potential to help resolve what he described as the central problem in international affairs, the Soviet-American relationship.

"For a long time, cold war and confrontation have made the international situation tense," Mr. Deng, the foremost Chinese leader, said. "This leads nowhere."

The summit meeting, the first between the two countries since 1959, is described by both sides as marking the beginning of normalization of relations. However, the domestic atmosphere in Beijing was decidedly abnormal because of continuing protests.

In a major loss of face for the Chinese leadership, Monday's itinerary had to be repeatedly adjusted to avoid 150,000 students and spectators who took over Tiananmen Square. While Mr. Gorbachev, the Soviet leader, did not directly refer to the student demonstrations in his meeting on Monday with President Yang Shangkun, the entire day seemed to be an exotic dance in which the Chinese side tried to shield Mr. Gorbachev from the protesters.

The demonstrations were doubly embarrassing for the Chinese leaders because of the obvious enthusiasm that many of the protesters felt for Mr. Gorbachev. Several had prepared banners in Russian hailing him as a great reformer, and a crowd of workers and bicyclists applauded when he drove past them on his way to the Great Hall of the People.

Mr. Gorbachev was to lay a wreath at a monument in the center of the square, but because of the crowds of protesters occupying the area, the Chinese Government canceled the event this morning.

Because of the demonstrations, the Chinese Government held its welcoming ceremony for Mr. Gorbachev at the airport, instead of on the edge of the square where the students gathered. Officials then had to drive Mr. Gorbachev by a back road to his guest house when students blocked the avenue that had been decked with Soviet and Chinese flags in preparation for Mr. Gorbachev's entry.

Later, the Chinese postponed the discussions between Mr. Gorbachev and President Yang by two hours, and then changed the site of his arrival at the Great Hall of the People from the main entrance first to a side door and then to a back door.

Despite the adjustments and confusion, Mr. Gorbachev seemed in good spirits on Monday on the few occasions when it was possible to catch a glimpse of him. His plane touched down at noon, and he and his wife, Raisa, stepped out to a 21-gun salute and a welcome from the Moscow-educated Mr. Yang, who later practiced his rusty Russian on the Soviet leader. When driving around the capital, Mr. Gorbachev was grinning broadly as he waved to bystanders along the roads.

The meeting and banquet with President Yang, an 81-year-old veteran revolutionary whose post is largely honorary, was cordial and took as its tone the need to forget past differences and begin a new chapter in bilateral relations.

"There is no need for us to recollect the past," Mr. Yang said, quoting Mr. Deng. Mr. Gorbachev agreed, saying, "That is an approach that we welcome."

The meetings of leaders were having an impact on the streets.

150,000 Lift Their Voices for Change
By Sheryl WuDunn

BEIJING, May 15—One after another today, groups of teachers, professors, museum workers, factory workers, writers, artists, scholars, entrepreneurs, low-level officials, middle-school students, and even journalists from the official *People's Daily* paraded into Tiananmen Square behind their own wide, colorful banners.

They sang the "Internationale" and chanted anti-Government slogans, while inside in the adjacent Great Hall of the People, President Yang Shangkun held a banquet this evening for the Soviet leader, Mikhail S. Gorbachev.

The ebullient crowd of about 150,000 protesters and spectators rallied to show support for a hunger strike on the opening day of the first Chinese-Soviet summit meeting in 30 years. . . .

"In the Soviet Union, they have Gorbachev," read a banner carried by students. "In China, we have whom?" . . .

"Sell the Mercedes-Benzes to pay the national debt!" shouted several thousand citizens as they marched into Tiananmen Square, where the hunger strikers, visibly weakened on their third day without food, lay sprawled in one corner under the scorching sun.

"This day will go down in history," said Zhao Xiaoyan, a reporter with *Science and Technology Daily*, who marched to the square with a large group of journalists. "Today, we have gone beyond the students. It it clear that the Chinese people believe that the Communist Party cannot continue to adopt the kind of attitude it takes toward its people."

The diplomatic business was completed.

Soviets and China Resuming Normal Ties After 30 Years; Beijing Pledges "Democracy"
By Bill Keller

BEIJING, May 16—If Mikhail S. Gorbachev were to stray from his diplomatically constrained itinerary for a visit to the unofficial festival of democracy under way on Tiananmen Square, he would surely be flattered by the banners in Chinese and Russian hailing him as a champion of political liberty.

But as a Soviet consumer, he might be more impressed by the slogans in Japanese—Nikon, Panasonic, Ricoh, Olympus—displayed on the cameras and tape recorders wielded in profusion by the protesting Chinese students and their sympathizers.

While Mr. Gorbachev and China's leaders learn to like each other better, the citizens of the two giant neighbors are beginning to envy each other. Russia is getting freer, China is getting richer, and at the human level far below the meeting of the leaders, the people of each country are demanding more of what the other has.

The experts have long recognized that economic change—the breakup of collective farming, the growth of private commerce, the decentralization of industry—has progressed a good deal farther in China, while political liberalization—a less inhibited press, a measure of democracy, a promise of civil rights—is far more advanced in the Soviet Union.

Mr. Gorbachev's visit here has helped advertise this to the ordinary citizens of each country, and has also raised hopes that each can learn something from the other.

In Moscow, extensive and positive press coverage has been given to China's experiments with private farming and stock markets, as Soviet journalists decided that Mr. Gorbachev's visit made China topical.

And in Beijing, a consumer attuned to the paucity of Soviet consumer choice can only marvel at the things money will buy.

Within earshot of the student brass band that blared the "Internationale" for the occupiers of central Beijing this afternoon, a shopper finds stores stacked to the ceilings with Chinese and imported electronics, private shops displaying stylish shoes turned out by China-Hong Kong joint ventures, street vendors peddling strawberries and watermelons, and restaurants where the meals are cheap and decent. What is more, there is often quick and cordial service, something as exotic to Muscovites as the Forbidden City.

A bit of that in Moscow, and Mr. Gorbachev would be almost as popular at home as he is on Tiananmen Square.

In Beijing, the student bullhorns and bicycle brigades have quickly spread the word that the Soviet Union is a center of something vaguely known as political reform.

The students, joined each day by droves of journalists, intellectuals and factory workers, demand greater press freedom, free speech, the recognition of their independent students' unions, an attack on official corruption and legal safeguards against an authoritarian Government.

"We have rice, but we need laws," said a Beijing University language student who was pleased to learn from a Chinese television documentary this week that Mr. Gorbachev graduated from law school. "Many, many laws."

Mr. Gorbachev is less the inspiration for this movement than an opportunity to flaunt its demands in a way the leadership cannot ignore.

"As a great political reformer, we urge Mikhail Gorbachev to talk to the Government on our behalf, for humanitarian reasons," Wang Dan, a student leader from Beijing University, said at a news conference today. . . .

According to Zhang Binjiu, a research scholar at Beijing University, another Gorbachev-era event that struck a powerful chord here in this corruption-conscious society was the bribery trial last December of the son-in-law of Leonid I. Brezhnev, the former Soviet leader.

Most Chinese know few details of the Soviet experiment, but they declare with pride that given the chance they will quickly surpass it.

"The flowers of political reform blossom in the Soviet Union," Mr. Zhang said. "But the tree will bear fruit in China."

In truth, the grass is not as green in either China or Russia as it seems from across the border.

The chanting crowds in the center of Beijing might be disillusioned to learn that similar demonstrations in the Soviet Union are some-times set upon by riot policemen, that Moscow intellectuals consider their democracy still tenuous and halfway, and that some of the new Soviet laws impose new restrictions on protest and expression.

The Muscovite, in turn, might be disenchanted to learn that the VCR's freely available in Chinese cities cost an average worker's annual paycheck, to see the occasional run on the banks when a wave of inflation fever hits, or to visit the squalid, tenement-style dormitories in which the protesting students live six to a room.

The disparity in the two countries' routes from Communist orthodoxy has its reasons. Deng Xiaoping, the senior Chinese leader, introduced his version of perestroika, called gaige, 10 years ago by freeing peasants to be private farmers. China started so far behind that things could hardly help but get demonstrably better.

The Soviet Union has implemented perestroika piecemeal, mostly in the last two years, and many of the proclaimed revisions have been thwarted by the dead weight of an outmoded industrial economy.

The Chinese, in turn, felt no pressure to democratize, and the aging leadership had no inclination to share the Communist Party's power.

Mr. Gorbachev, on the other hand, recognized that his sluggish and authoritarian bureaucracy was the worst impediment to modernization. That is why the Soviet leader came more quickly to the view that political and economic change must go hand in hand.

The Soviet Union, most Russians would agree, has not yet proved his point.

But the respective discontents of the Chinese and Soviet people have proven that neither economic freedom nor political freedom is wholly satisfying by itself.

Gorbachev Praises the Students and Declares Reform Is Necessary
By Bill Keller

BEIJING, May 17—Mikhail S. Gorbachev today portrayed the popular uprising that has engulfed the Chinese capital as part of a painful but healthy worldwide upheaval in Communist countries.

In his most extensive comments on the demonstrations that have disrupted and overshadowed the Chinese-Soviet reconciliation here, Mr. Gorbachev cautiously praised the students who began the huge vigil for greater democracy and repeatedly declared that economic change was impossible without political reform.

"I am convinced that we are participating in a very serious turning point in the development of world socialism," the Soviet leader said at a news conference when asked to assess the unrest here and in his own country.

All Communist countries, he said, are headed at different paces toward greater freedom of expression, democracy and individual rights.

"These processes are painful, but they are necessary," he said.

The Soviet leader was careful not to be seen taking sides in the domestic political struggle provoked by the unrest, but it now appears clear he has used his three days in Beijing to encourage political liberalization and indirectly to do what he could to promote the aspirations of the self-styled reformer, Zhao Ziyang, the Chinese Communist Party leader, in an internal power struggle.

Mr. Gorbachev's comments today, in a speech to Chinese intellectuals, a televised interview and the news conference, also included calls for patience and discipline, but he avoided any direct criticism of the students.

In a meeting with Mr. Zhao on Tuesday, Mr. Gorbachev reportedly expressed his distaste for "hotheads" who demand that change be accomplished overnight. Today he said he had received a letter from the students praising the Soviet moves toward political liberalization, and added, "I value their position."

He commended the Chinese leadership for opening a political dialogue with the students, a conciliatory approach that initially met firm resistance from some senior Chinese leaders. . . .

Those within the Chinese leadership who might have been hoping that Mr. Gorbachev's visit and the declarations of restored amity with Moscow would appease or divert the protesters had their hopes dashed very quickly. Instead of quieting down, the crowds became even more insistent.

A Million Chinese March, Adding Pressure for Change

By Sheryl WuDunn

BEIJING, May 17—Sirens wailed as ambulances whizzed by, carrying hunger strikers who have fainted after five days without eating, when the gray-haired schoolteacher suddenly pulled out her handkerchief and cried.

"Our hearts bleed when we hear the sound of ambulances," she said, her voice breaking. "They are no longer children. They are the hope of China."

The teacher, like more than a million other people in the capital, had taken to the streets to support the hunger-striking students and express her demands for democracy. When a group of students approached, passing around a cardboard box to collect money for their cause, she reached into her faded purse and pulled out the equivalent of $5—a week's wages for her—and put it into the box.

"I want to thank them," she said, sniffling. "They represent our hearts. They represent our hopes." Scenes like that near Tiananmen Square—the Square of the Gate of Heavenly Peace—occurred all over central Beijing today, as office clerks, factory workers, bank tellers, journalists and taxicab drivers fought through vast seas of people to get near the enclave of hunger-striking students, now the center of China's swelling democracy movement.

The twist and tangle of people, bicycles, pedicabs, cars and banners froze the steady flow of traffic, and when protesters had no room to march, they cheerfully walked around in circles.

But as confusion bordering on chaos spread across the capital, with more and more people leaving their dank offices and small homes for the open air, a certain order is evident on the streets, revealing the touch of a tightly run organization of students.

Specially designated students used long ropes to keep a single lane free on the otherwise jammed Avenue of Eternal Peace and on Tiananmen Square, so that spectators did not get in the way of ambulances carrying hunger strikers.

The result is that the ambulances dash by at 40 miles an hour, while all around them are pedestrians who struggle even to inch forward through the mass of demonstrators.

Just a week or two ago, many Beijing residents patronized the students, saying they were a bit too idealistic and too inclined to tie up traffic with their demonstrations. But now the city's citizens, from the young entrepreneurs in business suits to the old ladies sitting in front of their homes, compete in praising the students.

"The student movement is terrific!" an elderly police officer shouted to a group of high school students and workers who had gathered to listen. "If the Government commands a crackdown, will I obey their order? No, I will go against it."

Marchers and spectators, chanting and singing and screaming, shoved their way back and forth on the Avenue of Eternal Peace in front of Zhongnanhai, the Communist Party headquarters, where the country's leaders live. Even late at night, the entrance was packed with 2,000 workers, students, and other protesters shouting for the Prime Minister: "Li Peng, come out! Li Peng, come out!" In the afternoon, students formed a semicircular human fence to protect the leaders' compound from the possibility of being stormed by angry workers. Just inside the human ring, but outside the doorway, students turned the area into a place for resting and eating.

Deep in the heart of Tiananmen Square, the nation's political center that the democracy fighters have now invaded, inside several rings of students, is a heavily guarded, peaceful, airy enclave where the senior student leaders confer with the hunger strikers and where the containers of water and stacks of medicines—glucose and aspirins and salt tablets—are dispensed.

Here, the nearly 3,000 strikers—sprawling on the ground from exhaustion, heat, lack of food and sleep—are fainting more frequently as the sun sears the square throughout the day.

Every so often, bicycle riders carting wagons of soda water and bread are allowed to penetrate the outer layers of the rings to bring in nourishment for students who are eating but still showing their support by occupying a spot on the square 24 hours a day. Some rise in the early morning, carrying old, dirty banners that they use to help sweep away the litter of the previous day's thousands of spectators.

A makeshift loudspeaker system allows them to announce news of their latest plans or supporters—how much money they have raised, the condition of strikers, a letter of sympathy. They have a copying machine, and every time they distribute a stack of pamphlets, spectators fight for every scrap of paper.

The outpouring of sympathy stretches two miles in either direction, from the faces that peer out of office buildings, to the posters hanging out the windows, to the cars whose passengers lean out to wave banners or pictures of Zhou Enlai, the former Prime Minister who is now a hero for many young people.

Sensing that this is a historic time that they want to play a part in, many workers have come to help. Often that means buying food and drink for students, even if they don't ask for it.

"We're very moved by the people coming out to support us," said T. F. Wang, a Beijing University student who was carrying a watermelon and box of Popsicles that people had handed to him. "This turnout adds to the pressure on the leadership to come out and talk to us."

In the days that followed Mr. Gorbachev's departure the tempo of China's upheaval quickened and a sense of menace grew.

Crowds in Street Ask Deng's Ouster
By Nicholas D. Kristof

BEIJING, May 18—More than a million Chinese took to the streets of Beijing Wednesday in an extraordinary outpouring of support for more democracy.

The protests, amounting almost to a general strike, continued this morning and greatly increased the pressure on the Government to sacrifice one or more top officials and speed political liberalization.

In an attempt to defuse the situation, several of the nation's top leaders visited hospitalized students on a hunger strike early this morning to show their concern. But the crowds this morning seemed at least as militant as those on Wednesday, and many people said they would be satisfied only with the removal of the country's senior leader, Deng Xiaoping, or Prime Miniser Li Peng. . . .

Chinese Premier Issues a Warning to the Protesters
By Nicholas D. Kristof

BEIJING, Friday, May 19—Prime Minister Li Peng warned Thursday that chaos in Beijing was spreading all over the country, but his demand for restraint was ignored by up to a million people who braved a driving rain to demonstrate once more for greater democracy.

To defuse the situation, the Government capitulated on a key student demand by arranging a nationally televised meeting between Mr.

Li and leaders of the students' pro-democracy movement.

In another gesture of conciliation, Mr. Li and the Communist Party leader, Zhao Ziyang, went to Tiananmen Square in central Beijing before dawn today to visit some of the 3,000 hunger strikers whose protest has galvanized the nation into mass demonstrations of support.

"We've come too late," Mr. Zhao told the students, according to the official New China News Agency. "You have good intentions. You want our country to become better. The problems you have raised will eventually be resolved. But things are complicated, and there must be a process to resolve these problems."

Mr. Zhao added that "the whole of Beijing" was discussing the hunger strike, and he called on the students to end the fast. . . .

The Chinese leadership has been split about how to handle the challenge from the students. Mr. Zhao's comments appeared to be an attempt to win support from demonstrators and to put blame on other leaders for adopting a harder line and thereby complicating the situation.

The meeting today in Tiananmen Square appeared to be much more cordial than the students' televised encounter with Mr. Li on Thursday, in which the Prime Minister refused to discuss issues raised by the students and hinted at a crackdown if the disorder continued. . . .

"Most people didn't do any work today," said a graying, heavily callused worker of Beijing's No. 2 Chemical Factory. "You can call it a strike, and it will continue until the Government responds to our demands. We're terribly angry, because the Government won't agree to a meaningful dialogue with the students. What kind of a Government do we have?. . . ."

The demonstration in the capital on Thursday was noteworthy not only for the numbers of people who braved the rain, but also for the degree of organization. Many workers clearly had the support of their work units, for they carried the official banners of their factories. Several said Communist Party cadres had approved of the protest.

The degree of organization did not necessarily indicate some hidden hand encouraging the demonstrators to benefit a faction in China's leadership. The workers all denied that this was the case, and some said their local Communist Party cells had simply become sufficiently independent of the central party organization that they did not worry about disobeying higher officials.

As on Wednesday, the organizations represented in the demonstrations included an array of institutions that are close to the party and the Government. A few units from the army arrived in the square, and so did others from the police and several Government ministries.

The army was called in. Was this a prelude for a violent crackdown like the tank-led invasions that had crushed the Budapest uprising of 1956 or Prague's liberal spring in 1968? Or were the Chinese getting ready to spring the trap of martial law as Poland's General Jaruzelski had done in December of 1981, when thousands of members of Solidarity suddenly found themselves detained?

China Hard-Liners Send Troops to Beijing
By Nicholas D. Kristof

BEIJING, Saturday, May 20—The Government called troops into the capital this morning and imposed martial law in parts of the city to crack down on China's growing democracy movement. But tens of thousands of people rushed out of their homes to block troops from reaching student demonstrators in the central square.

"We must adopt firm and resolute measures to end the turmoil swiftly," Prime Minister Li Peng said in a speech broadcast shortly after midnight. "If we fail to put an end to such chaos immediately and let it go unchecked, it will very likely lead to a situation which none of us want to see."

Chinese with access to information at the highest level said the Communist Party leader, Zhao Ziyang, had been stripped of all power but retained his title of General Secretary of the party.

Mr. Zhao was apparently deprived of his authority because he was too conciliatory toward the demonstrators and because he lost a power struggle with Mr. Li. Chinese said the nation's senior leader, Deng Xiaoping, removed Mr. Zhao and put Mr. Li in charge of the party as well as the Government.

The Beijing municipal authorities imposed strict limits on the activities of foreign journalists, banning interviews or taping on the streets or at government offices, schools, factories and mines. "Any violators will be stopped according to the law," the order said.

The Government ordered the Cable News Network to halt transmissions, a move that also shut down transmissions by NBC News, which was sharing equipment with the cable network. CBS News and ABC News reported similar restrictions.

In mid-morning, loudspeakers on Tiananmen Square in the center of Beijing announced that martial law had been imposed in some parts of the capital. The announcement said this meant restrictions on movement within the city, but it did not give details. The crowd of workers and students in the square had welled by then to about 200,000. . . .

The announcement of a crackdown set the stage for a confrontation between the Government and the vast numbers of people who have joined demonstrations for more democracy in the capital and more than 20 other cities.

More than one million people demonstrated in Beijing this week for greater democracy—often calling for the resignations of Mr. Li and Mr. Deng—and many students seemed to think that the next few days would see an enormous uprising against the Government.

"This is a people's revolution, and the people will win," Z. G. Yang, a history scholar, said as he stood near the trucks immobilized at the western outskirts. "We will stay here around the clock, and we won't let them leave."

Many others were less optimistic about a short-run victory. A 33-year-old army engineer who had rushed out of his home to block the troops, said, "If the Government is determined to resort to violence, the people can't stop the army."

Before dawn, citizens hurried to Tiananmen Square or to places where they had heard that army convoys were approaching. Groups of students set up roadblocks every few hundred yards on the Avenue of Eternal Peace to stop private cars and demand a ride to the site where the soldiers were blocked. . . .

Sad but Defiant, Chinese Stand Up to Troops
By Sheryl WuDunn

BEIJING, Saturday, May 20—The 1,000 troops looked out in bewilderment from their immobilized convoy of 21 trucks in western Beijing today to find that their world had been turned upside down.

Rather than dispersing student demonstrators, as they had apparently been sent to do, they found themselves protected by students from throngs of residents who wanted to climb on the vehicles and let air out of the tires. The students linked arms and refused to let people through, except a handful who were assigned the task of making speeches imploring the soldiers to join the cause.

"You are our army," said a Chinese businesswoman who gave her name as Linda Liu and seemed near tears as she went from truck to truck pleading with the soldiers. "You are our brothers and sisters. You are Chinese. Our interests are the same as yours. We believe you have a conscience. You must not crush the movement."

Prime Minister Li Peng's speech calling for "resolute and powerful measures to curb turmoil" had barely concluded when students rushed from all parts of the capital to the central square and vowed they would continue their fight for democracy. Later in the day there were reports of violence in the outskirts of the city, but early this morning the confrontations were peaceful.

"Even if there is bloodshed, we are not afraid," said a 27-year-old teacher from Beijing University who then joined in singing the "Internationale" as he linked arms with his colleagues.

Throughout the capital before dawn today, tens of thousands of people, stunned and worried, emerged from their homes after seeing the speech on television—parents with children, workers on trucks, teachers, intellectuals and party officials. As they wiped their blurry eyes and clasped jackets around their nightgowns, many said that they would do what they could to overcome the planned crackdown.

"We're ordinary people, but we heard the speech and we decided we had to do something," said a young man whose body was one link in the human chain formed on Beijing's outer road to keep troops from passing through. "We'll keep this barricade up, because students are protesting for the things we want, and we must protect them."

Those forming the human cordon seemed somewhat disappointed that no troops were to be seen. All over the city, citizens were hailing down cars and trucks to take them to the site of the troops who they were told would remain in Beijing for at least a few days.

Chinese were treated to a rare scene on television in the early hours today. A usually calm and expressionless Mr. Li had given his sternest speech yet, clenching his fists at times and tensing his face in a display of emotion that few ordinary people had seen in him before. Throughout the day on Friday, the television had replayed portions of a critical speech by Mr. Li to hunger-striking students in a Thursday discussion.

The atmosphere all night was tense and excited, as workers defied the Government by jumping into trucks to stage demonstrations of support, shouting slogans and waving banners. Teachers rushed to Tiananmen Square to watch over the weakened hunger strikers and throw warm blankets over the students.

As the Prime Minister's speech blared again and again, the city's residents rushed to and fro in large packs, tilting their ears to catch a word from the nearest orator or passing on the latest rumor about the Communist Party leader, Zhao Ziyang, who had apparently fallen from power.

Many gathered in small groups at intersections or on the edge of Tiananmen Square to guess what might happen next and to denounce the Government action.

"This Government is crazy," said a law professor whose face was flushed with anger. "How does it think it can go against such a clear demonstration of the people's will? The more blood that is shed, the angrier people will get and the faster the Government will be overthrown. This Government is not worth dying for."

In the streets, along the human picket lines, in the tangles of bicycles, people were discussing the fate of the student movement and what it would mean for the battles the people seemed to have won for press freedom and the freedom to demonstrate and organize.

"China has a long history of submissiveness, and so the progress of this movement came as a surprise to many people," said Q. X. Chen, who had listened to Mr. Li's speech over the official loudspeaker in the central square. "But the people have gained confidence in the last few days, and they will not keep silent anymore."

Facing the People, the Soldiers Fall Back
By Sheryl WuDunn

BEIJING, May 20—When a small convoy of military trucks used to launch tear gas and to spray water on rioters rolled through eastern Beijing early this morning, the soldiers met their first unexpected challenge. An old woman street cleaner rushed up and lay down on the road in front of the trucks.

Several hundred students immediately dashed toward the convoy, and the soldiers found themselves surrounded by Beijing residents who showered them with questions about why they wanted to repress a democratic movement. The residents also offered the troops breakfast: bread, Coca-Cola and Popsicles.

"We absolutely won't repress the people," an officer told the crowd. "We are the people's soldiers." And then the soldiers, so moved that several were crying quietly, drove back the way they had come.

In an awakening of sorts, the Chinese people are tapping the only weapon they can to defend themselves and their struggle for democracy against the tens of thousands of military troops ordered by the Government to move into the city: what many residents were calling "people power."

Martial law in some sectors of Beijing went into effect at 10 A.M. today. But by late tonight none of the special troops that have been brought in from outside Beijing had made much progress into the city. All over the capital, China's "desperados" and "kamikazes"—as they call themselves—were emerging from their silence and standing up for the university students' protest for democracy.

"We have towels for tear gas and maybe buckets of cement to make road blocks, but besides that, we come just as we are—people," said Kong Lingqi, a 39-year-old worker at Capital Iron and Steel Company.

Mr. Kong and the people around him in the Haidian district of Beijing were preparing for the coming of the troops, who they said were based about seven miles away. They were hoping that every inch of the seven miles would be lined with people prepared to bodily block the convoy of military trucks.

The residents tried to obstruct the soldiers with persuasion. They tried to engage soldiers in discussions about the democracy movement, and often they found that the troops had no idea at all of their cause. At least some of the troops said they had been told by their leaders not to read recent newspapers or watch television news.

Flush with exuberance, crowds have massed along roads they think the troops may use to approach Tiananmen Square, the nation's political center. When five military helicopters encircled the area above Tiananmen Square today, thousands of fists went up in the air and angry shouts rose against the Government.

The crowd swelled at many intersections, and the hum of the crowd's voices rose into shrill shouts every so often when someone believed he had spotted the troops.

"We will lie beneath the wheels," said Wang Gang, a 30-year-old leader of a new workers' organization whose members have taken an oath to risk their lives for the students. These 300 "desperados," as they call themselves, wear white bandannas to distinguish themselves from the 400 "deputies" who wear red bandannas and take fewer risks because they have families to protect.

"We are not afraid of guns or bullets," Mr. Wang said. "But we are not allowed to smash glasses, flatten the trucks' tires or beat the drivers."

Mr. Wang, a sweater factory designer who has spent most of the last few days at Tiananmen Square, spent this morning planning where the men in his organization should be placed.

Similar volunteer groups have sprung up all over the capital as angry residents form neighborhood teams that link up with others to protect the area from soldiers.

Often these teams form spontaneously. In the predawn hours today in the southern suburbs of Beijing, 48 armed personnel carriers and 17 trucks holding about 850 policemen found their path impeded by a truck driver who parked his large vehicle right in front of them and then ran around the neighborhood to get the help of neighbors, witnesses said.

"I'll never come again," a lieutenant in the convoy was quoted as saying. "I'll never touch a hair of a student's head."

When troops parked three supply trucks near the Beijing Steel Institute, students drained the gas from the tanks and deflated the tires of the trucks.

This evening, people were out on the streets discussing the political state of affairs and waiting for the troops to come.

In the Xizhimen district, thousands of people crowded around the train station because they had heard that the soldiers may be forced to come in by train since they were having difficulty entering by truck or tank.

"We are waiting here," said a film worker, Wu Jianping, "because we hear there are tens of thousands of troops coming in by train."

Biggest Beijing Crowds So Far Keep Troops from City Center; Party Reported in Bitter Fight
By Nicholas D. Kristof

BEIJING, May 20—Huge throngs, possibly amounting to more than one million Chinese, took to the streets today to defy martial law and block troops from reaching the center of the capital, effectively delaying or preventing the planned crackdown on China's democracy movement.

Troops approaching Beijing on at least five major roads were halted or turned back by the largest crowds to have gathered so far in a month of almost continuous protests. Students and ordinary citizens erected roadblocks or lay in the path of army trucks, while others let the air out of their tires.

Reports from around the country indicated growing support for the democracy movement. The city of Xian was reportedly brought to a standstill by 300,000 protesters, and rallies were reported in Shanghai, Canton and at least half a dozen other cities, and even small villages.

A few clashes were reported, but the confrontations seemed to be mostly peaceful. More troops were reported to be making their way toward Beijing, however, and it was not clear that the people could continue to keep the soldiers out. So far, the troops have not tried very hard to enter Beijing, and a more concerted effort backed by the use of tear gas would almost certainly succeed. But after a full day of confrontation, questions were increasingly raised about the army's readiness to quell the protests. Prime Minister Li Peng, who early this morning ordered the military crackdown on the democracy movement, did not make an appearance or comment later today. Television stations repeatedly broadcast his speech calling for the military crackdown.

As the military crackdown seemed increasingly uncertain, there were signs that the Communist Party General Secretary, Zhao Ziyang, still had a chance of recovering his authority and elbowing aside Mr. Li and the senior leader, Deng Xiaoping, to become China's next leader in an intense and increasingly bitter power struggle within the Communist Party.

Communist Party officials with access to information at the highest level say Mr. Deng has stripped Mr. Zhao of his powers while leaving him with his title. In addition, they say a meeting of the Central Military Commission on Thursday effectively stripped him of his right to order troop movements.

Mr. Zhao submitted his resignation on May 17, after being out-voted 4 to 1 on the Standing Committee of the Politburo on his proposals to grant most student demands, the official said. The resignation was withdrawn the next day before it was acted upon. . . .

"Li Peng is now in charge of the party, so he'll be scheduling the meetings," an official said. "So if he thinks he might lose, he will delay holding a meeting." The harshness of Mr. Li's speech seems to have galvanized much of Beijing's population to support the student democracy movement, and Mr. Li and Mr. Deng are now openly referred to as public enemies.

Protesters in Shanghai today carried banners reading "Li Peng does not represent us" and "Li Peng, do not use the people's army against the people," Reuters reported. In most parts of Beijing, neither the police nor army troops could be seen today, but residents were in an exuberant frenzy to protect themselves from the threat of what is regarded as virtually an enemy invasion. All major intersections have been taken over by local residents who stand guard, waiting impatiently for the troops to arrive so they can implement careful plans to erect barricades and summon help.

"With the people behind us, we'll succeed," said Xu Shiyi, a student from Henan Province who has come to Beijing to support the movement. "No Government can survive by using the army against its own citizens." . . .

Truck drivers drove their vehicles in front of military convoys to block their way, and ordinary citizens lay down on the ground in front of army trucks. Many seemed to remember these tactics from the Philippine military coup that ousted President Ferdinand E. Marcos. Television footage of the "people power" revolution of the Philippines was widely shown in China at the time and now workers delight in saying that people power will defeat Prime Minister Li.

The most serious of the scattered clashes reported today occurred on a road in western Beijing, according to students, who said about 150 police officers used cattle prods to beat about 45 students blocking military trucks. . . . Nearly 100,000 people seemed prepared this evening to wait all night in central Tiananmen Square to protect student protesters from attack by troops. Even though there was no evidence of hostile troops within miles, many waited expectantly with cloths over their faces for the clouds of tear gas they have been told to expect.

The readiness to help has taken other forms. The Government today cut off the water supply to Tiananmen Square, but as word spread that the water fountains and taps in the area were no longer working, private business people from all over the capital contributed their motorcycles to carry buckets of water to the students.

There are still nearly 3,000 students engaged in a hunger strike on the square to back their demands for a dialogue with Government officials and for reappraisal of the student movement. After the harshness of Mr. Li's speech, the lack of any strong military follow-through has raised questions about the extent to which the Prime Minister can force his will. About 30,000 troops from Inner Mongolia and Shanxi Province reportedly have been deployed, but they are vastly outnumbered by the more than one million people who took to the streets today.

Some of the troops today could be seen with tear gas canisters, and some reportedly had guns, but they seemed decidedly pacifist. Most of the soldiers seemed unwilling to openly violate their orders to advance on Beijing, but they seemed quite happy to be blocked along the way.

Beijing Throngs Again Thwart Advances by Troops Amid Signs Military Balks at Crackdown

By Nicholas D. Kristof

BEIJING, Monday, May 22—Workers and students blocked new advances by army convoys today, preventing a military crackdown on China's democracy movement from taking effect, and several dozen top legislators quietly began preparing a strategy to revoke martial law.

There was exhilaration as well as exhaustion on central Tiananmen Square as dawn broke this morning, for many of the tens of thousands of students occupying the square had earlier written their wills after widespread rumors that brutal repression would begin during the night.

While many still fear that there will be violence, there is a sense of triumph in the capital that ordinary citizens have been able to prevent the Government from carrying out martial law more than two days after Prime Minister Li Peng ordered it.

It is not clear why the troops have not moved more aggressively to put martial law into effect. Several knowledgeable Chinese said the army did indeed plan a crackdown on Sunday night, and there are growing suspicions that the army's slowness has more to do with its own reluctance than with Prime Minister Li's.

The crowd this morning bellowed out a new slogan referring to the architects of martial law, Mr. Li and Deng Xiaoping, the senior leader: "Step down, or we will keep coming every day!" . . .

"Tiananmen Square has become a holy spot for Chinese democracy," a student leader, Wang Dan, told the crowd today. "If we stay here longer, we will contribute more to China's democratization and increase our influence. If we withdraw, we will let down the citizens who have defended us. We will stay until our victory."

Since Martial Law, Protest Crackles with Fury at Deng

By Sheryl WuDunn

BEIJING, May 21—As daylight wanes, a defiant exuberance seems to swell among the throngs clogging the intersections along roadways leading to Beijing's central square. But in the small homes of the capital, in the moments shared by friends away from the comfort of the masses, the darker side of what it means to live under martial law emerges.

"Don't you dare go out tonight," an official in a Communist Party organization said, his voice shaking, as he scolded his younger brother, who until Saturday had fasted for democracy with his university classmates.

"Mom spent her whole life raising us. The Government, those troops, if they come out, they will have no mercy," the official said as his brother, sinking into his chair, nodded. But the elder brother was planning to go to the square and spend several hours to support the students there.

Streets all over the capital were jammed with hundreds of thousands of citizens, many of whom were awakened politically by the call for greater democracy in China by hunger-striking students. . . .

The idea that tens of thousands or even hundreds of thousands of army troops, possibly carrying tear gas or guns, might close in on the unarmed students in and around Tiananmen Square is deeply troubling to many citizens. Some have forsaken sleep to spend the night on the streets waiting for the troops to arrive. Others have tried to persuade the students to be more careful.

"Please, those of you students who have no brothers or sisters, go home," a teacher implored his students on the square. "You must be prepared for the worst."

"I do not want to see these students killed by guns," said Li Xiaodong, a 22-year-old Government official. Like many other citizens, he accepted an assignment from the student organization to keep a lookout for troops at a particular location. "I was stationed at the Golden Water Bridge yesterday and I will be there again tonight," he said. "If and when the troops begin their action, they probably will come out over the bridge. We will perhaps be killed there, so we at least will die before the students." . . .

As tension grew, strategic concerns overtook idealistic visions.

Reporter's Notebook
By Nicholas D. Kristof

BEIJING, May 22—Throughout the capital, neighborhood residents have taken charge of local intersections. The people stay up all night, passing the time by exchanging increasingly implausible rumors about the imminent arrival and undoubted brutality of enormous numbers of troops.

Most of the corner-watchers are people who live nearby, but a few are sent by the central student organizing committee to make sure that all intersections are covered. The main strategy, if the troops come, is to block their path with people and obstructions like bicycles, bricks and anything else available. They also speak to the soldiers and try to convince them that they should not attack their fellow countrymen.

The students' latest concern is that the Government will use soldiers from remote areas because they speak different languages and may be unable to understand the students' pleas for retreat. So the student organizing committee now sends members of minority nationalities to all the major roads where it expects troops may arrive, so that they can function as translators and persuade soldiers to leave in any tongue.

"We can convince any group of soldiers not to attack us," Pa Hardin, a member of the Uighur minority, said the other day as he waited in front of the Beijing train station. He had been assigned to stand there in case Uighur soldiers emerged from the station to attack the students.

Another tactic has been adopted by the "kamikaze" group of workers who roam around the capital all night looking for invading army convoys to halt. Many of the kamikazes now carry knives, so they can puncture truck tires, and they often travel with their wives or girlfriends. The idea is that the woman will distract the soldiers while the man slashes the tires. . . .

Before the Communist victory in China in 1949, Mao Zedong and Zhou Enlai were famous for their accessibility and common touch.

When they conquered Beijing, they moved into the walled Zhongnanhai compound in the center of the capital, but for the first few years, ordinary Chinese could still stroll around the leaders' compound. As time passed, not only were ordinary Chinese barred, but a complex system of passes was devised so that permission was required to go from one part of the compound to another.

The students on Tiananmen Square have adopted a similar system.

71

The outside of the square is cordoned off by students, supposedly to protect those who are resting inside. Then there are several inner circles, each cordoned off by student guards who demand a pass to go through. To see the student organization's top leaders, a visitor must be escorted through four different checkpoints and present identification at each.

"We need to have a good system of discipline and organization," a student leader explained this evening. "Otherwise the Government will say we encourage chaos."

As the size of the crowds in the square rose and fell from day to day, so did the power struggle within the leadership. Seven military commanders warned against the use of military force by the soldiers who were still massing. But Li Peng, the known advocate of toughness, was seemingly gaining. For the fully committed students, the time for caution had passed, but for those who had spent their working lives aware of limits, the new conditions required a certain nimbleness.

Boldly and Subtly, China's Press Tests Limits . . .
By Sheryl WuDunn

BEIJING, May 23—Not many Chinese follow Italian politics, so perhaps it was a bit surprising for *People's Daily* to carry a small front-page article Sunday on the resignation of the Italian Government.

But in China, where subtlety is a way of journalism as of life, the message was obvious: China's Government should think about resigning as well. . . .

In the last five weeks, news organizations witnessed a startling transformation to what was for a Communist country a remarkably independent press. Then, on Saturday morning, came martial law, and all bets were off.

News organizations suddenly assumed a more cautious attitude, printing fewer articles that were not authorized, but it was not a full-scale retreat. Instead of openly criticizing the Government, newspapers tried more subtle tactics.

People's Daily on Monday published a front-page article about a Hungarian leader objecting to the use of army troops to solve domestic problems. That was a slap at Prime Minister Li Peng after his attempt to call army troops to the capital to suppress the democracy movement.

A journalist at the newspaper confirmed that the placement of the article was intended as a criticism of Prime Minister Li and his policies. He recalled the glee in the newsroom when the Hungarian leader's comment was found, and it was realized that it could be printed on the front page.

Television news and radio broadcasts have recently included daily reports on the student protests. In a subtle indication that army troops are dissatisfied with their mission to quell students, the television news today carried an illuminating interview with an officer in the military. The news tonight was clearly trying to embarrass Mr. Li by undermining the likelihood that his order for martial law would be carried out.

"As soldiers, it is our bounden duty to obey orders," the major told the reporter for the Central China Television news agency. "But we will never fire at the people."

Then, the television reporter asked the kind of leading question that is rarely seen, "Haven't you received an order to move away?"

The major answered, "Retreat, retreat."

As May entered its last week, successive headlines reflected how impasse was inching toward a violent resolution, how hopes were giving way to fears, and how the harsh counsel of Li Peng was holding sway.

Tide Turns Toward Chinese Hard-Liner

Students Plan for Hurdle: Zhao's Fall

Wishful Thinkers?

Chinese Hard-Liner Tightens Grip as Attacks on His Rival Multiply

Then the students, who had been massed in large but tensely quiet numbers, moved once more.

Students Renew Call for Change in Beijing March
By Nicholas D. Kristof

BEIJING, May 28—About 100,000 people on foot and on bicycles streamed through the capital today to demand more democracy and the resignation of Prime Minister Li Peng. The police and soldiers made no move to interfere despite martial law restrictions and the Government's strict warnings against demonstrations.

The students, who are increasingly aware of support from Chinese around the world, hailed the protest as part of an "international Chinese people's demonstration day" to put pressure on the Government. Other demonstrations were held in several Chinese cities, including the economic capital, Shanghai, as well as in Taiwan, Hong Kong, Australia and the United States.

One of the largest protests was in Hong Kong, which held a political rally with a crowd estimated at more than 300,000. Such protests are likely to put new pressure on the Chinese authorities, who are sensitive to turbulence in Hong Kong in the years before they inherit the British territory in 1997.

In Beijing, the demonstrators paraded along five different routes intended to maximize their exposure to the city's residents. Separate columns of protesters—mostly students but including some workers—passed by the Zhongnanhai compound, where Mr. Li lives, as well as the Dianmen neighborhood home of the 84-year-old senior leader, Deng Xiaoping.

"We love our country, but we do not love the puppet government of Li Peng," chanted the demonstrators as they waved red banners and sang songs that mocked the nation's leadership.

The demonstration in the capital was smaller than several previous marches, although it was difficult to calculate since the students took different routes and did not all pass by central Tiananmen Square. In particular, fewer workers joined in, although those who lined the route cheered the students and seemed enthusiastic.

"I see hope for China, which I didn't see before," said Yang Mei, an artist who joined the protesters. "The students already have won, because they have support from 90 percent of the population. And the greatest climax is yet to come. This is sowing time, and the harvest will come when Deng Xiaoping dies."

The demonstrations were smaller today for two reasons. The first is that the Government has been putting intense pressure on factories and universities to curb protests, and factory managers have warned workers that they will lose their bonuses and maybe their jobs if they join the students.

The second is that there is an air of apprehension in the nation these days, a fear that a violent crackdown and major political realignment will be announced in the next few days.

The demonstration today was not reported by the television news or the New China News Agency, a sign that the Government is tightening its control over the media. The official news media here have covered previous demonstrations, although with less and less interest in the last week following Prime Minister Li's announcement of martial law on May 20.

The Communist Party newspaper, *People's Daily*, was represented in today's march by a small group of journalists who demanded press freedom, but most journalists seem to have battened the hatches of their aspirations, in expectation of rough weather ahead.

"There's a spirit of depression that probably the conservatives have won and that there will be a settling of accounts," said a Western diplomat. "The mood is that there's trouble ahead."

Fates were being decided in party meetings but consciousness was being shaped on the street. Thousands of young people were living through events and emotions that they would one day tell to children as yet unborn.

In Quest for Democracy, a Mini-City Is Born
By Sheryl WuDunn

BEIJING, May 30—A few hundred yards from the center of Chinese bureaucracy, where the Communist Party leadership is engaged in a bitter power struggle, a smaller group of less experienced bureaucrats on Tiananmen Square is building its own society, a virtual city of protest.

The several thousand students who are occupying the square as a pro-democracy demonstration have established their own mini-government: a secretariat, a printing office, a financial affairs ministry, a goods and resources ministry, a propaganda ministry, a liaison ministry, a picket squad, a special action squad, a small loudspeaker broadcast station, a pharmacy and three clinics.

Instead of the nation's five-star flag, the students have hung a kaleidoscope of red, blue and white school flags from tall poles to represent their federation of universities from all over the country. Presiding over the scene is a large mascot, a 27-foot-high replica of the Statue of Liberty positioned so that it faces a large portrait of Mao Zedong.

"This is a holy land for democracy," said Zhou Chihui, a 22-year-old mathematics student from the central Chinese city of Wuhan. "It takes a lot of courage to continue to stay on Tiananmen Square. And we need to manage a life here."

Three rings of student picket lines surround the headquarters that house the ministries, and in the times of tight security, there were several types of special passes that students had to show to pass through deeper rings of student police. Even now, it is rare to be allowed to speak with any of the student leaders.

But if the students consider their own society on the square a battleground in the struggle for freedom and democracy, they have not produced defenses against the thousands of military troops on the outskirts of the capital.

The students say they plan to rely on local citizens to help them should there be a confrontation. If a military crackdown occurred quietly in the middle of the night, they acknowledge that they would probably be defeated, but they say this would anger citizens the next day and generate more support.

Even if the troops do not invade the square, it is not clear how long the students' small society can last. Already the numbers are dwindling sharply. Only a few thousand students are now camping on the square. While the students say they will maintain their occupation at least until June 20, when the standing committee of the National People's Congress is due to meet, the numbers are likely to shrink even more by then.

Because they have so effectively sheltered themselves from the Beijing authorities, the students have also lost some of the benefits from the city's social services, like garbage collection, continuous electricity and water supply. All this has made the square a less habitable place.

The ministries hardly resemble the halls of Government offices. Most of them are housed in red or light blue plastic tents that were sent as donations from Hong Kong. But also unlike the nation's formal ministries, these offices are open 24 hours a day.

Already, the financial affairs office has the equivalent of nearly $40,000 under its management, which it will begin spending more quickly as donations of food, drink and other supplies come in more slowly from local residents.

Money has been raised throughout the world for the students, and in one instance, a rock concert in Hong Kong reportedly raised the equivalent of more than $1 million for the students. But the students say they have not been able to receive money sent from overseas through the Government postal system, a common financial intermediary.

As a result, the student money managers have shied from parking their money in the Government banks or post offices. Instead, they keep it hidden in a place outside the square. They also plan to issue financial reports through posters, news conferences and loudspeaker broadcasts.

"You can say this place is like a city," said Mi Weizhuo, a 21-year-old statistics student from Hebei University who is in charge of financial supervision in the financial affairs office. "But it is a purely consumer's society because we don't produce anything."

Mr. Mi has helped allocate the money for food purchases, which the resources department is responsible for purchasing. To control how much food is bought daily, delegates from each university on the square are required to show the resources department the student identification cards of their students living on the square.

Even then, the food is mainly bread and drink. Students have already complained that they lack various vitamins and vegetables, as well as adequate hygiene. While the clinics are much emptier now than they were during a hunger strike two weeks ago, when tens of thousands more students lived on the square to show their support, most of the patients have minor ailments like the common cold, a sore throat or fatigue.

The clinics also have their specialties, according to their facilities and supplies. At one small clinic, which like the others is under the Red Cross, physicians mainly administer first aid. Severe cases are sent to the square's emergency clinic.

The pharmacy dispenses both Western and Chinese medicines that have been donated by factories. Many of the hundred-odd boxes of medicine that line the pharmacy tent have not been opened, and since the hunger strike, the supplies of glucose water, salt water and a popular Chinese nutritional medicine have hardly been used.

The anxieties and fears that were gripping Beijing were not limited to just one side of the conflict.

Why Deng Trembles: A Leader Equates Protest and Chaos
By Nicholas D. Kristof

BEIJING, May 31—For many Chinese and foreign viewers of the latest upheavals, China's script in the last few weeks has resembled a Greek tragedy: Deng Xiaoping is cast as the once-heroic leader whose intolerance and hubris caused him to destroy much of what he has accomplished.

What impels a man like Mr. Deng, China's senior leader, to undermine in a few weeks what took him a decade to achieve: a stable political order, respect in Hong Kong for China's good intentions, the preparations for a succession of power?

Mr. Deng's critics—and these days they are numerous—often assume that his decision to dismiss his chosen successor, Zhao Ziyang, and summon troops to crack down on the democracy movement simply reflects the tenacity of his ambition, an unwillingness or inability to share power. Mr. Deng is undoubtedly reluctant to give up the power he has grown used to, but there is an additional explanation to account for his horror of the democracy movement.

"If our country were plunged into disorder and our nation reduced to a heap of loose sand, how could we ever prosper?" Mr. Deng asked in a speech more than two years ago, on the eve of his last crackdown on a student movement. "The reason the imperialists were able to bully us in the past was precisely that we were a heap of loose sand."

He and others of his generation spent the first half of their lives in a China racked by division and chaos, where the hopes of modernizing movements always seemed frustrated by the country's disorder.

The lessons about chaos were burned into their psyches again when the Cultural Revolution began in 1966 and led to hundreds of thousands of deaths and other personal tragedies in their families.

"They have a deep-seated allergy to any form of disorder," a Western diplomat said recently in Beijing. "They have an intense belief that they need stability in order to have development."

The distaste for student unrest is perhaps accentuated because Mr. Deng's oldest son, Deng Pufang, was permanently paralyzed after being pushed from a window at Beijing University by student militants during the Cultural Revolution.

"While Westerners have tended to think of China as under firm rule, Deng tends to see the potential for chaos, and may often feel the central Government is hanging on by its fingernails," explained Kenneth G. Lieberthal, director of the Center for Chinese Studies at the University of Michigan. "He wants reform but not at the price of chaos."

While Mr. Deng is best known for his efforts to open China's economy, and, to a lesser extent, its political system, these are simply means to achieve his most cherished aim: modernization. And Mr.

Deng has made clear that he regards political protest as inimical to modernization. He seems to see bubbles of discontent not as a sign of China's resilience but as a sign of its growing malaise and weakness.

In a speech early in 1979, when he was cracking down on an earlier democracy movement, Mr. Deng warned that if it was allowed to continue, it would "inevitably lead to the unchecked spread of ultra-democracy and anarchism, to the complete disruption of political stability and unity, and to the total failure of our modernization campaign."

"China will once again be plunged into chaos, division, retrogression and darkness, and the Chinese people will be deprived of all hope," he said.

In addition to this fear of chaos, there seems to have been a naked fear of losing power. For a group of old revolutionaries, men in their 80's who have held power for four decades and see their interests as virtually identical with their country's interests, there was a deep-seated alarm at the possibility that the Communist Party would crumble the way that Chinese dynasties have fallen.

"To retreat means our downfall," President Yang Shangkun said in a speech to the Politburo now being circulated among party officials. "To retreat means the downfall of the People's Republic of China and the restoration of capitalism."

There is also evident in the leadership a deep resentment against Mr. Zhao's unwillingness to play by the rules. The old leaders constructed China according to their vision, and Mr. Zhao apparently came to threaten not only that vision but also their personal hold on power. Respect for the elderly is fundamental practice in China, and yet Mr. Zhao openly disagreed with Mr. Deng and other senior officials. While they warned of the dangers of unrest, Mr. Zhao hailed the patriotic spirit of student demonstrators.

President Yang, an 82-year-old veteran military figure, suggested in the speech that one of Mr. Zhao's offenses was a simple lack of respect, an unwillingness to be subdued even in the presence of Mr. Deng.

"He insisted on his own idea," President Yang complained in the speech, a copy of which was obtained from students and has been verified by people who heard it read in party meetings. "When Comrade Deng Xiaoping attended the meeting, he still insisted on his idea."

For Communist Party leaders, who for decades have felt secure when a single voice emanated from the party, there has been something deeply troubling about Mr. Zhao's unwillingness to be quiet. Mr. Zhao in his speeches never openly broke with his colleagues, but his televised speeches were more conciliatory toward the protesters than those of other officials, and President Yang appears convinced that this is what stimulated the democracy movement.

The old revolutionaries seem to regard the public as having little or no independent vitality, but are simply a weather vane to be directed by the force of the Communist Party or the force of opposing "bourgeois liberalism," whichever is greater. Their fear is that divisions within the party will strengthen the enemy.

China's former President, Li Xiannian, complained that "there are two headquarters" in the party, and that this confused people and encouraged unrest. While in the West there is a political tradition that glorifies the lone dissenter who sticks to his principles, in the Politburo Mr. Zhao's persistence came across as impudence and treachery.

Indeed, there may be more to the situation than is now known, and no one can rule out the possibility of Mr. Zhao plotting against Mr. Deng. A member of Mr. Zhao's camp confirmed that the party General Secretary had directly challenged Mr. Deng's authority, and there are some hints that Mr. Zhao's aides may have tried to stir up unrest in the belief that it would help their man.

In 1976, when it was to his advantage, Mr. Zhao reacted to the purge of Mr. Deng by calling on the masses to "thoroughly expose and criticize the crimes of Deng Xiaoping." On this occasion, once again, his own interests may have crossed Mr. Deng's.

Mr. Deng and his comrades may have felt they had little choice but to take the actions they did, if they were to hold on to the power they had grown used to. It was not necessarily a blunder—a miscalculation of the impact of suppression on Hong Kong, on the succession plans or on China's domestic political stability—but a response to a higher imperative, from the perspective of the old revolutionaries. They felt that it came down to the need to preserve their own power, and also the need to save China.

Few people, in China or abroad, seem to agree with Mr. Deng that his actions have helped. But even many of his detractors believe it was such calculations that drove him to rise in a fury and turn on his protégé and uproot the carefully laid plans for political stability and succession that previously had won him such acclaim.

Mr. Deng's actions have probably already cost him his reputation in China, for he is increasingly resented and disliked in the country he leads. Now the central question, which the coming months are likely to answer, will be whether his forceful intervention has staved off the chaos he dreads or merely worsened it.

Some troops started to move and the supporters of the students moved to parry them.

Beijing Residents Block Army Move Near City Center
By Nicholas D. Kristof

BEIJING, Saturday, June 3—Tens of thousands of Beijing students and workers surged onto the streets early this morning to turn back more than 2,000 troops who were marching toward Tiananmen Square.

It was the biggest outpouring of citizen support for the demonstrating students in more than a week, and it seemed possible that it would rekindle the student movement and present a new challenge to the Government.

The confrontation underscored the fragile and volatile nature of the situation in Beijing just when the turmoil here seemed to be subsiding after seven weeks of demonstrations by students and workers for democracy and against corruption.

[The Associated Press, in a report from Beijing today, said about 800 riot police officers fired tear gas to clear an area outside the Communist Party headquarters, just west of the square. Witnesses reported at least 30 people outside the Beijing Hotel were beaten by the police, who were said to be armed with truncheons and knives, the A.P. said.]

Students and local residents were convinced that the army troops planned to clear Tiananmen Square, which students have occupied for three weeks. All along Changan Avenue, the main east-west thoroughfare, local residents emerged in the pre-dawn hours to block nearby intersections and prevent troops from passing, after more than a week in which the streets were clear of such roadblocks. . . .

Local residents stopped every police and military truck they could find along Changan Avenue. They barricaded the vehicles and let the air out of their tires. Some also drove trucks across the avenue to create roadblocks.

Thousands of students and local residents also gathered at the site of the car accident, but the police left the scene and there were no conflicts.

The number of students occupying the square is down to a few thousand from the tens of thousands who camped there just a week ago. But on Friday evening, more than 100,000 people had gathered in Tiananmen Square to listen to a pop singer, Hou Dejian, who began a 48-hour hunger strike in support of the students. Mr. Hou was joined by two young scholars and an officer of a major computer company who were planning a 72-hour fast.

As a group, the students had made a powerful impression on a world that watched the mounting confrontation until television was prevented from transmitting its images abroad. They had appeared on screens all over the world speaking intensely, if often naively. They all made it clear that they were only spokesmen, not leaders, and with their modesty, it was hard to hear specific voices and accounts of individual lives.

A Portrait of a Young Man as a Beijing Student Leader
By Sheryl WuDunn

BEIJING, June 2—Four months ago a scrawny, scraggly-haired student gave speeches about human rights that baffled his classmates, who wondered how anyone could harbor such a passion for what was then a remote concept like democracy.

Now, Wang Dan, a 20-year-old history student at Beijing University, is a national figure. He carries a beeper and is accompanied by two bodyguards, signs of his new status as perhaps the single most prominent leader of the student democracy movement that has thrust the Government into a political crisis.

He is rather embarrassed to talk about how his personal life has changed. But when his mail is given to him, he lets on that he has already received a dozen love letters. Certainly he has been the subject of some wild rumors. Some people say he has taken part in Politburo meetings, while others say he has been martyred in various grim ways.

Two students from the eastern city of Suzhou, who arrived in Beijing the other day, were surprised to learn that Mr. Wang was still alive. They said they had held a ceremony in Suzhou to mourn his passing.

What emerges from the last seven weeks is a picture of a survivor: an intellectual lacking charisma or oratorical skill, but bold enough and determined enough to remain a student leader despite factional bickering and Government criticisms.

While other student leaders focus on tactics and mundane matters like where to obtain megaphones, Mr. Wang stands out as the leader who dares to articulate a world very unlike China today.

"I'm not afraid," Mr. Wang said. "I've nothing to be afraid of. I don't think they will be able to imprison me for as long as Wei Jingsheng." Mr. Wei is a dissident who was sentenced a decade ago to 15 years in prison.

There are other prominent student leaders, like Wuer Kaixi and Chai Ling from Beijing Normal University, but it is Mr. Wang who seems to have had the greatest influence. Mr. Wuer's popularity tumbled 10 days ago when he proposed leaving the square, and Miss Chai's role seems limited to the students now occupying the square.

Mr. Wang refuses to evaluate his own role as a leader, but admits there have been mistakes and lessons.

"I have one regret," Mr. Wang said. "I failed to persuade the elite intellectuals to give us direct support." Intellectuals should have been more involved in helping to lead the movement, he says.

Mr. Wang believes that the intellectuals joined too late, and he suggests that one of the results of this is that the students did not have coherent goals.

"I think that the student movements in the future should be firmly based on something solid, such as the democratization of campus life or the realization of civil rights according to the Constitution," Mr. Wang said. "Otherwise, the result is chaos."

Although many of the students' demands—press freedom, direct talks with the Government and the uprooting of corruption among officials—were more practical than in past demonstrations, they had no framework.

While certain themes, like opposition to official corruption, gained the support of workers, Mr. Wang says he believes the movement is not ready for worker participation because the principles of democracy must first be absorbed by students and intellectuals before they can be spread to others.

The recent student movement went way beyond just ideas, and Mr. Wang has learned that there are limits to how one can apply those ideas, especially the concept of democracy.

When students went on their hunger strike, any policy decision that was made had to be voted in unanimously by all the fasting students, whose numbers grew from 1,000 to 3,000.

Another difficulty was the election of a student leadership.

"You can't have direct democracy where everyone is electing leaders and trying to get involved because it only results in frequent changes of leaders and causes disorder," Mr. Wang said.

Another problem that hampered the student movement was the bickering among leaders. Most recently, a debate centered on whether to stay at or leave Tiananmen Square, which students invaded more than two weeks ago.

Mr. Wang and his fellow students from Beijing University and other colleges in the capital have essentially retreated from the square, which has lately been occupied mainly by students from outside Beijing.

Through all this, Mr. Wang has remained a leader, partly because he is from Beijing University, the nation's most prestigious school, and partly because he has become a nationwide figure who has been involved all along, from the hunger strike to the talks with the Government.

In part Mr. Wang seems to have held on to his constituency because he has learned to sense how far his supporters are willing to go.

Other times, he displayed a knack for public relations. Mr. Wang says he did not spearhead the hunger strike, but when the idea became popular and a list of participants was posted, his name was the first on the list.

"The hunger strike was significant," Mr. Wang said, "because it brought out the ordinary people's enthusiasm."

And then the army stormed the heart of the city, firing at protesters who tried to fight back as best they could.

Troops Attack and Crush Beijing Protest; Thousands Fight Back, Scores Are Killed
By Nicholas D. Kristof

BEIJING, Sunday, June 4—Tens of thousands of Chinese troops retook the center of the capital early this morning from pro-democracy protesters, killing scores of students and workers and wounding hundreds more as they fired submachine guns at crowds of people who tried to resist.

Troops marched along the main roads surrounding central Tiananmen Square, sometimes firing in the air and sometimes firing directly at crowds of men and women who refused to move out of the way.

Early this morning, the troops finally cleared the square after first sweeping the area around it. Several thousand students who had remained on the square throughout the shooting left peacefully, still waving the banners of their universities. Several armed personnel carriers ran over their tents and destroyed the encampment.

Reports on the number of dead were sketchy. Three Beijing hospitals reported receiving at least 68 corpses of civilians and said many others had not been picked up from the scene. Four other hospitals said they had received bodies of civilians but declined to disclose how many. Students said, however, that at least 500 people may have been killed in the crackdown.

Most of the dead had been shot, but some had been run over by armored personnel carriers that forced their way through barricades erected by local residents.

The official news programs this morning reported that the People's Liberation Army had crushed a "counterrevolutionary rebellion" in the capital. They said that more than 1,000 police and troops had been injured and some killed, and that civilians had been killed, but did not give details.

Changan Avenue, or the Avenue of Eternal Peace, Beijing's main east-west thoroughfare, echoed with screams this morning as young people carried the bodies of their friends away from the front lines. The dead or seriously wounded were heaped on the backs of bicycles or tricycle rickshaws and supported by friends who rushed through the crowds, sometimes sobbing as they ran.

The avenue was lit by the glow of several trucks and two armed personnel carriers that students and workers set afire, and bullets swooshed overhead or glanced off buildings. The air crackled almost constantly with gunfire and tear gas grenades.

"General strike!" people roared, in bitterness and outrage, as they ran from Tiananmen Square, which pro-democracy demonstrators had occupied for three weeks. "General strike!"

While hundreds of thousands of people had turned out to the streets Saturday and early today to show support for the democracy movement, it was not clear if the call for a general strike would be successful. The Government had been fearful that a crackdown on the movement would lead to strikes, but its willingness to shoot students suggested that it was also capable of putting considerable pressure on workers to stay on the job.

The morning radio news program reported that it would be "very difficult" to hold a meeting of the National People's Congress standing committee as scheduled. The committee, which had been scheduled to meet June 20, has the power to revoke martial law and oversee the Government, and many members of the panel are known to be deeply upset by the crackdown.

The announcement by the Beijing news program suggested that Prime Minister Li Peng, who is backed by hard-liners in the Communist Party, was still on top in his power struggle for control of the Chinese leadership. The violent suppression of the student movement also suggested that for now, the hard-liners are firmly in control, and that those who favor conciliation, like party leader Zhao Ziyang, at least temporarily have little influence on policy.

It was too early to tell if the crackdown would be followed by arrests of student leaders, intellectuals who have been critical of the Party, or members of Mr. Zhao's faction. Blacklists have been widely rumored, and many people have been worried about the possibility of arrest.

Students and workers tried to resist the crackdown, and destroyed at least sixteen trucks and two armored personnel carriers. Scores of students and workers ran alongside the personnel carriers, hurling concrete blocks and wooden staves into the treads until they ground to a halt. They then threw firebombs at one until it caught fire, and set the other alight after first covering it with blankets soaked in gasoline.

The drivers escaped, but were beaten by students. A young American man, who could not be immediately identified, was also beaten by the crowd after he tried to intervene and protect one of the drivers.

Clutching iron pipes and stones, groups of students periodically advanced toward the soldiers. Some threw bricks and firebombs at the lines of soldiers, apparently wounding many of them.

Many of those killed were throwing bricks at the soldiers, but others were simply watching passively or standing at barricades when soldiers fired directly at them.

Two groups of young people commandeered city buses to attack the troops. About 10 people were in each bus, and they held firebombs or sticks in their hands as they drove toward lines of armored personnel carriers and troops. Teenage boys, with scarves wrapped around their mouths to protect themselves from tear gas, were behind the steering wheels and gunned the engines as they weaved around the debris to approach the troops.

The first bus was soon stopped by machine-gun fire, and only one person—a young man who jumped out of a back window and ran away—was seen getting out. Gunfire also stopped the second bus, and it quickly caught fire, perhaps ignited by the firebomb of someone inside. No one appeared to escape.

It was also impossible to determine how many civilians had been killed or injured. Beijing Fuxing Hospital, 3.3 miles to the west of Tiananmen Square, reported more than 38 deaths and more than 100 wounded, and said that many more bodies had yet to be taken to its morgue. A doctor at the Beijing Union Medical College Hospital, two miles northeast of the square, reported 17 deaths. Beijing Tongren Hospital, one mile southeast of the square, reported 13 deaths and more than 100 critically wounded.

"As doctors, we often see deaths," said a doctor at the Tongren Hospital. "But we've never seen such a tragedy like this. Every room in the hospital is covered with blood. We are terribly short of blood, but citizens are lining up outside to give blood."

Four other hospitals also reported receiving bodies, but refused to say how many.

In addition, this reporter saw five people killed by gunfire and many more wounded on the east side of the square. Witnesses described at least six more people who had been run over by armored personnel carriers, and about 25 more who had been shot to death in the area. It was not known how many bodies remained on the square or how many people had been killed in other parts of the capital.

It was unclear whether the violence would mark the extinction of the seven-week-old democracy movement, or would prompt a new phase in the uprising, like a general strike. The violence in the capital ended a period of remarkable restraint by both sides, and seemed certain to arouse new bitterness and antagonism among both ordinary people and Communist Party officials for the Government of Prime Minister Li Peng.

"Our Government is already done with," said a young worker who held a rock in his hand, as he gazed at the army forces across Tiananmen Square. "Nothing can show more clearly that it does not represent the people."

Another young man, an art student, was nearly incoherent with grief and anger as he watched the body of a student being carted away, his head blown away by bullets.

"Maybe we'll fail today," he said. "Maybe we'll fail tomorrow. But someday we'll succeed. It's a historical inevitability."

On Saturday the police had used tear gas and beat dozens of demonstrators near the Communist Party headquarters in Zhongnanhai, while soldiers and workers hurled bricks at each other behind the Great Hall of the People. Dozens of people were wounded, but exact numbers could not be confirmed.

It appeared to be the first use of tear gas ever in the Chinese capital, and the violence seemed to radicalize the crowds that filled Tiananmen Square and Changan Avenue in the center of the city. The clashes also appeared to contribute to the public bitterness against the Government of Prime Minister Li.

The violence on both sides seemed to mark a milestone in the democracy movement, and the streets in the center of the city were a kaleidescope of scenes rarely if ever seen in the Chinese capital: furious crowds smashed and overturned army vehicles in front of Zhongnanhai, and then stoned the Great Hall of the People; grim-faced young soldiers clutching submachine guns tried to push their way through thick crowds of demonstrators near the Beijing train station; and the police charged a crowd near Zhongnanhai and used truncheons to beat men and women disabled by tear gas.

"In 1949, we welcomed the army into Beijing," said an old man on the Jianguomenwai bridge, referring to the crowds who hailed the arrival of Communist troops at the end of the Communist revolution. Then he waved toward a line of 50 army trucks that were blocked in a sea of more than 10,000 angry men and women, and added, "Now we're fighting to keep them out."

Most Chinese seemed convinced that the tanks and troops had been ordered into the city to crush the pro-democracy demonstrations once and for all. The immediate result of the first clashes was to revitalize the pro-democracy movement, which had been losing momentum over the last 10 days, and to erase the sense that life in the capital was returning to normal. But the use of tanks and guns came later, and it was not clear if they would succeed in ending the movement or would lead to such measures as a general strike.

The tension was exacerbated by an extraordinary announcement on television Saturday night, ordering citizens to "stay at home to protect your lives." In particular, the announcement ordered people to stay off the streets and away from Tiananmen Square.

"The situation in Beijing at present is very serious," the Government warned in another urgent notice read on television. "A handful of ruffians are wantonly making rumors to instigate the masses to openly insult, denounce, beat and kidnap soldiers in the People's Liberation Army, to seize arms, surround and block Zhongnanhai, attack the Great Hall of the People, and attempt to gather together various forces. More serious riots can occur at any time."

There were some reports that the Communist Party's ruling Politburo had met Friday and given the Beijing municipality the authority to clear the square and end the protests. The *People's Daily* and the television news on Saturday took a hard line against the unrest, and the evening news warned that "armed police and troops have the right to use all means to dispose of troublemakers who act willfully to defy the law."

The clashes and enormous outpouring of support for the students were an unexpected turnaround for the democracy movement. Just a few days ago, the number of students occupying Tiananmen Square had dropped to a few thousand, and students seemed to be having difficulty mobilizing large numbers of citizens to take to the streets. The Government's strategy, of waiting for the students to become bored and go home, seemed to be leading to the possibility of a resolution to the difficulty.

Then a police van crashed into four bicyclists late Friday night, generating new outrage against the Government. One cyclist was killed instantly, and two died in the hospital Saturday, while the fourth seemed less seriously hurt.

Rumors were less meticulous about detail, and word spread early Saturday morning through the capital that four people had been killed by the police. Tens of thousands of people took to the streets to protest, and immediately found themselves confronting more than 2,000 unarmed troops who were marching toward Tiananmen Square.

The troops retreated, but that confrontation seemed to set the tone for the massive demonstrations later Saturday and early today.

Crackdown in Beijing; In the Streets, Anguish, Fury and Tears

By Sheryl WuDunn

BEIJING, Sunday, June 4—As the crackle of automatic weapons filled the air today on the Avenue of Eternal Peace, tens of thousands of

Beijing residents, even elderly men and women, rushed out to see what they could do to turn back the troops.

"The citizens have gone crazy," said a driver watching as a tank plowed its way down the main thoroughfare. "They throw themselves in front of the tank, and only when they see it won't stop, they scatter."

The driver himself was shaken by what he had seen: A tank had rammed into an army truck used as a barricade. As the truck turned over, it crushed a man to death. Elsewhere, he had seen three bloodied bodies lying in the street. Several soldiers still standing in their trucks were crying.

Students and workers threw beer bottles, gasoline bombs, lead pipes, whatever they could find, at the tanks and armed personnel trucks, which nevertheless continued rumbling down the avenue. One truck drove back and forth along the east side of Changan Avenue, as the Avenue of Eternal Peace is known in Chinese, and did not stop when people stood in its path.

Amazement had already turned to fear and defiance earlier in the evening as citizens saw the military convoys entering the city. Some troops from other provinces practically paraded their AK-47 rifles as they stood in their trucks, stranded by the human blockades that had formed around the trucks.

By dark, tensions had soared throughout the city. Hundreds of thousands of people were impelled outdoors by their disbelief and anger, yet brought back to their homes by fear of the violence. The sound of tanks whizzing by and reports of open firing fanned their fears.

"You beasts! You beasts!" shouted the people at the troops.

Around a convoy of about 45 military trucks in the eastern part of the city, people pushed and shoved their way to the troops, shouting and urging them to consider their role as fellow citizens. But the sympathy that had characterized the troops last week was gone; the soldiers seemed to have a certain resolve.

"Will you shoot at us if they order you to?" was a question asked by many of the people surrounding the truck. The soldiers gave weak assurances to the people that they would not fire, but they also admitted that they had to follow orders.

"We have to obey orders because we are soldiers," said one uniformed trooper who was driving a truck. "Otherwise, we will be punished. In any case, there's no way they will order us to shoot the people."

His platoon commander was firm. "We don't fear being beaten by you people," he said as he climbed out of the truck. "We just fear that our guns will be taken and then we will have chaos." Everywhere in the vicinity of the convoy was the sound of hissing, as people let out the air from the tires of as many trucks as they could.

"Why do you have guns?" shouted one man.

"A man is not a soldier without his gun, is he?" came the reply of a soldier carrying an AK-47 automatic rifle.

An old man took up the cause. "I tell you, there will be no good end for you if you follow your order loyally," he screamed as though his life depended upon it. "You have parents, you have brothers and sisters. You should not beat your fellow citizens under any circumstances."

The nearly crazed citizens were climbing onto the trucks, trying to intimidate the soldier. But everywhere in the vicinity, anger was mixed with horror as the people saw how the soldiers handled their rifles and watched as several tanks pulled up.

"Is this the way Li Peng shows how martial law protects the people?" said an old man sitting on a rail.

Another young man said, "When they shoot with real bullets, it will be doomsday." Only hours later did the troops open fire.

In the afternoon, the scene near the walled-in Communist Party compound, where about 30 tear-gas bombs were released, had been the first site of violence. But now that seemed tame. A 20-minute conflict between 300 to 400 riot policemen and hundreds of citizens seemed to have galvanized the citizens. They began to believe that the Government was willing to use force—rubber bullets, broken bricks, truncheons—against the people.

"I couldn't keep my eyes open because of the dense tear gas," said Lu Baochun, a 26-year-old assistant engineer. "It was the troops that first used bricks and tiles to attack, and the citizens fought back."

Mr. Lu had rushed back out to the scene, a chaotic swirl of thousands of people darting back and forth inspecting broken bricks and glass and examining the white powder-like splotches on the street apparently from the tear gas.

"When I went into the house of a nearby citizen to wash my eyes with fresh water, I saw several children lying on their stomachs on a bed," said Mr. Lu, whose own face and neck were reddened from the gas. "They had wet towels covering their mouths, and an old woman was beside them weeping."

He was standing at the Communist Party headquarters shouting with rage now at the two dozen military troops with long truncheons and green helmets, sweating in their heavy green uniforms under the pelting sun.

Some citizens gathered in small huddles around people they thought had been witnesses to the attack. Others crowded together discussing the event, many apprehensive about how far the Government would go.

"They are simply ruffians and bandits," said a young well-dressed woman who had gotten caught in the cross fire of bricks and stones as she was on her way to the office. "They bit people just like mad dogs."

A Chinese journalist was trying to comfort her. "We are shocked," he said. "We thought that this kind of thing only happened during the reign of the corrupt Government of the Kuomintang. Yet this happened in our People's Republic. The troops and the police, they are supposed to be our brothers."

"Please, Tell the World," Students Beg
By Nicholas D. Kristof

BEIJING, Sunday, June 4—The violence against students and workers in Tiananmen Square was most obvious today, because for the most part they were the ones getting killed. But they, too, were violent against the police and army troops, although less effectively so.

Clutching iron bars and bricks, the students glared at soldiers 100 yards away on the other side of the square. It was dark, although the fire from an armed personnel carrier that students had set ablaze cast an eerie glow over part of the square, and the troops and their rows of vehicles could be dimly discerned in the haze.

From time to time, a group of them would advance on the soldiers to throw rocks and otherwise harass them. And then often, they would be shot and killed. It was an unequal competition.

Whenever the students got their chance, spotting an unarmed group of soldiers, they attacked with bricks and iron bars. However, the soldiers, most of whom had guns, tended to stick together.

Until now, students had emphasized the need for nonviolent tactics, and today some still begged their friends to put down their bricks and iron bars. But many students seemed to have crossed their personal Rubicon today, and those who previously had clutched leaflets and megaphones today picked up firebombs.

To be an American on the square this morning was to be the object of fervent hope and inarticulate pleas for help.

"We appeal to your country," a university student begged as bullets careened overhead. "Our Government is mad. We need help from abroad, especially America. There must be something that America can do."

Enraged and desperate as they saw their friends fall and crimson stains grow on their chests, students and workers rushed to any foreigner they could find to express such appeals for help. Almost nobody had any idea what the United States could do, and perhaps it was more a cry of outrage than a plea for help. But this sometimes wordless craving for an international response seemed almost universal on Tiananmen Square.

It was not that students wanted or expected foreign forces to actively intervene. Rather, it seemed to be a moral judgment that they sought, and especially the hope that the news of the bloodshed would reach the outside world and not be covered up.

Most were convinced that the Chinese authorities would never report an accurate toll of the dead and wounded, nor explain what had truly happened in the capital. The morning news programs seemed to justify their skepticism: a brief report said little more than that soldiers had successfully crushed a "counterrevolutionary rebellion."

Denied recognition at home, it became all the more important that the blood and sorrow and bitterness somehow find expression abroad. Even if it did not reverberate back home, students said, at least it could give some meaning to the sacrifices. And so they sought out foreign journalists, tugging them toward the corpses, showing them the blood on the pavement, and begging them to write about what had happened.

"You must tell the world what is happening," a long-haired university student urged, nearly incoherent with fury, "because otherwise all this counts for nothing."

Many asked that their appeals be transmitted to the United Nations, although none had a clear idea of what the United Nations could possibly do to help.

"Maybe it can discuss this situation," a student said impatiently. "Anyway, we have to do something."

While reassurances to the rest of the world that China welcomes foreign tourists and investment presumably remain a consideration, such matters seemed to take a back seat in this morning's military crackdown.

The diplomatic quarter in Beijing was roused from slumber this morning by the almost deafening rumble of seven armed personnel carriers rolling by on the way to Tiananmen Square. Then, truckloads of soldiers arrived and, directly in front of the Jianguomenwai diplomatic compound where many diplomats live, began firing their submachine guns in the air.

In front of the Friendship Store, where tourists go to buy souvenirs, students and workers had turned over an army van and set it ablaze. In the Sanlitun diplomatic compound to the north, opponents of the Government expressed their outrage by setting a police station on fire.

In the lobby of the Beijing Hotel, undercover police officers searched photographers for film they had taken of the clashes, and one photographer was beaten when he refused to hand it over.

While there were no direct attacks on foreigners, there seemed to be a hostility in the air from the Government toward Western influences that had helped the democracy movement. Student demonstrators may appeal to Americans for help, but the Government is suggesting that Americans keep their distance.

Beijing Death Toll at Least 300; Army Tightens Control of City but Angry Resistance Goes On
By Nicholas D. Kristof

BEIJING, Monday, June 5—Army units tightened their hold on the center of the Chinese capital on Sunday, moving in large convoys on some of the main thoroughfares and firing indiscriminately at crowds as outraged citizens continued to attack and burn army vehicles.

It was clear that at least 300 people had been killed since the troops first opened fire shortly after midnight on Sunday morning but the toll may be much higher. Word-of-mouth estimates continued to soar, some reaching far into the thousands. Outbreaks of firing continued today, as more convoys of troops moved through the city.

The bloodshed stunned Beijing and seemed to traumatize its citizens. Normal life halted as armored personnel carriers and troop trucks rumbled along debris-filled roads, with soldiers firing their automatic weapons in every direction. Smoke filled the sky as workers and students vented frustration and outrage by burning army vehicles wherever they found them separated from major convoys, in side streets or at intersections.

The area around central Tiananmen Square was completely sealed by troops who periodically responded with bursts of automatic-weapons fire whenever crowds drew close to the square.

By ordering soldiers to fire on the unarmed crowds, the Chinese leadership has created an incident that almost surely will haunt the Government for years to come. It is believed here that after the bloodshed of this weekend, it will be incomparably more difficult to rule China.

Many fewer people than normal were in the streets Sunday and today, and some of them ended up in the hospitals or in the morgues. The number of casualties may never be known, because the Government has asked hospitals not to report any numbers on deaths or injuries. However, based on accounts pieced together from doctors at several hospitals, it seems that at least 200 died in the hospitals and that many other corpses were probably left in the hands of the military.

'We had to concentrate on those who were still living," one doctor said today. "We had to leave behind most of those who already were dead."

When troops finally seized Tiananmen Square early Sunday morning, they allowed the student occupiers who held on to the center of the square for three weeks to leave and then sent tanks to run over the tents and makeshift encampment that demonstrators had set up. Unconfirmed reports rapidly spread that some students had remained in the tents and were crushed to death.

The troops sealed off Tiananmen Square and started a huge bonfire. Many Beijing residents drew the conclusion, again impossible to verify, that the soldiers cremated corpses to destroy the evidence.

The student organization that coordinated the long protests continued to function and announced today that 2,600 students were believed to have been killed. Several doctors said that, based on their discussions with ambulance drivers and colleagues who had been on Tiananmen Square, they estimated that at least 2,000 had died. But some of these estimates, based principally on antipathy for the Government, appeared to be high.

Soldiers also beat and bayonetted students and workers after daybreak on Sunday, witnesses said, usually after some provocation but sometimes entirely at random.

"I saw a young woman tell the soldiers that they are the people's army, and that they mustn't hurt the people," a young doctor said after returning from one clash Sunday. "Then the soldiers shot her, and ran up and bayonetted her. I ran away, so I couldn't tell if she lived or died."

News of the killings quickly spread to other parts of China, principally by radio reports from the Voice of America and the British Broadcasting Corporation.

Chinese-language broadcasts have been jammed recently, but not on all frequencies.

In Shanghai, some supporters of the democracy movement reacted to the killings in Beijing by going on strike, a diplomat there said in a telephone interview. However, few factories are open on Sundays, so the real test of a strike will come today, and many people doubt that a strike will be successful because of a lack of organization among workers.

In addition, Shanghai residents expressed protest by erecting barricades throughout the city to block traffic.

In northeastern China, small demonstrations to protest the killings in Beijing were held in Shenyang, Dalian and Changchun. However, in those areas there has not been much talk of a general strike, a diplomat said.

Huge convoys of scores of army vehicles, led by tanks, continued to roll through the main roads of Beijing this morning and early afternoon, skirting trucks that had been set on fire by civilians with Molotov cocktails. Troops in the vehicles fired their submachine guns constantly, mostly in the air. However, some casualties were reported.

Troops still fired periodically when clusters of people gathered near the Beijing Hotel, and several people were reported killed and injured. Among them was a middle-aged Western man who was hit in the leg and stomach, according to a witness. He could not be immediately identified and his condition was not known.

In a sign that the troops' mission is not over, the television news today broadcast a letter from the army headquarters to the soldiers, congratulating them on their "everlasting historic exploits in defending our republic" and warning that "the struggle is a long and complicated one."

"Arriving at the scheduled positions and restoring order at the square is only the first elementary victory we have achieved," the letter added, without elaborating. "More difficult and challenging tasks remain before us."

China's television news on Sunday night showed the army knocking down a replica of the Statue of Liberty that students had put in place on the square. The broadcast hailed troops for "victoriously crushing this counterrevolutionary rebellion."

The broadcast did not mention civilian casualties, but said that three soldiers had been killed and two were missing.

In fact, one of the three, a man who was described as "beaten dead by ruffians on Jianguomen Bridge," had actually been run over by an armored personnel carrier.

The official news also indicated that people had destroyed 31 military trucks, 23 police cars, two armored personnel carriers and 31 buses. But those numbers seemed much too low, for everywhere in Beijing people reacted to the killings by torching vehicles and creating blockades. The troops controlled only a few major thoroughfares, and elsewhere citizens continued to control the streets.

One soldier who had shot a young child was overpowered by a large crowd in the Chongwenmen district early Sunday, and then hanged and burned him as he dangled from a bridge. Troops later arrived at the scene and cut down his smoking corpse.

The Government issued an announcement calling for the return of weapons it said had been taken from the army, as well as demanding that "kidnapped" troops be returned. The announcement could be interpreted as preparing the way for an attack on several universities, on the ground of recovering stolen weapons.

Student leaders apparently have some submachine guns that were taken from soldiers or from supply trucks, but at least so far they have seemed more interested in displaying the weapons than in using them. Students at People's University also seized an armored personnel carrier this afternoon and drove it around their neighborhood, but there was no indication that they planned to use them against troops.

There was no announcement from the senior leader, Deng Xiaoping, Prime Minister Li Peng or other officials who presumably ordered the military attack on student demonstrators. Mr. Li is believed to be winning so far in a major power struggle with the Communist Party General Secretary, Zhao Ziyang, who favors a more moderate line toward protesters.

Some accounts had Mr. Deng in poor health, and even in a hospital, but diplomats noted that such rumors invariably surface whenever the 84-year-old leader has been absent from view for a period of time. Mr. Deng has not appeared in public since he met the Soviet President, Mikhail S. Gorbachev, on May 16. . . .

In Beijing, Rage and Despair over the Soldiers' Brutality

By Sheryl WuDunn

BEIJING, June 4—Her world collapsed early this morning, when she got a phone call that her husband was in the hospital fighting to survive the bullets that ripped through his midriff.

"He was convinced that by staying in the Communist Party, he was in a better position to contribute to the reforms," said the 30-year-old woman, whose puffed red eyes betrayed hours of weeping. "At the time, he said such a party could never hurt the people. But he was wrong. And so many party members think the same way he does. They are all deluded."

Despair seemed to silence the woman's sobs as she sat on an old bench outside the intensive care unit where her husband lay. The despair was accompanied by a fear that kept her from disclosing her name.

Throughout the capital today, untold numbers of people found their lives shattered by a similar grief. Their tales were all different, but they were bound by a common source of tragedy—the military crackdown against China's democracy movement—and by a common rage at the Government. Beijing today was nothing so much as a city of sorrow.

The woman's husband, a 31-year-old engineer who has seven Chinese patents to his name, had sensed that something would happen Saturday night, and he had made sure to carry a piece of paper with his name, address and phone number on it.

Early in the night, the two of them had gone out together and seen the troops chatting rather comfortably with local residents. She went home at 11 P.M. to care for their 4-year-old son and to wait for her husband. He returned around midnight after the first shots were fired at the crowd, but he left again almost immediately.

"There is violence out there and the students are poor and weak," she recalled him saying. "I must go out and help them."

Finally, at 3 A.M. this morning the Beijing Union Medical College Hospital called to say that her husband needed emergency surgery. It lasted seven hours.

The hospitals this afternoon were calmer than in the early morning, when wounded students and workers were brought in every few minutes. Several stretchers are still splotched with bloodstains, but the pools of blood on the hospital floors are gone and the frenzy has subsided.

The possibility that the bloodshed may continue alarms doctors, however.

"We have no more blood," said one doctor at the Union Medical College Hospital. "If there are many more wounded again in the next couple of days, we won't be able to handle them."

The growing expectation of a widespread crackdown frightens some hospital employees from revealing details about their patients or the number of deaths, and doctors at several hospitals say they have been told that visitors other than kin or close friends are not allowed through the gates.

This afternoon, sympathetic workmen led a reporter into the Union Medical College Hospital by an underground passage, past the guards at the gate.

A small crowd gathered in the center of one of the special wards, where the bloodied young men and women lay side by side on mattresses on the floor. Wives bent down over their wounded husbands to loosen a shoelace or just to reassure their loved one that the wounds would heal.

Citizens carried or carted to the hospitals many of the wounded found on the outskirts of the square, but ambulances were needed to enter parts of the Tiananmen Square area to pick up the wounded.

Doctors at different hospitals said today that they had often been restricted in collecting the wounded. Without the cooperation of the army, it was difficult to enter or leave certain parts of the Tiananmen area with the wounded.

One doctor who traveled in his hospital's ambulance to Tiananmen Square said machine guns raked the sides of the ambulance when it was making its way out of the square with several wounded citizens. He showed the bullet holes in the vehicle.

Everywhere in the hospital corridors there were stories of dashed hopes and lives that had been changed forever by a moment on Tiananmen Square.

A 24-year-old Government official was fleeing from a volley of bullets on a side street just northeast of the square when three men near him were hit with bullets. He went to help them, but a People's Liberation Army officer stopped him from tending the wounded.

"Don't stir or you will be dead," a soldier said as he pointed a rifle at the official's head. The official said a dozen soldiers then surrounded him and beat him with bricks, truncheons and the butts of their rifles.

"I never thought they would be so brutal," said the official, still wearing his bloodied clothes at a hospital where he is recovering from wounds all over his body. A friend had spent the afternoon with him, and now they were taking a walk around an area of the dark corridor, his friend supporting him.

A 28-year-old Government official stayed at home during the night and wandered out only at daylight to see what happened. When he strolled over at 9 A.M. to the Beijing Hotel, a few hundred yards east of the square, he was shot in the hip.

"I feel as though my leg isn't there," he moaned to a doctor beside him. The doctor assured him that he would survive, although she said nothing about his leg.

"I thought the Government would use only rubber bullets," he added, as his wife moved closer to comfort him.

One young man who had spent hours helping out at a hospital early in the morning returned home this afternoon only to find that his wife's younger brother had been beaten to death by the troops.

Shoppers on a major side street this afternoon also were shot simply because they were in the line of view when troops decided to open fire on Wangfujing, one of Beijing's most popular shopping districts.

A Chinese student studying in Japan had returned home to visit his wife and son. When he crossed the street, soldiers shot him in the back. Doctors say he will be paralyzed forever.

A Student's Body Is Honored with Tears of Horror and Cries for Revenge
By Sheryl WuDunn

BEIJING, June 5—For the dozen student pallbearers who walked solemnly into the university hall, it was a grim scene: The body of a friend lay wrapped in a red cloth and nestled in a bed of ice on a table.

The students, their heads bowed in silence, circled the table while another student with a megaphone tried to clear the crowds away. Next to the body someone had placed a white "A01" license plate, the code for a high-ranking military vehicle and now, for the students, a spoil of war.

"I want to take revenge," said a 22-year-old student, his voice choking and his eyes beginning to tear beneath his wire-rim glasses. "It will be blood for blood."

Hundreds of people had come to see the macabre exhibit, which the students had erected to expose the atrocities they say the Government has committed against its citizens. Students wept, and in hushed voices they constantly asked each other one question: How could the Government commit such a horror?

The air was heavy with the smell of death and the floor splotched with pools of water where ice had melted. The body, along with four others, had been carried by workers Sunday morning from central Tiananmen Square to a small alley in the western part of the city. From there, the bodies were transported by car to the dark, empty front hall at the University of Politics and Law, where the last one now remained.

For the visiting students, who were from the University of Aerospace and Aeronautics, the body was confirmation that their friend had been martyred for the democracy movement. The whereabouts of two other students, out of 100 in the department of engineering dynamics, are still not known.

Students say more than 2,000 of their classmates from universities all over the capital are missing and feared dead. Some may have gone home to the provinces, and some may have stayed with family or friends in central Beijing. Some may have been killed and their bodies burned by troops to destroy the evidence.

Throughout the universities in the capital, the color and zest of the protest movement has turned to deep bitterness. Now white banners of mourning cover the campuses, and black cloths frame the front entrances of the universities, where people have come to seek solace.

"The soil of our nation is fertilized by blood," read a banner at Beijing University. "In all the world, there is nothing more cruel than this."

Students hovered in small groups, sharing expressions of horror over the army's massacre and trying to dispel their anger and anxiety over rumors that the universities will be the targets of the next military attack.

At Beijing University today, teachers were urged by school officials to spread the word among the students not to stage any demonstrations. The university clinic was asked to prepare for first aid, and teachers and students were warned not to go out at night.

The authorities said troops had been ordered to kill anyone who tries to stop the army from entering the school, according to a teacher who attended the meeting. For those still at the universities, there was no place to hide.

"Many students have left the campus because it is dangerous here," said another young teacher, who spoke as she nervously fiddled with her bicycle in the center of the campus. The absence of so many students makes it difficult to account for those who may have been killed. Some teachers say that only one death of a Beijing University student has been confirmed, and some estimates put the number of those missing from the university at more than 200.

"The Government won't let Beijing University alone, because it knows that this university is a hotbed of activism," the teacher said. The prestigious school traditionally has been the focus of many student political movements.

"What can we do?" she asked. "We have nowhere to escape."

Artillery Firing in Suburbs Adds to Tensions in Beijing; Mystery on Leaders Grows
By Nicholas D. Kristof

BEIJING, Wednesday, June 7—Artillery fire reverberated through the capital Tuesday, and there were continued reports of clashes among rival military units.

The security situation seemed to continue to deteriorate, and today there were the first direct moves against foreign residents of the capital. Troops fired at the Qijiayuan Diplomatic Compound, where many diplomats and foreign journalists live, witnesses said, but no one was known to be injured.

This afternoon, troops sealed off the nearby Jianguomenwai Diplomatic Compound, which also houses thousands of foreign diplomats and journalists. Several soldiers with submachine guns guarded each entrance and refused to allow people to enter or leave.

Embassies of several countries were trying to arrange evacuations of their nationals in the compound, but it was not immediately clear if they would be successful.

Witnesses also said that soldiers had stopped two diplomatic cars on Beijing's third ring road, forced the foreign occupants of the car out at gunpoint and robbed them of all their belongings.

The sounds of artillery fire appeared to be coming from the western outskirts of the city, the general direction of the headquarters of the Beijing military region. But it could not be determined if the headquarters was involved in the fighting or who was firing the shells. Most diplomats and Chinese said they assumed that the shelling involved competing army units seeking a military solution to China's power struggle.

The evening news program denounced as "purely rumor" the reports of fighting between military units near the military airport in southern Beijing. It also offered an unusual denial of a report that Deng Xiaoping, China's senior leader, had died.

"That's a sheer fabrication intended to poison people's minds," the newscaster said, without shedding any light on Mr. Deng's situation or whereabouts. . . .

The air of unreality in the capital has been increased by the mysteries in the press. The newspapers have not appeared in several days, and state television has been growing increasingly peculiar. Tuesday's evening television news program never showed the faces of the news readers, for example, as if they were embarrassed to be seen. The English-language news was canceled, and all programming ended early.

Nobody interviewed seems to believe the Government propaganda, and it is so discredited that it seems to make most people even angrier than they were.

The Government spokesman said in his estimate of casualties that more than 5,000 soldiers had been wounded, compared with 2,000 citizens wounded. He said that the number of 300 killed included "troops, thugs and spectators," but did not indicate which were most numerous. But he said that only 23 students were known to have died. . . .

Foreboding Grasps Beijing; Army Units Crisscross City; Foreigners Hurry to Leave
By Nicholas D. Kristof

BEIJING, Thursday, June 8—As reports of clashes between military units on the outskirts of Beijing continued, a major convoy of tanks and trucks returned to the capital early today, dashing hopes that the unit responsible for large-scale killing might be withdrawing.

On Wednesday, three tank-led convoys headed out of the city toward the east. All were assumed to belong to the 27th Army, the unit most responsible for the killing of hundreds or possibly thousands of protesters and bystanders here since Sunday. Clashes were then reported in Tongxian County, about 20 miles east of Beijing, but like most such reports they could not be confirmed.

The crisscrossing of the capital by nervous military units compounded the sense of urgency at foreign embassies. The United States and other countries ordered an evacuation of diplomats'

103

families, and some embassies said they would also be sending staff members home. . . .

Everything about China is tinged with the surreal these days, even the troop movements.

"Down with chaos!" several thousand troops shouted in unison on Wednesday as they marched east along the Avenue of Eternal Peace, accompanied by scores of military vehicles. "Down with corruption! Fight the counterrevolutionaries! Fight the fascists!"

And then, fueling the chaos around them, the troops simultaneously began firing their submachine guns into the air, creating a deafening thunder that lasted several minutes and sent people diving to the ground. It was not clear if they were firing as a show of strength, to clear the streets of spectators, or for some other reason.

This morning, shortly before dawn, tanks escorted scores of troop trucks west along the Avenue of Eternal Peace toward Tiananmen Square, the clatter of tank treads softened slightly by a gentle rain. It was no clearer why the convoy was now heading west than why it had gone east the previous day.

It was similarly unclear who, if anyone, is running China. The country's pre-eminent leader, Deng Xiaoping, was last seen on May 16, and there were rumors that he is dead or dying. But the morning news programs and the Communist Party newspaper, *People's Daily*, which reappeared for the first time in several days, reported that Prime Minister Li Peng had held a meeting, suggesting that he still is in authority. . . .

The Government issued a statement attacking the decision to give refuge in the American Embassy to Fang Lizhi, the astrophysicist, who is China's best-known dissident.

"The refuge provided to Fang by the U.S. Embassy in Beijing is an interference in China's internal affairs," read the statement, issued by the official New China News Agency.

On the Surface, Beijing Starts to Appear Normal
By Sheryl WuDunn

BEIJING, June 8—A bitter memory lingers on a narrow street where soldiers opened fire on scores of citizens last Sunday, but even here on South Pond Street, life today seemed to be gradually returning to normal.

A man selling bananas now stands where neighbors say an old man was shot in the head Sunday morning, and part of the street has become a nursery for children who chase each other in circles a block away from the Avenue of Eternal Peace, or Changan Avenue, which is still controlled by troops.

Neighbors took their turns walking gingerly toward the avenue to peer beyond the police barricade at the troops. Just days before, few of them dared to venture that far.

The rumble of tank treads and the sporadic crackle of machine-gun fire continued in the capital today. But the atmosphere of fear and apprehension that cast a pall over Beijing earlier this week seemed to fade today as people on bicycles flooded the streets, mail trucks began to resume their rounds, and many Government offices resumed operation. People answered the phone at more than half of 26 Government offices called today. Today, much more than in previous days, there seemed a genuine possibility that life would soon return to normal—although there remains a deep bitterness against the Government.

But this calm may be only superficial. While people's activities may hint of normalcy, many citizens, like the residents of South Pond Street, still harbor a deep anger against the Government.

"The blood of those who were killed has already hardened on the gate down the road," said one woman.

The Government has blamed the chaos that has stricken the city on "a very small number" of counterrevolutionaries and thugs whom it accuses of conspiring to overthrow the Government.

"We are all counterrevolutionaries," said a 30-year-old woman, with some bitterness. "We are all thugs now."

Next to her, a young man said, "Only a very small number of people support the Government."

Although garbage lay scattered in the streets, the authorities had towed away many of the burned-out vehicles and buses that citizens used to make road blocks. Tonight's news program also showed soldiers sweeping the streets of debris from recent fighting.

For the first time since the military crackdown, troops even allowed citizens on Changan Avenue and on the north side of Tiananmen Square early this morning for about half an hour. The square had been the campsite of pro-democracy student demonstrators until soldiers cleared the area Sunday morning. Now the square is an encampment for thousands of soldiers and their tanks and trucks.

When the area was sealed off again this morning, it was by the police rather than by army troops, and the atmosphere seemed much less tense than before. Leaving one's home to buy vegetables still involves a risk, but it is smaller than it was a few days ago, and residents seemed to have stopped building barricades at intersections.

Groups of troops still patrolled the capital, as they marched in formation through neighborhood streets, and gunfire echoed periodically. But along major roads and bridges where armed soldiers had set up camp, citizens of all ages gathered and chatted with them.

The fervor of their appeals was gone, and instead the citizens were restrained and polite, taking care not to taunt or anger the armed soldiers.

"We hope you think of yourselves as the army for the people," a young man said calmly to one of the soldiers. "We hope you will protect, and not harm, us."

Some of the soldiers listened silently to the pleas of the people, while others laughed and joked. This group of troops said it was from the 39th Army, from the northeastern city of Shenyang, and some soldiers even said they did not approve of the massacre committed Sunday by troops widely believed to be from the 27th Army.

"They have tarnished the image of the army," said one soldier to a small crowd of citizens plying him with questions about his views on the 27th Army.

"We wouldn't kill people," said another soldier. "We are the people's army." But a woman hearing this turned away in disgust.

"That's what they've been saying all along, but look what happened," she said as she walked away. . . .

Democracy Movement: Over, for the Time Being
By Nicholas D. Kristof

BEIJING, June 11—The bloodstains are scarcely visible on the pavement now, the once ubiquitous posters calling for greater freedom are now only tattered shreds, and no one dares protest as the prisons open up for those who sought change.

The democracy movement, which in just eight weeks convulsed China and awakened aspirations throughout the nation for a more open political system, seems finally to have collapsed, for now. Even in cities around the country where protest reached a peak last week in reaction to the shooting of hundreds or possibly thousands of demonstrators in Beijing, resistance has collapsed and protesters are awaiting their fates.

The collapse of the movement suggests the difficulties that Chinese dissidents face in sustaining any organized opposition to the Government. The authorities apparently retain the loyalty of the security apparatus and the army, and the result is that they can intimidate an active opposition into at least a sullen acquiescence.

In the pre-dawn hours on June 4, when soldiers were firing their guns on demonstrators and the crowd was retreating down Beijing's Changan Avenue, anguished young men carried the bloodied corpses of their friends and bellowed their response: "Strike! Strike! Strike!" But there was no general strike. People stayed away from work for a few days—mostly because of fear of stray bullets—but there was never an organized strike. Now workers are returning to their factories.

Last week, many Chinese also hoped that some military units were ready to attack the 27th Army, which was responsible for most of the bloodshed, and depose the elements in the leadership that had launched the crackdown. There were some murky reports of military skirmishes, but it now seems increasingly unlikely that the army will intervene in support of democracy.

"There is no hope," said a Beijing University student who has been active in the democracy movement. A few weeks ago, he would have been happy to be quoted by name; now he is afraid to allow his name to be used.

"The movement is over," he continued. "Maybe it can come back later on, maybe there can be some underground organization, but essentially everyone is terrified into submission. Who can resist guns?"

The democracy movement has several times risen after what seemed to be fatal blows, and the situation in China is unstable. But for now, intimidation seems to prevail.

The tangible achievements of the last two months—a freer press, a network of student organizations, an unofficial student newspaper, an unofficial labor union, an immense number of ad hoc bulletin boards where people posted essays and articles from foreign newspapers—all have vanished. The exhilaration and boldness of the last two months have been replaced by pain and panic.

The university campuses are empty, the loudspeakers quiet, and the student organizations disbanded. Since all the students have gone home, it would be difficult to revive the student movement even if the atmosphere were more tolerant.

Still, beneath the surface and beyond the superficial expressions of assent there is a profound rage and bitterness at the nation's aging leadership. In some past crackdowns, such as the 1957 anti-rightist campaign, there was a reservoir of good will toward the Government, and so people wondered if maybe the leadership was right even when it did things that seemed on their face to be bad. But the good will has long since dissipated, and it is virtually impossible to find somebody who in private has anything positive to say about the Government.

Even if the democracy movement has lost this battle, this rage is likely to resurface. Both Chinese and foreign experts note that there has been a regular pattern of a period of growing tolerance followed by a crackdown and then crackdown followed by a steady increase in tolerance and democracy, followed by a new crackdown. Each time the flowering of ideas and enthusiasm for democracy has been greater than the previous one, and so most people expect that after a few months or years, the movement will re-emerge as vigorous as ever.

"Democracy is now engraved in people's hearts, so you can't say the movement is washed up," said a young worker who sympathized with the recent demonstrations but was not much involved himself. "Even ordinary people who don't really understand what the students want, they feel in their hearts a hatred for the Government that makes them support the students."

While most people believe that the democracy movement, as a mass campaign, has definitely lost the first round, many say the present leadership is unstable and could still be ousted by other elements within the Communist Party. The leadership still has not summoned a Central Committee meeting to ratify the dismissal of the party General Secretary, Zhao Ziyang, and most people believe that Mr. Zhao has a number of silent supporters on the Central Committee.

It is not yet clear how the provinces and localities will react to the political furor in Beijing, but so far they seem to be unenthusiastic about a retreat to the purges of the Maoist era.

Two years ago, the campaign against "bourgeois liberalization" collapsed partly because provinces did little to implement it. Now Chinese intellectuals are hoping that the same will happen this year, and they are fleeing to the provinces because they feel they are safer than the capital.

Almost anything seems possible, including some kind of a power play or revolt within the leadership that would bring less hard-line elements to the fore. And if this does not happen, many believe that the political problems and economic challenges that the Government faces will be so severe that Prime Minister Li Peng will be hard pressed to last a year.

SUMMER 1989

As the enthusiasm on the streets of China was turning into anxiety and then to despair, people in Poland, who had been through similar emotional cycles over the past decade, were embarking on something that had never happened before under Communism—openly contested elections for a parliament that was to be more than a rubber stamp. As agreed in the round-table talks held during the winter, the elections were organized in such a way as to assure the Communists a bloc of seats in the lower house, which along with those allotted to their docile allied parties would assure them a majority. In the newly reconstituted Senate, however, all 100 seats were up for grabs, and there, it was thought, the Solidarity-backed candidates would make the largest gains. From Solidarity's perspective the election turned out considerably better than this. As summer approached and the cherries blossomed, revolutionary élan was giving way to energetic political campaigning of the sort that had never been seen within any Communist country. Even though there was little tumult in the streets, it was nevertheless a remarkable season. People who until very recently had been in prison or hiding as fugitives were running for the highest offices as heroes of the nation. At the same time the leaders of the party were relinquishing power and prerogatives and were virtually shrinking in full view as the election approached.

Communist Wallflowers Join Democracy's Dance
By John Tagliabue

WARSAW, May 23—The Communist Party's candidates held an open house Saturday, and they were selling warm Coca-Cola, toilet paper and biographies of President Bush.

The Coke was a kind of refreshment. The toilet paper, a notoriously scarce commodity in present-day Poland, was a come-on for indifferent voters, and the Bush biographies were being autographed by the author, Longin Pastusiak, a Communist Party candidate for the Senate and one of the country's best-known America scholars.

For the first time since early postwar years, Poland's Communist Party is waging an election campaign, one that essentially pits it against the Solidarity trade union movement. But while Solidarity is fighting aggressively, the party has been a wallflower, trying to interest Poles in a party most of them hold responsible for 40 years of repression and mismanagement.

"I'll probably lose," said Jerzy Wojtysiak, a 46-year-old building contractor who is running on the independent list, which the Communist leadership hopes will siphon votes from Solidarity. "You know about the Roman Emperor Caligula, how they elected his horse to the Senate?" he asks. "Well, here, if they brought a cow with a sign that said Solidarity, it would get elected."

At a rally that was billed as an occasion to meet the candidates, Mr. Wojtysiak stood in a schoolyard out in the Wola district of Warsaw, amid gray apartment buildings, where children played games, sipped Coke and heard a group wail an American country-and-western tune that went, "I hope your dreams come true." None of the Solidarity people showed up since the union rarely sends candidates to such rallies because they seldom offer a chance for debate and the union resists giving any semblance of support to the party and its allies.

Few voters came, and those who did appeared very much more interested in toilet paper than politics.

Ireneusz Szrajner, a Communist candidate from a Wola housing project, uses none of the signs, symbols or slogans of the party. There are no endorsements from smiling party bosses, no mention of Gen. Wojciech Jaruzelski or the Prime Minister, Mieczyslaw Rakowski, on any posters or leaflets. The party organization in Warsaw has eschewed the hammer and sickle on streetcar advertisements, choosing instead a bright red-and-white stylized figure of a mermaid, the symbol of Warsaw, waving a Polish flag.

Mr. Szrajner, a 42-year-old engineer, is down-to-earth. "Do you want to have a telephone?" his election leaflets ask. "Then vote for Ireneusz Szrajner." That is because in his neighborhood, a cluster of high-rises housing 6,500 families, there are 200 telephones.

To offset the unpopularity of its leaders and record, the party has sought popular figures from the stage, television and public life. Poland's first astronaut, Miroslaw Hermaszewski, an Army officer who rode in a Soviet craft, is running for the Senate. In Wroclaw, an industrial center in Silesia, the local zookeeper, who also stars with his wife in a popular television show about animals, is a Communist candidate.

Whatever the outcome of the election, the party hardly forfeits its primacy. Though elections to the 100-seat Senate will be entirely open, the Communists and their allies in two smaller parties are guaranteed 65 percent of the seats in the more powerful lower chamber.

While in Warsaw, where Mr. Szrajner is running, the local party apparatus decreed that any party member who obtained 3,000 signatures would be on the ballot, party leaders in other regions established a process to assure selection of the party's preferred candidate.

Competitive caucuses and competition as in Warsaw were the means preferred by the party leader, General Jaruzelski, who appears to be following the lead of Mikhail S. Gorbachev in exploiting such competition to weed out old faces and inject new vigor into the prostrate party.

"The process is important not only for the elections, but also for the party," said Ludwik Krasucki, a leading party ideologist. "We need changes, and this creates a possibility for volunteers to come forward."

Fired by successes in these pre-election caucuses, liberal party thinkers like Mr. Krasucki, who is also the deputy editor of the party's ideological journal, muse about the day when the party may evolve into a "modern left-wing party."

The anguish over all this among the party's conservatives is threatening to split its ranks. Their anger is raised by Solidarity's campaign claim to an agreement the union says was struck with the authorities that while the present elections are limited, those in four years will be entirely free.

As the campaign heats up, those in the party averse to change show signs of the party striking back. In Warsaw today, a court angered students by refusing to fulfill agreements reached between the Communist authorities and Solidarity and register a Solidarity-affiliated student union. Some 200 students chanting anti-Government slogans tried to march on central Warsaw, and some fought with the police and shouted "Down with Communism!" About 20 protesters were detained.

This evening, television viewers were startled to discover that Solidarity's weekly election campaign program had been struck from the listing and replaced with a song-and-dance show. A speaker on the screen announced laconically that the program offended "the policy of reconciliation."

Mr. Krasucki said internal party studies showed about 10 to 12 percent of party members reject the changes represented by the balloting, while 23 to 25 percent fully supported them. "The majority are in the middle, and they are waiting to see whether the reforms will succeed," he said. "If they succeed, they will be with us."

"Both clear tendencies are playing a bigger role than the persons in the middle," he said. "What Poland needs is a return to the middle."

But if the still-ruling party was undergoing stress in the process, there were other Poles who were clearly euphoric as they watched their candidates campaign openly with speeches that a year earlier could have only appeared in the clandestine press.

In an Unpredictable Land, the Pariah as Candidate
By John Tagliabue

WARSAW, June 1—The indictment in Jacek Kuron's trial for anti-Government activity in 1983 describes him this way: "Not working, no estate, no decorations, nonassociated." Despite such meager qualifications, Mr. Kuron has been a favorite target of official repression over the years.

Twice he was ejected from the Communist Party: the first time in 1953, after six months' membership, for refusal to submit to self-criticism, and again in 1964. Once he was beaten senseless by the police and left with a concussion.

All told, the 56-year-old Solidarity leader has spent nearly nine years in prison for crimes ranging from attempting to overthrow the system to undermining the alliance with Moscow. Now he is a Solidarity candidate in the election on Sunday, Poland's first experiment in competitive elections in nearly half a century.

Yet Mr. Kuron's race is unusual for reasons other than his background, which has produced charges that he is a Communist and anti-Semitic slurs although he is not a Jew. It is perhaps the most intensely watched and compelling match in the country because his opponent is one of Poland's most distinguished lawyers and defenders of human rights causes, Wladyslaw Sila-Nowicki. Mr. Sila-Nowicki, once a chief Solidarity adviser, enjoys strong backing from some of Poland's Roman Catholic bishops.

On Wednesday night, the burly Mr. Kuron, clad typically in T-shirt, blue jeans and denim jacket, and clutching a microphone, paced like an aging warhorse in the cavernous basement of St. Zygmunt's Church, a cluster of concrete spires in Warsaw's lately patrician Zoliborz district. It is here that he is running against Mr. Sila-Nowicki.

The tall, 76-year-old lawyer fell from favor three years ago after agreeing to join an advisory council to Gen. Wojciech Jaruzelski, when the opposition was still boycotting the Communist leader. Though Solidarity is assured 35 percent of the 460-seat Parliament, it has declared the balloting for its seats free and democratic, opening the door to challengers like Mr. Sila-Nowicki, who for his part says he is running to give Solidarity voters a clear choice.

In response to the challenge, Mr. Kuron has plunged into a grueling campaign, rousing crowds that, night after night, jam local movie houses and church basements with impassioned defenses of his record and his vision of Poland's future.

The campaign tactics of the race are strikingly up-to-date by Western standards. Andrzej Anusz, a 24-year-old history student, commands an army of 100 volunteers, high school and college students who wallpapered Zoliborz with red and white posters proclaiming the time and place of Mr. Kuron's twice-daily public appearances. Others depict the burly, balding candidate side by side with Solidarity's leader, Lech Walesa. A minibus cruises the neighborhood, loudspeakers on its roof blaring the Kuron message.

Although he lacks the broad appeal of leaders like Mr. Walesa, Mr. Kuron has been called the godfather of Solidarity. A veteran of the Workers' Defense Committee in the 1970's, he organized an information service during the strikes that spawned Solidarity in 1980, and again last year during the labor unrest that led to its return, to keep reporters abreast of events. Last year, he was arrested.

Solidarity's intellectual roots go back to elaborate strategies Mr. Kuron developed in the 1970's with other independent leaders, like the essayist Adam Michnik, who calls Mr. Kuron a spiritual mentor.

These themes echo at his rallies. In response to a woman's question whether elections will be truly free in four years, as promised, he said: "Political agreements in which political forces divide power are not worth the paper they're written on. If an agreement is real, not fictitious, it is worth the strength of the partners that sign it."

"With the army, the militia and the bureaucracy, the party has about 65 percent of the power," he said, only half-joking, "and the accords we reached with the authorities take into account those circumstances. But those accords give us a chance to organize ourselves. In four years, we will create a new balance. Then we can approach a new agreement with a new balance."

"Is there any certainty?" he asks. "No. But we have a 35 percent chance."

Mr. Kuron spends much of his time seeking to exorcise what many Solidarity supporters see as the greatest sin of his past—his membership in the Communist Party. He explains that he was young—"I stemmed from a very strongly socialist family, my father was a socialist"—and how his membership in the party ended in 1965 when he was sent to prison for the heresy of charging that Poland was run by a "dictatorship of the political bureaucracy" that exploited workers under Communism as the capitalists had done earlier.

Some Zoliborz voters are unhappy about his professed agnosticism. Pamphlets that appear to have been the work of Solidarity's radical student wing, which opposes accommodation with the Communist Party, have appeared, denouncing "the Jew Kuron." Mr. Kuron's campaign managers believe them to be counterfeit, the work of the Government's security police.

For the authorities, Mr. Kuron has evolved from a dangerous enemy into something of a reasonable negotiator and supporter of compromise with the Communists. Still, a victory by Mr. Sila-Nowicki would not be unwelcome, weakening the opposition as it enters Parliament.

Yet Poland is an unpredictable place. Witold Trzeciakowski, a Solidarity economist who shares the Solidarity ticket with Mr. Kuron, gets up to tell one of the few jokes, a flash of black humor, that the campaign has spawned. "Kuron and Kiszczak are taking a walk," the economist says, referring to Gen. Mieczyslaw Kiszczak, the Interior Minister and the Government's negotiator with Solidarity.

"Kuron reproaches Kiszczak: 'Why did you have to demand 65 percent of Parliament?'

"Kiszczak replies, 'Why did you have to demand wage indexing?'

"A voice speaks out," Mr. Trzeciakowski says, " 'Recreation's over. Back to your cells.' "

Everyone, including Mr. Kuron, laughs.

On the very day that Chinese troops were shooting into demonstrators calling for democracy, Poles were lining up to vote in the freest elections ever held under Communism. By the time they ended, Solidarity-backed candidates had been swept in and the party was repudiated. In the weeks and months ahead, the processes unleashed by the elections would go so far that Jacek Kuron, former critic and gadfly of social change, was serving as Minister of Labor in a non-Communist government. But that is getting ahead of the story.

Poland Flirts with Pluralism Today
By John Tagliabue

WARSAW, June 3—Solidarity, born in 1980 as an independent trade union, is being reborn on Sunday as an all-but-official opposition party in the first openly contested election in Eastern Europe in more than four decades.

Four years from now, the movement's banners proclaim, Poland will see a genuinely free election. By implication, Solidarity is campaigning for votes this weekend by promising that limited power is within reach now while the prospect of real power is at least within sight.

For now, with only the Communist Party and its allies formally recognized as political parties, the union must field its candidates as independents, but there are 261 candidates running under a loosely knit organization called the Citizens' Committee of Lech Walesa, named after the union's leader. Mr. Walesa is not running himself, but appears to be waiting in the wings to negotiate for Solidarity in the likely event that the movement emerges with something of a parliamentary veto over the Government's initiatives.

Behind Solidarity's dramatic return to the political stage was the Government's realization that the country's economic problems are so severe that they cannot be resolved without the help of the union. But within Solidarity are conflicting views of how to deal with the crisis.

"Solidarity is itself a child of the system," said Marian Drozdowski, a historian at the Polish Academy of Sciences and a Solidarity supporter. "At heart, there is some kind of belief in a powerful state at the center of the economy."

Echoing other observers of the movement, Mr. Drozdowski predicted that "after the elections there will be a disintegration," as

116

Solidarity strategists more in favor of market economic solutions find it increasingly difficult to support the mainstream labor union orientation, with its focus on job security and maintaining standards of living.

In fact, since its restoration to legal status in April, Solidarity has been slow to sign up new members. It now counts about one million members, compared with the seven million it boasted when martial law was imposed in December 1981.

According to Jan Litynski, a Warsaw union leader who is running on the Solidarity list, this is partly because Solidarity has thrust its limited resources into running the election campaign. He conceded, however, that the relatively low membership is also partly a reflection of a stronger mood of caution and diminished optimism among workers burned once by the use of military force.

Mikolaj Kozakiewicz, a distinguished sociologist and incumbent Parliament deputy who is running for the lower house on the so-called national list of candidates proposed by the Communist-led bloc, believes that divisions after the election will not be limited to Solidarity.

"We can expect after the elections some kind of shifts within all the movements, including the Communist Party, maybe reaching a level as it was before the war when we had 12 to 15 parties," he said.

"As is normal, some will then die out, others will create new alliances, until a more reasonable number emerges at the next elections in four years' time," he added.

Mr. Kozakiewicz believes that Solidarity itself will split into separate groups, one carrying on the functions of a party while another focuses on trade union functions. Mr. Walesa is expected to seek his future in the union wing of Solidarity.

On the Government side, it appears that the Communist Party leader, Gen. Wojciech Jaruzelski, hopes that the balloting process sweeps away apparatchiks resistant to change so that new blood can be pumped into the party—a process employed by President Mikhail S. Gorbachev in March's voting in the Soviet Union.

But the balloting could have the opposite effect of dealing a serious blow to the party's liberal, change-oriented wing. That is because 35 leaders of the Communist-led bloc, including the Prime Minister, Mieczyslaw Rakowski, and Gen. Czeslaw Kiszczak, the Interior Minister who was the chief negotiator with Solidarity, have been put on a national list of candidates.

To win, these unopposed candidates must obtain the support of at least 50 percent of the voters, who must express their preference by not crossing out the candidates' names. Solidarity has mounted a campaign to have voters cross off Communist nominees.

Under sweeping accords concluded in April between Solidarity and the Communists, the union's candidates are in theory capable of sweeping all 100 seats in the Senate, where voting is open and competitive, and can win 35 percent of the lower house, where seats have been apportioned according to a complex formula agreed to at the negotiations this year between Solidarity and the authorities.

The Communist Party will have another 38 percent and parties aligned until now with the Communists the rest.

Runoff elections June 18 will decide any seats not won outright in the first round. Within days of that vote, a joint session of both houses is expected to select a President of the Republic for a six-year term. Given the Communist-bloc majority in the lower house, Gen. Jaruzelski is expected to be chosen. The bold experiment in democracy poses no immediate threat to the Communist Party's monopoly on power, but it will provide Poles with a clear public referendum on the Communists, who have ruled Poland since the country became the first in Eastern Europe to fall under Soviet domination after the war.

Understandably, the campaign has provoked varying official reactions throughout the Eastern bloc, deepening the ideological divide between countries fired more or less by the momentum for change coming from the Soviet Union.

In Hungary, where moves toward change are apace of those in Poland, attention in the official press and television has been rapt. Opposition forces in Hungary reached agreement this week to begin talks with the Communist leadership that could lead to balloting comparable to Poland's.

In East Germany and Czechoslovakia, where resistance to change is strong, reports on Poland were limited and hostile. East Berlin's Communist Party daily, *Neues Deutschland*, has published one report in the last two weeks, reprinting an article from Poland's Communist Party daily that scathingly attacked Solidarity. *Rude Pravo*, the Czechoslovak party daily, has contented itself with reprinting aggressively polemical reports from the Polish Communist press on Solidarity and its allies in the Roman Catholic Church.

The first major step toward institutionalizing democracy in the East bloc came in the Polish elections. Other steps were soon to follow, first in Poland, then Hungary, and then in those very countries whose leaders had been so contemptuous of Polish reforms—East Germany, Czechoslovakia, Bulgaria and Rumania. But as summer approached, Poland was out in front.

Big Solidarity Victory Seen in Poland

By John Tagliabue

WARSAW, June 4—In their first chance to express at the ballot box their feelings about 44 years of Communist rule, Polish voters today appeared to have voted overwhelmingly for candidates endorsed by the Solidarity opposition and to have endangered many unopposed Communists whose election was thought to have been insured by the intricate election rules.

Informal samplings by foreign journalists and exit polls conducted by the opposition raised the prospect that the Communists could fall short, in what would be a crushing setback, of the majority of 65 percent of the seats in the Parliament's lower house that had been guaranteed to them and their supporters by their agreement with Solidarity.

Communist candidates and their allies, running unopposed and on a separate election list from opposition and independent candidates, appeared to be failing in many cases to get the 50 percent of the votes cast that is required for their election to be certified. If they fail to get 50 percent, their seats are supposed to be declared vacant.

Although the system of separate lists was contrived to minimize comparisons between support for the Communists and support for Solidarity, it seemed clear that many more votes were cast for opposition candidates than for supporters of the regime.

By contrast, candidates endorsed by the Solidarity movement—which became a legal organization again less than two months ago—appeared to be rolling up huge majorities in races for the lower house, called the Sejm (Assembly), and the Senate.

The contest for the 100 seats in the Senate was an open one, conducted with a single list of candidates, and there Solidarity's nominees appeared to be on their way to a solid majority in the most open election the Soviet bloc has seen in more than four decades.

Official results were not expected until later in the week, but if the results for the Communists and their allies were as poor as the samplings and exit polls indicated, the opposition may have exceeded its expectations to such an extent as to endanger Solidarity's agreement with the regime of Gen. Wojciech Jaruzelski.

Under the agreement, the governing party needs its guaranteed 299 seats in the 460-member Assembly to assure General Jaruzelski's election as President in an indirect vote by the Parliament's two chambers. Communist officials have hinted that they might then seek to block the convening of the Parliament on constitutional grounds, pointing to a requirement that all 460 seats in the Assembly be filled.

The Solidarity leader, Lech Walesa, who was not standing as a candidate, expressed anxiety about the effects of lopsided results in favor of his movement. "I think that too big a percentage of our people getting through would be disturbing and might force a fight on us," Mr. Walesa said after casting his vote in the Oliwa district of Gdansk, his hometown, according to Reuters.

Though the day was sunny, voter turnout appeared low. The Government said that turnout by 7:30 P.M. varied considerably by province. Low attendance was marked in Lodz, where only 40.9 percent voted, and Bialystok, 50 percent. The largest turnout, according to a Communist Party spokesman, Jan Bisztyga, was in Wloclawek, in central Poland, at 70 percent.

Adam Szostkiewicz, the spokesman for Solidarity's organizing committee in Cracow, said by phone that an informal exit poll of about 100 people in each of the city's nearly 20 districts showed that 75 percent to 80 percent had voted for the union's candidates.

The Government appeared nervous that some of its best-known candidates, running unopposed on the so-called national list, might fail to receive the required 50 percent.

Major losses on the national list would be a blow to General Jaruzelski, who has sought to use the vote to sweep reform-minded leaders into key posts. Speaking in Gdansk, Mr. Walesa said one of the Communist candidates he had chosen was Tadeusz Fiszbach, the Gdansk party leader in the years 1980–81, when the accords that gave birth to Solidarity were signed. Mr. Fiszbach later left office in disgrace and was named Ambassador to Finland after hard-line party factions prevailed.

General Jaruzelski, while declining to say how he had voted, said he hoped that Poland "will get peace from these elections."

"This is a huge step toward democracy," the Polish leader said after casting his vote.

First partial returns were expected to begin arriving on Monday, but official results in most election districts were not expected until later this week, after hand counting of the ballots.

It was as Mr. Walesa feared. Solidarity's people had won everywhere. Moreover, many of the leading Communists who were running unopposed failed to get enough votes to assure victory. Now Solidarity's gravest problem was that society would be expecting their people to bring about real and rapid improvements in daily life, while technically power still lay with the party.

Stunning Vote Casts Poles into Uncharted Waters
By John Tagliabue

WARSAW, June 5—As the breadth and depth of Solidarity's overwhelming victory over the Communists in Poland's freest election in more than four decades emerged today, both the Communist leadership and Solidarity faced questions never confronted before in a Communist-ruled Eastern European country.

To be sure, the Communists have never relied on parliamentary majorities to maintain control. Yet neither had Communists ever resorted to competitive elections before.

For the Government, there was the question of how to continue governing when the results of the elections, though only partial and not official, showed that Solidarity enjoyed the support of the broad majority of Poles. . . .

What appeared to most upset the Communist leadership, as well as some of Solidarity's senior strategists, was the danger to a large bloc of unopposed Communist candidates whose election was supposed to have been assured under the intricate election rules. . . .

Thus the immediate concern was how to get these candidates into the lower house despite the results. To the end, senior Solidarity advisers were hoping they would surmount the 50 percent hurdle. "We would prefer they got 50.5 percent," a Solidarity strategist in Warsaw acknowledged.

"We are trying to shift the focus of power from the party to the Parliament," he explained, "and for that we need these people in Parliament. . . ."

Warsaw Accepts Solidarity Sweep and Humiliating Losses by Party
By John Tagliabue

WARSAW, June 8—As Government and Solidarity negotiators sat down tonight to map out potential fields of political collaboration, the

Government announced the official returns showing the extent of Solidarity's success in Sunday's national elections.

At the start of the talks with Solidarity this evening, Gen. Czeslaw Kiszczak, the Interior Minister who signed the arrest order for the union leader, Lech Walesa, when the Government imposed martial law to crush the movement in 1981, now shook his hand, and told him, "Lech, my hearty congratulations on your election success."

Mr. Walesa, who traveled by train to the talks from his home in the Baltic seaport of Gdansk, replied, "I want to use it for the benefit of Poland."

General Kiszczak, along with the Prime Minister, Mieczyslaw Rakowski, and other members of the Communist Party elite, failed to win seats in Parliament, although they ran as unopposed candidates whose election was thought to have been assured by the complex voting. The same humiliation befell six other members of the party's 17-member ruling Politburo.

According to the official figures, the vote swept in 92 of Solidarity's candidates to the 100-seat Senate, which was contested in open balloting. Eight seats in which none of the competing candidates obtained 50 percent of the votes will be contested in runoffs June 18. There appears to be only one seat, in Slupsk, in northern Poland, where the Communist candidate, a successful private businessman named Henryk Stoklosa, who made a fortune running what is reputed to be Poland's largest private enterprise producing animal fodder, is given a good chance.

In voting for the 161 seats accorded Solidarity in the lower house, the Sejm, only one of the union-endorsed candidates failed to be elected in the first round, necessitating a runoff.

By contrast, the electorate dealt a mortifying rebuke to the Communist Party and its allies. None of those candidates were elected outright to the Senate, and only three obtained enough votes to be certified the winners in the elections to the lower house, in which a complex apportionment assures the Communist-led bloc 65 percent.

Moreover, only two of the Communist-bloc candidates on a list of 35 unopposed nominees to the lower house took the requisite 50 percent of the vote to take their seats. One of them, Mikolaj Kozakiewicz, is a leader of the small Peasant Party, allied with the Communists. Mr. Kozakiewicz, a respected sociologist, has been one of the most scathing critics of the Communist regime in the present Parliament.

The second, Adam Zielinski, is a little-known law professor and chief judge of Poland's highest administrative court. One Communist Party official speculated that Mr. Zielinski may have been elected inadvertently, since his name stood at the bottom of the 35-place alphabetical listing, and some voters may have missed it as they crossed out the names by making a large "x" on the ballot.

Voters in most of the 108 districts gave the Communists dismal returns, ranging from 25 percent down to 5 percent or lower. In one of the most striking defeats, the Government's former spokesman, Jerzy Urban, who is widely known from regular television appearances, ran as an independent for the lower house head-on against a popular Solidarity-endorsed actor, Andrzej Lapicki, and suffered defeat with 15.6 percent of the vote, against his opponent's 77.8 percent.

Among Solidarity's candidates, some of the more prominent to win seats in the Senate included Adam Michnik, the essayist and a leading intellectual light of the opposition, and in the lower house, Jacek Kuron, whom Mr. Michnik has often described as his mentor, who got 65.8 percent of the vote to defeat his opponent, the human rights lawyer Wladyslaw Sila-Nowicki, with 21 percent.

The election paved the way for a bizarre period of parliamentary bickering and maneuver. Finding themselves with a larger and more powerful bloc in Parliament then they had anticipated, the Solidarity-backed representatives were divided as to how to proceed. There were some who wanted to use their new muscle to punish the Communists, for example, to defeat their old nemesis General Wojciech Jaruzelski as he sought parliamentary election to the new post of President. But there were others who cautioned that the still-fragile quest they were embarked upon would require the support of Jaruzelski and the army he commanded. They claimed that the old party liberals were needed to protect the process from party hard-liners who would love to topple it. In the end, Jaruzelski was elected to the post by one vote but only with the help of key abstentions by Solidarity members. Another debate among the Solidarity bloc concerned how they should use their windfall from the elections. Should they remain as an opposition for a while, learning parliamentary practices, or should they immediately vie for real power?

Solidarity Takes Its Elected Place in the Parliament

By Henry Kamm

WARSAW, July 4—Solidarity, vilified and outlawed for eight years until April, jubilantly entered Parliament today as the first freely elected opposition party to do so in a Communist country.

As the Assembly opened its session at noon, Lech Walesa, the Solidarity leader, sat in the place of honor of Poland's newest political institution—the opposition front bench. On the Communist front bench sat Gen. Wojciech Jaruzelski, the man who imposed martial law in 1981 to crush the movement Mr. Walesa founded and put him and his companions in prison.

Later in the day, the two men sat next to one another in the Senate. But at this first meeting, in the lower house, the general sat stolid and unsmiling, barely speaking to those near him and occasionally applauding politely. The Nobel Prize–winning union leader, at ease and visibly enjoying every moment, carried on an animated conversation throughout the formalities with his movement's parliamentary leader, Bronislaw Geremek, and occasionally exchanged jokes with those behind him. Mr. Walesa and General Jaruzelski took no note of one another.

The Solidarity deputies and senators, most of whom still sported the badges bearing the familiar red and white logo on their suits or dresses, took visible satisfaction in reflecting on how far their movement had come. They recalled its birth in the strikes of 1980.

They spoke of the national exhilaration that followed the union's legalization in August 1980 and its crushing and banning by the declaration of martial law in December 1981.

There was a sense of having earned the rebirth of their movement last year in the crucible of renewed labor unrest, which forced the Government to extend implicit and finally explicit recognition of the fact that Solidarity had never ceased to exist.

Today was for the Solidarity members a day of quiet but full triumph. Janusz Onyszkiewicz said this evening at an Independence Day reception at the American Embassy that "the big day for us was the opening of the round-table, when we forced them to talk with us after all these years."

In the afternoon, when the newly created Senate gathered for the first time in the same hall as the Assembly, Gen. Jaruzelski and Mr. Walesa sat together in the front row as guests of honor, smiling and chatting for a moment before proceedings began. The Senate offered no Communist bench to accommodate Gen. Jaruzelski, the party's leader, because Solidarity swept 99 of the 100 seats, losing one to an independent.

Neither General Jaruzelski nor Mr. Walesa ran in the general elections last month.

Many who did watched from the visitors' gallery, among them Prime Minister Mieczyslaw Rakowski, Interior Minister Czeslaw Kiszczak, Defense Minister Florian Siwicki, the official trade union chief Alfred Miodowicz, and several other Politburo members. The voters denied them the right to sit as members, striking their names from the list of 35 unopposed candidates that had been thought sure of election to the lower house.

The union movement won, in addition to 99 seats in the newly created Senate, all 161 seats in the Assembly that it was permitted to contest under the agreement reached with the Communist Party in April.

The losers sat quietly, occasionally conversing with one another and unsmilingly enduring the cameras that were constantly trained on them from the adjoining press box.

They looked down on those whom until recently their party and government had jailed as "dissidents." Elevated to the legitimate status of opposition deputies were such prominent former political prisoners as Jacek Kuron, Adam Michnik and Janusz Onyszkiewicz, as well as Mr. Geremek.

In the Senate, the Solidarity leaders who were honored by the presence of their former jailers as they were sworn in included Bogdan Lis, Karol Modzelewski and Jan Jozef Lipski. Andrzej Wajda, the noted film and stage director, also took the oath of office.

In Parliament today, Mr. Michnik, who unlike his colleagues continued to eschew suit and tie and took his oath in jeans and an open-necked shirt, challenged the lower house's Communist majority when it presented only one candidate for the post of marshal, the officer who presides over sessions.

"Let's have elections here and not just voting," he said in his first appearance at the speaker's rostrum. His demand for more candidates was ignored and the single nominee, Mikolaj Kozakiewicz of the Peasant Party, the only survivor from the "national list," was chosen.

Mr. Kuron, whose friends said he had worn a suit only once, to meet President Bush earlier this year, astonished supporters by appearing in unaccustomed elegance.

The new deputy strayed from the routine of the inaugural session by attacking the Government for Poland's dire economic crisis and denouncing its recent raising of a wide range of consumer prices. "This chaotic policy of the Government is alone responsible for social disturbances and deep public unease," Mr. Kuron said.

Although the Communists intend the "round-table" agreement to safeguard their party's control until fully free elections in 1993, the structure of the new two-chamber Parliament does not guarantee it. The Senate has the right to veto decisions of the lower house. The veto can be overridden by two-thirds, or 306 votes, of the 460-member Assembly. The Communists and their coalition partners, the Democratic and Peasant parties, hold only 299 seats.

As the new Parliament went about its business of establishing a government, it grew more and more apparent that the Communists would not be able to rule on their own. The small, once docile parties that associated with the Communists for so long were finding it advantageous to cut deals with the Solidarity bloc, thus depriving the Communists of the edge they needed to form a government. In this situation the Communists were hoping to entice the Solidarity people—including many they had arrested—to support them as junior partners in a coalition.

Walesa Rejects Offer of Coalition
By John Tagliabue

WARSAW, July 25—The Solidarity leader, Lech Walesa, said today that his movement would not join a grand coalition with the Communist Party, but would prepare instead for the "inevitable" day when it would form a government on its own.

In a two-hour meeting with President Wojciech Jaruzelski, Mr. Walesa spurned the general's offer of a Solidarity-Communist coalition, presenting a statement asserting that in the face of Poland's "continuously deteriorating economic situation," the "only reasonable decision" for the Communists and their minor-party partners would be to hand over running of the Government to Solidarity, which he described as "those forces that enjoy the support of a majority of society."

"Everything indicates, however, that the coalition exercising power now is not ready to accept such a solution," Mr. Walesa said. "In this situation, it must, as a result, take over the whole responsibility for forming a Government.'. . .

"Our philosophy, our attitudes toward the Government, are different," he said. In a Communist-led coalition, Mr. Walesa said, Solidarity would be a "mere floral decoration."

"We would take responsibility for many bad things, we would try to lead the country to reform and we would be buried," he said. . . .

The headlines of the days that followed told the story of a deepening parliamentary crisis and political impasse.

Jaruzelski Says Warsaw Pact Opposes a Solidarity Premier
By John Tagliabue

WARSAW, July 26—President Wojciech Jaruzelski has told Solidarity that he cannot allow it to form a government because Poland's Communist neighbors "would look at this askance," a Solidarity official who attended talks with him said today.

The official, Jozef Slisz, head of Solidarity's rural wing, said General Jaruzelski, in the talks on Tuesday, mentioned "in particular" the Soviet Union, East Germany and Czechoslovakia as opposing the formation of a Solidarity Government or the naming of a Solidarity leader as Prime Minister. . . .

Jaruzelski Quits as Party Leader
By John Tagliabue

WARSAW, July 29—President Wojciech Jaruzelski resigned today as the leader of Poland's Communist Party and was replaced by his close associate, Prime Minister Mieczyslaw Rakowski, the Government press agency said.

At the same meeting, the party's Central Committee shook up its leadership. Besides accepting the resignation of General Jaruzelski, it dismissed 4 others from the 17-member Politburo and 5 of the 9 high-ranking party secretaries.

General Jaruzelski's resignation from the post of First Secretary was expected; he had pledged to step down if elected to the new office of President. When he became President, he gained powers greater than those he held as party secretary. . . .

General Chosen as Polish Prime Minister
By John Tagliabue

WARSAW, July 31—The newly elected Polish Communist Party leader, Mieczyslaw Rakowski, nominated the Interior Minister today to be his successor as Prime Minister, the nation's official press agency said.

The choice of Interior Minister Czeslaw Kiszczak comes as Poland braces for a possible round of sharp food-price increases in the wake of a Government decision to move Tuesday to make food and other essential goods subject to free-market forces. Price increases are a particularly sensitive political matter here, for they set off riots or strikes that toppled party leaders in 1956, 1970 and 1980.

The selection of General Kiszczak was announced by Mr. Rakowski to the Communist parliamentary caucus. Afterward, the floor leader of the Solidarity opposition in Parliament, Bronislaw Geremek, met with General Kiszczak and told him that Solidarity would refuse to provide Cabinet ministers for his Government. . . .

Solidarity Seeks to Oust Warsaw Premier
By John Tagliabue

WARSAW, Aug. 7—Solidarity mounted an effort today to oust the newly elected Prime Minister, Czeslaw Kiszczak, by appealing to small parties allied with the Communists in Parliament to swing their allegiance to an anti-Communist coalition.

Solidarity appears to believe that it can persuade the small Peasant and Democratic parties, whose loyalty to the Communists has been wavering, to withdraw support from General Kiszczak and throw it behind a Solidarity nominee for Prime Minister. Lech Walesa, the Solidarity leader, said efforts by General Kiszczak to assemble a Communist-led cabinet had worsened "the crisis of confidence" and "reaffirmed society's fears that essentially nothing has changed, that hope for the future is nonexistent."

In a statement released to news agencies, the union leader said, "I once again categorically oppose the formation of a new Government by General Czeslaw Kiszczak.". . .

Peasant Party: New Kingmakers for a New Poland
By John Tagliabue

WARSAW, Aug. 10—The newly complicated task of forming a Polish cabinet has turned a little-noticed political party that was a steady satellite of the Communists into a maverick force familiar to millions of Poles.

Today, officials of the party, the United Peasant Alliance, met with leaders of the Solidarity opposition to explore Lech Walesa's appeal this week for the Peasants to desert the Communists and switch to the opposition. Afterward, the two sides announced only that they intended to meet again.

On Wednesday, Aleksander Bentkowski, the Peasants' floor leader in Parliament, shocked Poles by announcing on state television that when it came to a vote, his group could be expected to oppose a cabinet assembled by the Communist Prime Minister, Gen. Czeslaw Kiszczak. . . .

Poland's Premier Offering to Yield to Non-Communist
By John Tagliabue

WARSAW, Aug. 14—Under increasing Soviet pressure for an end to Poland's Government crisis, Prime Minister Czeslaw Kiszczak said today that he would resign and ask that the leader of a small party traditionally allied with the Communists be allowed to form a cabinet.

In a statement read on state television, General Kiszczak said a "new situation has arisen" that appeared to provide a chance for the leader of the United Peasant Alliance, Roman Malinowski, to form a Cabinet "in which representatives of all forces in Parliament would be included."

On the basis of that new situation, General Kiszczak said he would ask that President Wojciech Jaruzelski "draw the appropriate conclusion.". . .

Senior Solidarity Aide Says He Is Being Named Premier
By John Tagliabue

WARSAW, Aug. 18—A senior Solidarity official said today that he would be nominated as Poland's Prime Minister. He would be the first non-Communist head of government in Eastern Europe since the early postwar years.

Various reports in the capital said that the official, Tadeusz Mazowiecki, would be formally nominated by President Wojciech Jaruzelski on Saturday. The nomination would then face a vote in Parliament.

Mr. Mazowiecki, a close aide to the Solidarity founder Lech Walesa, met with General Jaruzelski today and said afterward that he expected to be nominated and that he would accept. . . .

And finally, there came the word that Mr. Mazowiecki, a prominent Catholic editor and Solidarity organizer, had indeed become the first non-Communist to head a government in Eastern Europe since Stalin had imposed Soviet-style Communism there after the Second World War.

Jaruzelski, Moved By "Needs and Aspirations" of Poland, Names Walesa Aide Premier
By John Tagliabue

WARSAW, Aug. 19—The Communist President, Wojciech Jaruzelski, today designated a senior Solidarity official, Tadeusz Mazowiecki, to be the first non-Communist Prime Minister of Poland since the early postwar years.

"The President believes," said a statement issued by General Jaruzelski's office, that the formation of a Government headed by Mr. Mazowiecki would be "conducive to expeditiously overcoming economic difficulties, continuing reforms . . . and satisfying the needs and aspirations of Polish society."

Recalling the year of Solidarity's birth, Mr. Mazowiecki said, "I think there are a great many historic moments in our life, in my lifetime, and I can mention here 1980, that show we can still achieve a lot.

"I think we can gather our strength from within ourselves," he said. "This is not easy, but it is possible if everyone begins to realize and to feel that we are now on our own, and that it all has some sense and can lead somewhere."

The nomination of Mr. Mazowiecki was expected. He is a 62-year-old journalist, a devout Roman Catholic and a close adviser to the Solidarity leader, Lech Walesa, since the union's birth nine years ago.

If he succeeds in assembling a cabinet, it will be a substantial change in the type of rule found in the Soviet bloc since World War II.

Bush Administration officials welcomed the selection of Mr. Mazowiecki as a historic step, but their reaction was muted rather than jubilant as they noted the immense economic challenges he faces. "There is no sense of gloating here," said a State Department official. The nomination was another major success in a series of Solidarity victories that began last year when the outlawed union led nationwide strikes against economic conditions. The strikes led to the union's legalization, to negotiations with the Communist Government, and that led in turn to the June elections in which Solidarity soundly defeated Communist candidates for the Parliament. This success made it impossible for the Communists to form a government and led to President Jaruzelski's decision to agree to a Solidarity Prime Minister. Earlier this week, Mr. Walesa rejected offers to take the post himself and proposed his old ally, Mr. Mazowiecki. . . .

The political structure in Poland was one of the first to be put under Soviet domination after the war. It now appears that General Jaruzelski, pressed by the prospect of political and economic chaos and taking advantage of liberal policies of the Soviet leadership under Mikhail S. Gorbachev, has decided to take the step that will push Poland's political system beyond anything being attempted elsewhere in the East bloc.

The Government's announcement came as the Communist Party Central Committee met in Warsaw to consider the changes.

Tonight, the Communist Party let it be known it intends to fight for more than just the two Cabinet seats Solidarity says it is willing to give it—the posts of Defense Minister and Interior Minister.

Slawomir Wiatr, a Central Committee secretary, said "two portfolios do not constitute a coalition."

Addressing a news conference after the session, Mr. Wiatr said the party favored a grand coalition, athough he did not explain how this differed from what Solidarity was about to assemble. The Central Committee session, he said, discussed the substance of policy, not the division of cabinet seats.

The Government announcement came in a statement released in English by the official Polish press agency reporting that President Jaruzelski, "as a result of talks and consultations with parliamentary and nonparliamentary representatives of social and political groups," had nominated Mr. Mazowiecki, who is the editor in chief of *Tygod-*

nik Solidarnosci, the Solidarity weekly newspaper.

The statement was later read in Polish on national television, a stunning event for Poles who have never seen opposition to Communist Party rule countenanced in the postwar history of their country.

Earlier, the press agency reported that the President had accepted the resignation of the incumbent Prime Minister, Czeslaw Kiszczak, whose efforts to form a cabinet stumbled over Solidarity's bitter resistance to the former Interior Minister. Many Solidarity supporters reject him for his role in engineering the imposition of martial law on December 13, 1981, and hunting down nearly all the union leaders.

In his statement, the President described Mr. Mazowiecki as a "longtime Catholic activist," who he said had been a deputy in the assembly from 1961 to 1972.

"Later he began his activities in Solidarity," the statement went on, describing the nominee as "one of the leading activists of this organization," and the editor of its weekly newspaper.

Mr. Mazowiecki, a graying man with an angular face and a dry sense of humor, spent the day in the gardens of a home for the blind in Laski, west of the capital, run by Franciscan sisters. He said he had gone "to concentrate a bit before facing what awaits me.". . .

In Moscow, Tone Is a Studied Calm
By Bill Keller

MOSCOW, Aug. 17—The Soviet Union reacted with deliberate equanimity today to Poland's movement toward a government led by non-Communists, declaring that developments there were strictly an internal affair.

"This is entirely a matter to be decided by Poland," declared Yevgeny M. Primakov, a chief legislative deputy to President Mikhail S. Gorbachev, when asked by a visiting United States Congressional delegation about the possibility of a Polish coalition government excluding the Communists.

Mr. Primakov described the proposal for a coalition involving Solidarity and two smaller non-Communist parties as "reasonable."

Yuri A. Gremitskikh, a Foreign Ministry spokesman, said, "We can only hope that the outcome will be in the best interests of the Polish people." He declined to make a detailed comment on the ground that events in Poland were its own business.

Western diplomats who have taken soundings among senior officials said they received nothing but clear signals that Moscow's policy of noninterference was firm.

Mr. Gorbachev has repeatedly disavowed intervention in Eastern Europe, and surely realizes that any Soviet interference in Poland would endanger the warm relations with the West on which his hope of a domestic economic recovery depends. . . .

As Poland was leading the way, Hungary was not far behind in moving toward pluralistic political institutions. One major obstacle was what to do about the recent past, notably the 1956 uprising against Soviet and Communist domination. Until very recently the party line had been that the uprising, which cost an estimated 30,000 lives, had been a counterrevolution and that those who led it were justifiably executed as criminals. They were buried in unmarked graves in an overgrown corner of a Budapest cemetery, and just two years earlier, people who put flowers on the mounds faced police interrogation.

Hungarian Who Led '56 Revolt Is Buried as a Hero
By Henry Kamm

BUDAPEST, June 16—Thirty-one years after he was hanged and his body thrown into a prison grave, Imre Nagy, who led the 1956 uprising against Soviet domination, was given a solemn funeral today on Budapest's largest square, followed by a hero's burial.

The ceremonies were organized by the opposition, which worships the former Prime Minister as a national hero, but four leading members of the ruling Communist Party came to pay tribute.

They were announced to the crowd by their Government titles, because it had been made clear that they would not have been welcome as party representatives. The Interior Ministry estimated the crowd at 100,000, nowhere near the quarter of a million the organizers had expected.

The four top party officials, Prime Minister Miklos Nemeth, Minister of State Imre Pozsgay, Deputy Prime Minister Peter Megyessy and Matyas Szuros, the president of Parliament, laid wreaths and stood briefly as honorary pallbearers flanking Mr. Nagy's coffin.

They left before a succession of eulogies to Imre Nagy that were unsparing in their condemnation of the Communist Party and its ally, the Soviet Union.

The Soviet Army crushed the uprising after feigning a withdrawal from Hungary on November 4, 1956. Its tanks began rolling after Mr. Nagy, yielding to an aroused nation, formed a coalition government to replace one-party rule, declared Hungary's neutrality and withdrew from the Warsaw Pact.

Moscow secretly put Janos Kadar, whom Mr. Nagy had earlier freed from prison, in full charge of the country, which he dominated until he was deposed last year. Mr. Kadar has been relegated to oblivion by his successor, Karoly Grosz, and is said by the party that for 32 years did his bidding to be physically and mentally ill.

Many in the crowd looked up in shock and seemed to be holding their breath to hear at so public a ceremony, in so sumptuous a setting, words of such astonishing candor. The Government network televised the ceremony live from 9 A.M. to 6 P.M.

Victor Orban, a spokesman for the Federation of Young Democrats, paid tribute to Mr. Nagy as a man who, although a Communist, "identified himself with the wishes of the Hungarian nation to put an end to the Communist taboos, blind obedience to the Russian empire and the dictatorship of a single party."

As though speaking of the party leaders who shortly before had bowed before the coffins of Mr. Nagy and his colleagues, Mr. Orban continued: "We cannot understand that those who were eager to slander the revolution and its Prime Minister have suddenly changed into great supporters and followers of Imre Nagy. Nor can we understand that the party leaders, who made us study from books that falsified the revolution, now rush to touch the coffins as if they were charms of good luck."

Sandor Racz, who led the Budapest Workers' Council during the uprising and spent seven years in prison, condemned the Soviet Army and the Communist Party as "obstacles for Hungarian society."

Looking toward the coffins, covered in wreaths and bouquets, as well as single flowers laid on them by a long procession of mourners, Mr. Racz said, "These coffins are a result of the presence of Russian troops on our territory."

He said the party was "clinging fearfully to power," although it was clear that "what it failed to achieve in the last 44 years cannot be remedied now." He continued, "They are responsible for the past. They are responsible for the damaged lives of Hungarians."

Budapest experienced a day full of anomalies and contradictions. No state funeral could have been more solemnly and publicly marked or held in a more prestigious setting, but for the Hungarian Government and the ruling party, Mr. Nagy and the four companions who were sentenced to death and now reburied with him remain traitors and counterrevolutionaries.

A review of their trial is under way, and after today's rites it can hardly end with anything short of restoration of their civil dignity and full rehabilitation as victims of judicial murder. But their sentences still stand.

As recently as earlier this year, Mr. Grosz still ruled out Mr. Nagy's rehabilitation. On the thirtieth anniversary of the hangings last year, the police broke up with considerable violence a small tribute organized by dissidents on a Budapest square.

It was an anomaly also that the Soviet Union and Hungary's other Communist friends sent diplomats, but not their ambassadors, to attend the ceremony, although it had no official character that would have obliged them to be there. But other Communist countries—China, North Korea, Rumania and Albania—stayed away.

The Heroes Square ceremony was staged, in one more irony, by the son of another executed Communist, Laszlo Rajk, who was Interior and Foreign Minister. Mr. Rajk, a loyal Communist, was hanged after a show trial in 1949 at the eight of the Stalinist period.

The younger Laszlo Rajk, an architect and movie set designer, draped the neoclassical facade of the art museum and a tall column in the center of the square's vast expanse fully in black and white, traditional mourning colors among the Hungarians of Transylvania, annexed by Rumania.

He devised strikingly modern wood and metal structures as a setting on which to display the five coffins, as well as a sixth, empty one commemorating the more than 300 victims of judicial retribution after the uprising.

Tall, flaming torches stood between the coffins, and a permanent rotation of honorary pallbearers—including widows, children and other relatives of the five victims being buried—flanked them. Each coffin was inscribed with the name of the executed man and his dates, all ending in 1958.

Like all of the victims, Mr. Nagy was a lifelong Communist and friend of the Soviet Union, where he spent nearly one-third of his 62 years. The others were his Defense Minister, Gen. Pal Maleter; Minister of State Geza Losonczy; Jozsef Szilagyi, the head of the Prime Minister's staff, and Miklos Gimes, a leading journalist and close associate of Mr. Nagy.

General Maleter and Mr. Gimes were executed with Mr. Nagy, Mr. Szilagyi was tried and put to death separately, and Mr. Losonczy died in prison.

Mr. Nagy was buried in secret in a prison lot while his wife and daughter were interned in Rumania. He was reburied, again in secret and in an unmarked grave, a few years later and exhumed this year when the party leadership finally yielded to demands for a decent burial.

Today, after the wreath-laying and eulogies, a procession of hearses, followed by cars and buses, set out for the huge public cemetery next to the prison where the hangings took place.

Plot 301, the once desolate potter's field that contains the graves of perhaps 260 of the victims, had been turned in recent weeks, since the reburial had been decided on, into a landscaped funeral park.

Fresh grass and trees now grow where only weeks ago there were only dirt and weeds. Paved paths led through the field to five open graves aligned in a row that had been dug for Mr. Nagy's companions and for the symbolic coffin.

Beyond them, in an adjoining field full of mainly unmarked graves, a tomb had been dug for Mr. Nagy. His daughter had requested that he be laid to rest amid the bulk of those who paid with their lives for following his lead.

Two actors read in alphabetical order the names of the 260 victims, who were executed from 1956 to 1961, their occupations and their ages. At each name, a torchbearer stepped forward, held high the flame and replied, "He lives in us; he has not gone."

When the name of one of the five was called, surname first, in the Hungarian fashion, like "Nagy Imre, Prime Minister, 62 years," his coffin was carried to the grave and a friend delivered a eulogy. Then, supporting one another, his nearest relatives stepped to the grave to put down flowers and stand, with bowed heads, allowed for the first time to mourn in public, together with those who share their grief.

The Hungarian summer rolled on and with it came the steady erosion of Communist power. First, the party leadership elected a four-man presidency, and then it virtually stripped one of the four, Karoly Grosz, who had succeeded Janos Kadar as party leader, of most his authority. The so-called party liberals were on the rise, while outside the party a variety of dissidents, cultural activists, defenders of the ecology and cultural nationalists were forming embryonic parties and coalitions for pluralistic free elections that many believed would take place in

1990. Indeed, such elections were later scheduled and by fall, the Communists were meeting to discuss the liquidation of party's assets and the changing of its name.

• • •

In the Soviet Union, the social trends set in motion by both glasnost and perestroika were also continuing through the summer. Some unfolded in troubling ways, while others offered hope of positive change. New institutions and beliefs were forming; old monoliths were weakening.

Enrollment Problems Increasing, Soviet Communist Party Admits
By Bill Keller

MOSCOW, July 11—The Soviet Communist Party is troubled by dwindling recruitment and a steep decline in prestige, according to an unusually candid collection of articles and letters published today in Moscow's main party newspaper.

The material included an article by a teacher at a top party training school who reported that many of the most active young party candidates are defecting to join informal political organizations, where the activities are "more relevant and effective."

Occasional letters expressing anguish about the condition of the party began to creep into the press last year, but the hand-wringing has become more pronounced since March, when many prominent party figures were trounced in the first competitive elections for a new national legislature.

In another sign of the party's distress, Mikhail S. Gorbachev, the President and party leader, today went to Leningrad, where voters rejected the six top Communists in the city's party organization. The defeated Leningrad officials have refused to give up their party leadership positions.

At the time of the elections, Mr. Gorbachev said the outcome was not a repudiation of the party. Emphasizing that nearly 90 percent of the winners were party members, he said the elections were a victory of fresher and more progressive Communists over conservative party functionaries.

But the party-controlled press is beginning to admit that the party itself is held in low repute.

The declining prestige of the party is most evident in statistics showing plummeting enrollment of new party members, despite the fact that membership has traditionally brought career advancement and privileges.

According to data published recently in the journal of the party Central Committee, induction of new members began to fall off in 1987, and last year plunged 20 percent. After years of steady growth, the total party membership barely held steady at 19.5 million.

The party does not publish statistics on the number of people who quit, but the letters published today in *Moskovskaya Pravda* indicated that this, too, has become a growing problem.

One writer, the party secretary at a Moscow metallurgical factory, reported that in the first six months of this year more workers in that factory had quit the party than had joined.

"The most active Communists often leave to 'do their own thing'— that is, they join more lively and flexible, more relevant and effective voluntary movements," wrote the teacher at the party training school.

Several writers said the greatest blow to the party's prestige was its decision to reserve 100 seats in the new 2,250-member Congress for deputies chosen by the party without a vote of the general public.

"No matter which way you look at it, the party still retains Stalin's pattern, a rigid, command-administrative structure," the teacher wrote. "It lags behind the changes in life. It cannot prevent undesirable changes and it lags behind the positive ones."

Among the older institutions still active under glasnost was the censor.

The Life of a Soviet Censor: Anything Goes? Not Just Yet
By Bill Keller

MOSCOW, July 17—Suppose an inquisitive Soviet reporter were to unearth evidence that a member of the Communist Party Politburo had a mistress. Could he publish it?

Vladimir A. Boldyrev, the chief censor of the Soviet Union, ponders the question for a long time. A very long time.

"Well, I think the answer is, yes, we are now approaching the stage where personal details can be made public that it was not customary to publish before," he replied at last.

Then he added, with a nervous laugh that suggested that the verdict was not final, "I hope this is just a hypothetical question."

Mr. Boldyrev is the keeper of a shrinking but still formidable catalogue of what the press cannot write, the publishing houses cannot publish, the movies cannot show, the libraries cannot put on public display, and the post office cannot deliver.

In his three years as chairman of Glavlit—the Administration for the Protection of State Secrets in the Press—Mr. Boldyrev boasts that he has cut the list by half, lifting the ban on such diverse secrets as the works of Aleksandr Solzhenitsyn, the bunnies of *Playboy* magazine, and the crime rate.

Indeed, it is difficult to extract from Mr. Boldyrev exactly what is forbidden anymore in the Soviet Union, in part because the boundary is moving so fast and in part because the idea of censorship has become so unfashionable in the day of glasnost that even the censor in chief finds the subject a bit distasteful.

"In the classical sense, it is no longer really correct to call us censors," he insisted in an interview at his office midway between the Kremlin and the K.G.B. headquarters. "Today we do not impose limits of a purely political or ideological character, which was one of our duties before."

Still, there is much room for discretion in Glavlit's current standard of what is prohibited, which Mr. Boldyrev recently elaborated to the newspaper *Izvestia* as follows: "The use of the press for purposes of undermining or eliminating the established socialist system in the U.S.S.R., to propagandize war, to preach racial or national exclusivity or hatred and violence on a national, religious or other basis, to damage the country's security interests or defense capability or public order, or to publish materials incompatible with the requirements of public morality and protecting the population's health."

Mr. Boldyrev said most of the thick catalogue of forbidden themes—a document that is itself restricted to a narrow circle of editors and publishers—consists of military and industrial secrets.

Glavlit's clout is such that it has occasionally overruled the Defense Ministry on what constitutes a secret, Mr. Boldyrev said, although it has never found occasion to overrule the K.G.B., the state security police.

His agency is also responsible for preventing the dissemination of pornography, which like many arbiters of official taste he has trouble defining.

"You probably have to see it," said the censor, who is 59 years old and an economist by training. Once resolutely puritanical, Glavlit has become more permissive. Soft-core erotica is now considered acceptable in films and publications, and formerly taboo themes like homosexuality can be discussed in a positive light, although an article on that subject is almost certain to pass Mr. Boldyrev's desk before it reaches the readers.

Despite his disclaimer about politics and ideology, Glavlit is also empowered to decide that hostile literature poses a danger to the state.

Mr. Boldyrev said Glavlit ruled last year that the works of Mr. Solzhenitsyn, the fiercely anti-Communist Russian living in exile in Vermont, were no longer a threat. Mr. Solzhenitsyn's epic labor camp memoir, *The Gulag Archipelago,* is to be excerpted next month in the magazine *Novy Mir*, and a publishing house has announced plans to publish seven volumes of selected Solzhenitsyn works.

"Regarding Solzhenitsyn, all debates are over," the censor said. "We released all of his works from the closed archives, and our publishing houses have the right to publish them—of course, without violating the copyright."

Mr. Boldyrev said the vast bulk of writings by émigrés and exiles, once banned automatically regardless of their content, have now been removed from the closed archives of libraries, and the rest are to be reviewed by the end of the year.

The liberated writers include some of the bitterest critics of Soviet authority, among them such émigré novelists as Vladimir N. Voinovich, Vladimir Maximov—who once damned Communism as "an evil ideology"—and Viktor Nekrasov, and the non-émigré Vasily Grossman, whose thinly fictionalized attack on Lenin, "Forever Flowing," was published last month in the magazine *Oktyabr*.

The books written by Trotsky before he was expelled from the country as a Bolshevik heretic are now open, but what he wrote in exile is still under review.

Also locked away are foreign works that Glavlit feels might "undermine" Soviet power or outrage public sensibilities.

Mein Kampf, the Hitler manifesto widely studied in other countries as a model of political pathology, is here banned as an offense to memories of the Great Patriotic War Against Fascism.

"I think it will eventually be published, but first we have to live through a certain period of time to absorb what is being done today," Mr. Boldyrev said of the book. "It would be wrong to overfeed the public."

The limits of contemporary writing are murkier.

"If some paper wants to publish a call to arms to overthrow the authorities, we will not allow it to be published," he said.

And what about a scathing satire of President Mikhail S. Gorbachev? Not likely, Mr. Boldyrev said.

"This affects not only the prestige of our country, but perestroika itself," he said. "If we trample on the leader of perestroika, how can we make any progress?"

He added, however, that an attack on the Soviet leader would probably be squelched long before it reached his desk. While Glavlit is the supreme court of censorship, the Soviet system has countless less formal ways of saying "nyet."

A magazine, for example, depends on the good will of the officially sanctioned organization that sponsors it, of the ideology department of the Communist Party, of the state committee that controls printing presses and newsprint, of the official writers' union, and of local authorities who sometimes block distribution of publications approved in Moscow.

Editors who rise in this system have cultivated a keen sense of protective self-censorship.

Thus while Glavlit says it has imposed no limits on writing about the recent bloody events in China, no Soviet publication has dared criticize the Chinese regime. On matters of foreign policy, editors take their cues from the party and Government leadership, which has been carefully nurturing its recently normalized relations with Beijing.

Mr. Boldyrev estimates that about half of the information dispensed for public consumption in the Soviet Union is reviewed in advance by Glavlit's agents. The rest—including reprints of literary classics, many local and regional newspapers of scant circulation, certain reference works, and publications with a demonstrated devotion to self-censorship—do not undergo prior review, but are spot-checked.

Periodicals that suddenly develop a free spirit may find themselves back under Glavlit's wing. That happened this year to *Twentieth Century and Peace*, a long-quiescent little magazine that fell into the hands of a free-thinking editor and began publishing critiques of the K.G.B.

Mr. Boldyrev explained to the disbelieving editors that the publication had been leashed because it wrote about disarmament, raising the risk that it would disclose some privileged detail of a Soviet negotiating position.

The reins on the press may be loosened further when the new legislature approves a long-awaited law on the rights and responsibilities of the press. But legislators say the new law is unlikely to curtail Glavlit's authority seriously or to permit a truly independent press. Mr. Boldyrev is not worried about job security.

"The system of protecting secrets was created by people who are not completely unreasonable," he said. "It was built up over time, and it has its rationale."

Much more troubling for Gorbachev than the drift from Communism of his Polish and Hungarian allies were the separatist feelings being articulated within his country's borders.

Annexation Void, Lithuanians Say
By Bill Keller

MOSCOW, Aug. 22—In a move that could lay the legal foundation for eventual secession from the Soviet Union, a commission of the Lithuanian Parliament declared today that Moscow's annexation of the republic in 1940 was invalid.

The commission, the first official body to challenge directly the legitimacy of Soviet rule in the Baltic republics, charged that Lithuania and its neighbors, Latvia and Estonia, were occupied and absorbed against their will as a result of a secret agreement between Stalin and Hitler.

The statement was published today in Lithuanian newspapers, as all three Baltic republics prepared mass demonstrations to mark the fiftieth anniversary of the accord.

The full Lithuanian legislature is expected to vote on the commission's declaration at its next session in early September, and approval is considered virtually certain.

"Stalinism and Hitlerism destroyed independent states by secret deals," the commission's statement released today said. "The independence of many of these states has been restored, but Lithuania, Latvia and Estonia still have not reacquired their independence."

The nonaggression pact reached in August 1939 by the Soviet Foreign Minister, Vyacheslav M. Molotov, and his Nazi counterpart, Joachim von Ribbentrop, included a secret protocol dividing Europe into Soviet and German spheres of influence, splitting Poland and giving the Soviets a free hand in Latvia, Estonia and part of Rumania.

142

A second secret protocol a month later refined the spheres of influence in Poland and gave the Soviets predominance in Lithuania, as well.

During the war, the Soviet Union annexed the three Baltic states and forced their puppet parliaments to seek admission to the Soviet Union.

The declaration made by the Lithuanians today directly contradicted the latest Moscow position on the Stalin-Hitler pact and its protocols. After decades of denying the existence of the secret deal, Communist Party officials now concede that such an agreement was signed, but they say that it had no bearing on the annexation of the Baltic states.

On Friday, Aleksandr N. Yakovlev, an influential Politburo member who is also chairman of a Government commission examining the history of the Stalin-Hitler pact, insisted that it was "farfetched to see some kind of interconnection between the present status of the three republics and the nonaggression treaty."

In an interview published on Monday, Valentin M. Falin, chief of the international department of the Communist Party Central Committee, warned that attempts to redraw the boundaries of Eastern Europe could have a dangerous destabilizing effect.

"If the striving to divide what cannot be divided continues, as was characteristic of the period before the previous two world wars, if lands and frontiers are being recarved while the lives and safety of people are neglected, the worst, and this time, the final disaster will be brought on," he predicted.

Residents of the Baltic republics are divided about the wisdom of separating completely from the Soviet Union, but there seems to be overwhelming agreement in the republics that their membership in a Soviet federation must be on their own terms.

The Soviet Constitution guarantees republics the right to secede, but this has always been regarded as symbolic and few doubt that Moscow would resist.

Popular Front groups that have amassed broad followings in the three republics have campaigned for invalidating the Soviet annexation, after which some favor a loose affiliation with the Soviet Union while others want independence.

Tonight in Vilnius, the Lithuanian capital, a crowd estimated in the tens of thousands roared approval as Vytautas Landsbergis, president of Sajudis, a Popular Front group, called for "a free Lithuania."

According to a Sajudis spokesman, Mr. Landsbergis rejected the Communist Party's proposal for a revamped confederation giving republics more, but still limited, freedom.

The sentiment for secession has grown with each expression of Moscow's resistance. Although the Soviet national legislature has approved in principle Baltic plans to experiment with market-style economies, the authorities have insisted that the republics be bound by the Soviet Constitution and laws.

Today, in laying the basis for a possible separation from the Soviet Union, the Lithuanian legislature said in conclusion: "The declaration of the People's Assembly of 21 July 1940 on the entry of Lithuania into the U.S.S.R., and the law of the Supreme Soviet of the U.S.S.R. of 3 August 1940 on the incorporation of the Lithuanian Soviet Socialist Republic into the U.S.S.R. are illegal."

AUTUMN 1989

Troublesome *as they were, the secessionist impulses in the Baltic were at least still largely a matter of debate and discussion. That was not so in the south, where the Kremlin was confronted with a bloody conflict between groups of citizens with very old grudges against each other.*

A Deadly Feud Tears at Enclave on Gorbachev's Southern Flank
By Bill Keller

BADARA, U.S.S.R., Aug. 29—From the windows of her living room, Galya Israelyan can look down over the rooftops of this Armenian village, out to the green and gold mountains and the clearing where a few days ago her husband, Ruben, was shot dead.

He was 32 years old and the father of five, including a newborn daughter, when he became a casualty in the Soviet Union's fiercest and most intractable nationalist feud in recent years.

Although the police say their investigation is unfinished, the victim's brother, a witness, identified the killer as an Azerbaijani farmhand from the neighboring settlement of Lesnoye.

"He had been a guest in our house for dinner," the widow recalled in a monotone bitter and hopeless from a dispute that is now more tribal than political.

This is Mikhail S. Gorbachev's Lebanon, his Cyprus: Nagorno-Karabakh—wild mountains of rugged beauty, riven by mutual hatred, partitioned by military force and governed, in reality, by no one.

In the 18 months since Armenians and Azerbaijanis began their struggle for custody of Nagorno-Karabakh, a predominantly Armenian enclave surrounded by the southern republic of Azerbaijan, the dispute has frustrated every attempt at settlement. Some say the demonstration of official impotence has encouraged outbreaks of unrest in other regions of the Soviet Union.

Military and civilian authorities sent from Moscow to oversee the territory say their greatest accomplishment has been to prevent all-out war between the two adjoining republics, Christian Armenia and Muslim Azerbaijan.

Now that nationalist tensions seem to tear at every corner of the Soviet Union, and the Communist Party awaits a special meeting to address the issue, Nagorno-Karabakh is a reminder of how limited Soviet power can be in the face of ethnic passion.

"For now, only Allah or God knows the answer," Mr. Gorbachev's special administrator in Nagorno-Karabakh, Arkady I. Volsky, told a reporter who was allowed a four-day visit to the tightly restricted region.

After a fresh outbreak of gun battles and highway ambushes, the Ministry of Internal Affairs moved in more troops in recent days to buy time while Mr. Volsky embarked without great optimism on the search for a new compromise.

For centuries before Nagorno-Karabakh became Mr. Gorbachev's affliction, the ancestors of today's Armenians and Azerbaijanis contested this mountainous land.

The successive masters of the region—the czarist empire, the Turkish Army, the British authorities after World War I, and then the Soviets—have placed Nagorno-Karabakh under Azerbaijani rule, primarily because of its geographic isolation from Armenia and its rail and economic links to Baku, the capital of Azerbaijan.

But the Armenian majority has usually retained a limited autonomy within the region, and has periodically defied Azerbaijani rule. Armenian passions are heightened by memories of the killings, starvation and forced resettlement inflicted on Armenian civilians in 1915 by the Ottoman Turks, the Azerbaijanis' ethnic cousins. The Armenians suffered losses on a scale that shocked the world, even during World War I. Inspired by Mr. Gorbachev's promise of greater democracy and by rising Armenian nationalism, Nagorno-Karabakh early last year demanded unification with the Armenian Republic.

Moscow, sensitive to the authority of Azerbaijan and the precedent of redrawing boundaries, refused and condemned the instigators as extremists. Tensions mounted. In February 1988, while the Azerbaijani authorities looked the other way, anti-Armenian riots broke out in the Azerbaijani port of Sumgait, on the Caspian Sea. This began a violent chain reaction that has left more than 100 people dead by official count—many more by unofficial estimates.

In hindsight, Armenians see Sumgait as a signal—and not just to Armenians—that Soviet power could not or would not protect them, that safety lay in the clan, the tribe.

Fearful minorities by the hundreds of thousands have fled the two republics, including a continuing Armenian evacuation of Baku, once a cosmopolitan, multinational city.

Trains and buses carrying refugees are regularly stoned as they pass through alien territory.

In Nagorno-Karabakh itself, there have been paralyzing strikes and huge demonstrations but, remarkably, no serious violence in the six months after the Sumgait killings.

Then last September, on two terror-filled nights, the neighboring cities of Stepanakert and Shusha erupted.

Scores of Azerbaijani homes were ransacked and burned in Stepanakert and scores of Armenian apartments in Shusha were destroyed before armored caravans escorted the two peoples to neutral corners.

Each side blames the other for the rampages. Each side insists it is the guiltless victim of a conspiracy.

"What happened here?" a visitor asked a group of Armenian men sharing a bottle on the sidewalk across from a burned-out Azerbaijani house in Stepanakert.

"The Azerbaijanis did it," one replied, "so the Armenians would get the blame."

Today, the 186,000 residents of Nagorno-Karabakh, about 80 percent of them Armenian, are almost completely polarized into Armenian and Azerbaijani sectors. They are guarded by troops of the Internal Affairs Ministry and by vigilante patrols, and ruled by a jumble of competing jurisdictions.

Stepanakert, the regional capital, is almost entirely Armenian, and is gradually cutting its ties to Baku.

Local factories that once worked as subsidiaries of larger enterprises in Baku have begun to realign themselves with Armenian companies in Yerevan, capital of the neighboring Armenian republic.

"Baku was just skimming off our profits, like tribute to the Azerbaijanis," said Boris S. Arushanyan, director of a lighting-fixture factory that now flies an Armenian flag over its main workshop.

The strike that had idled most of the city's factories since May ended a few days ago at the urging of Armenian nationalists, who decided that the tactic was self-defeating.

But the city is plagued by shortages of food, fuel and building materials. Supplies are delivered by armed convoy and airlift from Yerevan, the Armenian Republic's capital.

The seedy Hotel Karabakh is crowded with newly arrived refugees and shirtless soldiers, who roam the steamy corridors wearing their sidearms.

"We'll give it a year," said Lena Shakhgeldyan, who fled from Baku in December and now lives with her husband, mother and three children in a single room of a Stepanakert refugee hostel. "Then if it's still bad, we'll apply to go to America."

Four miles up the mountain, past a military checkpoint, is the main Azerbaijani stronghold, Shusha. Once it was a vacation mecca prized for its mountain springs and fresh air. Now the shady mountainside pavilion where Armenian and Azerbaijani Communist officials used to share long lunches is empty. The Armenian church and graveyard have been vandalized, and the holiday camps have been converted to refugee centers that fester with anger.

A children's camp on the outskirts of town is home for 100 Azerbaijani families who say they were driven forcibly from their farms in Armenia a year and a half ago.

They live jobless and in squalor, several generations packed into each small room, cooking communal meals over hot plates and washing at buckets because, local officials say, their water is often cut off at Armenian-controlled pumping stations.

They flock around a visitor, shouting their indignation. A current object of wrath is the United States Senate, which recently adopted a resolution expressing support for Soviet Armenians in the Nagorno-Karabakh dispute.

"If these young men were to take up guns and go off today to shoot Armenians, I could not sincerely tell them 'Don't do it,'" said Zakhid Abbasov, a local party official.

Not long ago, a Russian official in Stepanakert said, a reporter from the Soviet satirical weekly *Krokodil* visited Shusha, and word got out that he had an Armenian name. He was sitting in the office of the city's mayor when four men burst into the room, beat him to the floor and kicked him.

Local Azerbaijani officials abruptly canceled plans to let two visiting American journalists spend the night in Shusha when they learned that the photographer had an Armenian last name.

"You must understand we cannot guarantee your safety," said Rena A. Allakhverdieva, the Communist Party ideology chief for the

Shusha region. "When they see the name on your passport, the fact that you are American will not save you. It is out of our hands."

On the winding roads and in the mountain hollows, periods of false calm are followed by periods of reprisal.

"You cannot say who starts it, or who is more to blame," said Maj. Gen. Vladislav F. Safonov, the Internal Affairs Ministry troop commander in the region.

Early one morning, a bus from Yerevan, the Armenian capital, limped into Stepanakert with bullet holes in the side, and shattered windows.

The hysterically frightened Armenian passengers, huddled with their baggage in the lobby of the Hotel Karabakh, said they had been delayed at an Azerbaijani police post at Mir-Bashir, on the northeast border.

"It was a trap," one passenger said. "Young Azerbaijanis began arriving by the carload. Then someone shot at us from the roof of a garage, and the stones started flying. We screamed until the troops came."

The Armenians pointed to bloodstains on their clothes and held out rocks and handfuls of broken window glass they had scooped up as evidence of their ordeal.

"If the troops had not happened by, they would have burned the bus with us in it," a woman said.

In fact, General Safonov said, it was the outnumbered Azerbaijani police who called the special troops to rescue the Armenians. But no Armenian here seems to believe it.

The story spread quickly, and soon separate groups of Armenians and Azerbaijanis were on the highway armed with rocks and raising the level of violence, even stoning the military patrols sent to clear the roads. By the day's end, the authorities said the Armenians had smashed four buses, and each side had damaged a number of cars.

"We have a policy of not being the first to attack, but every action should have a concrete response," said Robert Kucharyan, the head of a local Armenian nationalist group, approving the day's reprisals.

"We know throwing rocks is not a civilized approach, but our neighbors are not civilized and they don't understand civilized language," he said. "From many years of living together, we learned to eat their bread and drink their wine. This month we've learned how to throw rocks at cars."

The next day, the commander of all troops of the Soviet Internal

Affairs Ministry, Col. Gen. Yuri V. Shatalin, arrived to survey the situation and announced plans to supplement the 4,500 soldiers in Nagorno-Karabakh with additional forces, mostly stationed in adjacent regions of Azerbaijan.

"The conflict has to be resolved by the two republics," he said in an interview. "There are two choices: begin talks or begin the bloodshed. And believe me, the number of victims would be in the hundreds."

In the mountains, villagers on both sides say they live in constant fear. Although the authorities have confiscated more than 3,000 hunting rifles and other weapons since the conflict began, enough remain in private hands to give the region a Wild West character.

In Lesnoye, a village of dilapidated houses isolated at the end of a road that passes through Armenian territory, 380 Azerbaijanis have lived the last year in a state of siege.

Once, the villagers say, they worked alongside Armenians in the nearby collective farm and in a woodworking shop. But after the "events" in Shusha and Stepanakert, Azerbaijanis say they were driven from their jobs.

Residents of Lesnoye get their flour, sugar and tea by helicopter from Azerbaijani authorities in Agdam, just east of Nagorno-Karabakh. Armenians are convinced they get weapons that way, too.

It is a war of attrition with the neighboring Armenian settlement of Badara. The villagers who used to attend each other's weddings now kill each other's livestock, stone each other's cars, cut each other's utility lines, and occasionally exchange gunfire in the woods.

A few days ago, Youssef Orudzhov was killed by an Armenian policeman at a makeshift guardpost at the edge of Lesnoye. The Azerbaijanis say that Mr. Orudzhov was shot in the back while fleeing into the woods so that the police would not confiscate his weapon. The police say it was a gun battle. Alysh M. Alyshev, a 39-year-old schoolteacher and Lesnoye spokesman, told a visitor that the Armenian policeman would be repaid.

"If I don't get him, the wife will, or the daughter will," he said calmly as he served tea and local honey. "If someone has to die, so be it."

A few miles away in Badara, the 850 Armenians seem more prosperous—the homes are well kept and a condenser factory in Stepanakert has just opened a branch here—but they are about equal in the purity of their hatred, in their determination to yield not an inch.

They have just buried Ruben Israelyan, and they mutter angrily that his killer will be "a national hero" in Azerbaijan.

Arshak Israelyan wears a snapshot of his dead brother pinned to his shirt.

"It is ridiculous to speak of peace," he said. "Maybe the only thing left is to poison the water and kill everybody.". . .

If old enmities and old yearnings for autonomy were surfacing through fissures pried open as a consequence of glasnost, there were also some basic institutional changes occurring. Among the more bizarre of these was the public relations drive to improve the image of spies and secret police.

The Soviets Proudly Present Their Friendly K.G.B. Agent
By Bill Keller

MOSCOW, Sept. 13—The K.G.B. stepped up its charm offensive today with the premiere of a new film on the benign patriotism and just-folks life-styles of the Soviet secret police.

The screening, before an audience consisting of a favorite K.G.B. target, the foreign press corps, was followed by a rare opportunity to question the chief of the K.G.B. investigations department and the operative who handled the agency's most stellar recruit, Kim Philby, the British spy who worked as a double agent before fleeing to the Soviet Union.

Neither the film nor the news conference provided any hard new information about the secret police, although afterward Mr. Philby's K.G.B. handler, a white-goateed colonel named Yuri Modin, told the correspondent for *The Independent*, a London newspaper, that there was an uncaught fifth mole in the Philby spy network. This information—or was it disinformation?—is sure to cause a minor tempest in London, where Mr. Philby, who defected in 1963 and died here last year, and "fifth man" conspiracy theories are subjects of boundless fascination.

The film, *The K.G.B. Today*, was intended to convince Soviet and foreign audiences that the agency long feared as an engine of repression has transformed itself into a rather likable law enforcement agency.

Today's skeptical full house reacted with smiles and occasional gales of laughter to the homespun glimpses of daily K.G.B. life.

K.G.B. cooking tips: Col. Igor N. Prelin, the K.G.B. press officer, escorts the camera crew through Lefortovo Prison, pausing at the kitchen where, viewers are told, the crew prepares a choice of vegetarian and nonvegetarian cuisine for lucky inmates.

"How do you manage to cook pearl barley this good?" Colonel Prelin inquires, dipping a spoon into an enormous vat of porridge. "Do you cook it over steam?" "Yes, I do," burbles the flattered chef. "I cook everything this way."

"I'll tell you one thing: my wife cannot do it right," the colonel confides as the cook ladles him a glutinous second helping.

K.G.B. grooming: "Is your haircut your own invention?" the narrator inquires of Sergei Savichev, a K.G.B. captain whose brush cut bears an eerie resemblance to the look of a recently liberated labor camp prisoner.

"I think it is the best for my head," the young officer explains.

And K.G.B. poetry: Colonel Prelin, an occasional scribbler of verse, recites for the camera his couplets about the crazy, cruel ironies of intelligence work: We wage a war with no rules / A snowstorm with no end. / We share a bottle with a foe / Or get a bullet from a friend.

Other highlights include a martial arts class at the K.G.B. Higher School; a clip of Mathias Rust, the young West German pilot who landed his Cessna uninvited in Red Square, giving a tour of his prison cell; and a seeming reenactment of the K.G.B. capture of an accused American diplomat-spymaster in Moscow.

The Novosti press agency, which produced the film, hopes for wide commercial distribution overseas. American television companies who inquired today were told that the opening asking price for North American rights was $100,000.

The 55-minute film will also be shown domestically in hopes of countering the outpouring of revelations here about repressions carried out during the decades of Soviet power.

"The K.G.B. is not what it used to be in the infamous 1930's," said Colonel-General Gennadi Ageyev, a K.G.B deputy director interviewed in the film. "Not a single member of the K.G.B. today has had anything to do with the events of that period."

Asked after the screening about the K.G.B.'s more recent role in repression of dissidents in the 1960's, 70's and 80's, Colonel Prelin neither denied nor apologized, saying all of those activities were conducted within Soviet law.

Col. Oleg Dobrovolsky, chief of the K.G.B. investigations department, also sidestepped questions about the agency's supposed use to this day of telephone taps and informants to monitor Soviet citizens of unorthodox views.

The K.G.B. officials declined to answer questions about the number of K.G.B. employees, the structure of the organization or K.G.B. methods.

Today's event was part of an intensive campaign to humanize the image of the K.G.B. and underscore its work against drug smugglers, terrorists and organized crime.

In recent months, the K.G.B. director, Vladimir A. Kryuchkov, has made himself briefly available to Western journalists and has met with the American ambassador in Moscow, Jack F. Matlock Jr., and with Robert M. Gates, a former deputy director of the Central Intelligence Agency.

In appearances before the new Soviet Parliament and in the Soviet press, the K.G.B. chief has sung the praises of glasnost, as President Mikhail S. Gorbachev calls his campaign for greater openness.

Colonel Prelin, who heads the K.G.B.'s recently opened press office, said today that the K.G.B. is cooperating in the production of two documentary films lionizing Mr. Philby and George Blake, another British intelligence officer who secretly served the K.G.B.

A recurring theme of the film released today is that all countries carry out intelligence work, and the K.G.B. is no worse—in fact, is more moral—than its Western rivals.

Using film clips and what appeared to be a reenactment, the film recounted the arrest of an American couple, Lon D. Augustenborg, a diplomat, and his wife, Denise, who were expelled from Moscow in 1983 on charges of collecting espionage data on the Soviet Navy.

The case received unusually detailed coverage in the Soviet press at the time, when the Soviets were intent on justifying their shooting down of a Korean Air Lines 747 that they suspected of a spy mission.

To accompany its movie, Novosti filmed the reaction of the K.G.B. director himself, Mr. Kryuchkov, who delightedly predicted the movie would help "to project an objective image of our work both at home and abroad."

With summer giving way to fall, people all over Europe were returning as they always did from their holidays. This time, however, the annual retreat was to lead to massive migrations and shifts of populations that changed governments and altered the political map of the continent. It began in Hungary, where for many years East Germans and West Germans would meet at vacation spots along Lake Balaton. In the past, the Hungarian border guards made sure that the East Germans went home to East Germany. This was the year when that changed.

East Germans Put Hungary in a Bind
By Henry Kamm

BUDAPEST, Sept. 1—At least 3,000 East German tourists, and possibly many more, are waiting in Budapest for permission from Hungary to cross into Austria on the way to West Germany.

Many say that if permission is denied, they intend to cross "the green border." This is a German expression for migrating illegally, through the forest.

Since the summer vacation period began, an estimated 6,000 East Germans have made it to the West German Embassy in Vienna in this way, passing under the willfully averted eyes of Hungarian border guards.

But as the vacation period ends and the tourists confront the choice between returning in time for the reopening of factories and schools or not returning, a diffuse flow has become a concentration and a diplomatic quandary that Hungary cannot pretend to ignore.

Officials from the West German Embassy here, which Bonn closed last month when it could no longer cope with an occupation by East Germans seeking to emigrate, have joined with a West German Catholic relief organization in an ad hoc refugee operation at the Roman Catholic Parish Church.

The tree-shaded streets around the church in the garden suburb of Zugliget are lined with hundreds of small cars with East German plates, and as one gets closer to the church, flashier cars from West Germany are mingled among them.

In the churchyard, about 600 East Germans, including the owners of the parked cars, are camping out under tents. At least 2,000 more are waiting in two other informal camps as well as in private accommodations.

This afternoon, the Hungarian Red Cross told West German reporters that a new camp was being opened on Lake Balaton, a favorite vacation area southwest of here.

Hungary appears to have conferred a kind of informal extraterritoriality on the spacious grounds around the neo-Gothic church, where the latest act in the drama of defying East German borders is being acted out. Few Hungarians are to be seen, and the prevailing language is German in the strong accents of Saxony and Berlin, whose people make up the bulk of East Germany's population.

To Budapest's embarrassment, thousands of East Germans are taking advantage of Hungary's new era of tolerance and its recent relaxation of controls along the Austrian border to turn their vacation trips to a fellow Communist country into permanent departures, by way of Austria, to the richer and freer Germany.

In addition to those who have declared their intention not to return home, more than 100,000 other East German tourists are thought to be in Hungary. How many of them will seek to join the mass migration is unknown.

The situation puts Hungary in a diplomatic bind. It is caught between its treaty obligation to East Germany not to allow East Germans to leave here for anywhere but home, and its need not to offend West Germany, its biggest Western creditor and trading partner, as well as its principal hope for future economic support.

Although Hungary calls it a problem for the Germans to resolve, Prime Minister Miklos Nemeth and Foreign Minister Gyula Horn visited Chancellor Helmut Kohl in Bonn last week in an effort to seek a solution. On Thursday Mr. Horn paid an unannounced visit to the East German Foreign Minister, Oskar Fischer.

No agreements were announced, although West German Government and opposition officials disclosed on Thursday that Bonn and Budapest had worked out a plan to let out all the East Germans who want to leave.

In addition, the Hungarian Interior Minister, Istvan Horvath, said in an interview with West German television on Thursday that he hoped "an acceptable solution, conforming to European norms and culture," would be found.

"We find the present situation at the country's borders highly unpleasant and inconvenient," said the minister, who is in charge of border forces.

Some would-be refugees took heart when told by a reporter that Mr. Horvath had said it was certain that Hungary would not return them to their country. In the East German penal code, "flight from the republic" is punished by long prison terms and followed by harsh discrimination in professional and social life.

"If nothing else works, our State Security Service does," a 27-year-old mechanic from Karl-Marx-Stadt said.

In a garage to the rear of the church, West German consuls, surrounded by a patient crowd of men and women shushing their bored and cranky children, are accepting applications for passports and, after a few days' delay, issuing them. Despite their valid passports, however, Hungary feels restrained from recognizing them because they lack entry stamps. The tourists entered Hungary with an East German travel permit valid only for this country.

East Germany demands that Hungary live up to the formal understanding between Warsaw Pact members not to abet "defection" of their citizens to the West.

The steady trickle of East Germans making their way to West Germany by way of Hungary intensified when ten days later the Hungarians removed the barbed-wire barriers at the crossing point to Austria and permitted East Germans to cross that frontier easily. The East Germans responded by limiting the access their citizens had to Hungary. At that point East Germans, mostly young, began showing up at the West German Embassy in Prague. Czechoslovakia was one of the few places in the world where East Germans could travel without hard-to-get documents, and more and more of them were flocking to the West German Embassy in hopes that they would be permitted to go to West Germany.

More Than 6,000 East Germans Swell Tide of Refugees to the West
By Serge Schmemann

HOF, WEST GERMANY, Oct.1—From early this morning, packed East German trains pulled into this border junction town at three-hour intervals, disgorging exhausted East Germans whose departure had been allowed only the day before through an extraordinary face-saving arrangement reportedly approved by Erich Honecker, the East German leader.

By day's end, more than 5,500 East Germans who had taken refuge at the West German embassy in Prague and 800 more from Bonn's embassy in Warsaw arrived at Hof, near the juncture of West Germany's borders with East Germany and Czechoslovakia, after a 10-hour trip that took them back through the country they were leaving.

In Prague, several hundred more East Germans eluded the Czecho-slovak police to gain sanctuary at the embassy. It was not clear whether the new arrivals would be covered by the agreement.

West German officials said the device that finally enabled East Germany to approve the departure was the detour through East Germany, proposed by Foreign Minister Hans-Dietrich Genscher on Friday. The arrangement enabled East Berlin to contend that the refugees had first come home, as it had repeatedly demanded of them, and on Saturday morning, the Communist Government agreed.

The deal also permitted stops in Dresden and Karl-Marx-Stadt, where more émigrés managed to climb aboard the train. According to the refugees, other East Germans gathered to wave as they sped past.

"This was the most moving hour in my political career," said Mr. Genscher, who himself fled from East Germany in the 1950s, in describing his trip to Prague Saturday night to tell the East Germans of their impending release. "You can see what people will go through so that they can live like we do—not in the material sense, but to have the right to decide for themselves what to do with their lives."

The development suggested that the summer-long exodus of East Germans and the occupation of West German embassies was far from over. "Our embassies will not be walled shut," a West German Interior Ministry official, Horst Waffenschmidt, said.

The arrangement to free the East Germans underscored the problem facing both Germanys as a result of the exodus, which began when Hungary dismantled the barbed wire from its border with Austria. More than 30,000 East Germans have fled illegally, most of them crossing from Hungary since September 10, when the Budapest Government lifted restrictions on westward travel. Those who arrived in Hof today were bleary after a sleepless night. For most there were still hours to go as they waited for trasnportation to reception camps.

Some had spent weeks at the embassy. Others had made the move at the eleventh hour. Heike Schubert, a 22-year-old hairdresser from Halle, and her boyfriend, Andreas Stolz, 20, took the plunge Saturday night on hearing on the radio that the Germans in Prague had been allowed to leave.

Miss Schubert, crying on Mr. Stolz's shoulder, described how they rushed to her parents, who were at a party, and how the parents had said: "You go on. We'd do the same if we were young and had the possibility." . . .

For East Germany, the flight has been a painful blow, for which any solution—whether to seal off borders with its East European neighbors or to allow the flow to continue—have been similarly untenable.

For West Germany, the flight has meant a flood of new settlers at a time when the country's capacity has already been strained by tens of thousands of ethnic Germans arriving from the Soviet Union and East European countries, as well as an estimated 100,000 East Germans expected to emigrate this year legally.

It is an article of political and constitutional faith in West Germany, however, that all East Germans are fellow Germans eligible for the benefits and privileges of West German citizenship.

Thus, while the exodus has provided something of a political boom to Chancellor Helmut Kohl and Mr. Genscher, it has also challenged the standing policy of seeking a gradual improvement in relations with East Germany.

The East German expectation that the flight of their young people would taper off were quickly proved wrong. The trail to the embassy in Prague grew congested as people made their way to sanctuary at the embassy. Eventually more special trains were organized. But as the numbers of refugees grew, the demands of those they left behind also grew more strident. Freedom of travel had been the first cry, but now people were taking to the street shouting that they wanted to stay but in a different sort of country than the one they lived in. In East Berlin, in Dresden, but most particularly in Leipzig, the calls for reform and democratic changes were being raised more and more loudly by greater and greater throngs. The headlines of early autumn reflect the feverish pace.

East Germans Line Émigré Routes, Some in Hope of Their Own Exit
By Serge Schmemann

EAST BERLIN, Oct. 4—Thousands of East Germans flocked to stations and junctions along the railroad line taking their compatriots from Prague to West Germany today in hopes of sneaking aboard. Conditions became so hectic that police had to clear the Dresden terminal by force and the doors of the trains were sealed from the outside to block them.

Security Forces Storm Protesters in East Germany
By Serge Schmemann

DRESDEN, Oct. 8—Protesters clashed with the police and security forces today in cities throughout East Germany as the Communist Government's efforts to celebrate its fortieth anniversary ignited rallies and demonstrations urging changes in the country's hard-line system.

Spurred on in part by the presence of the Soviet President, Mikhail S. Gorbachev, who came for the celebrations, protesters took to the streets late Saturday and again today, often mingling their calls for greater freedom with chants of "Gorby! Gorby!"

"In East Berlin, Dresden, Leipzig and elsewhere, the police beat back defiant protesters, swinging riot sticks and menacing them with water cannon. In East Berlin tonight, a candlelight vigil was broken up by the security police, who set upon some of the nearly 1,500 people there as the protesters shouted, "No violence!" and "We're staying here!" . . .

Two days later, the police stood by without interfering as large rallies took place. New Forum, an organization that arose out of the rallies, uniting people who wanted democratic change but who had little if any experience as dissidents, was gaining cohesion. The furor was mounting and the besieged party tried to sacrifice its leadership to save itself.

East Germany Removes Honecker and His Protégé Takes His Place
By Serge Schmemann

WEST BERLIN, Oct. 18—Confronted with increasing demands for change, the East German Communist Party today ousted Erich Honecker, its hard-line leader of 18 years, and named his 52-year-old protégé to replace him .

The new leader, Egon Krenz, had been the Politburo member charged with security and youth affairs. He was named to Mr. Honecker's three positions—party chief, head of state and chairman of the Defense Council—granting him the broad powers Mr. Honecker spent years accumulating.

Though the youngest member of the Politburo, Mr. Krenz is generally regarded as a tough and conservative leader in Mr. Honecker's mold but 25 years younger, more sophisticated and probably better aware of the scope and sources of popular discontent. . . .

Mr. Krenz underscored his difference in style from Mr. Honecker, who usually restricted public appearances to stiff, formal rituals, with an appearance on television shortly after his appointment. Smiling, Mr. Krenz said: "My motto remains work, work, work and more work, but work that should be pleasant and serve all the people."

In the evening Mr. Krenz delivered an hour-long nationally televised address in which he reaffirmed the standing policy of "continuity and renewal," but added that "within these bounds, the door is wide open for earnest political dialogue."

"It is clear that we have not realistically appraised the social developments in our country in recent months, and we have not drawn the right conclusions quickly enough," Mr. Krenz said. "We see the seriousness of the situation. But we also sense and recognize the major opportunity we have opened for ourselves to define the policies in dialogue with our citizens, policies that will bring us to the verge of the next century." . . .

It may not have been what Mr. Krenz had in mind, but an emboldened populace continued to speak out in large numbers. As reported in **The Times** *on October 19, meetings were being held at which people were publicly calling for the resignation of all the old guard and assailing the credibility of Mr. Krenz. At one meeting outside East Berlin's City Hall, citizens repeatedly challenged and attacked once-powerful figures, who listened meekly. One man stood facing the East Berlin party chief, Gunter Schabowski, and shouted, "You are finished! Give us Free Election!" Under such pressure something—in fact, many things—would have to give, among them the leadership and wall that symbolized the system that erected it to divide the continent.*

• • •

In early autumn, most of the world's attention was focused on East and West Germany. But the continuing erosion of Communist power was also occurring elsewhere. In Hungary, for example, the Communist leadership met with leaders of dissident groups and together they endorsed a plan calling for multiparty elections. Then, in anticipation that they would not do very well running as Communists against anti-Communists, the Communist party met in early October and decided to redefine itself.

Communist Party in Hungary Votes for Radical Shift

By Henry Kamm

BUDAPEST, Oct. 7—The Hungarian Communist Party voted today to transform itself into a socialist party and said it would strive to bridge the gulf between doctrinaire Marxism and European democratic socialism.

In a series of votes to change the party's name to the Hungarian Socialist Party and set general party direction, the delegates at an extraordinary party congress here greatly raised expectations that the reform-oriented leadership's entire program to overhaul the party would be adopted. Among the changes expected are more democratic procedures for choosing the leadership.

With Poland, Hungary is at the forefront of change in the Eastern bloc. But unlike Poland, where the Solidarity union has taken the reins of power with the Communist Party largely unchanged, Hungary is pushing through radical change from within its Communist Party. . . .

In a news conference before the voting, Imre Pozsgay, a member of Hungary's collective presidency and a leader of those advocating major change, said an overwhelming majority of the delegates supported the leadership's program so that the party can better confront new, independently formed parties in free parliamentary elections due to be held by next June. . . .

One key aspect of the changes in Budapest dealt largely with a semantic issue.

What's in a Name? Just Ask the Hungarians

By Henry Kamm

BUDAPEST, Oct. 10—Attila Agh, until last weekend a leading "reform Communist," was asked today what party members should be called now that their organization has become the Socialist Party. "Radical Socialists," he replied. For the first time in a Communist country, a ruling party has formally abandoned Communism.

In a four-day congress that ended on Monday, the party changed its name and structure, modeled closely on that of the Soviet Communist Party, and declared its eagerness to open friendly relations with reform-oriented Communist parties of East and West and beyond that with all leftist parties.

It expressed hope for contacts even with the organization that Communists demonize as an ideological enemy, the Socialist International.

The split between evolutionary and revolutionary Socialists after the Bolshevik Revolution of 1917 arrayed Communists in the Third International and Socialists and social democrats in the Socialist International.

Nonetheless, the Hungarian party president, Rezso Nyers, announced after his election Monday night that President Mikhail S. Gorbachev of the Soviet Union had waited only an hour or two to telegraph his congratulations.

Mr. Agh, a political scientist and drafter of the document embracing socialism, said that the new stance toward foreign parties showed how earnestly the newly baptized Socialists meant their break with Communism.

"We have given up the whole terminology of brotherly parties," he said.

Dogmatic Soviet and East European Communists take the terminology and protocol of their movement seriously, and consider it a faux pas to address a Communist as "Mister" rather than "Comrade." Such hard-liners are likely to consider the Hungarian party's turnabout as an act of treason.

Casual conversations with Hungarians, however, indicate that many remain unconvinced that the outward changes represent a change of heart of the party that under two earlier names has been the absolute ruler of their country since World War II.

At a news conference today, spokesmen for the Democratic Forum, considered the principal opposition party in the first free presidential and parliamentary elections to be held by next spring, made sport of the name change. With heavy irony, the opposition leaders showed their disbelief in the Communists' name change and conversion.

"It's strange, we are all liberals now," said Dean Geza Jeszenszky of the School of Social and Political Science at Karl Marx University, a leader of the Democratic Forum. "Their program is not just socialist, it's more liberal than that of traditional social democrats. As an admirer of nineteenth-century liberalism, I welcome this."

But, Mr. Jeszenszky said, the reform Communists needed to compromise with more dogmatic Communists to create the new Socialist

162

Party. Referring to Marx, he said, "They think the teaching of a nineteenth-century philosopher is still valid today." As an opponent, he said he welcomed the outcome of the congress because the party had not changed enough to win credibility with the voters.

Mr. Agh, however, said he was convinced that the majority of Hungary's 725,000 Communists accepted the conversion and that, little by little, symbols of Communism like red stars and portraits of Lenin would disappear.

He said he and his friends would have been happier had Mr. Nyers, who is regarded as a moderate reformer, adopted a stronger line against conservative party members and provoked more of them to leave.

Party officials estimate that about a third of the membership will choose not to register in the new group.

"If we are lucky, those who leave will found a big Communist Party," Mr. Agh said. "It will give us political credentials."

Mr. Agh said that only three of the new party Presidium's 23 elected members "may have a past," meaning a former association with more dogmatic Communism. "We have a very solid voting majority," he said.

And farther to the east, Mikhail S. Gorbachev was once again leading by retreating. This time it was in Finland that he delivered an unexpected message.

Gorbachev in Finland, Disavows Any Right of Regional Intervention
By Bill Keller

HELSINKI, FINLAND, Oct. 25—President Mikhail S. Gorbachev declared today that the Soviet Union has no moral or political right to interfere in the affairs of its East European neighbors, and held up neutral Finland as a model of stability in stormy Europe.

His spokesman embroidered the theme jokingly, saying that Moscow had adopted "the Sinatra doctrine" in Eastern Europe. "You know the Frank Sinatra song, 'I Did It My Way'?" said Gennadi I. Gerasimov to reporters. "Hungary and Poland are doing it their way."

"I think the Brezhnev doctrine is dead," he added, using the Western term for the previous Soviet policy of armed intervention to

163

prevent changes in the Communist governments of the Warsaw Pact. In talks with Finland's President, Mauno Koivisto, at the beginning of a three-day state visit, Mr. Gorbachev was reported to have said that the current political upheavals in the East bloc must be allowed to run their course.

Mr. Gorbachev has repeatedly pledged a policy of noninterference, but his emphasis on the point—and his lauding of the Finnish example—were striking in a week when Hungary was joining Poland in a retreat from orthodox Communist rule and East Germany was boiling with demands for political liberty.

"The events that are now taking place in the countries of Eastern Europe concern the countries and people of that region," the Soviet leader told the Finnish President, according to Mr. Gerasimov, whose formal position is that of spokesman for the Soviet Foreign Ministry. "We have no right, moral or political right, to interfere in events happening there. We assume others will not interfere either."

Finland, once an autonomous part of czarist Russia, gained its independence in 1917. It was invaded by the Soviet Union late in 1939, after the formal outbreak of World War II, and was forced to cede some territory to the Russians. The Karelian Autonomous Republic, which borders on Finland, is largely populated by Finnish speakers.

Today, as Mr. Gorbachev moved through largely friendly crowds, there were some cries of "Give us back Karelia," but no indication that he heard them.

Mr. Gerasimov, who served for many years as a correspondent for the Soviet news-feature agency Novosti in New York, has used the "Sinatra doctrine" expression before to explain the willingness of the Soviet Union to allow its allies to follow different political lines.

Mr. Gerasimov declined a direct answer when asked how Moscow would respond if its allies wanted to move toward neutrality. He noted that Hungary and Poland still have obligations as members of military and economic alliances with the Soviet Union.

"We may witness a change of government in Warsaw or Budapest, but international obligations do not necessarily go away with a change of government," Mr. Gerasimov said.

He added that Moscow has long proposed a mutual breakup of both the North Atlantic Treaty Organization and the Warsaw Pact, but he did not say how the Kremlin would react if the Warsaw Pact showed signs of breaking up on its own.

Still, Mr. Gorbachev's remarks today seemed to suggest that Moscow is open to more fundamental changes in its relations with East bloc allies.

Both Poland and Hungary have said they do not plan to leave the alliance, but some officials in both countries favor drastic military changes, including withdrawal of Soviet forces now based on their soil.

In recent months, Finland—with a largely free-market economy but reliant on Soviet trade, formally neutral but always attentive to Soviet security concerns—has loomed large in the minds of East bloc countries. Hungary has sent several delegations to study Finland's economy, its laws and its relations with Moscow.

Asked during a brief walk in downtown Helsinki this evening whether he considered Finland a model for countries in Eastern Europe, Mr. Gorbachev replied, "To me, Finland is a model of relations between a big country and a small country, a model of relations between states with different social systems, a model of relations between neighbors."

As if to underscore the advantages of good-neighborly relations, Soviet officials this week are to sign an agreement to sharply reduce sulfur emissions that have been poisoning Finland's forests.

Kaj Barlund, the Finnish Minister of the Environment, said in an interview today that it was "the most radical" anti-pollution agreement ever signed between a Communist and a non-Communist country, but he conceded that the Soviets would probably require costly technological help from the Finns to live up to their end of the deal.

The treaty calls for reducing the two countries' 1.4 million tons a year of sulfur-dioxide emissions by half before 1995. The largest share of the noxious emissions comes from two Soviet nickel smelters a few miles east of the Finnish border.

Mr. Gorbachev also made a significant concession to Finland's pride tonight when he said at a banquet speech, "I want to greet neutral Finland."

It was the first time that a Soviet leader had given full weight to this country's policy of neutrality in world politics. Moscow's reluctance to directly acknowledge that Finland is neutral has long been resented here as an implication that Finland owes special deference to the Kremlin.

In turn, Mr. Koivisto, the Finnish President, demonstrated the kind of sensitivity to the Soviet Union that the Kremlin prizes in this relationship. He included in his banquet speech an implicit but unmistakable message of nonsupport for separatist movements in Soviet Lithuania, Latvia and Estonia, across the Baltic Sea from Finland.

Mr. Koivisto said that although tensions are now erupting in the Soviet Union, "underneath the surface, there is every reason for confidence in the ability of this community of peoples to solve its problems in a way that enables the distinctiveness of the parts to be increased while strengthening the whole."

Finland and Estonia, which face each other across the Gulf of Finland, have longstanding ties that are now expanding. Direct air connections and a new, second ferry line across the gulf are due to open this winter, adding to an already fast-growing business and tourist traffic. Finnish bankers and businessmen say they see promising investment opportunities if Estonia gets greater economic independence from Moscow.

By mid-October, in the days just before and after Gorbachev delivered the Helsinki speech, the clamor for change that had arisen in Eastern Europe was centering on East Germany. Some East Germans were fleeing while others were trying to wield suddenly unleashed emotions and yearnings into an organization. Out of the milling and shouting—chaotic by German standards—emerged New Forum, which was to focus, if not fully lead, the mounting wave of demonstrations.

East German Movement Overtaken by Followers
By Serge Schmemann

WEST BERLIN, Oct. 15—It is a sign of the novelty of resistance in East Germany that the premier opposition grouping, founded only a month ago, provided a rallying cry in the streets even before it had time to become a movement.

Among the chants that echoed loudest through the streets of East Berlin, Leipzig and Dresden during last week's mass protests was "Neu-es Fo-rum! Neu-es Fo-rum!" But few of the demonstrators had met anyone from New Forum, and its leaders deliberately stayed clear of the marches.

On the eve of the Government's celebration of the fortieth anniversary of the Communist state, New Forum leaders had actually urged East Germans not to demonstrate, fearing that uncontrolled protests could turn violent.

As Sebastian Pflugbeil, one of the founding members, said on the eve of the anniversary, "We don't have any means of asking people to behave peacefully. We have no access to media, we don't have any organization, we have no group that could manage a demonstration."

That was 10 days ago, before tens of thousands of East Germans across the country took to the streets, and before the alarmed Politburo demonstrated a first, tentative readiness to discuss the problems that had fired the protest and the earlier mass exodus to the West. One hundred and twenty New Forum representatives from all parts of East Germany met and agreed to form a standing coordinating committee, to appoint a "spokesmen's council" to speak for the movement, and to publish a newspaper starting next month. They claimed to have 25,000 supporters.

New Forum also renewed its application for official registration as a political organization, which authorities rejected last month with a threatening denunciation of the fledgling group as "a platform hostile to the state."

To be sure, the Politburo made clear in its statement on Wednesday that it was prepared to have discussions only through existing channels.

But the newly stiffened New Forum declared that "real dialogue had to be institutionalized."

"With our first manifesto we tried to bring people out, to say to them, 'We want to stay,'" Barbel Bohley, the most vocal of the founding members, said in a recent interview. "Many agreed with that, but we can't remain at this point. We are interested in standing on our own feet."

Founded less than a month before the anniversary by a group of middle-aged, left-wing intellectuals and defectors from the ruling Communist Party, New Forum was born as a popular rebuttal to the mass exodus of East Germans to West Germany through Hungary, Czechoslovakia and Poland and to the talk of reunification this prompted in the West.

In their manifesto on September 12, the founders declared that they did not want to go West, they did not want German reunification, they did not want capitalism. They want to create a political platform for the "restructuring of the German Democratic Republic," for a democratic socialism.

At a time when the world's attention was focused on the exodus and the common joke was whether anyone would be left in East Germany to turn off the lights, the appearance of a group militantly bent on staying and changing the state from within attracted instant attention.

If the Government had simply ignored New Forum instead of denouncing the movement, it might have remained one of several pro-reform groups springing up in the fertile tumult of the exodus. Instead, its name spread through East Germany by West German radio and television, it became a rallying cry for the dissatisfaction catalyzed by the exodus.

"Things are moving much faster than we ever thought," said Mr. Pflugbeil. "Now even in small cities and in small factories people are joining New Forum. But you shouldn't overestimate what we are doing. You shouldn't compare us to Solidarity. This is only the beginning, on a very small scale."

With his tangled beard and large glasses, Mr. Pflugbeil seemed to fit well the profile of a New Forum founder. A physicist and at 42 a veteran of the East German peace movement, he had emerged like many other founders from the protective shadow of the Protestant churches, where East German dissenters had long huddled.

Teenagers when the Berlin wall was erected, they had cut their dissenters' teeth in the small anti-missile movements that rose after 1979 as an echo of the potent peace movement in West Germany, and the environmental activism of the early 1980's. Harassed constantly by the state, they had watched their leaders repeatedly expelled to the West, leaving their movement in a permanent state of disorganization.

Now, joined by Communist Party defectors inspired by the Soviet President, Mikhail S. Gorbachev, they represent a blend of perestroika Communism and environmentalism, a group in some ways reminiscent of the dissident writers and scientists in Moscow in the 1960's, or of KOR in Poland or Charter '77 in Czechoslovakia in the 1970's.

Speaking in a soft voice over tea in his book-lined apartment in central East Berlin, Mr. Pflugbeil talked of the difficulty of dissent in a nation still scarred by its past.

"We are now at the point where we have to openly discuss change," he said. "It is especially important that we speak openly and with no fear, because since 1933 we have forgotten that freedom of speech can be used. We all learned from our parents that to touch political things is dangerous. That is an attitude that has to change."

The attitude, it seemed last week, has changed more than New Forum or the church were prepared for. At one point during the demonstrations in East Berlin, several thousand protesters reached Gethsemane Church, a center of opposition, and filled the small square facing its entrance.

As the police advanced, the throng looked to the entrance glowing in the light of candles placed by dissenters, as if waiting for someone to appear and take charge.

Nobody did. Unlike the Polish strikers in 1980, the young East German demonstrators had neither militant workers nor an organization behind them. Their demonstrations seemed largely spontaneous eruptions of anger and frustration, catalyzed by the mass exodus and the gaudy celebrations marking the state's fortieth birthday. Mr. Gorbachev was in town, and an army of Western reporters had been reluctantly let in for the festivities.

For New Forum, the protests seemed to pose a critical challenge. To remain an intellectual forum was to risk irrelevance in the new mood. To try to take charge was to telescope an evolutionary process from intellectual dissent to power politics that had taken successful movements like Solidarity years to achieve.

"We move ahead, but we don't have an overview yet," Miss Bohley said. "We've grown up without democracy, and we honestly do not know this playing field, democracy. On one hand we reject the tutelage of the state, on the other we don't know how democracy really looks. Now some are calling for a program. We have to have patience."

As Mr. Gorbachev offered his assurances of nonintervention and the New Forum people drew more and more adherents, tens of thousands of East Germans had been streaming out of their country via Hungary and Czechoslovakia to West Germany. As numbers of these mostly young émigrés built up in the West German Embassy in Prague, the East Germans agreed to their transfer, but at the same time announced the border to Czechoslovakia would be sealed. But then in the face of protests, they relented, and once more people swarmed to Prague in growing numbers. And at home, huge rallies were taking place at which new demands were raised that went far beyond calls for freer travel.

300,000 Reported to March in Largest East German Protest
By Henry Kamm

EAST BERLIN, Oct 23—Hundreds of thousands of East Germans marched peacefully through Leipzig tonight, demanding democratic changes, including legalization of opposition movements, independent labor unions and separation of powers between the Communist Party and the state. . . .

An East Berlin worker complained not long ago that all his life he had been taught "to learn from the Soviet Union is to learn to triumph." Now that East Germans would like to follow the Soviet example, he said, they are being told that each country must follow its own path. . . .

The East German government was being forced into concessions.

East Germans Declare Amnesty for Those Who Fled
By Serge Schmemann

BONN, Oct. 27—East Germany announced an amnesty today for all citizens who have fled or tried to flee the country, as well as most of those arrested in the recent wave of anti-Government demonstrations.

The Government also announced that East Germans could again travel to Czechoslovakia without a visa. A ban was imposed on October 3 to halt a tide of East Germans fleeing to the West German Embassy in Prague hoping to win passage to the West. Almost 20,000 fled in this way before East Germany shut the border, the only one East Germans had been freely allowed to cross.

The Interior Ministry said today the ban would be lifted as of November 1. There was no indication whether the Government would take new steps to prevent another mass flight to the West German Embassy, which has continued to attract a trickle of East Germans. . . .

Another Big Rally in East Germany
By Serge Schmemann

LEIPZIG, EAST GERMANY, Oct. 30—Chanting demands for everything from free elections to the ouster of the secret police, more than

300,000 East Germans marched around Leipzig's old center in what has become the major weekly ritual of the growing popular movement for change.

A thicket of placards challenging the Communist Party's rule with slogans like "New politics with the old crowd?" offered evidence of how far the movement has evolved in the three weeks since the Communist Party first allowed a march in Leipzig to go unchallenged and so signaled a retreat from its hard line. . . .

As soon as they were able to resume their flight via Prague, they did, and on November 1 the very first day that the new rules went into effect, 8,000 crossed into Czechoslovakia, and even larger numbers swarmed in the days that followed. The policies of permissiveness were not stemming the exodus. The stream of émigrés was turning into a torrent, as was the surge of protest inside the country.

500,000 in East Berlin Rally for Change; Émigrés Are Given Passage to West
By Serge Schmemann

EAST BERLIN, Nov. 4—Four weeks to the day after a few thousand East Berliners took to the streets to demand political change, at least a half-million demonstrators jammed the heart of the East German capital today for the largest rally so far in what one speaker called a "revolution from below."

At the same time, reports from Prague, the Czechoslovak capital, said East Germany had agreed to let its citizens leave for the West from Czechoslovakia by simply producing their internal identity documents.

The decision marked the first time that East Germany allowed its citizens free passage to West Germany, and in essence it opened a door through the wall that for so long has stood as the foremost symbol of Communist control, the dividing line between East and West.

Ingrid Stahmer, the Deputy Mayor of West Berlin, who visited Prague today, indicated that she believed that the new measures meant that the Berlin wall had, in effect, passed into history. "It is just going to be superfluous," she said. The news did not seem to dampen calls for change as the throng in the East German capital marched down broad boulevards through the city center with a thicket of placards, finally engulfing Alexanderplatz, a vast plain of concrete at the heart of East Berlin, to hear a series of speeches. As the marchers passed the headquarters of the Council of Ministers, many demonstrators posted demands on the wall or laid them on the ground, and they remained there long after the demonstration ended.

Some estimates put the crowd at more than a million, and by any count it posted another milestone in a mass movement that has filled the streets of East Germany virtually daily in numbers unknown in its forty-year history.

And like all the demonstrations since the state first reined in the police on October 9 and allowed people to protest unmolested, the authorities did not interfere and the four-hour rally was disciplined and peaceful.

In the spirit of openness that has spread over the last four weeks, the demonstration was broadcast live on the East German radio and television.

Most of the placards, and the statements from the seventeen speakers that drew the loudest cheers, called for free speech, free elections, an end to the "leading role" of the Communist Party and—a demand that prompted the most boisterous whoops—a settling of accounts with the hated security police.

Only Gunter Schabowski, the Communist Party chief in East Berlin, referred directly to the renewed flight when he spoke of the "depressing news and pictures from Prague." There was also a banner linking "monopoly of power by the Communist Party" and "mass flight" by émigrés.

The agreement between East Germany and Czechoslovakia, first announced by West German officials, meant that an East German had only to show an internal identity document to cross Czechoslovakia to West Germany. Almost immediately, sputtering East German Trabant cars began arriving at the Czechoslovak–West German border, along with trainloads of East Germans who had thronged to the West German Embassy after East Berlin first lifted restrictions on travel to Czechoslovakia on November 1.

East Germans still could not travel directly to West Germany. But the announcement of the East German–Czechoslovak arrangement stressed that it would be in force only until East Germany enacts a promised new travel law, which reportedly will enable East Germans to travel abroad with relative ease.

The march in East Berlin had been organized by the official Union of Actors, and a cordon of actors and artists, wearing sashes that read "No Violence," helped keep order.

Most marchers seemed largely unimpressed by the promises of "far-reaching" changes and the dismissal of five Politburo members announced Friday evening by Egon Krenz, the new party chief. The new program and the resignations are to become formal at a meeting of the Communist Party's Central Committee next week.

It seemed a measure of the remarkable pace of events in East Germany that even while Mr. Krenz was announcing measures that would have been breathtaking only four weeks earlier, he now seemed to trail behind the demands of a popular movement still without real leadership.

"He's learned a lot, he's gaining pace, but I'm not sure whether he's quick enough to keep up with events," said Jens Reich, one of the founding members of the New Forum opposition group and a speaker at the rally. "He must become more bold."

Four weeks earlier, during celebrations of East Germany's fortieth anniversary that were attended by President Mikhail S. Gorbachev of the Soviet Union, a small group of demonstrators had begun chanting "Freedom!" and "Gorby!" on Alexanderplatz.

Before the night was over, about 5,000 demonstrators had clashed violently with the police, revealing to the Government the danger of the popular discontent and prompting the dramatic change of course both by the Communists and the public.

Many of the placards carried by the crowd were laced with a humor that seemed to reflect a growing confidence in the popular movement. "Always forward, never backward—Erich Honecker, roofer," read one, referring to the fallen party leader and his original trade. Some referred to Mr. Krenz's support for the Chinese after the June crackdown on dissent: "Krenz Xiaoping, no thanks."

Other banners called for dismantling the security police and demanded free trade unions and new faces at the top. One simply read, "Thanks, Hungary." It was Hungary's opening of its borders that prompted a mass migration last summer, which in turn was a catalyst for the movement for change at home.

The seventeen speakers included actors, opposition leaders, party officials, church leaders, writers and other prominent figures. Some drew cheers, some jeers and some both.

"I don't like the words 'change of course,'" said one of the most popular speakers, the prominent writer Christa Wolff, referring to the term by which the Communist Party has repeatedly referred to its new openness.

"It sounds like a sailor changing direction with the prevailing wind," she said. "I would rather say 'revolutionary renewal,' a 'revolution from below.' "

Some of the largest jeers were reserved for Mr. Schabowski, who has shown probably the least reticence among Politburo members in coming face to face with critics.

"What does a Communist think in the face of hundreds of thousands of demonstrators?" he asked, shouting into the microphones over a steady roar of whistles and jeers. "Bitter things have been said, directed to my address. But only if we speak to each other can we create a new East Germany."

Shouts of "Shut up!" rose from the crowd, drowning out all but snatches of Mr. Schabowski's address.

A prominent lawyer, Gregor Gysi, received a mixed reaction when he said it was Mr. Krenz, then the party secretary charged with security, who ordered the police not to interfere with marchers in Leipzig on October 9, and thus ended the violence that had marked demonstrations until then.

Among the last speakers was an elderly and popular actress, Steffie Spira, who alone stayed within the five-minute limit set on addresses and who raised a roar of laughter when she concluded her remarks by saying: "I want the Government to do what I am about to do. Step down." And she did.

The next week proved critical. Successive headlines reflected the quickening tempo.

10,000 More Flee as East Germany Vows Easy Travel
By Serge Schmemann

EAST BERLIN, Nov. 5—Thousands of East Germans left for West Germany today as the Government said that new laws making it relatively easy for citizens to travel to the West would be ready for Christmas.

The announcement by Interior Minister Friedrich Dickel on the evening news program seemed intended to halt another frenzied westward flight by East Germans afraid that the borders might once more close. . . .

A Draft Law Grants East Germans the Right to Travel or Emigrate

By Serge Schmemann

EAST BERLIN, Nov. 6—East Germany today published the draft of a law that declared for the first time that every citizen has the right to travel abroad or emigrate. But against the weekend backdrop of yet another surge of emigration to West Germany, the measure seemed to attract little excitement.

"Travel is not the primary problem anymore," said Sebastian Pflugbeil, a founding member of the opposition movement New Forum. . . .

Then on November 7 came word that the entire East German cabinet resigned and the next day the announcement was made that the Politburo was being reorganized to enable Egon Krenz, then still in his first month as party leader, to name what was described as a streamlined and younger party leadership. The day after that, on November 9, a Thursday, the East German authorities took the step that they had long thought unthinkable.

The Border Is Open; Joyous East Germans Pour Through Wall; Party Pledges Freedoms, and City Exults

By Serge Schmemann

WEST BERLIN, Nov. 10—As hundreds of thousands of East Berliners romped through the newly porous wall in an unending celebration, West German leaders today proclaimed this the moment Germans had yearned for through forty years of division.

At the same time, change continued unabated in East Berlin, where the Communist Party's Central Committee concluded a three-day session with the announcement of a program of radical changes. They included "free, democratic and secret elections," a "socialist planned economy oriented to market conditions," separation of party and state, parliamentary supervision of state security, freedom of assembly and a new law on the press and broadcasting.

"The German Democratic Republic is in the midst of an awakening," the Central Committee declared in the prologue to the newly adopted program. "A revolutionary people's movement has brought into motion a process of great change. The renewal of society is on the agenda."

Though the West Berlin police could give no estimate of the numbers of East Berliners who crossed over in the last 24 hours, the authorities said that only 1,500 so far had announced their intention to stay.

Beyond Berlin, only one of many points along the border between the two Germanys where people could cross, 55,500 East Germans crossed over the border between the two Germanys since the wall was opened on Thursday, and 3,250 remained in West Germany, the West German Interior Ministry said.

Chancellor Helmut Kohl, who interrupted a state visit to Poland to come to West Berlin, told an emotional crowd of East and West Berliners gathered outside the West Berlin city hall: "I want to call out to all in the German Democratic Republic: We're on your side, we are and remain one nation. We belong together."

Speaking on the steps of the city hall, from which President John F. Kennedy had made his "Ich bin ein Berliner" speech shortly after the wall was raised, Mr. Kohl declared: "Long live a free German fatherland! Long live a united Europe!"

All through the night and through the day, East Berliners continued to flood into West Berlin in vast numbers, filling the glittering Kurfurstendamm until traffic came to a halt, forming long lines to pick up the 100-mark "welcome money"—about $55—that West Germany has traditionally given East Germans on their first time in the West, gaping at shop windows and drinking in the heady new feeling of freedom.

A festive air seized the entire city. West Berliners lined entry points to greet East Berliners with champagne, cheers and hugs. Many restaurants offered the visitors free food. A television station urged West Berliners to call in with offers of theater tickets, beds, dinners or just guided tours of the "Ku'damm."

The Hertha soccer club, popular both in West and East, offered 10,000 free tickets to the game against Wattenscheid on Saturday.

Both West and East German television gave saturation coverage to the reunion, often under titles like "The End of the Wall," contributing to a widespread sense that a great moment was in the making.

In a development that gave further evidence of the figurative crumbling of the wall, East Germany announced the opening of five new crossings. One was at the Glienicke Bridge, famed as the site of past exchanges of captured spies between East and West, and another was at Potsdammer Platz, once the heart of Berlin.

The arrival of an army bulldozer at Eberswalder Strasse to drill another new opening quickly attracted a crowd on both sides and sent rumors through the city that the East German Army was breaking down the wall. When the machine finally broke through, West Berliners handed flowers to the driver and rushed to pick up pieces of the wall for souvenirs.

At the Potsdammer Platz crossing site, West Berliners mounted the wall to chip away pieces while East German workers laid paving stones in the no-man's-land, watched by about 50 soldiers.

The East German authorities also announced that bus shuttles would connect East and West Berlin.

In the giddiness of the grand reunion, German reunification was in the air. "We've done it! The wall is open!" proclaimed the popular tabloid *Bild* in a giant headline. "This is the first step to unity."

The conservative *Frankfurter Allgemeine* tempered its excitement with caution: "Since Thursday evening that monstrous construction and barbed wire no longer divide the people. But with the joy over the end of the torment of German division, we must realize that faster German rapprochement needs a faster consideration of how politically to handle a situation changing by the hour."

A group of young men walked down the Kurfurstendamm with the two German flags, identical save for a Communist emblem at the center of the East German banner, sewn together.

The theme was there, too, in the emotional speeches from the steps of city hall. Willy Brandt, the former West German Chancellor who was West Berlin's Mayor in 1961 when the wall was raised, declared in a choked voice: "This is a beautiful day after a long voyage, but we are only at a way station. We are not at the end of our way."

"The moving together of the German states is taking shape in reality in a different way than many of us expected," Mr. Brandt said. "No one should act as if he knows in which concrete form the people in these two states will find a new relationship. But that they will find a relationship, that they will come together in freedom, that is the important point."

Walter Momper, the Mayor of West Berlin, raised cheers when he declared: "The whole city and all its citizens will never forget November 9, 1989. For 28 years since the wall was built we have yearned for this day. We Germans are now the happiest people on earth. Yesterday was not yet the day of reunification, but it was a day of reunion."

The West German Foreign Minister, Hans-Dietrich Genscher, who returned with Mr. Kohl from Poland for the gathering, opened his address by recalling his roots in East Germany, from which he fled after the war.

"My most hearty greetings go to the people of my homeland," he said. "What we are witnessing in the streets of Berlin in these hours is that forty years of division have not created two nations out of one. There is no capitalist and there is no socialist Germany, but only one German nation in unity and peace."

Evidently anticipating the anxieties of other countries, Mr. Genscher added: "No people on this earth, no people in Europe have to fear if the gates are opened now between East and West. No people have to fear that liberty and democracy have returned to the G.D.R."

Mr. Kohl was met by loud jeers from the crowd, evidently reflecting his unpopularity among many West Berliners, as he declared this "a historic moment for Berlin and for Germany."

The Chancellor appealed to East Germans to stay in their country now that it was evidently firmly on the road to political and economic change. "We are sure that when these reforms come to pass, and if the G.D.R. goes forward on this path, our compatriots there who now think of leaving will stay in their homeland," he said.

Mr. Kohl flew from West Berlin to Bonn, where he will preside over an emergency Cabinet meeting on Saturday morning before returning to Poland to continue his official visit.

In East Germany, the conclusion of the Central Committee meeting was followed by a mass rally of Communist Party members that was addressed Egon Krenz, the new party leader.

"We plan a great work, a revolution on German soil that will bring us a socialism that is economically effective, politically democratic, morally clean and will turn to the people in everything," Mr. Krenz declared.

"That's why the Council of Ministers issued new travel regulations for all mature citizens in our country as an expression that we are serious in our policy of renewal and that we reach out our hands to everyone who wants to go with us," he said.

The "action program" adopted today, Mr. Krenz said, was "a program for our people to win back trust among the people."

"We want better socialism, we want free elections, we want our people to send their best representatives to Parliament," he said.

Mr. Krenz also reaffirmed his loyalty to Moscow, as he has taken care to do since he came to power. "Our close links to the Soviet Union make us strong, and give new meaning to our slogan, that to learn from the Soviet Union is to learn to win, especially in these days," he said.

The action program outlined by the official press agency A.D.N. followed the proposals first made by Mr. Krenz on the opening day of the Central Committee meeting. The three-day meeting proved a turning point in the dramatic upheaval that has seized East Germany over the last month.

The Central Committee issued only broad directives for change. On the economic front, it called for making the planned economy sensitive to market conditions, though it did not elaborate how this would be done. With an eye to the most widespread complaints, it said the economy would concentrate on areas such as consumer goods, meat, beer and spare parts.

The proposed election law promised to be the most fateful of the new measures. The West German radio said Hans Modrow, the new Prime Minister, had discussed with Mr. Krenz the possibility of forming a coalition government with some of the small parties, including the Social Democrats and the Liberals.

Mr. Modrow said the action program of the Communist Party would not be enough without the input of the other parties, which have become more independent and vocal over the last month.

The Central Committee also strongly censured Erich Honecker, the fallen party leader, and two Politburo members ousted with him, Gunter Mittag and Joachim Hermann. "The Central Committee has learned that serious mistakes of the previous General Secretary and Politburo led the party and republic into deep crisis," the final communiqué of the session said.

The committee reserved its sharpest criticism for Mr. Mittag, who had been the secretary charged with the economy. "Comrade Mittag was excluded from the Central Committee because of the gravest violations of inner-party democracy, against party and state discipline and because of damaging the reputation of the party," it said.

The program also called for approval of freedom of assembly, legalization of new political organizations, a constitutional court and changes in criminal law to include independent juries. It also said the party would immediately take measures to lift privileges held by party leaders.

It declared, too, that military policy would be publicly discussed, and that military spending might be reduced.

The program is expected to come under more detailed discussion when Parliament meets on Monday.

Amid the euphoria there were trickles of anxiety. Would a less divided Europe become a less peaceful place? How great would be the burdens of helping the poor Eastern cousins catch up with the West, and if they did not catch up, would they remain quiet and content?

Redefining Europe; As the Revelry Goes On, Politicians Ponder the Ramifications of Changes in Germany
By Craig R. Whitney

WEST BERLIN, Nov. 10—By the simple act of forcing their Communist rulers to open the Berlin wall and allow them to go wherever they wish, the people of East Germany have irrevocably changed the way Berlin, Germany and all of Europe have defined themselves for more than forty years.

Thousands and thousands of East Berliners celebrated their triumph today by promenading up and down the elegant, tree-lined shopping boulevards of the western part of the city, which most of them had never before been allowed to see. They made the Kurfurstendamm into a street festival this evening as church bells pealed joyously into the night.

Willy Brandt, who was Mayor of West Berlin when the wall was built in 1961, said at a rally this evening, "The moving together of the German states is taking shape in reality in a different way than many of us expected.

"No one should act as if he knows in which concrete form the people in these two states will find a new relationship. But that they will find a relationship, that they will come together in freedom, that is the important point."

But the entire postwar European order has been based on the assumption that Germany, and Europe, would remain divided, and the countries of Eastern and Western Europe firmly anchored in their respective alliances.

In that assumption the United States, in the NATO alliance, guaranteed the security of Western Europe. And in that same assumption

France, West Germany and the other major industrial countries of Western Europe began the economic and political unification of the European Community.

West German politicians, including Mr. Brandt and Chancellor Helmut Kohl, who interrupted an official visit to Poland today to fly to Berlin, all insist that West Germany's commitment to West European integration and the alliance remains.

But politicians, diplomats and business leaders all over Europe are considering new implications for both institutions now that the end of German partition is at last imaginable.

"Europe, though Europeans did not always appreciate it, has been a haven of order these past 44 years," *The Economist* wrote today. "For East Europeans the price of that stability has been high: a lifetime wasted under a government you loathed. For West Europeans the stability has been marvelous. They could get rich, and start to build a new unity, within a clearly defined zone which ended at the river Elbe and the Bohemian forest."

Now, a NATO diplomat in Brussels said, "The end of the wall raises questions of what's going to happen in Europe. The whole concept of the European Community now may have to change."

So would the concept of the NATO alliance, this diplomat conceded: "Our role will be to design a new role for the alliance—maintaining a balance of stability with the East while all this change is going on.

"There's a reassessment of the Warsaw Pact going on too," he said. "This organization we rejected over the years is beginning to be seen as a possible element of stability in the future, to prevent the Balkanization of Eastern Europe."

Rudolf Witt, a 32-year-old mechanic from East Berlin who crossed over this afternoon with his wife, Barbara Rieck, and their 4-month-old baby, Susanne, said on his way back home at the Invalidenstrasse crossing point, "We're the balancing scales of Europe, and we don't want to tip them with something like German reunification."

An American diplomatic expert on Germany said, "I think the orderliness of everything that has happened so far, and the great restraint shown by the West Germans, shows that there will be an orderly transition to something else."

"I think Kohl will make a great big pledge and West German industrialists will start rebuilding" East Germany, he said. "But the price will be more political reform than the East German leadership originally intended. If they follow the Polish model, East Germans would have eight or ten years to determine whether they wanted to remain a separate country," he said.

Such uncertainties have been far from the minds of the European Community politicians who have spent the last three years trying to agree on ways to closer economic and political unity among the twelve existing members.

Chancellor Kohl has been trying to persuade his fellow European leaders to agree to make the Community into a confederation, rather than the loose collection of cooperating sovereign states that is preferred by Prime Minister Margaret Thatcher of Britain.

Mrs. Thatcher is already regarded by the other leaders in the Community as an obstacle to greater unity among the twelve. At full steam only a year ago, omentum toward closer union could falter if much of West Germany's attention in the next few years is diverted to the East. On Wednesday, Mr. Kohl promised a "completely new dimension" of economic aid for East Germany if it went ahead with promised political changes.

But even if European integration is sidetracked for the time being, it may acquire a new direction if the peoples of Eastern Europe can go on forcing democratic change in their countries. Nations like Hungary, Poland and perhaps even East Germany could become associate members of an expanded European Community, if not full ones.

The challenge would be to allow them to flourish economically in association with Western Europe without upsetting the security interests of either the United States or the Soviet Union in the process.

Both superpowers, at the moment, look more or less like passive, though benevolent, bystanders as events in Eastern Europe unfold. Moscow no longer seems to see itself as threatened by radical political or economic change in Eastern Europe, and both the United States and the Soviet Union have an interest in achieving substantial cuts in their conventional armed forces on both sides of the German divide.

What is not so clear is where Moscow's strategic bottom line lies, and what the attitude of the United States—not just the Bush Administration, but Congress as well—will be if many Americans decide the cold war is over and their troops should all come home. There are about 300,000 Army and Air Force troops in Western Europe.

The American attitude is the key to insuring that Germany does not lose its Western orientation and that Europe manages an orderly transition to whatever new future awaits it, many Germans and Western diplomats agree.

"We are at present at the creation of a new postwar era," one American official said, "and I hope the people at home will see it that way."

Jubilation in Berlin; A Day for Celebration and a Bit of Shopping
By Ferdinand Protzman

EAST BERLIN, Nov. 10—Church bells pealed, long-separated friends and family members fell into each other's arms, people wept for joy and complete strangers pressed money into newcomers' hands or offered them rides to wherever they wanted to go.

It was a day that made an indelible imprint on Berlin's collective memory. Hundreds of thousands of East Berliners crossed into West Berlin today, according to police estimates.

"The mood is just fantastic," said a woman from East Berlin. "The West Berliners have been wonderful to us. I thank them all." The East Berliners, coming from a land where nearly all prices are kept artificially low by subsidies, were also greeted by price-tag shock.

"It's all quite lovely," said a young woman from Rostock as she gazed at the display window of a women's clothing store on the Kurfurstendamm, West Berlin's main street and the city's toniest shopping area. "But cheap it's not."

The sky was a high, clear blue and the "Berliner Luft"—the air of Berlin, that is lauded by natives for its invigorating qualities—overcame the usual pollution and lived up to its reputation. It rang with the sounds of celebration. The city center of West Berlin became a giant festival grounds, forcing police to ban auto traffic because of the press of pedestrians. Some restaurants gave out free food and drink. Bottles, cans and broken glass seemed to be everywhere.

"The wall is gone!" Those slightly hyperbolic words were uttered countless times here in the last 24 hours, by people in both sides of the city. Although the forbidding concrete barrier still stands, it has fallen in the minds of East and West Berliners alike.

"I knew as soon as I heard the news on the radio last night what it meant," said Stani, a 19-year-old East Berliner, as he jostled for position in a West Berlin subway packed with East Germans on their way to celebrate on the Kurfurstendamm. "There is no turning back from this now. Allowing people to travel freely is a step that our Government can never retract. We won't be closed in again. The people will simply not allow that. Now we know the way here." . . .

Ripples in Poland; Kohl Delivers Aid and Returns Home
By John Tagliabue

WARSAW, Nov. 10—Chancellor Helmut Kohl of West Germany told Polish leaders today that he was interrupting a five-day visit to their country for 24 hours, but not until he had signed accords granting Poland the largest amount of economic aid it has yet obtained from a Western nation.

The Chancellor, responding to the political changes in East Germany, then set off by aircraft for home, to attend a huge rally in West Berlin celebrating the end of the Berlin wall, to preside over an emergency session of his Cabinet in Bonn on Saturday morning, and to seek a meeting with East Germany's new leader, Egon Krenz. . . .

The changes were again spreading. They were occurring all over Eastern Europe. The success of marchers seeking reform in one place inspired marchers elsewhere. From Bulgaria came news that the man who had ruled that country for almost 35 decades was being forced to step down. Slightly more than a year earlier, the Warsaw pact allies of the Soviet Union had been ruled by old men who had seemed to have lifetime tenure. Now Janos Kadar was gone in Hungary, Erich Honecker was out in East Germany, and Zhivkov was on his way out in Bulgaria. In Poland, General Jaruzelski, the youngest of the lot, was President, but he was sharing power with non-Communists. Only in Czechoslovakia and Rumania were the old guard holding the same posts they had when the year began.

Bulgarian Chief Quits After 35 Years of Rigid Rule
By Clyde Haberman

SOFIA, BULGARIA, Nov. 10—Todor I. Zhivkov, Eastern Europe's longest-serving leader, resigned today as Bulgaria's President and Communist Party leader, after 35 years of guiding the country with old-line orthodoxy.

Mr. Zhivkov, 78 years old, was immediately replaced as the party's General Secretary by his longtime Foreign Minister, Petar T. Mladenov, who is viewed here as likely to take a somewhat more flexible approach toward economic and political restructuring. It will be up to the politically weak National Assembly to choose his successor as President.

Since Mr. Zhivkov and other top officials recently began to talk about the need to separate state and party roles, it seemed possible that someone other than Mr. Mladenov could be selected.

Mr. Zhivkov's resignation came as a surprise but not as a total shock to Western diplomats, who said that the Bulgarian leader had apparently fallen victim to the fast-paced changes elsewhere in Eastern Europe.

Bulgarian officials reportedly said in confidence that Mr. Zhivkov did not want to stay too long and risk being forced from power in disgrace, as were Janos Kadar of Hungary or Erich Honecker of East Germany.

There were strong rumors of more shifts to come in top party echelons, but the state press agency and television network made no announcements. The prospects for genuine change here, several diplomats said, are likely to be determined by the extent of any future shake-up.

Mr. Mladenov, who is 53 and was Foreign Minister for 18 years, wasted no time as the new leader in warning that "there is no alternative to restructuring" Bulgaria's struggling economy and tightly controlled political apparatus. The present system has "handicapped progress in our society in all spheres," he told the party Central Committee, adding: "We have to turn Bulgaria into a modern, democratic and lawful country."

Despite his words, however, many Bulgarians and diplomats were not convinced that rapid changes were on the way.

Mr. Zhivkov, they said, had filled the Central Committee with people who basically followed his version of orthodox Communism, and they did not regard Mr. Mladenov as a conspicuous exception. "He's generally perceived to be more liberal than Zhivkov but not markedly so," a Western diplomat said. "I would suspect that it means policies will continue."

Another reason for the cautious assessment is that Mr. Mladenov's remarks today echoed what Mr. Zhivkov had been saying for more than two years, if with meager results. Matching words with deeds eluded him. Official tolerance for dissent remains slight, and the economy has limped along with shoddy consumer goods, poor farm production and shortages of basic food items like butter and sugar.

Mr. Zhivkov acknowledged the failure in a report today to the Central Committee, in which he calls for broad political and economic adjustments, including more power for the National Assembly and clearer divisions between the party and the Government.

"In the final account, we were unable to make a significant breakthrough in any sector of our work," he said.

Thus far, Bulgaria has been in the rear guard of the Communist world, plodding along amid the rush of events sweeping the Soviet Union, Hungary, Poland and now even East Germany, which had also been a hard-line state. But it is not immune to events elsewhere, and in recent weeks a new breed of Bulgarian dissidents has begun to speak out to a degree rarely heard in this Slavic nation.

The first known demonstration in four decades took place last week in the center of Sofia, the capital, when about 5,000 Bulgarians marched on the National Assembly building to express their grievances on environmental pollution. For many, environmental concerns were merely an excuse to give vent to broader anti-Government frustrations.

It is not clear, however, that Bulgaria has turned the corner on dissent, for the Government permitted the demonstration primarily because an international environmental conference was under way in Sofia. Now that the foreigners have gone home, dissidents say they cannot be sure that another such protest would be tolerated.

Mr. Zhivkov became Communist Party leader in 1954, a year after Stalin's death, and in recent years he has been the Soviet Union's most faithful ally. Soviet flags often fly beside Bulgarian flags in the capital, and the anniversary of the Russian Revolution in 1917, observed last Tuesday, is a Bulgarian national holiday.

Over the decades, Mr. Zhivkov consolidated his power by purging opponents. The process continued as recently as last year, when he forced out a Politburo member, Chudomir A. Aleksandrov, who had been widely considered a possible successor.

In addition to his party post, Mr. Zhivkov became chairman of the Council of Ministers, the equivalent of Prime Minister, in 1962, a position that yielded in 1971 to the Presidency. Except for a failed coup attempt in 1965, there had been no serious challenges to his leadership. His health has suffered in the last few years, but before today there was no indication that he was in immediate danger of losing power.

Bulgaria's relations with the Soviet Union have weakened in recent years, partly because of Moscow's preoccupation with its own problems and partly because Soviet restructuring under Mikhail S. Gorbachev has outstripped the pace here.

Two years ago, a new economic program was announced by Mr. Zhivkov, laying the basis, it was hoped, for a thoroughly revamped economy. But the promise of more self-management for private businesses proved greater than the reality, and the economy has only bumped along since.

It suffered a further blow, as did Bulgaria's image, when 310,000 ethnic Turkish residents of the country fled across the border into Turkey last summer to escape a campaign of forced assimilation. Since then, 60,000 of them have returned, according to estimates, but their abrupt departure from a country of nine million people had already disrupted crop harvests and factory production in predominantly Muslim provinces in eastern Bulgaria.

Dramatic as the Bulgarian changes were, they were less riveting than what was going on in the very heart of Europe, in Berlin.

The Open Frontier; East Germans Flood the West, Most to Rejoice, Then Go Home; Kohl and Krenz Agree to Meet

By Serge Schmemann

WEST BERLIN, Nov. 11—A million East Germans streamed into West Berlin and West Germany today on foot and by car, subway and train, many passing through border crossings so new that the paint was not yet dry. More important for East Germany, most were going back.

In Bonn, Chancellor Helmut Kohl announced after a telephone call to Egon Krenz, the new East German leader, that he would visit East Germany before the year's end. Mr. Kohl also presided over an emergency meeting of his Cabinet before flying back to Poland to resume the state visit he interrupted after East Germany opened its borders on Thursday night.

In East Berlin, Mr. Krenz declared after the telephone call that "German reunification is not on the agenda." He said Mr. Kohl had touched on the provisions in the West German Constitution calling for the unity of Germany through self-determination, but "that is his business."

"My business as the representative of the German Democratic Republic," Mr. Krenz said, "is to point out that there are two wholly sovereign German states that have to get on well with each other."

At a news conference in Bonn, Chancellor Kohl said that his Cabinet supported the changes taking place in East Germany and that "we are ready to offer whatever help will benefit the people." But Mr. Kohl said West German assistance would help East Germany only if "the system of state-planned economy would be substituted by a socially responsible market economy."

After 40 years of being penned in by walls and barbed wire, the East Germans seized on their new freedom to travel, creating epic jams at border crossings, highways and train stations.

Officials said half a million flocked into West Berlin today and another 500,000 to other crossing points in West Germany. More were to come. The official East German press agency A.D.N. said 2.7 million visas had been issued for foreign travel since the Government announced the new travel regulations on Thursday.

First reports indicated that the large majority of visitors were returning home after a glimpse of the West and after lining up for 100 marks, about $55, in "welcome money" from the West German Government. Interior Minister Wolfgang Schauble said that of the first 125,000 visitors, only 5 percent, or some 6,000, had applied to stay. East German television said that of the first 206,000 visitors today, 2,866 had opted to remain in West Germany. An additional 8,000 had applied through East German channels to emigrate.

Though it was too early to draw firm conclusions, the figures suggested that the decision by Mr. Krenz to throw open the gates of his country may have succeeded in slowing the exodus that had drained East Germany of almost 300,000 citizens so far this year.

The images of the baptism in freedom mesmerized both Germanys, whether in the streets or in the endless coverage on television. For the third night a vast throng of people gazed at the bright lights of the Kurfurstendamm, West Berlin's celebrated shopping boulevard. Most stores stayed open long past the usual Saturday closing time of 2 P.M. and many offered discounts or gifts to the East Berliners.

Thousands more East Germans packed the Olympic stadium for a soccer game, while others explored a West they had known only from television. Young men swarmed through the BMW showroom, gazing at models whose 12-cylinder engines seemed light-years beyond their own antiquated little 2-cylinder Trabants. A few slipped into the luxurious Kempinski Hotel to grab a "Do Not Disturb" sign for a souvenir.

Then there were the epic lines. Human rivers formed at every border crossing, including two new gateways punched through the concrete Berlin wall overnight and a subway station reopened after being sealed off for 28 years. Workers were still painting the price schedule at the Jannowitz Bridge underground station when people began flooding down for the ride to the West.

Inside West Berlin, the lines formed again outside banks for the 100-mark welcome that the West German Government allows each visiting East German once a year. Many visitors who waited hours to cross and up to four hours at a bank simply returned home exhausted with their 100 marks, saying they would return to shop and sightsee another time.

Cars stretched three abreast for 40 miles back from the border crossing at Helmstedt, reaching beyond the city of Magdeburg, and motorists reportedly waited up to 11 hours to cross into West Germany.

Long lines formed for special trains to West Germany at Leipzig, Dresden and other cities, and the rows of smiling, waving travelers hanging out of open windows seemed an especially poignant contrast with the sealed trains in September and early October sent to transport East German refugees from Czechoslovakia to the West.

The invasion posed all sorts of problems. In the northern city of Lubeck, the city council ran out of cash to pay the welcome money and had to appeal to local banks and stores for more.

Not all was sweetness and light. At the wall before the Brandenburg Gate, across which people swarmed on Thursday night, a band of West Berliners managed last night to pry away one of the thick concrete panels of which the wall is built.

East German border guards drove the West Berliners back with water hoses and put the panel back. They then mounted the section of the wall in front of the gate.

The brief confrontation created a somewhat tense mood at the gate that persisted into the night. It also led to the first open contact between the police of both sides since the borders were opened. Their meeting at Checkpoint Charlie led to the East German border guards' retreating from the wall and the arrival of the West Berlin police to prevent more damage to it.

The curious image of West Berlin policemen guarding the wall was repeated at other openings, where security officers from East and West joined to maintain an orderly flow, often side by side.

In a poll taken in both Germanys by the Wickert Institute of West Germany, 91 percent of East Germans and 89 percent of West Germans responding said they believed that the border between them would remain permeable. But when asked if the border opening meant they could trust their new leadership, only 19 percent of the East Germans said yes. . . .

The meeting between Mr. Kohl and Mr. Krenz will be only the third summit conference between leaders of the two Germanys in the 40-year existence of the two countries. . . . The Chancellor also said that the right of Germans to self-determination had not yet been fulfilled.

"Freedom was, is and remains the heart of the German question," Mr. Kohl said. "That means above all that our fellow countrymen in East Germany must be able to decide themselves what road they want to take in the future. They do not need any instructions, from whatever side. They themselves know best what they want."

It was evidently this comment that prompted Mr. Krenz to declare that reunification was not up for discussion. The East German regime, both under Erich Honecker and now Mr. Krenz, has staunchly rejected any talk of reunification. . . .

A Day Trip Through the Wall; Family Says of the West, "It's a Dream"
By Ferdinand Protzman

WEST BERLIN, Nov. 11—In the midst of the carnival fever that seized West Berlin today, 4-year-old Gregor Stephan stretched out on a bench in a small inn just off the Kurfurstendamm where his family was having lunch, put his head in his father's lap and fell asleep.

Hans Schmalfeld, 51, put down his fork and stared at his slumbering grandson. "Gregor is taking a nap in West Berlin," he said in a hushed voice. "It's unfathomable. If you had told me that one week ago, I wouldn't have believed it. Mentally, I still can't. It will take a few days before what this means sinks in."

Gregor's weariness was understandable. His parents, Joachim and

Annette Stephan, had got Gregor and his older brother Robert, 7, out of bed at 3:45 A.M. An hour and a half later, the family piled into a Wartburg automobile along with Mr. Schmalfeld and his wife, Wally, 53, and headed for East Berlin, 40 miles west of home in Joachimstal, East Germany. Their destination was West Berlin.

They were not alone. Hundreds of thousands of East Germans poured into West Berlin today, taking advantage of the East German Government's new policy of allowing free travel to the West.

As they neared the Berlin wall, the family took one look at the crush of people streaming to the border crossing points and parked their car.

"Driving was hopeless, so we decided to go on foot," said Mr. Stephan, a 23-year-old cattle farmer. "From watching the news, we thought that crossing over wouldn't take much time, but there were so many people that it took three hours in line to get the visas stamped and our personal identity cards. They aren't letting people just walk through the border like they did last night."

The family crossed into West Berlin at Checkpoint Charlie, though that name, which is one of the symbols of Berlin's division in the Western world, meant nothing to them. "Is that what it is called?" Mrs. Schmalfeld asked later.

Once across, they did what all their countrymen do: they went straight to a bank to pick up the 100 marks in "greeting money" given by the West German Government to East Germans arriving in the West for the first time. The money goes to every man, woman and child from the East, but only once a year and each identity document must be stamped.

Mr. Schmalfeld, who operates a family-owned ice cream shop with his wife and daughter on the Werbellinsee, a large lake in the Schorf-heide forest east of Berlin that is a popular resort area, lived in what was then known as the Soviet sector of Berlin when the wall was built in August 1961. But he had not been back since, and the rest of the family had never set foot in the West.

After waiting three and a half hours, the family collected their money from the Deutsche Bank Berlin branch across from Check-point Charlie and headed for the Kurfurstendamm, the glittering shopping street in the heart of West Berlin. Although they did not want their picture in the newspaper, the family was happy to take a reporter they met outside the bank in tow.

The trip proved somewhat difficult. The crush of East Germans, most with the same destination in mind, overloaded West Berlin's usually efficient mass transit system. Subway trains were so packed that only a few people could squeeze aboard.

On the elevated S-bahn trains, the crowds were even thicker. A 20-minute wait proved futile. "Let's see if we can find a bus," Mr. Schmalfeld said. "There must be buses around here somewhere that go to the Ku'damm."

At the corner of Mehringdamm and Yorckstrasse, the family caught a No. 19 bus. As the brand-new double-decker bus rolled toward the city center, many of the East Germans on board stared out the window, eyeing the cars, stores and apartments like children at a candy counter.

A motorcyclist whizzed past, drawing oohs and aahs from passengers in the upper deck. "Woha! Hey, Achim, did you see that?" Mr. Schmalfeld yelled back to his son-in-law. Mr. Stephan groaned slightly and rolled his eyes.

Getting off at the city center, the family found themselves staring at the KaDeWe department store. "There it is," Mr. Schmalfeld cried. "I haven't seen it since 1961. The last time I was here was the day before the wall went up. Then, overnight, all this was gone for us." They wandered farther down the street, marveling at the crowds, the stores and the cars, then stopped for lunch.

"We were in church at a peace service Thursday evening when we heard the news," Mr. Stephan recalled. "I never really thought the wall would be open. Last year, we were just sitting around and I made a joke that soon people would be able to walk through the Brandenburg Gate. But I didn't really believe it."

His wife described their trip as "such a dream for us, a storybook tale. We'll look around slowly and carefully and see if there is anything we want. It's mostly the little things we don't have in East Germany, like fresh vegetables or tomato catsup. Supply has gotten a bit better lately. There is a little fresh breeze blowing, but there is still very much that must be changed."

A decisive factor in the family's decision to come today instead of waiting was mistrust of the East German Government, she added. "No one knows what will happen in the future and we were forbidden to travel to the West for so long that we wanted to take this opportunity now while it's there.

"We don't want to leave the G.D.R.," she said. "We love our home and we live quite well by East German standards. We work really hard and earn pretty well, but our money just isn't worth anything."

Mrs. Stephan also pointed out that there are many good things in East Germany that are often overlooked. Prices are state-subsidized, so the cost of living is very low. The nation also has an outstanding public health system, although it is suffering at the moment because so many doctors, nurses and nurse's aides have emigrated to the West in the exodus that began in May.

"What bothered us most was that they always treated us like idiots," she said of the Government. "That is really changed now. Before, it was always such lies. The newspapers said the plan had been fulfilled and still there was nothing in the shops."

The family viewed many of the things that the West takes for granted as luxuries. Returning from the restroom in the inn, Mrs. Schmalfeld said that she had never seen such a rest room, that even the toilets were beautiful. "Do they spin you around?" her husband joked.

Lunch finished, the family returned to the Kurfurstendamm, planning to go shopping. That plan was thwarted by one of the less free-market aspects of West German capitalism. The big department stores, like KeDeWe, were closed, despite recently passed legislation that would have allowed them to stay open.

The mood in the street was euphoric nevertheless. Cars had been banned, and East and West Berliners alike were strolling along, taking the air and window-shopping. The family looked at the Christmas displays in the show windows of the Wertheim department store, then moved on, looking mostly at household goods.

"We want to renovate our ice cream shop," Mr. Schmalfeld explained. He glanced up at a movie marquee and burst into laughter. "*Sex, Lies and Videotape*," he read aloud. "Unbelievable."

Gregor was wide awake now. In a kiosk on the sidewalk, he spotted a familiar figure. "It's Batman," he screeched, pointing to an array of Batman dolls. "It's Batman and Batman and Batman." He began humming the Batman theme song. Closed stores or not, his first day of freedom to travel in the West was made.

In Moscow, Soviet citizens drew hope from the collapse of the wall.

The Comrade on the Street; Russians See an Omen of Their Own Progress

By Francis X. Clines

MOSCOW, Nov. 11—Soviet citizens hailed the end of the Berlin wall today as an omen, if not an outright prod, for even faster Soviet progress toward genuine democracy and economic recovery.

"Every honest man wants socialism wiped out," said a strapping man talking loudly and happily near Pushkin Square. "You can't control a country with bayonets and walls."

Various countrymen easily agreed with him as they stopped to listen, to take hope from the failed wall and to express surprisingly little concern over the specter of a reunified Germany, the World War II enemy whose Nazi infamy has been inculcated for generations into the Soviet worldview.

"This is not 1941," said Vasily F. Simonenko, a 67-year-old veteran of the war, limping from old battle wounds as he took a sunny stroll on Gogol Boulevard and declared that he wished the best for East and West Germans.

"The war was horrible for us, but there is no Fascist country left there now," he said. He echoed the reassurances of other Soviet citizens that Chancellor Helmut Kohl of West Germany, as one of the earliest European leaders to support President Mikhail S. Gorbachev's liberalization proposals, would be even more helpful now toward the gasping Soviet economy because of the end of the Berlin wall.

"Political theory is one thing, and real life is quite another, and we must make practical decisions based on all these changes," Mr. Simonenko said.

In conversations around the city, ordinary Muscovites, and young people in particular, stressed that any benefits from the changes in Germany could not come fast enough to this demoralized nation.

"Even with this, it could take ten or twenty years for us to get as far," said one rather despairing student, 20-year-old Yuliana Pogosov, asserting that razing a wall, even one that was the symbol of the cold war, seemed a far simpler problem than resurrecting the depressed Soviet economy. "This is good news for Gorbachev, but I don't think such change can really happen here because he wants to do everything himself, without anyone else's help."

Her colleague, Natalya Demenko, 20, added, "And what our economy needs now is capitalist improvement."

Across from her in the garden quadrangle at the University of Moscow, another student, 17-year-old Andrei Rumyantsev, said the fall of the Berlin wall would not be likely to resonate this far into the Communist world. "There's such inertia here," he said, looking far too weary for his boyish face and crewcut hair. "We can see our Government is feverishly trying to adjust to all this."

"So far our own borders have not opened up," stressed his companion, Dmitri Zubov, 17. "This great wave of excitement seems to be going in only one direction, toward the Germans, not toward us."

"A lot depends now on what happens in our country," said Yelena N. Dobroditsky, a 66-year-old war veteran and invalid. "The problem here remains that individuals, not laws, rule our country."

Vladimir Porokhov, a 37-year-old economist, seemed to be mainly savoring the pleasing shock of the news about the wall, rather than joining in the day's running political dialogue amid the talkative crowd that always gathers lately outside the offices of *The Moscow News*. "Gorbachev could not have expected this outcome so quickly," he speculated. "His way is to go for gradual change, to pacify the people. Who knows whether such an unexpected change could happen here, too?"

But he could not resist his own question. "We have begun thinking beyond our daily bread," he said. "Take the miners' strike: They pushed for political change, not just for bread. Something similar can happen here, provided the Government does not decide to turn guns on the people."

Several people seemed to think the question of lost prestige from the Communist turmoil was one mainly for the Kremlin, not the ordinary Muscovite. "We're happy—what could be the danger in such good news?" asked Ilya B. Goldman, a 69-year-old retiree.

"We have too many real problems now," he said, dismissing national prestige as an academic aside when shop shelves are so empty.

The one noticeable note of suspicion to the news about East Germany was offered by a man who said he was an active member of the Communist Party. "It seems to have been a necessary thing, a matter of their internal business," said Nikolai D. Nekrasov, a 49-year-old Government executive. "But the role of our party remains strong here, and I don't think the wall will influence our life unless reunification actually happens. Then people would sense danger, and that would complicate life greatly for Gorbachev."

But Sergei S. Abelikchen, a 64-year-old factory inspector, disagreed. "I remember the war very well, with Moscow under constant threat, almost lost," he said.

"Germany is a different nation now based on different ideas, and by all means, the news about the Berlin wall can only influence us positively," he said, searching for fresh news from Germany amid the Moscow crowds studying newspaper bulletin boards.

From China, the official view of the events in Europe was quite different.

Disgust with the West Is Reported, but Beijing Ignores the Wall's End
By Sheryl WuDunn

BEIJING, Nov. 10—Newspaper readers in China learned of the remarkable resignations of East German leaders this week, but they also picked up another bit of news: two East Germans who had fled more than a month ago to the West found the new society too disorderly and so returned home.

Chinese official newspapers have regularly, if sparingly, reported the developments within the East German leadership this week. But the brief reports included no explanations of the pressures that led to the unusual collective resignations. Lately, there has been little coverage of the mass demonstrations for democracy or the exodus to the West.

Such matters are presumably regarded as too delicate, too reminiscent of the democracy movement in China in the spring. Instead of giving in to some of the demonstrators' demands, as the East German leadership has done, the Chinese authorities called in troops and crushed the movement.

Today, there was no mention in the press or the national television about East Germany's opening of its borders to the West, although the trip to Poland by Chancellor Helmut Kohl of West Germany was reported.

The recent articles—about one every two days, carried on the international news pages—have confined themselves to reporting excerpts from speeches by the new East German leader, Egon Krenz, about the necessity of reforming the party so that it can better exercise its leadership role.

"Democratic Germany is currently in a tense period full of contradictions," *People's Daily* today quoted Mr. Krenz as saying. "To make it through the difficult period, it is necessary to first carry out reform in the party itself." . . .

A Contrite Government; Contrite Deputies Say Party Failed the East Germans
By Craig R. Whitney

EAST BERLIN, Nov. 13—The East German Parliament, dormant and docile ever since it called the German Democratic Republic into existence 40 years ago, came to life today, with deputy after deputy agreeing that the Communist Party's failings were so great that it was no longer entitled to the leading role guaranteed in the nation's Constitution.

It was a day of contrition, anger and hangdog faces for the 478 legislators who were elected the old way, without opposition, three years ago. As one speaker after another acknowledged, they had only themselves to blame for letting the old leadership under Erich Honecker run the economy into the ground, creating a situation in which more than 200,000 people left the country in the last two months.

After hours of grim recitation of past failure, the members of Parliament did what the new Communist Party leader, Egon Krenz, had asked them to do. They elected Hans Modrow, the 61-year-old party chief in Dresden, as Prime Minister,though one lawmaker raised a hand in opposition.

Mr. Modrow, widely regarded as a proponent of liberalization, said he would lay out his new policy and name a coalition cabinet that would include members of East Germany's long-subservient non-Communist parties at the end of this week.

Last week, Mr. Modrow confided to a fellow member of the Central Committee that "I can see the end coming." His disgraced predecessor, Willi Stoph, who is 76 years old, took the floor earlier today to say: "I accept responsibility for all the failures of the former Government. We failed to account properly to Parliament and report shortcomings as they occurred."

Mr. Stoph blamed "decisions not made in the Council of Ministers"—presumably meaning interference by the Communist Party—for "severely" harming the economy.

"The deposed leadership was characterized by arrogance," said Werner Jarowinsky, the Communist Party leader in Parliament.

Mr. Krenz, who replaced Mr. Honecker last month, listened, apparently hoping that his party's promises of free elections, a freer press and freedom to travel would convince most of the country's 16.5 million people that the new leadership would earn their trust.

But in Leipzig, the hotbed of protest, mass demonstrations continued tonight. Huge crowds chanted, "We are the people!" and booed and hissed Mr. Krenz's promises of "free" elections.

Most of the one million or so East Germans who visited the West after the border was opened on Thursday night appeared to have gone back home to work today. The streets of West Berlin were almost normal this morning, although visitors from the East poured in again in smaller numbers than the vast crowds that thronged the shopping streets from Friday to Sunday.

Mr. Krenz, answering a question in Parliament, said he had told West Germany's Chancellor, Helmut Kohl, in a telephone call yesterday, "Unification, or reunification, of Germany is not on the agenda."

"I believe the existence of two German states, independent of each other, is a decisive question of stability in Europe, and that that is a decisive question of peace in Europe," he said. "Without peace there is nothing."

The East German authorities continued today to announce the opening of new border crossings up and down the 1,000-mile frontier with West Germany, and said East Germans living close to the line would no longer require special permission to have guests and visitors. The East German military authorities have also ordered troops to stop using weapons to prevent illegal border crossing.

After Parliament debated the critical situation in the country, the Communist Party Central Committee met late into the night to discuss Mr. Krenz's decision to hold the special party congress next month. He said he wanted it to elect a new Central Committee to support his program of change. Western diplomats and East Germans believe there is considerable skepticism about his sincerity among party members, who number about two million, as well as in the country at large.

All the speakers in Parliament today agreed on the need to strengthen Communism, to save the system, not abandon it, and to create what Mr. Jarowinsky called a "market-oriented planned economy."

"Our fatherland is in danger," said Hans-Dieter Raspe, a member of the small Liberal Democratic Party. "Our citizens have no confidence in the leadership of the country."

The former president of Parliament, Horst Sindermann, apologized for having waited too long to call the legislature into session after the mass emigration and police repression of demonstrators began early last month. He apologized for doing his job "not always well," but said he had tried to do his best.

Mr. Jarowinsky said: "Our party is determined to draw radical consequences from this bitter fact. We need changes in the Constitution."

The first article of the Constitution says East Germany is a Communist state of workers and farmers, "led by the working class and its Marxist-Leninist party." But speaker after speaker today agreed that the Communists had lost touch with the people.

"We see and hear encouraging things from New Forum," Mr. Jarowinsky said, referring to the biggest new opposition group. "It's time to come closer together."

Since 1950, the East German system has grouped four other parties with Mr. Krenz's Communists—officially called the Socialist Unity Party—plus the central trade-union organization, the youth league and various other political groups in a so-called National Front.

In a system that has not changed since the Communists came to power after World War II, East Germans vote every five years, with only candidates of the National Front on the ballot. The groups in the front, which all agreed in 1950 that the Communists would run things, then divide up the 500 seats, with the Communists getting the biggest share—127 seats in the current legislature, which was elected in 1986.

The Communists did not offer a candidate today for the largely ceremonial post of President of the People's Chamber. Manfred Gerlach, a 61-year-old leader of the Liberal Democrats since the beginning, was widely expected to win, since he had called for radical change before Mr. Krenz did. But in the second ballot, he lost, 230 to 246, to Gunther Maleuda, the little-known leader of the 120,000-member Democratic Farmers' Party.

The name on each of the nearly 480 ballots that were cast had to be read aloud to the chamber and the results counted by hand.

"Surely there must be more modern and scientific methods in the age of micro-electronics," the East German television announcer said to the national audience.

The chamber was closed to most journalists and to the general public.

The combustible nature of social change was reflected in the following story, which accurately captured the stolid mood of Prague. Unlike their neighbors in Poland, Hungary, and East Germany, the Czechoslovaks had remained impassive except for a handful of dissidents, mostly intellectuals. A week later things would be very different.

Little Change in Czechoslovakia; Maintaining Tight Control in Prague
By R. W. Apple, Jr.

PRAGUE, Nov. 13—Last month, 300,000 people staged a demonstration in Leipzig, East Germany's second city. Five days later, about 10,000 people gathered in Wenceslas Square, this capital's historic cockpit of protest, to call for change.

Only about 160 miles separate the two cities, and both have been ruled by Communists for four decades.

But while the protest in Leipzig and others that followed it resulted in a new East German Government, the opening of the Berlin wall and a promise of major political changes, the protest in Prague was followed by no others, provoking a show of force by the Czechoslovak Government and almost no political change. As a shopkeeper said today, "We have become the class dunces, the ones who learn their lessons slowly."

Milos Jakes, the Communist Party leader, ordered out heavily armed police officers, who bashed dozens of heads with their truncheons, to put down the October 28 demonstration. And he remains firmly in control at a time when his fellow hard-liners, Erich Honecker in East Germany and Todor Zhivkov in Bulgaria, have either stepped down voluntarily or been forced to resign.

"He will probably survive this year," a European diplomat said, "but he may not make it through the party congress next year, and he certainly won't settle in for five or ten years. He and his colleagues on the Politburo simply lack the flexibility and the intelligence to make the reforms and accept the changes that will be needed if Communism is to last here."

Shortly before the October demonstration, someone leaked a tape recording of a speech that Mr. Jakes gave at a provincial party meeting. Rambling and clumsy, the recording was broadcast into Czechoslovakia by Radio Liberty and other Western radio stations, providing what one dissident described as "a laugh a minute" that he said undercut Mr. Jakes's public standing.

200

Some opponents of the Government hope to stage a protest on Friday to mark the anniversary of the death of one of the political martyrs in Czechoslovak history. The protesters intend to commemorate the death of Jan Opletal, who was killed in 1939 by Nazi storm troopers while protesting the German occupation of Czechoslovakia.

Today four prominent dissidents went on trial in Bratislava on charges of sedition for urging Czechoslovaks to lay flowers for those killed in the 1968 invasion by the Soviet Union and its Warsaw Pact allies that crushed the movement for liberalization that became known as the Prague Spring. And in Prague another dissident, Jiri Jilinek, 22 years old, was sentenced to a year in prison for distributing leaflets urging a pro-democracy protest in May, the dissident Anna Sabatova said.

Mr. Jakes on Sunday told 900 delegates to a conference of the Socialist Youth Union in Prague, where other speakers were unusually critical of the regime, that he would not tolerate street protests or communicate with groups advocating abandonment of Czechoslovakia's form of Communism.

According to the official press agency, the party leader promised that restructuring of the Communist apparatus would continue. In a response unusual for Czechoslovakia but still timid by the standards common in Poland, Hungary and, of late, East Germany, Vasil Mohorita, a leader of the state-sponsored youth group, said that the Government's plans, which call for some important economic change but no real political evolution, "do not fit the expectations of young people."

"Some youths are losing faith in the possibility of Communist renewal," the official news agency quoted Mr. Mohorita as saying. "The reason for this weakening of trust is that an atmosphere of self-satisfaction has ruled in this country."

In recent months, the Czechoslovak Government had been attempting to forge closer ties with East Germany, working toward a kind of traditionalist caucus within the Warsaw Pact that would refuse to follow the lead of Poland and Hungary. Mr. Honecker had visited Prague, and Ladislav Adamec, the Czechoslovak Prime Minister, had visited East Berlin. Now those efforts are ruined.

"The way Honecker's world was swept away in two or three weeks, and the way the people got so far ahead of the leadership so fast, must have sent shivers up and down Jakes's spine," a leading Czechoslovak dissident said.

Bonn Outlines Aid for East Germany

By Henry Kamm

BONN, Nov. 14—West Germany made public the outlines of a possible economic aid program to East Germany today, but repeated a warning that the proposal would be adopted only if East Germany carried out a "thorough change" of its centralized economy and spelled out the changes it plans.

Economics Minister Helmut Haussmann said that if East Berlin met its conditions, Bonn would make loans available to West German entrepreneurs interested in investing in East Germany. The money would come from a European reconstruction fund totaling $2.5 billion.

He added that if East Germany allowed its citizens to engage in such ventures, they too might be eligible for loans from the fund.

West Germany also said it might offer tax advantages to investors in East Germany similar to those it provides for investors in West Berlin.

Other ways of helping the East German economy might include export credit guarantees for sales of capital goods to East Germany, investment guarantees for the West German partner in joint ventures and support for West German concerns acting as management consultants in East Germany.

The Economics Ministry announcement came six days after Chancellor Helmut Kohl said Bonn would be ready to provide "a new dimension" of aid to East Germany if it allowed political pluralism and made fundamental economic changes. But the statement today gave no indication of how much direct assistance Bonn was prepared to extend.

For the time being, "there are more questions than answers," Mr. Haussmann said. "Announcements of billions in aid at this time are devoid of sense."

In an "action program" adopted on Friday by the Communist Party's Central Committee, the new East German leadership under Egon Krenz said "fundamental changes" in economic policies were required and promised "far-reaching economic reform." The aims cited in the program were "constantly improving satisfaction of the real needs of the population," more honest reporting on whether the central plan's goals are being met and the speeding up of technological renewal of industry.

But neither the program nor the speeches of economists and industrial managers in the committee's three days of sessions suggested how those goals are to be achieved. Unlike other Communist countries, including the Soviet Union, whose economic reform programs have stressed the introduction of market conditions at the expense of central planning, East Germany continues to affirm the virtues of planning.

The "action program" espoused "a socialist planned economy oriented toward market conditions" but failed to explain how the two would coexist. The Central Committee said the Government, which is soon to be formed under Prime Minister Hans Modrow, named Monday, should work out plans and submit them for discussion.

Mr. Haussmann said a basic condition for West German assistance was greater freedom in East German social life and the economy. He cited difficulties experienced by West German businessmen in establishing direct contacts with their East German partners. Businessmen often complain of slow progress through a complex bureaucracy in their efforts to conclude deals in East Germany.

Mr. Haussmann also urged quick East German approval of a law governing the establishment of joint ventures.

In a television interview, Finance Minister Theo Waigel said he believed that West German capital would not flow into East Germany until a market economy was established.

Hans Peter Stihl, president of the German Industry and Commerce Organization, said, "Before we break our heads about it here, East Germany must spell out its concept for economic reform."

Mr. Haussmann announced that he would soon invite leading West German economic figures to discuss relations with East Germany and to sound out businessmen on conditions they would demand for active participation in East Germany's industry. He said that so far East Germany had failed to take full advantage of the special conditions for inter-German trade offered by Bonn and had prevented trade from rising above the level of barter.

The Minister said he was ready to meet with the East German Economics Minister and favored Mr. Krenz's suggestion for establishing a bilateral trade commission.

It was hard to imagine that the repressed calm of Czechoslovakia would endure forever as reform and democratic movements were sweeping all of the neighboring allied countries, yet this was the view to which Prague's Communist leadership was clinging despite warnings from Moscow.

Unease in Prague; A Soviet Warning on Foot-Dragging Is Given to Prague
By R. W. Apple, Jr.

PRAGUE, Nov. 15—The Soviet Union warned Czechoslovakia last week in a high-level message that further delay in introducing political change could cause serious trouble, Communist Party officials said today.

Perhaps as a result, the first major public signs of fear, tension and conflict are beginning to appear within the hard-line Czechoslovak Government.

According to reports circulating in party circles, Moscow cautioned Prague not to make the same mistakes made by Communist traditionalists elsewhere in Eastern Europe. Excessive caution or half-heartedness in putting political changes into effect, the Soviets are reported to have said, could lead to an uprising like the one that forced sweeping changes in East Germany.

The present Czechoslovak leadership descends from the one that was installed by the Soviets 21 years ago, at a time when the Brezhnev doctrine, since renounced by President Mikhail S. Gorbachev, sanctioned intervention by one Communist country in the internal affairs of another if necessary to prevent heresy.

A senior adviser to one Czech minister said that the message was similar to one sent to Bulgaria, which apparently helped to persuade Todor I. Zhivkov, that country's longtime party leader, that it was time to retire.

Although the position of Milos Jakes, the 67-year-old Czech party leader, is believed to have weakened somewhat lately, and although Prague is alive with speculation about his ability to survive until next spring's party congress, there is no sign that he plans to follow Mr. Zhivkov's lead soon.

Nonetheless, dramatic exchanges have taken place this week in Parliament here, centering on the question of political evolution. Last night, Prime Minister Ladislav Adamec quoted in a wrap-up speech to Parliament the formula repeatedly stated by Mr. Jakes, his boss: first major economic changes, and later—only later—minor political adjustments. Then, according to today's ssue of *Rude Pravo*, the official party newspaper, the Prime Minister explicitly challenged that position. The newspaper quoted him as having said: "We hold the view that economic progress cannot be separated from political progress. Economic reform cannot succeed without political reform. Especially in our situation, the political change should be somewhat in advance."

Prace, the trade-union newspaper, quoted a passage from Mr. Adamec's speech that *Rude Pravo* did not. In it, the Prime Minister went even further, asserting that "nothing can be ordered" by the Government, which, he said, "can only create favorable conditions." He added: "In the very complicated present conditions, it is possible to govern only provided that people have the necessary confidence in our central political organs."

A party official close to Mr. Adamec said today that he had "decided to throw the gauntlet down to Jakes on this, because he knows that his economic reform program has no chance unless there is some democratization."

One experienced politician who heard them said that the Prime Minister's words angered Vasil Bilak, the former ideological chief in Gustav Husak's regime, who is widely believed to have asked the Soviet Union to suppress the Government of Alexander Dubcek in the Prague Spring of 1968. The politician reported that Mr. Bilak said it sounded as if Mr. Adamec "thinks nothing good happened in this building in the last 40 years."

A motto in the chamber where the debate took place says, "All power resides in the people." Mr. Bilak reportedly pointed to it and demanded of Mr. Adamec whether or not he thought that had been true in the past.

When the outburst was over, the politician said, Mr. Bilak, once a very powerful figure, sat down, and no one paid the old-guard parliamentarian the slightest bit of attention.

Slowly, a party member familiar with the situation said the heretofor quiescent Parliament is moving—"not the way the Polish or the Hungarian Parliament has moved, toward real coalition government, not from black to white, not too far or fast, not everyone at once, but slowly and surely from black to dark gray."

What that might mean in terms of political change is not clear. Mr. Jakes has already made concessions on travel, cultural issues and religion, but he has yielded nothing to the dissidents, such as the playwright Vaclav Havel, and indeed has cracked down even harder on demonstrators and others who make their dissatisfaction public.

Mr. Havel, one of the original signers of the Charter 77 manifesto, was arrested last January and released in May after serving half his sentence. His trial helped him to become, like Lech Walesa in Poland, a powerful symbol of the opposition. But he is still seen here as more a moral force than a man likely to form a government.

"I think of him in terms of Jan Hus," said a Czechoslovak journalist, referring to the fifteenth-century church reformer who remains a national hero. "But maybe he has capacities we don't know about. Maybe he can someday become what he isn't yet—the leader of a mass movement, like Walesa, or like Tomas Masaryk, come to that."

Masaryk built and led the first Czechoslovak republic after World War I. Both Mr. Adamec, who at 62 may be a bit old, and Frantisek Pitra, 55, the party leader in Bohemia, one of the constituent parts of Czechoslovakia, are believed to be maneuvering to succeed Mr. Jakes if he steps down. Mr. Pitra is considered the more subtle, less confrontational of the two. Neither is thought by Western analysts to be an instinctive progressive; both are thought to be attempting to harness the current forces of change in Eastern Europe to help their careers.

But as East Germany showed, any change at the top can result in other, unforeseen changes at lower levels, as well as major shifts in policies.

Some Western diplomats believe that Mr. Jakes might try to save himself by throwing one of his colleagues to the wolves. If that happened, several of the diplomats said, a likely candidate would be Jan Fojtik, the tough current ideological chief. He was reported to be in trouble a year ago, but he was saved, some observers think, because events in China strengthened hard-liners and hurt reformers within the Communist Party here, as elsewhere.

As the pressure was mounting in Prague, Lech Walesa, the shipyard electrician who had first shown how Communist totalitarianism can be peacefully and successfully challenged, was in the United States, being cheered and celebrated as a prophet. The high point of his visit came when he addressed a joint meeting of Congress.

Gratitude and a Request; In Talk to Congress, Walesa Urges a Marshall Plan to Revive Poland

By Neil A. Lewis

WASHINGTON, Nov. 15—Lech Walesa, the founder of Poland's Solidarity movement, called for a second Marshall Plan today as he addressed a joint meeting of Congress. He warned that without the sort of commitment that helped rebuild Western Europe after World War II, the situation in his country could become dangerous.

The former shipyard electrician began by expressing his gratitude for the support his movement received from Americans in the years that it was suppressed and driven underground. He also gave thanks for the support the United States has given to more recent political and economic changes in Poland.

Nevertheless, to the accompaniment of repeated rounds of hearty applause, Mr. Walesa made it clear that more assistance would be needed to keep Poland from becoming so poor that it could destabilize the region.

"We are not asking for charity or expecting philanthropy," he said. "But we would like to see our country treated as a partner and a friend." He chided Americans for offering a surplus of good wishes but a paucity of money. "We have heard many beautiful words of encouragement," he said. "These are appreciated, but being a worker and a man of concrete work, I must tell you that the supply of words on the world market is plentiful but the demand is falling. Let deeds follow words now."

Mr. Walesa's entrance was announced in much the same manner reserved for the President before a State of the Union Address. "Mr. Speaker, the leader of Solidarity," said the doorkeeper. Mr. Walesa entered the chamber to a boisterous reception and as he made his way down the center aisle, members of Congress struggled to get close and shake his hand.

Among those vigorously applauding Mr. Walesa was Yuri V. Dubinin, the Soviet Ambassador to Washington, who was sitting in the audience. . . .

Senator Barbara A. Mikulski, a Maryland Democrat whose great-grandmother came from Poland to Baltimore for an arranged marriage, was one of those in the audience who wept during the address. "I never thought this day would come," she said afterward. "I just didn't think it was Poland's destiny to be free." . . .

207

Mr. Walesa, describing in his address the efforts of the new non-Communist Government in Warsaw, said, "Our task is viewed with understanding by our Eastern neighbors and their leader, Mikhail Gorbachev."

But he also said the imposition of a Communist economy on Poland for forty years had brought it to the "verge of utter catastrophe," and that "all the countries of the East bloc are bankrupt." He recalled that at the end of World War II, Stalin pressed Poland to reject an invitation to take part in the Marshall Plan.

"It is worth recalling this great American plan which helped Western Europe to protect its freedom and peaceful order," Mr. Walesa said. "And now it is the moment when Eastern Europe awaits an investment of this kind—an investment in freedom, democracy and peace, an investment adequate to the greatness of the American nation."

At a lunch meeting with Senators after his speech, he offered a gloomy assessment of the consequences if the new Solidarity-led Government fails to get control of the economy.

Speaking of his own turn of fortunes, which led him from the shipyard to the Nobel Peace Prize and a key political role, he said through a translator, "I was happier as an electrician and did not understand how difficult it was to make that jump to the public arena."

Mr. Walesa's remarks were underscored by reports from East Germany, which had always been regarded as the most successful of the East bloc economies, that the true state of the economy was ragged and getting worse.

Grim State of East Germany's Economy Is Disclosed to Parliament
By David Binder

EAST BERLIN, Nov. 15—East Germany's economy, battered by the flight to the West of more than 100,000 workers, many of them highly skilled, is in much worse shape than almost anyone knew, high-ranking Communist officials disclosed this week.

In the session of Parliament on Monday, the departing Finance Minister, Ernst Hofner, declared that East Germany's budget deficit amounted to 130 billion marks, causing gasps of amazement in the hall. The amount is about $70 billion at the official exchange rate of 1.85 marks to the dollar.

Mr. Hofner said further that the efficiency of factories producing goods for export had sunk by almost 50 percent in the last nine years and that this would lead to further deficits, perhaps 65 billion marks—about $35 billion at the official rate—in the 1990's. As a small consolation, he told the Parliament that East Germany's counties, cities and villages were debt-free.

The Finance Minister said he could not confirm an estimate by a member of Parliament that East Germany's inflation rate stood at 12 percent. But today a party economics expert said the rate was much higher than that. Gerhard Schurer, the departing chairman of the State Planning Commission, told Parliament that East Germany's foreign debt was a state secret. But today *Berliner Zeitung*, the organ of the Berlin party, cited the Swiss Central Bank as saying that East Germany's short-, middle- and long-term obligations to Western creditors totaled $20 billion. This sum would put East Germany's per capita foreign debt close to or ahead of those of Hungary and Poland.

Seeking to defend his performance as planning chief in the Government of the ousted party leader, Erich Honecker, Mr. Schurer said he had been unable to block excessive investments in the electronics industry and other areas of the economy.

Mr. Schurer said that all of his proposals to ease the economic situation were "rejected by the Central Committee Secretary for Economy, Gunter Mittag, with attacks and false accusation." Mr. Mittag, a Honecker associate, was dismissed from the Central Committee last week.

The planning chief was backed up by Willi Stoph, the former Prime Minister, who told the Parliament with bitterness in his voice that his own efforts in economic policy making had been subverted by Mr. Mittag, who he said had approved huge investments in the electronics and fertilizer industries without informing him or his aides.

The fresh gaps in the economy created by the flight of skilled workers and professionals was underlined in a report today by *Berliner Zeitung*, which said the departures registered since June included doctors and transport personnel. It named the Narva electrical products factory as one of the big losers. And a person knowledgeable about health personnel said today that more than 200 staff members had fled from the well-known Charité Hospital. About 1,200 East Germans fled to West Germany today, either directly or by way of Czechoslovakia.

Adding to these problems are the relatively new phenomena of large-scale smuggling and hoarding, according to Gunther Arndt, deputy head of East Germany's Customs Administration.

Edda Kaiser, an executive of the Centrum department store in Berlin, said in an interview about those problems, "It is an untenable situation for our house and surely for similar establishments, not only in Berlin." *Berliner Zeitung*, which quoted Mrs. Kaiser, said the offenders were mostly Poles and members of the American, British and French forces stationed in West Berlin. These people can purchase East German marks at a very low rate outside this country. Although the official exchange rate is 1.85 East German marks to the dollar, the currency can be exchanged outside at a black-market rate of over 10 marks per dollar.

The events in Germany were quite clearly exhilarating, spelling out as they did a further erosion of oppressive state power. They also signaled the approaching end of a divided Europe. But at the heart of any united Europe there had to be an undivided Germany, and given the modern history of Europe, this was a prospect that alarmed many. Moreover, the logistics of bringing together NATO's richest member with the Warsaw Pact's second-richest state after the Soviet Union were staggering. For one thing, West Germany was the home base to the largest concentration of NATO forces, while East Germany was the fortress of the Warsaw Pact. Sensitive to the fears of its allies, West German leaders, at first, took special care in their responses.

Kohl Says Bonn Will Not Press East Germany on Reunification
By Serge Schmemann

WEST BERLIN, Nov. 16—Chancellor Helmut Kohl presented today what has evolved into a broad West German consensus on how to approach the new developments in East Germany, declaring that Bonn would not try to influence the East Germans on reunification and would respect whatever path they chose.

Mr. Kohl also reiterated that any substantial economic aid to the East Germans would be given on the condition that they introduce a market economy.

Mr. Kohl addressed the Parliament in Bonn on the eve of a meeting of the East German Parliament at which the new Prime Minister,

Hans Modrow, is to make public an economic program that is said to call for a loosening of the central-planning system and greater possibilities for foreign participation.

Mr. Modrow is also expected to announce a new, streamlined government with almost half the ministries distributed among members of the four small parties traditionally allied with the governing Communists.

Mr. Kohl's speech, and the reactions of opposition parties to the right and left in Parliament, indicated that the Chancellor had achieved a consensus before any significant political disagreement over Bonn's policy toward the East emerged.

"We do not wish to force our conceptions upon anyone," Mr. Kohl said. "Nobody, however, could honestly argue that socialism has proven to be one single failure. It has failed throughout the world, not just in the G.D.R. By contrast, free enterprise means the freedom of decision, personal self-determination and broadly distributed wealth."

On the issue of German reunification, Mr. Kohl said, "Our compatriots in the G.D.R. must be able to decide for themselves which way they want to go in the future," and that West Germans would not try to influence their choice.

"Of course we will respect every decision that is being made by the people of the G.D.R. in free self-determination," he said.

But the Chancellor said economic assistance would be useless "unless there is an irreversible reform of the economic system, an end to a bureaucratic planned economy and the introduction of a market economy."

Mr. Kohl also sought to give strong reassurance to West Germany's Western allies that the developments in East Germany would not alter Bonn's commitments to the West. "We are and remain a part of the Western system of values," he said, adding that it would be a "fatal error" to slow the process of European integration.

Mr. Kohl's statements prompted almost no retorts from the opposition. "There is little room for party patriotism when what is being asked for is national responsibility and solidarity," said Willy Brandt, the former Social Democratic Chancellor. With their ideological affinities with socialist opposition movements in the East, the Social Democrats potentially have the most to gain from reunification.

In East Berlin, officials said that the 45 ministries would be reduced to 27, and that 11 of those would be filled by the "block parties"—

small organizations that were subsumed by the Communists when they seized power and survived to give the impression of pluralism to the one-party state.

Opposition spokesmen and Western diplomats were initially skeptical of Mr. Modrow's assertion to have formed a broad "coalition government," even though the block parties have tried to demonstrate a degree of independence in recent weeks.

They noted that no members of the new opposition movements were included and that the ministers were still drawn from a Parliament that until recently served as a rubber stamp for party directives.

"It is a beginning, but we have to wait and see how it works out," said Jutta Seidel of New Forum, the largest of the new opposition groups. "The other parties have never really been an opposition."

A.D.N., the East German press agency, said Egon Krenz, the East German leader, was also involved in the talks with the small parties. The Communist Party, which has about 2.3 million members, holds 127 of the 500 seats in Parliament, and the block parties, with a combined membership of 470,000, have 52 each. The 165 remaining seats are divided among mass organizations like trade unions and the Communist Youth League, many of whose delegates are Communist Party members.

Mr. Modrow is also expected on Friday to ask the Parliament to prepare a new election law and to form a commission to propose changes to the Constitution, which now in its first article guarantees the Communist Party a "leading role" in East German society. . . .

But just as the wall and the party that had built it were finally brought low not by the action of governments but by the assertion of autonomy by the millions who walked and chanted, so the prospect of reunification or reassociation of the Germanys lay in the action of people who were likely to join in thousands of private economic relationships, establishing and expanding networks embracing both East and West.

The Two Countries Are Likely to Join Their Industries Before Their Politics
By Craig R. Whitney

WEST BERLIN, Nov. 16—Foreigners who worry about "reunification" as an immediate and ominous consequence of the end of the Berlin wall overlook two things. One is that East and West Germany together only constitute about two-thirds of the prewar territory of the German Reich. Another is that East and West Germany have gradually been extending and broadening ties of all kinds ever since they established diplomatic relations with each other in 1972.

For Germans on either side of the border, what is at the top of their minds is not political reunification, but an economic growing together.

"Other models are conceivable, of course," said a Western diplomat in East Berlin. "It's possible to think of East Germany being annexed someday by West Germany, or of West Germany seceding from NATO and the European Community and coming together with East Germany as a neutral country. But neither of those seems anywhere near as likely as a gradual coming together of the two economies, with later political consequences."

Not all Western politicians would agree about the unlikelihood of the first two possibilities, but the two German economies have undoubtedly been coming together over the years. Trade between East and West Germany will amount to about $7.5 billion in both directions this year. And even though nearly four million East Germans have visited the West since the border barriers were taken down a week ago, more than 2.3 million East Germans visited West Germany last year, and 5.2 million West Germans visited the East.

Germans, East and West, will increasingly read even more of the same books if censorship in East Germany continues to be lifted at the current rate. Stefan Heym, who lives and works in East Germany, has been a best-selling author in the West for much of the last 40 years. East German television is now, at times, hard to distinguish from the Western stations.

Economic differences divide the two countries more than social or cultural ones. But West German business leaders and politicians are already thinking of ways to do it, and East German economic planners and politicians are already hoping they will be allowed to start soon.

"Nothing can happen until we have thorough political reform here," a leading East German lawyer said the other day, echoing Chancellor Helmut Kohl's conditions for providing massive economic aid to the East. "That means genuinely free elections."

"If we had free elections today, the Communist Party might win 5 percent of the vote," an East German diplomat said. "But then we might at least be able to start a genuine process of economic reform."

How difficult that would be can be seen on two levels. One is daily life. East Germans live in subsidized housing and the food they buy in state stores is sold at subsidized prices. A two-bedroom apartment in the Prenzlauer Berg section of East Berlin, for example, rents for 57 marks a month, about $31 at the official rate of exchange—and $3.10 at the rate East Berliners get when they go over to a bank in the West to change their money.

Right now, East German police and customs officials are barely checking people as they go back and forth across the border. But until apartments and loaves of bread and apples and oranges cost the same and are as freely available on both sides of the border, smuggling and black-market profiteering, not rapid economic growth, will be the result in East Germany, according to East German officials.

On a larger scale, West German businesses are ready to help develop the East German economy if they can be assured of the security for their investment and of a way to make profits and get them out in freely convertible currency.

"West German enterprises enter into cooperation agreements the world over," wrote Heinz Durr, chairman of the West German electronics giant, A.E.G., in *Der Spiegel* recently. "Why shouldn't they start cooperating with plants in the G.D.R. and offer joint products on the world market? We would have cost savings, and the G.D.R. would solve its convertible-currency problem, at least to a large extent."

"The same language and culture, the same mentality, even our tendency to perfectionism all speak for such a vision becoming reality," Mr. Durr wrote. "But the new model has to be wanted by the G.D.R."

However, a West German member of Parliament, Andreas von Bulow, pointed out that even then there would be many difficulties to overcome. Volkswagen, he said, had arranged years ago to build motors for its small cars in East Germany but the East German enterprise that built them had not yet been able to make them to standards high enough for any market except East Germany's.

Mr. von Bulow has produced a list of 35 steps for revision-minded Eastern European countries to take if they want to integrate themselves more closely into the Western economic system. They include steps like those taken by Ludwig Erhard in West Germany in 1948, when the Western allies introduced a new currency in their occupation zone—the West German mark—to replace the Reichsmark.

Many West Germans point to the history of the European Community as the best precedent for the kind of slow growing together of the two German states that they think is more likely than overnight reunification.

Economic integration has been underway in Western Europe since the Treaty of Rome was signed in 1957, they say. Political unification has been a much more difficult and slower process.

Prime Minister Margaret Thatcher of Britain said that even a common European currency would require a surrender of national sovereignty by the British Government because 12 European Community countries cannot have a common currency without a common monetary policy, probably run by a common central bank.

The borders among the 12 European Community countries have become far less important than they ever were in the past. On the Belgian border with West Germany, most cars pass through without a customs inspection and the police of both countries work side by side.

Since last week, East Germany's border has not been much more complicated to pass through than Britain's Heathrow Airport. The West Berlin and East Berlin Police have had their first contacts in 28 years about how to ensure order on both sides of the wall, and the mayors of both sides have shaken hands on the Potsdamer Platz.

Sometime in the next few weeks, Chancellor Kohl and Egon Krenz, the East German leader, will meet in East Berlin to talk about where things go from here.

"If it's true that the parts of Europe are coming closer to each other," wrote the former West German Chancellor Willy Brandt today in *Die Zeit*, "who could halfway seriously suggest that it would be justified to keep the parts of Germany out of it?"

The view from China remained deeply negative.

Chinese Premier Sees No Effect from Europe

RAWALPINDI, PAKISTAN, Nov. 16—Prime Minister Li Peng of China said here today that Beijing was watching events in Eastern Europe closely but that the surge of change in East Germany and other Warsaw Pact nations would not weaken China's commitment to Communism.

On his first foreign trip since Chinese troops crushed the democracy demonstrators in Tiananmen Square in June, Mr. Li said at a news conference with Western reporters that the "drastic changes" in Eastern Europe were attracting worldwide attention, and that "China naturally is also concerned" about them. The 61-year-old Prime Minister, who has given Western reporters few opportunities to question him since the Tiananmen crackdown, rejected any comparisons between Beijing's actions and the far-reaching concessions in East Germany.

Things were happening so quickly that it was hard to maintain perspective. At times it appeared as if people in the East bloc, notably in East Germany, suddenly became emboldened and that by marching and chanting they brought down the toughest and most absolute of rulers—men like Honecker—and that these emperors were revealed as naked. As the East Germans were now adding calls for justice and accountability to their cries for freedom, some of the inner circle were ready to offer the most prominent among them in their hope of salvaging some credibility for their wounded party and for themselves. In the process it was possible for outsiders to learn what exactly had happened in the innermost circles of power as their political control unraveled, at summer's end and most particularly after Mikhail Gorbachev's visit on October 6, when Honecker was thwarted from implementing what was termed "The Chinese solution."

How the Wall Was Cracked—A Special Report; Party Coup Turned East German Tide

Based on reporting by Craig R. Whitney, David Binder and Serge Schmemann and written by Mr. Whitney

EAST BERLIN, Nov. 17—The turning point came on October 7, after the Communist Party leader, Erich Honecker, ordered security forces to be prepared to open fire on demonstrators in Leipzig—a "Chinese solution" to the rising tide of dissent in East Germany.

But violence and killing were averted when Egon Krenz, then Politburo member in charge of security, flew to Leipzig on October 9 and canceled Mr. Honecker's order, allowing the protesters to march unmolested. Mr. Krenz became the new party chief on October 18.

What could have become a bloodbath as terrible as China's June crackdown instead became a peaceful revolution that is changing the face of East Germany and Eastern Europe. Within ten days, Mr. Honecker had resigned under pressure and the Communist Party was pledging profound changes. Within a month, the Berlin wall was broken.

Although this sequence of events would tend to bolster the image of Mr. Krenz, it is supported by the accounts of several members of the East German party, most of whom do not owe their current positions to Mr. Krenz.

They said Mr. Krenz reversed the order to shoot because he feared that hundreds of dead and wounded would be a fatal blow to the East German party's standing at home and abroad. . . .

On October 7, with Mikhail S. Gorbachev in East Berlin, crowds took to the streets of the capital, chanting "Gorby! Gorby!" and "We want to stay!" With many foreign reporters looking on, the police waded into the throngs, and their actions were recorded and immediately played back to the rest of East Germany on West German television.

More violence followed on Sunday, and by Monday, October 9, the suspense was tangible. A weekly Monday peace service, held in the Nikolai Church in Leipzig, had in recent weeks become the launching point for broad protests, and after the weekend clashes, huge crowds were expected at the church.

According to Manfred Gerlach, the leader of the small Liberal Democratic Party, and others, a huge force of soldiers, policemen and secret police agents was assembled in Leipzig and issued with live ammunition. Their order was to shoot if necessary, and the order had reportedly been signed by Mr. Honecker himself.

"There was a written order from Honecker for a Chinese solution," said Markus Wolf, the retired head of East Germany's spy agencies, who has emerged as a leading advocate of reform. "It could have been worse than Beijing."

But by then many in the Politburo had come to the decision that Mr. Honecker must go, and that the situation was explosive. In Leipzig, Kurt Masur, the director of the Gewandhaus musical theater, and some local party officials opened urgent discussions on averting a clash.

Finally, Mr. Krenz and Wolfgang Herger, the Central Committee department chief under him, flew to Leipzig's Schkeuditz Airport. They drove into the city to meet with local Communist officials at the home of Mr. Masur.

"I was in Leipzig," Mr. Krenz later said. "I helped there to see to it that these things were solved politically."

When tens of thousands took to the streets of Leipzig that night, the police did not interfere. The "revolution from below" was under way.

The frustration that erupted in October had been long in gathering. Mikhail S. Gorbachev, the Soviet President, had set loose yearnings for change throughout Eastern Europe, but in East Germany the old loyalists around Mr. Honecker sat entrenched in their isolated villas on Lake Wandlitz, refusing to acknowledge any reason to change.

The words perestroika and glasnost could not be uttered over the airwaves or printed in the East German press, either in Russian or German, and Soviet publications were banned.

East Berlin continued to flaunt its rigidity. Local elections on May 7 were plainly rigged. After the massacre in Tiananmen Square in Beijing on June 4, Mr. Krenz sent a message to the authorities in China congratulating them on their firmness. . . .

Mr. Honecker [after an operation] was back at work, and his attention was on the celebrations planned for October 7, the fortieth anniversary of the German Democratic Republic. Mr. Gorbachev was to lead a retinue of Communist leaders to East Berlin. . . .

Mr. Gorbachev seemed intent, publicly at least, not to inflame the opposition. But it did not take much. It was enough that he said that East Germany had to decide its own future to signal to many that Soviet troops would not interfere. When he said that those who did not change with the times would see life punishing them, the comment was seen as a direct reference to Mr. Honecker. Wherever he went, the crowds chanted "Gorby! Gorby!" Mieczyslav Rakowski, the Polish Communist Party leader, sat next to Mr. Gorbachev on the reviewing stand at the October 7 military parade. He later said with some irony that when he heard the chants he remarked to Mr. Gorbachev, "It looks as if they want you to liberate them again."

The Soviet leader was more direct when he met in private with the East German Politburo. An East German diplomat said Mr. Gorbachev did not try to prescribe what the East Germans should do. "He made it very clear that the spectacle of thousands of people running away from the country and of violence being the only way to keep them in was not helping him in his own difficult situation," he said.

According to a wide range of party insiders, Mr. Honecker was incapable of grasping the situation. He reacted with stubborn insistence that he was on the right course and would brook no leniency. He told a Chinese visitor that any attempt to change his course was "nothing more than Don Quixote's futile running against the steadily turning sails of a windmill."

On Saturday night, October 7, as Mr. Gorbachev was leaving for Moscow, tens of thousands of East Berliners moved from the anniversary ceremonies to Alexanderplatz, the vast square at the heart of the city. Bearing candles and torches, they began chanting slogans demanding change.

The East German police, armed with riot sticks, chased them out of the square and north into the heavily populated and dilapidated Prenzlauer Berg section, a hotbed of the growing New Forum opposition group. Hundreds were beaten and jailed. The scene was played out again on Sunday night in the same area of East Berlin, as well as in Leipzig and Dresden.

Mr. Krenz, at 52 the youngest member of the Politburo, was hardly a predictable architect of change. He had followed Mr. Honecker's path from the Communist youth league to take charge of security and youth affairs, and his statements had given no sign that he was anything but a hard-liner.

But he was considered sharp, and he was young. And it was he who took the fateful step on October 9 to avert violence in Leipzig.

Back in East Berlin, the Politburo gathered for its regular Tuesday meeting. Nobody knew how Mr. Honecker or his ideological allies would react to the unilateral order by Mr. Krenz barring the Leipzig crackdown.

It was Erich Mielke, the tough 82-year-old security chief, who told Mr. Honecker, "Erich, we can't beat up hundreds of thousands of people."

But the 77-year-old Communist leader would not be swayed. Earlier in the day, three members of the Central Committee had handed Mr. Honecker a report on the unrest among the country's youth and its causes, with a request for a special session of the leadership to deal with it. Mr. Honecker flew into a rage, calling the report "the greatest attack on the party leadership in 40 years."

Now Kurt Hager, the 77-year-old chief ideologist, raised his voice. The young people were right, he said. The mood on the streets was more defiant that he had ever seen it. Gunter Schabowski, the respected party secretary for East Belin, concurred.

Only two members firmly took Mr. Honecker's side: Gunter Mittag, the 63-year-old Economics Minister, who had dominated East German planning since the era of Walter Ulbricht, the first Communist Party chief, and Joachim Hermann, the 61-year-old secretary for propaganda.

Others wavered or kept silent. With the Politburo deadlocked, the secretaries of East Germany's 15 districts, including Hans Modrow, the party chief for Dresden who had a reputation as a reformer favored by Moscow, were called in for an unusual expanded meeting of the leadership. The meeting went late into the night of October 10 and continued on October 11.

"The district leaders said that the grassroots wouldn't stand for things to continue the way they were," a Central Committee member said.

The leaders began discussing a conciliatory statement to the nation. According to several accounts, Mr. Honecker resisted this too, fuming instead about his betrayal by Hungary.

Over his objections, the statement was issued October 11, declaring that the Politburo was ready "to discuss all basic questions of our society," and acknowledging that those who had fled may have had valid reasons.

From that day, the press suddenly became more open, with panel discussions on major public complaints. The small "parties," traditionally subservient to the Communists, suddenly gained a voice of their own, and Mr. Gerlach, the Liberal Party chairman, even suggested in his party paper that the "leading role" of the party should be reconsidered.

The Politburo met again on October 17. By now it was clear to most of the other seventeen Politburo members that Mr. Honecker no longer understood what was happening. One Communist official said Mr. Honecker had been so infuriated by Mr. Gerlach's statement and considered taking action against him.

This time, several Central Committee members said, only Mr. Mittag and Mr. Hermann still supported Mr. Honecker. Some officials said Mr. Mittag was holding out in the hope of securing the party leadership for himself, after having filled in for the ailing Mr. Honecker through the summer.

An important defector was Mr. Hager. "Without Hager, nothing would have gone through in the Politburo," a party official said.

Finally, Willi Stoph, the 75-year-old Prime Minister, told Mr. Honecker that the time had come for him to resign, a Central Committee member said.

That was the decisive push. On the next day, October 18, Mr. Honecker announced to the Central Committee that he was resigning for reasons of health, and the Politburo moved that Mr. Mittag and Mr. Hermann be ousted. Mr. Krenz was the new party chief, head of state and Defense Council chairman.

The meeting was brief. Mr. Krenz read a speech promising an "earnest political dialogue," and then urged the Central Committee to quickly close its proceedings so he could go on nationwide television.

Mr. Krenz immediately set about trying to establish himself, within the party and outside, as the leader of real change. "We see the seriousness of the situation," he said. "But we also sense and recognize the major opportunity we have opened for ourselves to define policies in dialogue with our citizens."

The pace quickened. Mr. Krenz and other Politburo members met people in factories and in the streets. On October 27, the Government announced that it would restore free travel through Czechoslovakia, for people wanting to go to West Germany. On November 1, Mr. Krenz flew to Moscow to meet Mr. Gorbachev and endorsed a version of perestroika—economic and social restructuring—in East Germany.

Still, demonstrations swelled. Huge crowds marched in Leipzig, East Berlin, Dresden and other major cities, and thousands of East Germans perhaps seeing this as their last chance to flee resumed their efforts to get into the West German Embassy in Prague.

Finally, on November 4, Mr. Krenz announced that East Germans who wanted to settle in West Germany could travel freely through Czechoslovakia. More than 10,000 a day began quickly surging across the border into the West.

That same day, more than a half million East Germans demonstrated for democracy in the largest protest that East Berlin or East Germany had ever seen. The crisis was not over.

Hoping to slow the exodus, the Government hastily drafted a law on travel that said East German citizens would be free to go abroad, but for only 30 days a year and after applying at police offices. The bill was promptly denounced, and in a sign of the rebellious mood, the Legal and Constitutional Committee of the normally docile Parliament dismissed it as unacceptable.

The pace of change gathered speed. On November 7, the entire Council of Ministers resigned and called on Parliament to choose a new government. The Central Committee convened on November 8, and this time the entire Politburo resigned, to be replaced by a smaller group, still headed by Mr. Krenz, with five new members. Among them was Mr. Modrow, the party leader from Dresden, who would soon become the next Prime Minister.

Thousands of Communist Party members demonstrated outside,

demanding a party congress to install an entirely new leadership.

On November 9, a Thursday, the Central Committee continued to sweep the ranks of the leadership. Four new members of the top leadership were swept out after their regional party organizations rejected them.

Mr. Mittag came under intense criticism and was expelled from the Central Committee for "the most egregious violations of internal party democracy and of party and state discipline, as well as damaging the reputation of the party."

In the evening, Gunter Schabowski came to brief reporters. Toward the end of the session, he announced that a new travel law had been drafted, giving East Germans the right to leave the country through any border crossings. The Berlin wall, already circumvented, was beginning to crumble.

The measures had been drafted by the Politburo, officials later said. It was still fresh, and the details were not immediately clear, although it later became evident that citizens did have to obtain exit visas from local police stations before going across. But when Mr. Schabowski was asked directly if East Germans could freely go West, his answer was yes.

Soon after, a young East German couple went to the Invaliden-strasse crossing to test the announcement. To their amazement, the guards, who had heard Mr. Schabowski and had no instructions, let them cross. After 28 years, 2 months, 27 days and, the deaths of 80 killed trying to cross it, the wall was open. The astonishing event was reported on West German television, and within an hour tens of thousands were streaming into West Berlin for one of the most extraordinary reunions ever held. Over the weekend two million visited the West, bought chocolates and for the most part, returned home to East Germany. Only a few thousand remained.

Not even the Soviet Government, one of the four World War II Allied powers who hold occupation rights in Berlin, was told of what the East Germans were doing, an East German Government official said. . . .

As events pressed forward, Hans Modrow, the man who by the virtual default of every other party figure, was leading East Germany, gave his own response to Chancellor Kohl on the question of reunification.

New Ties to Bonn Sought by Premier of East Germany

By Craig R. Whitney

EAST BERLIN, Nov. 17—Announcing a sweeping program of economic and political change, East Germany's new Prime Minister today held out the prospect of relations "on a new level" with West Germany.

In a speech broadcast live in East and West Germany, the new Prime Minister, Hans Modrow, said his nation stood by its commitments to the Warsaw Pact, but added:

"We are for supplementing the common responsibility of both German states with a complex of treaties that go far beyond the treaties and agreements signed up to now. This Government is ready for talks on this."

But Mr. Modrow, the 61-year-old former Communist Party chief in Dresden, said decisive change in East Germany would end "unrealistic and dangerous speculation about reunification."

The West German Government, which is sending an official to East Berlin on Monday to meet with the new Communist Party leader, Egon Krenz, reacted cautiously. Chancellor Helmut Kohl has promised West German economic aid on a vast scale if the East Germans carry out genuine economic and political change.

Mr. Modrow obtained unanimous approval from the 500-member East German Parliament for a streamlined, 28-member Cabinet in which the Communist Party kept control of the major portfolios, including defense, national security, foreign affairs, finance, heavy industry, planning and interior, which controls the police. . . . Twenty-seven members of the old Parliament, including the ousted Communist Party chief, Erich Honecker, and his wife, Margot, were replaced with new faces by unanimous consent this morning.

Several thousand East Germans demonstrated in front of the immense white Parliament building as deputies debated Mr. Modrow's statement of policy this afternoon. They carried banners including such slogans as "Socialism Is Dead! Long Live Socialism" and "Rehabilitate the Victims of Stalinist Show Trials." The demonstrations showed, as much of Mr. Modrow's speech did, both how far the country has come since Mr. Honecker was forced to resign a month ago and how far it has yet to go.

"A lot of things have stagnated here for a long time," said Steffen

Feiereis, one of the demonstrators. "There's been a lot of talk. Now it's time to do something." . . .

While fall was giving way to winter, radical political and social changes were underway in East Germany, Hungary and Poland. The course of reform was also zigzagging unevenly in different regions of the Soviet Union. All Europe was anticipating further changes. In this context, correspondents of **The Times** *interviewed three figures who were viewing the transformation from the perspective of dissidents, men who had spent years in jail for the efforts to bring about what now seemed to be taking place.*

Three Dissident Voices From Eastern Europe

Three Eastern Europeans with long careers as dissidents—a Pole, a Hungarian and a Czechoslovak—were asked in separate interviews what surprised them most about the recent events in East Germany, what they thought might be the next step in Eastern Europe and what they considered the greatest dangers.

Jan Litynski: Poland

Jan Litynski was thrown out of the mathematics department of Warsaw University in March 1968 and spent two and half years in jail for taking part in anti-Soviet protests. In the late 1970's he was a founder of the Committee to Defend Workers and edited underground papers.

He helped organize Solidarity, and when the movement was crushed under martial law in 1981, he was arrested and spent another year and a half in jail. He escaped into the underground when he was given a furlough to attend the communion of his daughter.

Mr. Litynski worked as an adviser to Silesian coal miners during the strike-filled summer of 1988. He was elected to Parliament as a candidate of the Solidarity-backed party.

"I guess what surpised me most is that I just did not think it would happen so soon," he said.

"The next major step? I think it should be real change in Czechoslovakia. For us, this is much more important than Germany, because it affords the chance of developing a common line for Hungary, Poland and Czechoslovakia. This would mean the end of Soviet domination in this region.

"By common line I mean we should work out a kind of common foreign policy. Now there are discrepancies, contradictions. I'm not talking about a confederation, as some have suggested, but simply to do our best to avoid the mistakes of the 1920's and 1930's.

"Dangers? Altogether, the economy, and especially the economic situation in the Soviet Union. I hope and think we can cope with our economic situation, and first symptoms are emerging that we will be able to do it. But there is the possibility of a crash in the Soviet Union, especially because of the nationalities problem. And then there is the situation in East Germany. If the Soviet Union lost its influence on East Germany it could result in a kind of military coup in Moscow."

Mr. Litynski was asked whether in his prison years he ever fantasized about the kind of changes that have taken place.

"Never, not at all. Even after I got out of prison, in the underground, I never dreamed of it. As for myself, I used to think maybe someday there'd be a role for me as a trade-union activist. But never as a politician, someone sitting in Parliament."

Miklos Vasarhelyi: Hungary

Miklos Vasarhelyi is a writer and former journalist who was sentenced to five years in prison for his role in the 1956 Hungarian uprising, which was crushed by the Soviet Army. Mr. Vasarhelyi, who was press secretary to the reformist Prime Minister Imre Nagy, was a defendant in the same secret trial in 1958 at which Mr. Nagy and three others were condemned to death. They were executed; he was sentenced to five years and released after four years.

Mr. Vasarhelyi lives in Budapest. He was interviewed in Washington, where he is doing research on the Western role and response to the Soviet invasion of Budapest in 1956.

Referring to the events in East Germany, he said: "What was most surprising was the speed with which it happened. Since last May we thought and we hoped there would be changes. But what's happening now and especially in Berlin is a major surprise. Nobody dared to think about such big changes. Even to have mentioned such things three months ago would have seemed crazy.

"What was so unusual is that it was all the will of the people. It was not figured out by intellectuals or politicians or diplomats.

"It's very different than in 1956. Then, we were crushed because we were alone. Hungary was isolated. This today is impossible to crush because it is going on almost everywhere behind the Iron Curtain. It is irreversible and I can tell you sincerely, I never expected to live to see it."

Asked what he thought would happen now, he replied: "First of all, there will really be a Europe again. The countries of Central and Eastern Europe will finally get an opportunity to unite with the West. We will begin to live under the same conditions.

"It will take time, but socially, politically and economically we will achieve what the Western countries have already achieved. The doors are open now."

On the question of dangers, he said they were fewer than they had been. "There are problems, but they don't worry me. What worried me was to live under a dictatorial system and foreign domination. All other worries are peanuts compared to that.

"Nor am I afraid of a united Germany. The Germans have changed very much. In the last century, the French wanted to take all of Europe. Now they are the most civilized and cultured of nations. The Germans had the terrible experience of Nazism for 10 years 50 years ago. Should we now have to say forever that we have to be afraid of the Germans?"

Jiri Dienstbier: Czechoslovakia

Jiri Dienstbier is one of the founders of the Czechoslovak human-rights group Charter 77. He was a Communist Party member and radio commentator on foreign affairs in 1968 when the Soviets invaded to crush the liberalization begun by the Communist Government of Alexander Dubcek. He spent three years in prison, lost his job and has not been allowed a telephone because of his work.

This is what he said in an interview this week at his home in Prague:

"What surprised everybody was the quick unraveling of things in East Germany. The opposition there wasn't very much bigger than in Czechoslovakia, which is pretty small. It was based almost completely on the evangelical church. In fact, the East German movement started outside the country, with the opening of the border between Austria and Hungary, which gave the East Germans an escape route. This shows that no matter where the rot sets in, the Communist system collapses very quickly.

"The next step? I hope it's Czechoslovakia. I think it could be. The leadership here is dead, only waiting to be carried away. Jakes is completely discredited. The party's only alternative to the status quo is to open up the system, but they know that once they open it up, they are doomed.

"As for dangers, the main problems are the potential economic collapse in Russia and Poland. Whether that pulls us all down would depend mainly on the scope and the nature of the collapse."

The enthusiasm of the three men was justified. Mr. Dienstbier's hopes that the next turn of the wheel would take place in his country was fulfilled within days of the interview. On the night of November 17, as students were taking part in a procession meant to commemorate the shootings of university students by Nazi occupiers, police attacked them. It was an officially sanctioned march, but presumably some authorities felt that what was needed was a preemptive show of force to thwart any attempt to march, chant and bring down the government on the East German model. If that was the intent, the policy backfired. For from that night on, daily rallies grew more massive with each day until in Czechoslovakia, too, the dissidents turned out the Communists. When Mr. Dienstbier gave his interview he was working as a coal stoker in a hospital, a job he had been assigned as a result of his protest. A month later, he was his country's foreign minister.

With Czechoslovakia on the verge of change, Rumania was the last holdout in the Warsaw pact. Nothing, it seemed, was likely to happen there to weaken the tight grip of its Stalinist leader, Nicolae Ceausescu.

Rumanian Leader Refuses Changes
By Alan Riding

BUCHAREST, RUMANIA, Nov. 20—Using the occasion of a major Communist Party congress, President Nicolae Ceausescu made it clear today that as long as he is in charge, Rumania will not follow other East European countries along the paths toward democracy or capitalism.

"Some socialist countries have adopted measures with a view to increasing the wealth of some people and increasing the number of poor," he said. "This focus is not socialist, and we cannot admit it in any way."

In a five-hour speech constantly interrupted by delegates who jumped up, chanted slogans, applauded and sat down in unison, Mr. Ceausescu singled out no particular Eastern bloc government for criticism, prefering instead to emphasize each country's right to pick its own political system.

But the 71-year-old President indirectly referred to widespread speculation about German reunification after the opening of the Berlin wall, noting that "the existence of two Germanys should continue to be a reality of Europe today and tomorrow."

He also raised eyebrows by calling for "the condemnation and cancellation of all the accords concluded with Hitler's Germany, practical conclusions being drawn to eliminate all the consequences of those accords and dictates."

One consequence of the Hitler-Stalin pact of 1939 was that Soviet troops occupied the Rumanian territory of Bessarabia. Although Rumania's Communist Government has never reclaimed what is now Soviet Moldavia, more than 90 percent of its population is still Rumanian, with nationalist sentiments one reason for recent unrest in the republic.

Most of Mr. Ceausescu's speech today, though, was dedicated to extolling the virtues and listing the achievements of the Government since he became General Secretary of the Rumanian Communist Party in 1965.

Only on two occasions did he abandon his prepared text and raise his voice almost to a scream to insure that Rumanians were in no doubt about his opinion of those East European Governments that are veering away from Communism.

"What do we say to those who want to lead the way to capitalism?" he asked. "What were they doing when they were in positions of responsibility? The answer is they used their jobs to block socialism and did not serve their people."

To underline his point, he said that the capitalist world was characterized today by unemployment, homelessness and growing illiteracy. "Adding to all this are crime and drugs, which have become national problems in many countries," he said.

While Mr. Ceausescu's orthodox stance came as no surprise, the long-scheduled party congress has underlined his hard-line Government's growing international isolation as well as its heightened sensitivity to foreign criticism.

With the exception of Yasir Arafat, chairman of the Palestine Liberation Organization, no prominent foreign dignitaries were present at the opening of the party congress, and other East bloc Communist parties sent low-level delegations. Western ambassadors boycotted the occasion to protest Rumania's human rights record.

In the days leading up to the congress, the Government also tightened its borders with Hungary, Yugoslavia and the Soviet Union to the point of turning away ordinary tourists. A French journalist was expelled last Friday, numerous correspondents from Western newspapers were refused visas, and reporters arriving here Sunday saw all their papers mentioning Rumania seized by customs officers at Bucharest airport.

At home, though, bolstered by a huge and notoriously effective security apparatus, Mr. Ceausescu still appears to be unchallenged, with dissidents numbering only a score of intellectuals and disillusioned party officials whose occasional protests are better known abroad than here.

Unlike other East European countries, Rumania also seems to be largely immune to pressure from the Soviet Union. Moscow has had no troops stationed here since 1957 and has viewed Mr. Ceausescu as something of a maverick ever since he criticized the Soviet invasion of Czechoslovakia in 1968.

Further, even though living conditions have steadily deteriorated over the last fifteen years, the Rumanian economy is less dependent on the outside world than that of, say, Poland because of Mr. Ceausescu's decision to dedicate the 1980's to paying off the country's $11 billion debt.

"The repayment of the foreign debt is a great success of our state's policy, and it puts an end to this country's long dependence on foreign monopolies and financial capital," he said today. "For the first time in its history, Rumania no longer pays either tribute or interest."

And although the Rumanian leader has lost much of the international influence that he enjoyed when he was viewed by the West as a critic of Moscow, Mr. Ceausescu urged the superpowers to move rapidly toward disarmament. Specifically, he called for the denuclearization of Europe by 1995 and the elimination of all nuclear weapons by the year 2000.

200,000 March in Prague as Calls for Change Mount
By John Tagliabue

PRAGUE, Nov. 20—More than 200,000 marchers called today for freedom and a change in government in the largest and most vociferous public demonstration since the euphoric Prague Spring that preceded the 1968 Soviet-led invasion of Czechoslovakia.

At the same time, party and Government officials pointedly reaffirmed their opposition to introducing political change in the face of the protests.

Nonetheless, they at least tacitly acknowledged a changed political climate by postponing an official visit here by Egon Krenz, the new East German leader, which was to have begun Tuesday. Prague's official press agency said that on the "basis of a mutual agreement," Czechoslovakia and East Germany had decided to call off the visit indefinitely.

The demonstrators, most of them young people, gathered initially at Wenceslas Square, the half-mile-long pedestrian plaza sloping down from the National Museum. The square has repeatedly been the forum for expressions of Czechoslovak nationalism. And today, the crowd waved flags and chanted anti-Government slogans.

As the group, which included striking university and high school students, set out to cross the Vltava River on the way to Hradcany Castle, which houses the President's office, their shouts became bolder. Cries demanding "freedom"and "free elections" mingled with calls for a general strike and chants of "Jakes out!," a reference to the country's orthodox Communist Party General Secretary, Milos Jakes.

The gigantic crowd moved slowly through the narrow, curving streets of the baroque city. But as the marchers headed onto several bridges, they were confronted by large numbers of heavily armed police officers. The protesters reversed course and dispersed soon after they returned to the north shore, avoiding the kind of violence with which club-wielding policemen scattered a smaller group of demonstrators on Friday night.

The march through Prague was reminiscent of the mass protests in 1967 that swept out Antonin Novotny, then the hard-line Communist leader, replacing him with the reform-minded Alexander Dubcek. . . .

Though the tremendous size of the crowds—which seeped through crooked squares and broad shopping streets, and then snaked along the open stretches of the river shore—made it difficult to determine how many people marched, the official radio estimated that more than 200,000 Czechoslovaks had taken to the streets.

National television, which reported extensively on the demonstration, also gave news of similar marches in at least three other cities— the northern center of heavy industry, Ostrava; the Slovak capital, Bratislava, and Brno, the site of the second-largest protest, with several thousand marchers.

In Prague, schools of the university were closed by striking students, and banners declaring sit-in strikes appeared at institutes of higher learning throughout the city.

Dissident leaders repeated a call for a two-hour general strike on November 27. Vaclav Havel, the playwright and leading Czechoslovak dissident, reported that he had received a message from coal miners at a small pit in northern Bohemia, who expressed support for the requested stoppage. But the extent to which industrial workers might join the swelling protest remained both critical and, as yet, unanswered.

Western diplomats and Czechoslovak dissident leaders believe that if workers were to join in with students and intellectuals, it would spell the almost certain collapse of the Government.

At various sites throughout the city tonight, groups of young people, students and workers could be seen milling around columns of police vehicles, in animated discussion with the young officers. Apparently, the security authorities had given orders for the police to use restraint today. But that decision did not appear to signal any lessening of the leadership's will to resist political change.

Mr. Jakes, in a statement that rang with a sense of warning, accused the protest-march organizers of "seeking to create chaos and anarchy."

Such efforts, he said, would "seriously endanger the implementation of necessary changes and bring socialism into crisis, with unforeseeable consequences."

Even more striking than the statement by Mr. Jakes, a widely acknowledged hard-liner, was another by the Cabinet today that endorsed the measures taken by the Communist Party leadership to put down protest last Friday. Many demonstrators were injured in that action.

The Cabinet said it approved of "measures whose purpose is to renew order, protect property and protect the lives of the citizens."

Its remarks were notable because Ladislav Adamec, the 62-year-old Prime Minister, has emerged in recent weeks as the principal rival to Mr. Jakes. He has adopted a relatively moderate stance in his apparent maneuvering to succeed the party leader.

An example of the Communist Party's declining authority came last Sunday, when the leader of the hitherto satellite Socialist Party, Jan Skoda, broke ranks and turned up along with Mr. Havel and other dissidents at the founding assembly of a new political group, the Civil Forum.

That gathering, held in a Prague theater, heard another leading dissident, the Rev. Vaclav Maly, a Roman Catholic priest banned by the state from performing his priestly duties, read a declaration calling for the removal of hard-liners like Mr. Jakes and threatening a general strike.

Earlier today, Mr. Havel announced that he had refused a Government offer of a passport to travel to Sweden and accept an award there "because the situation at home is becoming dramatic."

Prague's Premier Has Initial Talks with Opposition
By John Tagliabue

PRAGUE, Nov. 21—Czechoslovakia's Communist leaders held their first talks with representatives of a newly formed opposition movement today, while more than 200,000 people joined in a fifth day of street demonstrations sustaining pressure for political changes.

In developments that at times appeared to parallel recent East German events, dissident voices were raised in the streets while Communist leaders promised new approaches and the expansion of political life beyond the ruling party.

In a televised address tonight, Milos Jakes, the hard-line Communist Party General Secretary, appealed to citizens to "depart from this present, exacerbated situation." He warned, "There are boundaries that should not be overstepped."

Mr. Jakes's address offered somewhat stern counterpoint to the news that Prime Minister Ladislav Adamec had met with opposition figures. The party leader looked despondent, but he gave no sign that he was about to step down, while acknowledging that "more than one dialogue" lay ahead of him.

Earlier, the playwright Vaclav Havel, a frequently arrested dissident leader stood on a balcony and told a huge gathering in Wenceslas Square of the meeting between Prime Minister Adamec and a delegation of the Civic Forum, a recently formed opposition group.

Mr. Adamec also promised that the Government would not impose martial law. His comments were reported by the official press agency.

The demonstrators had at times cried "Punish, punish, punish!"— urging retribution for policemen who had used billy clubs to scatter protesters on Friday. As Mr. Havel spoke, some waved Czechoslovak flags and others applauded.

The show of enthusiasm continued as the Rev. Vaclav Maly, a priest who has been barred by the Government from wearing clerical garb or performing religious duties because of his involvement with dissident and human rights groups, read a letter from Frantisek Cardinal Tomasek, the 90-year-old Primate of the Roman Catholic Church in Czechoslovakia.

"There can be no confidence in the leadership of a state that refuses to tell the people the truth and give them the rights and freedoms that are common even in third-world countries," said Father Maly, quoting the Primate. "We can wait no longer." . . .

250,000 Czechs, Hailing Dubcek, Urge Ouster of Hard-Line Leaders
By John Tagliabue

PRAGUE, Nov. 22—More than 250,000 Czechoslovaks who gathered in Wenceslas Square for a sixth consecutive day of protest shouted "Resign! Resign!" today when speakers called for the country's hard-line Communist leaders to step down.

The loudest cheers came when the urging was made in the name of Alexander Dubcek, the reformist leader who was forced from power after Soviet tanks invaded Czechoslovakia 21 years ago. Mr. Dubcek emerged today from the obscurity to which he had been officially consigned to ask that President Gustav Husak and Milos Jakes, the party leader, give up their posts.

Mr. Dubcek also spoke in public today for the first time since his efforts to introduce "Socialism with a human face" were crushed in 1968. In Bratislava, he addressed 2,000 people protesting the trial of a human-rights advocate, urging calm. Mr. Dubcek, who has been officially ignored while working in a state forestry office for much of the last two decades, was shown on state television tonight as he met protesters. Mr. Dubcek's message, read to the crowd in Prague, noted that he hoped to visit the capital soon and to appear in person at Wenceslas Square. When this was announced, the crowd began chanting, "Dubcek, Dubcek." [The Associated Press reported that citizens were able for the first time to watch a live broadcast from the square on state-run television. But the broadcast, spliced with studio film of rock bands, was abruptly halted after 50 minutes when a worker interviewed by a reporter on the square accused the Government of lying. "What is the Government afraid of?" said the worker, identified as Honza Lexa. "They might be afraid because they are lying to us for 20 years." An announcer appeared to say the broadcast was temporarily halted because some unidentified television workers disagreed with it. The broadcast from the square resumed 35 minutes later. . . .

At today's rally, Vaclav Havel, the playwright and dissident, told cheering crowds that he sought to reach "especially all the workers in our country who are for reform."

As cheers of "Long live the workers" echoed through the floodlit square, Mr. Havel continued, "Those who have been taking bloody vengeance against all their rivals for so many years are now afraid of us."

"But we are not like them," he said, from a balcony high above the square. "We don't want to take vengeance on anyone. We only ask to take control of our country."

Students in Prague who have been striking since Monday, demanding free elections and a change in government, sent hundreds of their numbers into the countryside to visit industrial plants in an effort to enlist support for the general strike. . . .

The upheavals in the East bloc were not only raising hopes; they were raising some very tricky questions as well.

The New Europe: Will It Come Apart as It Comes Together?

By R. W. Apple, Jr.

VIENNA, Nov. 22—More than a century ago, the Hapsburg Empire, based in this grand old city on the Danube, stretched across Central and Eastern Europe from the Tyrolian Alps to the Carpathian Mountains.

In a sense, its collapse under the weight of emergent nationalism led to the two great twentieth-century conflicts. The assassination at Sarajevo of Archduke Franz Ferdinand, the heir to the throne, set off World War I, and Hitler's dismemberment of Czechoslovakia, one of the "succession states" created from the defunct empire in 1918, raised European tensions to the breaking point on the eve of World War II.

Now the East European region once contested by the Hapsburg monarchy and its neighbors, with its complicated patterns of tribe and language, is in turmoil once again, with consequences that are unpredictable.

The people of Poland and Czechoslovakia, of Hungary and Bulgaria, clearly hope that once their freedom is established, once the threat of war between East and West has truly receded, they will be able to restore long-ruptured links with the rest of Europe. As a Hungarian actor said last summer, "We want so much to be Europeans again, and we think that we really have a chance, if we cross our fingers and get our politicians going."

But at the same time, the sharp reduction in Moscow's sway over what used to be called the satellite nations in Eastern Europe, a unifying influence in some ways parallel to the old empire's, could give greater play to the centrifugal forces that have proved so destructive in the past.

In the new era, in other words, with the centripetal force of ideology weakened, Poles will be able to be more Polish, Hungarians more Hungarian.

Already the Hungarians complain bitterly about Rumanian treatment of ethnic Hungarians in Transylvania, Slovaks and Czechs are more vocal in expressing resentment of each another, East Germans grouse about the fate of ethnic Germans in the now Polish region of Silesia. Everyone complains about the Poles, who can find little in their own shops, sweeping into stores in neighboring countries and denuding the shelves of shops there.

Other ancient forces have also been liberated in the drive for pluralism and free speech. In at least some countries in Eastern Europe, there has been a rise in anti-Semitism, prominent Jews say, at the same time as there is a rise in the open expression of Jewish pride.

So far, though, nationalistic rivalries have been muted in the common struggle for freedom. In a striking example of that, Anna Masaryk, the 60-year-old granddaughter of the founder of modern Czechoslovakia, Tomas Masaryk, was seen among the demonstrators this week in Wenceslas Square in Prague.

On both sides of the rapidly disintegrating Iron Curtain, older people recall a day when there was one Europe, not two, and when intellectual and cultural currents flowed freely back and forth. They remember, as the younger ones often do not, that it was the Soviet Union and not so much the Eastern Europeans themselves who cut their historical links with the West—links that made the Polish scientist Copernicus and the Czechoslovak playwright Karel Capek and the Hungarian composer Bela Bartok part of Western civilization, not a part of a separate culture that stopped at the Elbe.

When the Berlin wall was finally opened two weeks ago, Neil Ascherson wrote in a commentary in *The Independent of London*, "It wasn't just the landscape of European politics that suddenly changed; it was the European cosmos." With that act, Europe started to become whole once more, with its eastern reaches no longer enshrouded, in Mr. Ascherson's vivid phrase, in "darkness and demons."

Even far across the Atlantic, the lesson will not be long in sinking in. Americans, after all, have ethnic and religious roots in Wittenberg and Bratislava and Lodz, not just in Naples and Athens and Munich and Dublin. One of their favorite beers is named after what was once Budweis, an ethnically German brewing town in the Bohemia region of Czechoslovakia that is now called Ceske Budejovice. The Bauhaus architectural style that shaped American cities after the war was developed in Dessau, in what is now East Germany, and Haydn, as mainstream a figure in Western musical history as it is possible to imagine, wrote many of his best symphonies while serving the Ester-hazy family as music-master in Hungary.

It is not so far, really, from Cracow to Chicago. At the height of the cold war, the gulf seemed enormous, but it does no longer, not with Lech Walesa drawing crowds in America and American busi-nessmen flocking to Budapest with deal-making on their minds.

For the Europeans, the distances have been reduced even more, and events are forcing fresh thinking to the fore. The Italians are talking about—and have even held a conference to discuss—a new economic alignment in which they, the Hungarians, the Austrians and the Yugoslavs could cooperate to create a balancing force to the German sphere of influence that many expect to emerge to the north.

The Swedes, who have maintained their neutrality throughout the cold war, now see less reason to do so. With that once-central idea not so gripping anymore, they are thinking again about the possibility of joining the European Community. In Britain, debate raging over how fully that country should take part in the tighter organization of the community scheduled to take effect in 1992 has been intensified.

"We have to build mechanisms to integrate this new Europe," says Gianni de Michelis, the Italian Foreign Minister. "The new realities are social, political, economic, artistic. For a thousand years, Euro-pean equilibrium was built in Central Europe, starting with Charle-magne. For the last eighty years we have lacked a workable system, with obvious results, but now we have a chance once again to build it."

In Czechoslovakia, as in East Germany, the party began to make concessions to placate the crowds. The crowds, meanwhile, kept asking for more.

Prague Party Leaders Resign; New Chief, 48, Surprise Choice; 350,000 at Rally Cheer Dubcek

By Steven Greenhouse

PRAGUE, Saturday, Nov. 25—Yielding to mass protests throughout Czechoslovakia, the Communist Party's leadership resigned on Friday, and the beleaguered Central Committee chose a younger, lesser-known Politburo member to replace General Secretary Milos Jakes.

But the election of the new chief, Karel Urbanek, a 48-year-old former party leader in Bohemia, was followed by the unexpected announcement early this morning that the moderate Prime Minister, Ladislav Adamec, was resigning as well. Mr. Adamec this week had met with dissidents calling for dialogue and had been considered a likely successor to Mr. Jakes as party leader; his departure was considered a setback to the movement for change.

The makeup of a new nine-member Politburo was also announced this morning, and the new body retained several hard-liners on the 13-member Politburo that resigned on Friday.

The replacement of Mr. Jakes on Friday came just hours after 350,000 protesters crowded into central Prague in the eighth straight day of huge demonstrations.

In a striking paradox, the throng was addressed by Alexander Dubcek, whose liberal regime was overthrown by a Soviet-led Warsaw Pact invasion in 1968, and replaced by hard-line Communists of whom Mr. Jakes was one of the leaders. It was Mr. Dubcek's first public appearance in Prague since 1968.

After the news of the resignations of the old leaders spread, there was singing and dancing and scenes of jubilation throughout the center of Prague, where just a week before the police had clubbed demonstrators in a vain effort to put down the protests.

"An old wise man said, 'If there once was light, why should there be darkness again?' " Mr. Dubcek had told the crowd. "Let us act in such a way to bring the light back again." . . .

Speaking about the Politburo changes, one Western diplomat said: "It was a generational change. It is still dominated by hard-liners. I can't say it is very positive." Several diplomats said the party might have been trying to make cosmetic changes to placate protesters. The diplomats said they doubted that the changes would come close to satisfying the dissidents. . . .

The diplomats were right.

Prague Opposition Mounts Huge Protest, Denouncing New Leadership as "a Trick"

By R. W. Apple, Jr.

PRAGUE, Nov. 25—Opposition leaders redoubled their pressure on the tottering Communist regime in Czechoslovakia today, staging an immense protest rally and insisting that the shuffling of the Politburo on Friday night and further resignations this morning had failed to move the nation far enough toward democracy.

"The new leadership is a trick that was meant to confuse," said Vaclav Havel, the often-jailed playwright who to many symbolizes political dissent here. "The power remains in or is passing into the hands of the neo-Stalinists."

"Shame! Shame! Shame!" shouted thousands of his listeners, part of a huge throng of protesters estimated by Czechoslovak officials at 500,000 to 800,000. The protesters filled a large field next to a sports stadium and near Letenske Gardens, on the north side of the river and across from Wenceslas Square. Hundreds of thousands of Czechoslovaks have demonstrated in the square, a blocks-long pedestrian plaza, each night this week.

Today's crowd was the largest in the nine straight days of demonstrations.

The throng provided a powerful symbol of continuing political dissent despite the resignation of Milos Jakes, the Communist Party chief, whose leadership crumbled under the pressure of the mass rallies, and a clear lack of support from Moscow.

Karel Urbanek, the little-known Politburo member who was made Communist Party General Secretary, said on television tonight in his first address to the people that "nobody manages to create miracles from day to day." He spoke for eleven minutes, in generalities, calling himself "an honest man" who was open to dialogue with his opponents.

Mr. Urbanek did not mention a two-hour general strike that is planned for Monday. The omission was considered significant by commentators here, who saw in it a possible attempt by the new party leader to identify himself with some of the opposition's goals.

More than 24 hours after the old regime came apart, it was still not clear whether the Communists were ready for significant changes, including the abandonment of their claim to permanent control of the Government, or whether they were trying to regroup behind a new facade.

Most outsiders, including Western diplomats, leaned to the belief that Mr. Urbanek was offering the appearance of change without the reality.

"It was impossible to give Jakes a soft landing," a European envoy said. "He had to be blamed at once, and when that happens in a Communist country, it means the party is in retreat. But it doesn't mean that they're ready yet for genuine competition with other parties for power."

This was another turbulent day, not only in this fine old capital but also in Bratislava, the principal city of Slovakia; in Brno, largest city in Moravia, and in other centers. A commentator on state television spoke tonight of power struggles in party organizations nationwide. . . .

Ladislav Adamec, who lost his Politburo seat, said he had submitted his resignation as Prime Minister, but he seemed still to be functioning in that capacity. At a news conference, he said that the commandant of paramilitary forces who beat protesters on November 17 would be disciplined. He also promised a new draft constitution by the end of the year, discussed an amnesty for all political prisoners and agreed to meet again next week with the leaders of protesting students.

Pronouncing himself ready to talk with the Civic Forum, the main opposition movement, Mr. Adamec said: "Last week, I undertook such dialogue, but we cannot leave it unfinished. We must meet again and solve problems with which both sides are concerned. I think we can do it sometime next week."

A light snow was falling on Mr. Havel and Alexander Dubcek, the 67-year-old Slovak who instituted the liberalization crushed by Soviet-led tanks 21 years ago, as they spoke to the vast throng at the stadium.

People in the crowd were in an exuberant if wary mood, their confidence buoyed by the departure of Mr. Jakes. They wore ribbons in red, blue and white, the national colors, and waved Czechoslovak flags as Mr. Havel told them that he was "profoundly disturbed" by the composition of the new Politburo named at 3 A.M. today. . . .

In addition to the mass rallies, other forms of organization and protest were being planned.

Students Ask Workers' Aid in Czech Rally

By Esther B. Fein

PRAGUE, Nov. 23—Jana Markvartova is the daughter of a doctor and a lawyer, a privileged child of Czechoslovakia's elite. Before this week, she had never really talked to any of the hundreds of thousands of people who are this country's manual laborers.

Today, Miss Markvartova stood before nearly 200 workers at the Domaci Potreby household appliance factory in the polluted industrial outskirts of the city and told them how the police here had violently broken up a peaceful demonstration by students last Friday night. Then tearfully, she asked the workers to support a two-hour general strike that the students have called for Monday to demand wholesale changes in the country's leadership.

"We need your help," Miss Markvartova told the workers. "It is your work that allows us to study and to develop our minds and our ideas. But alone our ideas are nothing. We need you. We need you to join our strike."

Her efforts paid off. The workers voted overwhelmingly to support the strike.

In the last week, Miss Markvartova and students like her at Prague's universities have realized that they must reach out to workers at factories, farms and industries if their demonstrations and strikes are to succeed in forcing change on their resistant Communist Government.

Unlike Poland, where the workers themselves began the Solidarity movement that eventually unseated the Communist Government this year, the opposition in Czechoslovakia since 1968 has always been a cause of the intellectual crafts, with practically no input from workers.

To insure the complacency of the workers, Communist leaders in Czechoslovakia have consistently provided manual workers with higher salaries and greater access to such things as private cars and weekend cottages than almost anywhere else in the Eastern bloc with the possible exception of East Germany.

"We won't win if the workers are not on our side," said Jiru Masek, a 19-year-old student of foreign trade at Prague University and one of the strike organizers. "To the leaders of our country, we students are nothing. But workers are the power here. To persuade them is critical to our cause."

After successfully shutting down most college classes, the students set up work battalions in classrooms, gymnasiums and lecture halls. Ragged from little sleep and sporadic eating, they spend their days and nights typing up declarations and appeals to their fellow citizens, painting posters that are then plastered in store windows and subway stations and editing videotapes that show the brutal events of November 18 and the mass rallies on Wenceslas Square that have been a daily event ever since.

Then they sent teams of students out to factories and enterprises throughout the city and in the countryside, trying to bridge the vast gap between Czechoslovakia's elite and its working class and to win the support of the laborers.

Tomas Zuda, a 21-year-old economics student and a strike coordinator, acknowledged that there was not a natural line of communications betwen the impassioned young students and the workers.

"Some of us work in factories in the summer to earn money, but this is the first time most of us have actually had a dialogue with the workers," he said. "Every student who has gone to a factory, and there are hundreds of us, has had to find a common language to make the workers understand. There has been a lot of skepticism to overcome and social barriers that are usually not crossed in this country, and we don't always have success. But I think the workers see that we are more sincere, than the Government when we say: 'We need you. We want you.' "

Miss Markvartova first went to the Domaci Potreby factory on Tuesday with Jan Novak, both unsure that workers there would listen to the radical pleas of two 21-year-old philosophy students asking them to stop working on Monday in a two-hour strike. They had already been thrown out of the Balirny factory across the street, where the conservative director of the packaging enterprise refused to let them speak with workers.

At Domaci Potreby, they were told to leave their literature and to come back today, when the workers would meet in the cafeteria and hear them out.

During the next two days, Miss Markvartova, Mr. Novak and thousands of students here circumvented the conservative official press to get their word out to the working people. They covered the walls of the city's subway system, bus windows, escalator railings, shop windows and street lamps with information on demonstrations and strikes and with posters proclaiming: "Workers Join Us for Freedom!" "Students Against Violence Ask for Your Help!" and "Strike for Democracy."

Overnight the students created their own "mass media" on the streets. These days virtually every public place in Prague is crowded with people reading notices, looking at pictures of the Friday night clashes and signing declarations, all surprisingly unhindered by the police.

When Miss Markvartova and Mr. Novak returned to the Domaci Potreby factory today, the workers rose in applause.

"My heart is with you," said Jitka Jeslinkova, a 30-year-old woman who has worked for two years at the plant. "I want my children to buy anything they need in the shops, to read any books they choose and watch any film they want. I want freedom for them and for me."

Monika Mlejnkova, a representative of the factory's Communist Party committee, objected to the call for a strike. "Maybe we should allow an investigation of the events on Friday, but I urge you not to strike," she said, as her colleagues began to bang the table and hiss. "The Communist Party is our strength."

Miroslav Nedorast, a burly man who has been a factory truck driver for 40 years, then shouted from the back of the room: "We want pluralism. We want free elections. I wouldn't be a Communist Party member even if I were forced. Your time is over."

The factory director called for a vote. Who supports the strike? he asked. Hands shot up across the room, already dim in the late afternoon. Who is against? Three hands were raised.

"Let's take another count," Miss Mlejnkova said.

That stirred a response from an older worker with thick glasses. "I have bad eyes," the worker said. "But it's clear even to me that most everyone here is for a strike."

But they voted again and the decision remained: Workers at the Domaci Potreby factory will join the students and lay down their tools from noon until 2 P.M. on Monday.

"This was not spontaneous support," said Jaroslava Fornuskova, a 38-year-old factory worker. "We talked about what would happen if the strike didn't work, what kind of repression there might be. But we decided we can't support a Government that beats its students. Next time it will be us, and then who will strike?"

The center of the ongoing Eastern European drama had shifted quite suddenly to Prague, but there were also major developments unfolding in Germany and gripping events almost everywhere in the bloc.

Reports of Corruption in East Berlin Shock Even the Party Rank and File

By David Binder

EAST BERLIN, Nov. 24—For the last two days, the East German press has been publishing accusations of corruption and profiteering by top officials of the former Communist leadership under Erich Honecker, and the reports are coming as a shock to the public here.

For the first time, East Germans have learned from reporters in *Neues Deutschland*, the main Communist paper, as well as *Berliner Zeitung* and *Junge Welt* about the extraordinary privileges accumulated by the Honecker regime, which was ousted a month ago. The shock is all the greater among ordinary party members because the former regime had presented itself for years as a model of Communist modesty and probity.

For the East German public, the most fascinating and revolting revelations are about Wandlitz, the heavily guarded compound of 23 houses for the Communist elite a few miles north of the capital.

A dozen or so East German reporters, photographers and television camera teams allowed into the compound for the first time disclosed such amenities as a swimming pool, a greenhouse, gardeners, maids, a tailor, a beauty parlor and a store where consumer goods unavailable to the general public in quantity or quality are abundantly stocked.

All of a sudden, the inhabitants of Wandlitz were subjected to the unwelcome scrutiny of the press. Foreign reporters are to be bused to Wandlitz on Monday for a look.

Gerhard Schurer, one of the three members of the new Communist Politburo who is still residing in the compound, though soon to move out, told a *Junge Welt* reporter that he was paid 4,735 marks a month, or about $2,250 at the official exchange rate and more than four times the average wage in East Germany. East German marks are being sold in the West for less than a tenth of that value.

Wandlitz, which East Germans have called Volvograd, an allusion to the Swedish automobile favored by the former regime leaders, is becoming a small pensioners' village. Mr. Honecker and most of his associates are apparently retaining their homes there for the time being, but without the extraordinary privileges.

Egon Krenz, who replaced Mr. Honecker on October 18, moved from Wandlitz, 15 miles northeast of Berlin, to a bungalow in the Berlin borough of Pankow earlier this week.

Equally upsetting for the public are the revelations of luxurious excesses enjoyed by other former leaders, who created their own private hunting preserves.

For example, Harry Tisch, the ousted Communist trade union chief, retained about 5,000 acres of hunting grounds in the Eixner Forest in Mecklenburg. There he maintained a preserve of about 200 acres for breeding wild boar. He also shot as many as 100 elk annually, according to *Neues Deutschland*, and maintained a richly appointed hunting ledge.

Near Gotha, in Thuringia, Gerhard Muller, a recently ousted party secretary, maintained a 700,000-mark hunting lodge. *Neues Deutschland* reported on Thursday that Mr. Muller also had a four-mile asphalt road laid into the hunting preserve to his lodge at a cost of 1.1 million marks. "We would have preferred to put the road where it was needed," said Georg Doring, the senior forest ranger in Luisenthal, site of the preserve.

In other cases related to the assertions of corruption, Gunter Mittag, Mr. Honecker's former chief aide, and the district party secretaries were expelled from the Communist Party on Thursday and apparently also face court actions.

According to *Berliner Zeitung*, Mr. Mittag had set up a dummy corporation called Commercial Coordination—it is not clear when it was established—which milked hard currency earnings from East German companies that exported valuable antiquities and books to the West.

In effect, said Gerhard Beil, the Foreign Trade Minister, the dummy corporation broke through the foreign trade monopoly of his ministry.

Among the East German enterprises named by Dr. Beil as having been co-opted by the dummy corporation set up by Mr. Mittag were Intrac Inc., Forum Trade Society, BIEC, Transinter and the International Trade Center.

Mr. Mittag apparently persuaded the directors of those enterprises to go along with his scheme by bribing them with hard currency, according to a party official.

The corruption cases were also a topic Thursday night in a public discussion in the Communist Central Committee Building in downtown East Berlin and also a subject of hundreds of letters sent to Communist Party newspapers.

Among the other new developments in the affairs of the party, the East German press reported today that the Writers Association of the German Democratic epublic had voted to readmit nine authors who had been expelled from the ranks for various transgressions ten years ago. Among those readmitted is Joachim Seyppel, who has made his home in West Germany since then. Mr. Seyppel was recently found guilty by a Hamburg court of libeling Hermann Kant, the head of the Writers Association.

In an interview with *Neues Deutschland*, published today, Mr. Krenz, who is head of state as well as head of the party, said, "We are not a corrupt party," but that mistakes had been made under the former leadership, of which he was also a member. "Those who violated the law belong in front of the court," he said.

Mr. Krenz said he was in favor of the proposal that the Communist Party give up its "leading role," which is enshrined in the 1974 Constitution approved by the rubber-stamp Parliament.

Tonight Mr. Honecker's name was woven into a play being performed by the Repertory Company of the Maxim Gorki Theater on Unter den Linden. The comedy, called *The Prussians Are Coming*, by Claus Hammel, has Martin Luther and Frederick the Great among its characters. "I know everything," says Frederick the Great in the first act.

"That is what Erich Honecker thought, too," Martin Luther replies. The audience responded to the exchange with a big laugh.

There were also smaller dramas taking place.

And for Two East Germans in Love, the Changes Spell Bliss
By Henry Kamm

ERFURT, EAST GERMANY, Nov. 20—The young man with a crew cut and his fiancee held hands at the restaurant table that they shared with a foreigner and, love overcoming timidity, hugged each other and giggled happily while they studied the lunch menu.

"It's hard not to see each other for six weeks," he explained when she left the table briefly. "I'm a soldier here. She had to get up at four-thirty this morning in Karl-Marx-Stadt, and at six this evening she has to take the train back."

"I should really be in uniform," he said, "but I guess it doesn't matter now." Nowadays East Germans put a special emphasis on the word "now," as if between yesterday and today their whole lives had been altered.

The young couple regretted that they had been too late to attend the Sunday rally for democracy in the main square of this capital of the Thuringia region. Of course soldiers can and do attend such meetings, he said. "I also go to church," he added. Yes, in uniform.

They said they wished they had enough time together to join the three million East Germans who once again streamed across the border between the two Germanys for weekend visits. They have never been there, they said, but there is no hurry, the borders will stay open. Soldiers are allowed to go, he said. "We were really surprised when that was announced."

"What is happening here can't be turned back," he said, and she agreed. What is new in their lives? the foreigner asked. "We have a future," the young woman, a physical therapist, replied. "A future here," he added. Yes, they said, they had thought of leaving for West Germany. "Everybody has been thinking about it," he said.

"And a lot of people are gone," the therapist added. "People where I work and many others. But now, after the turnabout, they are not leaving anymore. Maybe some will start coming back."

"Funny, a few weeks ago I wouldn't have talked like we do now," the soldier mused. "And now it's quite natural. It was always natural with friends who knew each other, but not with strangers, especially from the Federal Republic."

Learning that the stranger was not West German but American, the couple looked at each other and burst out laughing in wonderment at what they said; it was something that had never happened to them before.

"But now everything is possible," she said, and both looked pleased. Politically, the therapist said, East Germany is now a free country. "We say what we want and to whom we want," her fiancé said.

Not all is as it should be, he continued, as if to compensate for his euphoria. "What's happening should make the world more peaceful, but I'm told the English are stepping up rearmament by mounting medium-range missiles on planes, cleverly contravening the treaties," he said. "And the Republicans in West Germany are very strong," he said, referring to a right-wing party.

"Maybe they would be strong here, too," the therapist said. "A lot of people here don't like foreigners, just like the fascists over there."

The foreigners who are unpopular, they said, are students, especially from Arab and African countries, who show off their wealth in dollars and West German marks and deal on the black market, as well as Mozambican and Cuban workers who have been sent here to make up for a chronic labor shortage.

There are also many Polish black-market traders and Vietnamese workers, who the therapist said have discovered that by feigning illness one can be excused from work for weeks and then use the time to sew jeans and sell them at high prices. About 50,000 Vietnamese work in East German factories, and Vietnamese-sewn black-market jeans have become a desired, if expensive, fashion item.

"I guess you're right," the young woman said, when the foreigner asked whether to make jeans that people want to buy was not economically more useful than working in a factory that produces second-rate goods, as many state enterprises are known to do. "Our one-sided education has confused our minds."

They ordered the most expensive things on the menu, including bird's-nest soup for the young woman, which came in a demitasse cup. "It's not that we eat like that every day," the soldier said, as if to apologize for unearned luxury. Their pay is very low, they said.

"I earned a lot more as a building worker, without a specialized education, than she does after three years of school learning a difficult profession," the soldier said.

They said East Germany's economic problems would be much harder to solve than the political questions. "It's only now that we are learning how bad our situation is, and we don't know all of it yet," the therapist said. "We have been told so many lies," the soldier added.

The couple agreed that, bad as the economic situation might be, it was far better than Poland's deep crisis.

"Maybe that's because we made our revolution after working hours," the young woman said, voicing a widespread pride that East Germans have succeeded, unlike other Communist countries, in producing political upheaval without hampering economic production.

And there was the stuff of thrillers,

Old Master Spy in East Berlin Tells Why He Backs Changes
By Serge Schmemann

EAST BERLIN, Nov. 21—Among the artists, intellectuals, clerics and other former dissidents at the forefront of those in East Germany calling for changes, Markus Wolf clearly stands out.

A big, dapper man given to well-cut tweed suits, Mr. Wolf was for 33 years East Germany's master spy. In fact, he is one of the few East Germans who cannot take advantage of the new travel freedoms because his espionage coups in West Germany have made him a wanted man there.

But three years after his retirement from the Ministry of State Security, Mr. Wolf, 66 years old, has become a leading proponent of change, appearing on television talk shows and opposition panel discussions, and he was a featured speaker at the huge rally in East Berlin on November 4.

Now there is talk that the man who bedeviled the West German Government with his spies—including the celebrated Gunter Guillaume, who became a personal aide to Willy Brandt and whose uncloaking brought about the fall of the Social Democratic Chancellor in 1974—may himself become part of a new party leadership selected when the Communist Party holds its congress next month.

Mr. Wolf denies any such ambitions. But after decades of toiling in the shadows, he seems to savor the limelight, and he is not unaware that spymasters in both superpowers have risen to the top—his "good friend" the late Yuri V. Andropov in Moscow and President Bush in Washington.

His own emergence as a reformer, he insists, was not a metamorphosis. His position in the East German Ministry of State Security, where he headed foreign intelligence, gave him access to information and license to ponder the growing problems in his homeland.

And his wartime years spent in the Soviet Union left him friends among Russians who later emerged at the forefront of perestroika and glasnost, including Vladimir A. Kryuchkov, the man President Mikhail S. Gorbachev chose to head the K.G.B.

Through Mr. Kryuchkov, he knew what was happening inside Mr. Gorbachev's Moscow. And through him, Moscow evidently kept abreast of what was happening in East Germany.

"A year ago I was telling the Russians we could still turn things around here in respect to glasnost and perestroika," Mr. Wolf said in an interview, casually acknowledging a close working relationship with Moscow.

He was saying the same things at home. "From the beginning of this year I told all our leaders that this would happen," he said, reflecting on the dramatic demonstrations that had forced the Communist Party into retreat.

"I didn't know it would be so powerful, or that there was such pressure. But even a half year ago there was still a chance for the party to take charge of these events. As it turned out, it was impossible with the old leadership."

Mr. Wolf's public debut as a reformer was a book published this year. Called *The Troika,* it described the lives of three families who lived together in Moscow before World War II and followed separate paths during the war—the families of Mr. Wolf's father, Friedrich, the American historian Louis Fisher and Wilhelm Bloch, who fought in Hitler's army and ended up a businessman in West Germany. .

The biggest sensation, however, was that the celebrated spymaster took a highly critical view in the book of Stalinism, a view then still taboo in East Germany, and of East Germany's policies in the 1970's, when many artists were purged. Mr. Wolf became an overnight celebrity, now as a champion of change.

"The huge interest in my book was not linked to its content but to the new demand for the truth, not to hide past errors," he said. "These demands were very strong in the party. Whoever I met demanded change—I never met anyone, in fact, who did not demand fundamental reform. But we were unable to act in good time."

Mr. Wolf professes to be proud of the peaceful and disciplined way East Germans handled their quiet revolution.

"Gorbachev's was a revolution from above," he said. "Ours was from below. To those who know the history of Germany, this is a phenomenon, that the people have been so wise, so reserved."

His great regret, he insists, is that this initiative did not come from the party. He repeatedly refers to the Socialist Unity Party, as the East German Communist organization is formally known, as "my party," and when he talks of reform, he leaves no doubt that he is talking of changes that would preserve a Communist system.

"If we want to preserve socialism—and for that we'll fight—we must have a precise concept of how we should move ahead," he said.

Mr. Wolf said academics at Humboldt University in East Berlin were already at work on concepts for reforming the party and the economy, while the opposition, including New Forum, had no expertise in these matters.

"If the leadership of the party is capable of again taking charge of the party, I'm convinced the party will not disappear," he said.

In an interview with West German television on Monday night, however, Mr. Wolf acknowledged that the Communist Party might eventually be forced into opposition. "Considering that most opposition groups are aiming at some kind of socialism, whatever they understand by socialism, we might have to say goodbye to the thought that the future of socialism has to be bound to one single party," he said.

Mr. Wolf does not exclude his former organization from the need for change. He outlined several changes he would demand, including examination of every reported violation of law by the State Security organization and compensation for its victims; a "new thinking, especially in regard to dissidents," and tight controls over the security apparatus.

Rehabilitating the State Security apparatus stands to be a major challenge. The hated Staasi have been a major target of virtually every demonstration, and Mr. Wolf himself faced prolonged jeers when he rose to address the demonstration on November 4.

"Workers of my former ministry must appear in public and fight for public confidence," he said. "If the public believes that this organization really takes care of state security, and that the rights of individuals are protected, it should accept it."

Only in Rumania did it appear that the old guard was in full control.

In Rumania, the Old Order Won't Budge
By Alan Riding

BUCHAREST, RUMANIA, Nov. 24—In a huge display of government control, tens of thousands of workers were marched to a demonstration here today to celebrate the reelection of President Nicolae Ceausescu as General Secretary of the Communist Party.

But while flags fluttered cheerfully amid a sea of posters of Mr. Ceausescu and his wife, Elena, and of banners proclaiming the people's joy, the Government was unable to inject the least enthusiasm into the crowd, which stood solemnly in the cold awaiting the chance to go home.

Until the 71-year-old President had spoken, though, burly secret policemen, militiamen and members of the Patriotic Guard blocked all exits to the plaza in front of the Communist Party headquarters to insure that no one left. Finally, after a four-hour wait for a 10-minute message. the ritual was over.

Like everything else that occurred during this week's Communist Party Congress, the demonstration had gone as planned. Not a squeak of dissidence was heard, and tonight Rumanians could see television pictures of "the people" expressing gratitude for Mr. Ceausescu's willingness to remain in charge.

Earlier, the party congress also dutifully elected a new 467-member Central Committee, which named a 47-member executive committee, which in turn picked Mr. Ceausescu as party leader. The votes took place behind closed doors, but it was later announced that each election was unanimous.

The composition of the executive committee, which is equivalent to the Politburo in other Communist countries, and Mr. Ceausescu's final address to the congress both confirmed what had long been expected: After 24 years of what is known here as the Ceausescu Era, nothing had changed.

Only two new full members of the executive committee were named. As in the recent past, Emil Bobu, a longtime Communist leader, was listed immediately after Mr. Ceausescu, while Elena Ceausescu was ranked third in the party hierarchy. The President's son, Nicu, was also reelected as an alternate member of the committee.

In his closing speech to the 3,500-member congress, Mr. Ceausescu said the party had prepared a 20-year program that would lead the country to "shining horizons" as "multilaterally developed socialism" is strengthened. "By the beginning of the third millennium, we will be ready for the next stage, which is Communism," he said.

In contrast to his opening address on Monday, when he referred disapprovingly to those socialist governments that favor moving toward capitalism, Mr. Ceausescu avoided even indirect reference to events elsewhere in Eastern Europe today. But he stressed the need for "still greater unity" in the country's Communist Party.

In a meeting with foreign delegates attending the Congress on Thursday, though, he reiterated his call for the annulment of the Hitler-Stalin pact that led to the redefinition of some European frontiers, including those of Rumania with the Soviet Union, at the beginning of World War II.

Referring to the coming meeting off Malta between President Bush and the Soviet President, Mikhail S. Gorbachev, he added: "That is why today, too, mankind is highly sensitive to a possible new accord between the United States and the Soviet Union to the detriment of other peoples. And you know well that this is something of concern to many states."

In his address to the Congress today, he focused on internal affairs, leaving no doubt that he planned to continue ruling Rumania indefinitely. "Almost sixty years ago I first joined the party," he said, "and in the future I will always be a soldier in the ranks of the Rumanian Communist Party."

Interrupted constantly by well-orchestrated applause and chants of "Ceausescu Heroism! Rumanian Communism!" he went on: "The job of General Secretary is not honorific but one of great responsibility. It is not easy to be General Secretary of a party that wants to construct socialism. But I will respond with all my strength."

If at times the congress seemed to respond to him more out of discipline than spontaneity, the short, graying party chief gave every impression of believing what he was saying, holding up the "golden dream" of Communism with the energy and emotion of a fundamentalist preacher.

When the rousing sound of the Communist Party's anthem was piped into the congress hall, only Mr. Ceausescu seemed to be singing, drumming his fingers on the podium and waving his right arm to the rhythm of the song as if each epic phrase was something to be taken literally.

As the Czechoslovaks marched and threatened strikes and as the East German Communists purged their more prominent leaders, the Hungarians went about the business of dismantling communist forms. Earlier in the year the party removed its hard-line leader and then voted to abandon its communist name, effectively declaring itself bankrupt. Now the whole country was voting in a referendum to determine the manner in which it would choose its President. At issue was whether the planned free election was to take place before or after countrywide balloting to elect a parliament in fully competitive multiparty elections. The ruling party, the successor to the Communists, were hoping to have the presidential vote before those elections, when they would still control Parliament. To that end they were favoring a boycott of the referendum; if less than 50 percent of the electorate voted, then the results would be nullified, enabling them to be free to pursue their own schedule.

Hungarians Hold First Free Vote in 42 Years, Shunning a Boycott

By Henry Kamm

BUDAPEST, Nov. 26—In the first free national vote in 42 years, Hungarians went to the polls today for a referendum on when a presidential election will be held.

Contrary to pessimistic forecasts, they did so in sufficient numbers to make the referendum valid, insuring the failure of the ruling party's silent boycott of the referendum. The vote was forced by some of the country's new opposition groups, although it was opposed by others. . . .

Participation of at least half of Hungary's 7.8 million voters was required to make the referendum valid. Two hours after most polling stations closed, the national election commission announced that an estimated 53.6 percent of eligible voters took part.

Election officials said many people were unfamiliar with voting procedures and asked how to fill out the ballots. After four decades of one-party rule by the Communists, some even asked what answers to give to the questions on the timing of the election. . . .

And when the votes were counted, it was clear that the voters had dealt another rebuff to those who had so recently been Communist but were now calling themselves something else.

Hungarians Reject Election Timetable of the Ruling Party

By Henry Kamm

BUDAPEST, Nov. 27—Voters rejected the election timetable of the ruling party by the narrowest of margins in a referendum on Sunday, forcing it to abandon its plan to elect the first President of the republic while it retained full control of the Government.

In today's counting of Hungary's first free national vote since World War II, a narrow Government lead wilted steadily until Minister of State Imre Pozsgay conceded that the opposition proposal to delay the presidential voting had carried the day. Mr. Pozsgay was to have been the ruling party's presidential candidate. Under the plan adopted by the Communist-controlled Parliament, presidential elections would have been held on January 7, before a new, democratically chosen Parliament is elected. Parliamentary elections are to be held by June, with late March considered the most likely time.

The ruling party, which until last month was known as the Communist Party, has renamed itself the Socialist Party in an effort to remain in power despite the unpopularity of Communists in Hungarian society.

"We can be certain that the number of yes votes was higher than the no votes," Mr. Pozsgay said at a news conference. A yes vote was in favor of delaying the presidential election.

The mechanics of the referendum were complicated. The most important question the voters were asked to decide was whether the presidential election proposed for January 7 should proceed.

A turnout of less than 50 percent, regardless of the vote outcome, would have meant that the referendum was null and that the election would be held as scheduled in January.

Once it was clear that enough people had voted to validate the referendum, the question became whether they would confirm the election date or vote it down, in effect delaying the choice of a President until after Parliament is elected.

The cancellation of the January 7 election works in favor of the opposition and against the Government and its candidate, Mr. Pozsgay. If he had been able to run in January, he would have had the advantages of incumbency of the Government and party.

Now the choice of President appears to go to a new Parliament, once it is elected. Most of the opposition feels that this will make it easier for the opposition to field and elect its own candidate.

As Mr. Pozsgay conceded defeat, the official count still showed the no votes ahead with 50.2 percent of those counted. But the Hungarian state radio said that in the final count the yeses would carry by a few thousand.

"It's an enormous victory," said Miklos Haraszti, a leader of the Alliance of Free Democrats, the party that had imposed the referendum on the Government.

The Free Democrats, supported by three other parties, opposed the Government's schedule on the ground that it was undemocratic to choose so important an official while the ruling party still controlled all essential offices and access to state-run television and most of the press. . . .

In Prague, it was still too early for formal referendum, so opinions were being registered by shouts of acclamation, placards and graffiti.

If the Party Has Its Back to the Wall, It's a Wall with New Posters on It

By Esther B. Fein

PRAGUE, Nov. 26—The underground press is thriving in Prague these days. The rare clandestine documents of previous generations have given way to a flood of homemade handbills and posters that adorn the city's walls and windows, subway cars and stations.

If you want to know what is going on in Prague, you have to read the walls, and the windows, and the sidewalks, and the railings, and the bumpers of city buses, all of which are covered with print.

Typed by students on home computers and typewriters, or in some cases hand painted, this "subway samizdat" has been the most effective means of spreading the word about the opposition movement and of informing the public about coming events like today's human chain, Saturday's mass at St. Vitus Cathedral and the weekend change of venue for a daily demonstration.

Even the subway workers have got involved. Today, announcers in the stations let people know the time and place of the rally where people were to hold hands and form chains of human solidarity. The announcers, who normally give the routings of trains, added the information that subway workers would be honoring the general strike from noon till 2 P.M. on Monday.

"It's a war on walls," said Jan Urban, one of the leaders of Civic Forum, the recently formed umbrella opposition group. "In a system where the state owns and controls the mass media, this is the only way to begin a campaign against the regime." . . .

In the last 48 hours, state television has metamorphosed from a tool of the Government into a vehicle for the opposition. The daily mass rallies are televised live and uncensored, including calls for an end to the Communist Party monopoly on political power. The television even broadcast an interview with Ivan Lendl, the tennis star who defected from Czechoslovakia and now lives in the United States, saying he would be delighted to return for a visit if true change took root here.

But the most innovative and provocative program is one shown on a television set placed in the window at the Magic Lantern Theater, headquarters for the Civic Forum, and on one in the window at the Gallerie Manes, an art studio and another informal gathering place for dissidents.

255

Both sets offer regular showings of a student-produced video that depicts the violent breakup by police of a student demonstration on Friday, November 17. The video also shows the daily rallies in Wenceslas Square that followed that night of violence. Also included are interviews with opposition leaders and snippets from the official press that have been exposed as lies.

These new forms of expression, which just two weeks ago would have been cause for arrest, have become so widespread and accepted that a worker who attended the Prague Communist Party meeting on Saturday said he overheard one member of the leadership asking another what time today's demonstration was scheduled for.

"I don't know," the official was overheard to say. "Why don't you go outside and check the wall?" . . .

There is a small, poignant sign of the new mood here on the faces of public clocks in town. Many have been deliberately stopped at 5 minutes before 12, and there are posters around showing a clock with its hands in the same position.

"It is a symbol that time is up for the Communist Party," explained Petr Krechler, a student who has been attending the daily rallies. "It's time for a new shift to come on.". . .

Since the days of Franz Kafka into the time of Milan Kundera, Prague has been a literary city. Its best known dissident, Vaclav Havel, is a playwright known for works of irony. Therefore it was not so strange that a longtime resident used the imagery of fiction to explain that for the last forty years, since Communists came to power here, people have become soured, feeling like a woman forced to marry the wrong man.

"It is like a young woman who is very much in love but she is made to marry another man," said the woman. "But she lives, she has children and she carries on in a kind of muted way, as if it were a normal life, even though in her heart, she knows it isn't normal. Then one day she sees her youthful lover on a bridge and suddenly, she comes alive.

"We are like that woman, and our lover may still be on the other side of the bridge, but at least he is now visible."

Millions of Czechoslovaks Increase Pressure on Party with Two-Hour General Strike

By R. W. Apple, Jr.

PRAGUE, Nov. 27—Millions of Czechs and Slovaks walked off their jobs and into the streets at midday today, bringing Prague and the rest of the country to a standstill. It was a powerful demonstration of national solidarity in support of free elections and opposition to Communist domination.

Rivers of people flowed down boulevards and into main squares, not only here and in Bratislava, the nation's second city, but also in Brno and Ostrava and Rosice, industrial towns where the party ruled supreme until a week or so ago.

The meticulously organized and nonviolent general strike, which lasted from noon to 2 P.M., seemed a stunning rebuke to the Communists, whose legitimacy as a party is rooted in the support of those who laid down their tools in protest today. It was the largest outpouring of dissent in this country of 15 million people since February 1948, when demonstrations orchestrated by the Communists toppled what was then the only functioning multiparty democratic government in Eastern Europe.

"It has become an unstoppable wave," a senior Western diplomat said after viewing the throngs. "One wants to avoid overexcitement, but the party has clearly fallen apart, except for some cardboard faces who meet every other day. It has no program and no response to the strike, except wishing it away. Now it is in danger of crumbling like the Polish party and finding itself excluded from power altogether."

The Communist leadership, appearing to lose strength by the hour, seemed to be moving closer to talks with Civic Forum, the new opposition group led by Vaclav Havel, the playwright and longtime dissident, who was repeatedly jailed by the Communist authorities in the 21 years after the crushing of the liberal Government led by Alexander Dubcek.

Seeking to keep the pressure on while at the same time trying to reflect a sense of responsibility, Civic Forum said in a statement issued tonight that it would negotiate with the Government if the Government responded positively on Tuesday to its demands but that, if not, it would call for the Government's resignation. The statement said the organization had "come to the conclusion that the original demands made by Civic Forum have essentially been met or are being met," and it was time to move on to larger issues, like the Communist monopoly on power.

"What is needed is a cooling down of emotions," said Vaclav Maly, a spokesman for the Forum, but he and other representatives of the group said they could restart strikes and demonstrations at once if the negotiations proved fruitless.

It seemed highly unlikely that the talks could await the special Communist Party congress scheduled for January 26 that was announced Sunday night.

A second shake-up in the Politburo in three days, announced late Sunday night, appeared to have done nothing to halt the momentum of the opposition. Three hard-liners were dropped, leaving only one hard-liner and two relatively moderate members of the old guard on the thirteen-member body. Seven new members were named, including three or four who back pluralism in one way or another.

Prague Evening, the newspaper of the city community committee, said the party could not survive because it had no program.

Rude Pravo, the organ of the national party, spoke of the paralysis of the Central Committee and of "political mummies" who were blocking action. It urged the party to prepare for "free democratic elections" by developing a new program "that will be supported by all."

On a new television program called *The Government Speaks to You,* ministers said that they favored a free-market economy—yet another departure from party orthodoxy.

Some Communist elements, including grass-roots organizations, still seemed prepared to fight for survival, and Karel Urbanek, the new party leader, appeared on television tonight, urging a group of miners to stand fast.

But Prime Minister Ladislav Adamec—who seems to have become a rival of sorts to Mr. Urbanek and whose job is believed by some to be in jeopardy as a result—has already begun negotiations with Civic Forum, and is to report to the group on Tuesday on the Politburo's reaction to its demands.

Bitter strife between hard- and soft-line factions was reported at Sunday night's Politburo meeting, but no one proposed using violent means to suppress the demonstrations. Government figures said no one had urged that since last Friday, when the party leadership started to crack.

It was hard even to spot a Communist between noon and 2 P.M.

today. A whole nation seemed to be in the streets, with more than 900 factories and other businesses closed, urban mass transit halted everywhere and only hospitals, nursing homes, food stores and a few other enterprises continuing to operate.

At exactly noon, the lights went off and doors clanged shut in cafés, bookstores, souvenir shops and airline offices around Old Town Square, a baroque complex in central Prague considered one of the most beautiful architectural settings in Europe. High in the fantastic turrets of Tyn Church, a deeply toned melancholy bell tolled.

In the middle of the square, hundreds of young women with babies in carriages gathered around the statue of Jan Hus, the religious reformer. They had been sent there, where they could be protected, lest the babies be hurt in the crush elsewhere.

The pressure was greatest in Wenceslas Square, but there were throngs as well on Narodni Avenue, where the country's leading actors and actresses gathered to wave to the strikers and shout encouragement.

The distinctive Czechoslovak flag—a blue triangular field at the left, with a band of white and a band of red on the right—hung from balconies, fluttered from poles and decorated windows everywhere. Flag-colored ribbons were pinned to every lapel and even to the collars of dogs.

On every window—even that of the Beryiozka, a restaurant run by the Soviet Government, even that of the headquarters of Cedok, the state travel agency there were signs announcing "Generalni Stavka," general strike.

In Bratislava's main square, they danced. In the old ghetto in Prague, high school students marched beneath their banners, chanting slogans of freedom as they passed historic synagogues. At the Inter-Continental Hotel, they hauled down the foreign flags in the courtyard and ran Czechoslovak flags up all ten poles. A convoy of taxicabs, lights on and horns honking, snaked through the streets of the capital. . . .

"Today's events show that the whole nation supports the students," one of their leaders, Martin Mejstrik, said in a speech this afternoon.

State television carried pictures of the strike from all over the country—from the brewing town of Ceske Budejovice in Bohemia, the mining town of Banska Bystrica in the Tatra Mountains, and from Kavci Hory, the mountain overlooking Prague where the television transmitters are situated.

In East Germany, the disclosures about the private lives of the party oligarchs brought cries of shame and calls for punishment.

Where East Berlin's Elite Lived It Up
By David Binder

WANDLITZ, EAST GERMANY—For the last three decades, the ladder to the top of what might sarcastically be called a workers' paradise ended here in a heavily wooded compound surrounded by a 1.5-mile concrete wall. The compound was the home of the 23-member Communist Politburo that ruled this country until six weeks ago.

It was something highly unusual in the Communist world, a ghetto for the elite designed to protect the leadership from any rebellion or terrorist action.

The order for its construction a few miles north of the capital came from Walter Ulbricht, who ruled the German Democratic Republic from its inception until he was ousted in 1971. His successor as Communist Party chief and head of state was Erich Honecker, who was deposed on October 17 as a result of mass demonstrations across the country and the sudden flight—at that time illegal—of close to 200,000 citizens to the West.

The rationale for the compound encompassing 23 houses, a small department store, medical clinic, swimming pool and movie theater, as explained here today by a state security officer, was "the events in Hungary in 1956 and other factors that resulted from the cold war."

Although Gunter Wolf, who ranks as a lieutenant general in East Germany's State Security Service, did not touch on the subject, one of those Cold War factors was the popular uprising of June 17, 1953, which compelled Mr. Ulbricht and fellow members of the Communist leadership to flee East Berlin in the trucks of the Soviet Army, some riding to safety in Potsdam, others flying all the way to Moscow.

The Hungarian uprising, in which a number of Moscow loyalists were killed, was not something the East German leaders wanted repeated here.

Completed in early 1961, the so-called Wandlitz Residential Object Forest Settlement was in some ways a forerunner of the Berlin wall: the border fortifications begun on August 13, 1961, to seal in East Germany.

The difference is that the wall around Wandlitz, guarded at all times by 24 armed soldiers of the Feliks E. Dzerzhinsky regiment, named for Lenin's secret police chief, is painted forest green. The Berlin wall was not painted, except for graffiti.

In the low fog that hangs over the slush of a late German November, the Wandlitz wall is scarcely visible among the thick stand of white and red pines, beeches, birches and rhododendrons here.

So, how well did the Communist elite live all these years? The department store had Western electronic products and clothes and cosmetics and toiletries that were unavailable to the general East German public until last month. The narrow elite of 23 families wanted for nothing. Two maids were provided free for each house. The rents ranged from 300 to 600 marks a month, or $168 to $336 at the official exchange rate. They could choose to view Western movies banned for the East German public.

What is surprising about Wandlitz, which is the name of the nearest village on this sandy flatland, is its banality. It is as if every member of Germany's petite bourgeoisie had voted on the architecture and furnishings: red-tile roofs topping cream-colored stucco two-story houses, a few marble tiles, parquet floors, big (but not picture) windows, pink tablecloths in the restaurant and artificial palms and magnolias on the edges of the modest swimming pool.

There are narrow asphalt roads, few toilets or bathrooms, gateposts but no fences for the houses, several aquariums with exotic fish and a bronze sculpture of a waitress carrying a tray under her right arm in front of the department store—sculptor unknown.

"As you see," General Wolf said, "no Italian marble, no silk wallpaper, no African wood." In fact, he said, everything to be seen now in the Wandlitz was "made in the German Democratic Republic."

Only two members of the past and current Politburo are living here now, Gerhard Schurer and Werner Jarowinsky, and they are moving out soon, General Wolf said. Mr. Honecker and other former members of his Politburo will leave "soon," he said.

"It can only help us to expose this," General Wolf said. "I accompanied Erich Honecker on almost all of his foreign journeys, and I can tell you that I have seen far more luxury in foreign capitals than you see here. I was there at the home of the President of Mexico in Mexico City. He had a whole stable of horses. I can only say that, compared with that, we are, as we say, in German, orphans."

The lieutenant general, a slender man in his 60's, said that since he had been under military orders, he could not and did not raise his voice against the practices of Wandlitz. He said he was unable to estimate what the compound had cost because the files were in the hands of the ministerial consul of East Germany. But he estimated that its upkeep ran into several hundred thousand marks a year.

Until today, only a handful of foreigners had been allowed through Wandlitz's modernistic blue-and-black-painted gates. Last week, the Government admitted hordes of journalists from the country's Communist news media.

"The situation for us, women and men in Wandlitz, is not easy," General Wolf said.

They were marching and remonstrating all over the lands over which the Soviet empire had held sway since war's end. Old satraps who had ruled in ways learned from Moscow were being toppled and the dogma and ideology they had intoned were being ridiculed. In the heart of the empire, Mikhail Gorbachev, the man who had urged the old satraps to reform, now seemed concerned that too much might be changing.

Marxism Will Revive, Gorbachev Insists
By Bill Keller

MOSCOW, Nov. 26—Faced with a growing clamor from Communist Party conservatives, President Mikhail S. Gorbachev published a manifesto today insisting that Marxism will be revived in the Soviet Union, and under the leadership of the Communist Party.

With Communist governments in headlong retreat throughout Eastern Europe, the document, spread across two full pages of *Pravda*, was apparently intended to reassure the party faithful at this uneasy juncture that Communism is not collapsing, at least not here.

"Today we face the difficult challenge of reviving the authority of Marxist thought, the Marxist approach to reality," he wrote, and asserted that "at this complex stage" the party must keep its monopoly on political power.

Mr. Gorbachev described his goal as "humane socialism," a clear echo of the "socialism with a human face" promoted by the Communist liberalizers of the Prague Spring in Czechoslovakia in 1968.

Mr. Gorbachev's manifesto—essentially his revisionist view of Marxism—seemed intended to counter conservatives, who have recently shown signs of trying to consolidate their forces against what they view as heresies in the party.

Tonight, the central television showed excerpts from a rally sponsored last week by Leningrad party leaders in which the crowd poured out their anger at the Politburo and legislature for tolerating a drift toward capitalism.

As the crowd waved banners denouncing private businessmen as "crooks" and warning Mr. Gorbachev, "Mikhail Sergeyevich, pay attention to the party," speakers bitterly lamented the party's loss of authority.

"Maybe we're in this situation because of the coldbloodedness and absence of emotions that prevail in our Politburo," yelled one speaker.

The Politburo has had its chance, shouted another, "now let us steer."

Aleksandr N. Yakovlev, a Politburo member who is Mr. Gorbachev's senior ally in rethinking Communism, appeared to have the Leningrad gathering in mind when he told a Soviet television interviewer tonight that the country must guard against "these dangerous conservatives."

"When they say, 'let us steer,' sometimes I wonder if they're really saying, 'let us shoot,' " Mr. Yakovlev said.

In addition to the restive party regulars, Mr. Gorbachev has recently witnessed the growing influence of new "worker fronts." These groups, backed by party and trade union functionaries, are demanding protection against the economic insecurity certain to come with moves toward a market economy.

Responding to this new lobby, the Soviet legislature last week approved a freeze on the prices of soap, nylons, cigarettes and other consumer goods.

Mr. Gorbachev's article in the party newspaper was presented as "a synthesis and development" of several recent speeches, and was aimed at emphasizing his program's Marxist-Leninist roots and working-class orientation.

He said, however, that Lenin might have been wrong about one central point of his philosophy, that there can be no intermediate phase between capitalism and socialism.

This was Mr. Gorbachev's most explicit suggestion that the "new socialism" he has in mind for the Soviet Union will be a hybrid, incorporating aspects of capitalism.

Such speeches have little appeal to those who favor more far-reaching changes and who chafe at Mr. Gorbachev's caution. But the Soviet leader seems to feel a need to shore up his defenses against the conservatives as he heads off on visits to Italy and the Vatican and prepares for his Malta meeting next weekend with President Bush.

The article appeared as the Polish Prime Minister, Tadeusz Mazowiecki, the first non-Communist to lead a government in the Soviet bloc, was leaving Moscow after a remarkably warm reception, and as the Communist Party in Czechoslovakia was wobbling under public pressure.

Often criticized for falsely raising public expectations of quick results, Mr. Gorbachev today conceded that the remaking of socialism "is a process that will stretch beyond the decade into the 21st century."

For Kremlinologists, the television interview with Mr. Yakovlev tonight was a tantalizing hint of further shifts in the Politburo.

Mr. Yakovlev, regarded as Mr. Gorbachev's main intellectual ally, is nominally in charge of foreign affairs. But his comments tonight dealt exclusively with ideology, a portfolio that belongs to the more conservative Vadim A. Medvedev.

Mr. Medvedev has recently been under open attack for trying to fire the editor of the country's most popular newspaper, and for intervening to limit the freedoms outlined in a new draft law on the press.

As in East Germany, the crowds in Prague also prevailed.

Czechoslovakia's Moment in Time
By Serge Schmemann

PRAGUE, Nov. 28—It seemed somehow appropriate that when the old regime in Czechoslovakia formally agreed to cede its monopoly on power, the deed was done between a caretaker Prime Minister and an opposition lacking even a formal headquarters.

So dizzyingly swift was the downfall of Milos Jakes and his associates in the Communist leadership that when Prime Minister Ladislav Adamec met today with Vaclav Havel and the other opposition leaders of the Civic Forum, the participants seemed to be sweeping away some unpleasant remnants before plunging into the next and far more complex phase in the shaping of a post-Communist Czechoslovakia.

As a Civic Forum representative told a news conference today, "The meeting of the demands today is just a recognition of the de facto situation on the part of the Government."

To be sure, much remained to be resolved and prepared. Mr. Adamec's pledge to delete the "leading role" of the Communist Party from the Constitution still left the Communist apparatus very much in place, running the factories, schools, courts and Government bureaus. There were still free elections to secure, ministries to fill, economic plans to forge.

But the vast force of humanity so strikingly mobilized over a week and a half of demonstrations and yesterday's two-hour general strike—a power manifest in the red, white and blue ribbons worn by every second Czechoslovak, in the flags decorating every house, in the myriad notices plastered to the shop windows of Prague and in the jubilant air pervading the old capital—seemed to preclude any chance of a comeback by the old guard.

Twenty-one years earlier, it required Soviet tanks to stifle the Prague Spring reform period. Now the Kremlin seemed almost irrelevant, Russians totally absent from the demonstrations or the slogans except for the rare tribute to Mikhail S. Gorbachev. And without Moscow, the old guard had proven to be only a flimsy facade.

Just as the Czechoslovaks followed their neighbors in the march to freedom, so too did they copy them in savoring their moment of triumph. Like the East Germans dancing through the newly opened Berlin wall, or the Hungarians cheering the restoration of the republic, Czechoslovaks also found themselves at that euphoric moment in their revolution before the heady wine of freedom began to exact its inevitable price.

The glow was almost tangible in the streets. People seemed unusually polite, even affectionate toward one another. At an impromptu public discussion in the small Ypsilon studio theater, an actor drew laughs when he said he saw a tram grind to a halt and come back in reverse to pick up a tardy passenger.

Students went around to shops with razor blades and sponges to rub off dated notices from among the hundreds plastered in virtually every shop window. Others posted large signs urging people not to spray-paint slogans onto walls.

"Democracy is fine," said 21-year-old Pavel Strida as he looked at the word "democracy" sprayed onto a stucco wall, "but it's the people who will have to clean and repaint the walls."

The Czechoslovak colors seemed to be everywhere, demonstrating a welling up of national pride. The symbol for the Civic Forum, the umbrella group of the opposition, included a leaf from the national tree—the lime in its design.

"Before this, I was afraid of what would come next, afraid that we would become poor like the Poles," Mr. Strida said. "Our professor told us recently that our country was turning into a memorial display of Communism. But now we have taken our own way."

At any rate, they had taken the first step along the way, shedding the yoke of a system that had dragged Czechoslovakia from the front ranks of industrialized Europe to the sidelines.

But already now, even while the Civic Forum searched for a headquarters and Mr. Adamec looked for new ministers, the faint outlines of the future were taking shape—pointing, many here thought, to a pluralistic social democracy and a market-oriented economy.

A central role in the future seemed likely for Walter Kamarek, the director of the Economic Forecasting Institute, who had argued for years that Czechoslovakia needed to inject market forces and to accept democratic pluralism if it was to reform its economy.

Another economist, Vladimir Karlez of the Academy of Sciences, was reported preparing a plan for the opening of the economy to domestic entrepreneurs and foreign investors.

How Czechoslovakia would fare in a post-Communist order was, at this stage, impossible to predict. But in comparison with Poland, Hungary and East Germany, at least, it seemed reasonably well positioned.

Czechoslovakia could not boast of East Germany's special links to a prosperous Western patron. But that also safeguarded it from the rush for West German marks and goods that has seized the East Germans since the border between the two Germanys fell open.

A well-developed industrial base, even one allowed to grow decrepit under forty years of Communist mismanagement, still afforded the Czechoslovaks a disciplined labor force and a base to build on.

With the population at a manageable 15 million and a foreign debt nowhere near the level of Hungary's or Poland's, Czechoslovakia seemed free of imminent economic crisis.

And a rich cultural tradition, coupled with a lingering faith in socialism, seemed to preclude any major social problems—at least in the immediate future.

The very swiftness of its revolution seemed to be in Czechoslovakia's favor. Though the bloodshed during the police attacks on November 17 still hung heavy in the public memory, the subsequent pace of events gave these days an improvisational character that seemed to sustain idealism and a party-like atmosphere.

There was not the fatigue of Poland's long series of strikes, nor the demoralizing exodus of East Germany. Rather, there was still energy to burn and the glow on the horizon was still bright.

By one of those lovely quirks so prevalent in these heady days, Civic Forum was given the Magic Lantern experimental theater for its temporary headquarters. For their evening news conferences, leaders of the opposition sat before a newly built set representing the last tunnel of the Minotaur—a maze guarded by a mythical creature with the head of a bull and the body of a man—with the light at the end of it glowing behind.

They had not planned it that way, nor had the theater, nor had Czechoslovakia. But in the spirit of the moment, improvisation and destiny seemed to blend in wondrous ways.

And, in the city that was Kafka's birthplace, the bargain was sealed by an often-imprisoned ironic playwright.

Prague's Unlikely Collaborators for Change: Party Stalwart and Ex-prisoner Havel, Often-Jailed Dramatist, Became Symbol of Dissent
By Serge Schmemann

PRAGUE, Nov. 28—If proof is needed that the pen is mightier than the sword, then Vaclav Havel is a veritable smoking gun.

In and out of prisons over the last twenty years, his plays banned in his native land, the playwright today accepted the figurative surrender of his tormentors at a meeting with Prime Minister Ladislav Adamec.

In a coincidence that seemed to close the symbolic circle, it was also today that *Rude Pravo*, the main party newspaper, announced that the Czech and Slovak ministries of culture had lifted twenty-year-old bans on many works of art, including the writings of Mr. Havel.

Mr. Havel, to be sure, did not achieve his role in a vacuum. There is a tradition in this part of the world that intellectual integrity and independent art translate into raw political power.

Writers and artists have played major roles in dissident movements in the Soviet Union and throughout Eastern Europe. In Prague, the release of censored works also freed, for example, the writings of Milan Kundera, and among several prominent Czechoslovaks returning from exile was an actor, Pavel Landovsky.

"In our country there has been a tradition since the nineteenth century that social movements were always ignited by the intelligentsia," Mr. Havel said in an interview in the current issue of the West German weekly magazine *Spiegel*. "That was the case in 1968, and this time is no different."

But few writers or intellectuals have been thrust to the forefront of their nation's destiny quite as dramatically as Mr. Havel, the sardonic 53-year-old playwright and essayist. As uncompromising in his resistance to the totalitarian state as he is in his ironic plays, he withstood censure, prison and the muzzle to become the premier symbol of Czech dissidence in the years after the Soviet Union intervened to crush the Prague Spring of 1968.

Active in 1968 as chairman of an unsanctioned Club of Independent Writers, he subsequently helped found the Charter 77 dissident movement and through his clashes with the authorities was repeatedly sent to prison.

Mr. Havel was on one of his stints in prison only last May, this time for trying to lay a wreath at the grave of Jan Palach, a student who burned himself to death when the Warsaw Pact forces invaded in 1968. As recently as a month ago, the police dragged Mr. Havel from his sickbed to put him in detention on the eve of anticipated demonstrations marking the October 28 National Day.

Now, at the huge demonstrations that have abruptly routed Czechoslovakia's neo-Stalinist regime, the crowds have chanted "Havel! Havel!" as the writer has proclaimed the demise of the system he fought with pen in hand and his willingness to join a government that would guide Czechoslovakia to democracy.

"If someone spends his life writing the truth without caring for the consequences, he inevitably becomes a political authority in a totalitarian regime," Mr. Havel said in the magazine interview. "I am willing, and may be able, to assume a role for a short time. This transitional phase may need symbolic representatives, who are not politicians but who represent the hopes of society."

What was good for democracy, however, was not conducive to his art. "I confess I'd like to arrange with the Interior Ministry to be free three days a week and to go to prison for two days a week to take a break from freedom," he said in the interview.

Vaclav Havel was born on October 5, 1936, in Prague, where his father was a well-to-do building contractor and restaurant owner. Legend holds that his father tried to evict the Soviet newspaper

Pravda from one of his buildings. Mr. Havel stlll lives in a building built by his father.

The "bourgeois" background blocked Mr. Havel in his education, and his early postwar years included work as a taxi driver and study of traffic-control automation. But from his early years he wrote, and in June 1967 he caused a stir at a writers' congress when he criticized as absurd censorship and the Communist apparatus.

After the 1968 invasion, he left Prague and settled in a remote farming village near Troutnova, where he worked in a brewery. His growing body of plays was banned across East Europe, but they rapidly gained him critical notice in the West.

Mr. Havel was among the chief theoreticians of the movement, and his essay setting out his ideas on national resurgence in a totalitarian state, "The Power of the Powerless," was widely studied inside and outside Czechoslovakia. In it, he argued that citizens "living in truth" could successfully confront and overturn dictatorial rulers.

His involvement with Charter 77 led to the first of Mr. Havel's several stints in prison. The longest was from October 1979 to February 1983, for founding a group called the Committee for the Defense of the Unjustly Persecuted and for "keeping up contacts with émigrés." He later collected the letters he wrote from prison to his wife in a widely read volume, *Letters to Olga.*

Last January, Mr. Havel was sentenced to eight months in prison for trying to lay the wreath at the tomb of Jan Palach. But after an international outcry, the sentence was reduced to four months.

The authorities also tried to get Mr. Havel to emigrate, but he refused. He refused even to travel abroad to accept international drama prizes in the Netherlands and Sweden for fear he might not be permitted to return home.

At one point, the recently ousted Communist Party leader, Milos Jakes, privately admitted that the harassment of the playwright had only made him better known. The comment was secretly taped and further added to Mr. Havel's renown.

Mr. Havel's plays—the better-known include *Protest*, *Temptation, The Saviors* and *Audience*—are generally marked by strong irony, which sometimes strikes audiences as absurdist.

Many of these satirical comedies center on the dumb mechanization of man in a totalitarian world. In an interview last March, Mr. Havel said his satires should not be understood as "satire coined to some concrete conditions," but rather as "parables for human life itself."

In a very short time Europe had become an uncertain place. As Communist power eroded, new possibilities emerged for those people and states that had until recently been subject to predictable rigors. Political aspirations often translated into geographic visions. The old postwar Europe was giving way to a new, not yet clearly defined continent. The shaping of this emerging Europe was proving to be the critical issue, supplanting earlier concerns with disarmament, the third world and regional conflicts. What were the competing visions of Europe that were forming in Moscow, in Western Europe and Washington as the binding force of Communism weakened?

Gorbachev's Hope for Future: "A Common European Home"
By Bill Keller

MOSCOW, Nov. 29—When it comes to the future of Europe, no one accuses President Mikhail S. Gorbachev of lacking vision.

The Soviet leader's vision—he calls it "a common European home"—is in some respects utopian. It has been shaped in large part by the tumult of events beyond the Kremlin's control, including economic desperation at home and explosive popular aspirations in Eastern Europe.

From the time Mr. Gorbachev first broached the "common home" notion on a visit to France in 1985, it has been regarded in the West as more a speechwriter's conceit than a basis for serious discussion.

But as Mr. Gorbachev and President Bush prepare to survey together the wreckage of the postwar order in Europe, both Soviet and Western specialists have begun to look more seriously at the Soviet leader's vision of what might replace it.

In interviews conducted as successive spasms of democracy struck Eastern Europe, Soviet officials and scholars and Western diplomats here said the West had not yet grasped the magnitude of what Mr. Gorbachev wants in Europe, of the overall vision toward which he would like to maneuver Mr. Bush in their meeting this week.

In effect, what Mr. Gorbachev seeks is a huge exchange, in which Moscow surrenders its costly ambitions of expansionism—at least beyond its postwar borders.

In return, Moscow wants admission to the club of Western industrial countries, bringing with it technology and a period of calm in which to focus on the problem that really threatens Soviet security:

an economy that cannot compete in the world or satisfy the growing wants of its own people.

"The common European home means decomposition of the empire, in our own interest," said Andranik Migranyan, an analyst at one of the most influential research groups, the Institute for the Economy of the World Socialist System.

"In the end, it means the return to a single European civilization," said Fyodor M. Burlatsky, chairman of the human rights panel of the parliamentary committee on foreign relations.

As Mr. Burlatsky suggests, this Europe is not so much a geographical concept as a cultural one—it means Western civilization, including the United States. What follows is a rough floor plan, based on these interviews and Mr. Gorbachev's own comments, of the Soviet leader's European home.

The first and most startling feature of this new Europe is the breakup of the Communist bloc.

"Of course, there is still a bloc of Eastern European states, in which the Soviet Union is clearly the most formidable partner," said a Western European diplomat. "But it is no longer uniformly Communist, and it seems even Communist parties within those countries are not bound by Moscow."

Although Soviet officials do not like to advertise it, they agree that the freedom of Eastern European countries to run their own affairs includes the right to reject Communism altogether, to adopt multiparty democracies and market economies and even to call themselves capitalists.

"Once you've determined the principle of freedom of choice, I don't see how any limit can be set," said a Foreign Ministry official, interviewed on the condition he not be named. "You cannot say 'This is socialism; this line you cannot cross.'"

Mr. Gorbachev has been increasingly categorical about a policy of noninterference in the internal affairs of his allies, and has backed up his words by accepting—even applauding—the dislodging of Communist regimes in Poland and Hungary.

"One can argue about the degree to which Gorbachev had a choice, and about his motives," said a Western diplomat. "But it is hard to make the case any longer that he doesn't mean it."

This diplomat speculates that if Mr. Gorbachev had any lingering qualms about a hands-off policy, they were erased this year as he watched the horrified reaction to China's suppression of its democracy movement, and the bitter domestic backlash after troops killed demonstrators in Soviet Georgia.

At the same time, Soviet officials and Western diplomats generally agree that Mr. Gorbachev had not engineered the tumbling of Eastern Europe's dominoes, nor foreseen the pace and sequence of events.

He has, rather, played the role of catalyst, both publicly, by opening a vigorous debate of Communism's failures at home, and privately, by making it clear Moscow would not intervene to prop up old regimes.

"A signal may be either indirect or indirect," Gennadi I. Gerasimov, the Foreign Ministry spokesman, observed the other day when asked to describe Moscow's role in Eastern Europe. "We are not waving a conductor's baton."

Perhaps the best metaphor for Mr. Gorbachev's approach to his restive allies is the opening of the Berlin wall.

Just as East Germany opened its borders to slow the headlong defection of its citizens—by assuring them they could wait awhile, size up the changes at home, and leave whenever they wanted—Mr. Gorbachev's policy is to open the bloc in hopes that the members will remain together voluntarily.

So far the more independent voices in Eastern Europe have been careful to pledge their allegiance to the Warsaw Pact and to the postwar boundaries of Europe—and not only because they worry how Moscow would respond if a country bolted from the pact.

"Now the governments in Poland and Hungary have changed," said Marshal Sergei F. Akhromeyev, the former chief of the armed forces general staff and now an adviser to Mr. Gorbachev in the Soviet legislature. "There are non-Communists at the heads of the governments. But the state interests of Poland and Hungary have remained the same, to a significant degree."

"First of all, there's the stability of the territory and state boundaries," he continued. "Second, there are the economic interests of the states. After all, they've been linked for many decades. That is why the military-political alliance remains."

The next stage, already under way, is a transformation of the eastern military and economic alliances—the Warsaw Pact and the Council for Mutual Economic Assistance.

While Soviets once talked of disbanding NATO and the Warsaw Pact simultaneously—a bluff the West did not take seriously—they now tend to agree that it is better to preserve the alliances for the foreseeable future, since on its own each country might be tempted to renew historical disputes with its neighbors.

In Mr. Gorbachev's vision, the military alliances that now face off across a central European front will evolve into political alliances, in which the military role has withered.

Beginning with a meeting of Warsaw Pact leaders in Bucharest, Rumania, last July, where the group for the first time declared a policy of noninterference in its members' internal affairs, the Eastern alliance has begun to take on some trappings of a more political, NATO-style fraternity.

According to Western and Soviet specialists, the Soviet side has signaled that it will accept changes in the Warsaw Pact Constitution that would ban use of troops in internal affairs, declare that the pact does not include promoting Communism, and make membership more equal and voluntary.

In the Soviet vision, the remaking of the pacts would include a rollback of military forces on both sides.

"The state interests of both alliances still remain, and the contradictions remain," Marshal Akhromeyev said. "And a certain quantity of arms and armed forces will remain. But what matters is that it be such a quantity which would not permit the country to start a war, even if it wanted to."

Mr. Akhromeyev and Mr. Gorbachev publicly insist these reductions must be mutual, worked out at the conventional arms talks under way in Vienna between the sixteen NATO allies and the seven members of the Warsaw Pact.

But among the Soviet researchers, some theorists now argue openly for more dramatic, one-sided moves.

Vladimir N. Chernega, vice rector of the diplomatic academy of the Soviet Foreign Ministry, suggests that the Soviet Union could withdraw its troops entirely from Eastern Europe without demanding that America match it.

"If the governments of Eastern Europe want it, we must withdraw our troops from their territory," he said, stressing that this was a personal opinion. "We can do this even unilaterally. As for American troops—I would leave that up to the Western European governments. I know that some circles in Western Europe feel their security is greater with American troops. It's an understandable position. Let them have it."

"We have a historical chance now and we have to make the most of it," he said. "In this context, a certain presence of Americans troops—a limited presence—poses no danger."

Like Mr. Gorbachev's own series of announced military budget cuts, "the pact will dissolve, that seems irreversible," said a Polish journalist who visited Moscow last week with Tadeusz Mazowiecki, Poland's new non-Communist Prime Minister. "So why waste our energy pushing it? The only thing we have to do is avoid posing a threat to the Soviet Union, and we are not that stupid."

"For us, this is not just reducing military spending and reallocating resources to civilian purposes," Mr. Chernega noted. "It is a matter of structural reorganization of our whole economy. Forty percent of our machine-tool industry and 75 percent of our spending on science go to the military. This is no basis for a normal economy."

Ultimately, after the withering of military confrontation, some Soviet analysts expect that some of the Soviet allies will become neutral-but-careful neighbors like Finland.

On his visit to Helsinki in October, Mr. Gorbachev hailed Finland as a model neighbor. Mr. Migranyan predicts that Finlandization of the Eastern bloc will come more quickly than anyone in the West anticipates.

Mr. Burlatsky, a legislator close to the leadership, is more cautious, but he says neutrality is entirely possible.

"If Austria can be neutral, then why not Hungary?" he said. "But that's in the future, after radical structural changes in the two blocs."

If the Warsaw Pact is being revamped, the Eastern economic alliance seems to be quickly coming apart, as budding market economies like Hungary and Poland find it harder to coexist with the older, planned economies.

The more market-minded members of the alliance, including the Soviet Union, are aggressively seeking to open new relationships with the European Community, and with individual Western countries.

But the Eastern European countries are so bound together by common backwardness and mutual trade dependencies that economic integration with the West may prove more difficult than reducing military confrontation.

"There is an asymmetry between the disintegration of Eastern Europe and the growing integration of Western Europe," Mr. Burlatsky said, noting the Western European countries' planned 1992 market consolidation.

"It seems there is a danger of Eastern Europe and the Soviet Union turning into an economic appendage of the West, a supplier of raw materials," he said. "That would create political problems, because a great superpower such as the Soviet Union will not feel comfortable in such a role."

Mr. Burlatsky argues for "a common market on the entire European continent," but he predicts a difficult decade or two before that is possible.

In the meantime, Mr. Gorbachev seems to accept, even welcome, the flow of Western credits, guarantees and investment to Eastern European countries. Although he warns against "exporting capitalism," he realizes that Western capital relieves him of an unbearable economic burden, and he hopes that it will help Eastern Europe become a bridge by which the Soviet Union can reach Western technology and markets.

Some portions of Mr. Gorbachev's design remain deliberately unfinished.

One is Germany. The Soviets are uneasy about the potential clout of a reunified Germany, and they are reluctant to be seen undermining the authority of their allies in East Berlin.

But some Soviet analysts say privately they are not alarmed about some new arrangement short of complete reunification, with security guarantees to reassure the neighbors.

And Soviet officials say they do not rule out reunification in the future, after "overcoming the division of Europe," as the Foreign Ministry spokesman Yuri Gremitskikh said today.

Another gray area in the blueprint is the fate of the Baltic republics, Lithuania, Latvia and Estonia, which yearn to rejoin Europe as independent states. Moscow is willing to concede these republics greater autonomy and closer economic links with the West, but balks at complete independence.

So far, most Western governments seem to accept this as Mr. Gorbachev's domestic problem, and they have not pressed him on behalf of the Baltics. But the three republics are pushing ahead without foreign encouragement.

The overriding question about Mr. Gorbachev's vision is how widely it is shared within the Soviet power structure. Clearly there are conservatives here who chafe at the retrenchment of Soviet power and the flouting of Communist verities, but they are understandably quiet about it.

Mr. Migranyan, for one, contends that the collapse of territorial ambitions has now very nearly reached the point where it would be impossible to reverse even if Mr. Gorbachev were replaced by a conservative.

"Even the most conservative government here will have to accept the changes in Eastern Europe," he said. "It would cost too much to reverse them."

The concerns and visions in Western Europe varied considerably.

Unease Fills Western Allies over Rapid Changes in East
By Craig R. Whitney

LONDON, Nov. 28—The joyous revolution of freedom sweeping Eastern Europe is confronting Western Europe with some of its gravest decisions in forty years.

Among the most daunting challenges is how to maintain the movement toward European unity if, as most Western European leaders expect, the West Germans become distracted from that old goal by the newly aroused prospects of achieving German unification—a vision spelled out by Chancellor Helmut Kohl in Bonn on Tuesday.

Another concern questions where the United States and the Soviet Union will fit in the suddenly shifting European landscape. Many Western Europeans think the natural course of events will bind them more closely to the new Soviet Union, which after all shares the same continent, and pry them loose from their security and economic ties to the United States.

The biggest worry of all, to many Europeans, is West Germany itself, increasingly inclined to take charge of its destiny in ways that would have been unthinkable a decade or even a year ago. Mr. Kohl, for example, outlined his ideas for German unification Tuesday without any prior consultation with his allies, though the United States, Britain and France share with the Soviet Union a treaty responsibility for "Germany as a whole" that dates back to 1945.

Conversations with politicians, business leaders, students, writers and ordinary people from Wales to West Berlin in recent weeks leave a clear impression of unease, a sense that without wise actions the dream come true in Eastern Europe could easily turn into unpleasant realities.

What is also becoming apparent is that rapid changes can bring long-submerged cultural, historical and political differences of the twelve members of the European Community to the surface. Indeed, this risk has appeared just as those nations are poised to eliminate the remaining trade barriers among their 320 million people by the end of 1992.

The unease is compounded by a feeling that Western leaders have not been saying what they really think about the central problem of a united Germany. For four decades, when reunification appeared impossible, all of them implicitly accepted it by saying that a truly free, united Europe, East and West, was the ultimate goal. Now that the reintegration of Europe and the Germanys no longer looks so distant, said Klaus Bolling, a former head of West Germany's mission to East Berlin, "We're seeing a tremendous outbreak of hypocrisy."

"It seems a little bit insulting to Germany to say that it needs to be anchored into Europe," Prime Minister Margaret Thatcher of Britain said on BBC television Monday night, clearly hoping to anchor the West Germans even more firmly with such expressed sentiments.

"I am not afraid of reunification," President François Mitterrand of France said in Bonn earlier this month. "If the Germans want to be a single nation in a single state, this must be founded on the will of the German nation, and nobody can oppose it." But officials in Paris now explain that what the President intended by the statement was to calm the fears of many French people over unification, and to encourage the Germans not to be distracted from the unfinished work of building the European Community.

Mr. Kohl tried to reassure other European leaders, in Paris on November 18, that West Germany saw "no alternative" but to work for German unity within the existing European context.

"We agreed not to raise the question of the existing borders," Mrs. Thatcher acknowledged, but diplomats in Bonn, Paris and London all agree that the reason German reunification was left off the agenda was the fear that forcing the issue could bring down President Mikhail S. Gorbachev, on whom they think all the fragile changes in the Soviet Union and Eastern Europe continue to depend. All the Western European leaders agreed over dinner in Paris on November 18 that Mr. Gorbachev was at a critical juncture and that they should do nothing to undermine his position.

Officially, reunification will not be on the agenda when President Bush sees Mr. Gorbachev off Malta this weekend, but hardly anyone in Europe thinks it can stay off forever.

"To talk about the breakup of NATO does no one any good at all," Mrs. Thatcher said Tuesday night. But questions are even beginning to surface at the popular level all over Western Europe about whether there will be any need for an American-dominated military alliance against possible Soviet attack, when or if that threat no longer exists.

Ordinary people, as well as their political leaders, sense that a historical turning point is being reached. "We thought we had everything perfect in the Common Market," said Janet Semper, who lives in Westminster Abbey with her husband, Colin, a resident canon there. "We were letting in one country at a time—Spain, Portugal, Greece, and then in comes this wonderful rabble through the Berlin wall and now we have to rethink the whole thing."

"The instant the Berlin wall comes down, France is no longer the center of Europe—it's on the periphery," said François Barbey, a 48-year-old real estate salesman in Paris. "People say we've won. We've come to the end of one world, but we haven't found the key to the next."

John le Carré, whose master spy George Smiley got his Soviet counterpart, Karla, to defect across the Berlin wall in his 1980 novel, *Smiley's People,* put it this way in a recent essay: "Smiley had won, as the West has won now. But the sweets of victory elude us—as they eluded Smiley, partly because he had forgotten what he was fighting for, partly because he feared that his masters preferred the comforts of permanent aggression to the hardship of new choices and alignments."

"We really invent the enemies we need," the novelist, whose real name is David Cornwell, explained later. "We could be making the discovery that Russia, once the military threat is removed, is a huge, untidy third world problem that will demand time, effort and money—lots of money—to fix. It could be a terrible headache."

To many people, the German question already is "I don't know what will become of this land," Mr. Bolling said in his home in West Berlin. "There'll be bound to be a cooling off vis-à-vis America as the prospect of a united Germany comes into view. Already the people of West Berlin are complaining about how the three allied military commanders have just bought ten new Mercedes cars with their money, and they're asking how much longer they have to go on paying for such things."

Already Lufthansa, the West German airline, is demanding that Britain, France and the United States relinquish their monopoly on flying between West Germany and West Berlin.

"The division into Eastern and Western Europe was a construction of the cold war," Heinz Ruhnau, Lufthansa's chairman, told *Die Welt* the day before the wall came down. "East and West have to recognize that their status positions can't be maintained any longer after forty years."

"We all want a relationship with the United States," said Sergio Romano, a former diplomat who was Italy's Ambassador to Moscow until earlier this year."But I imagine we would all prefer that it not be so hierarchical as it has been."

NATO diplomats in Brussels say that the organization, like the Warsaw Pact, will have to convert itself into an instrument for managing change and monitoring complex negotiated arms control agreements over the next few years, but in London, Paris and Bonn, diplomats complain that such thinking is only in its embryonic stage, and not well coordinated.

If events in Eastern Europe are only beginning to spark a rethinking of NATO's role, they have uncovered contradictions about the European Community that have existed since the Treaty of Rome established it in 1957. In those early days, President Charles de Gaulle of France insisted that Europe not be federation but a collection of sovereign, cooperating nation states. De Gaulle called it "l'Europe des patries," and used it as an excuse for keeping out Britain in the early 1960's, because he feared the British would turn the European Community into an Anglo-Saxon United States of Europe.

Now all the European leaders but one—the British Prime Minister—have agreed that the changes in the East require urgently forging ahead to more federalism in the community. "For the European Community to remain the center of gravity that it is, we must accelerate," said Jacques Delors, its executive president, two weeks ago.

Mrs. Thatcher wants to complete the 1992 program, but is wary of surrendering more British sovereignty to the community's executive commission in Brussels, which she says is not fully accountable to any democratic parliament. As Eastern European countries evolve toward political and economic democracy, her close advisers believe, the community should stay loose and flexible. "This isn't the time to become more exclusive," one of them explained.

"I do not believe in a federation of Europe, a United States of Europe," Mrs. Thatcher said again on television Monday. "I believe it will work far better if we cooperate together as twelve sovereign states."

French officials expect that Mrs. Thatcher will be alone in opposing a call at the next European Community summit in Strasbourg, France, December 8–9, for a conference that would consider changes in the Treaty of Rome to permit full monetary union, though they say they are not sure the Germans will not have developed second thoughts as well.

But if changes in the East continue, the European Community will no longer be limited to the twelve, and one of the main subjects on the agenda in Strasbourg will be how to respond to the clamor in Eastern Europe to get in on the prosperity.

The twelve agreed in principle in Paris earlier this month to provide economic aid to all Eastern European countries, but only if they make clear progress toward economic and political democracy. Separately or together, *Le Monde* calculated the other day, the Europeans and the other industrial democracies have given or pledged more than $6 billion in aid or loans to Eastern Europe, mainly Hungary and Poland, this year.

West German and French officials believe that Bonn is prepared to offer even more than that to East Germany. "It wouldn't be hard to make a success out of East Germany," one French diplomat observed. "It could be more prosperous than Portugal in five years."

The larger question behind this is whether Poland and Hungary, and now possibly East Germany and Czechoslovakia, should be allowed or encouraged to join the European Community, with associate membership as a first step.

"The E.C. already has various bilateral 'association agreements' with other countries; more can be struck in Eastern Europe as reform takes hold," *The Economist* newspaper wrote last week, a suggestion that was endorsed by Mrs. Thatcher. A former President of France, Valery Giscard d'Estaing, has suggested that the community tailor these association agreements country by country, and tie them to price reform, privatization and currency convertibility in each one.

Some European leaders speak of a Marshall Plan for Eastern Europe, with a leading role for the West; *Le Monde* said that Marshall aid from the United States from 1947 to 1948 totaled $13 billion, worth $171 billion today.

"A Marshall Plan now is impossible," Prof. Alfred Grosser, a French expert on Germany, said. "You have hardly anyone in the Soviet Union, and not many in Eastern Europe, who know how to manage a market economy."

In addition, all Eastern currencies have been pegged at wildly artificial rates against Western ones for years, and to get them down to realistic exchange values will be painful. In West Germany, the mark, now one of the world's strongest currencies, was introduced in June 1948 at a rate of one for every 10 old German reichsmarks, causing tremendous resentment and pain until people regained confidence in their money and the economy started functioning again.

Representatives of 24 industrial democracies, including the European Community, the United States, Japan and South Korea, will meet in Brussels on December 13 for more discussions about how to help. "The socialist models are collapsing," said François Perigot, head of the French employers' federation in Paris. "If all they get from our system is black markets, petty corruption, unemployment and social indifference, they could turn away from our model. Europe shouldn't give them a bad example."

But essentially Europe is confused. No journalist, politician, professor or economic expert saw that change would come so suddenly to so many countries all over the East. What has happened has left many of them in breathless bewilderment.

All ordinary people can see for sure is that a Soviet threat that made them dependent on the United States has receded, and that for better or for worse the Europe they have known for forty years will rapidly change into something else.

"Everyone everywhere is talking about it, of course," said Raymond Kingsley-Taylor, chapter clerk of Hereford Cathedral. "There's relief, sheer stunned surprise, and apprehension."

"Europe will become more and more aggressively competitive against Japan, and distance itself from the Americans," said Jacques Seguela, a French advertising executive and author in Paris. "The Soviet Union will be part of this new Europe." He will open an advertising agency in Moscow January 1 and two in Hungary and Poland.

Anke van der Valk, a 38-year-old social worker in Delft, the Netherlands, agreed. "Those Eastern lands belong to Europe," she said. "I think they should join the Common Market." But, she added, "I'm a bit afraid of a united Germany. Better for the two Germanys to remain separate, and let both of them be members of the European Community."

"All the French public opinion polls show that between 60 and 70 percent of the French people say German reunification wouldn't bother them," said Professor Grosser, France's leading expert on

Germany. But in the Quai d'Orsay, some diplomats speak of the shelling of Rheims Cathedral in the Franco-Prussian War of 1870 as if it were yesterday.

"National pride caused all the problems we're seeing today," said Markus Doll, a 22-year-old student in Hamburg. "The people who used to say 'We are Germans' now say 'We are Europeans.' For me it's no better. They should say 'We are people, just like everybody else.' "

In Washington the realization was dawning that while the Soviet Union would remain in Europe as at least a neighbor whether it had troops in the East bloc or not, the U.S. role on the continent was becoming less obvious in the new configurations of power. In the beginning of December, President Bush had met with Mr. Gorbachev in Malta to discuss essentially European issues.

Changes in East Call for a U.S. Balancing Act
By Thomas L. Friedman

WASHINGTON, Dec. 6—A senior policy maker was explaining the other day that the Bush Administration had two sets of policies for Eastern Europe—one for that night's network news and one for the year 2010. But the real challenge for Washington, he said, will be developing approaches to Europe not for tonight and not for the next century, but for next year, 1992 and 1995.

"Our internal debates are either very technical or very cosmic," the policy maker said. "Look, our long-term goal, the 'vision thing,' is obvious. It doesn't glitter. It doesn't blind you. It isn't a new Jerusalem. It is something very simple: all the countries in Eastern Europe should have democratic institutions and not go to war with each other. It isn't any more complicated than that."

"What is complicated," he said, "is getting there. It is that middle distance—the policy for 1995—that's the problem. It has to be something more than a Polish aid package and something less than the vision of a 'Europe whole and free.' "

Ultimately, it will be policies for the middle distance that will determine how effectively the United States can help Europe make its transition from the barbed-wire-divided landscape of the recent past to a continent whole and free. In addressing the NATO allies in Brussels this week after his meeting in Malta with President Mikhail

S. Gorbachev of the Soviet Union, President Bush acknowledged this challenge.

"The United States will remain a European power, and that means that the United States will stay engaged in the future of Europe and in our common defense," Mr. Bush said. But he was quick to add that the task required a reversal of old approaches almost as great as that being tried in Moscow.

"As I watched the way in which Mr. Gorbachev has handled the changes in Eastern Europe, it deserves new thinking," the President said. "It absolutely mandates new thinking."

But if the United States is to be involved in drawing the Europe of the 1990's, as the President vowed, what are the immediate goals it is seeking there? With budgetary pressure mounting for a reduction in the number of American troops in Europe, what form will the United States presence take over the middle distance? At a time when American officials themselves admit they have little leverage to influence the pace and scope of change in Eastern Europe, how can the United States develop a blueprint for the future that will not be overwhelmed by events? Finally, is there a threat that the emerging unity of Eastern and Western Europe may lead to a growing disunity in the Western alliance?

The time available for answering these questions may be less than anyone imagines. Administration officials say that although President Bush and Mr. Gorbachev never really got around to exchanging detailed plans for a new Eastern Europe, what the Soviet leader did say left the Bush team feeling that he was not only pleased with the nature of change there, but intended to continue promoting it. In other words, events are likely to move faster before they move slower.

The fact that senior Administration decision makers have not yet produced clear-cut blueprints for the middle distance appears to be more a result of their being overwhelmed by events than a lack of imagination. It seems that too much is changing too fast in too many unexpected ways for the leadership to get too far beyond the day-to-day.

"I don't think people genuinely have recovered their breath from what has happened," said a top Administration policy maker. "I have spent my entire grown-up life not knowing the difference between Latvia, Lithuania and Estonia. They were like Central African lakes to me. There was never any reason to think about them. If you had told me two years ago that I would now be drawing careful political distinctions between Estonia and Lithuania, I would never have believed it."

Nevertheless, interviews with a range of officials, scholars, policy analysts and historians made clear that there is no shortage of ideas on how the Administration should act toward Europe in the middle distance.

At the heart of all the "new thinking" about Europe in Washington lies the German question. How the United States relates to the North Atlantic Treaty Organization and the European Community will be shaped to a large extent by whether East and West Germany are reunited and if so, how.

The Bush Administration has made a strategic decision in recent months not to oppose German unification in principle provided it is done through free elections. But in his Brussels speech the President sketched out for the first time other conditions Washington would insist on.

"Unification should occur in the context of Germany's continued commitment to NATO, an increasingly integrated European Community, and with due regard to the legal role and responsibilities of the Allied powers," Mr. Bush said. "In the interest of general European stability, moves toward unification must be peaceful, gradual and part of a step-by-step basis. And lastly, on the question of borders, we should reiterate our support for the Helsinki Final Act"—which declared that Europe's postwar borders were inviolable.

But the question remains how the Administration should go about imposing these conditions.

"We would be nuts to try to oppose German reunification—there is nothing to be gained by antagonizing Germany—but we would be equally nuts to keep our hands off and say that German reunification is only a question for the German people," said Burton Yale Pines, an expert on Europe at the Heritage Foundation, a Washington-based conservative research center.

"Because of the instabilities a united Germany has created in this past century, it is absolutely appropriate for Moscow and Washington to begin talking now, along with Britain and France, about how Germany should be reunified—what sorts of weapons it should be allowed to have, what limitations on its troops should be imposed and how it would relate to its neighbors."

Administration officials say they are concentrating their energies now on insuring that there is a unified Western approach to the

German question before they begin talking with the Soviets. Washington's nightmares here are two. The first is that East Germany will literally collapse tomorrow, fostering a popular momentum for unification and possibly prompting the Soviets, who have some 400,000 troops in East Germany, to intervene to halt the process.

The Administration's view is that keeping East Germany propped up so that it can make a gradual transition to unification is primarily the job of West Germany, the only country with the resources and contacts to make it happen.

Which leads to the Administration's second nightmare: As East and West Germany inexorably grow closer together, even if step by step, deeply rooted fears about a united Germany will set off an earthquake in the NATO alliance, with its epicenter in London, where Prime Minister Margaret Thatcher has opposed unification at this time.

Secretary of State James A. Baker 3d will be going to Europe next week for meetings in Bonn and Brussels with the aim of obtaining a NATO consensus on Mr. Bush's approach. At the last minute he added London to his itinerary to try to ease Prime Minister Thatcher's anxieties.

In Bonn, Mr. Baker will try to continue the Administration's approach of hugging the West Germans to the Western camp. That means, an official said, letting Bonn know that Washington has "total confidence" in the prudent way West Germany has handled the situation up to now and wants to consult with Bonn at every step of the way. At the same time, the official said, Washington will need to reaffirm by words and with arms around the shoulder that it believes Bonn must continue consulting with the West and reiterating its unshakable ties to NATO and the European Community.

Such commitments are necessary both to reassure the rest of Western Europe and to send a signal to Mr. Gorbachev. Administration officials left Malta with a sense that while the Soviets continue to oppose total German unification, they too may be starting to recognize that it may be inevitable and hence they may begin insisting that such a unified entity be "neutral."

In London and in Brussels, Mr. Baker will try to promote Mr. Bush's position that German unification in the context of continued membership in NATO and the European Community is nothing the allies need to fear.

"This is a policy that is going to require a lot of handholding," a

State Department official said. "Once we have a framework agreed on with the British, French and West Germans, then we can start talking to the Soviets."

The longer-term question, policy analysts say, is how can the United States insure that a unified Germany is firmly anchored in the Western alliance when the lessening of the Soviet threat will feed budgetary momentum in Congress to bring the bulk of the 317,000 American troops in Europe home?

The answer, said Stephen F. Szabo, a German expert at the National War College, is for the United States to take a much more active role in promoting European integration, not only the plans of the twelve members of the European Community to turn themselves into a single market by the end of 1992, but also their proposals for a European monetary union and for a defensive structure of their own to augment NATO. This would both dilute the power of a unified Germany and keep it enmeshed in the West.

"We are going to be playing a declining military role, so we better have something there in place when we leave that can both maintain an overall balance of power with the Soviets and at the same time be a firm anchor holding Germany to the West," Mr. Szabo said. "This means trying to promote more European control of NATO."

Even over the long term, Administration officials are convinced that Mr. Gorbachev does not want the United States out of Europe, but instead sees a continued American presence there as the ultimate guarantor that neither the German question nor intra-European antagonisms will get out of control. Administration officials say it is premature to even begin talking about a changed American relationship to NATO, let alone the United States' leaving Europe.

"NATO provides the single greatest institutional tie the United States has to Western Europe, and no one wants to see that relationship attenuated," said Deputy Secretary of State Lawrence S. Eagleburger. "Over time I am sure we will have to adjust our relationship, but we are not there yet. I don't think anyone at this point can envisage how the relationship will change."

If there is any real threat from Eastern Europe to American interests in the middle term it is no longer the threat of a Warsaw Pact invasion but rather a Warsaw Pact economic collapse. When Administration officials talk about their "worst case scenario" for Eastern Europe, it always begins with economics, not politics.

"The worst case," a senior State Department official said, "is that the Eastern Europeans get bogged down and can't make the structural changes in their economic and political systems and then you see pessimism and cynicism set in. That could get ugly."

It is often forgotten that in the first few years of the cold war, American policies in Europe were not primarily military but economic. The Marshall Plan was intended primarily to strengthen European countries, which had been devastated by the war, so that they could resist decay, instability and Communist subversion. NATO and the policy of military containment came into their own only after the Korean War raised the specter of a Soviet-led strike across Central Europe.

"With the diminished threat from the East, American European policy no longer has to emphasize military containment," said Michael Mandelbaum, an expert on East-West relations at the Council on Foreign Relations. "We are back to the situation of 1947—helping fledgling democracies, devastated in this case by the calamity of forty years of Communist rule, trying to get on their feet."

For the short term, the Bush Administration, prodded by Congress, has come up with a package that provides $938 million in grants, investment funds, bank credits, scholarships, job-training schemes and environmental protection projects for Poland and Hungary. But this package will expire in three years, and does not even address changes in Czechoslovakia, Bulgaria and Yugoslavia.

For the middle distance, Felix G. Rohatyn, a senior partner in the investment bank Lazard Frères & Company, has suggested that the United States should take the lead in creating a permanent Eastern European Development Bank.

"For the longer haul," Mr. Rohatyn said, "it seems to me that some kind of multinational development institution should be created by the Europeans, Japanese and ourselves along the lines of the Reconstruction Finance Corporation of the 1930's."

The capital, Mr. Rohatyn said, should be held by Japan, the United States and the European Community.

"I would begin with $5 billion, which would allow them to borrow much more, and put the bank in Vienna," he said. "Any country that has made the political reforms—that is, free elections and recognition of the principle of private property—but not yet the economic ones could apply."

Such a bank, he said, would act as a permanent provider of financing for infrastructure projects, like telecommunications and irrigation systems, and for developing free-market instruments and skills, like accounting systems, mortgage institutions, copyright laws, credit and banking systems.

To transform the economies of Eastern Europe in a stable manner from planned economies to more free-market systems "is going to take a long time, so we need institutions that can work over the long haul," Mr. Rohatyn said.

And there is the rub, some American officials say.

"I represent a great power and we reach into our pockets and all we have is loose change," a State Department official said. "I am not saying you should substitute check writing for policy making. But let's face it: student exchanges, leadership grants, banking credits, new consulates—these are the network of things that bring us influence on the ground. You have to put your money where your mouth is, and we're broke."

Administration officials concede that they will have to influence economic development in Eastern Europe with a small purse, at best. Their policy for the middle distance is to make a virtue of necessity and share leadership on the aid front with both the European Community and the group of 24 leading Western industrial nations.

"There is a lot we can do without money—providing technical assistance, or incentives for reform or intellectual capital," an Administration official said. "We're going to have to do more of that. Look at all we offered Gorbachev in Malta. Did that cost us any money?"

Out of all these loose threads today's decision makers will somehow have to weave a policy for the middle distance. Those who will have to carry it out greet the task with excitement and humility, dread and awe, said Raymond G. H. Seitz, the Assistant Secretary for European Affairs, whose father was a United States Army general in command of American forces in Munich when the Berlin wall went up in 1961.

"When I was 20, I came home from college for the summer to visit my family in Munich," he recalled. "I remember very well the night when the red phone in the house rang and my father was told that the East Germans are putting up a wall in the middle of Berlin. Now his son is one of those dealing with the implications of that wall coming down."

"I guess history comes in waves," he added, "and this is one that is clearly cresting. It is not coups we are talking about. It is mass movements, people in the streets. What it has lacked up to now, thank goodness, is a feature that always gives history its real pungency, though. That is violence and barricades—*Les Misérables.* So we may not get on-Broadway plays out of this moment, but we'll definitely get off-Broadway."

When asked how he was instructing his staff to go about planning for the middle distance, Mr. Seitz mulled the question over for a moment before answering.

"Everything goes back to square one now," he said. "No assumptions are valid, nothing is ruled out anymore. Of course that is exciting. Bureaucracies are meant to operate within a framework. In terms of European policy we have had that framework established for a very long time. There was NATO, the Warsaw Pact, the wall, the spending levels. They were all thought to be immutable."

"The bureaucracy is not like academe, where you are trained to question assumptions," he continued. "Around here you don't have time to question assumptions, and anyway you know that they are valid. Right? Now everything is back to square one. Nothing is immutable. It requires a total intellectual retooling."

On his way to Malta, Mr. Gorbachev stopped in Italy, where he was cheered wildly by people who regarded him as the man who more than any other had brought about the piercing and toppling of Europe's divisions. But the highlight of this part of the trip was the first meeting ever between a Soviet leader and a Pope.

Gorbachev Lauds Religion on Eve of Meeting Pope
By Clyde Haberman

ROME, Nov. 30—On the eve of an encounter with Pope John Paul II, President Mikhail S. Gorbachev said tonight that the Soviet Union had erred in long rejecting religion and now needed its moral force to help make his plans for a restructured society work.

"We have changed our attitude on some matters, such as religion, for example, which admittedly we used to treat in a simplistic manner," said Mr. Gorbachev, whose meeting with the Pope on Friday will be the first between a Soviet Communist leader and the spiritual guide to the world's 850 million Roman Catholics.

"Now we not only proceed from the assumption that no one should interfere in matters of the individual's conscience," he said. "We also say that the moral values that religion generated and embodied for centuries can help in the work of renewal in our country, too."

289

"In fact," Mr. Gorbachev added, "this is already happening."

His thoughts on religion came in a multi-themed speech that was as much a philosophical reflection as a political statement. In it, the Soviet leader offered a vision of a new Europe, one that would be "a commonwealth of sovereign democratic states," based on spiritual values, pluralism, religious tolerance and mutual understanding. . . .

The Kremlin and the Vatican; Gorbachev Visits Pope at Vatican; Ties Are Forged
By Clyde Haberman

ROME, Dec. 1—With an agreement to begin official relations and a pledge of expanded religious freedom for Soviet citizens, President Mikhail S. Gorbachev joined hands today with Pope John Paul II.

Seven decades of spiritual and philosophical conflict came to a symbolic end as the two talked for more than an hour in the heart of Vatican City, the first encounter between a Soviet Communist leader and a Pope.

Both men agreed in principle to establish diplomatic ties, and Mr. Gorbachev invited the Pope to make a return visit to the Soviet Union.

The Pope's reply to the invitation was noncommittal. It appeared that before saying yes, he intended to keep on pressing Moscow to restore religious liberties to Soviet Catholics. According to a spokesman, the Pope "cordially thanked" his guest, and said he hoped that "developments would make it possible for him to accept."

Much will apparently depend on what happens to the four million to five million Eastern Rite Catholics in the Ukraine, in which the Polish-born Pope has a special interest. Much of the western Ukraine was once part of Poland, until it was incorporated into the Soviet Union after World War II.

The Ukrainian Catholic Church was driven underground by Stalin in 1946. It was forcibly dissolved, and its parishes were closed or merged into the Russian Orthodox Church. Centered in the western Ukraine, the Ukrainian Catholics follow the Eastern liturgy but profess allegiance to the Pope.

The Pope has insisted repeatedly that the Ukrainian Catholic Church be made legal again, and he got an important start toward that goal when Mr. Gorbachev promised him today that a new law guaranteeing freedom of conscience would soon be enacted.

In turn, the Soviet leader won something he had come for: legitimacy from the leader of the world's 900 million Roman Catholics. It came in the form of a papal blessing for his plans to restructure Soviet political and economic life. John Paul said the Holy See "wishes you success and declares itself ready to support every initiative that will better protect and integrate the rights and duties of individuals and peoples."

But the Pope's main concern was religious liberty, and he stuck to that point tenaciously, reminding Mr. Gorbachev that Moscow had signed international treaties guaranteeing freedom of worship. "I express the fervent hope," he said, that Catholics in the Ukraine, the Baltic republics and Armenia will be able "to practice freely their religious life."

In his brief remarks, the Soviet leader said all believers "have a right to satisfy their spiritual needs." On Thursday, he told Italian leaders that his country had made the mistake of treating religion in "a simplistic manner."

Developments such as these, the Pope said to him today, "lead us to hope that the situation will change."

Indeed, in the Ukrainian city of Lvov, the layman who leads the Ukrainian Catholic Church reported that a major shift had already occurred. The leader, Ivan Hel, said that Ukraine officials had announced that the church could register like any other accepted religious organization.

Beyond the immediate agendas of each leader, the meeting today in the ceremonial library of the Vatican's Apostolic Palace contained a symbolism of almost epic proportions.

At an earlier time, Stalin had scornfully asked how many divisions the Pope had. Now, a successor intent on undoing Stalin's legacy has crossed St. Peter's Square in open recognition that he must reckon with the Vatican as a moral and political force.

Certainly, the significance was not lost on either of the participants, who have many points in common. Both are Slavs. Both say spiritual values must go hand in hand with material gains. Both talk of a Europe unified by a common civilization despite political diversity. And both can maintain, in different ways, that their separate visions helped trigger the tumultuous changes under way across the Continent.

The two symbol-conscious men were also aware of the power of photographs and televised images showing them clasping hands and appearing in the relaxed company of each other.

"A truly extraordinary event has taken place," said the Communist leader, who was baptized as a boy in the Russian Orthodox Church. "It has become possible due to the profound changes that are sweeping many countries and nations. What is more, we can expect it to help assure their positive continuation."

"Our meeting today," the Pope said, "will hardly fail to have a powerful impact on world opinion. Not only is it something new and unusual, It will also be interpreted as singularly meaningful, a sign of the times that have slowly matured, a sign that is rich in promise," he said.

For the Vatican, the Gorbachev visit crowned a year of dramatically improved relations with the Eastern bloc.

The church has been permitted to make long-prohibited ecclesiastical appointments in Czechoslovakia and in the Soviet republics of Lithuania and Byelorussia. Four months ago, it established diplomatic relations with Poland, its first with a Warsaw Pact nation. Last week, Hungary announced that it was ready to follow suit.

But full Vatican relations with the Kremlin are expected to take considerably more time. Even so, it was a giant stride today when Mr. Gorbachev said, "We have reached agreement in principle to give official status to our interstate relations."

Asked later if this was a move toward full diplomatic relations, the chief Vatican spokesman, Dr. Joaquin Navarro-Valls, said it was.

While the meeting today was friendly—punctuated with smiles and occasional laughs—the two leaders did not show true warmth in public. Still, the special nature of the occasion shone through, even in small gestures.

Mr. Gorbachev called the Pope "Holy Father." For his part, John Paul varied his routine in a significant way.

Normally, he greets visitors at the door of his library, which is on the second floor of the Apostolic Palace, one floor below his private apartment. To show his esteem for this guest, he came out several dozen yards from the library, to the Throne Room.

Then they entered the library, sitting on either side of a wooden desk during a 70-minute conversation. For the first five minutes, according to Dr. Navarro, they were alone, speaking in Russian. But then they brought in interpreters, with Mr. Gorbachev continuing in Russian and the Pope alternating between Polish and Italian.

While the two men talked, Mr. Gorbachev's wife, Raisa, toured the Sistine Chapel and the Raphael rooms of the Vatican Museum. Then she returned to meet the Pope, raising eyebrows by turning out in a bright red suit. It is customary for women to wear black at private papal audiences. But if the Vatican was displeased, it kept its feelings to itself.

In an exchange of gifts, John Paul presented Mr. Gorbachev with a reproduction of an early Christian mosaic showing Christ on St. Peter's tomb, and gave Mrs. Gorbachev rosary beads of gold and mother of pearl. In return, he received two fourteenth-century Psalm books from Kiev.

Just before this exchange, Dr. Navarro said, the Soviet leader told the Pope, "Holy Father, we are aware that we are dealing not only with the highest religious authority in the world but also someone who is a Slav."

"Yes, I'm the first Slav Pope, " John Paul reportedly replied, adding, "I'm sure that Providence paved the way for this meeting."

After the meetings in Rome Mr. Gorbachev went on to Malta to discuss matters of European security and Soviet plans for progress and modernization with President Bush in a stormy setting that contrasted with the developing show of superpower amity.

The Malta Summit; Bush and Gorbachev Proclaim a New Era for U.S.-Soviet Ties; Agree on Arms and Trade Aims

By Andrew Rosenthal

VALLETTA, MALTA, Dec. 3—President Bush and President Mikhail S. Gorbachev ended their first summit meeting today with an extraordinary public affirmation of the new relationship between their countries.

Mr. Gorbachev said he and Mr. Bush agreed that "the characteristics of the cold war should be abandoned."

"The arms race, mistrust, psychological and ideological struggle, all those should be things of the past," he said.

Mr. Bush said: "With reform under way in the Soviet Union, we stand at the threshold of a brand-new era of U.S.-Soviet relations. It is within our grasp to contribute each in our own way to overcoming the division of Europe and ending the military confrontation there."

In the most substantial agreements reached at the meeting, the two leaders said they would strive to conclude treaties on long-range nuclear weapons and conventional arms in 1990. They also agreed to hold another summit meeting in June in the United States.

But the significance of the first summit meeting between the leaders seemed to lie more in the tone than the substance.

They ended their rain-soaked two-day meeting with the first joint news conference by Soviet and American leaders.

There had been some annoyance aboard Mr. Gorbachev's ship, the *Maxim Gorky*, on Saturday night when Mr. Bush canceled an afternoon session and a dinner because of a gale. The tension lingered in the background today but it melted under the television lights in a 65-minute display of cordiality that ended with Mr. Bush reaching over to grasp Mr. Gorbachev's right forearm. The news conference was remarkable for its lack of conflict over issues that have long divided East and West, including arms control, the Middle East and economic relations.

For all the cordiality, the meeting did not produce any new treaties or specific agreements, or even a joint statement.

After eight hours of intimate discussions, the two leaders were still far apart on the issue of sea-based nuclear cruise missiles, a major point of disagreement on a strategic arms treaty. They remained at odds on Central America, and Administration officials said Mr. Gorbachev did not give a definitive answer to Mr. Bush's proposals on an agreement reducing chemical weapons.

But Mr. Gorbachev, clearly pleased that Mr. Bush had shown some initiative on economic issues, registered approval on most of the proposals offered by Mr. Bush on Saturday, and the two leaders expressed broad optimism about the course of their relations.

Although they said they did not reach any specific accord on how to deal with the unraveling political power structure in Eastern Europe, Mr. Bush and Mr. Gorbachev seemed optimistic even about that problem.

"We searched for the answer to the question of where do we stand now," Mr. Gorbachev said. "We stated, both of us, that the world leaves one epoch of cold war and enters another epoch."

The two leaders did not dwell on Eastern Europe at length in their news conference, and American officials said the subject did not take up as much of the summit talks as they had expected. In response to a question about the two Germanys, Mr. Bush adopted what had long been the Soviet position. He said the conference on European security that began in Helsinki "spells out a concept of permanent borders."

Mr. Gorbachev said "any artificial acceleration" of the unification process would make it more difficult to carry through the changes taking place in Eastern Europe.

At times, the cautious Mr. Bush seemed to make an effort to show that all was not settled between the two nations. Even then, the statements from both sides were far more mild than the political oratory that has characterized the Soviet-American relationship for much of the last four decades.

Mr. Bush said his conversation with Mr. Gorbachev stayed cordial even on human rights. "I remember a time when I first met Mr. Gorbachev and we talked about human rights and he became visibly agitated with me for raising it," Mr. Bush said.

"And I think there's been a great evolution in his thinking on that question, and certainly on his relations with the United States, just as there had been an evolution in my thinking," Mr. Bush said, noting that he had once opposed holding the very type of meeting he had with Mr. Gorbachev here.

Indeed, when it came to what American officials said was the most troublesome policy dispute between the two leaders during the shipboard meeting—American charges that Nicaragua is sending arms to the leftist rebels in El Salvador—Mr. Gorbachev said, "We understand the concerns of the United States."

Mr. Bush, for his part, said he was "angry" about the issue but was not accusing Mr. Gorbachev of anything. Noting that Nicaragua had assured the Soviet Union that the arms shipments had ended, Mr. Bush said, "I do not believe the Sandinistas have told the truth to our Soviet friends."

Mr. Bush and Mr. Gorbachev talked to reporters aboard the *Maxim Gorky*, a Soviet cruise liner, before Mr. Gorbachev returned to Moscow.

Later in the day President Bush flew to Brussels, where he is to meet with heads of state and government of the North Atlantic Treaty Organization on Monday. At the airport this evening, he paid tribute to NATO's role in maintaining stability in Europe, noting that "this alliance of free nations remains the bedrock of peaceful change in Europe." . . .

On Saturday, Mr. Bush outlined 18 proposals to Mr. Gorbachev that ranged from nuclear arms control to educational exchanges. A senior American official who sat in on the talks said Mr. Gorbachev responded positively to almost all of them.

The notable exceptions, he said, were Mr. Bush's proposal that the two nations negotiate and sign an agreement in 1990 limiting their chemical arsenals to 20 percent of the present American level and that they call jointly for the holding of the 2004 Olympic Games on both sides of Berlin.

The official said that Mr. Gorbachev did not give Mr. Bush a clear no on those points but rather did not register the approval that he offered on the other issues.

In the news conference, Mr. Gorbachev said he had agreed with a suggestion by Mr. Bush that Secretary of State James A. Baker 3d and the Soviet Foreign Minister, Eduard A. Shevardnadze, meet in the Soviet Union in January to discuss arms control issues in preparation for a summit conference in the United States that the two leaders agreed to hold in the last two weeks of June.

He reaffirmed Mr. Bush's hope that the two leaders could sign a strategic arms control treaty, cutting long-range nuclear arsenals in half, at the next summit meeting. Barring that, he said, he hoped the two ministers would be able to resolve enough outstanding problems that at the next summit they could "agree on the provisions of the treaty and later in the coming months it might be ready for signature."

Mr. Gorbachev said he also hoped that a treaty limiting conventional weapons in Europe could be signed in 1990 in Vienna. Mr. Bush told reporters that he and Mr. Gorbachev had discussed in general what further cuts might be made in conventional arms, but did not talk about specific numbers.

On strategic arms, Mr. Gorbachev outlined some major obstacles to an accord. He said he was particularly concerned about remaining differences on air-launched cruise missiles and added that he had not dropped his insistence on opening negotiations on sea-based nuclear cruise missiles. Noting the progress that has been made in a number of other areas, Mr. Gorbachev said, "The time has come when we should begin discussing naval forces."

Mr. Gorbachev did not make it clear whether he was still setting forth a side agreement on naval weapons as a condition for concluding a strategic arms treaty. But Mr. Bush did suggest that he has not eased his opposition to negotiating about such weapons.

"The chairman knows that I could not come here to make deals in arms control," said Mr. Bush, who has repeatedly promised to consult his allies before making any major new treaty proposals or reaching any substantive agreements with Mr. Gorbachev on reducing nuclear or conventional arms.

Mr. Gorbachev was especially appreciative in public—and in private too, American and Soviet officials said—about Mr. Bush's proposals on trade and economic relations, which included his expression of support for Soviet observer status in the General Agreement on Tariffs and Trade. Mr. Bush also said he would begin immediate negotiations on lifting American barriers to trade with the Soviet Union and would recommend most-favored-nation status as soon as new Soviet emigration laws are enacted.

Mr. Gorbachev, who has long been seeking these moves and had viewed the lack of progress on economic issues as a major problem in the superpower relationship, said Mr. Bush's ideas and the discussion in Malta "could be regarded as a political impetus which we were lacking for our economic cooperation to gain momentum."

Mr. Bush called trade "one of the most fruitful parts of our discussion" and said he would "like to have a climate in which American businessmen can help with what Chairman Gorbachev is trying to do in terms of reform and glasnost."

On Central America, Mr. Bush said there were still clear differences between himself and Mr. Gorbachev. But he said, "I'd like to feel that if there are some differences between the two of us, then they have been narrowed."

Turning to the Middle East, Mr. Bush moved away from the often-expressed American view that the Soviet Union is impeding the peace process or, at best, trying to gain influence in the region at American expense.

"The Soviet Union is playing a constructive role in Lebanon and there is common ground there," Mr. Bush said, noting that it had "not always been the case in history" for an American President to take such a position.

New Spur for a New Journey Together
By R. W. Apple, Jr.

VALLETTA, MALTA, Dec. 3—George Bush finished one political journey today and started another.

Mr. Bush began his Presidency seeming more skeptical than his predecessor, Ronald Reagan, of Mikhail S. Gorbachev and his ideas. But the meeting in September between the Soviet Foreign Minister, Eduard A. Shevardnadze, and Secretary of State James A. Baker 3d marked a turning point, and two days of meetings here apparently convinced Mr. Bush and Mr. Gorbachev not only that they could trust each other but also that they needed each other to achieve their political goals.

So what their foreign ministers began amidst the scenic splendors of Wyoming in September was completed this weekend in the gales of Malta, as the leaders agreed to link their political fortunes in an effort to build a world free, as Mr. Gorbachev put it, from the "psychological and ideological struggles" of the last four decades.

No formal agreements were reached here; there was not even a written joint statement, let alone anything as formal as a communiqué. But the summit conference generated a sense of momentum, an intangible but important dynamic element, that the Soviet-American relationship had heretofore lacked.

As he had promised before arriving, Mr. Bush took the Soviet leader to task for his nation's Central American policy. But at the joint news conference given by the two men in lieu of individual sessions, the American President vividly demonstrated how eager he is to make the new relationship work.

Mr. Gorbachev had denied sending arms to El Salvador, Mr. Bush noted, while the United States had hard evidence that Soviet arms were reaching the insurgent forces there. Other American Presidents might have left the matter there, with the implication that the Soviets were being less than candid. But Mr. Bush reached a completely different conclusion.

The Sandinista Government in Nicaragua, the President said, must have shipped the Soviet weapons to El Salvador and then lied about their activities "to our Soviet friends."

Only at a time when the American attitudes are undergoing a profound change, with more and more Americans looking upon the Soviet Union not as an enemy but almost as the ally that it was during World War II, could Mr. Bush so clearly signal his willingness to give Mr. Gorbachev the benefit of the doubt. It will be more difficult now for his critics at home to accuse him of halfheartedness in his approach to the changes wrought by the Soviet leader.

The most important achievement here, one of Mr. Bush's advisers said, was to put "a new political impetus, a new impetus of personal leadership," behind United States–Soviet relations. The clear feeling among White House staff members and senior Kremlin officials was that this, plus an accelerated timetable for two sets of arms-reduction talks, plus good chemistry between the two leaders, made success in their summit conference next year in the United States a probability, not merely a possibility.

"I couldn't have asked for a better result from this non-summit summit," President Bush said. For Mr. Gorbachev, the broad spectrum of economic assistance offered by his friend in the White House, from better access to the Western trading bloc to lower tariffs on Soviet products in the United States to (improbably enough) American help in setting up a Soviet stock market, could not have been more welcome as the Soviet Union begins a long, cold winter.

Most of all, a Soviet official said, Mr. Gorbachev was greatly relieved that Mr. Bush now seemed fully engaged in the relationship in a way that he had not been before, and seemed disposed to look for ways he could help the Soviet program of perestroika, or restructuring, toward success.

In the early months of the Bush Administration, some officials questioned whether Mr. Gorbachev was really a reformer and asked whether the White House should help him. Those in favor of Mr. Gorbachev argued that Ronald Reagan, in the last years of his Presidency, had become more trustful of Mr. Gorbachev.

The mood generated here may prove less transitory than earlier waves of good feeling generated by summit meetings, but there are still problems with regard to regional conflicts, as in Central America, and with regard to arms control, with both sea-launched cruise missiles and chemical weapons.

"Look, we've got some differences," President Bush acknowledged. Both leaders seemed eager to sidestep the German question, for an evident reason: any move by the two Germanys to amalgamate or confederate will tend to undercut the North Atlantic Treaty Organization or the Warsaw Pact or both, and Mr. Bush and Mr. Gorbachev are counting on those two organizations, perhaps in changed form, to give them leverage in Europe.

Mr. Bush, furthermore, was at some pains to avoid giving offense to the Western Europeans—at least according to the accounts of his aides. He may have told Mr. Gorbachev of plans to cut United States troop strength in Europe; if so, he will presumably tell his allies in Brussels on Monday.

The plan to hold the conference on board Soviet and American warships, which was a White House idea, designed perhaps to generate public-relations echoes of the Roosevelt-Churchill talks during World War II off Newfoundland, didn't work out as planned, having failed to take into account the unpredictability of the weather. The meetings had to be shortened and moved to the cruise liner *Maxim Gorky*, docked nearby, because of mountainous seas.

Unlike Mr. Gorbachev, President Bush made no claim that the cold war was over, and unlike Mr. Reagan, he made only modest claims for the nature of his relationship with the Soviet leader.

"I don't think that he has me down as a total negativist," said Mr. Bush of Mr. Gorbachev, "and I certainly don't have him down as one."

In the end, Mr. Bush proposed more here than his staff had indicated that he would, and Mr. Gorbachev proposed less than expected. But then, it was Mr. Bush's turn, since the Soviet leader has been springing surprises almost weekly in recent months, and Mr. Bush must have been dying to do something unexpected, given his almost obsessive delight in keeping secrets.

Surprising as the turnaround in superpower relations had been, they were still not as startling as the almost daily events taking place in Eastern Europe. It appeared at times that the all the countries except Rumania were leapfrogging each other as they raced to democracy. Poland had been the first to challenge the party's political power; Hungary had been the first to have its party rename itself. Bulgaria was the first to take up the elimination of constitutional guarantees of the Communist Party's leading role. Under such onslaughts, the once all-powerful Communists were abasing themselves, offering concessions and self-criticism and sacrificing their more prominent leaders in vain attempts to appease the crowds who were calling for the end of a system. One of the more bizarre developments came when the Czechoslovak Communists moved to condemn the very act that gave them their authority.

Czech Party Calls '68 Invasion Wrong
By Serge Schmemann

PRAGUE, Dec. 1—The new Politburo of the Czechoslovak Communist Party declared today that the Soviet-led invasion that choked the Prague Spring of 1968 was wrong.

"We are of the opinion that the entry onto our territory of five armies of the Warsaw Pact in 1968 was not justified, and the decision to do so was wrong," said Vasil Mohorita, one of the reform-minded officials elevated to the 13-member Politburo last weekend, reporting at a news conference on today's meeting of the party's ruling body.

As the Politburo made the declaration, President Mikhail S. Gorbachev of the Soviet Union acknowledged that the Czechoslovak uprising of 1968 resulted from a yearning for democracy, and East Germany joined Hungary and Poland in apologizing to Czechoslovakia for participating in the military attack.

Mr. Gorbachev told a news conference in Milan, Italy, that the Czechoslovak reform movement in 1968 was "a process of democratization, renewal and humanization of society."

"It was right at that time and it is right now," he said.

But he stopped short of condemning the Soviet intervention, saying that the action had to be seen in the context of the tense East-West relations of the time.

By their condemnation of the Warsaw Pact invasion, the ten new appointees and the three Politburo holdovers basically undermined the position of all the Communists who have ruled here until last week. None of the members are old enough to have profited directly from the invasion, but their elders and patrons in the party were installed in their posts by the 1968 intervention that Moscow described at the time as "fraternal assistance."

One of the principal beneficiaries of this action was Gustav Husak, long the party leader and now Czechoslovakia's head of state. . . .

Four days later, the '68 invasion was formally condemned by the invaders.

Warsaw Pact Condemns '68 Prague Invasion
By Bill Keller

MOSCOW, Dec. 4—The Soviet Union and four Warsaw Pact allies made a common break with the past today by jointly condemning the Soviet-led 1968 military suppression of the Czechoslovak experiment in political liberalization called the Prague Spring.

The Kremlin also agreed today to open discussions with Czechoslovakia on the withdrawal of Soviet troops from that country, linked to broader East-West disarmament negotiations.

Meeting as several of their governments were still reeling from democratic upheavals, the leaders of the Eastern bloc called the 1968 invasion "illegal" and pledged a strict policy of noninterference in each other's internal affairs, the Soviet press agency Tass reported tonight.

The statement was signed by the five countries that took part in the invasion: the Soviet Union, East Germany, Poland, Hungary and Bulgaria. The Soviet Union also issued its own, separate declaration of repentance for contriving to stifle change in Czechoslovakia, its first official admission that the invasion was wrong. The Warsaw Pact statement today was in contrast to one issued on August 21, 1968, by the same countries saying they had sent armed forces to Czechoslovakia at the invitation of the Czechoslovak Communist Party and Government leaders to deal with "the threat emanating from the counter-revolutionary forces that have entered into a collusion with foreign forces hostile to socialism."

The crushing of the Prague Spring had already been condemned by the two alliance members that did not take part, Rumania, which refused to join the invading force, and Czechoslovakia itself. They reportedly endorsed today's statement by the invaders.

Rezso Nyers, chairman of Hungary's Socialist Party, told Hungarian journalists tonight that the declaration marked a formal repudiation of the Brezhnev doctrine, the Kremlin principle of intervening to prevent a retreat from Communism. . . .

Admissions of error and concessionary promises of freely contested elections, an end to the legally entrenched dominance of the Communist Party and the withdrawal of Soviet troops, while welcome, failed to silence the clamor of aroused nations. In East Germany, the party was withering in plain sight.

East Germans Fear New Freedom Could Outstrip Ways to Control It
By Craig R. Whitney

EAST BERLIN, Dec. 2—The position of Egon Krenz, who took over as Communist Party leader on October 18, appeared to be unraveling rapidly tonight on the eve of an emergency meeting of the party's Central Committee, scheduled for Sunday.

A crowd outside party headquarters this evening demanded Mr. Krenz's resignation and that of the rest of the Politburo, booing Mr. Krenz when he arrived. Many in the crowd said the new leadership under Mr. Krenz had failed to react strongly enough to reports of corruption and misuse of office by the country's old-guard leaders.

News of the growing clamor for Mr. Krenz's departure was broadcast on the East German television, which said the demonstrations would resume on Sunday night if the leadership did not quit.

Mr. Krenz, hearing the calls for his resignation, said, "I will report to the Central Committee of our party about the atmosphere here." He was sweating in the cold night air.

The demonstration reflected an intensifying mood of anger and disgust at a spate of revelations of abuses of power and authority. Mr. Krenz, responsible for internal security under Erich Honecker, the party chief ousted in October, has been criticized as one of the "new old men," as one party critic put it in an article published on Thursday in the East German newspaper *Berliner Zeitung*.

The Central Committee meeting was called without explanation on Friday. Several members said tonight that they expected Mr. Krenz and the entire Politburo brought in with him in the last month to resign, staying in office in a caretaker role until a special party congress, which begins on December 15.

A wide range of party members, diplomats and others here say the only figure who appears to have enough authority to take Mr. Krenz's place is Hans Modrow, the former party leader in Dresden, who became Prime Minister on November 13. The youngest member of the leadership, 37-year-old Hans-Joachim Willerding, a nonvoting member of the Politburo, resigned tonight, saying he no longer felt able to represent the party membership adequately, East German television reported.

The growing political crisis makes it clear that the Communist Party leaders, trying to save the system that has run the country for forty years by opening the Berlin wall and lifting most restrictions on public debate, set off a chain reaction that rapidly escaped their control, diplomats, party officials and ordinary citizens here say. . . .

The collapse of the authority of the Communist Party is accelerating, and its constitutionally prescribed leading role was eliminated on Friday by the East German legislature after forty years. The newspapers and television, newly free to report and comment on the failings and even crimes of its leading officials, are doing so with a vengeance, astonishing even longtime observers of the country's affairs. . . .

In Czechoslovakia, the Communists having promised to share power with non-Communists, came up with a coalition that reserved the lion's share of power for themselves while promising to do better and condemning the '68 invasion. This approach was denounced and essentially vetoed by the people, who once again turned out in Wenceslas Square.

Protest Rallies Resume in Prague in Effort to Oust New Government
By Henry Kamm

PRAGUE, Dec. 4—About 200,000 people poured into Wenceslas Square today to shout their rejection of a new Government formed on Sunday and to applaud a call for a general strike next Monday if it is not replaced.

Renewing protests suspended last Monday after Prime Minister Ladislav Adamec promised a multiparty Cabinet and other concessions, the marchers denounced the new Government as a betrayal.

The Cabinet presented by Mr. Adamec on Sunday is made up of sixteen Communists, two members of parties that had historically been aligned with the Communists and three independents. Opposition spokesmen said the Cabinet would keep intact the "leading role" for the Communist Party that Parliament struck from the Constitution last week as part of the concessions.

Responding to Sunday's announcement, student opposition leaders today reversed a decision to scale back a strike that is keeping all places of higher learning occupied and inactive. Actors and other performers called off an announcement that theaters and concert halls would reopen tonight. Since last month, theaters have been used for political discussions in which members of the Civic Forum opposition group replace actors onstage and discuss the upheaval with the public.

"We are forced to continue our strike," Miroslav Machacek, an actor and director, said in remarks to the demonstrators today.

"Long live the actors!" the protesters replied.

For the first time, a representative of industrial workers called for the formation of independent trade unions. The workers' representative, Igor Pleskov, said committees maintaining a strike alert throughout the country should be converted into the cores of independent unions. "Let's take our affairs into our own hands," he said.

In addition, leaders of Civic Forum, the main opposition group to emerge from the demonstrations of recent weeks, declared for the first time that it would function like a political party. Forum leaders and representatives of Public Against Violence, a similar organization that emerged in the Slovakian region of the country, announced at the rally that they would be offering a common list of candidates for parliamentary elections that the opposition has demanded for no later than July. The crowd cheered in the cold and darkness of the afternoon.

It was the first time Civic Forum representatives spoke publicly of turning the group into a competitive political party. Forum leaders had insisted that the group saw its role solely as stimulating free political expression and assisting fledgling political groups. . . .

The gathering today turned into a passionate dialogue, in which speakers' demands and declarations were greeted not with chants or slogans, as before, but with pointed comments from those gathered in front of the balcony. Those words were taken up by others standing farther away, until they rolled to the farthest fringes.

"Undoubtedly a number of members of Parliament have betrayed our confidence," said Radim Palous, a spokesman of Civic Forum. Then he began reciting a list of offenders. "Jakes," he began, referring to the deposed Communist chief, Milos Jakes.

The crowd responded, "Throw him out immediately."

He continued, naming Vaclac David, a former Foreign Minister; Jan Foitik, the ousted curator of ideology; and Alois Indra and Vasil Bilak, former party presidium members who had supported the Soviet-led invasion of 1968.

"Send them to work" came the chorus.

At Mr. Palous's next listing of deputies, the crowd roared, "Give them a shovel."

"They have lost the right to be deputies," the speaker said. "Mafia," the crowd responded. "You no longer have our mandate," the speaker said of the deputies.

"They don't have it," the chorus crowed.

What was happening in Prague was that the crowd was coalescing into a political force. Unlike Poland, where Solidarity had forged programs and structures during nearly a decade of clandestine activities, Czechoslovakia had no mass dissident movement. Nor were the churches able to serve as sanctuaries for protest, as was true in both Poland and East Germany. Essentially there were only a handful of often-persecuted dissidents associated with groups like Charter 77 and the Committee for the Defense of the Unjustly Accused. And yet, when the dam of repression began to give way, these few people—a playwright. a priest, and a number of coal stokers—formed a political nucleus that very quickly attracted a mass of followers.

Civic Forum: Politics on a Shoestring
By Henry Kamm

PRAGUE, Dec. 5—Civic Forum, which in scarcely two weeks has assumed the mantle of Czechoslovakia's political opposition, is a mass movement whose members simply declare themselves by shouting for freedom at demonstrations and whose leaders serve by acclamation.

And yet despite such loose organization, the group has forced and shaped greater changes in the country than what has taken place in two decades.

The group has no master plan, no bylaws, and its strategy is not drafted by professional consultants. Instead, its leaders, a group clustered around Vaclav Havel, the dramatist and human rights campaigner, conduct marathon crisis sessions in temporary headquarters in a dingy downtown theater, altering their plans from hour to hour. The group is in the process of moving to quarters that until recently housed the Czech-Soviet Friendship Society.

As the discussions continue into the night, new people come in while weary participants head elsewhere. For instance, as Mr. Havel and some others crossed the Vltava River to meet with Prime Minister Ladislav Adamec, others headed to a balcony on Wenceslas Square to address crowds or to attend concerts to be cheered by young supporters, or to go to news conferences and interviews.

The atmosphere is hectic and informal. Even distinguished visitors get only cursory attention. When Alexander Dubcek, who led the Prague Spring of 1968, called on Mr. Havel last week, the playwright, who had others waiting for him, had Mr. Dubcek sit in on a staff meeting. The former leader listened to the discussion, which continued as if he were not there, for two and a half hours and then left quietly.

Meals are taken on the fly or not at all. Most participants are clearly in need of sleep. The wife of a principal leader, asked if she needed anything available from the West, replied, "We're running short of vitamin pills to keep him going." The Forum is run on a shoestring, with all of its leaders and volunteer workers paying their own way. They all continue to go to their regular jobs while they debate and shape the future of their nation.

One example of the activities that have been going on in the basement of the Laterna Magica theater is reflected in the efforts of three men who have been pondering and discussing what kind of program and what kind of priorities Forum should propose to the nation, once the machinery is set up for national dialogue and public discourse.

"In three days—which for this period is a very long time—of very intense discussions, we worked out our principles," said Josef Vavrousek, an economist and ecologist, who worked with Petr Pithart, a lawyer and political scientist, and Ivan Havel, Vaclav's brother, a computer specialist.

The principles, made public last Wednesday, state broad goals under the headings of law, politics, foreign policy, economy, social justice, environment and culture. The statement sets the objective of turning Czechoslovakia into a democratic state of laws that will "again assume its honorable place" in the world.

Currently nine subcommittees are at work to put flesh on these bare bones. In addition to the seven principles, there is one charged with recording today's history and that of 1968 and the Soviet-led invasion, and another that is concerned with planning the internal organization of Forum.

In an interview in a café above his windowless "office," Mr. Vavrousek emphasized that there would be no revenge. "We don't want another genocide of the Czech intelligentsia," he said, referring to the mass firings and expulsions of professionals who refused to approve the invasion in the months after the tanks arrived. He also referred to the purges and persecutions of intellectuals in the last fifty years, the first carried out by Nazis in 1938–39, and the other by the Communists in 1948.

"We can't say, 'You're a Communist, so you're no good,' " Mr. Vavrousek said. "There are 1.7 million party members. That would mean another decline of Czechoslovakia."

Mr. Vavrousek added that of the various impulses that have brought the adherents of Forum together "the ethical level is the most important consideration." He noted that the group, which came together so quickly and suddenly, embraces many different points of view. "Ethics is the integrative factor for all of us," he continued.

Moreover, said Mr. Vavrousek, ethical pressure is the major mechanism by which the mass membership influences those who have assumed leadership. "They criticize extremely hard" when they believe a speaker for the Forum is showing intolerance, he said.

He said Mr. Havel held a special position. "We are respectful to each other, but he gets slightly more respect than all the others," said Mr. Vavrousek, attributing the high esteem for Mr. Havel to the commitment to moral positions that the playwright showed through years of imprisonment.

"We can only understand this by the history of Czechoslovakia," he said when asked to explain the exceptional tolerance shown to representatives of a repressive regime during its decline. He said it grew from "a culture of mutual understanding" that kept the Czech nation alive in three centuries of subjugation to Austria.

Mr. Vavrousek said Mr. Havel was directly linked to the ethics of Thomas G. Masaryk, the founding President of Czechoslovakia, who anchored the nation's political character in the tradition of humaneness.

He said the Communist regime had driven people into "inner emigration" by violating these values. To be in contact with those of common values, which was politically impossible, Mr. Vavrousek said, people found each other in churches or sports clubs and other innocuous groups. "Even people in the party joined," he said.

"These became the cells of the Civic Forum," said Mr. Vavrousek. "Together, they have set off a chain reaction of mutual trust."

On December 6 Egon Krenz, who had replaced Erich Honecker as a younger, ostensibly less tainted, more acceptable leader, bowed out like his predecessor, who by this time was under detention facing charges of abusing his power and enriching himself. In Prague, Ladislav Adamec, the new and ostensible liberal Communist Prime Minister, threatened to quit. And Vaclav Havel, the ironic playwright and much imprisoned dissident, declared that he was willing to serve as President.

East German Out as Chief of State; Party in Disarray
By Serge Schmemann

EAST BERLIN, Dec. 6—East Germany's fallen Communist chief, Egon Krenz, gave up his remaining state positions today amid the continuing political turmoil. The foundering Communist Party advanced its emergency congress to Friday and is expected to shed its Stalinist structures and even its name.

The developments added to a sense of a political whirlwind, fed by the rapid disintegration of the Communist Party before the anger of the nation over revelations of widespread corruption at the top.

Mr. Krenz was replaced as the head of state on an interim basis by Manfred Gerlach, the head of the small Liberal Democratic Party, which until recently was subservient to the Communists but like other small parties has broken away. . . .

The caretaker committee formed Sunday to steer the Communist Party toward the emergency congress announced today that the meeting would start Friday instead of December 15.

The committee gave no reason for the shift, but several party members said a tide of resignations by members, coupled with the collapse of party authority, had made it imperative to hold the congress as soon as possible. Delegates have already been selected by local organizations.

Members said the congress would almost certainly change the name of the Communist Party, whose official name is the Socialist Unity Party, and could well transform it along the lines of Western social democracy, possibly abandoning the factory cells that have traditionally been its primary base.

Neues Deutschland, the official Communist organ, asked in an editorial whether the party needed a Politburo any longer and urged the congress to "radically end structural Stalinism." The *Berliner Zeitung* urged a new name for a "new socialist party."

But given the tempo of the time, no one dared to predict what the congress would do, or how long it would last. . . .

At the East Berlin City Hall, a government committee opened public hearings on the violent clashes between the police and demonstrators in early October. The clashes led to the mass demonstrations that toppled Mr. Honecker.

At today's session, the East Berlin Police Chief, Friedhelm Rausch, said the former Minister of State Security, Erich Mielke, had given the direct order "under all circumstances not to permit demonstrations and to disperse them."

Czech Premier Quits as Dissidents Press to Control Cabinet
By John Tagliabue

PRAGUE, Dec. 7—Ladislav Adamec resigned today as Czechoslovakia's Communist Prime Minister and was replaced by his relatively unknown 43-year-old deputy. Mr. Adamec reportedly felt that the new leader would find it easier to put together a cabinet acceptable to the opposition led by Civic Forum.

The 63-year-old Mr. Adamec announced his resignation as he met with the increasingly independent members of once-docile parties allied to the Communists. According to some of these non-Communist politicians, Mr. Adamec told them that a new, younger leader would be better able to achieve a compromise on the composition of a Government.

Shortly thereafter, President Gustav Husak, among the hardest of Czechoslovak hard-liners, asked Marian Calfa, a Slovak, who was named deputy Prime Minister when the current Government was empaneled five days ago, to take over for Mr. Adamec and continue seeking a solution.

In the meantime, Civic Forum sustained its pressure on the Government, once again raising the prospect of renewed mass demonstrations and a general strike, as its leaders publicly offered the names of recently imprisoned and ostracized dissidents on lists of those it wanted to be included in a Government that would diminish the power of the Communists.

Spokesmen for the Forum said that shortly before Mr. Adamec resigned he had been given a list of people favored by the Forum for ministerial appointments that included Jiri Dienstbier, a man who has spent most of the last two decades forced to work as a coal stoker; Jan Carnogursky, a Catholic human rights campaigner released from prison two weeks ago; and Petr Miller, a worker at a large industrial plant in Prague.

The opposition group spokesman said the group had nominated Mr. Dienstbier to be Foreign Minister, Mr. Carnogursky to be deputy Prime Minister, and Mr. Miller as Minister of Social Affairs.

As pressure on the Government mounted, some people within the small People's Party, which has recently allied itself more and more with Civic Forum, said that the goal of negotiations between the opposition and the Government should be the replacement of the Communist President, Gustav Husak, and the formation of a cabinet in which Communist Ministers would be a minority.

As the demands on the Government seemed to increase, Civic Forum leaders renewed their warnings that a general strike, similar to a two-hour nationwide work stoppage they staged last week, would be held this Monday unless talks produced some significant progress. . . .

Havel Makes It Official: He'd Accept Top Billing
By Henry Kamm

PRAGUE, Dec. 7—Vaclav Havel, the playwright and opposition leader, declared his readiness tonight to become President.

His announcement, in reply to a barrage of questions at a news conference, marked a quantum jump in a meteoric political career. In less than a month, the modest 53-year-old writer has gone from being a bookish and persecuted symbol of resistance to totalitarianism to become the acclaimed leader of the Civic Forum mass movement, which is shaking the foundations of a 41-year-old Communist regime.

The boyish-looking Mr. Havel, who until recently was often conveyed in police cars and police wagons, has since last week been riding in chauffeured Government limousines to meetings with the top leaders of the Communist Party and state structure.

And tonight, after fencing wittily with several reporters and refusing to deny his availability, he finally owned up to it.

"I have repeatedly said my occupation is writer," he replied to an American correspondent. "I have no political ambitions. I don't feel myself to be a professional politician. But I have always placed the public interest above my own.

"And if, God help us, the situation develops in such a way that the only service that I could render my country would be to do this, then of course I would do it." . . .

The whirlwind pace of change had most Czechoslovaks concentrating on where they were headed, wondering what new twists lay ahead. But from the west of the country came a story that underscored how far they had already come.

For Hidden Slovak Dissidents, a Guide
By Brenda Fowler

BRATISLAVA, CZECHOSLOVAKIA—When a visitor rings the doorbell at the apartment of Bishop Jan Korec, there is no sound inside, but a small light goes on in the kitchen. He would not want frequent ringing to be heard by the neighbors upstairs, who for the last eight years have been assigned to keep tabs on Bishop Korec, the leader of the underground church in Slovakia.

Prohibited from celebrating Mass because his secret ordination in

311

1950 is not recognized by the state-sponsored organization of priests, the 64-year-old Bishop has worked quietly since then, waiting for a time when he might openly practice his faith again.

His life underground parallels that of many dissidents in Slovakia, where 60 percent of the population is Catholic. Less oriented toward the West and its media than their statesmen in Prague, many Slovaks have worked quietly within the Catholic Church, publishing illegal books and newspapers and sometimes going to prison. Unlike best-known opposition figures in Bohemia—the region that includes the capital—such as the Civic Forum leader Vaclav Havel, few Slovak dissidents are members of human rights groups like Charter 77.

"In Slovakia, the leaders of the movement were ordinary people in the church and only a few intellectuals," said Jan Carnogursky, a Catholic dissident here who was the only person from Slovakia at a meeting between Mr. Havel and Government officials in November.

"And even the intellectuals weren't interested in publicity," Mr. Carnogursky said. "Mostly they were just interested in working among young people and they felt that publicity would hurt them."

The most common form of protest in Slovakia is the pilgrimage, dozens of which are held each year, he said. Last year, 500,000 Slovaks took part in pilgrimages, and one to the thirteenth-century town of Levoca drew more than 100,000 people.

But there have also been demonstrations. Slovak Catholics maintain that the student protest on November 17 in Prague was not the first occasion that police intervened brutally at a large demonstration in the last twenty years.

In March of last year, they said, several thousand Catholics, including many elderly people, gathered with candles in front of the National Theater here to call for greater religious freedom. The police closed off the area and began harassing the protesters, finally using water cannon to disperse them.

For Bishop Korec, the mass demonstrations and changes in the Communist Party and Czechoslovak Government have brought a sense that his own personal struggles and those of all Slovak Catholics may finally be nearing an end.

As a young seminary student in 1950, he was briefly interned when the Government liquidated all monasteries and seminaries. An interned bishop secretly ordained him a priest in 1950. Less than a year later his superiors decided to make him a bishop, and he was secretly consecrated on August 24, 1951.

"Then I began fulfilling my mission," the Bishop said, though at that time not even his mother knew he was a bishop. He spent the next ten years doing manual labor until he was arrested in 1960 on a charge of treason for having helped to educate seminary students. Sentenced to 12 years in prison, and led out of the court handcuffed to a murderer, Bishop Korec worked on a lathe shaping crystal for chandeliers, a job that ground away the fingertips of those not trained for such a craft.

During the liberalization movement of 1968 he was released from prison and met Pope Paul VI at the Vatican, though he was still not allowed to work as a priest. Since 1970 the Bishop has lived in the apartment of a friend, working in a small room crammed with books. In that time he has written the bulk of his 65 manuscripts and books, most of them published abroad.

The authorities have continued to harass him, and he has been interrogated by police 30 times in the last ten years. This interview, Bishop Korec said, indicating his informant-neighbors upstairs, was only the second time in eight years that he has spoken in a normal voice.

Then, his voice dropping to a whisper, his eyes opening wide, he asked, "Can you imagine what kind of a total physical stress it was to speak like this? Can you imagine?"

Farther to the northeast, another people were pursuing their own plans for establishing democratic pluralism. The Lithuanians were advancing their challenge not on the streets but through parliamentary and Constitutional means.

Lithuania Legalizes Rival Parties, Removing Communists' Monopoly
By Esther B. Fein

MOSCOW, Dec. 7—Lithuania became the first Soviet republic to abolish the Communist Party's guaranteed monopoly on power when its parliament voted overwhelmingly today to legalize rival political parties.

Rejecting repeated Kremlin pleas and warnings to curb its political defiance, the Lithuanian parliament changed the republic's constitution to abolish the guarantee of power for the Communist Party.

With the vote of 243 to 1 with 39 abstentions, Lithuania, one of 15

Soviet republics, joined the majority of Eastern bloc nations in legalizing a multiparty system.

In neighboring Estonia, the central committee of the Communist Party agreed at a meeting today that Article Six of the republic's constitution, which guarantees the Communist Party's pre-eminence, should be annulled, setting the stage for a similar constitutional amendment in that republic.

Both decisions today are clear signs that the tensions tearing at the former strongholds of Communist power elsewhere in Eastern Europe are growing in the Soviet Union itself.

The actions are sure to anger President Mikhail S. Gorbachev, who while not interfering with such moves by the Soviet Union's East European allies, has said the Communist Party is the only force capable of seeing the country through its current economic and political crises.

A leading Lithuanian Communist Party official said today that Mr. Gorbachev had "without a doubt" contacted the Lithuanian party leader, Algirdas Brazauskas, to try to prevent the legislature's move and to censure it. But Mr. Brazauskas clearly resisted the pressure, which Mr. Gorbachev has brought to bear on several previous occasions, and voted for the constitutional amendment.

The parliaments of Poland, Hungary, Czechoslovakia and East Germany have all voted recently to deny the Communist Party its long-guaranteed "leading role" in political, educational and social spheres.

According to people who attended or listened to the Lithuanian parliamentary session today, several deputies spoke of the changes elsewhere in Eastern Europe and urged the legislators to continue the progressive path that Lithuania had already begun. . . .

Amid the decay so evident in the Communist world, the only appeal for the retention of orthodoxy came from an island ninety miles from Florida.

Castro Says He'll Resist Changes Like Those Sweeping Soviet Bloc
By Larry Rohter

MEXICO CITY, Dec. 8—In his bluntest public rejection yet of the profound political and economic changes now sweeping the rest of the

Soviet bloc, President Fidel Castro of Cuba has vowed to resist all such reforms even if it means a parting of the ways with his allies.

"If destiny assigns us the role of one day being among the last defenders of socialism in a world in which the Yankee empire has succeeded in embodying Hitler's dream of world domination, we will know how to defend this bulwark to the last drop of blood," President Castro said in a speech delivered on Thursday in Havana and monitored here.

Mr. Castro's remarks were his first public comment on the state of East-West relations since last weekend's summit talks between President Bush and President Mikhail S. Gorbachev of the Soviet Union and reflected his growing ideological isolation within the Eastern bloc. At the meeting off Malta, Mr. Bush called on Mr. Gorbachev to do more to prevent Cuba from shipping arms to Nicaragua and to leftist guerrillas in El Salvador and also offered to assist Mr. Gorbachev in carrying out economic reforms.

Speaking at ceremonies honoring Cuban combatants killed in the course of "internationalist missions" in Angola, Ethiopia and other African countries, Mr. Castro did not criticize Mr. Gorbachev or any Eastern European leader by name. But he complained of the difficulty of building a Communist state when others are "slandering socialism, destroying its values, discrediting the party and liquidating its leading role, doing away with social discipline and sowing chaos and anarchy everywhere."

Mr. Gorbachev's policies of perestroika and glasnost, or restructuring and openness, have aroused interest in Cuba, which experimented briefly with a degree of economic liberalization early in the decade but then reversed course with a "rectification" program after Mr. Castro decided that some people were making too much money and egalitarianism was eroding. The Soviet leader received a warm popular welcome when he visited Cuba in April, but Mr. Castro has rejected many of Mr. Gorbachev's innovations as violations of Marxist-Leninist orthodoxy.

The transformations taking place elsewhere in the Soviet bloc coincide with Cuba's most serious political and leadership crisis in years. In July, several senior Cuban military officials were executed for drug trafficking in circumstances that have yet to be fully explained, and economic and morale problems have also forced Mr. Castro, who is 63 years old and has been in power for more than thirty years, to shake up his Cabinet.

The Cuban leader has long feared that the lessening of tensions between the United States and the Soviet Union will translate into changes in the military status quo in Europe that would increase Washington's ability to impose its own views elsewhere, including the Caribbean. He also remains firmly committed to the principle of "proletarian internationalism," a justification for intervention abroad that he fears is on the wane elsewhere.

According to reports from Managua, the Soviet Ambassador there met with Nicaraguan and Cuban officials on November 28, just days after Mr. Bush had blamed the Soviet Union for supplying arms to Mr. Castro that eventually ended up in the hands of rebels in El Salvador. "We are hearing that he really read them the riot act," said a European diplomat based in the Nicaraguan capital.

The official Cuban news agency Prensa Latina reported on Thursday that American forces at Guantanamo Bay Naval Station had fired twice on Cuban sentries outside, calling the incident "serious and of unpredictable consequences." Today, a Pentagon spokesman denied the charge, saying "no weapons or rounds ever crossed the fence line."

In his address, Mr. Castro justified the prohibition in Cuba of some Soviet publications, such as *Sputnik* and *Moscow News*. He said the measure was necessary because such publications were "filled with venom against the U.S.S.R. itself and against socialism" and have "demanded the cessation of just and equitable commercial relations between the U.S.S.R. and Cuba."

Since the early 1960's the Soviet Union has heavily subsidized the Cuban economy through such measures as the purchase of Cuban sugar at prices well above market levels and the sale at bargain rates of petroleum, some of which Cuba then resells to gain hard currency. Those subsidies, amounting to as much as $5 billion a year, have increasingly been questioned by Soviet officials as part of the economic restructuring that is under way.

"From the crisis that has emerged in the socialist camp, we can only expect negative economic consequences for our country," Mr. Castro said.

Just hours before Mr. Castro's appearance at the war commemoration ceremonies, during which he was accompanied by President Jose Eduardo dos Santos of Angola, the Cuban Government for the first time announced casualty figures for the more than 400,000 soldiers and "technical advisers" it has sent to fight in Africa over the last fifteen years. According to official statements, 2,289 Cubans have died abroad, more than 2,000 of them in Angola.

If there were any in East Germany who heard Mr. Castro's counsel, they may well have regarded the advice as either outdated or absurd. Instead of resorting to old slogans, the beleaguered party hunkered down in an emergency congress, and after rejecting a motion to dissolve itself, voted in Gregor Gysi as its new leader, citing among his virtues the fact that as a lawyer he had defended members of the amorphous New Forum opposition when they were persecuted three months earlier.

• • •

The paramount issue for those who had marched to bring down old Communist leaders had been liberty. The paramount issue for the leaders still plying their trade in both the East and the West was becoming the maintenance of stability, limits and borders. At the heart was the German question, and Helmut Kohl, who had earlier offered his vision of an amalgamated German nation without consulting any allies, now spoke in less definite terms.

Bonn Leader Softens His Plan for German Unity
By Craig R. Whitney

WEST BERLIN, Dec. 11—Taking account of foreign concerns, Chancellor Helmut Kohl of West Germany softened a vital element of his vision of German unity today as representatives of the four wartime occupying powers met here and insisted on "the importance of stability" in Eastern Europe.

In a speech to members of his Christian Democratic Party, Mr. Kohl eased away from his notion of an early "confederation" of the two German states—an idea that has worried the European allies, the United States and the Soviet Union by suggesting that German reunification could come without international approval.

"For several reasons, I am consciously not talking about a 'confederation,'" he said. "One of these reasons is that such a step raises questions that we cannot yet answer today because of the fact that both states in Germany belong to different alliances."

Mr. Kohl, who now says West Germany will not move toward unification without consulting with the Western alliance and the Soviet Union, said, "The goal of our policy never has been and never will be to establish an overpowerful Germany in the middle of Europe, as many in the Council of Europe, in London, Rome and Paris fear—just look at the newspapers," he said. But he added, "Reunification—that

317

is, regaining the state unity of Germany—remains our political goal."

While openly acknowledging the uneasiness of Germany's neighbors, Mr. Kohl also spoke with a view toward domestic politics on the issue of unification, which has become the central theme of West Germany's 1990 election campaign. As the Chancellor encouraged his Christian Democrats to run as the party that encouraged East Germans to march for freedom, the Social Democratic opposition in Bonn announced its own plan for a confederation of the two Germanys and accused the Kohl forces of plagiarizing its ideas. Mr. Kohl suggested today that many people had misunderstood his proposals, but he also said that German policy was being made not in the chancelleries but in the streets. And in protests tonight in the East German cities of Leipzig and Dresden, as many as 300,000 people took to the streets in a huge demonstration marked by insistent calls for unification, more so than in previous weeks. . . .

Since the upheavals began, the United States had been either slow or deliberate in its reactions. But as the year was ending, Secretary of State Baker visited both Germanys and outlined a comprehensive plan reaffirming a U.S. role in the new Europe that was yet to emerge.

Baker, in Berlin, Outlines a Plan to Make NATO a Political Group
By Thomas L. Friedman

POTSDAM, EAST GERMANY, Dec. 12—Seeking to give some American direction to the rapidly changing events in Europe, Secretary of State James A. Baker 3d today outlined proposals for transforming NATO from a primarily military organization to a political alliance.

Mr. Baker's proposal, made in a speech to the Berlin Press Club in West Berlin, was part of the most comprehensive and detailed set of ideas to emerge from the Bush Administration to deal with the upheavals that are reshaping the European political landscape.

Mr. Baker said he hoped that his ideas for recasting existing institutions like NATO, the European Economic Community and the Helsinki process could help channel the "peaceful revolution" under way in Europe into a stable, democratic new order.

Mr. Baker, in his speech, also proposed that the United States and the European Community work together to strengthen their ties. He urged support for changes in Czechoslovakia, Bulgaria and East Germany and suggested that the 35-nation Conference on Security and Cooperation in Europe be reshaped into a framework for "openness" between NATO and the armies of Eastern Europe.

Directly after his speech, Mr. Baker slipped into a Mercedes limousine and traveled to East Germany to deliver another message in a previously unanounced round of talks with East Germany's Communist Prime Minister, Hans Modrow, as well as with several East German opposition leaders.

Those talks were held in Potsdam, not far from the hall where Truman, Churchill and Attlee gathered to meet with Stalin in 1945 to frame Germany's postwar occupation, and they were made at the first visit of an American Secretary of State to East Germany. Potsdam lies just 20 miles southeast of Berlin.

While American officials would not say so explicitly, they left a clear impression that Mr. Baker's primary purpose in seeing Mr. Modrow was to do what he could to shore up his Government in the hope that it might survive long enough to conduct free elections, now scheduled for May. In other words, after refusing to visit East Germany for 45 years because it was considered to have an illegitimate, unrepresentative regime, an American Secretary of State finally made such a trip. Officials also said that Mr. Baker wanted personally to urge the opposition to keep its movement nonviolent and to approach the issue of German reunification with sober restraint. . . .

At about the same time, Mikhail Gorbachev was analyzing the tumult in Eastern Europe for his own Central Committee.

Excerpts from Speech by Gorbachev on Bloc

MOSCOW, Dec. 11—Following are excerpts from the speech by President Mikhail S. Gorbachev to the Communist Party Central Committee last Saturday, as translated by the Soviet press agency Tass:

Comrades, implementation of the long-term course of perestroika not only exerts a revolutionary influence on all the spheres of life of Soviet society, but also influences other socialist coutries and developments in the world. At the same time, perestroika itself comes under the influence of the world, and needs favorable international conditions.

This year signified major changes in Eastern Europe. In fact, processes there are developing swiftly. . . . The truth, about which we spoke so often in the past few years, has been reaffirmed once again: Where there is a delay in dealing with overripe problems, excesses are inevitable.

What is taking place in socialist countries is the logical outcome of a certain stage of development which made the peoples of these countries aware of the need for change. This is the result of internal development, the result of choice by peoples themselves.

For all the specificity of deep changes in socialist countries, one cannot deny the fact that they proceed in the same mainstream as our perestroika, although we in no way encouraged these processes.

In some socialist countries the situation has been unconventional. Fraternal parties are no longer ruling in Poland and Hungary. Our friends in the German Democratic Republic and Czechoslovakia have largely lost their positions. New political forces have emerged on the arena. They include both those who support the socialist idea and those who seek other ways of social development. . . .

The Soviet Union is building its relations with East European countries—whether they have been carrying out transformations for quite some time, or have only embarked on that road, or are yet to do it—on a single position of respect for sovereignty, noninterference and recognition of freedom of choice. We proceed from the fact that any nation has the right to decide its fate itself, including the choice of a system, ways, the pace and methods of its development. . . .

We firmly declare that we will see to it that no harm comes to the G.D.R. It is our strategic ally and a member of the Warsaw Treaty. It is necessary to proceed from the postwar realities—the existence of the two sovereign German states, members of the United Nations. Departure from this threatens . . . destabilization in Europe.

Naturally this is not to say that relations between the G.D.R. and the F.R.G. cannot change. Peaceful cooperation between them can and must develop. As for the future, it will take shape in the course of history, in the framework of the development of the general European process. . . .

Despite the image of tractability that Mr. Gorbachev was so eager to project abroad, at home he was growing more and more impatient with those who wanted to move faster and further than he thought appropriate.

Gorbachev Blocks Debate on Ending Party Supremacy

By Francis X. Clines

MOSCOW, Dec. 12—President Mikhail S. Gorbachev, appearing wary and temperamental, today beat back attempts by the national Congress to question the Communist Party's constitutional monopoly on power and politics in the Soviet Union.

In the vote rejecting the proposal to take the issue up now rather than later, Mr. Gorbachev was supported by 1,139 deputies, while 839 others favored enlarging the agenda to include debate over the existing Article Six, which gives Communists dominance. Fifty-six other legislators abstained.

The issue, an echo of the rush from Communism now under way in the Soviet Union's once-obeisant Eastern European satellites, was settled early and quickly by Mr. Gorbachev in the Congress's opening winter session.

The Soviet leader's obvious concern veered toward testiness at times, as he allocated most debating time to his own insistence on the party's necessary primacy and cut off some speakers, waving his hand dismissively and snapping, "That's all, that's all."

The debate demonstrated Mr. Gorbachev's overwhelming, near-bullying parliamentary dominance of the 2,106-member assembly. The Congress of People's Deputies, the nation's new lawmaking forum, is trying to come to grips with the limited democratic initiatives introduced last spring by Mr. Gorbachev in the nation's first partly competitive elections under its one-party system.

Only a few deputies came forward to present a call for multiparty politics and an end to Communism's seven decades of monopoly over society.

Among them was Andrei D. Sakharov, the Nobel laureate and human rights champion, who was unceremoniously cut short by Mr. Gorbachev. But the final vote still managed to put a considerable measure of minority interest in the issue on the public record, indicating, as Mr. Gorbachev conceded, that it likely would return if only as part of a less timely, more drawn out attempt to revise the Constitution.

"I think a way will be found," he declared, while tenaciously defending for now the party supremacy that the Eastern European nations have been typically shedding in their first days of poltical revolt.

321

The vote took place in the Palace of Congresses.

In a long, emotional, at times desk-slapping defense of Communist hegemony, Mr. Gorbachev contended the issue was a choice between remaining on an intensified quest for his perestroika program of national review while guided by the party, or veering off on a "hasty" political tangent.

"We would be making the biggest mistake," he said. He argued that he did not necessarily disagree with the proponents of change in the long run, but that changes should come "in the framework of the normal constitutional process."

That is a framework for procrastination, in the view of critics, but Mr. Gorbachev dismissed their attempt to raise the issue in the Congress as a "bell-ringing" fire brigade.

"We must not involve society in clashes," he told the lawmakers, some of whom predicted there would be repeated future attempts to debate the party's privileged status.

One leader of the nationalist movement in Estonia, Marju Lauristin, cautioned Mr. Gorbachev that the issue, now flaming with popular sentiment in Eastern Europe, had arrived. "It has ripened for discussion," she said in a direct, brief summary. "It's obsolete for our political system and now has become an obstacle."

Mr. Gorbachev, a lawyer and ever-vigilant master of the Congress's agenda, worked hard to hold the debate to the procedural question of changing the agenda and to rule out substantive statements questioning the party's monopoly on politics and power.

"I'm asking you two to leave," he told two deputies, ruling even before they spoke that their points were not germane.

"All deputies who do not have something new to propose may return to their seats," he announced, waving his hand in frowning contrast to the beaming, cooperative summit leader that so recently was on display in his role more familiar to the outside world.

One deputy who did reach the rostrum, Yevgeny Yevtushenko, the poet, spoke directly as a non-party member to the many Communists in the hall, warning them that in these times the party would be wise to take up the fight to open up the pluralism debate.

"You cannot gain prestige from a single paragraph," he said, referring to Article Six. "Such authority should be earned daily."

At the last minute, after Mr. Gorbachev had winnowed the speaker's line away, Dr. Sakharov arose from his sixth-row seat and walked slowly toward the microphone.

His approach prompted groans from some party stalwarts as he advanced to speak. Leaning to the microphone, he pleaded in his characteristic sharp-toned voice for the fullest congressional debate of such amendments crucial to revamping Communism as property ownership and party pluralism. "We have to open up a way for the Parliament to adopt these laws without amending the Constitution," Mr. Sakharov said, speaking of the urgency of the nation's needs.

"This will not do," Mr. Gorbachev interrupted at one of Dr. Sakharov's points, for a brief moment no longer taking his usual care to appear courtly toward a man respected in the West as a voice of conscience.

Dr. Sakharov sought to raise Article Six by citing telegrams from the public, but Mr. Gorbachev, unimpressed, interjected: "I can show you three folders of them with thousands. Let's not manipulate public opinion."

"That's all," he said, waving Dr. Sakharov back from the microphone.

That exchange marked the last public appearance by Dr. Sakharov. The old dissident, human rights campaigner and renowned physicist died of a heart attack two days later.

Government That Exiled Him Hurries to Mourn Sakharov
By Francis X. Clines

MOSCOW, Dec. 15—The Soviet Government, which once exiled Andrei D. Sakharov for being a human rights champion, today embraced him in death. President Mikhail S. Gorbachev mourned the national loss of "a man of conviction and sincerity."

The Government moved swiftly to seek a state funeral and marshal Politburo tributes for the tart-tongued humanist who died on Thursday night, only hours after delivering another denunciation of the Communist monopoly of the nation.

But the Sakharov family was reported working on other plans for the burial of the 68-year-old Nobel laureate and deputy to the new national legislature who collapsed from a heart attack and died alone in his study.

The sudden news swept this hard-pressed nation with much of the political and emotional power that Dr. Sakharov wielded in two decades of singular criticism of the Kremlin.

Many Soviet citizens felt that with his death President Gorbachev had lost a badly needed, greatly respected moral goad. And Dr. Sakharov's nation had lost another embattled individualist who demonstrated the virtue of resisting the regime at personal risk in the service of others' freedom.

"As long as he was alive, we all felt safe," said a woman who stood mourning on the street below his apartment, her face wet with tears and snow.

"Uzhasna," she muttered in Russian: terrible.

No less lamentable than the death of the physically frail, spiritually relentless man were the political ironies that ensued before the eyes of Muscovites: guards of the K.G.B., who once kept Dr. Sakharov at bay in his apartment, cleared a path to his front door this afternoon so a quickly assembled Government funeral commission could express sad-faced grief to his widow, Yelena G. Bonner.

Tass, the Government press agency, which once denounced Dr. Sakharov as a traitor deserving his six years of internal exile in Gorky, issued warm posthumous descriptions of him as a civil rights battler and even offered videotapes of his final days for sale to foreign correspondents at $1,500.

Dr. Sakharov's death was the opening story on the evening television news program *Vremya*. The account focused briefly on the moment of silence observed in the Congress rather than on a detailed biography of Dr. Sakharov and his long history of resisting the Kremlin. *Izvestia,* the Government newspaper, had no mention in its evening edition.

Zglyad, the alternative Friday television program of current events, now the most popular in the nation, devoted considerable time and sympathy to Dr. Sakharov in the recollective style reminiscent of American television's treatment of the assassination of Senator Robert F. Kennedy and the Rev. Dr. Martin Luther King, Jr. Most poignant was a moment when Dr. Sakharov's widow paused in midinterview as it dawned on her what she was discussing.

"My God," she said, her eyes welling with tears. "My God."'

"They did all they could to kill him," lamented Boris Fayants, one of the many ordinary Soviet citizens who seemed clearly to feel that Soviet political life, with its fresh seeds of hope born when President Gorbachev ended Dr. Sakharov's exile, had been drastically altered by the death.

"For us, it was wonderful to see him elected to the Congress, but for him it was a terrible mistake," Mr. Fayants, a mathematician, said, grasping at his own heart.

Mr. Gorbachev said, "This is a big loss," choosing to comment not from the Congress rostrum but in a corridor outside in a brief interview with reporters. "This was not some sort of a political intriguer, but a person who had his own ideas, his own convictions, which he expressed openly and directly."

The death of Dr. Sakharov, a physicist who evolved from designing the Soviet hydrogen bomb to leading the nation's antiwar movement, deprives the Soviet leader of a badly needed force for credibility.

Mr. Gorbachev was obviously peeved at times to see Dr. Sakharov arise regularly from his sixth-row congressional seat to deliver sharp-toned blasts at Gorbachev programs. But the President seemed far more mindful of the fact that he gained credit for having invited such political change and goading in the first place.

It was credit from the outside world more than from the members of the Communist majority in Congress. After Dr. Sakharov's death, they all had to stand for a moment of silence in his memory this morning.

Sakharov associates complained that the funeral commission included prominent party officials who did nothing to help him a decade ago when the Government ostracized him for refusing to cease his criticism of the Soviet combat role in Afghanistan, and he was exiled to Gorky.

The body of the slender, stoop-shouldered physicist was discovered by his wife. He had returned to their eighth-floor apartment near the center of the city after another long day of congressional debate and caucusing with the opposition group he helped to found.

Needing to work further on a congressional speech on the economic crisis, Dr. Sakharov had gone down to his study, a separate apartment on the seventh floor.

"He was in his undershirt, probably getting undressed, and he fell to the floor with a heart attack," said a friend, the poet Vladimir Kornilov.

Dr. Sakharov's body, wrapped in a green sackcloth and strapped to a stretcher, was carried down to a waiting ambulance at 1:30 this afternoon. Wet, thick snow fell on the city. "There is no one in the Congress to take up his leadership," said Igor Belkov, a passerby watching the scene. "He was the real leader in the real perestroika."

In Congress, Dr. Sakharov's admirers had the same thought. Anatoly A. Sobchak, normally a steely-eyed analyst of things politic, was teary-eyed in conceding the enormous loss of Dr. Sakharov.

"This was a man whose uncompromising fight in the period of

stagnation—one on one against the whole Government apparatus, beaten down, betrayed—was maintained with all his strength so that this day, today, would come," he said. . . .

Dr. Sakharov died in the midst of a campaign to demonstrate to the nation the value of opposition voices in the one-party legislature. The stilling of his own special voice now makes this point most dramatically, but raises questions of how the nebulous early opposition caucus he helped found, the Interregional Group, will carry on without him.

Both the opposition and Mr. Gorbachev seemed to benefit from Dr. Sakharov's treks to the rostrum. The last public exchange of the two men on Tuesday was typical. Legislators groaned as Dr. Sakharov came up to speak. Mr. Gorbachev had been busy brushing aside other speakers, but not Andrei Dmitrivich.

In one sentence, squinting and craggy-voiced, Dr. Sakharov ripped into the Government's failure to move toward its promises on land reform. In the next, he turned toward Mr. Gorbachev wielding a sheaf of telegrams like a fiery sword, speaking for citizens demanding that Congress repeal the Communist Party's power monopoly.

"That's all," Mr. Gorbachev snapped, growing short with the man he freed from exile. Dr. Sakharov retreated from the uncertain new legislature for the last time looking unsurprised and unsatisfied, as if he harbored every intent of complaining another day.

Despite the changes that have already taken place in East Germany, the level of national yearning had not abated. Though travel restrictions had been removed, the pace of emigration to the West had not slackened once the novelty of free movement wore off. In the face of this, the Communists followed the same general formula that had been pursued first in Poland and Hungary and was now also taking place in Czechoslovakia—that is, they gave up their monopolies in successive stages. They abandoned the leading role that they had held by fiat, they changed the symbols, they eased censorship, they tinkered with economic reform, in some cases they even changed the name of the party. With each such step came the hope that since they had lost de jure omnipotence, society might now be willing to grant them some de facto credibility. Indeed, what seemed to be happening was that society was simply demanding unlimited freedoms.

Berlin Communists Outline Platform
By Craig R. Whitney

EAST BERLIN, Dec. 17—Acknowledging a struggle for the country's continued existence as well as its own, the Communist Party of East Germany said today that it would give up the formal trappings of power and declared itself ready to compete in elections next May with other emerging democratic forces.

And the Communist-controlled Cabinet, acknowledging the failure of an earlier plan to rename the Ministry of State Security, one of the most feared institutions of control, announced today that it would dissolve the secret police agency.

It said a new civilian administrator would be named to supervise the assignment of legitimate intelligence functions to two new and separate organizations reporting directly to Prime Minister Hans Modrow.

Today's developments seemed to reflect a turning point in the way the East German authorities have responded to the revolution on the streets that swept the country's hard-line leader, Erich Honecker, out of power in October. They apparently realize that the popular mood will not accept superficial changes, but demands real ones.

Egon Krenz, who briefly replaced Mr. Honecker, tried the first course, failed and was forced to resign along with the entire party leadership on December 3.

And both Gregor Gysi, the 41-year-old lawyer who became Communist Party Chairman last weekend, and Mr. Modrow also recognize that their country could quickly be swallowed up by its larger, economically more powerful Western neighbor unless they can persuade East German voters next spring to stand by their country as a separate, "socialist" alternative.

"Like it or not, the election campaign has already begun," Mr. Gysi said today in a speech outlining policy positions to 2,654 delegates at a resumed special party congress here. "On December 3," he concluded, two and a half hours later, "a party leadership that had failed resigned, and there was a serious danger that the party, and with it the country, could go under."

To a standing ovation before the delegates ended the congress by singing the "Internationale," he said, "We're all ready now to raise our heads high and fight for the party and for the country."

They also decided to drop the party statute defining the Communists as "the conscious and organized shock force of the working class," and on Saturday night amended the party's formal name to add a commitment to socialist democracy, producing the jawbreaking title of Socialist Unity Party of Germany–Party of Democratic Socialism, or, in German, S.E.D.-P.D.S., for short.

Mr. Gysi read a remarkable catalog of confessions of past party and state failures, and the delegates eagerly assented to all of the criticisms.

By way of giving up the trappings of power, he proposed turning part of the giant party headquarters in East Berlin into a public conference center with a library, a movie theater and hotel rooms. He called for dissolution of established party organizations in the armed forces, and he said military uniforms should be replaced because they resemble those of the Nazi Wehrmacht. Military parades and goose-stepping, he suggested, should also go.

"And we'd be doing not only ourselves, but more important all soldiers, a favor," he said.

Concern over the danger to the continued existence of East Germany as a nation was never far from Mr. Gysi's mind in his long speech this morning.

"Supporting the Modrow coalition Government is of life-and-death importance for our country and our citizens," he said. "We all have to be clear that whether our ship of state can steer clear of the reefs of anarchy and annexation by West Germany depends essentially on this Government." Mr. Modrow, a Communist, formed the Cabinet last month with twelve non-Communist members from previously subservient smaller parties. . . .

Mr. Gysi was applauded when he criticized East Germany's professional sports machine, a source of Olympic medals, international recognition and prestige under the Honecker leadership.

"In sports we see an important, but no longer the only cultural achievement of our country," he said, "and we urge that it be supported but not elevated to a question of national prestige."

More important for his party's future constituency, he seemed to say, were things like grocery stores. "After forty years, it must be possible for us to have vegetable stores that it's a pleasure to go to and, more important, to come out of," he said to laughter. "And for that, the permanent choice between cabbage and apples just won't do."

WINTER 1989-90

Within the last two weeks of the year, the general pace of reform seemed quick and steady throughout the East bloc. In Poland, where the non-Communist-led government was completing its fourth month, the emphasis shifted from political reforms to the massive reorganization of the economy. A proposal was drafted and enacted just before the new year calling for an end of subsidies, a free float of prices and other measures that would be certain to bring painful unemployment and high prices, at least in the short run. The plan was being sold to the nation as the bitter medicine needed to finally escape from the stranglehold of central planning and structural inefficiency. Implementation of the package was certain to prove the greatest challenge for the new government but if it worked, Poland, the first of the bloc countries to have moved toward pluralism and democracy would be the first also to achieve an economy where the value of money, time and labor as well as goods would be determined by markets and not fiat.

In Czechoslovakia, the pressure from the nation was forcing the leaders of party and state to concede on the composition of the newly emerging government and to move toward free elections. Facing the prospects of strikes and demonstrations, the Communists in the parliament were preparing to accept as the country's leaders two men whom their party had persecuted and scorned for more than twenty years— Alexander Dubcek and Vaclav Havel.

These events were all remarkable, but they were no longer quite so startling for a world that had seen the Berlin wall come down. The bloodless revolutions of the East bloc appeared to be playing themselves out with a steady march toward greater democracy and freer markets.

Leaders of the Two Germanys Meet; Symbolic Reconciliation Cheered

By Serge Schmemann

DRESDEN, EAST GERMANY—The leaders of the two Germanys met today for the first time since the East fell into the throes of protest and change, and in a symbolic reconciliation agreed to reopen the Brandenburg Gate in Berlin and introduce free movement across their border for all Germans by Christmas.

The announcement was the centerpiece of the first official visit to East Germany by Chancellor Helmut Kohl, an emotional journey on which he was greeted at every stop by thousands of East Germans, many waving West German flags and clamoring for the reunification still opposed by their leaders.

In the sort of public adulation that has usually eluded him at home, the crowds often broke into chants of "Helmut! Helmut!" Their cheers were loudest when the Chancellor mounted a platform in front of the memorial ruins of the Frauenkirche at dusk and declared to a throng of about 10,000:

"My goal, when the historic moment makes it possible, is the unity of our nation. I know we can reach this goal. It is a difficult way, but it is a good way in our common future, though it won't happen overnight."

At the end of his address, Mr. Kohl wished the East Germans a merry Christmas and then, his voice breaking, concluded, "God bless our German fatherland."

At a news conference earlier, the East German Prime Minister, Hans Modrow, announced that he and Mr. Kohl would join the mayors of the two Berlins to inaugurate a pedestrian crossing at the Brandenburg Gate. East German state television later said the ceremony would take place on Christmas Eve.

The eighteenth-century triumphal arch has stood for the last 28 years as the premier symbol of German division, a war-damaged relic of past glory stranded in the no-man's-land on the eastern side of the Berlin wall. The West German President, Richard von Weizsaecker, once declared that as long as the gate was closed the "German question" would remain open.

The opening would unite the divided halves of what was once Berlin's premier boulevard, Unter den Linden. The avenue is still among the most elegant in both Berlins, lined with embassies in the

East and with parkland in the West, where it was renamed "17 June" in honor of the 1953 anti-Communist uprising in East Berlin.

Mr. Modrow and Mr. Kohl also moved up the ending of all restrictions on the movement of West Germans across the border, originally scheduled for January 1, to Christmas Eve. That would effectively end any hindrance to the free movement of Germans across the line that has divided their nation for the last forty years.

The two leaders also announced plans to sign a treaty by next spring establishing future forms of social, economic, cultural and other ties. The treaty plans are a response to Mr. Modrow's call for a "community of treaties" between the two Germanys, as well as to Mr. Kohl's call for the establishment of "confederative structures" as a prelude to reunification. . . .

The chants of "Helmut! Helmut!" were not only a personal tribute, they were also typical of the familiarity East Germans have come to feel for West German public figures. Similar cheers have met Willy Brandt, the former Chancellor; Hans-Dietrich Genscher, the Foreign Minister and President von Weizsaecker.

Mr. Kohl, who rarely prompts such a spirited reaction in his own Germany, seemed to revel in the televised cheers, especially with West German national elections now less than a year away and German unity looming as the dominant issue.

Before the ruins of the Frauenkirche in this city, which was destroyed by Allied bombers in 1945 and then painstakingly rebuilt, he said: "I stand here to bring the greetings of fellow citizens in West Germany, and also to express my recognition and admiration for the nonviolent revolution in the G.D.R. It is the first time in German history, and I thank you for it."

While most of Eastern Europe was approaching the year-end holidays with an enthusiasm touched off by the accelerating pace of social and political change, another sudden and unexpected event erupted in Rumania, the country that until then had seemed impervious to the reforms sweeping Europe's Communist states, remaining in the very tight grasp of its Stalinist dictator, Nicolae Ceausescu. The first news of any stirrings there reported that on December 17 security forces were battling protesters in the city of Timisoara, near the Yugoslav border. As details slowly emerged, it turned out that a pastor of the Hungarian Reform Church, a man named Laszlo Tokes, was about to be forcibly deported from his home for having openly preached against the Ceau-

331

sescu policy of razing old villages and replacing them with agricultural factories where families were to live in giant dormitories. As the police came to seize him, his Hungarian-speaking parishioners sought to protect him and they were joined by students and others from the city's Rumanian majority. There was a protest rally. The security forces fired into the crowd. Ceausescu went on a state visit to Iran. The protests continued and intensified. The security forces received orders to kill. Ceausescu returned and summoned another of his state-managed demonstrations in the capital. This time when he denounced counterrevolutionaries, he was booed. The shock on his face was shown on television just before the transmission was cut off. Very quickly, the Rumanian revolution had begun and the clamor for freedom had spread to the last holdout in the Warsaw Pact.

Hatred of Security Forces Growing as Rumanian Atrocities Increase

By Celestine Bohlen

ARAD, RUMANIA, Dec. 23—"It's the Securitate," yelled a burly man, leaning out of the open door of the small white car as it careened, horn honking and lights blazing, down a dark and empty boulevard. "They're shooting again, the bastards."

It was after midnight and fighting had broken out between the security forces and the army in Rumania outside the capital city of Bucharest. After a day of euphoria of celebrating the fall of the hated tyrant, people stood silently in knots, listening to the spates of gunfire and the air-raid sirens. One woman sobbed. A young man clenched his fists.

"This is just another case of the Securitate to fight and kill more people," he said fiercely.

In the last few days, with former President Nicolae Ceausescu in hiding, the people's fear, anger and hatred has concentrated on his security forces, the main corps of forces now fighting the provisional government. The most despised group is the Securitate's black-shirted elite, said to number 10,000 to 15,000.

As they fight from hidden perches, machine-gunning the population from helicopters, rooftops and running cars "Capone-style," as one witness described it, the Securitate's reputation for brutality has only grown. The odd part is that this hated group still hopes to regain control of the country even as evidence of its atrocities are being brought to light.

In Timisoara, a city to the south of here where the revolt began last Friday, citizens early this morning silently filed by a gruesome lineup of naked corpses, dug up the day before from one of several mass graves for the victims of last Sunday's massacre, now estimated here at 4,500.

Given the horrors of this scene—a pregnant woman's belly ripped open, scars from barbed wire on the bodies' bare legs—the people's grief seemed strangely contained. But as a visiting Hungarian noted, these things are not new for Rumanians.

No one knows why, but it seems that people picked up from the demonstrations last Sunday were tortured before they were killed. Those who found the bodies, after getting tipped that trucks had appeared at a potter's field late last Sunday night, say the torture must have taken place in a pink stucco house at the back of the cemetery, on a makeshift autopsy table.

"They're worse than Hitler," said a middle-aged man who had helped to dig up the 23 bodies found in the potter's field grave. "Compared to them, Hitler looks wonderful."

One man, giving further testimony, described how agents of the Securitate went to local hospitals after Sunday's bloodletting, collected some of the wounded and took them to a morgue where they were killed. He quoted irate witnesses who said the security forces, mingling with regular army soldiers, could be seen executing those soldiers who refused to fire on the crowd.

In the days since the collapse of the Ceausescu regime, people are wary about saying that the Securitate's days are over.

"Be careful," an old man warned two travelers as they drove through the deserted, dimly lit streets of Arad after 3 A.M. this morning. "Remember, they are like a snake."

In this western Rumanian city as in other populated centers outside of Bucharest, the dreaded security forces—well trained, well paid and intent on keeping the population in fear—waited until the dead of night to strike back at the popular revolution that had defeated them and their patron, Mr. Ceausescu.

In Timisoara, they laid low until midnight. Then as bells, horns and sirens sounded in honor of the thousands they had killed last Sunday, the Securitate agents fired into a crowd of more than 100,000 people gathered on Opera Square, killing an estimated 160 people.

Even today, as crowds gathered anew in the square, the shooting continued. One witness said the Securitate's forces were even shooting at ambulances as they attempted to approach victims lying on the ground.

Stories of the Securitate's cunning and resourcefulness continued to spread. One report circulating in Timisoara told of a woman Securitate agent who smuggled arms in her small Rumanian-built car to the children's hospital, where "terrorists," as the security forces are now called, were gathering.

This and other reports of arms smuggling are cited as reasons for the dozens of roadblocks that have been set up on roads leading to the battle-scarred urban centers by young supporters of the new Government.

In Arad, one family spoke of how the Securitate had infiltrated a Red Cross convoy, using one of its trucks to store guns.

"They have secret apartments, secret caches of ammunition, places where they can hide all over the country," said Alexander Hernea, a chemical engineer who today for the first time set aside the fear instilled by this awesome police force and invited a foreigner to his apartment.

The fighting between the Securitate and the army, which has now come out in support of the anti-Ceausescu revolution, seems shrouded in mystery. Accurate body counts are hard to come by and the fighting is so scattered that many people continue to go about their daily business as though a civil war were not taking place in their midst.

In Timisoara, the Securitate forces were holed up in several central locations—a fourteenth-century castle opposite the opera house and the Botanical Gardens, the Children's Hospital and a downtown fashion store where a handful were flushed out earlier today.

On December 23, as Western correspondents were still trying to get to Bucharest, East bloc correspondents reported that Nicolae Ceausescu, who fled from his besieged party headquarters in a white helicopter, had been captured. Meanwhile fighting was continuing between the Securitate people and units of the army that joined the revolutionary effort.

Rumanian Army Gains in Capital but Battle Goes On

By John Kifner

BUCHAREST, RUMANIA, Dec. 24—Bursts of gunfire sounded through this exultant but tense capital today and into the night as secret police officers loyal to the ousted dictator, Nicolae Ceausescu, held out and harassed the new provisional government claiming power in what had been the most rigorously controlled state in Eastern Europe.

Heavy-weapons fire echoed through the university district around the Inter-Continental Hotel throughout the night.

There were also reports tonight that widespread shooting had resumed after a lull during the day in the western city of Timisoara, where the uprising began nine days ago.

In Timisoara as well as in Bucharest, army units siding with the insurgents clashed with members of the Securitate, the secret police who carried out the Ceausescu policies of terror.

Somewhat incongruously, as shots rang out and sniper attacks continued in the capital, the state television tonight broadcast Christmas carols for the first time in more than four decades of Communist rule.

"But it has been bloody," a Rumanian said, staring at the unfamiliar televised image of Christmas tree bulbs on an evergreen.

It appeared certain that thousands have been killed in the fighting here, with some reports putting the toll of the dead in Bucharest at 5,000 since Friday. Rumanians are only beginning to calculate the number of dead in the countryside.

There were indications that the provisional government, calling itself the Council of National Salvation, was gaining the upper hand. The international airport, the scene of heavy fighting in recent days, where the cafeteria had been turned into a morgue, was reported reopened tonight.

Mr. Ceausescu's whereabouts remained uncertain today.

On Saturday afternoon, the state radio and television said he had been captured by the army, but the television has yet to show pictures of him.

Yugoslav press reports said that in Timisoara about forty secret policemen had surrendered and that the army had prevented people from lynching them.

The new government's radio and television stations, protected by army tanks, stayed on the air.

335

The state television repeated assertions that the army was in control of the city. The state television and radio carried a communiqué by the provisional government calling on the holdouts to turn in their arms by Monday or "face the consequences."

In the broadcasts, the provisional government urged calm, saying there should be no retribution because "enough blood has been shed."

The decree further declared that the "downfall of the odious dictatorship of the Ceausescu clan" had taken place but that "elements who had remained loyal to the tyrant were trying to go ahead with the terrorist practices of the old regime."

The television, which regularly displays its new name—Free Rumanian Television—has become a symbol of revolution here, having broadcast almost continuously since Friday. Before then, state television programming was limited to two hours a day, devoted almost entirely to the activities of Mr. Ceausescu.

Now the screen is filled with scenes of battles and demonstrations in the streets, interviews with excited citizens, musical programs and round-table discussions with intellectuals and suddenly reformed Government officials, all wearing armbands of red, yellow and blue, the national colors. Tonight scenes were shown from churches.

Earlier the television showed images of Zoia Ceausescu, the dictator's daughter, who was reported captured today. Nicu Ceausescu, a son of the deposed leader, had been shown after his seizure on Friday, his face bearing the signs of beating.

The 71-year-old former dictator and his wife, Elena, who had served as his chief deputy, have not been shown. But a spokesman for the Council of National Salvation said the couple were in custody and would be given a "strict and fair" trial. . . .

On Christmas Day the Ceausescus were executed by firing squad and the fighting began to wind down.

Army Executes Ceausescu and Wife for "Genocide" Role, Bucharest Says

By John Kifner

BUCHAREST, RUMANIA, Tuesday, Dec. 26—Nicolae Ceausescu, absolute ruler of Rumania for 24 years, and his wife were executed on Monday by the army that he once commanded, the Free Rumanian Television of the new provisional government said.

A first brief announcement said an "extraordinary military court" had tried Mr. Ceausescu and his wife, Elena, who was widely viewed as the country's second most powerful figure until widespread demonstrations forced the pair to flee the capital on Friday morning. They were reportedly captured on Saturday in Tirgoviste.

At 1:30 this morning, a few hours after the report of the executions, the television showed its first footage of the Ceausescus in captivity.

Some of the footage appeared to be from Monday's trial. The words "condemned to death" were barely audible on the fuzzy sound track. At one point, Mr. Ceausescu slammed his fur cap on the table. At times he seemed contemptuous. His wife appeared frightened.

The film, which opened with a doctor taking Mr. Ceausescu's blood pressure, was the first solid evidence that he had indeed been captured. The sound track also referred to the billion dollars he was said to have secreted abroad.

"The sentence was death and the sentence was executed," said the television announcement. It was proclaimed in the name of a largely faceless revolutionary government, the Council of National Salvation, which took power after the Ceausescus fled. It has not been made clear exactly when, where, how or on whose authority the Ceausescus were put to death, and their bodies had not been shown.

The charges against the Ceausescus, according to the television announcement, included the "genocide" of 60,000 people, many of whom died in the last week of fighting; undermining state power; destroying the country's economic and spiritual values; and trying to escape the country to claim $1 billion reportedly hidden abroad.

The Rumanian television said this morning that fighting near its studios in the capital was preventing staff members from getting footage of the execution on the air, Reuters reported.

The television studio has been the focus of heavy fighting between the Rumanian Army, which has sided with the popular uprising, and the security police, which is loyal to the Ceausescu regime. It is not known whether the security forces will fight on after the death of their leaders, but the insurgents clearly hope to demoralize them by showing proof of the executions.

The announcement of the execution came as Rumanians celebrated a bittersweet Christmas, treasuring their newfound and tentative liberties but mourning the many hundreds and perhaps thousands slain in the uprising.

The capital was calmer on Monday, with Rumanians strolling the boulevards and only an occasional burst of gunfire. The army appeared to be consolidating control over the remaining bands of now-renegade secret policemen, the backbone of the old order.

A Christmas tree stood on the balcony of the Communist Party headquarters this afternoon. It was placed in the spot where only last Thursday Mr. Ceausescu was hooted into shocked silence, jeered by a crowd that had been summoned to hear him condemn protests in a western city, Timisoara.

Sightseers wandered where fighting took place over the weekend between diehard security forces, who had sustained the reign of the Ceausescus, and a spontaneous coalition that united army units and irate civilians. Among those who turned out were several hundred people who gathered in front of party headquarters early this morning chanting, "We want Ceausescu hanged here at the palace!"

New newspapers have been printed in the last few days with names like *Freedom*, *Liberty* and *Free Rumania*. One paper that appeared as *Spark* when it was put under sanctions by Mr. Ceausescu renamed itself *Truth*. On Monday, when truckers drove by tossing out copies of the new papers, crowds rushed into the streets to grab them. "We had cold, hunger and terror" was the way one of the papers, *Free Youth*, described the past regime.

At a Christmas Mass at the Rumanian Orthodox Cathedral, the center of the major religion, Patriarch Teoctist Arapafu hailed "these brave young people, these young boys and girls who have died for freedom."

"They will live in our hearts forever," he said. At the same time, the Patriarch, who had cooperated with Mr. Ceausescu's Government, acknowledged that despite what he called shocking times, "I did not have the courage these children have shown."

Although orthodox, the Rumanian Church observes the same calendar of holy days as does Catholicism, the next-largest denomination in the country. But under the old regime, observances of Christmas were celebrated in private or in secrecy.

The reported execution of Mr. Ceausescu and his wife, along with the capture of his brother, son and daughter, ended nearly a quarter-century of absolute power. Mr. Ceausescu was routinely idolized as the "leader for life," with accounts of his daily routine dominating the local newspapers and the two hours each day that Rumanian television was on the air.

His harsh rule, enforced by a hated secret police and a system in which one in four Rumanians was said to be an informer, included drastic measures to pay off the foreign debt. Those included cutting off heat and electricity during the fierce Central European winter and exporting harvests of food while keeping citizens on meager rations.

But as in other Communist countries, a privileged inner circle of the party elite enjoyed amenities like ski and hunting resorts and special food shops.

The television made much of the luxurious circumstances in which Zoia Ceausescu, the ousted leader's daughter, lived, noting that $100,000 had been found in her home after she was captured over the weekend.

As in several other parts of the Soviet bloc, rigid and seemingly entrenched one-man and one-party rule has collapsed in the face of popular protest. Here the process was tougher and more violent both during the years of oppressive rule and in the days that have seen it toppled. . . .

The membership of the new government has not been made public for what its spokesman says are security reasons. But it is known to include a number of members of recent governments, some of whom had fallen out with Mr. Ceausescu.

Those include Corneliu Manescu, a former Foreign Minister; Ion Iliescu, a onetime member of the Politburo who had quarreled with the former President; and two top military figures: the chief of the general staff, Gen. Stefan Gusa, and the Deputy Foreign Minister, Ion Stanculescu.

All along the main boulevard, thousands of people strolled today, pausing to look at handbills hailing the revolution that were posted in store windows. They barely flinched as bursts of gunfire sounded a few blocks away, although at one point a group took refuge in doorways when the gunfire sounded too close.

As the new year approached, the revolutionary government gained breathing room and a modicum of legitimacy, calling for elections to be held in the next year. The leaders, men and women who were hardly well known when the revolt erupted, were making their case to the nation through television, which, it turned out, had been the most powerful of weapons.

The Airwaves; Rumanian Revolt, Live and Uncensored

By John Kifner

BUCHAREST, RUMANIA, Dec. 27—"This is the first revolution on live television," said Ion Todan, proud and tired this afternoon amid the chaotic but businesslike clutter at the heart of the videocracy that has replaced the dictatorship of Nicolae Ceausescu.

Studio 4 of Free Rumanian Television, a chamber about 12 feet square with antiquated cameras and black-and-white monitors, has been the real seat of power since Mr. Ceausescu tried to bolt the country on Friday after 24 years of harsh, absolute rule.

Rapt audiences watched again and again as the television studio repeatedly broadcast videotape of the military trial of Mr. Ceausescu and his wife, Elena, and showed the pictures of the executed ruler's body.

The broadcasts are profoundly political acts, calculated to consolidate support for the provisional government, the Council of National Salvation, and to show that further resistance by die-hard security agents is pointless.

Beginning with the poet Murica Dinesco's sudden appearance on the air on Friday morning, shouting, "We've won! We've won!" the once-soporific state television has become the pivotal instrument and embodiment of the revolution. It has struggled against sniper fire, commando attacks and its own outdated gear to keep broadcasting.

Even today, two days after Mr. Ceausescu and his wife were executed, his security police again tried to storm the station. The Bucharest radio said the agents were beaten back after a half-hour firefight.

"We knew we had to stay on the air," said Eugenia Bogdan, her face lined with fatigue, as she spoke of the station's importance to the uprising. Like the other workers, she has been living in the station since Friday. "If television falls, the revolution falls," she said. "That's for certain."

Outside, the blocks of luxurious villas and embassy buildings in the station's neighborhood sit empty, bullet-scarred and broken from the fire of the tanks and soldiers who have defended the broadcasting center. Inside, the monitors showed scenes unimaginable in Rumania just a week ago. Among them were people singing Christmas carols.

The tale of Studio 4 reveals much about power in the electronic age. Once, those who plotted revolutions and coups took aim at radio stations to gain a monopoly on the flow of information. In the Iranian revolution, new technology spread the word of Ayatollah Ruhollah Khomeini, first through tape cassettes telephoned from abroad and played over mosque loudspeakers. Later, when Khomeini was in power, the state television became his pulpit.

Conversations with ordinary Rumanians underscored the impact of the news broadcasts, not only in the last two weeks in Rumania but throughout Eastern Europe, where images of popular uprisings have penetrated borders, apparently sharpening yearnings for freedom and shaping official and public action.

Small shortwave radios can pick up foreign broadcasts. And in relatively prosperous East Germany, the people for years caught seductive glimpses of a richer society, as depicted on the West German television.

Here, where Rumanian television was once so dull that the schedules for Bulgarian programming, which can be tuned in, are a hot item for smugglers, the new freedom in the rest of the Eastern bloc could be seen on broadcasts from neighboring countries.

"The whole people see changes coming in Eastern Europe," Sergei Secuescu, a student, said on the street the other day. "We can see TV from Bulgaria, from Yugoslavia. We listen to the foreign radios, to Voice of America, Radio Free Europe, BBC. The phone was working. People have brothers, friends."

But the impact of television in the last two weeks goes far beyond that level. Viewers have seen the formation and defense of a revolutionary government, often as it happens.

For a week, Rumanians huddled around television sets and watched the demonstrations and gun battles between the army, which is supporting the popular revolution, and the renegade security forces, who propped up the old order. Then they saw the first tentative steps of the provisional government.

In a sense it was like watching live coverage of the storming of the Bastille or the Battle of Yorktown, interspersed with debates from the Constitutional Congress. But in this case the focus of the violence and struggle was the television studio itself. Sovereignty, it seemed, was reduced to the ability to convey what was happening just outside the studio door.

Early on Saturday morning, as security forces loyal to Mr. Ceausescu began their first attacks on the station, a family in the western city of Arad sat spellbound before their television, watching announcers force smiles as gunshots echoed in the studio. Soldiers were battling the security police, or Securitate, in the lobby of the television station.

Behind the announcer, a helmeted soldier with a rifle stood watch. Paratroopers who repelled the attack were brought to the studio as heroes. The announcer broadcast an appeal for help.

The television screen showed a panel of revolutionaries sitting around tables draped in red, yellow and blue, the national colors. The panel included a tank driver, two men in suits, one in a denim jacket and a student in a parka and turtleneck. At 3 A.M., the student was reading from a new broadsheet issued by an angry group of students. He stopped and began singing a song, only to be interrupted by the appearance of one of the country's biggest soccer stars.

In Arad, 265 miles northwest of Bucharest, the mother of the family watching the televised revolution—she would give only her first name, Ann—said, "We will not sleep tonight"

At another point, the television showed ten soldiers in a circle with their rifles pointing at the building's elevators, fearful that the security police had infiltrated. And in another remarkable segment, the anchorman on the news during much of the Ceausescu era told his audience that he had been forced to lie for years. He apologized and stayed on the air.

Mr. Todan, who in earlier times bought and translated the station's meager store of foreign films, recalled that on Friday morning, "The first mass movement was for the youngsters to come to the television, and Studio 4 became the heart of the revolution."

"But in the evening, the shooting started and we called for help," he said. "Crowds were surrounding the station and thousands of students were sitting under fire. If we went off the air, it meant it was over."

Perhaps the greatest threat to those inside the station came on Saturday, when security policemen assigned to the television suddenly turned on the workers. Six paratroopers were killed inside the station by knives or silencer-equipped pistols. One of the policemen got into the basement and cut off the electricity, which was restored only ten minutes before air time.

Besides bullets, the television workers had to worry about their outmoded equipment, sometimes shutting it down to avoid overheating.

"We have no spare parts," said Mikhail Bucauanu, the technical chief. "We just patch what we have." "We recently got three new cameras," he said. "They were only for filming him." He was referring to the late Mr. Ceausescu, whose activities dominated the few hours a day the television was on the air under the old regime. Now it is on long into the night.

The last few days of broadcasts have been dominated by Christmas programs.

"It was the first time we were even allowed to pronounce the word on television," Mr. Todan said. "Before, if it was in a foreign film, and somebody said 'Merry Christmas,' we had to translate it as 'Happy New Year.' "

A scrawny Christmas tree, tinsel in its few branches, stood in one corner of Studio 4 this afternoon, behind two peasants wearing knee-high boots, wide leather belts, smocks and high fur hats and carrying huge loaves of bread, proclaiming loyalty to the new Government.

The programming also included a speech by the Rev. Laszlo Tokes, the ethnic Hungarian clergyman whose persecution set off the initial protests; Christmas carols by teenage girls walking through the snow; new government decrees calling for military trials and executions of any secret policemen who did not turn themselves in by tomorrow, and the Chicago Philharmonic Orchestra playing the overture to *The Flying Dutchman*.

"At Christmas, for 17 people, we had just a round of cheese, some crackers and 200 grams of salami," Mr. Todan said. "The terrorists had infiltrated and the fight started inside the building. It was the most fantastic Christmas of my life."

In the final days of the year most attention was focused on Rumania, where revolution had flared so suddenly and violently. But in Czechoslovakia another great drama was also coming to a remarkable, though far less bloody resolution. Faced with the prospect of continuing protests and strikes, the Communist-dominated parliament gave the nation's top two posts to the two most prominent opponents of the old regime. First, Alexander Dubcek was named as Premier, and then just before the year lapsed Vaclav Havel was chosen to be President.

Czechoslovakia: Havel, Long Prague's Prisoner, Elected President
By Craig R. Whitney

PRAGUE, Dec. 29—Vaclav Havel, the Czechoslovak writer whose insistence on speaking the truth about repression in his country repeatedly cost him his freedom over the last 21 years, was elected President by Parliament today in an event celebrated by the throng outside the chamber as the redemption of their freedom.

In a speech formally nominating the 53-year-old playwright who until May 17 was serving a jail term, the country's Communist Prime Minister, Marian Calfa, praised Mr. Havel.

"He has won the respect of all," Mr. Calfa told the legislators assembled in the medieval Hradcany Castle high above the city. "He never accepted the suggestions of friends or foes that he go into exile, and bore the humiliation of a man oppressed and relegated by those in power to the margins of society. Your vote for Vaclav Havel will be a vote for insuring the human rights of every citizen of our country."

Mr. Calfa said Mr. Havel had insisted on free parliamentary elections next year as a condition for accepting the mostly symbolic post and would serve only until a new Parliament could be elected to choose a new President for a regular five-year term.

Alexander Dubcek, the country's Communist leader during the liberalizing Prague Spring of 1968 and now rehabilitated as the chairman of Parliament, called for other nominations. But there were none; Mr. Havel's election had been agreed to beforehand by the Communist leadership and the opposition Civic Forum.

Completing the formality, all 323 deputies in the heavily Communist legislature voted for Mr. Havel, Czechoslovakia's first non-Communist President since 1948.

Mr. Dubcek and Mr. Calfa left the sixteenth-century hall to fetch the new President, somber in a dark blue suit, and swear him in with an oath revised by Parliament on Thursday to delete a promise of loyalty to the cause of socialism.

After a 20-gun salute and a military parade, he addressed the joyous crowd that thronged the castle courtyard.

"Dear friends," he said. "I promise you I will not betray your confidence. I will lead this country to free elections. This must be done in an honest and calm way, so that the clean face of our revolution is not soiled. That is the task for all of us. Thank you."

After his short speech, Mr. Havel went into St. Vitus Cathedral, within the castle walls, for a Te Deum Mass presided over by 90-year-old Frantisek Cardinal Tomasek, the country's Roman Catholic Primate and Archbishop of Prague. The Gothic cathedral was jammed with people of every age. The Czech Philharmonic Orchestra and choir performed Dvorak's *Te Deum*.

Cardinal Tomasek, who celebrated the Mass, said, "We have come today to the cathedral to thank God for the great hope that has opened up for us in the last few days."

This evening, tens of thousands of people streamed into the center of Prague's Old Town in what amounted to a street celebration of Mr. Havel's election. He appeared along with the visiting Portuguese President, Mario Soares, and greeted them.

Mr. Havel, son of an upper-class civil engineer, was not allowed to go to university by the Communist Government after he finished his compulsory schooling in 1951, because of his class background. Today the students of Prague, many of them children of the Communist ruling class, have made Mr. Havel their intellectual hero, and they have been on strike since demonstrations on November 17 sparked the peaceful revolution that overthrew the long repression.

"Havel is the only guarantee that the changes here will be of a permanent character," said one of them, Ludek Vasta, 21, an economics student.

The student strike was expected to end today with his election.

President Havel, whose most recent prison term was for participating in a demonstration last January in memory of a student who immolated himself in protest against the crushing of the Prague Spring of 1968, is expected to address the nation by television on New Year's Day. He has told friends he will not move into the splendid presidential residence in the castle as his retired predecessor, Gustav Husak did, but will remain in the flat in the center of town where he and his wife, Olga, have lived for years, and commute to work in his car.

He is a man who wrote, in a 1984 acceptance speech for a French university award that the Czechoslovak authorities would not allow him to pick up, "The slogan 'better Red than dead' does not irritate me as an expression of surrender to the Soviet Union, but it terrifies me as an expression of the renunciation by Western people of any claim to a meaningful life and of their acceptance of impersonal power as such. For what the slogan really says is that nothing is worth giving one's life for."

Through much of Mr. Havel's work runs the thread of what he calls "the absolute horizon"—the moral and philosophical judgments that give human life its meaning. He repeatedly warned his persecutors that by their repression of human freedom they were ultimately undercutting their own existence as well.

When the Soviet-led invasion began in August 1968, Mr. Havel took part in Free Czechoslovak Radio broadcasts. A year later, he signed a declaration condemning the post-Dubcek policy of "normalization." His published works were withdrawn from public libraries, and his new works were banned.

In April 1975, he sent a letter to the man he has now succeeded as President, Mr. Husak, warning that ultimately a repressed people would demand a price for "the permanent humiliation of their human dignity."

"I fear the price we are all bound to pay for the drastic suppression of history, the cruel and needless banishment of life into the underground of society and the depths of the human soul, the new compulsory 'deferral' of every opportunity for society to live in anything like a natural way," he wrote then, more than a decade before the facade crumbled in Czechoslovakia and elsewhere in Eastern Europe.

"No wonder, then, that when the crust cracks and the lava of life rolls out, there appear not only well-considered attempts to rectify old wrongs, not only searchings for truth and for reforms matching life's needs, but also symptoms of bilious hatred, vengeful wrath and a kind of feverish desire for immediate compensation for all the endured degradation," he wrote.

For writing that letter, and for organizing the Charter 77 human rights movement at the beginning of January 1977, Mr. Havel was arrested and charged with "subversion of the republic." Convicted that October, his fourteen-month sentence was conditionally deferred, but he was in and out of jail again until arrested in May 1979 for supporting the Committee for the Defense of the Unjustly Accused. With Jiri Dienstbier, now Foreign Minister of Czechoslovakia, and four other defendants, he was tried again for subversion that October and sentenced to four and one-half years in prison, but he was released for health reasons in February 1983.

His refusal to break with the Charter 77 movement led to other brief periods of detention in jail. But in January of this year, defying police orders to stay away from a demonstration in memory of Jan Palach, the young man who burned himself alive in protest after the 1968 invasion, cost him four months' imprisonment.

After his release, Mr. Havel called for restraint in commemorating the invasion's twenty-first anniversary in August, but he had to hide from the police anyway to keep from being arrested. He and three associates organized a petition, called "A Few Words," which soon gathered tens of thousands of signatures, calling for the release of all political prisoners and an end to discrimination on religious and other grounds.

The presidency of independent Czechoslovakia was first held by Tomas G. Masaryk, from 1918 to 1935. Eduard Benes, his successor, resigned in 1938 when the Western Allies signed Czechoslovakia over to Nazi Germany in the Munich Pact, but served again from 1946 to 1948. After that all presidents had to be members of the Communist Party, and they were until President Husak resigned on December 10.

As the new year unfolded, the essential impulse away from Communist Party control continued to make itself felt in the more remote backwaters of the old system. Appeals for democracy and political pluralism were to be uttered and acted upon in Albania and Yugoslavia, each in its own way an eccentric heretic of European Communism. Further afield, the leaders of one-party African states who had shaped and justified their rule on the basis of Communist models were to be confronted by popular movements demanding greater political freedoms. As Soviet power weakened, Moscow's old beneficiaries in places like Angola and Afghanistan would find their own strengths ebbing. In Nicaragua, the Sandinistas, whose party and slogans had been significantly modeled after the Cuban strain of Communism, would agree to face the challenge of internationally monitored democratic elections, which they would then lose.

The political and social processes that had been generated so suddenly in Eastern Europe in 1989 were obviously continuing to develop and diverge over the following 12 months. As the various societies struggled to free themselves, It was easy to see what they were eager to shed; it was harder to determine where exactly they all were heading. The escape route they had shared in their first steps quickly split into many rough, unmarked tracks.

For those states where the break with the past had come earlier, euphoria was increasingly giving way to anxieties. Economic problems were looming larger and larger even when political progress was being registered. At the very heart of Europe's transformation were the crucial events taking place in Germany and the Soviet Union. Just as 1989 was the year when the Communist systems of Eastern Europe finally crumbled, so 1990 was to be dominated by the coming together of East and West Germany and the apparent coming apart of the Soviet Empire. As the year opened, the pace of these processes was uncertain.

It was by then obvious that the destiny of East Germany was leading to unification with West Germany, though no one had a clear idea whether the timetable would involve years or decades. More specifically, no formulas were being offered to explain how exactly any fusion was to take place when the respective forces of the Warsaw Pact and NATO, the military alliances whose rivalry had defined the postwar period, were facing each other across a divided Germany with more might than had ever been assembled in such a small region.

East Germany: Berlin Communist Urges Troop Cuts
By Serge Schmemann

BONN, Jan. 6—The head of East Germany's Communist Party proposed today that all NATO and Warsaw Pact forces quit both Germanys within a decade, adding spice to an already bitter political struggle shaping in East Germany.

The proposal by Gregor Gysi, the new party chief, was not likely to become Government policy or be accepted by NATO or the Warsaw Pact any time soon. But as a political ploy it played directly into a conflict between the Communists and the opposition that has soured East Germany's euphoric march toward democracy.

According to A.D.N., the East German press agency, Mr. Gysi proposed at a party meeting that all allied troops leave by 1999 and that both Germanys cut their armies in half within a year.

"Without an end to military rivalry between the two German states, any talk of the unity of the nation is not credible," Mr. Gysi said in introducing a program he dubbed "Security 2000."

Mr. Gysi is not in the Government, and the Communists may lose control of the Government when free elections are held May 6. But diplomats saw the proposal as an effort to position the Communists as champions of disarmament and national unity as part of an aggressive new campaign by the party to revive its fallen fortunes.

According to a recent public-opinion poll conducted by sociologists from the East German Academy for Social Sciences, support for the Communists has grown to 34 percent, far more than that of any opposition party. The accuracy of the poll could not be checked, but the newly active Communists have alarmed both the opposition and the West German Government.

Over the past week, East German opposition groups have accused the Communists of manipulating their control of the Government and the press to gain unfair advantage, and of trying to reconstruct the security apparatus, using purported neo-fascist incidents to justify doing so.

The incidents, including anti-Soviet slogans painted on Soviet war memorials, were given extensive publicity in the East German press, and the Communists held a mass anti-fascist protest on Wednesday. But many in the opposition charged that the government had deliberately sensationalized the incidents to foment fear in the population and strengthen the Communists' hand.

One theme that was to grow stronger as the collapse of Communism grew more and more apparent was that as the bonds of totalitarianism loosened, old repressed hatreds and ethnic rivalries rose to define political activity. Class identity and class solidarity, by which Communists since Lenin had hoped to unite nationalities, was proving far less tenacious than ethnic ties. Instead of defining themselves as the industrial proletariat, people were now proclaiming themselves to be fundamentally Bulgarian, Turk, Moldavian, Lithuanian, Hungarian or Rumanian, and in virtually each case, affirming one nationality meant confronting and disdaining others.

Voices of Bulgaria Tell Story of Hate
By Clyde Haberman

SOFIA, BULGARIA, Jan. 8—Around the equestrian statue of Czar Alexander II, the 19th-century Russian liberator of Bulgaria from Turkish domination, the talk today was of civil rights and racism, of patriotism and perfidy.

The Turks are arming themselves to take over the country, said Ivan Kamishev, a construction engineer who stood amid a knot of people on this numbingly cold afternoon. He said he had heard that some Bulgarian Muslims who migrated to Turkey last summer had tried to smuggle in weapons when they returned.

"Do you really believe that?" asked someone at the edge of the crowd.

"I am convinced of it," Mr. Kamishev said.

Nonsense, replied Alexander Drensky, a physician who has worked for the last three years near Kirdzhali, a southeastern Bulgarian city with a large ethnic Turkish population.

"The Muslims living in that region are not going to tear the country apart," he said. "They are not going to fight against Bulgarians. They only want their rights restored."

"If they're deprived of their human rights," Mr. Kamishev shot back, "how come their pockets are full of money? They are richer than Bulgarians." So it went, back and forth, as Bulgarians grappled with serious ethnic divisions that have resurfaced in recent days, producing anti-Government rallies, strikes and floods of invective. These tensions, born of centuries-old hatreds, have created an important first test for both the country's Communist leadership, which promises democratic change, and the burgeoning opposition, which has made the ethnic issue a priority.

Protests began last week after the Communist Party jettisoned a six-year program of forced assimilation that had required Bulgaria's large ethnic Turkish minority to take Slavic names. Under this policy—begun by the recently ousted party leader, Todor I. Zhivkov, and endorsed by some of the same men who now hold power—use of the Turkish language was banned in public, as were some Muslim practices like ritual circumcision.

The entire region of Eastern Europe was full of reassertive nationalities and ethnic minorities. Their strivings for greater autonomy or, in some cases, full independence, were most apparent in those federations of ethnically based Republics such as Czechoslovakia, Yugoslavia and most of all the Union of Soviet Socialist Republics. There the national tapestry was fraying badly around the edges.

Lithuanians Cry "Freedom!" on Eve of Gorbachev Visit

By Esther B. Fein

VILNIUS, LITHUANIA, Jan. 10—A day before President Mikhail S. Gorbachev is to arrive in Lithuania, tens of thousands of Lithuanians gathered here today in the center of their capital, carrying signs calling for "Independence for Lithuania," and chanting, "Freedom!"

Mr. Gorbachev decided to visit the republic to assess the mood among Lithuanians, particularly Communist Party members, after the local Communist Party voted last month to secede from the Soviet Communist Party.

Speakers and demonstrators at the rally today said they wanted Mr. Gorbachev to know that the decision by the Lithuanian Communists was wildly popular in the republic and that many hoped it presaged a future break of the republic from the Soviet Union.

Speaker after speaker acknowledged that one goal of the demonstration, which was called by the popular political organization Sajudis, was to show through the Soviet and foreign press that an overwhelming majority of Lithuanians support the call for independence.

Buying Time in Lithuania; His Choices Severely Limited, Gorbachev Is Forced to Sell the Virtues of Federation
By Bill Keller

MOSCOW, Jan. 12—Barnstorming across Lithuania this week, President Mikhail S. Gorbachev has undertaken the most desperate diplomatic endeavor of his career: a campaign to preserve the integrity of the Soviet Union by personal persuasion.

Facing a Lithuanian separatist movement that could present him with a test in a matter of months, Mr. Gorbachev is appealing for time to broker the creation of a new, freer Soviet federation in which, he promises, Lithuanians and other independence-minded republics would have real economic and political liberty while remaining at least nominally tied to Moscow.

At each stop in the streets and auditoriums of the Baltic republic, Mr. Gorbachev has encountered the polite but glacial determination of the Lithuanians, who doubt that Mr. Gorbachev can deliver on that promise. Many are already treating him as the leader of a friendly but foreign country.

Mr. Gorbachev is jawboning his way through Lithuania—his encounters with the defiant populace played out to incredulous television audiences across the country—because he has apparently accepted that he has no other attractive options for preventing a first, precedent-setting breach in the union.

What Mr. Gorbachev is attempting to achieve by exhortation, any previous Soviet leader would almost surely have handled with brute force.

But forcible repression of the peaceful Lithuanian independence drive would be a devastating setback for Mr. Gorbachev's foreign and domestic policies, and would probably be met with massive civil disobedience.

Even a top conservative of the Communist Party Politburo, Yegor K. Ligachev, has ruled out the use of force to contain the errant Lithuanians, telling a Swedish newspaper this week that "tanks cannot solve such problems."

As Gorbachev moved to placate the Lithuanians, he was confronted by a new challenge, this time in the south.

Soviet Azerbaijan in Ethnic Turmoil
By Bill Keller

MOSCOW, Jan. 14—The southern Soviet republic of Azerbaijan has erupted in civil violence, leaving at least 25 people killed in the capital city, Baku, and several towns in disarray, official reports and residents reached by telephone said today.

Witnesses said Azerbaijani mobs broke away from a huge rally in Baku on Saturday night and rampaged through the streets, using mimeographed address lists to find the homes of Armenians and drive them outside.

Gangs continued to roam the Armenian quarter today, committing what the official press agency Tass described as atrocities and pogroms despite the presence of a division of Interior Ministry troops flown in to control the violence.

In one rural district of the republic, the entire Communist Party leadership has reportedly been held hostage for five days. In another area, heavily armed vigilantes were said to have attacked a military patrol and stolen its armored vehicles. Two cities along the Caspian Sea were reported to be under nationalist control after officials and the police essentially abdicated.

President Mikhail S. Gorbachev, who just returned to Moscow from Lithuania, where he tried without apparent success to head off a peaceful secession campaign, sent delegations of senior Government and Communist Party officials to Azerbaijan and neighboring Armenia.

The two nationalist crises—the deliberate, ballot-box independence campaign in the Baltic region and the eruptions of ethnic hatred in the Caucasus Mountains—could hardly be more different, but both contribute to the impression of events spinning out of Mr. Gorbachev's control.

The central issue in the Caucasus is the status of Nagorno-Karabakh, a mountainous region of western Azerbaijan where the Armenian majority demands to be annexed to Armenia.

The central television tonight portrayed Nagorno-Karabakh and the area around it as verging on civil war, with armed crowds of both ethnic groups converging on the area and federal peacekeeping troops under frequent attack.

The authorities in Moscow have not allowed foreign journalists to travel to the southern republics during the current unrest.

Tass reported that at the Saturday rally in Baku, a crowd of about 130,000 people roared its support for a demand that the republic's Parliament conduct a referendum on withdrawing Azerbaijan from the Soviet Union.

The disturbances in the south are the worst outbreak of the centuries-old antagonism between the predominantly Islamic Azerbaijanis and the mainly Christian Armenians since anti-Armenian riots two years ago in a Caspian Sea industrial city, Sumgait. The authorities say 32 people were killed in that rioting, although Armenians say the toll was much higher.

Azerbaijani bitterness about the political stalemate over Nagorno-Karabakh has been compounded by economic and political grievances against Moscow and local Communist Party rulers.

The terror in Baku, a city once touted by Moscow as a cosmopolitan model of inter-ethnic coexistence, reportedly began several days ago with Azerbaijani gangs going from house to house throwing Armenians from their apartments and building bonfires of their possessions.

One of the problems that beleaguered those who took over in the East Bloc after the professed Communists were toppled was the question of what to do with the networks of secret police that had sustained the old regimes. Should their leaders be prosecuted? Should informers be revealed? Should files be destroyed?

Angry Crowds of East Germans Ransack Offices of Spy Service
By Serge Schmemann

EAST BERLIN, Jan. 15—Crowds of angry protesters invaded the 3,000-room state-security headquarters today, destroying files and furniture in a show of popular frustration with the pace of change.

Opposition leaders and the Communist authorities, who were holding roundtable discussions when the rampage broke out, suspended their talks and drove to the scene, appealing through loudspeakers for calm. They were joined by Prime Minister Hans Modrow, a Communist.

"I've come to call for reason," Mr. Modrow told the demonstrators. "I hope we can continue to forge the path of democracy."

Much of the rage of recent days has found its focus in hatred for the remnants of the "Stasis," the Office of State Security and its discredited agents. For many years the Stasis spied on and repressed East Germans, and the word Stasi is a bitter epithet.

The crowd at the Stasi headquarters had gathered today for a demonstration called by the opposition movement New Forum. They were to demand faster dissolution of the political and police apparatus.

But ignoring New Forum's calls for a peaceful demonstration, hundreds of protesters stormed the building, breaking down doors, smashing furniture and windows and scattering files. Thousands more thronged outside, chanting "Stasis out!"

The East German television showed people rummaging through the litter of rooms that appeared to have been largely emptied earlier, vandalizing offices and defacing portraits of Erich Honecker, the fallen Communist leader, and Erich Mielke, the former Minister of State Security. The state prosecutor announced earlier that both men might be charged with treason, although Mr. Honecker is in a hospital being treated for cancer of the kidneys.

A woman could be seen writing on the wall, "Stasi, Gestapo, K.G.B., Securitate: all bloodsuckers."

In Azerbaijan, Soviet force appeared to have crushed the uprising.

Soviet Military Takes Control of Baku; Scores of Azerbaijanis Killed; Coup Averted, Gorbachev Says
By Bill Keller

MOSCOW, Jan. 20—Soviet troops claimed control of the Azerbaijani capital of Baku today and began settling in for a probable long-term occupation after a night of urban conflict that left scores of civilians and several soldiers dead.

The military commandant in the stunned Caspian Sea port said 60 people had died as columns of tanks and soldiers crashed through the barricades erected by Azerbaijani insurgents and suppressed scattered resistance.

Baku residents reached by telephone, citing estimates by local health officials and hospitals, gave death tolls ranging up to several hundred.

Several witnesses described army and Interior Ministry soldiers blazing their way through the city before dawn, firing into apartment balconies and at bystanders who rushed from their apartments out of curiosity.

The taking of Baku climaxed a week of turmoil that began when deadly anti-Armenian riots broke out in the city on Jan. 13.

President Mikhail S. Gorbachev, who signed the order that launched the midnight assault on the city, appeared on television tonight and said the military intervention had been taken to prevent an attempted coup by the Azerbaijani Popular Front.

"There were growing calls for a seizure of power by force," Mr. Gorbachev said.

Despite a reported heavy martial presence in the city, Popular Front leaders rallied supporters this morning for a demonstration in front of the Communist Party headquarters in Baku and vowed to defy the military with a campaign of strikes and civil disobedience.

"We will fight until we win," said Yussef Samadoglu, a poet and Popular Front leader. "The goal is to drive out the army, liquidate the Azerbaijani Communist Party, establish a democratic parliament."

In East Germany those who were ruling without much legitimacy decided to accelerate the timetable for democratic elections. It was the first of what would be many accelerations on the road to unification.

Vote Is Moved Up by East Germans; Coalition Widened

By Serge Schmemann

EAST BERLIN, Jan. 28—Meeting late into the night, the Government and all major political groups in East Germany agreed today to hold the country's first democratic elections on March 18 instead of in May, and to form a coalition government until then.

The announcement, which came after a seven-hour emergency

meeting, reflected a growing anxiety that an increasingly restive and frustrated public was not prepared to wait another two months for a representative government, and that a rapidly disintegrating Communist Party lacked sufficient credibility to govern alone.

The development also marked a sharp new turn in the tortuous development of the East German revolution, the acceptance of a share in power by the opposition forged in the peaceful revolution of last fall and the effective surrender by the Communist Party of its control of the Government.

Emerging at about midnight from a smoke-filled room of the Johanneshof Government guest house in central East Berlin, Martin Zeigler, a Protestant church leader who chaired the talks, told reporters that elections to a new Parliament would now be held March 18, and that local elections would be held instead on the original date, May 6.

In the meantime, he said, a "government of national responsibility" would be formed, with each of nine opposition groups sending one minister without portfolio into the existing government.

If the East German Communists were looking to enter into coalitions to gain credibility, their Polish counterparts, who had been under attack much longer, opted for a more radical solution.

Polish Communists Vote to Disband
By Steven Greenhouse

WARSAW, Monday, Jan. 29—Poland's Communist Party voted early today to dissolve itself after party members decided to create a new democratic and left-of-center party in the hope of winning public support.

But the new party got off to a traumatic start when a group of 100 dissidents broke off to form a competing party along social-democratic lines.

The disbanding of the Communists, who ruled Poland for 45 years before giving up power to the Solidarity movement last year, was foreshadowed in recent days as delegates gathered over the weekend to criticize their past and debate a more populous future.

The party finally ended its turbulent existence early today when party delegates approved a resolution saying that it was proper to dissolve "because of the impossibility of the party's regaining the public's confidence."

356

Just about everywhere in Eastern Europe outside the Soviet Union, the turmoil on the streets had crested. The tasks now were to find ways in which new political and economic systems could be institutionalized. In East Germany, the prevailing hope was that rescue would come from West Germany and that it would come quickly.

In Suspense, East Germans Await Capitalism
By Serge Schmemann

MAGDEBURG, EAST GERMANY, Jan. 30—Some are anxious, some can hardly wait, but it seems that everyone here is waiting for the West Germans.

The Government in East Berlin may be dragging its feet on legalizing foreign investment, but the rambling, sooty factories ringing the city have already begun laying off workers—something unthinkable under the old order—to make themselves more attractive as joint ventures.

Skilled workers are quitting factory jobs to set up independent garages and shops in anticipation of the West German wave. Seven dating services have been founded in recent months.

Pensioners and unskilled laborers, meanwhile, tremble for their once-sacred social benefits, and obsolete factories fear for their survival in this grimy industrial center of 290,000 set in flat country between Berlin and West Germany.

At the weekly demonstration last Monday, the theme was no longer "Reunification" or "Communists Out." This time, the posters read: "Protect Our Social Benefits," or "No Unemployment"—signs of a spreading apprehension about the side effects of a capitalist invasion.

The West Germans, in fact, are already here. Scores of latter-day carpetbaggers come daily, scouting possibilities for investments. Mayor Werner Nothe said he has had to restrict his meetings with West German entrepreneurs to 15 minutes each.

Outside the City Hall, a Jaguar sport sedan disgorges a West German in shiny gray suit, alligator briefcase and heavy diamond ring.

"I probably should not talk to you," he said with a conspiratorial wink, "But I'm here to set up a casino and some video-game parlors." But what about the absence of laws on foreign investment? "If you wait for those to start, you'll be last in line," he said, walking off briskly down Karl-Marx Street.

Not all the carpetbaggers are entrepreneurs. There are also the West German politicians who have been sucked into the political

357

vacuum of the post-Communist German state, and who have now effectively declared East Germany's March elections a dry run for West Germany's own elections next December.

By all accounts, the East German Social Democrats have taken a long lead and are stretching it fast. At their new Magdeburg headquarters, in offices recently vacated by Communists, the shelves and desks are still bare. But stacks of freshly printed posters stand on the floor alongside a new copying machine, all courtesy of the West German Social Democratic Party.

The West German party also sends over two experts every week to hold seminars on campaigning, organizing, marketing and all the other unfamiliar rules of the game of democracy. Not long ago Willy Brandt, the former West German Chancellor who is likely to become the honorary president of the East German Social Democrats, drew 60,000 to a rally on the Cathedral Square—more than a fifth of the city's total population.

Similar scenes are increasingly common across East Germany, signs of a profound change that has come over the East German revolution over the past month.

If on New Year's Day the Germans were still reveling in their unexpected reunion, the last month has witnessed a shift in mood and expectations as uncharted as the popular revolution of last fall.

The change has included a precipitous collapse of Communist authority, an outbreak of insecurity and a recognition across the entire spectrum of East German society that union with West Germany is inevitable, near and necessary.

The most dramatic prod has been the continued exodus to the West of almost 2,000 East Germans a day. Among those who stay, feelings have been ambivalent—on the one hand an anticipation of sharing in the wealth of West Germany, on the other the fear that jobs, social security and savings are all threatened.

In a nation that places a great premium on security and order, the suspense has been troubling. Last week the Government and opposition in East Berlin were forced to join hands and move up elections to March. Prime Minister Hans Modrow, not long ago a critic of reunification, has now been forced to present his own plan for unity, and President Mikhail S. Gorbachev has had to give a reluctant endorsement to the process.

Under terms of the peace that followed World War II. any change in the status of the divided Germany needed the approval of the major allied powers who had met at Yalta and Potsdam. Clearly, the United States, France and Britain were willing to endorse what would amount to the absorption of East Germany by West Germany, but how would the Soviet Union respond? Would it insist that this new enlarged Germany had to be demilitarized? Would the new state be linked to NATO as Washington insisted? What kind of arrangements could Moscow accept and what might the Kremlin want in exchange for its assent to any formula?

West Germans Assert Gorbachev Has Cleared Way to Reunification
By Serge Schmemann

BONN, Jan. 31—President Mikhail S. Gorbachev's recognition that pressure is growing for German reunification was seized upon in West Germany today as the lifting of the last major obstacle to unity.

The paper *Bild,* an unabashed booster of reunification, splashed the Soviet leader's name across its front page in the German national colors of black, red and gold, followed by the headline, "He Said Yes."

The sagging stock market in Frankfurt rose a notch on the news and politicians from both left and right greeted Mr. Gorbachev's statement with enthusiasm.

Most analysts in West Germany saw Mr. Gorbachev's attitude as recognition that the Germanys had embarked on an immutable drive toward unity and that to stand in the way was to risk losing any input into the process.

"There are no longer any differences between our and the Soviet General Secretary's views," said Egon Bahr, a senior member of the opposition Social Democratic party. "It is no longer a question of if, but when, how and what form a unified German state might take."

That was probably the message taken to Mr. Gorbachev by the East German Prime Minister, Hans Modrow. Mr. Modrow traveled to Moscow on Tuesday, two days after agreeing to move up the East German elections to March 18.

Most current analyses hold that the East German Social Democratic Party will emerge dominant, sparking a rapid increase in the creation of economic, political and social links with West Germany.

From East Germany, the lame-duck Prime Minister Hans Modrow kept insisting that the process of unification would have to be slow and gradual and that the single state that emerged would have to be neu-

359

tral. On the heels of Modrow's suggestion came one from the Soviet Foreign Minister.

World Vote Urged by Shevardnadze on German Unity

By Francis X. Clines

MOSCOW, Feb. 2—Foreign Minister Eduard A. Shevardnadze, expressing concern over "the revival of sinister shadows of the past" associated with German unification, proposed today that the issue be put to an international referendum.

"All peoples, especially those of the Soviet Union, must have a guarantee that the war threat will never come from German soil," Mr. Shevardnadze said in an interview with Soviet reporters that appeared intended to slow the momentum for reunification growing in the two Germanys.

President Mikhail S. Gorbachev, after a meeting with the East German Communist leader Gregor Gysi, also expressed some concern, saying that he viewed German rapprochement "with understanding" but cautioning that "forcing passions and simplified approaches to the problem could be pernicious."

Earlier in the week, Mr. Gorbachev seemed to soften his objections to German reunification during a meeting with Prime Minister Hans Modrow of East Germany. That in turn led to reports in both West and East Germany that Mr. Gorbachev was now backing reunification.

Today's comments by Mr. Gorbachev and Mr. Shevardnadze suggested that they might have felt that Mr. Gorbachev's comments were misinterpreted as expressing more support for reunification than was the case.

With Communist dogma in ruins throughout Eastern Europe, Gorbachev sought to modify the basic tenets by which he and his predecessors had ruled.

Gorbachev Calls on Party to Forgo Power Monopoly; Meets Hard-Line Opposition
By Bill Keller

MOSCOW, Feb. 5—President Mikhail S. Gorbachev called on the Communist Party today to forswear its constitutional monopoly on power and to accept the prospect of rival political parties.

Speaking to the party's governing Central Committee, the Soviet leader vowed that the Communists would give up "any legal and political advantages," apparently including the party's nearly unlimited power to fill important jobs in government, industry, news organizations and other major social institutions. Mr. Gorbachev immediately encountered fierce opposition from hard-liners who warned that political pluralism would lead to the extinction of the Communists.

In his opening speech to the two-day gathering, the Soviet leader urged that a nationwide congress on the future of the party be moved up to next summer, because the party is in danger of losing its initiative.

He also proposed, in a draft of a party program, the most sweeping internal reorganization of the party structure since Lenin's day. And he urged the party to consider broader but unspecified powers for the recently created post of presidency.

Shadow of Eastern Europe Looms in Nightmares of Soviet Speakers
By Bill Keller

MOSCOW, Feb. 6—As the leaders of the Soviet Communist Party labored over their future course today, they confronted the tumult of Eastern Europe as a lesson and a threat.

Throughout a day of impassioned debate, fears of Eastern Europe surfaced again and again—stark fears that the new shape of Europe, and especially Germany, could menace Soviet security, and more subtle fears that the Soviet Union may not be immune from similar upheaval.

Vadim A. Medvedev, the party's ideology secretary, said that unless the Communists continue to open democratic channels for the public's discontent, the Soviet Union will go the way of Eastern Europe.

"During the decades of distortions and stagnation, such a critical

361

mass of explosive material has accumulated that further delay could have resulted in a shock of enormous strength," Mr. Medvedev said. "Today we can see this clearly in the example of the countries of Eastern Europe."

The ideologist said that in order to "prevent a catastrophe" in the Soviet Union it was necessary "to transform the impending explosion into a controlled reaction."

Justas Paleckis, a guest representing the Lithuanian Communist Party, said the tone of urgency at the party meeting was heightened by the recent memory of collapsing Communist governments from East Germany to Rumania, and the nagging worry that the Soviet Union may not escape a similar fate.

"Without a doubt, events in Eastern Europe gave a push to the plenum," Mr. Paleckis said. Foreign Minister Eduard A. Shevardnadze insisted fervently that the demise of Communism in Eastern Europe was not Mr. Gorbachev's fault, implicitly acknowledging that some hard-liners in his audience think otherwise.

"Perestroika should not be blamed for the destruction of the political structure of Europe," said the Foreign Minister, one of Mr. Gorbachev's closest confidants in the ruling party Politburo.

"It has been destroyed by the will of peoples no longer willing to put up with violence," he said. "The undermining of faith in a Socialism based on suppression and violence began in the 1940's, not in 1985," when Mr. Gorbachev came to power.

Mr. Shevardnadze said the leadership foresaw the coming changes in Eastern Europe and fashioned a new policy of noninterference because "it is easier to change our policies than their people."

The old guard and new guard of the Soviet leadership were evenly matched today in their horror of German reunification, which Mr. Gorbachev has faced with growing acquiescence.

Yegor K. Ligachev, the Politburo's pillar of the orthodoxy, said Europe was speeding toward "a new Munich."

"It would be unforgivable shortsightedness and error not to see that a Germany with huge economic and military potential is looming on the world horizon," Mr. Ligachev said, in an address guests said was interrupted three times by ovations.

"I think it is the time to recognize this new danger and loudly proclaim it to the party and the people," he added, implying that Mr. Gorbachev had failed to do so.

"The ghost of revanchism is roaming Europe, hand in hand with the ideas of unity and unification," agreed Mr. Shevardnadze, whose world outlook often seems diametrically opposed to Mr. Ligachev's. "The hunger for justice is diluted by the hunger for political revenge. The new status of the German question has raised dangerous hopes for redrawing of borders."

Mr. Gorbachev has been publicly cautious about reunification, stressing primarily his concern about the sanctity of postwar borders in Europe—including Soviet borders—without dwelling on the more visceral fear of a warlike, united Germany.

The idea emerging among the party leadership in Moscow was to have Gorbachev consolidate his party and government powers under a Presidential canopy.

Party Maps Plan to Give Gorbachev Broader Powers
By Bill Keller

MOSCOW, Feb. 8—The Communist Party leadership has mapped out a strategy to endow Mikhail S. Gorbachev with broad new presidential powers, probably without forcing him to undergo a popular election, party officials said today.

One day after the party's governing Central Committee agreed to forfeit the Communist legal monopoly, officials said the moves to consolidate Mr. Gorbachev's government powers could be enacted by a special parliamentary session in a matter of months.

In a draft Communist platform approved on Wednesday that opened the way for multiparty politics, the party leadership called for establishing something resembling a Western-style presidential government with a strong executive and separation of powers.

Ivan T. Frolov, editor in chief of *Pravda* and a Gorbachev confidant, indicated today that the party hopes to have Mr. Gorbachev named to the enhanced post without facing a general election. But that idea is likely to face resistance from some legislators who already worry about too much power being concentrated in the hands of one unelected man.

While party leaders touted the Central Committee meeting as a big advance for Mr. Gorbachev's perestroika program, insurgents in the Communist Party said today that the new platform did not go far enough toward democracy. They said that a formal split of the party seemed unavoidable.

Members of one party faction, including Yuri N. Afanasyev, the historian, announced plans to meet this weekend to consider whether to break off and form their own party or to focus their energies on a Communist Party congress scheduled for the summer.

Critics said the platform was too vague about the legalization of new political parties, that it failed to assure the removal of party domination of the army and the police, and that it fell short of opening the party to internal, grassroots democracy.

Boris N. Yeltsin, the unorthodox Communist who cast the only vote against the platform in the 249-member Central Committee, told The Associated Press today that the platform was "a half-step forward" that would relieve tension until the summer congress.

But he said he would favor the creation of a breakaway party if the congress failed to expel hard-liners and adopt a more far-reaching program.

According to many opposition figures, the obstacles to building new political parties from scratch are so formidable that such a schismatic party is the most likely route to creation of political competition in the Soviet Union.

Mr. Gorbachev, in closing remarks on Wednesday to the three-day party meeting, warned that such divisions would be fatal for the country.

"We should not start breaking up into clans and groups," Mr. Gorbachev said, in remarks distributed tonight by the official press agency Tass. "This is the road to destroying the party and the country."

As he sought to cope with unrest at home, Gorbachev was increasingly accommodating toward Chancellor Kohl, establishing a pattern that would continue in the months ahead.

Kohl Says Moscow Agrees on Unity Issue
By Craig R. Whitney

MOSCOW, Feb. 10—Chancellor Helmut Kohl of West Germany said today that he and President Mikhail S. Gorbachev of the Soviet Union had agreed that it was "the right of the German people alone to decide whether to live together in one state."

But Mr. Gorbachev's comments on German self-determination were not unqualified. After three hours of talks with Mr. Gorbachev in the Kremlin, Mr. Kohl quoted him as saying the Germans should take the security interests of "our neighbors, friends, and partners in Europe and the world" into account.

Soviet officials said foremost among their concerns was that German unification not put the postwar European boundaries in question. That left open the possibility of extended discussions to insure that the various interests are taken into account.

"General Secretary Gorbachev assured me unmistakably that the Soviet Union would respect the right of the German people to decide to live in one state, and that it is a matter for the Germans to determine the time and the method," Mr. Kohl said at a late-night news conference.

"The German question can be solved only on the basis of reality," he said. "That is, it must be embedded in the architecture of all Europe. We must take into account the legitimate interests of our neighbors, friends, and partners in Europe and the world."

Today's comments suggested that Moscow has now agreed to let talks on German reunification go ahead. A plan for unification is to be considered at a 35-nation East-West summit meeting this fall.

Shortly after the Berlin wall was opened on November 9, Mr. Gorbachev said the question of German reunification was "not on the agenda." Since then, the accelerating collapse of authority in East Germany has apparently forced Soviet leaders to revise their view and accept reunification as something they must quickly help to shape.

Last week, Mr. Gorbachev first indicated acceptance of the idea by endorsing the plan of the East German Prime Minister, Hans Modrow, who called for a unified, demilitarized, neutral state to be achieved in stages.

Mr. Kohl and his Foreign Minister, Hans-Dietrich Genscher, said that they expected an accelerated round of consultations between East and West Germany, and between the two Germanys and their allies, from now until next fall, when the 35-nation summit meeting of the Conference of Security and Cooperation in Europe can discuss the question of German unity.

Mr. Kohl declined to set a date for reunification, but he said, "We are facing a very, very difficult, critical situation in the German Democratic Republic. I only know one thing: there could be very dramatic developments there." . . .

With unification taking shape more rapidly than anyone predicted, the main Soviet concerns are security and the inviolability of the postwar European borders.

"This is the question of questions," the Soviet Foreign Minister, Eduard A. Shevardnadze, said earlier this morning.

On Friday Mr. Gorbachev and Mr. Shevardnadze discussed the unification issue with Secretary of State James A. Baker 3d.

Mr. Shevardnadze said that the Soviets were willing to listen to various approaches, but stood behind the proposal by Prime Minister Modrow for gradual unification with both German states detaching themselves from their respective military alliances.

Somewhat surprisingly, the breakthrough on a formula was announced at a conference in Canada.

West and Soviets Agree with 2 Germanys on Rapid Schedule for Unification Talks; Gorbachev Accepts Bush's Troop Ceiling
By Paul Lewis

OTTAWA, Feb. 13—The four major World War II Allies and East and West Germany agreed today on a framework for negotiating German reunification after 45 years of division.

The agreement, announced at the end of an East-West conference of foreign ministers here, came as Moscow accepted President Bush's proposal last month on Soviet and American troop reductions in central Europe and elsewhere in Europe.

This represented a sudden reversal by President Mikhail S. Gorbachev of the Soviet Union, who only last Friday had insisted on absolute parity in troop strengths. Under the plan agreed to here, Soviet and American troop levels in central Europe would be limited to 195,000 but the United States could have an additional 30,000 troops in other parts of Europe, in accord with Mr. Bush's original proposal.

Although some difficult issues remain to be negotiated, the swift pace of agreements suggested that the unification of Germany, once thought to be a remote goal, could be achieved much sooner than anyone had anticipated. It also suggested that the major powers were on the verge of an agreement to reduce conventional military forces in Europe after more than 15 years of fruitless negotiations.

The agreement on German unification set up a two-stage process by which West and East Germany would first discuss the domestic details of unification and then meet with the United States, Britain,

France and the Soviet Union on more controversial questions relating to postwar security issues. A central issue is whether a united Germany would remain a member of the North Atlantic Treaty Organization alliance, as West Germany and its allies want, or be neutral, as the East Germans and the Soviet Union prefer.

The turnaround on the issue of troop reductions was striking. Last week in Moscow, Secretary of State James A. Baker 3d was told by President Gorbachev that the two sides could each have 195,000 troops or 225,000 troops, but the United States could not have 30,000 more than the Soviet Union, as Mr. Bush proposed.

The meeting of the foreign ministers here had originally been called to begin negotiations for an "open skies" agreement between the two alliances under which each side would open its airspace for aerial inspection by the other. But the talks quickly became dominated by Western efforts to negotiate German reunification.

Under the plan for reunification, the two Germanys would work out internal aspects of unification themselves as soon as a democratic government comes to power in East Germany after elections on March 18.

The Germanys would then start to negotiate their future security arrangements with Britain, France, the United States and the Soviet Union—the four World War II victors who still retain legal rights over Germany.

Despite the importance of the agreement, the announcement was brief. It said that the foreign ministers of West and East Germany would meet with their counterparts from the United States, the Soviet Union, Britain and France at an unspecified time and place "to discuss external aspects of the establishment of German unity, including the issues of security of the neighboring states."

It said that "preliminary discussions at the official level will begin shortly."

It is expected that if an agreement can be forged by the major powers and the two Germanys, it would be formally approved by an East-West conference of the 35 nations that originally met in Helsinki in 1975.

The three Western powers and the Bonn Government want a united Germany to remain in NATO, but on terms that "satisfy the legitimate security interests of the Soviet Union and Poland," as the British Foreign Secretary, Douglas Hurd, put it today.

Mr. Hurd said at a news conference that non-German NATO

forces would be barred from present-day East Germany. But he said the Soviet Union would be permitted to retain some of its troops stationed there for an agreed period.

In addition, a united Germany would "give a clear and binding agreement to respect Poland's present-day frontiers," which include land that was once German.

The West German Foreign Minister, Hans-Dietrich Genscher, said the four powers had made an "unconditional, formal commitment to the reunification of Germany." As a result, he said, whether Germany remains in NATO or becomes neutral is not a condition for its unification.

Asked today whether a united Germany could remain in NATO, Foreign Minister Eduard A. Shevardnadze of the Soviet Union merely shrugged his shoulders and declined to reply.

On Monday, however, he said that "the most sensible way" to reunify Germany was to neutralize the country, although he acknowledged that this was "not the only way."

Throughout the meeting, the Soviet Union and its East European allies had appeared uncertain and divided over the Western proposals on German unification, their unity clearly under strain as a result of the political changes under way in Eastern Europe.

Western officials maintained that the Soviets had been less rigid in private than in their public stance.

During the talks here, the three Western powers said that they have told the Eastern Europeans in particular that a united Germany firmly anchored to the NATO alliance would be less threatening than if it is left on its own as neutral.

Today, the British Foreign Secretary said "a useful weight of opinion" against the idea of a neutral Germany had formed among Eastern Europeans during the conference. He cited Poland and Hungary as two leading opponents. The East German Foreign Minister, Oskar Fischer, he pointed out, was the only Eastern European minister to call openly for neutrality.

Mr. Genscher also sought today to reassure officials from the Soviet Union and Eastern Europe that they have nothing to fear from a larger and united Germany.

Echoing the German author Thomas Mann, he said, "We seek a European Germany, not a German Europe," adding that the two Germanys would unify themselves in consultation with the four Allies.

"We respect the rights and responsibilities of the four powers," he said, adding that "unification will not take place behind the backs of the four powers."

On German ground, things were moving even faster.

Germans Move to Unite Economies, As Kohl Leads and Modrow Follows
By Serge Schmemann

BONN, Feb. 13—After meeting with the caretaker leader of East Germany, Chancellor Helmut Kohl announced today that a joint committee would start immediate preparations for currency and economic union, the first major step in Mr. Kohl's drive toward rapid reunification.

"This offer by the federal Government means that we are willing to give an extraordinary, even revolutionary response to extraordinary, even revolutionary events and challenges in East Germany," Mr. Kohl said at a news conference.

The Chancellor, however, gave no new details about how the West German mark would replace the East German currency, and he said the union in any case would not take place until after the elections in East Germany on March 18. Mr. Kohl also rejected East Germany's appeal for 15 billion marks, or $9 billion, in special emergency aid, saying that about $3 billion was already being spent on East Germany from a supplementary budget.

Hans Modrow, on his first and probably last visit to Bonn as the East German Prime Minister, formally acquiesced to forming the committee. But it was evident through the day that Mr. Modrow had little influence left, either in the negotiations in Bonn or over events in East Berlin.

He and his delegation of 17 Cabinet ministers were met at the airport by low-ranking protocol officials. At the news conference, Mr. Modrow sought to defend East Germany's integrity, saying that East Germans were not coming to reunification empty-handed, but carried "spiritual and cultural values," and that the state carried a net worth of 1.4 trillion marks.

West German economists said the figure was of little value, since it was denominated in East German marks, and since holding these assets did not change the fact that the economy was rapidly deteriorating.

At the end of the news conference, listening to one of Mr. Kohl's

369

Government ministers describe Bonn's "good will" in helping East Germany, Mr. Modrow sardonically interjected, "Good will was the main topic today."

Mr. Kohl, by contrast, spoke as if he were already the chancellor of all the Germans and their guide toward rapid reunification, and he used Mr. Modrow's visit largely as a platform to press his case.

"Until the unity of Germany is fulfilled, we have a difficult way ahead of us," he said. "But we are not heading into uncertainty, because the light at the end of the tunnel is clear even today."

A month after violence erupted in Azerbaijan, foreign journalists were able to visit the still-tense area.

A Once-Docile Azerbaijani City Bridles under the Kremlin's Grip
By Bill Keller

BAKU, U.S.S.R., Feb. 16—Four weeks after troops swarmed into this seaside city to suppress a nationalist uprising, the most popular excursion for classes at local schools is the hilltop park where the city has buried its dead.

Each day the schoolchildren come by the busload from around the Republic of Azerbaijan to study the row of graves heaped with red carnations, to honor those who died under Soviet tanks and gunfire and to absorb new lessons about their country.

"The soldiers came and killed them," said Ali, a 10-year-old boy from School No. 27 in the nearby industrial center of Sumgait. "They wanted our Azerbaijanis to die. Because they said we were savages."

"Gorbachev is to blame," added his 13-year-old schoolmate, a soft-spoken girl named Rukhangiz. Teachers and children murmured their agreement. As if reciting a lesson, she added: "It will not happen again. The blood of the victims will not remain on the earth. Those who did it will pay for it."

The acute mourning is over and a veneer of normalcy prevails in Baku, which was reopened to foreign reporters two weeks ago for the first time since mid-January. Stores are open. Buses are running. The soldiers who occupy the city keep a low profile.

But since the taking of Baku, a resentful loathing of Moscow and of President Mikhail S. Gorbachev has penetrated the culture of Azerbaijan, completing the alienation of this once docile colony. . . .

370

The anti-Azerbaijani prejudice of Moscow, the duplicity of Mr. Gorbachev, the imperial nature of Communism, the sly intrigues and insolent territorial demands of neighboring Armenia—these are now the daily themes in classrooms where children once memorized the doctrines of their loving Grandpa Lenin.

"I do not believe in the party any longer," declared Niyar Nezarova, 16 years old, the leader of her 11th-grade Communist youth league at Baku School No. 83.

"Nobody does," her classmates say, chiming in.

"The party cannot lead our people," the girl continued, her light brown eyes blazing with the fervor of a convert. "The party led us to this tragedy."

Brushing aside whatever reservations were still coming from the Kremlin, Chancellor Kohl took his case and timetable for unification to the people of East Germany.

The Germans; Kohl Stumps As If Germanys Were One

By Serge Schmemann

ERFURT, EAST GERMANY, Feb. 20—Chancellor Helmut Kohl of West Germany, introduced to a cheering throng as the "Chancellor of our German fatherland," today plunged into the intense political campaign for East German elections now less than four weeks away.

"Here in Erfurt you do not have to argue that Germany is one fatherland," Mr. Kohl declared, basking in the roar of "Helmut! Helmut!" rising from the sea of faces and West German flags spread across the spacious square under the Gothic cathedral. "We are one Germany. We are one people."

Less than two months earlier, Mr. Kohl had paid his first official visit to East Germany as the West German Chancellor.

Now, in a demonstration of the rapidity with which the politics of the two Germanys are being melded, he made no acknowledgment that he had crossed into a separate state or that he was campaigning in a foreign election, uninvited by the Government. When he referred indirectly to Prime Minister Hans Modrow at all, it was in the spirit of criticizing a competing politician.

In East Berlin, Mr. Modrow showed irritation at Mr. Kohl's treatment of his Government, telling the East German Parliament that despite Bonn's apparent conviction that reunification will come quickly on its own terms, his country would not enter a united Germany "as a beggar." Mr. Kohl's appearance in Erfurt was the first of six campaign stops he plans in East Germany in the four weeks remaining before the first free elections there since 1933 on March 18.

His schedule underscores the degree to which the West Germans have adopted the East German campaign as the first round of an all-out race for the leadership of a united Germany. The final round will be the West German elections on December 2. But by then, if the current race to unity continues, the Germanys may already be one, and the elections nationwide.

Accordingly, organizers and politicians from all major West German parties have already been crisscrossing East Germany for weeks. Campaign posters have sprouted in every village, and West German campaign vans have become a fixture on cobbled market squares, distributing leaflets, stickers and plastic bags. The first campaign spots appeared today on West German television, which a large majority of East Germans can watch.

In Leipzig, even the weekly demonstration that until recently had been the vanguard of the East German "quiet revolution" has been transformed into a campaign rally for all major contenders.

Mr. Kohl will not hold the limelight for long. Later this week, the East German Social Democrats hold a party congress in Leipzig at which all the West German Social Democratic luminaries will be present, from the venerable Willy Brandt to Oskar Lafontaine, the challenger-designate to Mr. Kohl.

Last weekend, Foreign Minister Hans-Dietrich Genscher, a leader of West Germany's Free Democrats, launched his campaign for a coalition of liberal parties at an emotive mass rally in his home city of Halle.

Political parties other than those backed by the major West German parties are involved. But it is the mainstream West German parties, with their ample war chests and smooth organization, that have emerged as the real contenders, with the Social Democrats in a strong lead.

An illustration of just how complex the European situation was became strikingly apparent when Vaclav Havel, the Czechoslovakian President who for so long has struggled against Soviet-style Communism, addressed a joint meeting of the American Congress urging legislators to show sympathy for Moscow.

The once-imprisoned playwright-turned-President declared: "I often hear the question: How can the United States of America help us today? My reply is as paradoxical as the whole of my life has been: You can help us most of all if you help the Soviet Union on its irreversible but immensely complicated road to democracy." As he made his plea the Soviet predicament was steadily worsening.

Lithuanians Vote Strongly for Independence Backers; Soviet Crowds Ask Change
By Bill Keller

MOSCOW, Feb. 25—The Communist establishment suffered a double blow today as protesters across the country thronged the streets in a defiant call for a share of power while one republic, Lithuania, voted to end Communist rule.

In at least 20 cities from the Baltic Sea to the Sea of Japan, citizens braved an official scare campaign, registering their impatience and anger with President Mikhail S. Gorbachev's pace of change through quiet demonstrations.

The peaceful rallies, the first nationwide independent show of strength by the country's pro-democracy opposition, were held to promote insurgent candidates in next Sunday's elections for control of the three largest Soviet republics, Russia, the Ukraine and Byelorussia, and to demand an Eastern European-style round table with the Kremlin on a transfer of power from the Communists.

Lithuania held its vote on Saturday, the first multiparty contest in the Soviet Union since just after the Bolshevik Revolution. As expected, the voters soundly rejected the Communists and a gave the Lithuanian parliament a strong mandate for independence from the Soviet Union.

Candidates backed by the Lithuanian independence movement Sajudis swept 72 of the 90 seats decided in the new 141-seat parliament. Sajudis candidates are expected to win more seats in runoff elections scheduled for March 10 in the 51 districts where no candidate received a majority of the vote.

The 72 seats are enough to guarantee a majority in the Baltic state's new parliament. The Sajudis slate was a mix of pro-secession Communists, independents and newly legalized Social Democratic, Christian Democratic and Green parties.

Only 29 of the winners were Communist Party members. Of those, only seven belonged to the loyalist group that pledged allegiance to Moscow.

The Communist Party has not given up its legal monopoly in the rest of the country, but the party regulars face challenges from non-party members and Communist insurgents, many of them fighting uphill races against machine tactics and news blackouts.

Voters also went to the polls in the Moldavian republic, where the first free elections under Soviet rule were expected to benefit another front seeking autonomy from Moscow. No results were available today.

The protest rallies across the Soviet heartland may prove to be an even greater humiliation to the Communist Party than the loss of Lithuania, because the authorities used everything from warnings of bloodshed to an appeal by the Russian Orthodox Church to keep people at home.

The scare tactics surely reduced the turnout, but in Moscow at least they left many residents wondering, What is this opposition that has Mr. Gorbachev so frightened?

"Authorities: You don't frighten us; you're just frightening your-selves" was the message an elderly protester scrawled on cardboard and wore around her neck as she moved through a crowd that was predominantly mainstream and middle-aged.

Judging from photographs made from above, about 50,000 people jammed into a stretch of Moscow's broad garden ring road, although the police claimed that twice that number turned out, and organizers inflated the figure by several times.

Soviet press agencies reported crowds ranging from a few hundred in Tashkent, the capital of Uzbekistan, where the rally was banned, to tens of thousands in Minsk, the Byelorussian capital. Major cities in most regions of the Slavic vastness reported preelection gatherings in the thousands.

In Moscow, the attitude toward Mr. Gorbachev in the speeches and crowd remarks varied from disappointment to bitterness. Participants scorned the Soviet leader as a halfhearted reformer, as a captive of a Stalinist system and as out of touch or hungry for power.

"Oh, I am so sick of him," said Tamara N. Zveryeva, a pensioner, when asked about Mr. Gorbachev's proposal to fashion himself a more powerful presidency. Wordy and arrogant was her verdict.

Then she relented a bit and added: "We have to admit it is tough for him. He took on all this himself, and he is still the only Communist leader we can trust."

The main purpose of the rally today was to tout candidates for the Russian parliament who have been endorsed by a makeshift alliance of pro-democracy groups inside and outside of the party.

But hostility to the Communist Party was unusually open, in some of the speeches and in placards waved above the crowd. "C.P.S.U., Nuremberg awaits you," said one. "Corruption and the party are twin brothers," said another.

The only party functionary who dared to climb aboard the podium, placed in the bed of a truck, was the ideologically ambiguous Communist chief for the Sevastopol neighborhood of Moscow. He was booed and heckled.

Sergei Kuznetsov, a dissident journalist released last month from a jail in Sverdlovsk, delivered one of the angriest speeches, denouncing Lenin as a "totalitarian" and Mr. Gorbachev as his heir.

"What can we expect from a round table between democratic forces and a criminal Government?" he asked, to loud applause.

Other candidates called on the Communist Party apparatus at all levels to step down. . . .

This morning Moscow was reinforced by thousands of unarmed police and troops who blocked routes to the Kremlin and contributed to an early tension as the crowd gathered. The protesters and the police soon relaxed, and the day passed without a serious incident being reported anywhere.

Television tonight gave a reasonably straightforward account of the meeting, showing the impressive crowd but omitting the anti-Gorbachev speeches.

Oleg Rumyantsev, one of the rally organizers, charged that the fear campaign in recent days was organized by party apparatchiks in an attempt to diminish opposition chances in the elections and to bolster Mr. Gorbachev's campaign for new presidential powers.

"Since 1937, there has not been such an unprecedented campaign of hysteria, rumors, fear, slanders and provocations," said Gavriil K. Popov, an economist and rally organizer.

On the eve of parliamentary elections—still a novelty in the Soviet Union—one man was casting himself as a serious political alternative to Gorbachev.

Moscow's Maverick with a Purpose

By Francis X. Clines

MOSCOW, March 2—Boris N. Yeltsin, the virtuoso in the evolving Communist art of campaigning against Communism, is in the thick of it again with a bold election stratagem to craft a shadow presidency for himself, the better to challenge the nation's President, Mikhail S. Gorbachev.

Mr. Yeltsin, the former Moscow party chief who has become a leader of the Soviet Parliament's opposition, has been roaming the troubled heart of this nation, the Russian republic, campaigning for near-certain victory on Sunday as a candidate for the republic's parliament.

He hopes to use this as a springboard to be chosen as republic president and chief executive of what he intends to turn into a showcase alternative to Mr. Gorbachev's foundering plan of national renewal.

"This is a chance to form a core of legislators with a better, far different, more progressive outlook directed at the deeper life of Russia," said the ubiquitous politician, who has been pioneering a Western political touch, using his much-sought coattail power to travel around the republic and be photographed with like-minded candidates for their campaign pamphlets.

Delighted, he slaps his palm to symbolize the insurgents' collective handbill and pantomimes pasting the challenge squarely on a campaign wall, beaming as if at the Kremlin wall: Yeltsin redux.

"I am undergoing personal perestroika," he declared with impish ebullience, appropriating Mr. Gorbachev's patented buzzword for change to describe his chesslike move at jumping from Moscow, where he is currently a deputy in the national parliament, and challenging Mr. Gorbachev obliquely from the grass roots.

Mr. Yeltsin is perhaps the best-known candidate in the elections on Sunday, when the most populous republics—Russia, Byelorussia and the Ukraine—vote for local officeholders and members of republic parliaments.

Mr. Yeltsin's choice is impressive, for Russia contains three-quarters of the land and almost half the population of the Soviet Union. It also includes more than a fair share of popular unrest over the failed economy and national anxiety over sagging morale.

And his timing seems impeccable, for the change of Soviet politics begun by Mr. Gorbachev is fast coming to focus on a struggle for power between the traditional fortress, the central Government, and the separate republics epitomized by Russia, newly awakening to promises of some autonomy.

Mr. Gorbachev himself has provided a new flashpoint for this issue by demanding the emergency creation of a popularly elected national presidency with greatly increased executive powers, a role tailored to his strategy of shifting his seat of power from the party to the Government.

Mr. Gorbachev hurriedly moved the measure establishing this proposed presidency through the Supreme Soviet standing legislature this week. But the plan is being denounced by opposition critics, led by Mr. Yeltsin, as a betrayal of perestroika's promise of balanced self-government.

"We must make Russia and all the republics more independent and at the same time give the center government a good push to become more progressive," said Mr. Yeltsin, an avid politician who garnered daredevil fame in 1987 by being cast from the ruling Politburo for criticizing the party establishment, a role he has since honed into an open challenge of his one-time mentor, Mr. Gorbachev.

"The critical mass is growing," said Mr. Yeltsin, who started his move from his old power base in Sverdlovsk, at the nation's working backbone in the Urals, where he first rose from factory worker to party prodigy.

His strategy is to bring enough insurgents into the Russian parliament to stop the central party's anti-Yeltsin campaign there and guarantee his success in the deputies' election of one of their members as republic president.

"It's not that I need a higher post," protested Mr. Yeltsin, looking delighted after a day at his current job as the unofficial opposition leader in the National Congress of Peoples Deputies. . . .

"So far Mr. Gorbachev cannot easily pronounce the word 'opposition,'" Mr. Yeltsin said of the Soviet leader's thin-skinned performance in pushing the presidency bill to initial passage. In that confrontation, Mr. Gorbachev dismissed the minority opposition as "demagogues" for having questioned his devotion to power sharing.

"He is getting very nervous," said Mr. Yeltsin, who feels that Mr. Gorbachev's pride is getting in the way of democratization. "I can read between the lines."

In some major cities of the Soviet Union, other radical reformers were gaining with elections.

Reform Majorities Likely in Moscow and in Leningrad
Bill Keller

MOSCOW, March 5—Independent Soviet pro-democracy groups today celebrated what appeared to be major gains in elections Sunday, including the election of several former political prisoners and the probability of gaining outright control of local governments in Moscow, Leningrad and some other cities.

Although runoff elections will be required within two weeks to decide most races, the opposition groups seemed assured of sizable minorities in the parliaments of the Russian, Ukrainian and Byelorussian republics.

Potentially more important, the insurgents expected to win majorities on district and city councils in several cities, and to transform them into bastions of real democracy.

Opposition strategists said this would give them a chance to dislodge the Communist-appointed government managers and to create showplaces of political pluralism and market economics.

"In the larger cities, at least, there should now be a chance to speed up democratic change," said Vasily S. Shakhnovsky, a dissident Communist who was favored to win a runoff for a seat on the Moscow city council.

It was the first time voters in the three Slavic republics were offered a choice of candidates from rival political movements, and opposition leaders said their slates of dissident Communists and non-party independents could well become the basis of alternative parties. No other groups formally constituted as parties took part in the elections.

In each republic, Communist Party regulars were challenged by an alliance of dissident Communists and non-party candidates, united by a disenchantment with the pace at which President Mikhail S. Gorbachev has introduced democracy and market economics.

The elections on Sunday included many races in which numerous candidates competed for one seat. To win, a candidate had to take at least 50 percent of the vote. Thus, many races were thrown into runoffs, which will be held on March 18.

Outright winners included Boris N. Yeltsin, the populist opposition leader in the Soviet Parliament, who rolled over 11 other candidates and won more than 80 percent of the vote to represent Sverdlovsk in the parliament of the Russian Republic. He has promised to run for president of the republic.

But for the Soviet leaders, the most pressing problem they had to confront was coming from Lithuania.

Gorbachev Wants Lithuania to Pay Billions to Secede
By Bill Keller

MOSCOW, March 7—President Mikhail S. Gorbachev has demanded that Lithuania pay compensation equivalent to $33 billion if the republic goes ahead with plans to secede from the Soviet Union, Lithuanian officials said today.

Mr. Gorbachev also challenged Lithuania's boundaries for the first time, suggesting that the republic must surrender the major Baltic port city of Klaipeda and other territory before going its own way.

Lithuanians rejected the demands but said Mr. Gorbachev's readiness to begin negotiating the terms of separation was a clear sign that the Kremlin had accepted in principle the republic's right to leave the union.

The Lithuanian Parliament has scheduled a meeting Sunday at which it is expected to declare the restoration of the independent nation that existed before the Baltic republics were forcibly annexed by Stalin in 1940. In an interview tonight on Lithuanian television, Algirdas Brazauskas, the Lithuanian President and Communist leader, said Mr. Gorbachev had told him that Moscow's financial claims would have to be paid in Western currency rather than Soviet rubles.

"We don't have this kind of hard currency, and to be sure we won't have it for some time," Algas Zukas, an aide to Mr. Brazauskas, said in a telephone interview.

The Soviet ruble is nonconvertible—that is, its exchange is strictly controlled by the Government. Western currencies like the American dollar, the Japanese yen and the West German mark are all hard, or convertible—their value is determined by market forces and they can be freely exchanged for other currencies.

It could not be learned what hard currency, if any, the Lithuanians now have. But if they become sovereign, the Lithuanians could conceivably try to borrow from Western banks, countries or international lending agencies.

Mr. Brazauskas, who has generally supported a gradual, negotiated secession, bristled tonight when the television interviewer suggested that he and Mr. Gorbachev were trying to frighten Lithuanians into postponing independence.

The people in Vilnius did not appear to be cowed.

Parliament in Lithuania, 124–0, Declares Nation Independent
By Bill Keller

VILNIUS, LITHUANIA, March 11—Lithuania tonight proclaimed itself a sovereign state, legally free of the Soviet Union, and named the leaders of a non-Communist government to negotiate their future relations with Moscow.

The Lithuanian Parliament voted 124 to 0, with 9 abstentions and absentees, to restore the independent statehood ended by Soviet annexation 50 years ago. The Lithuanian Communist Party, which won only a minority of seats in parliamentary elections last month, joined the non-Communist majority in the vote, and in an outburst of songs and embraces that followed.

"Expressing the will of the people, the Supreme Soviet of the Lithuanian Republic declares and solemnly proclaims the restoration of the exercise of sovereign powers of the Lithuanian state, which were annulled by an alien power in 1940," said a resolution passed late tonight. "From now on, Lithuania is once again an independent state."

It was not immediately clear what the full implications of the Lithuanian action were. According to Lithuanian leaders, Mikhail S. Gorbachev, the Soviet President, has indicated a willingness to negotiate the conditions of independence. But there was no immediate reaction to the declaration of independence either from Mr. Gorbachev or the Soviet Government.

Tass, the Soviet press agency, issued a factual report of the Lithuanian action without comment. Reports on national television were similar.

Hundreds of Lithuanians gathered outside the Parliament building, singing national hymns and chanting independence slogans, as the legislators changed the name of the Lithuanian Soviet Socialist Republic to simply the Lithuanian Republic and ordered the hammer and sickle replaced by the old Lithuanian coat of arms.

At one point, people in the crowd outside used screwdrivers to pry the copper Soviet insignia from the front of the building, to a roar of approval.

But behind the united front, many legislators and ordinary citizens voiced deep worry about how Moscow would respond to this precedent-setting breach in the union. The most common fear was a wave of economic reprisals that could produce fuel shortages and unemployment, threatening the state with chaos.

Other legislators worried that such a dramatic act of defiance, especially on the eve of an important Soviet congressional gathering, would weaken President Gorbachev, who has so far generally acquiesced to Lithuania's drive for freedom.

Before approving the law completing the political break with Moscow, the parliament elected as Lithuania's new President Vytautas Landsbergis, a soft-spoken music professor who led the pro-independence movement called Sajudis from an eclectic band of dissidents to a legislative majority.

By a vote of 91 to 38, the Sajudis-dominated legislature elected Mr. Landsbergis over Algirdas Brazauskas, the Lithuanian Communist Party leader, whose personal popularity has soared since his party broke with the Soviet Communist Party in December, but not enough to overcome the Communists' association with decades of occupation.

Mr. Landsbergis urged the 3.7 million citizens of the republic to be calm and united as they enter a period of tense negotiations aimed at persuading Moscow to treat them as a friendly neighbor. On Monday the Parliament is to consider an appeal to Mr. Gorbachev asking for withdrawal of the more than 30,000 Soviet troops based in Lithuania and the speedy repatriation of Lithuanian men serving in the Soviet Army.

"We cannot ignore the interests of our neighbors, particularly our neighbors to the east," the new Lithuanian President said. "But we will not be asking for permission to take this or that step." . . .

Mr. Brazauskas is an economist by training, and supporters said the Communist leader would be a more reassuring presence at the bargaining table where details of the disengagement are to be worked out. But Mr. Landsbergis represented a clean break with the 50-year period that Lithuanians regard as an armed occupation.

The neighboring Baltic republics, Latvia and Estonia, are also moving toward secession.

"It will be contagious for other republics," said Mr. Brazauskas, who voted for today's decision but had earlier argued for a more gradual separation. "Perhaps some will follow our example. But a great state like the Soviet Union will not collapse easily."

As national unity seemed to be giving way on a daily basis, the Soviet Parliament granted Gorbachev the special powers he had been seeking.

Parliament Votes Expanded Powers for Soviet Leader

By Francis X. Clines

MOSCOW, March 13—The full Soviet Parliament voted overwhelmingly today in favor of Mikhail S. Gorbachev's plan for a strong presidency and ended the Communist Party's seven-decade monopoly of political power in the Soviet Union.

The decisions opened the way for a popularly elected chief executive eventually, although the first person to hold the new post will be chosen by Parliament, probably later in the week, and is likely to be Mr. Gorbachev. Some legislators, however, upset at some of Mr. Gorbachev's parliamentary tactics, threatened to try to block his election.

The presidency bill was approved by a vote of 1,817 to 133, with 61 abstentions. Much of the opposition bloc in the Congress of People's Deputies, the Parliament, was won over by concessions by Mr. Gorbachev. The opposition had demanded that the Soviet leader's new powers be more limited and subject to oversight.

The oversight concessions apparently eased many of the doubts expressed previously by critics concerned that the new presidency might usher in a new dictatorship.

The changes came in a long day of political bargaining and fencing.

"This decision is the most significant in the history of our Government." Mr. Gorbachev said in steering the presidency bill through the congress. Mr. Gorbachev is chairman of the Supreme Soviet, the standing legislature, and has been called "president" to indicate his duties.

"This is an important and powerful step on the road to democracy," Mr. Gorbachev declared.

In the past, power in the Soviet Union was controlled by the party, in particular the General Secretary, the ruling Politburo and the Central Committee. Under Mr. Gorbachev—who is also General Secretary, or head of the party, and a member of the Politburo—power gradually has been transferred from the party to the Government. Today's actions further reduce the influence of the party oligarchy. . . .

"Everything is in flux," said Yegor K. Ligachev, once considered the hard-liner in the Politburo devoted to braking Mr. Gorbachev's early democratization moves. "Everything is changing, and pretty quickly, too. We're politicians. We have to take reality into account. But as I see it, this will only rouse us to work even more effectively." . . .

The main advantages in the new presidency are to free Mr. Gorbachev of power struggles with the party, eventually provide him the strength of a popular mandate and afford "working space," said Roy Medvedev, a congress member who is an independent.

"This is the first time we're introducing a presidential form of government, and we can't know in advance how it will function," Mr. Medvedev said.

"Besides, it depends on the new president's personality," he added, citing differences in American presidents. "We can't expect everything from the president here, either, and we can't think that he alone will be the answer to all our problems."

"Gorbachev is closer to full control in a country that never was democratic," said Vitaly A. Korotich, a deputy and magazine editor. He was merry-eyed in dubbing him "dictator officially," but quickly adding, "I believe that Gorbachev, who destroyed totalitarianism in this country, will not be the man who will try to be a dictator himself."

Gorbachev Takes New Post and Pledges to Speed Move Toward a Market Economy
By Bill Keller

MOSCOW, March 15—Mikhail S. Gorbachev assumed the Soviet Union's new executive presidency today, and vowed to use his added powers to move his reluctant country more rapidly in the direction of a market economy.

In an acceptance speech that was remarkably free of Marxist terminology and did not mention Lenin's name, Mr. Gorbachev said his priorities would include liberalized pricing, breaking up state monopolies, free trade in surplus commodities, and creation of stock markets.

His usual references to the leading and unifying role of the Communist Party also disappeared, amid strong indications that later this year he would give up his position as party chief for a more symbolic party post.

Aides said he would begin using his new power of presidential decree almost immediately to force through changes that have been stalled by bureaucratic resistance, including leasing of factories and farmland, new forms of ownership, reining in the state role in pricing and marketing, and strengthening private enterprise.

The Soviet leader was elected by the Congress of People's Deputies without an alternative candidate, but attracted only 59 percent of the vote because of opposition from deputies unhappy with Mr. Gorbachev or with his unwillingness to face a nationwide election.

"The laws cannot work all by themselves, and grass-roots initiative and enterprises will die unless we foster the appropriate economic environment," Mr. Gorbachev said. "We must get down to creating a full-blooded domestic market."

"I think we need decisive moves to radicalize economic reform," he added.

He was approved with 1,329 votes for and 495 against, while 54 ballots were ruled invalid and 122 deputies carried away their ballots in protest to show voters they did not take part in what some called an undemocratic spectacle in the voting, which took place on Wednesday night with results announced this morning.

With the old division of Europe fading fast, the once-vaunted vanguard troops of the Warsaw Pact were losing their rationale, their identity and their esprit de corps.

In East German Army Ranks, a Headlong Farewell to Arms
By Serge Schmemann

SCHWERIN, EAST GERMANY, March 5—On paper, the mission of the East German Army's Eighth Motorized Rifle Division has been to strike into West Germany at the outbreak of war and to seize Hamburg, 60 miles to the west.

The trouble these days is that soldiers from the division pop into Hamburg pretty much whenever they feel like it. And that, in a nutshell, is the source of the identity crisis that has left the once-acclaimed National People's Army in disorder.

NATO and West German intelligence officials say discipline has disintegrated, desertion is rife and the officer corps is demoralized. East German soldiers in this garrison city 25 miles from the border confirm this information.

Strikes and demonstrations by soldiers have become common as many balk at exercises and discipline they find increasingly irrelevant. Tanks and other weapons have been placed in storage.

The official strength of the East German Army, 170,000, has dropped below 100,000, and many soldiers are working in the civilian economy—in hospitals, as bus drivers or on farms—in place of East Germans who have fled west. Now that alternative service to the draft has been introduced, officials expect the number to drop even further at the next call-up in May, probably below 70,000.

"The N.V.A. can't be used in war anymore," said Egon Bahr, a prominent Social Democrat and director of peace research at Hamburg University.

The Eighth Motorized Rifle Division in Schwerin used to have a reputation as one of East Germany's finest units. But only this morning members of a communications unit at the Stern-Buchholtz barracks refused to go out on exercise. A rainstorm was blowing, and when roused at 4 A.M. the soldiers simply said no.

It took seven hours before the troops agreed to move out, and two soldiers were arrested, but Lieut. Col. Bodo Schwarzer, the press officer in Schwerin, acknowledged that nothing was likely to happen to them.

"A year ago, they would have been sternly advised of the consequences and turned over to the military prosecutor," Colonel Schwarzer began. Then he stopped and shrugged, "A year ago this was unthinkable."

A year ago, a recruit like Pvt. Tomas Stefan, manning the gate at a firing range across the road from the Stern-Buchholtz barracks, would probably have panicked if two Westerners had pulled up in a Mercedes. Now the 26-year-old soldier from Halle made no effort to challenge the visitors or to hide his disdain for what he considered to be an utter waste of time.

"All we do is just stand on guard all the time," he complained. "What for? There's no enemy anymore. They don't know what to do with us. They don't talk to us. They just push us around and make us stand guard."

Like many of the current lot of conscripts, Private Stefan was drafted into the army early in November, just before the Berlin wall came down. Defying orders, soldiers flocked with civilians to visit West Germany. Some went over to stay, while others began openly joining the anti-Communist demonstrations at home.

Before long, they were finding it increasingly difficult to think of the

West as an enemy, and as the old order crumbled so did the authority of the officers and the ideology they were supposed to defend.

A large mural over the gates of the Ernst Burger Barracks in the center of Schwerin still carries the old military oath, "I pledge always to faithfully serve the German Democratic Republic, my socialist fatherland, and always to follow the orders of the workers' and peasants' Government."

But the mood of servicemen ambling out of the barracks was anything but faithful. One said troops refused to shoot at mock-ups of West German Leopard tanks.

"Everyone talks of 'brothers and sisters' in West Germany, and we're paid to practice shooting them," he said.

Judging by the results of the first free election in East Germany, there was no identity crisis among civilians. They strongly supported a group of conservative parties that were backed by Chancellor Kohl and were ready to back him given the chance.

Mandate for Unity "As Soon as Possible"
By Serge Schmemann

EAST BERLIN, Monday, March 19—In their surprising endorsement of a conservative alliance led by the Christian Democrats, the East Germans declared loudly that, as a young voter named Susanna Frank put it, "We should get out of this mess as soon as possible."

The large vote for the Christian Democrats and more generally for parties backed by Bonn was in effect a death sentence for the German Democratic Republic and an endorsement of absorption, as quickly as possible, into big, rich West Germany.

Even those worried about their jobs and social benefits seemed to accept that unification was like an injection—painful, frightening, but unavoidable and so best gotten over with.

"Every day we waste not having reunification just makes matters worse," declared Miss Frank, a 25-year-old East Berliner who seemed to echo the sentiment of hundreds who flocked to a discotheque in the center of the city on Sunday for an exuberant celebration by the Christian Democratic Union of a victory that no polls and no pundits had really anticipated.

Even many East Germans probably did not know for sure how they would vote in the first free election in their state. The one consistent thing polls had shown was that many voters were undecided, and in the weeks before the election the public mood seemed to lurch daily from hope to despair.

When they went behind the voting partitions—borrowed from West Berlin—the majority of the 12 million voters decided that they saw no point in clinging to any vestiges of the system that had left them poor, shabby and suffering from pollution. More than 40 percent voted for the C.D.U., and three-quarters cast their ballots for parties backed by counterparts in West Germany.

The first free election in East German history, many pointed out, was likely to be its last. The next election in which East Germans vote, possibly within a year, is likely to be an all-German ballot.

In effect, the election of a Parliament dominated by West German–backed parties marks the real beginning of German unification. Whatever pace it assumes, the process can lead to only one conclusion now.

One international effect is likely to be felt at the talks between the two Germanys and the four major victors of World War II in Europe—the United States, the Soviet Union, Britain and France—which will soon begin in earnest. The Germanys will effectively speak with one voice.

The Soviet Union in particular has tried to slow the process toward unification and has resisted efforts to place a united Germany in the Western camp. But a pro-Western government in East Berlin will make Moscow's case harder to maintain.

Sunday's vote was a major milestone in the tumultuous but peaceful revolution that for the East Germans began last May, when East Germans began trickling west through newly opened gates in Hungary. By fall, the trickle was a flow that undermined the hard-line Communist regime of Erich Honecker and led his retreating successors to open the Berlin wall. . . .

The exact timetable for unification remains unknown. Obviously relishing a victory for which he could claim the major credit, Chancellor Helmut Kohl of West Germany declared that the East Germans had rejected socialism of any sort, and that "the voters showed they want to go the way of unity with the Federal Republic."

The vote in effect gave Mr. Kohl the possibility of extending considerable influence over East Germany and pursuing his goals of swift currency and economic union. But he left unclear when he expected political union.

One possible factor in his hedging was a growing resistance in West

Germany to hasty union. A West German television poll showed that 66 percent in West Germany favored taking time in unifying the Germanys.

But as Ibrahim Bohme, the chairman of the Social Democratic party in the East, acknowledged, what is clear is that, in East Germany, "the people have voted for a quick path to unity."

Outside the C.D.U. celebration, the sentiments were more blunt. "If I could do it, I'd have unity overnight," declared Hans Neubauer, 51 years old. "A lot of us older people want to live our lives now. We've had the Reds long enough. Just look at the outcome."

SPRING 1990

As the seasons changed, several interlocking dilemmas affecting the fate of Europe were steadily impinging on Mikhail Gorbachev. He clearly wanted and needed to transform the political and economic culture of the Soviet Union in ways that would stimulate growth. But as was becoming daily apparent in Lithuania, the drive toward greater local initiative that was needed to inspire greater growth hardly encouraged political stability. The Kremlin could, of course, still resort to even harsher measures than it had so far employed to suppress regional yearnings for autonomy. But if it did that, it would jeopardize any help from the West, on which it was counting to modernize the country or placate the yearnings of its consumers. Here is where Germany came in. If the West, notably West Germany and the United States, were unsympathetic to him and his handling of Soviet problems, he could at the very least delay the process and maybe even derail it. If on the other hand, the rich countries of the West showed understanding and were likely to offer material assistance, he could be more accommodating. In the meantime, he could hope that whatever prestige he gained abroad might be converted to improve his standing at home. And it would buy him time, as he sought to implement his new presidential powers.

Gorbachev Tells the Lithuanians to Turn In Arms
By Francis X. Clines

MOSCOW, March 21—President Mikhail S. Gorbachev made use of his new executive powers tonight to tighten Soviet resistance to Lithuanian independence, ordering civilians in Lithuania to surrender private firearms to representatives of the central Government, and putting foreigners under stricter controls in traveling to the increasingly anxious republic.

The order, announced on the main evening television news program, was notice that Mr. Gorbachev did not intend to remain passive in the face of increased announcements by the Lithuanian authorities of measures to secure the independence from Soviet authority that they declared 10 days ago.

Mr. Gorbachev said he was obliged to issue the decree because the Lithuanian legislature continued "passing bills that violate the rights of Soviet citizens and the sovereignty of the U.S.S.R."

The Lithuanian authorities have called for volunteers for a "territorial defense system" and have been planning for a separate currency, international trade links and management of Soviet enterprises in the republic, measures that Moscow on Monday sought to counteract by ordering its ministries to protect national industries in Lithuania.

The new President of Lithuania, Vytautas Landsbergis, issued a statement late tonight saying that the Gorbachev decree had no authority. "It can be enforced only through brutal, armed force, and if the Soviet Union wishes to openly continue the aggression of 1940 against Lithuania," he said. "The ghost of Stalinism is walking in the Kremlin, and the shadow of it lies far to the West."

Moscow's Forces Step Up Pressure Across Lithuania
By Esther B. Fein

VILNIUS, LITHUANIA, Saturday, March 24—The Soviet authorities sent a column of tanks and paratroopers rumbling past an all-night session of the Lithuanian Parliament early this morning, in what witnesses described as the strongest attempt yet to intimidate the republic into abandoning its declaration of independence.

More than 100 tanks and trucks, and more than 1,500 soldiers armed with automatic weapons thundered by the Parliament building in central Vilnius at about 3 A.M. as legislators worked through the night to complete the creation of an independent government.

The Parliament broke off from its work to pass an emergency resolution declaring that it would transfer all authority to its representative in Washington in the event that legislators were arrested or martial law was imposed.

The column proceeded through the town, stopping at an army base inside the city limits after passing the Parliament, and there were no signs that the central Government was trying to take power in Lithuania, where independence was declared on March 11.

Soviet Troops, Storming Hospital, Seize Lithuanian Army Deserters

By Francis X. Clines

VILNIUS, LITHUANIA, Tuesday, March 27—Armed Soviet troops stormed a psychiatric hospital early this morning and arrested a group of Lithuanian deserters from the army who had taken refuge there since the republic's proclamation of independence on March 11, witnesses said.

Some of the deserters were beaten as the troops routed them from the hospital, the witnesses said. Blood stained the stairway, and smashed glass and upended furniture littered the ward that had been the Lithuanians' sanctuary since late last week.

The action against the deserters followed conflicting signs from the Soviet military over the standoff in Lithuania, including the first meeting between Lithuanian leaders and military representatives on Monday.

A doctor who was present during the confrontation at the hospital estimated that about half of the 39 deserters fled down a fire escape.

Awakened at home early this morning, the Lithuanian President, Vytautas Landsbergis, said, "Now we can expect anything, that Parliament will also be arrested. The Western states raised hopes that there would not be force. They can say all they want, but Gorbachev does what he wants."

During the night a small group of Soviet troops also moved into the headquarters of the Lithuanian Communist Party in Vilnius. The move appeared to be related to a series of seizures of party property instigated recently by a Communist rump group that has remained loyal to Moscow.

In Kaunas, 65 miles west of Vilnius, Soviet troops took control of a second hospital that Lithuania's government had set up for "deserters," the Associated Press reported, quoting a police official. It was not immediately known if anyone was taken into custody there.

Lithuania Offers to Discuss a Vote on Its Sovereignty

By Francis X. Clines

VILNIUS, LITHUANIA, March 29—Leaders of this republic's embattled independence government sent a signal of compromise to the

Kremlin tonight, saying they were ready to discuss the difficult issue of a referendum on secession if President Mikhail S. Gorbachev agreed to talk with them.

The Lithuanian President, Vytautas Landsbergis, conceding that the Kremlin had greeted his pleas for negotiations with a "concrete wall," appeared to be searching openly for a conciliatory note that might entice Moscow to the negotiating table.

"There are no questions that cannot be discussed except the question of Lithuanian independence," Mr. Landsbergis said at a news conference. "The problem of the referendum could also be discussed."

The republic's Parliament declared Lithuania independent of Soviet rule 18 days ago without holding a referendum among Lithuanian citizens. This has been a particular complaint of Mr. Gorbachev as he continues to denounce the republic's secession as illegal and therefore nonnegotiable.

Mr. Landsbergis had previously belittled the referendum issue. He has said that Lithuania is not seeking permission to secede, but rather reclaiming the independence it lost 50 years ago when it was forcibly annexed by Stalin as a result of a Soviet nonaggression pact with Hitler.

An additional suggestion of compromise today was the outright endorsement of an independence referendum by Algirdas Brazauskas, the leader of the Lithuanian Communist Party, which broke away from the Soviet Communist Party in December. Mr. Brazauskas, also a Deputy Prime Minister of Lithuania, is viewed by the public as one of the few accomplished politicians here capable of dealing with the Kremlin.

"A referendum would be an additional ace in our negotiating position," said Mr. Brazauskas, who appeared at the Lithuanian President's side to propose that the independence issue be put to the voters.

Moscow's Forces Seize 2 Key Sites from Lithuanians

By Francis X. Clines

MOSCOW, March 30—Soviet forces took over the State Prosecutor's Office in the Lithuanian capital today and seized the printing plant where the republic's main independence newspapers are printed, Lithuanian officials said.

No resistance or injuries were reported in the raids by Soviet paratroopers. But the moves are the most serious so far in a week of steady harassment by Kremlin forces intent on forcing Lithuania to retreat from the declaration of independence approved on March 11 by the republic's Parliament in Vilnius, the capital.

The heightened Soviet pressure on Lithuania was reported as the Parliament of a neighboring Baltic republic, Estonia, mindful of the independence crisis in Lithuania, approved a slower, more deliberate path toward restoring full sovereignty. The third Baltic republic, Latvia, is expected to pursue its own independence plan next month at a Parliament meeting.

The Prosecutor's Office in Lithuania was the first government building to be seized in the continuing campaign of nighttime raids in the republic.

Earlier in the day, a Deputy Prosecutor from Moscow, Aleksei Vasilev, arrived at the office and criticized the breakaway republic for appointing a new Chief Prosecutor, Arturis Paulauskas, without Moscow's approval. Mr. Vasilev brought with him another Lithuanian, Antanas Petrauskas, to replace Mr. Paulauskas.

After staff members reacted angrily to the move, Lithuanian officials said, the soldiers took over the building.

The printing plant, like the other half-dozen properties occupied by Soviet forces this week, was a Communist Party enterprise that printed various publications, including the main organ of the Sajudis independence movement and the chief daily newspapers that carry the Lithuanian Government's news and statements at length.

The latest reports from Lithuania came on a day when most foreign correspondents there were ordered out of the republic, and the movements and reporting efforts of those who remained were severely limited.

The authorities in Vilnius said there were no immediate signs of other raids by the paratroopers, who move about the Baltic capital at double-time and in full battle gear. Vulnerable sites include the republic's television center and the Parliament, the seat of the breakaway government. Lithuanian militiamen were stationed at both places, armed only with nightsticks.

"The intimidation and takeovers picked up remarkably," said William J. H. Hough 3d, a New York lawyer who is in Vilnius advising the fledgling government of President Vytautas Landsbergis.

He said the troops had in both cases seized buildings already under Soviet sway. No one was being allowed into the printing plant, and there was no immediate word on whether the presses would be permitted to operate for the papers that support the republic's two-year-long separatist drive.

Far away from the Baltic, Yugoslavia, which like the Soviet Union is a federation of republics based on nationalities, was experiencing tugs and pulls on its unity. Democracy was expanding and people were using their electoral rights to vote against the center and against unity.

Yugoslavia Holds Free Vote for First Time since 1940's

By Chuck Sudetic

BELGRADE, YUGOSLAVIA, April 8—Slovenes lined up patiently at polling stations in a cold rain today to vote for a new President for their republic, members of a new collective presidency and representatives to two of three parliamentary chambers. The voting marked the first free multiparty elections in Yugoslavia since Tito took power here after World War II.

Preliminary results from balloting today are expected on Monday. The final outcome will not be known until after two more rounds of voting, on April 12 and 22.

Once a new government is formed in Slovenia, in northern Yugoslavia, the country will have a Western-style democracy in one republic, with deeply divided, indirectly elected Communist governments ruling the rest of Yugoslavia, which consists of a loose federation of six autonomous republics and two provinces.

How this inconsistency is resolved in the coming months will to a great extent determine whether Slovenia becomes Yugoslavia's Lithuania.

While the reassertion of relatively small nationalities was continuing to undermine old political arrangements, the most challenging issue facing Europe was Germany. While there was virtually universal agreement that the two German states ought to come together, there were major differences as to the pace and form of union. The stickiest issue concerned what was to be done with the armed forces of the two Germanys when they became one. Would they be in NATO? Would they be in both NATO and the Warsaw Pact? What roles would the old military alliances play in the new Europe?

The Armies: As Germany Reunites, East and West Seek a System for Future Security on Continent
By Serge Schmemann

BONN, April 9—If current thinking prevails, a year from now a NATO country might be paying Soviet troops to stay on its soil alongside American forces.

That NATO member is a united Germany, and that bizarre possibility is one arrangement under consideration as the Germans and their allies in the East and West begin to ponder the shape of a new security order in Europe now that the Warsaw Pact is disintegrating and the Germanys are reuniting.

Given the pace and confusion of developments in Eastern Europe, much of the thinking in Bonn, as at NATO headquarters in Brussels, in Moscow, Washington or the capitals of Europe, has been largely exploratory.

But already the broad outlines of the debate are taking shape on a system that can maintain the European peace, counter Soviet nuclear power, satisfy the Soviets' demands for security and influence, and accommodate a united Germany while reassuring its nervous neighbors.

A consensus in Europe—stated publicly by Chancellor Helmut Kohl and last Friday by Foreign Minister Eduard A. Shevardnadze of the Soviet Union—is that a united Germany must not become neutral. A large, wealthy Germany concerned only with its own security, according to this thinking, would become a "loose cannon" in the center of Europe, reviving the instabilities and insecurity that led to the world wars.

"All of our history tells us that our collective defense is an extremely stabilizing factor," a German diplomat said. "We would be stupid to give that up."

A NATO restructured to ease Soviet fears, the argument goes, would provide the most viable home for a united Germany, and an American presence is crucial to prevent the fragmentation of the Continent and to balance Soviet nuclear power.

Less openly, diplomats acknowledge that the Americans would also help alleviate fears on the Continent of the potency of a united Germany.

The obvious problem is how to sell this to the Russians. Last week, Moscow dropped its opening demand that a united Germany should be neutral, but that is still far short of accepting Germany's membership in the Western alliance.

Western diplomats at NATO headquarters in Brussels believe that Mikhail S. Gorbachev might conceivably accept the idea that keeping Germany in the NATO fold, and American troops in Europe, could be the most practical way to prevent the fragmentation of Europe or the growth of a dominant Germany. But Moscow would not accept the arrangement unless it was guaranteed security and a continuing role in European affairs.

The thinking now predominant in the West holds that the most likely intermediate solution will be for a sharply reduced American force to remain in what is now West Germany, while an equally downscaled Soviet force stays in what is now East Germany.

The huge Soviet force in East Germany is financed in part by East Germany, and the bill for any future Soviet presence would probably have to be picked up by a united Germany, a dues-paying member of NATO.

Other questions abound: What will be the role of the West German Army? How will German public opinion cope with such an arrangement? Would the superpowers be allowed nuclear weapons? Where will the other East European countries fit?

These are the issues that are likely to be at the center of the "two plus four" reunification talks between the two Germanys and the four World War II victors—the United States, the Soviet Union, Britain and France. The issues are also likely to play a major role in the Vienna talks on reducing conventional arms and in the American-Soviet summit meeting in late May. . . .

One idea often heard in Europe, especially in West Germany, is that both military alliances should eventually be dissolved into a new "European Security Order" under the umbrella of the Conference on Security and Cooperation in Europe, whose 35 members include all European nations except Albania, plus the United States and Canada. Set up in 1975, the conference was intended as a forum for "confidence building" not only on security issues, but on human rights as well.

The United States, however, has argued against abandoning NATO, saying the security conference is an unwieldy arena of disparate members in which all decisions must be unanimous. The United States, in effect, could be vetoed by Malta.

Proponents of the idea say that with time the organization could be adapted to the new function.

The idea has found particular favor in West Germany, where popular opinion is growing against the military blocs. Many West German politicians say they believe it is unlikely that citizens of a united Germany will long tolerate a continued presence of troops from both East and West on their soil.

Foreign Minister Hans-Dietrich Genscher, the most influential voice in shaping German foreign policy, spoke in a recent speech to the Western European Union in Luxembourg of tranforming NATO and the Warsaw Pact into "cooperative structures" with "special political control functions," and then to turn these "into an interlocking system of mutual collective security."

But Mr. Genscher also made clear that NATO must be retained, at least for the foreseeable future. That poses the problem of how to adjust an alliance formed for a Europe in which East was East and West was West.

Some diplomats say that the very uncertainty of the processes under way in Eastern Europe argue for the retention of an organization that has proved itself effective.

One diplomat said German unity "is happening not in a Europe that's growing together, but a Europe in which one power has suddenly collapsed, leaving chaos in its wake."

That is the main reason, he said, why NATO must be retained, adding, "This is when we need as much stability as we can get, and NATO and the European Community are the only structured sources of stability that exist in Europe."

The arguments for keeping NATO include the fact that the Soviet Union remains a major nuclear power, that it would calm worries about a united Germany, and more broadly that NATO was intended not only as a military alliance but as a community of shared values.

There is no question that the NATO of the future will be far smaller militarily, with a greatly reduced American presence. The talks on reducing conventional arms in Vienna envision reducing Soviet and American forces in Europe to 195,000 each, and there is already talk of far deeper cuts.

But major questions remain, including how long the forces would stay and whether German public opinion would tolerate nuclear weapons. A move to strip NATO of nuclear weapons, while the Soviet Union maintains its arsenal, some diplomats argue, would in effect finish NATO as a military alliance.

"There's a lot of thinking and discussing about the way ahead," a senior diplomat in Brussels said. "In a curious way, it's almost too soon to talk of lobbies. People are still trying to sort out their own ideas. Events are moving so fast it's quite hard to catch up with them."

Moscow, which had backed down from its earlier insistence, offered a new approach on the question of military alliances.

Soviets Flesh Out View on Germany
By Craig R. Whitney

MOSCOW, April 10—Providing the first details of a proposal broached last week, a top adviser to President Mikhail S. Gorbachev says the Soviet Union would accept a united Germany's membership in both NATO and the Warsaw Pact for a five- to seven-year transitional period leading to a new European security system.

Valentin M. Falin, chief of the international department of the Soviet Communist Party Central Committee and a former Ambassador to West Germany, said: "We need to arrive at an all-European security system in a few years, through some transitional steps. The idea that for a certain time a unified Germany could remain with its Western part in NATO and its Eastern part in the Warsaw Pact, as a modus vivendi for a few years, would probably be acceptable to our side."

But, he said, "the most important thing would be that Germany then become a motor to help to extract the best out of these two organizations and then meld them into an all-European security structure."

Last week the Soviet Union abandoned a demand that a united Germany be neutral.

Confirming the new stance, Mr. Gorbachev said tonight that the reunification of Germany should be synchronized with the formation of what he called "new structures of security for all of Europe, from the Atlantic to the Urals." The Soviet press agency Tass quoted Mr. Gorbachev as telling the visiting British Foreign Secretary, Douglas Hurd: "In the meantime a transitional stage is possible. We are prepared for a constructive search."

And, very quickly, Washington rejected the notion.

White House Bars a United Germany in Both Alliances
By Thomas L. Friedman

WASHINGTON, April 11—In its first detailed comment on a Soviet proposal that a unified Germany belong to NATO and the Warsaw Pact, the Bush Administration rejected the idea today as a guise for making a united Germany neutral. . . .

Nevertheless, Administration officials understand that if they want Moscow to accept a united Germany in NATO, they are going to have to provide President Mikhail S. Gorbachev with some sort of political cover so that he can move from his present position to one acceptable to the West.

They see that being done through a package of ideas that would disguise and make more palatable a united Germany in NATO. Among the alternatives being discussed would be that NATO become a more political, less military alliance and that the 35-nation Conference on Security and Cooperation in Europe, of which the Soviets are members, would take on some functions, like serving as a clearing-house for troop movements and for other confidence-building measures.

Other ideas are that the Soviets be allowed to station troops in East Germany for a transitional period, that the united Germany give the Soviets specific security guarantees regarding what weapons it will maintain and where its army might be deployed and, finally, that NATO agree not to extend its forces into East Germany.

Once more, the tensions were intensifying in Lithuania. Again the headlines seemed to resemble daily if not hourly temperature readings tracking the course of an inflammation.

Gorbachev Warns Lithuania of Ban on Major Supplies
By Francis X. Clines

MOSCOW, April 13—President Mikhail S. Gorbachev issued an ultimatum to Lithuania today, saying that if the republic does not rescind its strongest independence measures within 48 hours, he will order other republics to start cutting off needed supplies.

In his harshest attempt at pressure so far, the Soviet leader warned the rebellious republic that its independence campaign had degenerated into "an ever tighter knot, assuming the nature of a political dead end."

"Other constitutent republics are asking quite aptly why they should continue supplying products to Lithuania at the expense of their own needs," he declared in a letter to the leaders of the Lithuanian government, which declared its independence on March 11 in Vilnius.

Lithuanians Offer New Compromises to Avoid Blockade (April 16)

Lithuanians Say Moscow Has Cut Main Oil Pipeline (April 18)

Toughening Stand, Moscow Cuts Back Gas for Lithuania (April 19)

Lithuania Considers Delaying Full Independence (April 20)

In Poland, where the struggle against Communist rule had been won, the struggle to transform the economy, though more advanced than in any of the other Eastern European states, was running into difficulties.

Polish Free-Market Planner Comes under Solidarity Fire

By Stephen Engelberg

GDANSK, POLAND, April 23—The chief architect of Poland's transition to a free-market economy was questioned sharply today by a skeptical audience of Solidarity members, and he emphatically rejected calls for Government intervention to ease the hardships caused by his plan.

The official, Finance Minister Leszek Balcerowicz, stood firm as delegates at the Solidarity convention pelted him with questions and qualms for more than an hour about the Government's program of "shock therapy" for the economy.

"After 45 years of Communism, it was very difficult to find a program for the short term that would not lower living standards,"

Mr. Balcerowicz said. "I know people are suffering a lot, sometimes approaching the limit of patience."

But Mr. Balcerowicz appealed to the delegates for more time, and said he could not take any steps that would risk a return of high inflation.

He preached the Government's new gospel, saying the program had entered a crucial new phase in which the nation's economic rebirth would depend on the efforts of individual entrepreneurs.

The delegates—workers, doctors, lawyers and union activists from every region of Poland—said they saw scant evidence that capitalism was taking root to lessen the disruptions prompted by the first few months of the economic plan. They said factories remain largely state-owned and banks are still virtually nonexistent and they questioned whether more than a few Poles had enough money to become investors.

"How can you be sure the program will not end in social upheaval?" one delegate asked. "Do you realize that you are being criticized by old-age pensioners, farmers, single mothers, jobless? You speak of change. Can you tell me when people will feel things are getting better?"

The questioning of the Finance Minister came a day after Jacek Kuron, the Labor Minister, acknowledged to the delegates that Poland had not yet developed a social safety net for those dislocated by the economic changes.

Mr. Balcerowicz has the reputation of being a financial technocrat without political ambitions. He gives few speeches and his appearance today at the convention was a calculated risk, an effort to quiet a rising chorus of dissatisfaction over economic issues within the ranks of Solidarity. Polls show that the Solidarity-led Government enjoys significant, but declining, support for the economic plan. . . .

Since January 1, Poland has been in the midst of the most ambitious restructuring ever of a centrally planned, formerly Communist economy. While other nations in Eastern Europe have chosen less drastic measures, Poland has tried to wipe out almost overnight the system of subsidies and central control that characterized 45 years of Communist rule.

In Moscow, where the leaders wanted to find a way out of the economic morass, they were paying attention to what the Poles were doing and carefully calculating the risks involved.

Gorbachev Is Said to Delay Soviet Economic "Shock Therapy" Plan

By Bill Keller

MOSCOW, April 24—President Mikhail S. Gorbachev has ruled out a Polish-style economic "shock therapy" for the Soviet Union this year because the Government does not have the popular support for such drastic change, Mr. Gorbachev's main economic advisers say.

In a series of major interviews in the Soviet press in recent days, the economists and other senior officials said the Kremlin was still committed to creating a market-style economy and would undertake what were called radical measures this year to break down the state's economic monopoly.

But they said the main ingredient of a market economy, the introduction of free prices, would be postponed until at least next year because the Soviet public would not tolerate it.

"The Poles prefer high prices to empty counters," Nikolai Y. Petrakov, Mr. Gorbachev's personal economic adviser, said today in *Rabochaya Tribuna,* a Communist Party daily. "In this country, all the opinion polls show quite the opposite. People accept rationing coupons and standing in line—especially during work time—but not price increases."

The Soviet Government sets and subsidizes prices on most items, many of them extremely low. Bread is about 35 cents a loaf, potatoes 10 cents a pound, and cabbage 6 cents a pound. Other prices are similar to those in the West, including chicken at $1.90 a pound and butter $2.50 a pound at Government stores, while prices at farmers' markets, where goods are abundant and prices are deregulated, are far higher.

. . . Speaking at his inauguration into a newly enhanced presidency on March 15, Mr. Gorbachev stressed the urgency of the Soviet economic plight and vowed to take painful measures to move the country toward a market economy. Articles praising the Polish strategy suddenly blossomed in the Soviet press.

But in the last few weeks, the Kremlin has been waffling, and after an economic strategy session of Mr. Gorbachev's Cabinet last week, the tone of public pronouncements turned abruptly more conservative.

On Friday, Aleksandr N. Yakovlev, one of Mr. Gorbachev's closest confidants in the Communist Politburo, was quoted in *Moskovskaya*

Pravda as telling a voters' meeting that "the shock therapy that people are talking so much about will not happen."

The next day it was Stanislav S. Shatalin, an economist in Mr. Gorbachev's Cabinet and an ardent proponent of change, telling the Government daily *Izvestia* that the country must first take time to create a banking system, fiscal and monetary policies and other measures.

"Without all of this, to introduce a market today would only be suicide," he said.

Today Mr. Petrakov, with striking candor, underscored one major difference between Moscow and Warsaw: the Polish Government headed by Prime Minister Tadeusz Mazowiecki was popularly elected with a mandate for change.

"The Mazowiecki Government's program, even if it is bitter medicine, is implemented on the basis of a social consensus," the Kremlin economist said. "The situation in our society is completely different."

In the Soviet Union, he said, Gorbachev opponents would be quick to exploit any unpopular economic measure to challenge the Government.

While the Soviet leaders debated what offered the best escape from economic stagnation and decline, Gorbachev tried again to convince his nation how urgent the matter was.

Gorbachev Urges New Economy, Otherwise "Our Society Will Die"
By Francis X. Clines

MOSCOW, April 26—President Mikhail S. Gorbachev and his chief advisers resorted to the ultimate warning today and said the life of the nation would be at stake in the coming attempt to reverse the decline of the Soviet economy.

"If we do not get out of the system we're in—excuse my rough talk—then everything living in our society will die," Mr. Gorbachev said on the second day of his traveling campaign to stir public support for his plan for changes. "We will begin to asphyxiate."

The Soviet leader, spending another day in the industrial heartland of the Urals, was asked the most basic questions the public has about the economic plan he has been agonizing over.

"Will there soon be plenty?" a worker in Sverdlovsk asked.

Mr. Gorbachev did not reply directly. Instead he complained about the current system and urged the public not to tolerate its continuation, a theme heavily stressed in the Government-controlled television news that carried the account of his visit.

At the same time, one of his chief economists, Stanislav S. Shatalin, was warning in *Pravda,* the Communist Party newspaper, that if economic change did not take place, "We will find ourselves in a common grave."

"While private ownership has already proved socially useful throughout the world, our state ownership has only proved that it can land the country in a mess," Mr. Shatalin said.

But while the Gorbachev Government was clearly using its most unrestrained polemics in its drumbeat for revisions, the campaign still suffered from a lack of precise information about what the plans finally will be.

Gorbachev, still hailed abroad for his innovations, was finding that at home his critics were growing more vocal and aggressive.

Gorbachev Jeered at May Day Rally
By Bill Keller

MOSCOW, May 1—President Mikhail S. Gorbachev and the Kremlin leadership were jeered today by throngs of protesters who were allowed to march through Red Square at the end of the annual May Day parade.

The Soviet leaders watched in evident amazement from the top of Lenin's mausoleum as a shouting, fist-shaking column milled underneath waving banners that condemned the Communist Party and the K.G.B., and supported Lithuania's declaration of independence.

Chants of "Resign!" and "Shame!" were largely drowned out by the blare of parade music, but foreign visitors who watched from the reviewing stand said they could clearly hear the shriek of hoots and whistles that rose up from the cobblestoned square as Mr. Gorbachev led the others off the mausoleum after enduring 25 minutes of protest.

It was the first time the May Day demonstration, traditionally an orchestrated show of worker solidarity, had been opened to unofficial organizations, and several of the Kremlin officials seemed startled at the vehemence of the angry display. . . .

Organized by Moscow trade unions, it became a show of blue-collar concern about the threats to their security that might come with a market economy.

The banners and speeches warned against unemployment, private property and unregulated prices, and one placard called for the removal of Prime Minister Nikolai I. Ryzhkov for failing to lift the country out of its economic misery.

The Government trade unions, trying to halt a sharp decline in their credibility, have recently staked out a position opposing economic changes that might disrupt the traditional security of Soviet workers.

Mr. Gorbachev's economic advisers say the threat of a worker uprising is the main reason they have pulled back from a "shock therapy" transition to a market economy.

Several Soviet cities, including the capitals of the Baltic republics and the Caucasus republics of Georgia, Armenia and Azerbaijan, canceled their May Day festivities altogether as holdovers from a discredited past. In Kiev, the Ukrainian capital, the usual worker brigades were joined by demonstrators protesting Government handling of the Chernobyl nuclear accident in 1986.

Moscow Communist Party officials announced last week that the annual parade would be thrown open to all comers as a sign of increased pluralism. Officials may also have feared a repetition of last November's revolution day, when the official march was upstaged by a huge counterprotest at a soccer stadium.

In another gesture to the new realities of politics in the capital, the insurgent chairman of the Moscow City Council, Gavriil K. Popov, a free-market economist, joined Government and Communist Party leaders atop the mausoleum today.

The unofficial section of the parade was organized by the Moscow Voters Association, which was instrumental in the takeover of the city government by Mr. Popov and other candidates eager to hasten the demise of the Communist monopoly.

As the crowds of factory workers organized by the unions emptied Red Square, they were abruptly replaced by a scene that has become familiar at protest rallies in the city but must have seemed shocking to the assembled Kremlin hierarchy.

The columns included Hare Krishnas and anarcho-syndicalists, social democrats and anti-Stalinists, and at the front a monk from the Russian Orthodox monastery at Zagorsk who held up a nearly life-sized rendition of Jesus on the cross and called out to Mr. Gorbachev, "Mikhail Sergeyevich, Christ is risen!"

"Down with the red fascist empire!" said one placard that bobbed conspicuously before the marble mausoleum where the leadership stood. "Down with the cult of Lenin!" read another, its letters painted to simulate bloodstains.

One group of marchers waved the red-green-and-yellow flags of Lithuania and held up signs saying, "Gorbachev: hands off Lithuania," and "the blockade of Lithuania is the shame of the President."

They got an appreciative roar from other unofficial protesters as they entered Red Square and took up a position directly in front of the leadership.

The Kremlin has embargoed fuel and other products to Lithuania and demanded that the republic back down from its declaration of independence, made March 11.

"Lithuania is a bellwether of what is happening in our society," said Aleksandr Guryanov, a Russian physicist, who paraded with a home-made pro-Lithuania placard fixed to a hockey stick. "Their freedom is our freedom."

Television viewers watching the live coverage of the parade were given only fleeting glimpses of the protest placards, and the broadcast, which normally runs until the parade is finished, was cut off about 15 minutes into the unofficial portion.

Security was unusually tight around the official reviewing stand, but the police made no noticeable attempt to restrict access to the square. Several foreign correspondents and a few Western tourists crossed the square with the flood of marchers.

Atop the mausoleum, Marshal Dmitri T. Yazov, the Defense Minister, glared grimly. Mr. Gorbachev alternately bantered with colleagues and stared out over the heads of the crowd. After the unofficial marchers strode into view, he seemed to make a point of chatting with Mr. Popov.

The interplay between the Soviet Union's economic problems and the role Moscow had as a superpower, albeit a fading one, was made clear as the "two plus four" talks opened to formally pave the way for a new Germany and a new Europe. Three of the "four"—France, Britain, and the United States—were in close agreement on most matters. The "two"—East and West Germany—were rapidly drawing together. The major unknown was what Moscow would ultimately do and what it might demand for going along with the others.

Soviets' Price on Germany

By Serge Schmemann

BONN, May 6—If the opening session of the "two plus four" talks made one thing clear, it was that the real bargaining would be not between the victors and losers of World War II, but between a fairly unified West—now including both a prosperous West Germany and a democratized East Germany—and a battered, weakened and troubled Soviet Union using one of its last levers of power in Europe to exact the highest possible price for its final exit from the scene.

That was clear in the blend of carrots and sticks offered by Soviet Foreign Minister Eduard A. Shevardnadze, who staked out a tough posture in his formal comments, which were made available only to Tass and the East German press agency, and assumed a conciliatory stance at a subsequent news conference.

But it was probably more evident in the extent to which he went in his remarks to the closed gathering of foreign ministers. In his speech, he took pains to convince the other participants that the unification of Germany had a significance for the Soviet Union beyond the technical and logistical problems that the ministers had come to Bonn to discuss.

"We are not talking about Germany alone," he said at one point. "We are not resolving only German problems. What we are talking about is the final termination of the division of Europe."

"We are dealing here with an issue of special importance to Soviet people, to our whole society," Mr. Shevardnadze declared later, invoking the 20 million Soviet dead in World War II. "Neither this nor any other Soviet leadership could disregard public opinion. The Soviet people must see that the line under the past is being drawn in a just and worthy manner."

There was almost a plaintive character to these assertions, as if Mr. Shevardnadze wanted to impress on the West how difficult and fateful was the endorsement that Moscow was being asked to give.

The venue was the opening session of the two-plus-four talks between the two Germanys and the four victorious powers of World War II—the United States, the Soviet Union, Britain and France—on clearing away remaining obstacles to German unification.

The process was initially intended as a way for the victorious powers to arrange for the return of a chastened and reunited Germany into the family of nations. Instead, it has evolved into bargaining over the price for Moscow's withdrawal from the scene.

It was this dimension that Mr. Shevardnadze seemed to underscore. In being asked to sign off on German unity, he seemed to say, Moscow was in effect being asked to sign off on the vast influence, power and prestige it had won through the war and maintained by military power for four decades.

In the end, the core issue, as one tired Soviet journalist put it after a long day of speeches and news conferences, was "What do we get for getting out?"

The price was certain to be the object of hard bargaining in coming months, involving not only the Soviets and the Germans, but all the Western powers as well. At stake were "reliable guarantees for the stability and security for decades to come," as Mr. Shevardnadze put it.

The issues were likely to loom large over Mr. Gorbachev's summit meeting with President Bush beginning on May 30 and over continuing arms negotiations, most notably the Vienna talks on conventional arms and the Geneva talks on strategic weapons.

Diplomats say Moscow's concerns are of three sorts.

One is the political problem outlined by Mr. Shevardnadze: that the Soviet Union, and in particular its army, could not countenance the surrender of territory won through such sacrifice unless the Kremlin could show that it had received something worthwhile in return.

Mr. Shevardnadze's invocation of this problem, however, was not entirely guileless. Most Western diplomats discerned a thinly veiled threat that unless the West came through, the liberal forces now in power could be replaced by something considerably less favorable to Western interests.

The second area of Soviet demands is deemed to be economic. Specifically, Moscow wanted assurances from West Germany that it would provide concrete assistance to the Soviet economy.

Before the two-plus-four talks, Mr. Shevardnadze met with Chancellor Helmut Kohl, and one area reportedly under discussion was that a united Germany would fulfill the long-term contracts between the Soviet Union and East Germany. East Germany supplies 40 percent of all farm machinery to the Soviet Union, 40 percent of its cosmetics and medicine, 30 percent of imported clothing and an untold amount of military equipment.

Moscow would also like West Germany to increase scientific and technological cooperation. The Kremlin presumably would also want a united Germany to assume at least a large part of the expense of keeping whatever Soviet troops remain in Germany for a transitional period.

The third area of concern is probably the most problematic. The evaporation of the Soviet bloc has roused anew the historic Russian fear of being excluded from Europe, and in seeking a new "security order," Moscow will be certain to demand a role for itself.

That is where East and West are most likely to clash, and where the Germans will come under the sharpest pressure.

The United States and other major NATO countries have made it clear that they would like a united Germany to remain in NATO. Mr. Shevardnadze made it clear today that the Soviet Union finds this intolerable, and he proposed instead a center in Berlin to control all forces in Germany.

Further on, the Soviets have spoken of a new "European security order" based on the Conference on Security and Cooperation in Europe, which joins 33 European states, the United States and Canada. The West German Foreign Minister, Hans-Dietrich Genscher, has expressed similar proposals, but other Western leaders have been reluctant to consider any immediate attempts to supplant NATO.

The bottom line in all this is whether the Soviet Union has any real bargaining power left.

Moscow's only real weapon, diplomats believe, is to try to delay the process of unification. Mr. Shevardnadze, however, seemed to take pains to reassure the Germans that even if there were "serious differences," these "need not be dramatized."

At the same time, he declared that the Soviet Union would agree only to a "package approach," adding, "Nothing is agreed unless all aspects of unification are agreed on."

By most accounts, Moscow's hand is not a strong one. So far, the West has found an unusual degree of solidarity on the issue of unification, and a confident Chancellor Kohl did not seem likely to panic.

But there was also the sense at the talks that nobody wanted the Soviet Union to leave humiliated. That could not only affect Mr. Gorbachev's domestic position, with unknown consequences for security and stability elsewhere, but it could also derail the broader process of disarmament and liberalization.

In any case, it was clear to everyone at the talks that the process of German unity was under way. Perhaps it could be slowed a bit, but it could not be stopped.

Bonn Official Sees Rapid Unification

By Serge Schmemann

WEST BERLIN, May 7—Foreign Minister Hans-Dietrich Genscher said today that the "two plus four" talks had brought a "historic turnaround" that cleared the way for rapid German unity, and politicians in Bonn renewed calls to hold all-German elections as soon as possible.

In a radio interview, Mr. Genscher elaborated on his assertion that the Soviet Foreign Minister, Eduard A. Shevardnadze, had in effect cleared the way for quick reunification when he said in Bonn on Saturday that domestic and foreign aspects of reunification did not have to be resolved at the same time.

Mr. Genscher's interpretation was not fully shared by other Western participants in the negotiations, in which the victorious powers of World War II met with the two Germanys to negotiate an end to vestigial Allied controls.

But his optimistic assertion, with a renewed endorsement of unification in the second round of East German elections, gave a sense of quickening momentum to the merging of the Germanys.

In terms of the nuts and bolts of the German merger, things were proceeding swiftly.

2 Germanys Draw Up Pact to Merge Their Economies

By Serge Schmemann

BONN, Sunday, May 13—Experts from West and East Germany last night completed their work on a treaty to merge their economies and currencies, clearing the way for the two Governments to debate the first major step on the way to reunification.

A spokesman for the West German Government said today that the negotiators finished their work shortly before midnight. The Finance Ministers of both states are expected to begin discussing the financial aspects of the treaty on Monday, with approval by the two Governments possible on Friday.

But officials said West Germans still required accurate financial information from East Berlin, including the size of the budget deficit, before they could complete the financing of the treaty.

Details of the draft were not immediately available, but the West German spokesman, Dieter Vogel, indicated that some of the most complex issues under discussion—agricultural and industrial restructuring, as well as property rights—had been separated from the treaty and would be covered in additional agreements. . . .

Several of the most important aspects of the treaty, most notably exchange rates, have been known for some time now. The two Governments have agreed to exchange East German marks for West German marks at a rate of one to one for wages, pensions and savings up to 4,000 marks, and at a two-to-one rate for any additional savings. At the current rate of about 60 cents to the Western mark, 4,000 marks is about $2,400.

The Governments have also agreed that West Germany will assume responsibility for unemployment benefits. East Germany will agree to adopt West German monetary, economic and tax policies and shift from a centrally planned to a market economy.

The major problems remaining to be worked out center on property ownership, specifically how to settle the claims of former owners to properties in East Germany and how to dispose of state-owned properties. In agriculture, the discussion centered on ownership and farm subsidies.

Last Friday, East German farmers, most from state-owned or collective farms, blockaded several border crossing points to back their demands for market protection during the transition to Western-style agriculture. The East Germans have complained that the unregulated import of West German produce threatens to push their produce off the market. They are also afraid of being stripped of subsidies and of losing their land.

In general, the monetary and economic union has raised considerable anxiety in both Germanys. East Germans fear that the conversion of their socialist economy to a competitive market economy will create massive dislocation and unemployment. They also fear that a land rush by West Germans could effectively dispossess them of their homes and bankrupt their businesses.

Though the problems that had accompanied democracy and liberalism were evidently multiplying everywhere, the allure of such goals remained great enough to reach deeply into what had been the most tightly quarantined Communist state.

Albanian Leader Says the Country Will Be Democratized but Will Retain Socialism

By David Binder

TIRANA, ALBANIA, May 13—In his first encounter with foreign journalists, President Ramiz Alia said on Saturday that his policy of democratizing this isolated Communist country could not be stopped.

"All the processes of development of Albania are unstoppable," he said. "Albania can never be stopped on the path of freedom, independence and socialism. It is the desire of the Albanian people, won with the bloodshed of the Albanian people, and the Albanian people will march on the road they themselves have decided."

The informal news conference before about a dozen journalists was a reflection of Mr. Alia's efforts to open up Albanian society over the last six months.

But in his remarks to the journalists and in comments to the visiting United Nations Secretary-General, Javier Perez de Cuellar, that were published in the Albanian press today, Mr. Alia indicated that he intended to retain socialism and that he would not follow other East European countries in dismantling Communism altogether.

"As a small country, we need to have strong unity," he told Mr. Perez de Cuellar, the first United Nations Secretary-General to visit this country. "We cannot accept divisions as it may be the case with a big country. I think it would be absurd to recommend the French or English pattern of democracy."

He noted that the British Parliament was hundreds of years old, while in Albania "it is less than 50 years ago" that a Parliament was created, "and in what conditions!"

In developments here that would have been almost unthinkable in Albania a few years ago, the People's Assembly, or Parliament, approved laws last week authorizing freedom to travel and freedom for individuals to practice religion.

In addition, Prime Minister Adil Carcani declared Albania's intention to establish diplomatic relations with the United States and the Soviet Union. . . .

It is unclear where and when Mr. Alia's program of democratization, as he has called it, will stop.

Still, he and his allies, who now seem to be in the majority in Albania's political apparatus, are evidently determined to bring this country out of its self-grown shell and to expose its 3.3 million people to the West.

Before departing tonight, the Secretary-General said that in discussing human rights issues with his Albanian host, he was told by Mr. Alia that the Government was considering "reopening houses of worship," which were shut down in 1967. At that time, Albania was declared to be the world's first atheist country.

With the screws of an embargo tightening and the limits of Western backing becoming apparent in Vilnius, the Lithuanians started to pull back.

Lithuania Agrees to Suspend Laws on Independence
By Bill Keller

MOSCOW, May 16—The Lithuanian government formally agreed today to suspend all laws it has passed since its declaration of independence on March 11 and to discuss a transition period to full separation from the Soviet Union, officials of the republic said tonight.

The offer, prepared in a closed-door session of the Parliament and Cabinet, was the Lithuanians' most concerted attempt so far to persuade President Mikhail S. Gorbachev to lift his partial economic embargo and begin negotiations.

The Lithuanian Prime Minister, Kazimiera Prunskiene, was to fly to Moscow on Thursday bearing the government declaration and a letter to Mr. Gorbachev. It was not clear whether she would be met by Kremlin officials or whether Moscow would accept the gesture as an opportunity to end the standoff.

Mr. Gorbachev would presumably welcome a chance to end the economic sanctions against Lithuania, which could cast a pall over his meeting with President Bush in Washington. That meeting is to begin May 30, about the time that Lithuania expects to exhaust the last of its oil reserves.

As the Lithuanians met, Secretary of State James A. Baker 3d and Foreign Minister Eduard A. Shevardnadze of the Soviet Union started talks in Moscow on obstacles blocking a series of arms control agreements in advance of the summit. But the increasingly unstable situation in the Soviet Baltic republics threatened to derail their efforts. The proposal by the Lithuanians essentially embraced a compromise proposed last month by France and West Germany, which called for Lithuania to suspend the enforcement of its independence proclamation without actually repealing it.

When the proposal was made by President François Mitterrand

413

and Chancellor Helmut Kohl, President Vytautas Landsbergis of Lithuania and a Kremlin spokesman both praised it as a possible escape from the deadlock.

But since then, Mr. Gorbachev has insisted that Lithuania return to its status of March 10, the day before it broke with Moscow, and follow secession procedures spelled out in a new Soviet law. This would require approval of independence by referendum, a transition period of up to five years, and final approval by the Soviet Congress of People's Deputies. . . .

An estimated 30,000 people in Lithuania have been laid off or sent on unscheduled vacations since Mr. Gorbachev cut off oil, most natural gas and various other supplies to the republic.

The Lithuanians declined to disclose the text of their offer, but as explained by officials, it called for the suspension of the secession laws after Moscow agreed to begin negotiations and provided assurances that it would make no moves to supplant the current leadership of the republic.

Among the measures that would be suspended are several that Moscow has cited as particularly offensive, including those abolishing the Soviet military draft and laying claim to national property.

Gorbachev Meets with Lithuanian; "Big Step" Is Cited

By Bill Keller

MOSCOW, May 17—President Mikhail S. Gorbachev met with the Prime Minister of Lithuania in the Kremlin tonight and agreed to begin talks with the breakaway republic if the Lithuanian Parliament suspends its declaration of independence.

The official, Kazimiera Prunskiene, said tonight that the meeting, the first face-to-face encounter between Mr. Gorbachev and a leader of the Baltic republic, was a significant move toward negotiations that could lower the tension surrounding Lithuania's claim of sovereignty, made on March 11, and possibly end the limited economic blockade that Moscow has imposed in retribution.

Both the Lithuanian Prime Minister and the Soviet press agency Tass, reporting on the meeting tonight, said a serious hurdle remained in the way of beginning talks.

Lithuania has offered to suspend the application of its independence proclamation, including laws repealing the Soviet military draft and laying claim to national property, but the republic has previously insisted that suspending the act itself might jeopardize its status as an equal partner in talks with Moscow.

Mrs. Prunskiene indicated that this difference should not be insurmountable. She said she would offer a version of a new compromise that might be considered by the Lithuanian Parliament as early as Saturday.

She emphasized that she had told Mr. Gorbachev that independence itself was not negotiable, and said he did not dispute the point.

"He said the fact that we met, that we discussed the issues, that we made progress from our previous positions—this was a big step forward," Mrs. Prunskiene said. . . .

The meeting, which lasted an hour and 40 minutes, also appeared likely to ease the threat that the Lithuanian conflict could overshadow Mr. Gorbachev's meeting with President Bush in Washington, beginning May 30.

Secretary of State James A. Baker 3d, reached tonight in Moscow, said that, from what he had heard of the Kremlin meeting, "it would be a very encouraging step."

Mr. Baker is scheduled to see Mrs. Prunskiene on Friday after a meeting with Mr. Gorbachev, a session that tonight promised to be a bit more relaxed.

"One of the things we have wanted to see throughout this was the two sides talking face-to-face," said a senior American official who is here with Mr. Baker. "Here, you have them not only talking face-to-face, but at a high level."

The official added: "We're pleased. You don't want to get carried away with it, either. But it's a real positive step in the right direction." . . .

Mrs. Prunskiene, now a seasoned diplomat after her missions to the White House, Canada and European capitals, appeared buoyed by the Kremlin reception.

"Now we know to what the extent the other side has moved ahead, that there has been major progress, and what are the sticking points on the main issues," she told reporters tonight at the Lithuanian mission in Moscow. "We can say quite clearly that the desire and intentions to begin a discussion on the entire range of issues, within a framework of interests on both sides, have been expressed."

Mrs. Prunskiene said that while the Soviet leaders seemed eager to end the stalemate, they were far from enthusiastic about the idea of

Lithuania actually getting its freedom from the Soviet Union.

"Do they want or welcome the independence of Lithuania?" she asked rhetorically. "I not only doubt this, but I am sure they have no such desire. I confirmed once again today that they have trouble with this kind of decision, when a people independently decides an issue without the involvement of the Kremlin."

In terms of global politics, the Lithuanian conflict might have seemed parochial to many. But as French, German and American leaders understood, its escalation into bloody violence could spoil the atmosphere and undermine the sudden progress being registered on a wide diplomatic front.

U.S. and Soviets Close to a Pact on 30% Cut in Nuclear Missiles; Agree on Chemical-Arms Curbs

By Thomas L. Friedman

MOSCOW, May 19—American and Soviet officials announced major progress today toward a treaty reducing long-range nuclear weapons. They also said they had concluded an agreement to end their chemical-weapons production and sharply reduce their chemical stocks.

Secretary of State James A. Baker 3d spoke to reporters at the end of four days of talks with his Soviet counterpart, Eduard A. Shevardnadze. Mr. Baker said that the progress made in their negotiations left the two sides "in a position" to declare, at the coming summit between President Bush and President Mikhail S. Gorbachev, that they had resolved all major obstacles to a strategic arms reduction treaty. The treaty would cut their nuclear missile arsenals by about 30 percent. The completion of the strategic arms treaty would be the superpowers' first agreement to cut long-range nuclear weapons. The agreement would permit Moscow and Washington to deploy new generations of strategic weapons based in the air, on land and at sea. Arms control advocates have urged the two sides to seek deeper cuts as part of a Start 2 agreement. Start stands for Strategic Arms Reductions Talks.

Mr. Shevardnadze expressed confidence that the treaty itself would be completed by the end of the year.

As a result of compromises by both sides, the two officials said, two of the most difficult issues standing in the way of a strategic arms reduction agreement were finally resolved late today—how to limit air-launched cruise missiles and sea-launched cruise missiles. But for Presidents Bush and Gorbachev to be able to say when they meet on May 30 that the accord is basically finished, a variety of other, lesser, outstanding differences, which could not be settled here, will still have to be negotiated. . . .

Mr. Baker said a team of Soviet arms control experts would be coming to Washington in the middle of next week for more talks in hopes of wrapping up the strategic arms reduction treaty, which has been in negotiations since 1982.

"These have been some of the most intensive discussions we have had with our Soviet counterparts during this Administration," said a weary Mr. Baker. "In the end game of negotiations, it is reasonable to expect both the intensity and difficulty of the work to increase. In short, we have been engaged in some heavy lifting to lock in agreements by the summit between President Bush and President Gorbachev. I think our discussions have resulted in some real accomplishments, and the progress we have made here makes me optimistic that we will have a productive summit in Washington."

Mr. Shevardnadze in his news conference agreed that "there were moments when it seemed that our packages would fall apart." But he predicted with confidence that the two Presidents would be able to declare at their summit that "agreement has been reached on a radical reduction in nuclear arms."

"Of course there are still several remaining questions, details," he said. "They are not simple ones. They demand fundamental work. But now we are confident that a treaty on strategic weapons can be finished for signing by the end of this year."

The one area where the two sides made no progress was in their talks on how to limit conventional weapons in Europe. The 23-nation conventional arms negotiations in Vienna have been stalled now for months, largely because the Soviet-led Warsaw Pact has collapsed and Germany has been moving quickly to unification. This has left Moscow uncertain as to how fast and to what extent it wants to pull its conventional forces from central Europe. . . .

Under the accord, which is expected to be signed at the summit, the United States and Soviet Union will immediately cease production of all poison gas and reduce their respective stockpiles to 5,000 tons. The United States currently has about 25,000 tons and the Soviets about 50,000 tons. Once a multilateral agreement is reached in Geneva the two sides will reduce their chemical stocks over an eight-year period down to 500 tons each. These they will be allowed to maintain until every nation capable of making chemical weapons signs the worldwide ban.

The resolution of the two strategic arms issues also came about after a day of intense horse-trading. On air-launched cruise missiles the United States agreed to the Soviet demand that cruise missiles that can fly from 375 miles and up be covered by treaty limitations, but the Soviets agreed to exclude from this range limit a new, high-tech American conventional cruise missile now being tested and known as Tacit Rainbow.

On sea-launched cruise missiles, the Soviets basically accepted the American argument that they will be dealt with in a "politically binding" declaration that the two sides will make outside the treaty to limit submarine-launched cruise missiles to 880 each.

Obviously aware that the Lithuanian issue could be a burden during his upcoming visit to Washington and could even capsize a series of pending initiatives in the West, Gorbachev held out some carrots to the nationalists in Vilnius.

Gorbachev Offers Deal to Lithuania
By Esther B. Fein

MOSCOW, May 24—President Mikhail S. Gorbachev said today that Lithuania could be independent in two years if the republic suspended its declaration of independence, Lithuanian officials said tonight.

The officials said they were invited this afternoon to an unscheduled meeting with Mr. Gorbachev, at which he told them that the Kremlin's economic sanctions against Lithuania would be lifted "immediately" and that independence negotiations between Moscow and the republic would begin as soon as the declaration act was frozen.

Despite prodding from Washington and warnings from Moscow, Lithuania has refused to suspend the independence declaration it made March 11, although the Parliament voted on Wednesday to freeze legislation enacted after the act of independence if Moscow begins formal talks on the issue.

But before Gorbachev would meet Bush, there were still some hurdles he had to clear at home. For one thing, the economic plan charting the retreat from old policies was to be unveiled. With its announce-

ment, anxieties were certain to spread and intensify. Moreover, Boris Yeltsin, Gorbachev's main rival, was preparing for an election that could provide him with a post from which to stalk and challenge the Soviet President.

Soviets Unveil Limited Plan Toward "Regulated Market"
By Celestine Bohlen

MOSCOW, May 24—Prime Minister Nikolai I. Ryzhkov proposed a package of changes for the Soviet economy today that combine a small dose of free-market liberalization with continued heavy Government regulation.

The plan, which has been several months in the making, would raise prices across the board on both the retail and wholesale levels, but it stops far short of the kind of systemic transformation that many experts say is needed to halt the Soviet Union's worsening economic crisis.

In a speech to the Supreme Soviet, the standing Parliament, Mr. Ryzhkov set a "regulated market economy" as the goal. He said a more radical move toward a free market, similar to the "shock therapy" now being applied to the Polish economy, would produce hyper-inflation and damage the future of reform in the Soviet Union.

"Great hardships would befall the people, who are entirely unprepared for such a turn of events," he said. "The Government would also not be ready to help them, since in such a situation, it could not halt the inflationary spiral."

Government officials said they are confident that the plan will be endorsed this week by the Supreme Soviet. Several deputies, however, were more doubtful that the program's major elements could win approval in a popular referendum, likely to be held sometime this summer.

Many members of Parliament, both liberals and conservatives, said they themselves were not satisfied with the plan, which they said would be both unpopular and ineffective.

"The Government plan is a camouflaged attempt to double state retail prices, while making no real progress toward a market," said Gennadi Filshin, a member of the Interregional Deputies Group, an opposition faction that called today for a vote of no confidence in the Government led by Mr. Ryzhkov.

Pavel G. Bunich, a leading liberal economist and a member of Parliament, criticized the plan for raising prices without freeing them from state control. When the bulk of the price increases go into effect in January, only 15 percent will be set by the market, with the rest regulated by the state.

"There's shock therapy, which they say is bad," said Mr. Bunich. "Then there is just therapy, which is undergone willingly. Then there is shock without therapy. This is shock without therapy."

Other deputies said there would be resistance to sharp rises in prices, especially to those on food. Price increases are to begin under the plan on July 1 with a tripling of the price of bread and continue on January 1 with increases on a wide range of food and goods. This and many other details of the plan were disclosed before Mr. Ryzhkov's speech today.

"What concerns me is the retail prices," said Ravmer Khabibullin, a member of Parliament and First Secretary from Bashkiria. "This is a difficult and complicated question that needs to be thoroughly examined."

Answering questions after his two-hour speech, Mr. Ryzhkov, a former factory manager who has been a voice of caution and restraint in the economic debate, gave a sense of the protracted struggle over economic change inside the Communist Party leadership for the last few years.

"We should have done this two years ago," he said, when asked if the increase in bread prices would not adversely affect the Communist Party congress scheduled to convene here in early July.

"But every time, there was always some subjective reason not to—a congress, a session, something," he said. "Either we show some courage and bravery now and decide this question, or we will always find some reason to delay."

Mr. Ryzhkov, speaking with reporters in the corridor outside the Supreme Soviet, confirmed that the price increases, together with a compensating package of salary increases, would be put to a popular vote.

"Of course, it will be very difficult for the people to accept the proposals that were made now," he said. "The people are not informed. There is a lot of talk, a lot of rumors, so our first task is to explain it to the people. We have to speak to them honestly."

At a press conference on Wednesday, Yuri D. Maslyukov, the First Deputy Prime Minister, said the package would be put to a referendum, but today Mr. Ryzhkov said he was reluctant to use the word, since the Soviet Parliament has yet to adopt a law regulating referendums.

"We are purposely bringing out the section on retail prices and social security for general discussion among the people, and the results should be expressed by each citizen," he said. "It will be called something else, not a referendum, but the idea is the same."

President Mikhail S. Gorbachev, who attended as Mr. Ryzhkov made his long presentation this morning, has stayed aloof from the plan's debut, although his handpicked presidential council this week gave it approval.

Price increases are the central feature of the plan, and the section most likely to capture popular attention. Besides food prices, which are to go up between 100 and 200 percent, the cost of consumer goods will rise by an average of 30 percent.

Tackling a pricing system that he described as "a kingdom of curved mirrors," Mr. Ryzhkov today said that wholesale prices would rise by an average of 46 percent, with the largest increase, 82 percent, pegged for fuel and energy supplies.

Although those increases will make prices more accurately reflect costs, and bring down state subsidies, critics have complained that the new price list is as artificial as the old one.

A pound of beef, which now costs about a ruble, will cost 2.75 rubles after prices go up, although the cost to produce it has risen to 4.50 rubles. But, said Mr. Ryzhkov, charging Soviet customers that high a price is out of the question.

Still, he said, the cost of food subsidies will drop from 130 billion rubles—now a fifth of the budget—to 45 billion.

Mr. Ryzhkov said 70 percent of the money raised from the higher prices would be returned to the public through higher salaries or stipends—either as a 15 percent increase in salary or as a minimum lump-sum payment of 40 rubles a month. The plan also calls for a cost-of-living index to protect workers against inflation.

Gorbachev Issues Appeal for Calm amid Panic Buying
By Celestine Bohlen

MOSCOW, May 27—Faced with deep popular anxiety over a Government proposal to more than double food prices, President Mikhail S. Gorbachev made a nationally televised appeal to Soviet citizens tonight to stay calm during a "tense, difficult and, frankly speaking, dangerous" period.

Delivered two days before he leaves for a trip to Canada and the United States, Mr. Gorbachev's somber, unscheduled 45-minute address came after a weekend of panic buying in Moscow and other cities, where consumers reacted with alarm and distrust to the Government's move to what it calls a "regulated market economy" that starts July 1 with a tripling of bread prices. Other price increases are due to follow on January 1.

The economic crisis was not the only problem facing Mr. Gorbachev. New violence broke out today in Armenia on the eve of mass celebrations scheduled for Armenian Independence Day. Six people were killed in a clash between Soviet troops and a crowd at a railroad station in Yerevan, the capital of Armenia.

On the economic situation, Mr. Gorbachev said: "I ask you, dear comrades, don't succumb to panic, don't succumb to panic. Let us look at all this realistically and soberly and we will solve the problem." . . .

The new economic program, still under discussion in the Supreme Soviet, or Parliament, has been under attack from all sides since it was announced on Thursday. Liberal economists have criticized it as timid, while some politicians, including Mr. Gorbachev's rival Boris N. Yeltsin, have attacked its reliance on the highly unpopular price increases. In the Ukraine, miners have reacted by threatening to strike in protest. . . .

As Mr. Gorbachev's political and economic problems continue to mount, the summit meeting in Washington, which starts on Thursday, has receded into the background. Mr. Gorbachev made no reference tonight to the meeting with President Bush in his speech, which was devoted entirely to a stern lecture on the need for economic reform.

Until tonight, Mr. Gorbachev had kept his distance from the economic plan, which was presented by Prime Minister Nikolai I. Ryzhkov. Now, the President has put his own authority behind the measures, which he described as inevitable after earlier attempts at economic change failed to produce results. . . .

Today, with most stores closed, the sense of anxiety about the food supplies seemed to ebb somewhat in Moscow. In the farmers' market, where the prices are well above the average family budgets, strawberries and cherries, priced at 15 rubles—$2.40 at the tourist exchange rate—for 2 pounds, drew no more customers than usual.

For some people out strolling through the city on a bright, windy day, this week's political and economic tensions are now par for the course. "The situation is pretty normal," said Rushan, a 28-year-old bureaucrat who did not give his last name. "There are just some problems with the food supply."

Yeltsin Is Elected Russian President on 3d-Round Vote

By Celestine Bohlen

MOSCOW, May 29—Boris N. Yeltsin, the maverick politician who has spent three years fighting the Communist Party establishment, today became President of the Russian republic, overcoming a last-ditch effort by President Mikhail S. Gorbachev to block his election before departing for visits to Canada and the United States.

Mr. Yeltsin, whose popular following makes him a clear threat to Mr. Gorbachev's authority as leader of the Soviet Union, won the presidency of the nation's largest republic on a third round of balloting in the republic's Parliament with a final tally of 535 votes, 4 more than the required majority. His opponent, Aleksandr V. Vlasov, the choice of the party and Mr. Gorbachev, trailed with 467 votes.

When the final count was announced this afternoon to the tense and excited gathering at the Grand Kremlin Palace, deputies rose to their feet to give a standing ovation to Mr. Yeltsin, the former Moscow Communist Party chief who was thrown out of the leadership after a disagreement with Mr. Gorbachev over the pace of change.

Outside the Kremlin gates, hundreds of Yeltsin supporters, waving red-white-and-blue prerevolutionary Russian flags and carrying pictures of the new President, gathered to wait for a glimpse of the tall, 59-year-old Siberian, a popular hero who has become a symbol of the promise of real change.

Speaking to reporters after his election, Mr. Yeltsin said he wanted to build relations with Mr. Gorbachev "not on confrontation, but on a businesslike basis, dialogue and talks, on a principled basis, not to the prejudice of Russia's sovereignty and interests."

Mr. Gorbachev, on his arrival in Ottawa for a stop en route to Washington, was asked about the election. The Soviet President said he applauded reports that Mr. Yeltsin had said he was willing to "work fruitfully with the President of the Soviet Union," and then added: "If, however, he is indeed playing a political game, then we may be in for a difficult time. So we will wait and see. Life is richer than any teacher." . . .

Mr. Yeltsin, asked if he expected to receive a message of congratulation today from his longtime foe, said after a dramatic pause, "Yesterday I could not imagine it, but today it would be the politically correct step."

In contrast to the acrimony so obvious in Moscow, at the Washington summit there seemed to be nothing but sweetness and light.

Summit in Washington; 2 Leaders Spend Day in Relaxed Talks at Camp David
By Bill Keller

WASHINGTON, June 2—President Bush and President Mikhail S. Gorbachev withdrew to the relative informality of Camp David, Md., today and applied their growing rapport to such problems as regional conflicts, Soviet emigration and anti-Semitism.

The Presidential spokesman, Marlin Fitzwater, said the two leaders doffed their coats and ties and had a "relaxed give and take" on a range of regional issues, including Afghanistan, Cambodia, the Middle East, Cuba and Nicaragua. He said they then discussed human rights and anti-Semitism in the Soviet Union before moving into a more "philosophical" conversation.

Mr. Fitzwater said the two men did not resume their discussion on the major unresolved issue of the summit talks, the future of Europe after German reunification.

In his most upbeat comments of the week on this issue, the Presidential spokesman said that in their earlier meetings Mr. Bush and Mr. Gorbachev had laid the groundwork for an eventual convergence of views on the German issue.

American and Soviet officials said the two sides remained far from a breakthrough on the central issue of whether a united Germany will be integrated into the military structure of the North Atlantic Treaty Organization, but had come to a much closer understanding on ways to make Germany's future less threatening to the Soviets.

At Camp David, the presidential retreat 50 miles northeast of Washington, the two men spent the morning reviewing the world's hottest trouble spots, then took a short break and cruised the Camp

David grounds in a golf cart, with Mr. Gorbachev at the wheel at one point. After lunch they resumed their conversation with no specific agenda.

American officials today recounted how Mr. Bush tried to cement the kind of personal trust he prizes in his relations with world leaders by responding on Friday to Mr. Gorbachev's appeal for a trade pact, the first surprise of the summit meeting.

Mr. Bush had said before the summit meeting that the Kremlin's harsh resistance to Lithuania's drive for independence could impede a trade agreement, and members of Congress warned today that Congressional approval of the accord would hinge on an end to Moscow's economic crackdown on Lithuania. In what Soviet and American officials said was an example of the commercial contacts that would prosper under the trade accord, the Chevron Corporation signed an agreement today that could open the way for a major expansion of its activities in the Soviet Union. Discussing the two leaders' meeting this week, an American official said that Mr. Gorbachev brought up the issue of the trade accord in each of his encounters with Mr. Bush.

"He made it a personal thing between him and the President," the official said. "Chemistry played a big role in it, because Bush is very high on personal diplomacy."

At the same time, the official said, the Soviet side began dragging its heels on signing a new long-term grain agreement greatly desired by American farmers, implicitly signaling that the grain and trade deals were linked.

"They wanted to show they were bargaining hard too, that they were not groveling too much," the American official asserted.

The official said that after sounding out Mr. Gorbachev personally on his willingness to seek a peaceful resolution of the Lithuanian issue, and after having aides check for possible repercussions on Capitol Hill, Mr. Bush agreed to sign the treaty. It is to be sent to Congress as soon as the Soviet Parliament approves a new emigration law, a step that is expected soon.

"Gorbachev had a track record with us, and we calculated that he was going to need something to take back with him from Washington," the American official said. "That was in our interests too, because we need his acquiescence, at the very least, in Europe and his help on arms control and other issues."

The Administration's version of this exchange may have been

aimed at preempting criticism from American conservatives, who have already begun to complain that Mr. Bush failed to extract concessions from the Soviet leader on Lithuania. . . .

After two days of talks in the capital focused on arms accords and on trade and European security, the two Presidents flew by helicopter from the White House lawn to the Presidential retreat in the Maryland mountains this morning.

Yevgeny M. Primakov, a close adviser to Mr. Gorbachev, told reporters in Washington that the rustic setting of Camp David was conducive to reflection on broader philosophical questions: "You cannot talk very well in tuxedoes." . . .

The Soviets contend that a united Germany fully integrated into the NATO military command would be perceived at home as tilting the balance decisively against Soviet security.

As Germany reunifies, Moscow wants the rival military blocs gradually supplanted by a more collective European security structure that would protect existing boundaries, limit the size of the German army, and prevent Germany from becoming a nuclear power.

The United States contends that Germany's membership in NATO is virtually inevitable, and the only issue is how to make that fact politically, economically and militarily palatable for the Soviets.

Mr. Primakov said the issue of Germany's membership in NATO is "far from being settled," but he said the United States "understands much better than before" the Soviet desire for international structures to diminish the danger of military confrontation.

When a reporter asked what leverage Moscow had to prevent Germany from reuniting and joining NATO, Mr. Primakov said: "I don't think for that we would have to send tank divisions to the territory of Germany.

"As for other questions, the Soviet Union, if its security interests are not taken into account, then will have to consider on a unilateral basis a whole series of measures that will enable it to insure its own security," he said, without elaborating.

While in Washington an aide to Mr. Gorbachev was asked what the Soviet leader most wanted from America. He answered, "Understanding." This is what he seemed to have gotten from a Bush Administration that was aware how badly Mr. Gorbachev needed assurances that a new Europe would not leave the Soviet Union isolated and feeling threatened. If Gorbachev was hoping that the respect he received in

426

Washington would prove to be political capital back in Moscow, he had reason to be disheartened, for within days of his return, Yeltsin's supporters fired off a parliamentary challenge not just to Presidential authority but to the notion of federal supremacy.

Russian Republic Asserts Its Laws Have Primacy over Kremlin Rule
By Bill Keller

MOSCOW, June 8—The Parliament of the Russian Federation directly challenged central authority over the largest and richest Soviet republic today by asserting that Russian laws take precedence over Soviet laws.

But the resolution fell short of the two-thirds majority of the full Parliament needed to change the Russian Constitution, raising doubts among the deputies about whether the declaration would ultimately be put into binding form.

The declaration, which asserts the right to veto any federal law on Russian territory, was approved by 544 members, with 271 voting against and the rest absent or abstaining.

Russian sovereignty is a central plank in the platform of the republic's new President, Boris N. Yeltsin, who advocates a number of measures like the private sale of farmland and republic control of oil and gas resources that would directly contradict federal law.

Mr. Yeltsin has also announced his opposition to the Soviet Government's economic plan, which includes price increases on bread and other foods, and it is possible that he would urge the Russian Parliament to defy those measures if they are enacted.

Mr. Yeltsin's margin of victory on the question today is indicative of what many lawmakers believe will be a difficult task as he tries to govern Russia with a Parliament in which he controls a little more than half the votes.

The statement was adopted as part of a broad, nonbinding sovereignty declaration that is expected to be put to a final vote next week.

Several other republics, including the three Baltic states, have incorporated the right of veto in their constitutions. But a claim of sovereignty by Russia, which encompasses three-fourths of the country's territory—from Europe to the Pacific—more than half its population and most of its mineral wealth, would raise the issue of federalism to a new level.

President Mikhail S. Gorbachev discounted the prospect of conflict with the Russian republic, saying at a news conference that he was "100 percent certain" that its Parliament would pass no laws harmful to the creation of a new Soviet federation.

"The Russian Parliament has not taken any steps that contradict the Constitution of the Soviet Union," Mr. Gorbachev said, possibly alluding to the nonbinding nature of the measure adopted today.

The Parliament stood for a rousing ovation after its show of independence today, prompting Mr. Yeltsin to grin broadly and say, "I understand your emotional mood, but the Presidium must remain impartial."

Members of Parliament who supported the sovereignty move said their joy was tempered by the knowledge that it would take a two-thirds vote to incorporate the veto provision in the republic's Constitution.

Vladimir A. Zhenin, a member of Parliament from Mr. Yeltsin's home region of Sverdlovsk, said opponents of veto power for the republic might try to require a two-thirds vote next week on final approval of the sovereignty declaration itself, on the ground that it relates to a constitutional question.

"We can celebrate today's decision, but there are still serious complications ahead of us," Mr. Zhenin said.

For more than a year the flight from Communism in Eastern Europe had grown from a trickle to a flood. But in Bulgaria, where changes had come later than elsewhere, it turned out that many citizens were not quite so eager to turn their backs on the politics of the past.

Bulgarian Voting Stuns Opposition
By Celestine Bohlen

SOFIA, BULGARIA, June 11—Stunned by the Bulgarian Socialist Party's decisive victory in Sunday's parliamentary elections, leaders of the main opposition group told a rally today that they would keep up their fight against the former Communists, refusing all offers to form a coalition government.

"We will enter the National Assembly as an opposition that will confront the Communist Party with its crimes, and insist that it take responsibility for everything it has done under its rule," vowed Zhelyu Zhelev, head of the Union of Democratic Forces, before a crowd of about 50,000 people who gathered to protest the election results.

Official results on the elections to the 400-seat Grand National Assembly were not complete today. But preliminary results show the Socialists ahead with about 48 percent and the Union of Democratic Forces with 34 percent.

Many Bulgarians are still absorbing the news that after 45 years of Communist rule, almost one in two voters gave the Communists' successor, the Socialist Party, a mandate to lead the country again.

Although Bulgarian Communists have shed their old name and eased their grip on economic and political life, their victory still set a precedent—it was the first time that a ruling Marxist party has competed in multiparty national elections and won since the collapse of Communist rule began in Eastern Europe last year.

In a television appearance tonight, Andrei Lukanov, the Socialist Prime Minister and an architect of the party's changes, appealed for calm. He called the election "the first step toward the creation of a democratic society."

At a news conference, representatives from several international observer teams declared that the elections had been free and fair, although a separate, unofficial group of monitors, led by Americans, maintained that "fear is still a factor."

As the tempo of movement toward German unification was quickening from that of a pastoral ballad to a brisk march, a pattern of Soviet response was emerging. First, Gorbachev raised conditions, holding to them to establish that he and his nation were pivotal in whatever was to happen. Then, as the prospect of direct economic assistance to Moscow surfaced and just before the Soviet position was about to be flattened by the momentum of change, the Soviet leader, making a virtue of necessity, withdrew his objections.

Gorbachev Yields on Alliance Roles in a New Germany
By Bill Keller

MOSCOW, June 12—President Mikhail S. Gorbachev today removed one of the main conditions that his country had imposed on German unification. He agreed for the first time that West German troops could remain in the North Atlantic Treaty Organization without a corresponding role for the East Germans in the Soviet-led Warsaw Pact.

His offer, made during a report to the Soviet Parliament on his talks with President Bush in Washington, falls short of Western demands that a united Germany be allowed to remain in NATO without conditions.

Mr. Gorbachev proposed that East Germany retain a vaguely defined "associate membership" in the Warsaw Pact, and that a united Germany "honor all obligations" inherited from the two Germanys.

But Mr. Gorbachev's remarks clearly showed that he was striving to find a formula that would allow a united Germany to join NATO, and to prepare his Parliament and public opinion for such an eventuality. (In Washington, Bush Administration officials assessing Mr. Gorbachev's statement said they were growing increasingly convinced that the Soviet leader was slowly reconciling himself to the idea that a united Germany would be in NATO, provided that Moscow's economic, political and security concerns are met.) Before Mr. Gorbachev spoke today, Soviet officials had previously suggested various approaches intended to prevent German unification from tipping the military balance in NATO's favor. They had proposed a neutral Germany, joint membership for Germany in both alliances, and the dismantling of the alliances, all ideas rejected by the West.

Today the Soviet leader renewed his call for a broad, general security structure to supplant the two alliances, but he conceded that the rival blocs would continue to exist "for longer than might be imagined."

He again called for "dual membership" for Germany in the competing alliances, but this time it was clear that he was not insisting on an equal membership. The West German Army, or Bundeswehr, would belong to NATO, he said, while the East German Army would answer only to the unified German government, not to either alliance.

"United Germany could declare that for this transition period, it would honor all obligations it inherits from the Federal Republic of Germany and from the German Democratic Republic," Mr. Gorbachev said. "For this period, the Bundeswehr would, as before, be subordinate to NATO, and the East German troops would be subordinate to the Government of the new Germany."

That proposal would evidently leave a united Germany free to use East Germany's Army any way it saw fit—including, as some West Germans have proposed, abolishing it.

The Soviet leader said he had proposed to President Bush that during that period, Soviet troops would remain stationed in East Germany, a condition the West has already accepted, and Moscow would agree to the continued presence of American troops in Europe.

"I told the President that I think that the American presence in Europe, since it fulfills a certain role in maintaining stability, is an element of the strategic situation, and does represent a problem for us," Mr. Gorbachev told his Parliament.

Mr. Gorbachev's carefully worded statement on the intricacies of the German question was so murky in places that many diplomats spent the day puzzling over it before recognizing the new elements.

Western diplomats here said Mr. Gorbachev's comments reflected a rapid narrowing of the conceptual differences between East and West on the future of Germany, although the negotiations on concrete proposals remain excruciatingly complicated.

"He is no longer insisting that united Germany can under no circumstances be a member of NATO, something he had said two months ago was absolutely excluded," said one European diplomat.

But the two sides remain mired in the complexities of such questions as the number of troops, the command structure, compensation of the Soviets for possible loss of East German trade, and the creation of new political organizations that would give the Soviets some say in European affairs.

"Given the circumstances, it would be unreasonable to expect him to show more of his cards now," the diplomat said. "He is still waiting to see some concrete proposals from us at the NATO summit," a meeting of the Western leaders scheduled for July, the diplomat said.

Mr. Gorbachev's main concern is that German reunification not add to the threat—or the fear among his countrymen—of a decisive shift in the military balance, with NATO strengthened by the gain of a united Germany, while the Eastern alliance disintegrates.

If Mr. Gorbachev is not careful, his supporters say, hard-liners in the Government and military might use the loss of Germany to undermine the Soviet leader by asserting that his foreign policy is selling out Soviet security.

In the Communist Party daily *Rabochaya Tribuna* today, Oleg Baklanov, the Communist Party official responsible for the military industry, warned that the Soviet Union was rushing into a position of disadvantage in Europe.

"In short, we are leaving and NATO is staying behind and, as far as I can judge, growing stronger every day," Mr. Baklanov said, in an interview reflecting the hard-line pressures on Mr. Gorbachev. "I think we should stop and look around for a moment to understand the disposition of forces in Europe, and it is not tending toward parity."

In a gesture apparently toward the hard-liners, Mr. Gorbachev today tersely rejected a written suggestion from one member of Parliament that Communist Party political cells in the military be abolished to make the army more independent of party control. "No, I don't think so," he said. Mr. Gorbachev today also dismissed speculation that Moscow would welcome a united Germany that would be, like France, linked politically to NATO but not formally integrated into its military structure.

During the summit meeting in Washington, President Bush renewed the American insistence that Germany should remain in NATO, but offered a package of nine measures with a goal of alleviating Soviet security fears.

They included a promise not to extend NATO troops to East German territory, maintenance of 300,000 to 400,000 Soviet troops in East Germany at West German expense, revamping the NATO force structure to make it less threatening to Moscow, future discussions on limiting the German Army, and ways to institutionalize the 35-nation Conference on Security and Cooperation in Europe, which would give the Soviets a voice in general European security affairs.

Mr. Gorbachev today welcomed those proposals as a show of good faith and said that if NATO continued to remake itself into a more purely political alliance, the unification of Germany may be accomplished without bitterness.

Soon after the Bulgarian voters revealed countercurrents in the anti-Communist trend, Romanian workers streamed into Bucharest to beat up critics of the Government and attack the offices of the political opposition.

Rumanian Miners Invade Bucharest
By Celestine Bohlen

BUCHAREST, RUMANIA, June 14—Responding to an emergency appeal by President Ion Iliescu, thousands of miners from northern Rumania descended on the capital city today with wooden clubs and rubber truncheons and sought crude revenge for anti-Government rioting Wednesday.

In grimy work clothes and helmets, their faces blackened by soot, the miners took control of Bucharest's main boulevard and central square, menacing and beating passersby whom they apparently suspected of having tried to bring down the Iliescu Government.

Their suspicions appeared to be indiscriminate; motorists in their cars, well-dressed professors, students, photographers, reporters, mothers with children and girls walking their dogs were chased off the street, sometimes hit across the shoulders with rubber hoses.

By evening, the miners had emptied University Square, which was the setting of a marathon anti-Government demonstration that was broken up in a police raid before dawn Wednesday.

Summoned by Mr. Iliescu to save the Government from a "fascist rebellion," the miners joined other workers loyal to the governing National Salvation Front early this morning and ransacked the headquarters of the two main opposition parties, setting fires, breaking windows and carting off or destroying equipment and documents.

The miners' arrival in the city came the day after soldiers opened fire on anti-Government demonstrators outside the Interior Ministry, killing at least four and wounding scores in the worst violence in Eastern Europe since December, when Nicolae Ceausescu was overthrown in a popular revolt.

In the violence today, pro-Government workers laid siege to the apartments of prominent Government opponents and halted the publication of *Romania Libera,* the main opposition newspaper.

By the afternoon, the miners were still in control of the headquarters of one opposition party, the Peasants Party, lounging in the courtyard and on the balconies amid broken typewriters and piles of trash. At the Liberal Party headquarters, militiamen guarded the doors, while party members stayed away.

"We took a common decision to stay home and stay in touch by telephone," said Sorin Botez, a spokesman for the Liberal Party. Other critics of the Government also stayed off the streets today.

The rampage by the miners and other workers, tolerated by the few policemen visible today in Bucharest, came just as Rumania's new Government, headed by Mr. Iliescu and the front, is about to take office. Although bitterly opposed by students, liberal intellectuals and the so-called historical parties, the front won the May 20 election by a landslide, buoyed by Mr. Iliescu's personal popular appeal.

The extent of the Government's role in bringing the miners to the city, beyond Mr. Iliescu's appeal, was not known. A Government spokesman, Ion Pascu, said the police and the army had not responded to save the Government in what he called a coup attempt by opposition forces. The spokesmen said that in the absence of an adequate police force, the Government would continue to rely on the miners, who he said might stay in the capital for another two or three days. The miners are thought to number about 7,000.

Although the miners said that they came to Bucharest spontaneously after Mr. Iliescu's summons, the Government has clearly taken responsibility for them. This afternoon buses arrived at University Square to take the miners to an exhibition hall where they watched the World Cup soccer match before being bused back to the square and then to some location in the city where they were spending the night.

Mr. Botez criticized the attacks against the Government on Wednesday, but said they did not justify Mr. Iliescu's call to the miners. "It is not a good beginning for a new Government to start with acts of terrorism," he said. "It is a unique case in European history, a world premiere, for a president to incite one part of the population against the other."

Like a bandleader on a podium, Chancellor Kohl once again stepped up the beat of his orchestration of unification.

Kohl Sees Ballot by Two Germanys Before End of '90

By Serge Schmemann

BONN, June 18—Chancellor Helmut Kohl said today that a December date for the first all-German elections in more than 50 years was "coming near to being very, very likely."

Mr. Kohl's comment, in a television interview, was his most assertive to date on the possibility that German unity could become a reality by the end of the year.

The Chancellor has pressed for several weeks to expand the West German parliamentary elections scheduled for December 2 into an all-German vote, which he originally planned for next year.

The election could amount to political reunification, since the West German Constitution envisions direct accession by former German states into the Federal Republic. But the number of internal and foreign arrangements that remain make December a difficult deadline.

Internally, East Germany must still reconstitute the five former states abolished by the Communists in 1953, and the two Germanys must still reconcile their legal systems, property laws and the differences developed over four decades. Prime Minister Lothar de Maiziere of East Germany has called for a second treaty between the Governments to cover those issues before unification.

The Germanys must also reach agreement with the four victorious World War II Allies—the United States, the Soviet Union, Britain and France—in the "two plus four" talks on German unity.

The talks are being held to end the four powers' occupation rights in Germany and to devise new security arrangements for Central Europe. The two Germanys have said that whatever the legalities of the situation, they do not want to proceed with unification without four-power approval.

Bonn hopes to reach an agreement in time to present it to the 35 nations of the Conference on Security and Cooperation in Europe for endorsement by November, but negotiations with Moscow over compensation for the loss of East Germany as an ally have been difficult.

Foreign Minister Hans-Dietrich Genscher of West Germany held his eighth round of talks in two months today with Foreign Minister Eduard A. Shevardnadze of the Soviet Union, and they will meet again on Friday at a foreign ministers' session of the two-plus-four talks in Berlin.

Mr. Kohl, however, declared at a conference of his Christian Democratic party in Bonn earlier today that 1990 would be "the year of German unity."

His party set October 1 as the formal date to merge with the Christian Democrats in East Germany, who are led by Mr. de Maiziere. The Social Democrats and the small Free Democrats have also set dates next fall to merge with their East German counterparts.

Mr. Kohl's prediction that all-German elections can be held in December draws on several developments in the Germanys that give a sense of momentum.

The Parliaments of both Germanys are to vote this week on the treaty, signed last month, uniting their currencies and economies as of July 1. The move is the first big step toward merging the two countries.

The legislatures are also scheduled to pass matching resolutions on Tuesday renouncing any designs on German territories ceded to Poland after World War II, a measure that will clear one of the foreign obstacles to unity.

The most formidable obstacle, however, is the Soviet Union's concern over its economic and military security once East Germany is out of its sphere.

As before, Mr. Genscher and Mr. Shevardnadze gave little indication of the substance of their talks, but the frequency and intensity of the meetings suggest that they are working hard to fashion a compromise, possibly in time for the next session of the two-plus-four talks on Friday.

The most immediate reason for Mr. Kohl's optimism was apparently the debate he witnessed on Sunday in the East German Parliament on an unexpected motion to proceed immediately to unification. The motion was diverted to a committee by a large majority, but the debate revealed a readiness in East Germany and in the West to move up actual unification.

Mr. Kohl said his visit to East Berlin left him "with the firm impression that the wish exists there to vote with the Federal Republic." . . .

The negotiations between the Germans and the Soviets have become the focal point of the two-plus-four talks, in which the participants are working to lift the last vestiges of military occupation and to resolve the place of a united Germany in the European security structure.

Mr. Shevardnadze said the meeting was constructive and useful, but added: "I don't want to create the impression that everything proceeded smoothly, that all outstanding issues were resolved. Some thorny problems remain."

The Germans are rumored to be preparing a major package of financial aid and trade and security guarantees to gain Soviet support for unification.

SUMMER 1990

As the season changed, the West Germans, in their pell-mell rush for unity, appeared willing to spend whatever it cost, not only to buy the enthusiasm of their poorer cousins in East Germany, but also to gain Moscow's support of their objectives and their agenda.

2 Germanys Adopt Unity Treaty and Guarantee Poland's Borders
By Serge Schmemann

BONN, June 21—The Parliaments of the two Germanys adopted matching measures moving them another step closer to union today, one a resolution guaranteeing Poland's existing borders and the other the treaty on monetary and economic union.

The outcome of the votes was never in doubt, but both measures carried a burden of hope, anxiety and controversy. The debate in both Parliaments was at times strident and emotional.

The sessions in Bonn and East Berlin also marked the first time that the Parliaments approved matching measures, and the act joined a flurry of activities that gave a sense of quickening momentum to unity. . . .

There was less debate on the Polish border resolution. But in his speech Chancellor Kohl delivered a strong condemnation of the post-war border shift that transferred a broad stretch of German land to Poland and resulted in the expulsion of millions of Germans.

The issue became a heated dispute earlier this year when Poland demanded that the two Germanys guarantee that a united Germany would not claim the territories.

Mr. Kohl initially resisted, largely for fear of alienating the powerful lobby of the Germans expelled from those territories, but he retreated before an international outcry and agreed to the matching resolutions that were adopted today.

"Let no one be mistaken," Mr. Kohl said. "Today we face an absolutely clear choice. Either we confirm the existing border, or we gamble away the chance of German unity."

European Leaders Back Kohl's Plea to Aid Soviets
By Craig R. Whitney

DUBLIN, June 26—Leaders of the European Community, under pressure from Chancellor Helmut Kohl of West Germany to help speed German unification, agreed today on steps that he requested to reassure the Soviet Union.

Giving qualified endorsement to the Chancellor's appeal for billions of dollars in aid to help President Mikhail S. Gorbachev transform the Soviet Union from Communism to a market economy, the 12 leaders called for more detailed proposals for short-term credits and long-term economic aid.

They said they would consider the proposals at another meeting of European leaders expected to be held by October.

They also decided to propose November 19 for a gathering in Paris of the 35-nation Conference on Security and Cooperation in Europe, a meeting of leaders from East and West that Moscow wanted this year.

The United States has opposed using economic aid to prop up Soviet reforms. Defense Secretary Dick Cheney said on Monday that substantial economic aid would subsidize the Soviet military.

Mr. Kohl, announcing the decision today, said negotiations on the terms of German unity would have to be completed before the Paris meeting, a position supported by the United States and other members of the NATO alliance.

Mr. Kohl, who with the help of President François Mitterrand of France was the most insistent backer of the Soviet aid proposal, pronounced himself "very, very satisfied" at the end of the two-day meeting.

He made little secret of West Germany's reason for deciding last week to guarantee up to $2.9 billion in German private bank credits to the Soviet Union.

"In this connection," he wrote to the President of the European Community's executive commission, Jacques Delors, "I would urge the Soviet Union, for its part, to adopt a constructive approach to questions arising on the path toward German unity—and this applies in particular to anchoring a future united Germany within the North

Atlantic Alliance and the European Community."

At a news conference after the meeting today, Mr. Kohl dismissed the idea of a link between his proposal for further aid and the goal of ending Soviet objections to NATO membership for a united Germany. But his spokesman, Hans Klein, said the Chancellor had raised the possibility of Western aid amounting to many billions of dollars with Mr. Gorbachev in Moscow last winter and by telephone several times since. The Soviets had suggested a figure of $15 billion, he said.

The crisis over Lithuania seemed to subside, at least for the summer.

Lithuania Agrees to 100-Day Delay on Independence
By Bill Keller

MOSCOW, June 29—Lithuania agreed today to suspend its declaration of independence for 100 days in exchange for negotiations with Moscow and the lifting of economic sanctions.

The moratorium, which would begin as soon as any talks got under way, was formally proposed by the Lithuanian President, Vytautas Landsbergis. The resolution was approved by Parliament by a vote of 69 to 35, with 2 abstentions.

There was no immediate response from Soviet officials. But Lithuanians said they were confident that President Mikhail S. Gorbachev would accept the compromise as sufficient to end the impasse and to resume delivery of oil and other products that were cut off 10 weeks ago.

"If the members of Parliament were not sure that was the case, they would not have approved the moratorium," said Rita Dapkus, a spokeswoman for Parliament.

So far the movement on merging the two Germanys had been largely juridical and diplomatic. Now, for the men and women in the streets of the two countries, there would be concrete changes.

Germans Revel As Economies Unite
By Serge Schmemann

EAST BERLIN, Sunday, July 1—At the stroke of midnight, East Germany today formally ceded its currency and economy to West Germany. Thousands of East Germans gathered in the center of the city broke into cheers, firecrackers popped and car horns blared.

It was not yet formal reunification, but in effect it marked the end of the unsuccessful economic experiment that the former Communist Government forcibly imposed on the East German people for 40 years, until the regime fell amid the wave of change sweeping Eastern Europe last fall.

As the East German economy came formally under the control of West Germany, the West German mark became the legal tender of both Germanys, all protective tariffs were lifted and East Germany came under free-market rules.

At a new branch of Deutsche Bank, West Germany's largest commercial bank, on Karl-Marx Allee in the heart of East Berlin, several thousand people whooped and pushed forward as the manager opened the doors precisely at midnight to admit the first East Germans.

As it turned out, the process went quite smoothly.

In a Leap Toward Unity, 2 Germanys Meld Currencies

By Serge Schmemann

EAST BERLIN, July 1—East Germans formed orderly lines across the land today to get their West German currency, irrevocably throwing in their lot with the capitalist world and turning into the home stretch toward reunification.

The official economic and social merger of the two Germanys essentially terminated East Germany's 40-year attempt to build a separate, Communist state, leaving only the hope that the disintegrating old structures would be replaced by a new prosperity.

As the new order went into effect at midnight, tens of thousands of East Berliners in the central Alexanderplatz cheered, popped champagne corks, tooted horns and lit firecrackers.

Thousands pressed toward a new branch of West Germany's Deutsche Bank, which had decided to open at midnight to start distributing West German marks. The crush grew so heavy that some people fainted and several glass panes shattered, but there were no serious injuries.

The distribution of money continued more sedately when the 15,000 special distribution centers around the country opened at 8 A.M. Armored vehicles escorted by police cars churned around the city delivering money where needed, and few people reported standing in line for more than 20 minutes.

The Berlin subway system, severed when the Berlin wall was raised in 1961, was relinked today, enabling people to travel freely on public transport throughout both halves of the city.

"This is a great day in the history of the German nation," declared Chancellor Helmut Kohl of West Germany, who was the leading force behind the decision to meld the two economies quickly.

"The State Treaty is an expression of solidarity among Germans," he said, referring to the agreement that went into effect today. "Germans in the G.D.R. and in the Federal Republic are now again indissolubly linked. For now they are connected by a common currency, by the common order of the social market economy. But soon they will be linked in a free and unified state."

Mr. Kohl has been pressing to hold the first all-German elections by December so the process of unification can be completed. But the economic merger effectively means that East Germany has already surrendered economic sovereignty to West Germany. Nothing stands in the way of West German entrepreneurs seeking to plunge into ventures in the East.

Appearing on a televised panel discussion, Prime Minister Lothar de Maiziere of East Germany seemed to share the mixed excitement and anxiety of his countrymen as he described how he spent his last East German marks in a restaurant and then went home to toast the historic day.

"We face difficult weeks," he said. "For a certain time there will be lower wages and we will have to work harder."

Currency union promises access to places and goods that have been denied to East Germans for more than 40 years. But at least in the short run, it also threatens massive unemployment and dislocation as uncompetitive ventures restructure or fold. . . .

A major element of the economic merger was the transformation of East Germany's 8,000 state-owned companies into joint-stock ventures. Under the privatization plan, a special Government trust is to guarantee liquidity through October, when the companies are to present survival plans.

The East German Government has estimated that 30 percent of the companies will have virtually no problems, 50 percent will be rescued and 20 percent will probably collapse. Estimates vary widely on how many people will be thrown out of work and for how long. By all accounts, the pinch would turn especially painful in October.

For some planners, the more absorbing question is how long it will take the East German sector of the economy to turn around. Helmut Haussmann, the West German Economics Minister, said in an interview that he expected East German companies to post no profits in the next year. But beginning in 1992–93, he predicted, "good money will be made."

The merger plan freezes rents, energy costs and fares on public transport through the end of the year. Goods sold in East Germany are now subject to the West German value-added tax of up to 14 percent, and new taxes have been imposed on gasoline, tobacco, alcoholic beverages, coffee, tea, salt, sugar and light bulbs.

While the Germans were rushing off hopefully into a future few could envision, in Moscow the Communist elite were, with far less enthusiasm, addressing their party's own uncertain fate.

Soviet Communists Convening Today on Party's Future
By Bill Keller

MOSCOW, July 1—The Communist Party of the Soviet Union, divided, demoralized and endangered by democracy, is convening Monday for its 28th congress, where the main issue will be not so much where the party will lead the country but whether it will lead the country at all.

The congress, the highest authority of the party, promises to be more contentious than any such meeting since Lenin's day, if only because the presence of television cameras and the passion for gloves-off debate have become routine since the last congress in 1986.

In choosing a new leadership and adopting a new platform, the 4,700 delegates, with a high proportion of professional party functionaries alarmed over their slipping power, will be rendering their verdict on President Mikhail S. Gorbachev and his program of market-oriented economics and political pluralism.

The congress is opening with a report by Mr. Gorbachev, who seems assured of reelection as general secretary. . . .

The 28th congress is the first one since the Seventh Congress in 1918 in which the party is not confident that it is the dominant political force in the country. In February, the Central Committee agreed to surrender party monopoly on political power, which was guaranteed in the Soviet Constitution.

Nothing the congress does is likely to restore the party's credibility, which is lower than it has ever been after five years without an improvement in the standard of living.

Gorbachev Urges a Fractious Party to Pull Together
By Bill Keller

MOSCOW, July 2—President Mikhail S. Gorbachev fought to hold his crisis-ridden Communist Party together today with an uncompromising defense of his economic and foreign policies, but the performance left most of his fractious audience cold.

Opening the party's 28th congress, the first since 1986, Mr. Gorbachev pressed his beleaguered campaign for the creation of a market economy. He rejected charges from hard-liners that he had been the cause of humiliating setbacks in Eastern Europe. The most unpopular of his Government's recent economic initiatives, the attempt to raise food prices as a first step toward a free market, he disavowed as "absurd," evidently trying to shift the blame for that political blunder to Prime Minister Nikolai I. Ryzhkov.

While he made no concessions on policy to the party's resurgent hard-liners, neither did Mr. Gorbachev spell out any specific new initiatives, and he was rewarded with the most cursory of seated ovations.

Mr. Gorbachev pleaded with the insurgent wing not to abandon the party, as many have threatened to do, but he spurned their demands for sweeping internal reforms of the party. He specifically rejected calls for the withdrawal of party cells from the army, security police, courts and industry, and the right of dissenters to organize formal factions within the party.

The congress, the Communists' highest authority, is expected to adopt a new party program and select a new leadership in the course of a 10-day meeting that is sure to include a boisterous airing of grievances against Mr. Gorbachev's team.

Mr. Gorbachev got a foretaste of the raking to come in the opening minutes, when Vladimir Bludov, a delegate from the Far East city of Magadan, rose at a floor microphone to demand that the entire leadership resign at once for failing to "fulfill the food program."

Despite disenchantment, Mr. Gorbachev is considered a safe bet to retain his post as party leader, but his supporters said the governing bodies of the party, the Politburo and the Central Committee, will probably have a more orthodox cast than he would like. . . .

Before recessing for the night, the congress also listened in stony silence to Nikolai Ryzhkov, the Prime Minister, then clapped derisively during a speech by the ideology chief, Vadim A. Medvedev.

Mr. Ryzhkov is faulted for the troubled economy, Mr. Medvedev for the party's loss of ideological moorings.

Earlier, Mr. Ryzhkov sat grim-faced on the dais behind Mr. Gorbachev, as the party leader disparaged the Government's proposal to raise prices on bread and other food.

Mr. Gorbachev himself had endorsed the price increases, but he now argues that putting them at the front of the new program had alarmed consumers and undermined popular support for the whole idea of free markets.

"To begin the transition to a market economy by raising prices—this is absurd!" he said.

The Soviet leader focused his ire almost exclusively on conservatives, warning of "dark days" if they succeed in slowing his program and calling "simply rubbish" attempts to blame perestroika for all the country's ills.

Mr. Gorbachev's opening report, two hours and 20 minutes long, was criticized in the corridors by delegates from across the party spectrum who said they had hoped for concrete new proposals to resolve the economic woes that threaten to engulf them.

"My workers ask me, 'Are we going to live better?' " said Nikolai M. Simkin, the chief of a railroad depot, and a 25-year party member.

"Oh, they've heard of the various platforms, but the bottom line is 'Are we going to live better?' " he said. "But I can't say that this congress so far gives me any hope for that."

The congress takes place as the party tries to redefine itself in light of the Central Committee's vote in February to surrender the Communists' constitutionally guaranteed monopoly on power, and as Mr. Gorbachev seeks to shift power from the party to the presidency. But those who had thought Mr. Gorbachev would give up the party leadership to concentrate on the presidency now say that the party is too conservative and conditions are too potentially dangerous for that step.

The Congress got off to a tempestuous start as the conservative pillar of the Politburo, Yegor K. Ligachev, roused delegates by deploring the five years of President Mikhail S. Gorbachev's rule as a period of wavering and "blind radicalism." His lament for the undermining of old values was reinforced by the chief of the K.G.B. and the defense minister, who both warned against efforts to divorce their institutions from the party. But as the party was thrashing about attacking its leader, Gorbachev was given a remarkable boost as the leaders of the NATO Alliance, the Soviet Union's most feared adversaries, declared a new era of European amity.

NATO Allies, after 40 Years, Proclaim End of Cold War; Invite Gorbachev to Speak

By Craig R. Whitney

LONDON, July 6—President Bush and the other leaders of NATO today issued a declaration to end four decades of cold war by proposing to act jointly with Moscow and other East Europeans in stating that "we are no longer adversaries."

Inviting President Mikhail S. Gorbachev to travel to Brussels to speak with them, the Western leaders promised a new defensive strategy that would make their nuclear forces "truly weapons of last resort." They assured Moscow and the other Warsaw Pact nations that "we will never in any circumstance be the first to use force" and proposed that NATO, the Warsaw Pact and European states outside the two alliances join in a "commitment to nonaggression."

"Our alliance will do its share to overcome the legacy of decades of suspicion," they said.

NATO's Secretary-General will fly to Moscow to discuss the declaration with Mr. Gorbachev, whose own policies are under attack in the Soviet Union. Unspoken in the declaration is a desire by most NATO leaders to give Mr. Gorbachev striking evidence to demonstrate to his critics that his conciliatory policy toward the West is bringing results.

Mr. Bush said at a news conference that he thought the declaration would help Mr. Gorbachev deal with his "hard-liners." But he continued to oppose direct American economic aid to the Soviet Union.

The steps taken today were also aimed at making it easier for Mr. Gorbachev to acquiesce to the unification of the Germanys, something specifically called for in the declaration.

In what was called the London Declaration, drafted over the last two days by their foreign ministers in the palace of Lancaster House, the NATO leaders were clearly trying to speak to history in the same ringing tones that the North Atlantic Treaty sent out from Washington at the height of the cold war when the alliance was formed.

"The Atlantic Community must reach out to the countries of the East which were our adversaries in the cold war, and extend to them the hand of friendship," they said, inviting the members of the crumbling Warsaw Pact to join in a declaration solemnly stating that the era of mutually hostile blocs was over. "The walls that once confined people and ideas are collapsing," the allied heads of government said. "As a consequence, this alliance must and will adapt."

In a wide-ranging review of alliance strategy and force levels, the NATO leaders promised to prepare a new defensive approach, using small, multinational light forces stationed far from the former front lines instead of "forward defense." They also pledged to reduce the reliance on nuclear weapons now enshrined in the strategy of "flexible response." . . .

"As our alliance enters its fifth decade," the Western leaders said in their declaration, "it must continue to provide for the common defense."

"Yet our alliance must be even more an agent of change," they said. "It can help build the structures of a more united continent."

Reaffirming that "security and stability do not lie solely in the military dimension," the allies declared:

"We will remain a defensive alliance and will continue to defend all the territory of all of our members. We have no aggressive intentions and we commit ourselves to the peaceful resolution of all disputes. We will never in any circumstance be the first to use force." . . .

Manfred Worner, NATO's Secretary-General, will fly to Moscow on July 14 to explain the new NATO stance to Mr. Gorbachev and other Soviet leaders. Before departing for the United States this afternoon, President Bush said he expected to discuss the new position over with Mr. Gorbachev by telephone, "perhaps within the next couple of weeks."

"I think they have to sort it out now," the President said. "They have to decide what they want—how much of their gross national product ought to go into arms, whether the threat is much less than they have historically perceived. And once they take that decision, then we in the West will stand ready to work very cooperatively with them."

But, he said, the alliance has made no decision to send money to the Soviet Union, and the United States does not want to. "One problem is that a great percentage of their gross national product is going into the military," he said; another was "spending $5 billion a year on Cuba, for example, to sustain a totalitarian regime that is highly critical of the Soviet Union from time to time."

"If the Germans decide they're going to do that, that's their business," Mr. Bush said. Asked what message he thought the alliance was sending to the Soviet leader, the President replied, "I think it should be clear to Mr. Gorbachev, to his adversaries and to his friends inside the Soviet Union, that NATO is changing, and to the degree that they had seen it as a threat to their borders, they should look at it not as a threat to their people."

Moscow's reaction was quick and warm.

Shevardnadze Says the Measures Herald "A Safe Future" for Europe
By Bill Keller

MOSCOW, July 6—The Soviet Government reacted with enthusiasm today to Western proposals for a new order in Europe, and said the moves would strengthen President Mikhail S. Gorbachev at a time when he is under increasing attack from hard-liners.

Foreign Minister Eduard A. Shevardnadze said the measures approved by the London meeting of the North Atlantic Treaty Organization "pave the way to a safe future for the entire European continent."

"In London it was declared that the West extends its hand to the East," Mr. Shevardnadze said, in a five-page official statement that treated the NATO meeting as a landmark. "For our part, we are ready to extend our hand toward them."

The NATO proposals, which include a joint nonaggression declaration, new restrictions on the deployment and use of nuclear weapons, and a meeting of Mr. Gorbachev with NATO leaders, came as Soviet military officers and civilian hard-liners have tried to make the loss of Eastern Europe an angry theme at the Communist Party's nationwide congress.

"Now we can tell them they are wrong," Gennadi I. Gerasimov, the Foreign Ministry spokesman, said today, adding, "This has come at a good time, because he is being criticized."

Never before has a Soviet leader's foreign policy been the object of such controversy at a congress of his party.

Since the party congress opened on Monday, the withdrawal of Soviet troops from Eastern Europe, unconditional arms cuts and acquiescence in the unification of Germany have been attacked from the podium and in corridor interviews as part of a humiliating retreat.

The criticism has alarmed party liberals, some of whom have responded to the oratory of the generals by raising the specter of a military coup.

There is little evidence that the public is upset about the tumbling of Communist Governments in Eastern Europe by democratic movements. But among the generation that remembers World War II, the loss of Soviet influence and the resurgence of Germany have stirred old fears.

Mr. Shevardnadze has likened the attacks on Mr. Gorbachev's Eastern Europe policy to the period of McCarthyism in the United States in the decade after World War II, when accusations were raised that the Truman Administration had "lost China" by allowing the Communists to win the civil war against Chiang Kai-shek.

"Strange as it may seem, we hear similar accusations in this country," he said, in a response last week to letters from readers of the Communist Party daily *Pravda*. "It seems as if some people here would like to ferret out those who 'lost Eastern Europe.'"

The latest blast from the military came on Thursday, when Maj. Gen. Ivan Mikulin, a party delegate, accused Soviet diplomats of "seeing the world through rose-colored glasses" and of rushing recklessly to withdraw troops from Eastern Europe.

"What can I say to those who ask why we allowed changes in Eastern Europe and agreed to withdraw our troops?" Mr. Shevardnadze said of such critics. "They mean to ask why we did not use tanks to 'restore order.'"

Valentin M. Falin, chief of the international affairs department of the Communist Party Central Committee, tonight dismissed the speeches of the military delegates in a news conference, saying, "These people have no power."

But it is striking that top military officials have not taken the podium to defend Mr. Gorbachev and his policies. . . .

The Foreign Ministry statement praised each of the Western initiatives, and pointed out that many of them had originated as Soviet proposals.

Mr. Shevardnadze's statement was clearly intended to trumpet the NATO meeting as a triumph for the diplomacy Mr. Gorbachev calls "new political thinking," and to assure the Soviet public that the Western threat is continuing to dissolve.

The Foreign Minister said the Soviets "attach extremely great importance" to the NATO statement disavowing aggressive intentions and forswearing the first use of force, and approved of the proposal that NATO and the Warsaw Pact sign a joint declaration on that principle.

"This creates a fundamentally different political climate in Europe and, given its consistent implementation in life, may form a conceptual foundation for a new security system in the continent," he said.

Mr. Shevardnadze praised as "potentially important" NATO's offer to revise key aspects of the West's military defense, including the doctrine of "flexible response," which reserves the right to make first use of nuclear weapons in some circumstances. The new policy would describe nuclear arms as weapons of last resort.

"The invitation to speak in Brussels at a session of the North Atlantic Council, the proposal to establish diplomatic liaison with NATO and develop contacts in the military field are, in our view, important changes in NATO's stance," Mr. Shevardnadze said.

On one issue that has divided the Western alliance, financial aid to repair the Soviet economy, Mr. Falin said that it would be in the interest of the West to integrate the Soviet Union into the Western economy.

"If we want to avoid a split, you need to include the Soviets in the world system," he said.

Now, as the Party Congress continued, Gorbachev, strengthened by the London Declaration, was able to head off attempts to turn procedural debates into a vote of confidence on his programs.

Confronting Foes, Gorbachev Keeps Party Leadership
By Bill Keller

MOSCOW, July 10—Mikhail S. Gorbachev swept confidently to re-election as head of the Communist Party today, after confronting the party's hard-liners with a militant defense of the changes he has ignited in his society.

The party's nationwide congress chose Mr. Gorbachev, who is also President of the Soviet Union, overwhelmingly over the only other candidate who stayed in the race, a Western Siberian party official best known for helping lead a coal mine strike a year ago.

Before the voting today, Mr. Gorbachev shed his conciliatory tone and lashed out in a fighting speech at hard-liners who had vociferously criticized his economic and foreign policies at the congress.

Either they must learn to live with liberty and the free competition of ideas, or the party is doomed, he declared, adding that the party is now in crisis because it has moved too slowly toward democracy and a market economy.

"There is no way to bring back the past, and no dictatorship—if someone still entertains this crazy idea—will solve anything," he thundered.

Although the congress is to continue for a few more days, Mr. Gorbachev seemed to have it now firmly in hand and appeared to have headed off for now any danger of a major split in the party.

He has forcefully tamed the hard-liners and then, with his speech today, reached out to party radicals who want even faster change in hopes of keeping them from deserting the party in huge numbers. . . .

Implicitly confronting the military officers who have challenged his handling of foreign policy, Mr. Gorbachev warned that those who work for the state must carry out Government policies or resign.

"People ask if our policy not to interfere in the processes in Eastern Europe was correct," he added. "Well, do you want tanks again? Shall we teach them again how to live?"

But just as it appeared that the Congress would end without great surprise or mishap, Boris Yeltsin made his move.

Kremlin Maverick Leaves the Party; More May Follow

By Serge Schmemann

MOSCOW, July 12—Boris N. Yeltsin, the popular maverick of Soviet politics, announced today that he was quitting the Communist Party, dealing a sharp new blow to the once-monolithic force even as it struggled to stay united.

The brief announcement by the recently elected President of the

Russian republic sent gasps through the vast auditorium of the Palace of Congresses in the Kremlin, where 4,700 delegates have been arguing and maneuvering for 10 days over the future of their badly mauled organization.

Isolated shouts of "Shame! Shame!" competed with a smattering of applause after Mr. Yeltsin declared that he was resigning from the party—in which he once held a seat on the all-powerful Politburo—to concentrate his efforts on running the Russian federated republic, the largest of the 15 that make up the Soviet Union.

The resignation could lead to mass defections and was a serious blow to President Mikhail S. Gorbachev, who had managed to triumph over earlier challenges at the party congress.

Mr. Yeltsin gave no indication that he would form or join another political movement, and his statement included no criticism of the party or its platform. Concluding his announcement, he marched out of the hall, refusing to answer any questions.

Soon after his statement, however, leaders of the Democratic Platform faction announced their intention to create a new "democratic coalition" this fall, effectively breaking with the party. The faction claims about 100 of the 4,700 delegates, but it was not immediately clear whether all its members supported the decision.

Vyacheslav Shostakovsky, rector of the Moscow Higher Party School and one of the faction's leaders, said he and his colleagues had reached the decision because "the congress did not realize our hopes for the separation of party and Government functions."

Mr. Shostakovsky said his appeal had been signed by several leading members of the Democratic Platform, including Anatoly A. Sobchak, chairman of the Leningrad City Council; Yuri Boldyrev, a prominent member of Parliament from Leningrad; and Vladimir Lysenko, who has advocated reforms.

Mr. Yeltsin's announcement came in response to his nomination to the Central Committee of the party, the 396-member body that is chosen to guide the party between congresses.

"In view of my great responsibilities toward the people of Russia and in connection with the move toward a multiparty system, I cannot fulfill only the instructions of the Communist Party," he said, reading from a prepared statement. "As the highest elected figure in the republic, I have to bow to the will of all the people."

The decision by Mr. Yeltsin, long one of President Gorbachev's most nettlesome critics, was not entirely unexpected. He had previously declared his intention to create a multiparty system in the Russian republic, and he has campaigned to eliminate party influence over state administration.

Immediately after his announcement, Mr. Gorbachev, the party leader, said from the dais, "That ends the process logically."

Expected or not, Mr. Yeltsin's resignation was deeply unsettling for a gathering whose members so recently wielded unchallenged power that many of them are unprepared to cede their authority.

To be sure, Mr. Gorbachev himself has fought to loosen the party's grip on Soviet life, and he has shifted considerable power to his other office as President. But he has also said that it is too early to split from the Communists, and he and other top party leaders have publicly professed allegiance to socialism and the party.

Mr. Yeltsin broke that allegiance, not only by declaring that the party took up too much of his time, but by signaling to Soviet citizens that Communism is no longer the only arena for political action. His announcement was broadcast later on national television.

The development was a setback for Mr. Gorbachev, who had succeeded in preventing a schism between hard-liners and reformers at the congress and in imposing his authority on much of the battered party.

Earlier in the day the congress heard a formal announcement of the vote on Wednesday marking the overwhelmingly defeat of Yegor K. Ligachev, the tough-talking leader of resistance to Mr. Gorbachev's reforms, as the deputy chairman of the party.

Mr. Ligachev received only 776 votes to the 3,109 cast for Vladimir A. Ivashko, the Ukrainian leader who was Mr. Gorbachev's choice.

As the two-week-long Congress came to an end, the leaders of the Leningrad and Moscow City Councils also resigned from the Communist party, and insurgent forces began moving slowly toward forming a national opposition coalition. Meanwhile, Gorbachev responded to the defections with heat. "Those who reject our socialist past I view with contempt," he declared in an interview, adding, "I am not veering from my course, and I have many supporters."

Mr. Gorbachev was clearly eager to put the Congress behind him and move on to the next challenge of a summer filled with challenges—the visit of Chancellor Kohl.

Kohl Sees Soviets amid Upbeat Mood

By Serge Schmemann

MOSCOW, July 15—Smiling and bantering like old friends, President Mikhail S. Gorbachev and Chancellor Helmut Kohl of West Germany said today that they expected major progress in their talks on lifting the last obstacles to German unity.

First in Moscow and later in Stavropol, Mr. Gorbachev's hometown in southern Russia, the two leaders seemed eager to demonstrate confidence and comradeship as they tackled the critical issues of Germany's future membership in NATO, the size of the future German army, future European security structures, economic assistance to the Soviet Union and a comprehensive treaty next year defining Soviet-German relations.

Soviet and German officials said the upbeat mood on the first day of the leaders' two days of talks derived from several developments in East and West that Mr. Gorbachev evidently expected to enable him to sell German unification to the Soviet public.

The developments included the Soviet Communist Party congress last week, at which Mr. Gorbachev scored an impressive victory over hard-liners, and the summit meeting of the North Atlantic Treaty Organization in London early this month, at which the Western leaders moved to alter the alliance fundamentally and to end formally the adversarial relationship with the Warsaw Pact.

"I told Mr. Chancellor that as the ancient Greeks said, everything flows and everything changes, and we live in a dynamic time when change is very rapid," Mr. Gorbachev said at a joint news conference in Moscow. In the last month, he said, there had been "many substantive developments" in East-West relations, and "the new context opens new prospects for entering into new understandings."

Later, walking with Mr. Gorbachev through Stavropol, where they flew together after three hours of private talks, Mr. Kohl told West German television that they had already touched on all important issues, "and I think that by noon tomorrow we can come up with some very good results."

Mr. Gorbachev shared the sentiment, albeit in a more colorful formulation: "We began putting nuts in our mouth and testing them on our teeth, and I must say our teeth are strong. We'll crack them."

And evidently the nuts were cracked on schedule.

Gorbachev Clears Way for German Unity, Dropping Objection to NATO Membership

By Serge Schmemann

ZHELEZNOVODSK, U.S.S.R., July 16—The Soviet Union and West Germany agreed today to let a united Germany join NATO and to lift virtually all other remaining barriers to German reunification.

The breakthrough was announced at this spa in the foothills of the Caucasus Mountains by President Mikhail S. Gorbachev of the Soviet Union and Chancellor Helmut Kohl of West Germany after two days of talks marked by unusual displays of harmony and confidence.

Making no effort to conceal his jubilation, Mr. Kohl told West German television, "This is a breakthrough, a fantastic result."

Mr. Gorbachev, who opened the news conference on the accord with a promise of "interesting news," declared, "We are leaving one epoch in international relations, and entering another, a period, I think, of strong, prolonged peace." The agreement, announced after talks in Moscow and at a mountain hideaway, ends months of maneuvering and sparring between Moscow and the West over German unity. After Moscow's initial resistance to Western demands that a united Germany remain in NATO, a variety of formulas were proposed to enable the Soviets to withdraw from East Germany with dignity and some assurances for their economic and military security.

In the accord, Mr. Gorbachev effectively agreed to surrender all of the Soviet Union's remaining claims as an occupier of Germany and to renounce any restrictions on Germany's sovereignty, including its right to join whatever alliance it prefers.

Mr. Kohl said he had told Moscow that a united Germany would seek to become a member of the North Atlantic Treaty Organization.

In exchange, Mr. Kohl said, the Germans agreed to negotiate a treaty with the Soviet Union covering all aspects of their relations—political, economic, military, cultural and scientific. No details were immediately available, but officials said the treaty would include provisions for wide economic and technical cooperation.

The Soviet-German agreements make it virtually certain that the Germanys will be able to hold all-German elections and to reunite formally by the end of this year.

The Germans also agreed to restrict the future German military to 370,000 troops, compared with about 667,000 now for the two German armies combined. West Germany currently has about 494,000 active forces and East Germany, 173,000.

The Germans also pledged to allow Soviet troops to remain on East German territory for a three- to four-year transition period. Mr. Kohl said Germany would help pay for the maintenance and the withdrawal of the 350,000-strong Soviet force, and that American, British and French troops would remain in Berlin until the Soviet troops had withdrawn.

The Germans further agreed that no NATO troops, nuclear weapons or German forces assigned to NATO would be deployed on what is now East German soil during the transition period, and probably not afterward.

"We were unanimous that on the key questions we achieved a far-reaching success," Chancellor Kohl said at the press conference. "This breakthrough was critical because both sides are aware that the historic changes happening in Europe, Germany and the Soviet Union place special responsibility on us."

The arrangements were designed to satisfy Moscow's concerns over the strength of a future Germany and the problem of repatriating a large military contingent for which the Soviet Union has neither barracks nor jobs.

Officials said details of the agreements would be worked out at various forums, including the "two plus four" talks among the Germanys and the World War II Allies, scheduled to resume on Tuesday in Paris, and the Vienna talks on reducing conventional arms in Europe.

Mr. Kohl said the Soviets had agreed to conclude the series of two-plus-four talks in time for a meeting of the Conference on European Security and Cooperation in November, at which European countries, the United States and Canada will effectively give international endorsement to Germany's reunification.

The agreement marked a major personal triumph for Mr. Kohl, who sat throughout the press conference with a broad grin across his face. Two weeks after achieving the monetary and economic union of the two Germanys, Mr. Kohl now faces an unobstructed home stretch toward unity.

The two-day display of his personal rapport with Mr. Gorbachev, underscored by the invitation to join the Soviet President in his native regions in southern Russia, seemed certain to strengthen further Mr. Kohl's already strong chances of being elected the first chancellor of a reunited Germany.

Mr. Gorbachev treated Mr. Kohl with an intimacy that no other Western leader has enjoyed with the Soviet President. The two traveled together on a tour of Stavropol, which was long the Soviet leader's home, and then spent the night in a lodge in Arkhyz, a resort in the Caucasus Mountains.

"Our talks were very candid and marked by understanding and personal sympathy," Mr. Kohl said. Mr. Gorbachev said the discussions had been conducted in "the spirit of that well-known German word 'realpolitik.' "

German and Soviet officials agreed that the breakthrough was made possible by the series of meetings of Western leaders in recent weeks, including the European Community session in Dublin, the United States–Soviet summit meeting in Washington, the gathering of the seven leading industrial powers in Houston and above all, the NATO summit meeting in London. In these meetings, the officials said, the West effectively agreed to eliminate the vestiges of the cold war and to consider ways to help Mr. Gorbachev's program of perestroika.

"We could not have reached this agreement without the context in which the visit took place," Mr. Gorbachev said. "In recent months we've had tens of summit meetings, at which all these burning questions touching on the fundamental changes in Europe were discussed."

He specifically referred to the NATO summit in London this month, in which the alliance formally agreed to a reconciliation with the Warsaw Pact, to restructure NATO thoroughly and to invite Mr. Gorbachev to address it. NATO leaders also gave Mr. Kohl the go-ahead to set a specific ceiling on the size of a unified Germany's forces in his talks with the Soviet President.

"We received an impulse from London, the last meeting of NATO, where important and positive steps were made," Mr. Gorbachev said. "We do not say we applaud everything. Far from it. But a movement began, a historical turn in the development of this very important organization."

NATO's decisions enabled Mr. Gorbachev to tell his nation that Moscow was not giving up positions won through the sacrifices of World War II, but moving to a new stage of cooperation and development.

In comments clearly aimed at his audience at home, the Soviet President tried to argue that a united Germany's membership in NATO would have advantages. "Whether we want it or not, the day will come when the reality will be that a united Germany is in NATO," he said. "And if that is its choice, then it will still make

456

formal arrangements to cooperate with the Soviet Union, and that's to our advantage."

Both Mr. Kohl and Mr. Gorbachev gave credit to their Foreign Ministers, Hans-Dietrich Genscher and Eduard A. Shevardnadze, who met at least eight times in recent weeks to hammer out the agreement.

The two ministers left directly from their meetings here for Paris to attend the "two plus four" talks. Interviewed on West German television while en route to Paris, Mr. Genscher declared, "The message of Moscow is: Germany will come together this year."

Although the agreement involved a major Soviet concession, it was viewed as a personal success for Mr. Gorbachev, a reflection of the new authority gained through his triumph last week over hard-line forces at the Communist Party congress. . . .

Mr. Gorbachev emphasized repeatedly today and on Sunday that the two Germanys are Moscow's largest trading partners in their respective camps, and that a united Germany is therefore destined to play a major role in the Soviet Union's economic future.

Many of his statements at the press conference seemed intended to allay a widespread feeling at home that Moscow is abandoning the security and influence for which 20 million Soviet citizens died in World War II.

"They accept that the Germans, bearing on their shoulders the lesson of history, a dramatic, traumatic history, have in both their states reached certain conclusions," Mr. Gorbachev said.

"They have shown in their postwar history that they are for democracy, that their policy is that no war should arise from German soil, that they are open to cooperation with other nations. Without this nothing could have happened."

Meanwhile, the Ukraine became the seventh Soviet republic to set off in search of greater autonomy.

Ukrainians Declare Republic Sovereign Inside Soviet System
By Francis X. Clines

MOSCOW, July 16—The vast and rich Ukraine, one of the largest and most important republics in the Soviet Union, became the latest to declare its sovereignty today, challenging the Gorbachev Government to a larger share of self-determination and natural resources.

The new, democratized Parliament of the Ukraine adopted a declaration of sovereignty that stopped short of claiming full independence. But it served notice that the Ukrainians felt their laws took precedence over Moscow's authority, even to controlling troops on Ukrainian territory.

Galvanized by Rukh, the Ukrainian popular front, the republic's politics have become more separatist in the last year, electing a new Parliament in Kiev that endorsed the sovereignty declaration by a vote of 355 to 4.

With 50 million people and significant farming, resources and industry, the Ukraine is the second largest of the 15 republics in the Soviet Union.

It joins the largest, the Russian federated republic, in pressing President Mikhail S. Gorbachev to decentralize authority from the Kremlin.

Seven Soviet republics have approved variations of the separatist challenge that is fast becoming the major political problem facing the Soviet leader.

The decisions reached at the Kohl-Gorbachev meeting were an obvious watershed of postwar European history. What remained a subject for debate, however, was the question of how and to whose benefit those initiatives were likely to play out.

Bowing to the Inexorable; Soviets Make the Best of New German Might

By Serge Schmemann

MOSCOW, July 17—It will long be debated who won and who lost when Mikhail S. Gorbachev gave his blessing to the reunification of Germany.

Some will argue that the Soviets were humbled, others that Germany took its first step out of the West. Still others will invoke history, recalling previous Soviet-German pacts with muddled legacies: Brest-Litovsk, Rapallo, Molotov-Ribbentrop.

But it was probably the Soviet President himself who gave the closest approximation of the realities behind the agreement announced Monday in the Caucasus spa of Zheleznovodsk, when he said that what he and Chancellor Helmut Kohl had practiced was that old German game, Realpolitik.

Through two days of unusual chumminess in the sylvan setting of the northern Caucasus, Mr. Gorbachev virtually insured the election of Mr. Kohl as the first Chancellor of a reunited Germany, and in the process he gained probably his most important ally in the flagging campaign to revive the Soviet economy.

Mr. Gorbachev is an acknowledged master at Realpolitik, the politics of expediency. Much of his career, and much of his legend abroad, have been built on what amounts to making virtue of necessity, on recognizing the inevitable and claiming it for his goal.

And that was largely what he did with Mr. Kohl. According to Germans familiar with the process, Mr. Gorbachev recognized that he could do no more than delay the unification of Germany as a member of NATO, and that there was no question that the Soviet forces there would have to withdraw. It also looked increasingly likely that Mr. Kohl, a firm Atlanticist, would end up the first Chancellor of the reunited Germany.

Against this, Mr. Gorbachev weighed the fact that a united Germany held the key to his program of perestroika, the stalled campaign to stoke and Westernize the Soviet economy. The two Germanys, he noted more than once, are already the Soviet Union's largest trading partners. Together they hold the key to the Soviet Union's economic future and to its continued presence in Europe.

True, the Germans had made clear that no more billions in hard currency were immediately forthcoming. But the West had pledged in Houston to keep the question open, and the Germans were prepared to cooperate in phasing and financing the return home of the 380,000 Soviet troops in East Germany.

Moreover, the Germans were prepared to sign a major treaty on all facets of German-Soviet relations, with contractual guarantees of scientific, technological and commercial cooperation.

Finally, at the NATO summit in London earlier this month, the Western powers lifted a major obstacle when they agreed to terminate the adversarial character of the alliance, inviting the Warsaw Pact to sign a nonaggression statement and inviting Mr. Gorbachev to Brussels.

The choice seemed obvious. But by Soviet and German accounts, the real hurdle was domestic—the resistance of hard-liners in the Soviet Communist Party, who had found in German unity the one issue on which they thought they could rally popular opposition to Mr. Gorbachev and perestroika.

In an impassioned speech to the party congress that ended last week, Mr. Gorbachev asked the delegates whether they were prepared to stop German unity with tanks. In a key test vote last Thursday, the conservative standard-bearer, Yegor K. Ligachev, mustered barely a sixth of the delegates.

It was on that day, German officials said, that Mr. Gorbachev invited Mr. Kohl to add a southern side trip to his Soviet itinerary. The way was clear, and the Soviet leader apparently wanted to waste no time in securing Mr. Kohl's, and Germany's, good will.

Thrusting aside all reservations, he accepted the German package virtually intact, NATO membership and all, and he lavished on Mr. Kohl a welcome no other Western leader has enjoyed. Emulating the homey touch that has become increasingly popular in Western summits, Mr. Gorbachev took Mr. Kohl to his native southern Russia and to a mountain hideaway.

Mr. Kohl could not conceal his glee. All through the press conference at Zheleznovodsk, he sat with a broad grin. Meeting with the press in Bonn today, he acknowledged that he had not expected so broad an agreement—at best, he said, he had expected Mr. Gorbachev to agree to the NATO membership.

"These last 24 hours were among the important experiences of my life," the Chancellor said.

The haste with which Mr. Gorbachev dispatched the German question left diplomats surmising that he intended an equally swift assault on the economy now that Mr. Ligachev and his resistance to a market economy were subdued. German officials involved in the negotiations said Mr. Gorbachev repeatedly spoke of plans for such an offensive.

At his news conference in Bonn today, Mr. Kohl said Mr. Gorbachev "made it clear especially in private talks—and it's not indiscreet if I quote him here—that the way of the Soviet Union into the future must be a pluralistic way, not only in politics, but especially in economic preconditions."

Mr. Kohl is also no slouch at politics, and much of his career, like Mr. Gorbachev's, has been made by his instinct for the popular mood. He was among the first to sense that the fall of the Berlin wall would begin a process ending in unification, and he was quick to claim the process as his own.

Mr. Kohl also sensed that Mr. Gorbachev's problem was largely political, and with his Foreign Minister, Hans-Dietrich Genscher, he worked hard to persuade the Western allies to soften their stance toward Moscow, and to demonstrate that Germany was a potential boon, not a threat.

"It is interesting to see that the opinion comes through in Moscow now that it is useful, and not damaging, to have good relations with Germany," Mr. Kohl said in Bonn. "I say Germany here consciously."

Realpolitik, it seemed, had triumphed for the moment. It was not without precedent. From the time of Peter the Great, the Russians have looked to the Germans for technology and organization, and thousands of Germans migrated east to serve in the army and economy of the Russian Empire.

Yet the very effort Mr. Gorbachev and Mr. Kohl required to achieve their breakthrough underscored their awareness of the lingering pall that a more recent history of brutal conflicts still cast on all Soviet-German relations.

The pains Mr. Gorbachev took to seem friendly with Mr. Kohl were not solely intended to court the future all-German leader. They were also needed to demonstrate to the Soviet peoples that their President was prepared to accept a German as a personal friend.

The demonstration was not lost, at least on two decorated war veterans who met the two leaders. Mr. Kohl said he had been particularly moved by a comment one of them made to Mr. Gorbachev: "It is good, Mikhail Sergeyevich, that you talk to the Germans, so that our grandchildren will not experience what was in our time."

Whatever economic benefit Gorbachev hoped to reap from his West German connection lay off in the future, while in the Soviet Union the material conditions of everyday life were bad and growing worse. In an effort to either reverse the trend or share the responsibility, Gorbachev joined with Boris Yeltsin, his main rival, to establish a joint 12-member commission that was charged with preparing a program of economic change by the beginning of September. Essentially, the appointment of the commission fully established that the Ryzhkov plan, that earlier blueprint for moving toward a more market-oriented economy, assailed by Yeltsin as too timid, was languishing if not yet dead. But as the economists debated approaches and hoped for help from abroad, consumers were grumbling and smokers took to the streets in a fury of nicotine deprivation.

Soviet Smokers Vow Strikes as Cigarettes, Too, Disappear

By Celestine Bohlen

MOSCOW, Aug. 2—It happens like clockwork, all over the city. A truck pulls up to a boarded-up kiosk, unloads its wares, the sale window opens and within minutes smokers appear out of nowhere to take places in line, hopeful that for this day, anyway, their addiction can be fed.

Along with other ills, the Soviet Union is now in the throes of a nicotine fit, brought on by a painful and puzzling withdrawal of cigarettes from a nation of heavy smokers.

In many parts of the country, the cigarette shortage—caused by a series of typical economic lapses—has galvanized the patient, line-suffering Soviet consumer into action.

In the city of Perm last week, a demonstration that began in front of an empty tobacco shop spilled into downtown streets, ending in a rally outside City Hall, where 2,000 people chanted and waved banners, badgering the Communist Party for cigarettes. "Hey, you up there, your people have nothing to smoke as well as nothing to eat," one banner read. "Party, have you got a smoke?" asked another.

In Kuibyshev, smokers at an aircraft plant threatened a strike over the cigarette shortage and protesters mounted a daily vigil at a local tobacco plant that had been shut for repairs.

Warning strikes have also been reported in Ulyanovsk and Ufa, while in Voronezh and Orel, angry smokers have smashed the windows of tobacco kiosks. This month, at the height of the harvest in the Krasnador region, combine operators brought their machines to a stop with a nonnegotiable demand: "No tobacco, no work."

At the start of August, Iraq invaded Kuwait. In terms of geography, the conflict was far removed from Europe and, on the face of it, seemed to have little to do with the decline and collapse of Communist power. However, the world crisis that developed provided Moscow and Gorbachev an opportunity to prove their good faith within the newly emerging international order. Indeed, the Soviet Union had been Iraq's major arms supplier. Moscow had worked for years to develop close ties with Saddam Hussein in Baghdad. But as hostilities erupted, Foreign Minister Shevardnadze joined Secretary of State Baker in issuing a condemnation of Iraq that was read by Mr. Baker as he stopped in

462

Moscow on his way back from a trip to Mongolia. In the months that
followed, the Soviets would join in a naval blockade and would vote
along with the United States on the United Nations resolutions leading
to sanctions and then war against Iraq.

Moscow Joins U.S. in Criticizing Iraq
By Bill Keller

MOSCOW, Aug. 3—The Soviet Union and the United States joined
tonight in urging a worldwide halt of arms deliveries to Iraq after
what they called "the brutal and illegal invasion of Kuwait."

The coordinated effort by the superpowers to mobilize world pressure against Iraq, a longtime Soviet ally and arms customer, came
after hastily arranged consultations between Secretary of State James
A. Baker 3d and Foreign Minister Eduard A. Shevardnadze at
Vnukovo-2, the V.I.P. airport here.

"Today, we take the unusual step of jointly calling upon the rest
of the international community to join with us in an international
cutoff of all arms supplies to Iraq," said the statement.

U.S. and the Soviets as Allies: It's the First Time since 1945
By Bill Keller

MOSCOW, Aug. 7—In the five days since Iraq occupied Kuwait, the
Soviet Union and the United States have begun testing a new working
relationship that is without precedent since the outset of the cold war.

Their remarkable joint venture in foreign policy began last Friday
when Secretary of State James A. Baker 3d and Foreign Minister
Eduard A. Shevardnadze emerged from an airport meeting here to
call for a worldwide arms embargo against Iraq.

By today, Bush Administration officials were indicating that the
United States was prepared to invite the Soviet Union to join any
international naval force assembled to enforce sanctions against Iraq.

"For the first time since World War II, we are virtually acting as
allies," said Maksim A. Yusin, who has been covering the story for
the Soviet Government newspaper *Izvestia.*

Moscow's approach to the crisis has been more low-key than Washington's.

While the United States has pressed for the most sweeping United

Nations embargo in history against Iraq, the Soviet Union initially favored holding some sanctions in reserve.

While the United States has flaunted its military potential, a Soviet spokesman cautioned today against "muscle-flexing" and played down the Soviet decision to dispatch a destroyer and an antisubmarine ship to the Persian Gulf to protect Soviet merchant ships.

While the White House has reportedly contemplated ways to unseat the Iraqi leader, Saddam Hussein, Moscow has met regularly with Iraqi officials here and in Baghdad, in hopes of keeping a dialogue open with its erstwhile client.

But behind such tactical differences is a degree of coordination that is all the more significant because the Middle East has long been an arena of superpower rivalry.

Throughout the crisis, the two countries have kept in frequent contact in Washington, Moscow and New York.

Yesterday Mr. Baker and Mr. Shevardnadze talked by phone for half an hour, discussing the plight of their citizens trapped in the region and agreeing to support strict sanctions in the United Nations Security Council. Today Jack F. Matlock, the American Ambassador in Moscow, paid a call on the Foreign Ministry to discuss the gulf conflict.

Soviet officials have publicly ruled out joint Soviet-American military actions against Iraq, but they have suggested that they do not consider a blockade of the Persian Gulf to fall into the same category, and as a rule the Kremlin is a strong supporter of international peacekeeping efforts.

Mr. Yusin, the *Izvestia* correspondent, said he believed the Soviet Union would cooperate in an international naval blockade if such a strategy had United Nations approval.

"If it is done under the flag of the United Nations, the Soviet Union might participate," Mr. Yusin said in an interview. "But it is my personal feeling, based on some informal conversations, that they would do it only under the U.N. flag."

As the explosive conflict in the gulf was commanding much of the world's concern and attention, the thrust toward German unity, set into motion by equally dramatic events of less than a year before, was forging ahead in somber if not quite boring precision.

Germanys Codify Details of Union
By Serge Schmemann

EAST BERLIN, Aug. 31—After weeks of intense political maneuvering, representatives of the two Germanys signed a treaty of almost 1,000 pages today detailing the mechanics of reunification, now only 33 days away.

The document covers all aspects of unification, from the merger of the two nations' social and legal systems to specific questions like abortion, the fate of former secret-police files and the site of the capital: Berlin.

Leaders of both nations dutifully declared the treaty yet another historic moment on the road to unification. But the drafting of the document was accompanied by such openly partisan haggling, especially in the final days, that to most Germans in East and West the conclusion was mostly a source of relief.

In general, the entire process of unification has lost much of its luster in the public perception as the realities of its costs and complexity have been driven home.

In East Germany in particular, the mood has soured as economic union has led to mass layoffs and closures. Unemployment has soared from 7,440 in January to 350,000 at latest count and climbing. Hundreds of thousands of others have been put on short hours and could well be laid off by the end of the year.

The increasing problems are one of the reasons all political parties have been anxious to move up the date of unity. On the practical side, there is the hope that formal unity will improve the investment allure of the East. On the political side, both major parties hope to gain from early unification—the governing Christian Democrats from the advantages of incumbency, the Social Democrats by pinning any economic turmoil on their opponents.

The final negotiations over the treaty, in fact, took place not between the two Germanys, but between the two major parties in West Germany, since the Social Democrats' agreement was needed for the two-thirds majority in Parliament necessary to make constitutional changes.

The final dispute, resolved at midnight last night, was over abortion, which is available on demand in East Germany but is restricted in West Germany. The final compromise was that the East German laws would remain in force for at least two years and West German women would be able to have legal abortions in the East.

But the widespread perception was that the Social Democrats, under their candidate for Chancellor, Oskar Lafontaine, had seized on abortion because it was the issue likely to cause Chancellor Helmut Kohl and his Christian Democrats the most grief with their conservative constituents.

The debate thus only contributed to a sense that the momentous issue of reunification had been hijacked by the political campaign for all-German elections on December 2.

Despite such politicking, the "unification treaty" represented a considerable organizational step in the complex task of melding the widely disparate social and political systems of the two Germanys less than a year after the breach of the Berlin wall. . . .

The unification treaty was signed by its two primary drafters, Interior Minister Wolfgang Schauble for the West and State Secretary Gunther Krause for the East. The East German Prime Minister, Lothar de Maiziere, attended the ceremony. But Mr. Kohl canceled his appearance, setting off speculation that he wanted to be seen as leader of all Germany, and not just of the West. His office said only that he was not able to leave Bonn for the signing ceremony, which was held at the Palais Unter den Linden in East Berlin.

The treaty was the last major internal preparatory step before formal unity, which the East German Parliament voted last week to effect on October 3.

The last external hurdles are to be cleared when the World War II Allies meet in Moscow on September 12, and when their decisions on ending all vestiges of occupation are endorsed by the 33 members of the Conference on European Security and Cooperation on October 2. No major problems are anticipated, since Mr. Kohl agreed on Germany's role in NATO and other major issues with President Mikhail S. Gorbachev of the Soviet Union in July.

The bulk of the treaty amounts to a contract for the orderly absorption of East Germany by the Federal Republic. It covers matters ranging from property through sports, the environment, financing, culture, health care, education, science, postal and transport systems, energy supplies, national debt, external commitments, income sharing with the states, election procedures and the like.

The treaty called for all East German laws not covered by the Constitution, the European Community or the treaty to be made consistent with West German law within five years. These were some of the other key provisions:

- The West German Basic Law, or Constitution, was amended to declare that unity has been achieved. The change ended any claims to former German territories now belonging to Poland or the Soviet Union.
- The treaty resolved the question of property rights in East Germany by recognizing the land reforms between 1945 and 1949, when most major agricultural estates were broken up, and by declaring that the Government would guarantee compensation in any disputes.
- The treaty established hefty incentives for investing in the East. But it also decreed that the East German states would have to pay back half of the East German debt that a united Germany was assuming. And it put the new states on a lower level of income-sharing. West German states now divide proceeds from sales taxes according to their needs. But the western state governors had feared that the bankrupt new states would take most of the money.
- Berlin was declared the official German capital. But the treaty also said that an all-German parliament would decide on the seat of government and parliament, leaving open the possibility that Bonn would retain at least some functions of the federal government.
- One of the last issues in dispute with East Germany was the fate of the files of the old Ministry of State Security, whose secret surveillance probed into every corner of East German life. The final compromise called for the files to come under an administrator selected by the East Germans.

In Moscow, the program to shift and accelerate the economy, which had been promised as a Gorbachev-Yeltsin joint venture, was being described, at least by Yeltsin, as a crash course leading to growth, profits and prosperity.

Soviet Agreement Reported on Plan for Free Markets
By Bill Keller

MOSCOW, Sept. 1—President Mikhail S. Gorbachev and Boris N. Yeltsin, whose rivalry has sometimes seemed to threaten the integrity of the Soviet Union, have agreed on a plan to dismantle central economic controls and move to free markets in 500 days, leaders of the Russian republic said today.

As described by Mr. Yeltsin and his aides, the program would cede nearly total economic autonomy to the 15 constituent republics, freeing them from the dictates of central planning and state ownership.

In turn, the republics would participate in a coordinated emergency program to curb inflation and stabilize the economy.

In the first 100 days, the plan calls for the preparation of laws expanding the rights of private ownership, creating a banking system and stock markets, and establishing a social safety net for those with low incomes. The republics and central government would begin to bring inflation under control by selected wage and price controls and an infusion of imported consumer goods to absorb loose cash.

Mr. Yeltsin, who is President of the Russian republic, the Soviet Union's largest political subdivision, said at a news conference that the plan departs so radically from Mr. Gorbachev's previous reform attempts that it is expected to win approval even in the Baltic republics, where the governments are committed to full political independence and capitalism.

"This will be a sort of net that will preserve the union," as a common market if not necessarily as a political entity, Mr. Yeltsin said.

There was no immediate confirmation from Mr. Gorbachev's delegation that an agreement had been reached, and doubts remained about just how firmly Mr. Gorbachev was committed to the deal after the Soviet leader told a news conference on Friday that serious issues remained to be resolved.

He said it would take another week of work to reconcile differences between two competing blueprints for the economic future of the country.

One is the radical program prepared by a committee of Yeltsin and Gorbachev economists under the leadership of Stanislav S. Shatalin, an economic adviser to Mr. Gorbachev, and the other a more moderate version devised by Prime Minister Nikolai I. Ryzhkov and his aides.

But according to officials of the Russian republic, the choice is already made and Mr. Gorbachev is stalling because he is reluctant to repudiate Mr. Ryzhkov, who has been his loyal Prime Minister for five years.

"Gorbachev has agreed to the program worked out by academician Shatalin,'" said Ruslan I. Khasbulatov, Mr. Yeltsin's first vice president. "I can't say anything about the details or dramatic conflicts, because certain clever people made us swear that we would not talk about how it all came about.

"But I want to tell you unequivocally that the program that the Shatalin group proposed will be adopted."

Mr. Yeltsin said the plan could be put into effect beginning October 1, after review by each of the republics.

The two rivals reportedly reached agreement on the plan Wednesday in five hours of private meetings.

Then, during two days of sometimes stormy meetings with his top advisers and representatives from the republics, Mr. Gorbachev seemed to waffle, evidently hoping to find a broader consensus that would include Mr. Ryzhkov.

"The President is showing his indecisiveness," Mr. Yeltsin said of Mr. Gorbachev. . . .

The completion of a Yeltsin-Gorbachev economic deal would represent a stunning political achievement for Mr. Yeltsin, who was drummed out of Mr. Gorbachev's Politburo two and a half years ago for complaining too stridently about the slow pace of change.

Mr. Yeltsin, who was elected Russian President in May, seemed fully aware of the triumph today. Brimming with self-confidence and humor, cheerfully deriding Mr. Gorbachev's team as faint of heart and slow of mind, he was a startling contrast to the Soviet leader, who seemed fatigued and evasive during his news conference yesterday.

The completion of a market economic plan would also be a breakthrough for the free-market advocates in Mr. Gorbachev's own camp—including Mr. Shatalin and another adviser, Nikolai Petrakov—who have been engaged in what they consider a battle for Mr. Gorbachev's centrist soul.

For his part, Gorbachev was once again concentrating on international affairs, this time joining with President Bush during a summit meeting in Helsinki to affirm common objectives in the Persian Gulf.

Bush and Gorbachev Say Iraqis Must Obey U.N. and Quit Kuwait
By Bill Keller

HELSINKI, FINLAND, Sept. 9—President Bush and President Mikhail S. Gorbachev issued a joint pledge today to act "individually and in concert" to reverse Iraq's conquest of Kuwait, even if that cannot be accomplished by peaceful means.

After seven hours together devoted almost entirely to the Persian Gulf crisis, the two leaders reported no new agreement on specific measures to achieve their aim. But they said the meeting had underscored a remarkable political collaboration by the Soviet Union and the United States at a time of crisis.

"Our preference is to resolve the crisis peacefully, and we will be united against Iraq's aggression as long as the crisis exists," the statement said. "However, we are determined to see this aggression end, and if the current steps fail to end it, we are prepared to consider additional ones consistent with the U.N. Charter."

During an hourlong news conference, however, the two leaders often differed on how to pursue the campaign against President Saddam Hussein of Iraq. Differences emerged over the possible use of military force, over Soviet participation in policing the embargo, over the linkage of Iraq's aggression with other Middle East conflicts, over the Arab role as possible brokers of a compromise, and over the presence of Soviet military experts in Iraq.

The meeting, the first the two leaders had held during a time of world crisis, seemed to underscore the new international situation created by the improved relations between Moscow and Washington.

Mr. Gorbachev alluded to this in an interview over Moscow television after the meeting had ended. He said that during the Middle East war in 1967, the United States and the Soviet Union "were on the brink of war" because they supported different sides in the conflict between Israel and the Arab nations of Egypt, Syria and Jordan.

Mr. Bush, speaking to reporters on his flight back to Washington tonight, said he "couldn't be more pleased" by his talks with Mr. Gorbachev and the "clear signal" they sent to President Hussein. . . .

Mr. Gorbachev will apparently not take home any tangible commitment for American economic assistance. During their afternoon meeting, Mr. Gorbachev described his plans to move the Soviet Union toward a market-oriented economy, and Mr. Bush reiterated his willingness to give American technological help.

"I think this remarkable cooperation that has been demonstrated by the Soviet Union at the United Nations gets me inclined to recommend as close cooperation in the economic field as possible," the American President said.

Mr. Gorbachev, however, quickly interjected that Soviet cooperation in the gulf crisis was not tied to economic aid.

"It would be very oversimplified and very superficial to judge that the Soviet Union could be bought for dollars," the Soviet leader said.

Back from Finland, Gorbachev was immediately drawn into the grow-ing furor over how and how quickly the economy should be overhauled, and beneath these arguments lay a quarrel over who should lead the way, he or Yeltsin.

Gorbachev Endorses a Proposal for Free Enterprise in 500 Days

By Francis X. Clines

MOSCOW, Sept. 11—On a day of disarray in the Kremlin, President Mikhail S. Gorbachev finally endorsed a national economic reform plan today but was quickly upstaged as the Parliament of the Russian republic rushed the plan to approval to prod the central Government to more decisive action.

In the Kremlin, angry members of the national Parliament spent the day confronting the Gorbachev Government and urging it to make a choice and get the stagnant economy moving toward free-market innovations after months of indecision.

But across town, the legislature of Russia, the largest and richest of the nation's republics, enthusiastically approved the plan of the dominant insurgents to scrap the Communist economic monolith and install a free-enterprise economy within 500 days.

The two actions displayed the heart of the revision struggle in this deeply troubled nation. The national Government is anxious about yielding its powerful central economic controls, while the nation's 15 republics are rushing to take the free-market bit into their teeth.

The Russian Parliament's vote was 251 to 1. The fast action was engineered by Boris N. Yeltsin, President of the Russian republic, the chief proponent of the 500-day plan and a political rival of President Gorbachev who has struck something of an alliance with the Soviet leader on the economic crisis.

The legislative quickness of Russia, with three-quarters of the na-tion's land, more than half the population and most of its natural resources, only added to the sense of frustration among members of the national Parliament.

"Where's the program?" said a member of the national Parliament in the raucous Kremlin session, as the Gorbachev Government failed to meet an earlier promise to resolve its internal disagreement over the economy and present a full-scale proposal today. Demands increased for the resignation of Mr. Gorbachev's Prime Minister, Nikolai I. Ryzhkov.

As he finally committed himself publicly, Mr. Gorbachev appeared to surprise Mr. Ryzhkov. The embattled head of the Gorbachev Cabinet has been championing the alternative plan, which would take a slower, far more cautious retreat from central control as the most socially prudent course to free-market changes.

"I'm listening and I can't understand what's going on," a lawmaker said, and soon President Gorbachev stepped in, angrily demanding that the Parliament be patient and behave.

"All these charges, insults, innuendo—it smells bad, very bad," Mr. Gorbachev said. "Why are there attempts to corner us today? Wait a little bit. The process is under way."

The critical event in a day of heated, confused Kremlin wrangling was that Mr. Gorbachev, after considerable hesitation, finally committed himself to the 500 days proposal for moving toward free enterprise.

"If you ask me, I am more impressed by the Shatalin program," the Soviet leader said, referring to Stanislav S. Shatalin, an economist who is chairman of a crisis study commission that created an economic revision plan that is faster and presumably more traumatic than an alternative proposal.

"It brings together the republics on the basis of what we need," the Soviet leader said of the Shatalin plan. Mr. Gorbachev has been pressed by the republics for greater sovereignty and has promised them far more initiative in national recovery.

At issue in the choice between the plans was just how much inflation and social disruption each might bring to a nation already reeling from widespread shortages in consumer goods and a state economy stultified by seven decades of central bureaucratic dictates. The Ryzhkov proposal would resist the wholesale denationalization plans of the Shatalin proposal and be slower to ease the existing price and currency controls.

After committing himself at the parliamentary session, Mr. Gorbachev then characteristically sent Kremlin planners back for another attempt at what thus far has proved impossible, blending the Shatalin and Ryzhkov proposals into a single plan.

"The fact that the country's biggest republic will accept our plan will settle everything," Mr. Shatalin said. He insists that the great economic problem can be solved from the outside in, if the republics adopt and enforce the 500-day plan even as the central Government continues to struggle indecisively.

Some members of the national Parliament complained bitterly that they had been kept in the dark about all but the general direction of the rival plans.

"Shatalin has been working in Mozambique and Ryzhkov in New Zealand," a lawmaker said.

By the end of the day, there were promises to have copies of the revision ideas available to the Parliament on Wednesday. Mr. Gorbachev confused some members by stipulating, after personally embracing the Shatalin plan, that "one program on the basis of the two" rival plans be again attempted.

The confusion remained considerable as the lawmakers left the Kremlin for the day. The precise parliamentary method is difficult to predict, since the general plan is to have the proposals for changes considered by the legislatures in the other republics before the national Parliament takes final action.

The Shatalin plan, as described by Mr. Yeltsin and his aides, would give the 15 Soviet republics almost total economic autonomy, and the republics would take part in an emergency program to curb inflation and stabilize the economy. The plan would expand the rights of private ownership, create a banking system and stock markets, establish ways to protect low-income people, set selected wage and price controls in its early stages and include an infusion of imported consumer goods to absorb loose cash.

Eventually, according to the plan, subsidies to industry and agriculture would be ended, most ministries that regulate industry would be abolished, state controls over most prices would end and farmland, housing and businesses would be extensively privatized.

Mr. Ryzhkov's plan is a refined version of the program that the Soviet Parliament rejected in May. He proposed keeping much more central authority in Moscow, with tighter state controls on prices and property ownership.

Mr. Ryzhkov drew the most anger at the Kremlin session as insurgent lawmakers insisted that after five years of the Gorbachev Government's failure to stir major economic change, he had no credibility.

"Are you capable of bringing this country out of crisis?" a lawmaker said to him. By the end of the day, Mr. Ryzhkov was denying newspaper accusations that despite his policy doubts about private property he tried to purchase his Government dacha. . . .

There were no such moves against Mr. Gorbachev, who defended Mr. Ryzhkov.

Mr. Ryzhkov said his disagreements with the stronger features of the Shatalin plan were rooted in concern that the beleaguered Soviet consumer be protected by the Government from even greater trauma in the transition to free enterprise.

As the clamor mounted, it almost drowned out a ceremony that would have been unimaginable just a year earlier.

A Historic Moment Slips By, Overtaken by Other Events

By Serge Schmemann

MOSCOW, Sept. 12—For an event of such historic dimensions, the signing today of the final settlement between the Germans and the World War II victors seemed almost lost in the tumult of more immediate concerns.

Moscow was gripped by suspense over a grand new economic plan promised by President Mikhail S. Gorbachev. The Germans fretted over the rising cost of unification and braced for the actual moment of unity, now only three weeks off. Americans and Western Europeans were preoccupied by the standoff with Iraq.

And yet the "Treaty on the Final Settlement with Respect to Germany," to give it its full title, arguably had a significance akin to agreements familiar from every high school history text—the Versailles Treaty of 1871, from which a united Germany first emerged; and the Potsdam conference of 1945, from which the Germans emerged severed in two.

Now, after 45 years, the victorious allies were finally resolving the "German Question" and putting an end to the last formal remnants of occupation.

They were restoring full sovereignty to a nation that had savaged Europe a half century earlier. In exchange, the Germans were renouncing all claims to ancestral lands east of the Oder and Neisse Rivers lost to Poland and the Soviet Union, restricting their military and pledging that hereafter only peace would emanate from German soil.

More broadly, the European powers were laying the groundwork for a new European order, with a potent, wealthy Germany at its heart. Perhaps more clearly than any previous event, the treaty demonstrated the retreat of Communism from Europe. Not only the West German mark had gone East—the full Western package of liberal democracy, free-market economy and the North Atlantic alliance were being voluntarily accepted by the bankrupt rump of the "first state of workers and peasants on German soil."

Yet it was probably the first modern peace treaty that took pains to leave no winners or losers. The Germans, in fact, were insistent that it not be called a "peace treaty" at all, to underscore that it had been achieved in peace. In 1871, by contrast, a united Germany was proclaimed by Bismarck after a war against France, and in 1945 the victors had met in the midst of the smoldering ruins of the Third Reich.

But this, Chancellor Helmut Kohl declared, was "the first unification of a country in modern history achieved without war, pain or strife."

The statement invited a quick knock on wood, but it did reflect what the six signers—the United States, the Soviet Union, Britain, France and the two Germanys—all agreed had been a harmonious and creative negotiation.

FALL 1990

*A*s *attacks on him grew increasingly strident, a visibly angered Gorbachev moved to extend the legal limits of his rule.*

Soviet Parliament Grants Gorbachev Emergency Power

By Celestine Bohlen

MOSCOW, Sept. 24—The Soviet Parliament granted President Mikhail S. Gorbachev emergency economic powers today, but put off, at his request, answering the critical question of how to move to a free market.

The Supreme Soviet granted Mr. Gorbachev his request for additional authority by an overwhelming vote of 305 to 36, despite warnings from the giant Russian republic that it will not tolerate any infringement of its sovereign rights.

The vote in the national Parliament, reflecting the country's vacillating and uncertain political mood, seemed to defy the trend that in recent months has drained power from Moscow toward republic and regional centers.

In an angry, impatient speech, Mr. Gorbachev challenged the lawmakers to give him special powers over the next 18 months to pull the country out of its mounting crisis.

"Everybody agrees that a more effective functioning of government, especially of executive power, is needed," the Soviet President said. "The fact that this hasn't happened has given rise to distress and much criticism."

The resolution approved by the national Parliament today would give the Soviet President authority to put into effect policies on wages, prices, finances and the budget and also the "strengthening of law and order." The Supreme Soviet would have the right to challenge the President's directives, but its approval in advance would not be required.

Parliament today also accepted Mr. Gorbachev's proposal to create a compromise between two opposing views on the country's future economic course, averting a showdown between the more conservative approach advocated by Prime Minister Nikolai I. Ryzhkov and a swifter, radical transition favored by Mr. Gorbachev's top economists.

The compromise, to be worked out by October 15, should include elements of both plans, Mr. Gorbachev told lawmakers today.

"No single plan can be finally adopted," he said. "It is my deep conviction that we have to unite forces at this decisive moment. If we split up, if we clash, we will ruin this historic turning point." . . .

As the Soviet Union heads into a period of wrenching economic change, it also faces unresolved questions about the redistribution of power—between the central Government and the republics, between the presidency and the legislature, among newly emerging political factions.

Mr. Gorbachev has put his political skills to the test by trying to accommodate opposing points of views. In the economic debate, he managed to back both sides, defending Mr. Ryzhkov's beleaguered Government while seeming to push for the more radical program proposed by one of his top economic advisers, Stanislav S. Shatalin.

In the debate today, Mr. Shatalin compared Mr. Gorbachev to the captain of a football team, who tries to fix the game so that both sides win. Mr. Ryzhkov, emerging from the Parliament chamber, echoed the same thought by declaring that today's vote had left "no winners, and no losers."

But in his bid for additional powers, Mr. Gorbachev also showed impatience for opposing views. In a scathing speech, he scorned his critics, dismissing their objections as "juridical" and their concern about his accumulation of power as "political speculation."

Meanwhile, the countdown to the final act of the great drama of German reunion had begun.

On Unity's Eve, Subdued Mood Replaces Euphoria
By Serge Schmemann

BONN, Sept. 29—On the eve of German unity, large crowds have been drawn to a major exhibition in West Berlin devoted to Otto von Bismarck, the original architect of German unity.

It was the Iron Chancellor who first united the Germans into a state

120 years ago "by blood and iron." But organizers of the exhibition are quick to note that it was planned before the Berlin wall came down, and that the intention is only to provide a "moment of critical reflection," not to suggest parallels.

The disclaimer is understandable. The period of unity ushered in by Bismarck, from 1871 to 1945, was the most terrible in German history, and its legacy was to make "German nationalism" into a fearsome specter at home and abroad.

Such reflections alone might be enough to explain the subdued mood, almost anxiety, among the Germans on the threshold of a reunion that in West German mythology, at least, had been the premier goal of the nation.

It is also true that another round of euphoria may simply be too much to expect after 11 months of regular "historic moments" in the Germanys and across Eastern Europe, even if this may be the most historic moment of them all.

Besides, the more tangible elements of unity—the opening of the border, economic union—have already happened, and Germans on both sides have begun to feel the economic and social costs of the undertaking.

Faced with the prospect of higher taxes, West Germans grumble about the "Ossies" as a drain on their prosperity. The East Germans, facing swelling unemployment, rankle at their lot as second-class citizens in a state they fought to join. By any measure, things will get worse before they begin to get better.

Cynics may argue that such hand-wringing is innate in the Germans, that unification is actually taking place with exemplary Teutonic orderliness. This is, after all, a family affair, and all the grumbling and anxiety will not prevent some heady emotion and jubilation at the Brandenburg Gate when unity comes at 12 A.M. on Wednesday.

Yet the apprehension is tangible, and at its core lies a sense that becomes increasingly apparent browsing through the displays of Bismarck's life and times: neither Bismarck, nor the Weimar Republic, nor Hitler's Third Reich provides signposts for the Germany waiting to be born.

There are not many who fear that the new German Reich will revive the militance or aggressive nationalism of its predecessors. The conditions are far different, and the new Germany is being formed on the basis of a Federal Republic that has shaped a reliable democracy and a formidable economy that has found an identity and security in the West. It is a Germany that has accepted permanent limits on its military, that has forsworn all claims to former territories, that has pledged fealty to European unity and the Atlantic alliance.

Perhaps more important, the West Germans, at least, have shown a readiness to confront their past. The bitter "historians' dispute" of the 1980's delved into the cardinal question of responsibility for Auschwitz and all it stands for, and it concluded with President Richard von Weizsacker's declaration that "Auschwitz remains unique. It was perpetrated by Germans in the name of Germany."

"The time of marching armies in Europe is over," said Vernon A. Walters, the United States Ambassador to Bonn. "This is the smallest Germany in 1,000 years, and the richest and the furthest West. It is a nation that has learned it doesn't need space to be rich."

Yet it is also true that unity has come to Germans by surprise, long before any expected it, before they had sorted out where they were headed.

The bloodless upheavals of last fall have nurtured their own myth, that the Germans were brought together through the "peaceful revolution" in East Germany and the "democratic choice" of its people.

In fact, the original demonstrators chanted "We are the people" and demanded a reformed socialist state, and the vote that threw them into West German arms was less for unity than for the German mark. It can also be argued that West Germany's push for rapid monetary and political union was less due to a yearning for national unity than a panicky attempt to block the flood of East Germans threatening to overwhelm West Germany's cherished social security system.

In any case, it is clear that unity is coming not as the end of a search for a new German identity, but more as the beginning.

At one extreme, embodied in the pronouncements of the writer Gunter Grass, the process is viewed with open alarm. From this perspective unification is nothing more than the violent subjugation of a fledgling democracy and the start of an "irrepressible expansionism."

"I wish I could share the feeling that we are now practically harmless," Mr. Grass wrote in the French left-wing daily *Liberation*. "But when I weigh up the process of German unification, it re-arouses all my fears."

Objections have also come from a younger generation of West Germans who grew up with few feelings of kinship for the East Germans, and unconvinced that unity has any practical value.

"Just when we thought we had come to terms with our existence and knew at least in rough terms what it's going to be like in the future, out of the blue a mid-life crisis descends on us in the disguise of German unity," the popular 40-year-old West German writer Patrick Süskind wrote recently in *Der Spiegel.*

Such open objections, however, are overshadowed by the broad acceptance of unification as a German duty, and at best as the beginning of the restoration of health to the nation.

Many intellectuals initially skeptical about unity have found a certain reassurance in the absence of flag-waving nationalism, violence or bitterness.

Theo Sommer, editor in chief of the weekly *Die Zeit,* said such skepticism fed a determination that the new Germany not become overbearing or self-centered again.

"I think there is no 'hurrah' patriotism, no nationalism, no orgy of chauvinism," he said, "but rather a certain diffidence and apprehension about the future, and I think that's a better mood to enter unity than flag-waving."

Chancellor Helmut Kohl, the rough-hewn politician who has cajoled and maneuvered Germany toward rapid unity, probably speaks for a silent majority of Germans when he declares that his greatest hope for a united Germany is simply that it will become accepted as normal.

"I think it is possible, even probable, that the Germans will now find this inner balance that is characteristic of the casual self-confidence of other European nations," the Chancellor said in a recent interview.

Behind such hopes is the notion that the Germans are finally resuming the process of nation-building raised in the failed uprisings of 1848, when the German colors of black, red and gold were first raised and rebels fought for a unified Germany under a constitutional, parliamentary government. Once again, some argue, unity is rising from below, breaking ground for a new, shame-free patriotism.

However, the more immediate problem is how to manage the merger of two disparate states and peoples. While the cost of unity is probably the major source of grumbling, most Germans seem confident that West Germany's wealth and organizational genius will bring East Germany into the fold soon.

East Germans, for their part, have felt spurned and neglected by the rich Western kinsmen. "The countless embraces at the wall were fired by alcohol, and ended that way, in headache, broken glass and broken bones," wrote the East German writer Rolf Schneider. "Ever since then, the man from the West has appeared to the G.D.R. Germans as someone perfectly equipped with the strange character of a man-eating shark, 'Carcharodon carcharias,' as the force behind rising rents, eviction orders, as an arrogant know-it-all, as a babbling salesman."

Such initial stereotyping and complexes, however, may be only another example of the angst and self-searching that is inherent in the culture. One indication that the clash of East and West may not be all that critical is that it has also found its way into the repertory of East German satirical cabaret, a Berlin tradition that thrived even under the Communists.

At the Kartoon, a two-week-old cabaret in East Berlin, one skit has a West German chicken proposing a joint venture to an East German pig. "Let's make ham-and-egg sandwiches," proposes the chicken. "Wait a minute, that means I'd have to die," protests the pig. "Hey, it's not my fault you can't make eggs," says the chicken.

Carnivorous and powerful as the "Wessies" may appear to the "Ossies," the question is still open whether the Germans can handle the influence and power they will gain through unity, whether they can overcome their image as economic giants but political midgets. With every announcement of another troop withdrawal by the superpowers, it becomes evident that the Germans are destined to play a central role in the new Europe, ready or not.

The recent debate in Bonn over whether to join in the military action in the Persian Gulf demonstrated that the Germans are still squeamish about military force. Yet Mr. Kohl and his Foreign Minister, Hans-Dietrich Genscher, have shown an increasing readiness to play a role in global politics.

As these and other aspects of German and European realignment swirl through the press, even nations less given to worry would be forgiven bouts of apprehension. But for reformed skeptics like Mr. Sommer, the debate is a source of assurance.

"The point to make is really that we don't know some of the answers yet, and that's a positive thing," he said. "At least we're not goose-stepping where angels fear to tread."

What had until so recently been unimaginable became a cause for celebration.

Evolution in Europe; Two Germanys Unite after 45 Years with Jubilation and a Vow of Peace

By Serge Schmemann

BERLIN, Wednesday, Oct. 3—Forty-five years after it was carved up in defeat and disgrace, Germany was reunited today in a midnight celebration of pealing bells, national hymns and the jubilant blare of good old German oom-pah-pah.

At the stroke of midnight Tuesday, a copy of the American Liberty Bell, a gift from the United States at the height of the cold war, tolled from the Town Hall, and the black, red and gold banner of the Federal Republic of Germany rose slowly before the Reichstag, the scarred seat of past German Parliaments.

Then the President, Richard von Weizsacker, drawing on the words of the West German Constitution, proclaimed from the steps of the Reichstag: "In free self-determination, we want to achieve the unity in freedom of Germany. We are aware of our responsibility for these tasks before God and the people. We want to serve peace in the world in a united Europe."

With that, a throng estimated at one million joined in the West German national anthem, now the anthem for united Germany: "Unity and justice and freedom for the German fatherland . . ." The words are from the third stanza of the prewar anthem, whose opening verses, now banned, began, "Deutschland, Deutschland uber Alles."

The moment marked the return of a nation severed along the front line between East and West to the center stage of Europe, this time as an economic powerhouse vowing never again to bring grief to a continent it had so terribly ravaged in the past century.

It is the smallest unified German state to rise in the 119 years since Otto von Bismarck first gathered the Germans under the Prussian crown.

Hundreds of German flags waved and firecrackers snapped in the chilly autumn night. Beer and sparkling wine flowed freely and the strains of divergent bands mingled in a rowdy cacophony. Soon bottles began smashing on the pavement and celebration turned to intoxication, and by early morning the center of the new capital was deep in smashed bottles and weaving revelers.

A force of about 5,000 police officers had been massed in case radicals tried to disrupt the festivities, and the police reported seven arrests. But what protests there were passed with no major incidents.

Unity essentially meant that the German Democratic Republic with its 16 million citizens acceded to the Federal Republic of Germany, which expanded to become a state of 78 million souls and 137,900 square miles. The accession meant that the name, anthem, Constitution and Government of the Federal Republic became those of all Germany, that Chancellor Helmut Kohl became the first Chancellor of the reunited state and Mr. von Weizsacker the first President.

Berlin, a city divided by the infamous wall into a gray Communist capital and a glittering capitalist enclave, became once again the political and spiritual capital of Germany.

"Everybody should know: Germany will not go it alone, there will be no unilateral nationalism and no 'restless Reich,'" vowed Mr. Kohl in an article written for the *Frankfurter Allgemeine* newspaper.

It was also a moment of poignant lasts. The German Democratic Republic, founded by Soviet occupiers as the "first state of workers and peasants on German soil," expired bankrupt but not entirely unmourned.

At the final session of Parliament, Jens Reich, a leader of the citizens' movements that led demonstrations a year earlier to bring down the Communists, assailed the first and only democratic legislature of East Germany for having done nothing but surrender the state to the West. "Unity must not become a memory of a stab in the back," he said.

But a more prevalent note was struck by the East German Prime Minister, Lothar de Maiziere, at the final "state act" of the East German Government in the grand Schauspielhaus concert hall, attended by the political and cultural elite of the nation.

There, the first and last democratically elected leader of East Germany committed his state to history with the words: "In a few moments the German Democratic Republic accedes to the Federal Republic of Germany. With that, we Germans achieve unity in freedom. It is an hour of great joy. It is the end of many illusions. It is a farewell without tears."

Then Kurt Masur, the conductor from Leipzig and a hero of the peaceful revolution last fall, rose to conduct Beethoven's Ninth Symphony, with the grand "Ode to Joy" in the final movement that for Germans stands as a spiritual hymn to hope.

Mr. Kohl, capping a year of political successes, addressed the nation on television several hours before unity.

"In a few hours a dream will become reality," Mr. Kohl said, his eyes turning misty. "After 40 bitter years of division, Germany, our fatherland, will be reunited. This is one of the happiest moments of my life. From the many letters and conversations I have had, I know the great joy also felt by the vast majority of you."

Many Germans, in fact, had spent the last several weeks complaining of the cost and dislocation of unity. But at the moment of unity, Mr. Kohl seemed correct in finding that it was a moment to celebrate.

The Chancellor also made a point of thanking and reassuring Germany's allies and neighbors. "In particular," he said, "we thank the United States of America and above all President George Bush." Mr. Bush was among the first world leaders to abandon reservations about German unity and endorse Mr. Kohl's efforts.

In recent weeks, the process of unity had drawn growing grumbles from both East and West as Germans came to realize the huge cost of the undertaking. But for the hundreds of thousands who had gathered from across Germany and abroad, this was a night not to moan, but simply to celebrate.

"It is really moving," said Heinz Schober, a Berlin shopkeeper who had come with his wife. "We were here when the wall went up and we were here when it came down, and now we see something children will read about in history books."

Hundreds of stands along the Unter den Linden peddled everything from bratwurst and beer to "Day of Unity" T-shirts and chunks of the Berlin wall. Musicians ranging from rock bands to a Soviet military band to Wolf Biermann, a onetime East German dissident, blared from 16 stages set up among the beer and sausage stands, and all along the mile-long avenue the mood was festive and joyous.

At one point, revelers before the Reichstag pressed hard against the steps, where Chancellor Kohl and other political leaders were gathered, but no problems developed.

The most serious trouble was reported in Gottingen, a West German city near the former border, where about 1,000 radical youths went on a rampage, smashing windows and denouncing unity.

Unity came to the Germans barely a year after streams of East Germans began pouring out through newly porous borders in Hungary and Czechoslovakia, forcing the East German leader, Erich Honecker, to confront a crisis just as he prepared to preside over the celebrations of his state's 40th anniversary.

A year before unity came, on October 3, 1989, a flood of East German refugees had all but overwhelmed the West German Embassy in Czechoslovakia, and the East German Government finally gave permission for the refugees to go west. It also closed its borders, touching off new discontent and disorders.

The celebration of East Germany's anniversary four days later marked the beginning of the state's undoing. The Soviet leader, Mikhail S. Gorbachev, gave the first indications that he was not prepared to prop up the East German Government, and waves of demonstrators clashed with the police in East Berlin and other cities.

The demonstrations rapidly grew, driving the Government into disarray until it took the fateful action on November 9 of opening the Berlin wall a crack, touching off a rush to unity. By March 18 East Germany held its first democratic elections, and by July 1 its economy was merged into West Germany's. The pace accelerated through the summer, bringing formal unity up to October 3 and setting the scene for the celebration.

The pace of events also required a rapid termination of the vestigial occupation under which both Germanys and Berlins existed, and the moment of unity was preceded by a flurry of final arrangements and actions to end the Allied controls.

The commanders of the Western Allied forces, the United States, Britain and France, which merged their occupation zones of the city after the war to form West Berlin and defended it against Communist encirclement in ensuing years, met for the last time and ceded authority over the city.

"I now close this final meeting of the Allied Kommandatura with a good, solid bang," said the British commander, Maj. Gen. Robert Corbert, pounding the gavel at the Allied headquarters with a solid thump.

Amid all the jubilation, there were some nagging doubts.

Unity in Pensive Key
By Craig R. Whitney

BERLIN, Oct. 3—Germans, whether they had lived in East Germany or West Germany, woke up this morning in Germany, a country nobody had known since the end of World War II.

In a way, after the fall of the Berlin wall and the rest of the Iron Curtain last year, the events seemed anticlimactic, though they set the formal seal on the end of the cold war and brought an end to the division of Europe that began with Yalta and Potsdam.

But the division really began with Hitler and the war he launched in 1939, as President Richard von Weizsacker reminded Germans in a speech today on the day of unity, a glorious day of warm summerlike sunshine and golden autumn leaves. His was one of many appeals to Germans today to be "nachdenklich," a word meaning reflective, meditative and subdued that seemed to capture the national mood.

Germany's Western allies had reason to feel the same way today, as unification marked the formal end of the long cold war. By the logic of that struggle, West Germany had devoted itself to democratic political and military integration with the West.

But in the logic of peace, when the remaining 360,000 Soviet troops pull out of what was East Germany in four years, what will insure that Germans will still want American troops here, even in reduced numbers? President François Mitterrand has already announced that the 50,000 French troops in Germany will leave before Germans get tired of having them here.

A Western diplomat here wondered if or how the United States would move to preserve its security interests in Germany if, as expected, the Soviet Union continued to disintegrate.

"The major American asset—a security guarantee for Europe—is a wasting asset," the diplomat said. "I'm not sure the United States wishes to or can sustain a long-term interest in Central or Eastern Europe. Germany is the only country that can."

Now that Germany has achieved unification, it is unclear whether it will eventually turn its gaze from the West and resume—or is forced by default to assume—its former position as the dominant power of Central Europe.

But even if it does, a united Germany today has a chance to be a profoundly different country than it ever was before, as Mr. von Weizsacker pointed out. For the first time in German history, he said, unity had not come at the expense of Germany's neighbors, but was the freely accepted result of peaceful international agreement and a peaceful German revolution in the streets.

In Leipzig, where that revolution was born only 12 months ago, the mood was not only reflective but even brooding on the eve of unification, despite the German flags that hung from a few buildings.

The atmosphere in Bach's St. Thomas Church there, on the eve of unification, spoke eloquently. Inside, visitors from all over Europe had posted a whole bulletin board with prayers that things would turn out better this time than they had the last time Germany was united.

One, from a German man from Dusseldorf, said: "God give the German people an understanding of their past mistakes. It must not happen again."

On the organ, a Bach chorale-prelude on the hymn "Now Thank We All Our God" echoed through the sober Gothic nave, the cantus firmus melody seeming to speak through the plaintive minor-key accompaniment of struggle and doubt, rather than thanksgiving.

The nearby St. Nicholas Church, from which the Monday demonstrations for democracy and human rights of a year ago started out, was closed today, its bells silent.

"There are some people for whom we could hold a service of thanksgiving," said the pastor, the Rev. Christian Fuhrer, "to celebrate the fact that the borders are open and the state security police is gone.

"There are others for whom we could better hold a service of intercession—the people who have lost their jobs already or are about to, and don't have any idea what's to come. There are still others, triumphant nationalists, for whom we could hold a service of penitence. So instead we will simply keep quiet, and let the silence move people to think."

The difficulties that lie ahead are more evident to Germans from the East than those in the West, but they affect both.

Hans-Joachim Richter, a sports instructor whose brother served a year and a half in prison in East Germany for hanging a banner outside his window demanding human rights and freedom to travel, said that he was glad things had changed but that he was worried about how he could earn a living. "I wake up every morning with a knot in my stomach," he said.

His sports job, like many tens of thousands in East Germany, is being done away with next month as the artificial state structures of Communism continue to wither away.

"You have to realize that not only did people have to learn to deal with a new political system and a new currency overnight," said Heinrich Lehmann-Grube, who gave up a job as city manager of Hanover, in the West, to become mayor of Leipzig in June. "They also have to learn to deal with a new system of banking, insurance, apartment leasing, and everything else we in the West learned to take for granted over the past 40 years. It's a lot to deal with in a short time."

"This is only the beginning of a long and difficult task of rebuilding, not the end," the Mayor said of unification. "I hope we will have the financial help and the time we need to digest what has happened so far, let alone to do what we need in the future."

A Western diplomat predicted that unemployment would soar to 30 or 50 percent of the Eastern German labor force over the next year, in a population of something more than 16 million. And to give an idea of the scale of the necessary reconstruction of the former East Germany's dilapidated and worn-out capital structure, Mayor Lehmann-Grube said that in Leipzig, a city of 556,000, 30,000 apartments need urgent renovation to become habitable again, and 100,000 others are in scarcely better shape.

Some Germans and others think that this task of reconstruction, enormous as it is, is easy and manageable compared with what needs to be done to keep the Soviet Union, Poland and some other Eastern European countries from becoming dangerous sources of economic and political instability just as menacing as Soviet military might seemed during the cold war.

"We're in the process of seeing one power rise while another disintegrates," said a diplomat with long experience of Germany. But the Soviet Union, which exercised a veto on German unification until July, may have lifted it precisely because it is counting on a new alignment of forces in which a German-Soviet reconciliation, on a bigger scale than any seen heretofore, is the central element.

In that case, the question might become whether the many recent expressions of gratitude for United States support and encouragement to Germans and Berliners during the cold war years were only a last hurrah.

If the mood in Berlin was one of celebration with some anxiety, in Moscow it was a case of just clouds with no silver linings.

Amid Many Mirages, Russians Feel Lost
By Celestine Bohlen

MOSCOW, Oct. 11—Two items on Moscow Radio: The first, an old chestnut, announces that workers at a factory in Smolensk have donated a day's wages to veterans of the Great Patriotic War. The second describes the dismantling of yet another Lenin statue, in yet another Soviet city.

Two thoughts on the front page of the Communist Party newspaper

Pravda: Above the paper's name, the old motto, unchanged, "Workers of the World Unite." Farther down the page, a headline: "Can the Communist Party Hold Together?"

Two features of the Soviet consumer market: The introduction of Dick, the Soviet Union's first dog food, offered by a joint venture at 1.5 rubles a can, just as eggs disappear from state grocery stores already stripped bare of chicken, sausage, beef—in short, virtually all meat fit for human consumption.

Two aspects of the much-debated shift from a command to a market economy: A bevy of well-heeled Wall Street bankers, lawyers and accountants gather in a downtown hotel for seminars on how to set up a stock exchange, while in fields outside Moscow, office workers, doctors, professors, city hall bureaucrats and party bosses wade through ankle-deep mud to rescue a potato harvest that has become a metaphor for the country's economic quagmire.

In this quirky transition period, as a dark, rainy fall turns into winter, the Soviet Union seems suspended between two world views.

One, proceeding from the notion that all was, is and will be normal, proposes a smooth transition from Marxist slogans to capitalist comforts, to be accomplished with something simple like a "500-day plan."

The other is based on life as it already is for most people—chaotic, irrational, impenetrable, where goods run out, accidents proliferate, violence and disease break out, holes appear in the roads and neighbors get into arcane arguments over K.G.B. plots and ethnic quarrels that date from the fourth century.

Soviet reality has always been split on two levels. Television boasted of economic achievements while people continued to live in state-subsidized poverty; Intourist guides rattled off statistics on the number of hospitals, doctors, libraries and theaters while the population's health declined and cultural life receded into isolation and stagnation. People thought one thing, and said another.

The difference is that now both versions of reality have come into focus on the same screen, at the same time. Newspapers and television no longer try to hide the truth. Empty stores, rotting potatoes, angry customers, collapsing buildings—little about the harshness of Soviet life is left to the imagination anymore.

What people think of their leaders and what they read are no longer at odds. A cartoon in a republic newspaper this week had a picture of President Mikhail S. Gorbachev, under attack for his indecision, with the birthmark on his forehead shaped as a question mark.

A newspaper ran a cartoon picturing the Soviet Prime Minister, Nikolai I. Ryzhkov, knee deep in a puddle of his own tears, with Boris N. Yeltsin, the President of the Russian Republic, in a rowboat offering him a handkerchief.

But despite the rising decibels of the democratic debate, certain things remain unchanged, at least in the minds of some who still cling to their old jobs.

The Government newspaper *Izvestia* reported this week that soon after a law protecting the press went into effect this year, a document—marked "secret"—was published by the Central Department for the Protection of State Secrets, listing subjects that are still off limits to the press. They include statistics on livestock diseases, on disciplinary and moral problems in the Soviet Army, and on the inventory of rolling stock owned by the Ministry of Transportation.

Since these subjects have been written about in newspapers recently, the instructions can apparently be ignored. But other such throwbacks continue to surface, like the Tass press agency's recent full account of the meeting of the Canadian Communist Party's Central Committee.

The juxtaposition of life's mounting chaos and Soviet formalities still scrupulously observed can be bewildering. Officials at news conferences talk sanguinely about prospects for a functioning central bank, under conditions of a virtual breakdown of Soviet power. Traffic policemen chide drivers for one nonfunctioning windshield wiper at a time when breakdowns and accidents are commonplace on increasingly dangerous city streets.

Every week on Friday night, Mr. Ryzhkov goes on national television for a chat probably meant to be reassuring—as a normal head of government might do in a normal country in normal times.

But Mr. Ryzhkov's hand-wringing performance, his foot-stamping protests against criminals in the "shadow economy," separatists, saboteurs, unseasoned reformers and others identified as the source of the country's ills only reinforces the image of a Government with no one in charge.

For the last few weeks, even the transition has been in transition. A final adoption of an economic program that will lead the country out of its mess has now been delayed until October 15, a deadline that has been steadily moved forward in the hope that a consensus can be found between profoundly different points of view.

The consensus itself is probably a mirage, a goal that might have been reachable in the days of the Politburo, when a dozen men, meeting deep in the recesses of the Kremlin, would hammer out agreements on how to run the country. But now, when almost every week another region declares itself a Soviet Socialist Republic with sovereignty over all it surveys, such unanimity seems less and less possible.

In fact, many Soviet citizens now see the fight over the various economic plans as nothing more than a finely woven web of words to hide a struggle for power between the center and the republics, between the Soviet Union as it was and whatever creature will take its place.

For the Soviet citizen trying to decipher between the debate and the reality, the question is which is the one they are living in now.

For almost a year, Soviet citizens had been waiting for Gorbachev to choose the path of economic development. Would it be the Ryzhkov plan or the more radical approach favored by Shatalin, or would it be a combination synthesizing the two conceptions? Would it call for harsh and speedy implementation? Finally, if not quite decisively, Gorbachev declared himself.

Gorbachev Offers His Plan to Remake Soviet Economy, but Includes No Timetable
By Bill Keller

MOSCOW, Oct. 16—After months of wavering, President Mikhail S. Gorbachev sent the Soviet Parliament a compromise economic reform program today that calls for dismantling the state's economic monopoly, but sets no timetable.

The document embraced the broad principles of a revolutionary program devised by a team of radical economists in September: selling state property into private hands, lifting Government price controls and handing over many economic decisions to the governments of the country's 15 republics. But the Soviet leader called for a more gradual transition, dropping the 500-day timetable that the radicals said was necessary to ram the plan past Government bureaucrats' resistance.

Mr. Gorbachev was also vague in spelling out the rights of his increasingly assertive republic and local governments in setting economic policy.

Under his plan, many important sectors would remain under the control of the central Government, with its accompanying bureaucracy. These would include transportation, communications, defense industries, energy, banking and foreign trade. In addition, the Government would continue to regulate the prices of certain goods and services. Representatives of the republics would take part in a joint "interregional economic committee."

Stanislav S. Shatalin, the economics professor and Gorbachev adviser who promoted the radical free-market plan, said tonight that he was "not very" happy with the final version. In a telephone interview, he declined to discuss the Gorbachev plan in detail. But asked if it would lead to a real market economy, he said simply, "No."

Legislators said Mr. Gorbachev's plan was likely to be approved by the Soviet Parliament, which is desperate to be seen doing something to remedy the worsening shortages in the stores and the mounting anxiety of consumers. But the Soviet leader faces a far more difficult task in getting the 15 republics to go along with it.

Boris N. Yeltsin, the President of the Russian republic, tonight denounced the Gorbachev plan as a tactical retreat that would allow the central bureaucracy to retain its monopoly on power indefinitely. He said that like earlier Government economic plans, it was bound to fail in a matter of months.

The Russian republic has already approved the Shatalin 500-day plan, and the three Baltic republics also favor it.

Mr. Gorbachev's plan, completed in a final brainstorming session that ended after midnight, was billed as a synthesis of two rival proposals—a gradualist draft by the Government of Prime Minister Nikolai I. Ryzhkov and the more radical plan, devised in September by a panel of economists representing Mr. Gorbachev and Mr. Yeltsin, chaired by Mr. Shatalin.

It is the fourth proposed "market transition" program presented to Parliament since December, but the first to have Mr. Gorbachev's full endorsement. He is scheduled to present it personally to Parliament on Friday.

As a declaration of intentions, the Gorbachev plan is a sharp departure from the values and mechanics on which the Soviet economy was built. "The whole world experience has proved the vitality and efficiency of the market economy," the preamble declares. Mr. Gorbachev has dropped his earlier reference to a "regulated" market, and he uses the word "socialist" only once, saying, "The transition to the market does not contradict the socialist choice of our people."

But it is uncertain whether Mr. Gorbachev and Mr. Ryzhkov have the political influence to win public compliance with the decrees and laws needed to make the plan work. Its success will depend in large part on the cooperation of such popular elected figures as Mr. Yeltsin and the radical mayors of Moscow and Leningrad.

Mr. Gorbachev said in September that he favored Mr. Shatalin's radical alternative, but in the end he evidently decided he was not prepared to risk the degree of shock therapy and the surrender of central economic control embodied in that plan.

Critics said the Shatalin plan would lead to rocketing inflation and large-scale unemployment, economic chaos and political anarchy.

Embracing that plan would almost certainly have meant repudiating his loyal Prime Minister and building a new coalition government including more independent political figures.

It had been almost a year since the enthusiastic wave of protest and democratic yearnings had crested over Eastern Europe. In that time the dreams of many had been fulfilled, but now, having escaped from what was widely regarded as a dreadful past, they felt a rising discomfort about the immediate future.

For Eastern Europe Now, a New Disillusion
By Serge Schmemann

PRAGUE—A group of Czechoslovak students, veterans of the demonstrations a year ago that brought down the Communist Government, issued a statement recently urging that the anniversary not be marked this year, because "we don't want former Communist officials coming out cheering and laughing in our faces."

Complaining that the hopes and expectations of the student-led protests of a year ago had become mired in half-measures and disputes, and that old bureaucrats still held sway throughout the Government, they declared, "There's no reason to call our revolution a 'velvet' one."

However profound and indelible the changes that have swept their nation and the rest of Eastern Europe, theirs was a disappointment and disillusionment that could be felt to varying degrees from the rusty shipyards of Gdansk in Poland to the frequently darkened streets of Timisoara in Rumania.

All through the region, newly liberated people face recession, unemployment and insecurity. Obsolete industries crumble on exposure to free markets, energy shortages loom with the shrinking of Soviet supplies and the crisis in the Persian Gulf, and Western investments are slow in coming.

It is arguable that the extraordinary pace set last fall could not have been sustained and that the revolutions could not be completed without a heavy price. To anyone returning to the Czechoslovak capital or to any of the Eastern European countries a year after the last of them broke with Soviet-imposed governments, it is also evident that history has known few shifts as dramatic and swift as the disintegration of Eastern European Communist rule.

Free elections have been held at least once in every country of Eastern Europe. Reformers, former dissidents or elected politicians have taken over all the citadels of fallen tyrants. Free newspapers—like *Lidove Noviny,* the influential Prague daily in which the Czechoslovak students published their statement—have proliferated.

Borders have opened, public debate has flourished, and all across the land, Soviet occupation troops have begun a humiliating homeward trek, peddling uniforms and shedding discipline as they go.

Despite the grousing of the students, the "revolutions" of last fall—the wave of mass protests that pushed out faltering governments—stand as proud national myths. Germans play and replay the scenes of dancing on the Berlin wall the night it fell open on November 9. Bulgarians celebrate the fall of Todor Zhivkov on November 10. Czechoslovaks light candles to the students beaten on November 17. Rumanians commemorate the shooting of protesters in Rumania on December 17.

Nonetheless, as hardships mount, so does social unrest. Taxi drivers in Budapest blockade the city to protest fuel price increases, protesters march through Bucharest, and refugees and black marketeers threaten to swell into a huge revival of the medieval movement of tribes across the Continent.

Ancient ethnic rivalries, suppressed but hardly erased by 45 years of imposed Communist "internationalism," resurface with a vengeance.

And everywhere the refrain is "We never thought it would go so fast."

To revisit Eastern Europe a year after is to discover people who have lost their chains, but also their security, their illusions and often their bearings.

These are some images of peoples in transition.

In Bratislava, the capital of the Slovak minority in Czechoslovakia that has unexpectedly raised a cry for independence, an intellectual tries to explain why an ethnic group of 5 million with no outstanding grievance has suddenly become seized with nationalist fervor.

"The Slovaks are a peasant people who have spent most of their history under someone else, mostly Hungarians," said Boris Lazar, a professor of philosophy and member of Public Against Violence, the Slovak citizens' movement associated with President Vaclav Havel's Civic Forum. "They have a deep inferiority complex. The thinking is if we don't make a pitch for independence now, nobody in the world will know we exist."

Now, freed from the constraints of the enforced internationalism of Communism but remote from the anti-nationalist trends of the West, the Slovaks and similar minorities across Eastern Europe have tried to fill the vacuum left by Communism with reassertion of nationalism and revival of ancient feuds.

The Slovak rallying cause, fanned by the nationalist movement Matica Slovenska, is that some of the 600,000 Hungarians who live in Slovakia refuse to speak Slovak. In fact, several studies have shown that the strongest sentiments thrive in communities where there are the fewest Hungarians, suggesting that the nationalism has less to do with language than with a new assertiveness.

"Suddenly set free, people are looking for anything to grasp on to," Mr. Lazar said. "Here, in the Soviet Union, in Hungary, all over, nationalism has become one of the authentic expressions of post-Communism."

At the Rumanian-Yugoslav border on the road from Belgrade to Timisoara, Soviet cars are backed up for miles into Rumania. Many have trailers and tanks of gasoline lashed to roof racks. Angry drivers confront nervous Yugoslav border guards. "Bring in the army!" shouts a red-eyed, unshaven Russian.

The Yugoslavs watch anxiously while officers talk to representatives of the Russians. Across the border, Rumanian border troops are reinforced by soldiers with dogs as tensions rise.

For about two months, Russians had driven across Rumania in ever-growing numbers to peddle goods in Yugoslavia—instruments, clothes, fur hats. They would then convert the Yugoslav money into dollars and return with Western goods. The trip was long and difficult. Soviet customs agents charged $100 to $200 in "duty" on the way out, and drivers brought enough gasoline to make it to Yugoslavia and back.

But without notice on the evening of November 4, Yugoslavia shut its borders to Soviet citizens. "If they're going to shut the border, they should've let us know before we left the Soviet Union!" an infuriated driver shouted.

The scene is hardly unique. Ever since their borders opened, East Europeans by the millions have flocked west—first to gawk, next to barter, then to work illegally, finally to try to stay.

A year ago it was the East Germans fleeing through Hungary to West Germany, and the West blinked away its tears at the image of people celebrating their newfound freedom. Then swarms of Poles descended on West Berlin, then Czechs and Hungarians flooded into Vienna, and then Rumanians and Bulgarians began a westward trek. Most Western nations have now reinstated restrictions on travelers from the East, and in September, Austria sent troops to patrol its eastern borders.

The real fear among West Europeans is that the first waves of black marketeers and refugees are only the vanguard of a mass westward migration as Eastern societies, and especially the Soviet Union, disintegrate.

In Budapest, everyone talks anxiously about "the events last weekend." On October 27 and 28, after the Government abruptly raised fuel prices by 60 percent, taxi drivers virtually blockaded Budapest, some other cities and some border crossings until the prices were lowered.

The demonstration supplied a brutal jolt to a country that had become accustomed to the highest standard of living and the most open society in the East, but which under democracy had become mired in political haggling that often seemed oblivious to the looming economic crisis.

"The blockade was a traumatic demonstration of a sense of disenfranchisement," said Jozsef Martin, an editor of *Magyar Nemzet.* "The question it raised was whether the Government was capable of modernizing, of raising prices. We have to modernize, but the question is, can we cope with the social side effects? There seem to be no resources left in the tolerance of the people."

There had been signs of frustration before, especially in the shrinking turnout for each of the six rounds of voting Hungary has had in less than a year. Less than 30 percent of registered voters turned out for the recent municipal elections.

By all accounts, the real test is still to come, for Hungary as for its neighbors. As of January 1, the Soviet Union will charge convertible currency for its oil, and even then it may not have enough to meet East European demand. At the same time, the crisis in the gulf has pushed the price of oil beyond the means of most states.

"Every increase of $1 in the price of a barrel of oil translates into a loss of $70–80 million in our economy," said Andras Vertes, head of the Economic Research Institute in Budapest. The institute has predicted that the crisis will become worse in 1991. But then the institute has not tried to forecast beyond that for now. "There are just too many uncertainties," Mr. Vertes said.

The greatest variable is the huge, chaotic land to the East, the Soviet Union, on which all the Eastern European countries had been compelled to depend to varying degrees. The question is not only how much oil the Soviet Union will produce and how much it will charge, but even more what will survive of the disintegrating empire.

"The collapse of Russia hangs over us all," Mr. Vertes said.

In Prague, a visitor inquires about a dissident who had been forced to wash windows and tend boilers after his fall from grace when Soviet tanks ended the "Prague spring" of 1968. "Lubos Dobrowsky?" a friend of his says, "He was appointed Defense Minister last week."

Rushing out of a Cabinet meeting later that day, Mr. Dobrowsky paused briefly in the hallway of the Government building. The call came suddenly, he said. He was in Poland in his earlier function as a Deputy Foreign Minister when President Vaclav Havel, a friend, called at 2 A.M. and asked him to become Defense Minister.

A year ago that might have been the opening of a leisurely chat in Mr. Dobrowsky's small basement room next to the boilers, where the former journalist filled his time between checking gauges by translating Russian and Polish literature into Czech. But now he had no time to talk. A chauffeured car was waiting outside, and there were crises to tackle, a country to run.

The story is hardly unusual in Prague, where Mr. Havel has drawn liberally on fellow signers of Charter 77, a human-rights document produced by prominent dissidents in 1977, to staff the new Government. Jiri Dienstbier, the Foreign Minister, was also recently a boiler-tender.

In the majestic Hrad, the castle overlooking Prague that serves as the seat of government, Mr. Havel's press spokesman, Michael Zantowski, still greets visitors tieless and in jeans. Mr. Zantowski, 41 years old, was trained as a psychologist, then worked for two years at the Reuters news agency before heeding Mr. Havel's summons to the Hrad.

"At first we were all admittedly amateurish," he said of the early days. "There were a dozen of us here, and we couldn't find any help from the people here; most of the time we couldn't find the people. We were inexperienced, understaffed, underequipped, overworked. It's much better now. We no longer have to wonder who'll open the mail."

Mr. Zantowski may still wear jeans, but the palace guards outside stand in spiffy new uniforms designed by Teodor Pistek, a costume designer and friend of Mr. Havel's who created the costumes for the show *Amadeus*.

The theatrical touch by the playwright-President contributes to a sense that the people running the newly liberated countries are far from professionals. One consequence is that the new leaders often have been compelled to keep on former Communist managers, sometimes to public dissatisfaction.

"It's important to remember the dimensions," Mr. Zantowski said. "The Communists had 1.7 million members last year, plus another 500,000 to 600,000 members who were expelled in 1968. With families, that's about 5 million out of a total population of 15 million. So it's just not possible to pretend that they don't exist, to screen them out. Besides, we are principally opposed to collective guilt."

Yet throughout the region, the abrupt collapse of Communist governments has left a sense of unfinished business. In societies where thousands of people served the oppressor and tens of thousands informed or otherwise collaborated to survive, feelings of guilt mingle murkily with a need for vengeance.

In Timisoara, where on December 17 security forces opened fire on demonstrators in an incident that catalyzed the fall of Nicolae Ceausescu, people say that neither the identity of those who did the shooting nor even the number of victims has yet become known.

"There's an investigation, but people are still afraid to give evidence," a resident said, pausing by a memorial to the victims on the Opera Square. "Besides, we're not so sure the Securitate is gone."

There are indications that much of the old Securitate, Mr. Ceausescu's feared political police, has survived in the new Rumanian Information Service. More broadly, the political situation of Rumania under President Ion Iliescu—a former reform Communist who emerged from political oblivion to take charge of the National Salvation Front that came to power in December after the fall of the Ceausescus—is far from settled.

The reluctance to take action against former Communists, however, has not been limited to Rumania. In fact, the execution of Mr. Ceausescu and his wife, Elena, last December, and the subsequent trial of their son Nicu, have been among the few measures taken against former leaders anywhere in Eastern Europe.

The only other Communist official to face justice so far has been Miroslav Stepan, the former party chief in Prague. But even he has yet to go to jail.

Erich Honecker, the former party leader of East Germany, sits in a Soviet military hospital, while two of his comrades—Erich Mielke, the former Interior Minister, and Harry Tisch, the former head of trade unions—are in prison hospitals. None has been tried. In Poland, two senior officials of the Interior Ministry were recently arrested in connection with the slaying of the Rev. Jerzy Popieluszko, a dissident, but both have been released.

"There's pressure for a reckoning, but it's hard to see how this can be accommodated other than in a symbolic way—perhaps some form of collective condemnation, or some sort of moral tribunal," Mr. Zantowski said. "But we don't want a witch hunt."

As the troubles deepen, the eyes of Eastern Europe turn increasingly to the West. A widespread faith prevails that the West will never abandon these fledgling democracies after preaching for so long the merits of free enterprise and human rights.

"We will not be able to sustain democratic order without Western countries," said Mr. Martin of *Magyar Nemzet*. "Without Western aid, people will head West. But thank God, it's in the long-term interest of the West that East Europe should not become a volcano."

It is a faith born of long years in which the West wrestled fiercely with the Soviet Union for ideological and territorial dominion and greeted any stirring of independence in the East with hurrahs and rewards. But now that neither Marx nor Moscow stirs the fears they once did, even that assumption seems no longer secure.

"What you see is not a nostalgia, just a recognition of how far we still have to go," said Miklos Haraszti, a novelist and leader of the opposition Alliance of Free Democrats in Hungary.

"Post-Communism is all the real problems coming to the surface," he said. "But I believe the people are ready for hardships, once they are given a clear scenario. I believe that there's an almost invincible desire to maintain democracy, to remain in the West. In fact, for me one of the greatest surprises of the past year is how wise the people have been."

In Western Europe, too, there were mounting worries about the consequences of the changes that had been so enthusiastically applauded a year earlier.

Surprise for Western Europe: Eastern Kin Come Knocking
By Craig R. Whitney

LONDON, Nov. 14—A year after freedom began sweeping through the countries of Eastern Europe, the full implications, including some unpleasant surprises, are beginning to sink in for their rich Western neighbors.

Eastern Europeans used to be the distant, poor relatives they felt sorry for and sent presents to on holidays. On rare visits behind the Iron Curtain, they could feel good about themselves by deploring conditions there and issuing invitations that could never be taken up to come and visit.

Now that the poor relatives are suddenly free to travel, it is as if they are not only showing up on the doorstep but camping out in the spare bedroom for weeks on end and cooking meals in the bathroom. Next they threaten to bring scores of distant cousins and friends to sleep on the living room floor while they all look for work.

Their wealthier Western uncles and aunts have offered the ragged invading hordes long-term loans and stakes to start new businesses at home, but not enough. Now they are unlikely to come up with much more, because of worries about economic recession, rising oil prices, and the threat of a Middle East war.

One result, in the Western countries nearest the border with Eastern Europe, is a rising tide of anti–Eastern European popular sentiment.

On Mariahilferstrasse, one of the main shopping streets in prosperous Vienna, electronics and jewelry stores have hired hawkers who solicit Czech, Slovak and Hungarian customers in their languages. In the more upscale stores on the street, those customers are tolerated but not preferred, one clerk said, perhaps because of police statistics that showed that 34.3 percent of all shoplifting last year was perpetrated by "foreigners."

500

And on tree-lined Herbststrasse, near the state employment office in the 16th district, hundreds of foreigners mainly from Poland stand at the curb every weekday morning. They hope somebody in need of casual labor will pick them up and give them a few hours or days of employment.

The Poles work without benefit of health or unemployment insurance, so the labor is cheap—and illegal.

"You should see the street at 7 A.M.," a clerk in Karl Rath's hardware store, Beate Seidel, said the other morning. "You can't even see the other side of the street."

Therese Jonas, out for a walk with her poodle, has lived in the neighborhood since her parents moved to Vienna in 1912 and finds the Eastern European influx a menace.

"They use the lobbies of my apartment building as toilets and make a mess," she said. "They shouldn't let so many Poles come here, that's all."

Responding to the public pressure in the campaign for national elections in October, Austria's coalition Government reimposed visa requirements for Poles—though not for Hungarians or Czechs—on September 7.

Also in September the Austrians began sending patrols to catch illegal immigrants along the Hungarian border. The hunt there is not for Hungarians, Czechs or Slovaks, who need no special permission to enter, but mainly for unwanted visitors from Rumania, who do require visas.

"I am ashamed that Austria wants to erect a new Iron Curtain on its borders," the Roman Catholic Bishop of Graz, Johann Weber, said then. Some Austrian politicians also acknowledge embarrassment.

"We just need a breathing space until these flows are regularized," said a former Austrian Foreign Minister, Dr. Peter Jankowitsch, who said the rule would probably be lifted "in six months or a year."

The presence of so many unwanted foreigners gave a surge to the right-wing Austrian Freedom Party, which increased its share of the vote, from less than 10 percent in 1986 to 16.6 percent in October, with a xenophobic campaign and advertisements proclaiming, "Vienna must not become Chicago."

Similar feelings exist in Germany, but there they have so far been submerged politically in the general jubilation over unification, which took effect on October 3 and is the most spectacular byproduct of the revolutions in Eastern Europe.

Chancellor Helmut Kohl's long reluctance to guarantee the Oder-

Neisse line as the permanent German-Polish border, which he formally abandoned this month, put a strain on Bonn's relations with Warsaw that is only beginning to ease. The two countries signed a border treaty today, but Prime Minister Tadeusz Mazowiecki of Poland said in a meeting with Mr. Kohl at the border on November 8 that the old East-West political divisions should not become divisions between rich and poor. But Poles keep flocking west to find work, money and goods while their own economy undergoes the wrenching transition to market principles.

Germany, which also does not admit Polish visitors without visas though Poland admits former East German citizens without formalities, hopes to drop the requirement soon because it has become superfluous. More than 1.7 million visas were issued to Poles by the former West and East German Governments during the last year, according to the Foreign Ministry in Bonn.

Asked if the German authorities did not fear a flood from the East when the requirement was lifted, a Foreign Ministry official, Jurgen Chrobog, repeated last year's figures and said, "The flood has already arrived."

But so far, at least, it still ebbs and flows. All but a few hundred of the Poles who come return home after they've done their shopping or earned some spare Western currency by working.

Ethnic Germans from Poland, Rumania and the Soviet Union, on the other hand, number in the millions and all of them would be among the first potential immigrants to Germany if economic trends in those countries do not soon improve, Western officials fear. One consequence has been a move in Germany and Austria to redefine and restrict the laws on political asylum to clearly exclude economic refugees.

What happens if the Soviet economy disintegrates is now a problem preoccupying NATO and European Community officials in Brussels. Some of them have begun to talk of the possibility of millions of Soviet refugees on the roads by next spring, but there is no clear idea of what the West should do if that happens. . . .

To make Eastern European industry viable will take at least $135 billion per year of capital investment for at least a decade, which could only come from Western countries, according to a report by the London-based Center for Economic Policy Research. But except for West German firms pouring money into eastern Germany, it has not been happening.

"At present, I believe we are not doing anywhere near as much as is required, either in the short run or in the long term," said Prof. Richard Portes, the center's director. "I'm very conscious of the experience of Poland in 1981, when a nascent movement towards democratic structures broke down because of the collapse of economic structures. We could have a similar pattern in Hungary, Poland, and Bulgaria, which are already heavily indebted. The democratic structures are there, but they're fragile."

Meanwhile. Gorbachev continued to issue new initiatives as he sought to regain the credibility he had when his "new thinking" was truly new and novel. Shortly after he had disclosed his latest refined scheme for reshaping the economy, he announced he would shake up his most senior military and civilian advisers. Then, a day later, he unveiled his formula for power sharing between Moscow and the increasingly fractious republics.

Soviets Adopt Emergency Plan to Center Power in Gorbachev and Leaders of the Republics
By Bill Keller

MOSCOW, Nov. 17—Warning that the country was sliding toward chaos, President Mikhail S. Gorbachev today announced the creation of a new emergency power structure in which he will govern along with leaders of the republics.

The measures, promptly and overwhelmingly approved by Parliament, would abolish the post held by Prime Minister Nikolai I. Ryzhkov, who is seen by critics as a chief obstacle to the rapid introduction of free markets.

Mr. Gorbachev said the Federation Council, now a purely advisory body made up of the leaders of the 15 republics, would be transformed into the chief executive agency, a move that would co-opt Mr. Gorbachev's most troublesome rivals into sharing responsibility for the union.

But the final word would belong to Mr. Gorbachev, whose powers would be enhanced by a new security council overseeing the army, the police and the K.G.B., and by a network of presidential representatives around the country to enforce orders from the center.

"I propose carrying out an urgent fundamental reorganization of executive power in the center by subordinating it to the President, directly to the President," he said.

The Soviet leader also announced that within two weeks the Government would announce an emergency food program to supply the public through the winter and dispel fears of hunger. He provided no details.

While Mr. Gorbachev in theory has already accumulated vast powers, his decrees aimed at economic change and civil order have frequently been countermanded by republic and local government or neutralized by the balky Government bureaucracy.

The initial reaction was overwhelmingly positive—not only from hard-liners alarmed by increasing instability, but from some of the democratic insurgents, who said it could form the basis for a coalition government of consensus.

But there was no reaction from President Boris N. Yeltsin of the Russian republic, who on Friday called on Mr. Gorbachev to share power with the republics in an emergency anti-crisis committee. An aide to Mr. Yeltsin said he wanted to study the proposals and would probably not comment until the next session of the Russian Parliament on Tuesday.

Some allies of Mr. Yeltsin said the Gorbachev proposal was close enough to the Russian leader's scheme for a coalition government that it might be acceptable, while others said his suspicions of the Soviet leader run so deep that he could never agree to a subordinate position. . . .

The changes outlined by Mr. Gorbachev were interrupted by hearty applause and later approved by a vote of 316 to 19, with 31 abstentions. . . .

A close aide to Mr. Gorbachev, Georgy K. Shakhnazarov, said the introduction of direct presidential rule had been in the works for some time, but the impatience of the legislators on Friday had convinced him to move sooner.

"He was going to move in this direction sooner or later," Mr. Shakhnazarov told reporters. "Yesterday served as a turning point, and it pushed him to do this."

After his chilly reception in the Parliament on Friday, Mr. Gorbachev reportedly had a general conversation in the afternoon with Mr. Yeltsin. That night he discussed the state of the union with Communist Party leaders at a meeting of the party's governing Politburo, according to Vladimir A. Ivashno, the deputy party chairman.

Mr. Shakhnazarov said Mr. Gorbachev planned to put most of the new scheme into effect by decree in a matter of days. It would remain in force until enactment of a new "union treaty" that Mr. Gorbachev has proposed as the basis for a redesigned Soviet federation.

With many republics skeptical or flatly opposed to his draft of the new union, the prospects for approval were murky at best.

Mr. Gorbachev's measures announced today would leave the Parliament intact, but would dissolve much of the existing executive branch. The position of Prime Minister would be abolished, and his Cabinet, the huge Council of Ministers, would be demoted to a "working apparatus" of the new leadership, according to Mr. Shakhnazarov.

Mr. Ryzhkov, who has been Mr. Gorbachev's loyal but increasingly unpopular Prime Minister since 1985, said he did not know if there was a place for him in the new scheme, but other deputies predicted he would retire from government.

Using much more whimper than bang, Todor Zhivkov, the once widely feared Communist strongman of Bulgaria, talked of his years in office as prosecutors prepared to place him on trial.

Bulgarian Communist Stalwart Says He'd Do It All Differently
By Chuck Sudetic

SOFIA, BULGARIA, Nov. 27—Todor Zhivkov, Bulgaria's deposed Communist dictator, long regarded as the East bloc leader most subservient to Moscow, looked back on his long political career during an interview here on Monday and said it was all a big mistake.

"If I had to do it over again, I would not even be a Communist, and if Lenin were alive today he would say the same thing," said Mr. Zhivkov as he sat in his granddaughter's luxurious villa on a hillside above Sofia, where he remains under house arrest.

It was hardly surprising that the biggest winner in the all-German elections was the man who had been among the first to foresee them.

Kohl's Coalition Elected to Lead Unified Germany
By Serge Schmemann

BONN, Dec. 2—Chancellor Helmut Kohl claimed the reward for his stewardship of German unity today with a victory for his coalition in the first free all-German election in 58 years.

The results of the parliamentary elections were generally interpreted as an endorsement of German unification and the role played in it by Mr. Kohl, leader of the Christian Democratic Party, and Foreign Minister Hans-Dietrich Genscher of the Free Democratic Party.

The parties that had wavered or opposed unity—the Social Democrats, the Greens and the East German Communist Party, now called the Party of Democratic Socialism—all fared badly.

"If there is a general significance to the result, it is that unity is now being ratified by the people," said Johannes Gross, a prominent political commentator.

In elections in Poland, however, there were considerable surprises. In the first phase of the voting, Stanislaw Tyminski, a total outsider who had spent the Solidarity years as a businessman in Canada and Peru, acquired enough of a following to place second, knocking Prime Minister Tadeusz Mazowiecki out of the race and out of the office. In the runoff, the warring factions of the old Solidarity coalition were able to patch up their differences to rally behind Lech Walesa.

Poland Elects Walesa President in Landslide
By Stephen Engelberg

GDANSK, Dec. 9—Lech Walesa, the charismatic leader of the Solidarity movement for a decade, won a landslide runoff victory today in Poland's first direct presidential elections, according to exit polls and early returns.

In voting for Mr. Walesa, Poles chose a 47-year-old electrician with a vocational school education and a sure touch for mass politics to guide this formerly Communist nation through the next phase of its difficult transition to capitalism.

Mr. Walesa, the winner of the 1983 Nobel Prize for his role in the Solidarity labor union, soundly defeated Stanislaw Tyminski, a previously unknown émigré businessman from Canada and Peru whose pledge to improve Poles' lives within a month carried him into the runoff, ahead of the sitting Prime Minister, Tadeusz Mazowiecki.

Infas, a West German polling company, which has accurately forecast every election in Eastern Europe this year, said Mr. Walesa would finish with 74.7 percent of the vote and Mr. Tyminski with 25.3 percent.

"I will do everything so that every Pole owns a share of Poland in his hands," a jubilant Mr. Walesa said at a news conference tonight at his headquarters here, a few blocks from the shipyard where the Solidarity movement was born a decade ago. "As far as Mr. Tyminski is concerned, I think as quickly as he was born he will fade out, because truly he did not propose anything tangible. They were just slogans."

As the holidays approached, there was yet another surprise from Moscow.

Shevardnadze Stuns Kremlin by Quitting Foreign Ministry and Warning of "Dictatorship"
By Bill Keller

MOSCOW, Dec. 20—Foreign Minister Eduard A. Shevardnadze, President Mikhail S. Gorbachev's closest confederate in negotiating an end to the cold war, abruptly resigned today with an impassioned warning that "reactionaries" threatened his country with dictatorship.

"I cannot reconcile myself with what is happening in my country," Mr. Shevardnadze told his stunned audience at the Congress of People's Deputies, adding that he was weary of defending his policies against hard-liners.

Mr. Gorbachev, who said he was not warned of the resignation, sat frozen on the dais of the Kremlin Palace of Congresses. He still seemed distressed hours later when he took the podium to accuse his colleague in perestroika of deserting him at a time of political and economic crisis.

"Now, perhaps, is our most difficult time, and to leave at this time is unforgivable," he said. "This must be condemned."

Mr. Gorbachev disclosed that he had planned to recommend Mr. Shevardnadze for the new post of Vice President, where he could apply his artful diplomacy to healing the country's internal divisions. But Mr. Shevardnadze had already said publicly that if offered the post he would decline.

Electrified by the unparalleled spectacle of a top Soviet official resigning on principle, the Congress voted overwhelmingly to reaffirm the course of Soviet foreign policy and to urge that Mr. Shevardnadze reconsider. The Foreign Minister's spokesman, Vitaly Churkin, said the decision was final.

Mr. Shevardnadze said he would stay on until the Supreme Soviet, the standing Parliament, approved the change. The Parliament is not expected to meet before the new year.

Some legislators wondered if Mr. Shevardnadze might return to his native Georgia, where as Communist Party chief he had a reputation as a ruthless fighter of corruption and an early economic liberalizer. The republic is currently under control of a separatist government that regards Mr. Shevardnadze as a foe of Georgian nationalism because of his close ties to Mr. Gorbachev, who is a Russian.

Mr. Shevardnadze's announcement today seemed especially addressed to the bickering supporters of reform—perhaps including Mr. Gorbachev himself—as a warning to unite against those pressing for a return to authoritarian rule backed by force.

"The reformers have gone into hiding," Mr. Shevardnadze said, his voice taut with emotion. "A dictatorship is approaching—I tell you that with full responsibility. No one knows what this dictatorship will be like, what kind of dictator will come to power and what order will be established."

Mr. Shevardnadze spoke angrily and without notes, and except for allusions to a few outspoken critics of his policies he did not spell out what he regarded as the threat to democracy.

Although his resignation was clearly a major political problem for Mr. Gorbachev, Mr. Shevardnadze stressed that his devotion to Mr. Gorbachev and his policies remained strong, and voiced no criticism of the Soviet leader's plan, now before the Congress, to enlarge his presidential powers.

No one among numerous legislators and officials interviewed today said they believed Mr. Shevardnadze's speech meant dictatorship was imminent, in the sense that there would be some early return to the tight controls of the past.

Now in his sixth year of an enterprise that has remade the world order, Mr. Shevardnadze has for some time seemed tired and frustrated by the sniping of hard-liners who blame him for the contraction of Soviet power.

One of the hard-liners who provoked Mr. Shevardnadze's wrath, Col. Viktor I. Alksnis, hailed Mr. Shevardnadze's departure as a triumph for those who want order restored.

"Personally I am very satisfied," he said.

Today Mr. Shevardnadze lashed out at critics who have accused him of putting the Soviet Union at risk of war by siding so closely with the United States in the Persian Gulf crisis. He also defended the

Government's policies in favor of unification of Germany against those he said had accused him of "unilateral concessions."

The President's spokesman, Vitaly Ignatenko, rushed to tell reporters that there would be no changes in the foreign policy course that Mr. Shevardnadze helped draw up and execute.

"Our foreign policy does not change in one minute," Mr. Ignatenko said. "It does not depend on one person." . . .

Mr. Shevardnadze has been a target of personal invective from those who view the retrenchment of Soviet power as a humiliation.

Over the last year he has been openly attacked in the Communist Party and the Congress for tolerating the reunification of Germany and the collapse of satellite governments in Eastern Europe, for rushing the military forces home to languish in squalid tent cities, for negotiating arms treaties with the West that cut disproportionately into Soviet missiles and tanks, for accepting food aid from the West, and most recently for following too closely the American lead on policy in the gulf.

Mr. Shevardnadze has fought a fierce battle in public, and reportedly inside the leadership, to keep his country aligned with the American-led alliance that is isolating Iraq.

A hard-line parliamentary faction, Soyuz, has complained despite numerous reassurances that Mr. Shevardnadze is risking having Soviet troops drawn into a war in the gulf to protect American interests.

"Charges are made that the Foreign Minister plans to land troops in the Persian Gulf, in the region," Mr. Shevardnadze said today, in a tone of exasperation. "I explained that there are no such plans. They do not exist. Nobody is going to send a single military man, or even a single representative of the Soviet armed forces there."

WINTER 1990

In *Poland, where much of the process of renewal had begun, a formal changing of the guard was taking place. First, General Wojciech Jaruzelski, the last Warsaw Pact leader besides Gorbachev still to remain in office, walked away from his post.*

As Jaruzelski Leaves Office: A Traitor or a Patriot to Poles?

By Stephen Engelberg

WARSAW, Dec. 21—There was no fanfare or ceremony today at the Belweder Palace as Gen. Wojciech Jaruzelski, the last of Eastern Europe's old-guard Communist leaders, stepped down as Poland's President.

Nonetheless, this snow-swept winter day marked the passing of an epoch in which the general presided over the long retreat of the Communist Party.

As he steps down, the ambiguous record he leaves behind has become the object of a growing debate. Was he essentially a Soviet satrap who happened to be in office when Moscow's power ebbed, or was he primarily a Polish patriot who actively and cunningly set the pace of the transition from totalitarian rule?

As the Communist leader who imposed martial law in December 1981 to crush Solidarity as a free trade union, General Jaruzelski was widely condemned by Poles as a traitor. Yet eight years later, after Mikhail S. Gorbachev loosened Moscow's reins on Warsaw, it was General Jaruzelski who steered Poland's Communist Party as it became the first one in Eastern Europe to relinquish power to the opposition.

For most of his tenure he has maintained the posture of a stiff military man who kept his feelings behind the dark glasses he wore as a result of retinal problems. The corset he wore to ease old war wounds added to the impression of unyielding rigidity. But in taking his leave over the last few weeks, the stoic military officer for the first time offered his countrymen some sense of his emotional responses to the storms of the last decade.

In a televised address last week, the general declared that the suffering caused by his decisions "hurts me like a thorn in my flesh."

"As a soldier, I know that the commander is responsible for every man and every thing," he continued. "The words 'I apologize' may sound banal. But I cannot find any other words."

Lech Walesa then assumed the office of President with its newly expanded powers.

Tearful Walesa Is Sworn In as President
By Stephen Engelberg

WARSAW, Dec. 22—Lech Walesa, the 47-year-old shipyard electrician and founder of the Solidarity movement, was sworn in as Poland's President today in a day of pageantry that evoked this country's centuries of struggle against dismemberment and domination.

Blinking back tears, Mr. Walesa took the oath of office at noon at the lectern of Parliament and promised to shake this nation of 38 million from "passivity and discouragement."

"With this moment, the Third Republic of Poland is solemnly beginning," Mr. Walesa told the legislators. "Nobody, nothing can lessen this fact. The bad time, when the authorities of our state were elected under pressure from aliens or in effect of imposed compromises is coming to an end."

In Moscow, delegates to the Congress of People's Deputies considered Gorbachev's pleas to restructure the country's overlapping and competing institutions of power.

Gorbachev Given Direct Authority over His Cabinet
By Bill Keller

MOSCOW, Dec. 25—President Mikhail S. Gorbachev won general approval today for his plan to remake the Soviet Government, but he suffered an embarrassing setback when the Congress of People's Deputies denied him important new enforcement powers.

The Congress, the nation's supreme constitutional authority, agreed to give the President more direct control over the legal machinery of the executive branch by making Cabinet ministers directly subordinate to him and by creating the post of Vice President.

But Mr. Gorbachev's proposals to create a "Supreme State Inspectorate," a sort of presidential police force to assure that official decrees are carried out, was narrowly rejected after some deputies asserted that it might concentrate dictatorial powers in the hands of one man.

The mood of the Congress as it ended offered an overarching metaphor for the passing year. Enthusiasm and euphoria had flagged over twelve months and the familiar devils of cynicism, fear and indecision were reasserting themselves. The tendency was evident all over Eastern Europe, but it was most strongly felt in Moscow.

Mourning Soviet Reform
By Bill Keller

MOSCOW, Dec. 28—If the First Congress of People's Deputies, a year and a half ago, was a baptism of infant democracy and an exorcism of Stalinist demons, the fourth Congress, which ended on Thursday night, was a wake.

With desperate noise and little cheer, it marked not only the passing of this year of sunken spirits, but in the minds of many participants, the end of the period of great advances.

"The Congress reflected the trends that have been developing in the society around us, the sunset of democratization and the onset of conservative forces," said Aleksei M. Yemelyanov, a professor of agricultural economics and an opposition deputy.

President Mikhail S. Gorbachev emerged from the Congress more isolated than ever from the innovators who helped him remap Soviet society, and dependent on traditional institutions of power—the Communist Party, the military-industrial complex, the K.G.B.—for his chosen priority of the moment, which is order.

He seems to have run into the limits of what he started. Trying to unleash the creative energy of a suppressed society, he set loose forces that threaten the union.

Trying to break the paralysis of fear, he now finds himself afraid of the consequences. The word he used repeatedly on the closing day was "razval"—breakdown, disintegration, collapse.

People argue whether Mr. Gorbachev has reached his own personal limit, or is accommodating the hard-liners panicked by the mess of democracy; whether this is a temporary cooling-off period or the beginning of a more drastic retrenchment.

Mr. Gorbachev's spin controllers, who now adroitly work the press corps in the Kremlin lobbies, proclaimed the Congress a victory because the Soviet leader got most of what he wanted: a reorganized Government, his choice as Vice President, and a rousing endorsement of the general idea that the Soviet Union should continue to exist.

He won these victories because the Congress as a whole was not very assertive, and had no consensus of its own about how to confront the problems of economic decline and clashing sovereignties. He won because he catered to the Communist Party bloc, the military officers and military-industrialists and other hard-liners who make up a majority in the hall.

Even so, as American pols say, he won ugly.

It took him two ballots and a temper tantrum to win approval of his undistinguished vice presidential choice, a lifelong apparatchik named Gennadi I. Yanayev, whom he plucked from the Communist Party Politburo after two candidates of stature had publicly spurned the post.

The Congress refused to give him the one element of his proposed government reorganization that actually conferred upon him a conspicuous new power—a presidential Supreme State Inspectorate that was to police compliance with orders from Moscow.

What he won was a streamlining of the Government that theoretically makes it easier for him to call Cabinet members and other obstructive bureaucrats to account. This is useful for political infighting, but it is hard to see how it helps resolve the great power struggle going on outside the Cabinet, between Moscow and its rambunctious republics.

As the Congress ended, the Russian republic calmly announced that it would not pay its usual share of the federal budget. This was a challenge as real as the Boston Tea Party, and nothing in Mr. Gorbachev's ostensible new powers equipped him to solve it.

This was the Congress that witnessed the breakup of Mr. Gorbachev's original team, the strong and independent thinkers who helped shape the reforms.

Eduard A. Shevardnadze, the Foreign Minister who helped win his President the Nobel Peace Prize, quit his post, saying he could not stand to watch the country lurch toward dictatorship—although the hard line on domestic affairs seems to have no effect on the improvement in Soviet relations with the United States.

The Shevardnadze resignation remains such a sore point that the broadcasting authorities today canceled tonight's post-Congress edition of the irreverent, late-night weekly show "Vzglyad," or "View," which was to be devoted to Mr. Shevardnadze. The program has been a periodic target of censorship by broadcasting officials sensitive to Kremlin moods.

"People like Shevardnadze would never have turned away from Gorbachev unless they felt they weren't needed anymore," Mr. Yemelyanov said.

Three other key figures lost their places in the inner circle, at least for now, when the Congress abolished the Presidential Council. They are Aleksandr N. Yakovlev, a co-architect of perestroika; Vadim V. Bakatin, who battled the Communist Party for control of the Interior Ministry; and Stanislav S. Shatalin, the economist who almost persuaded Mr. Gorbachev to try a 500-day demolition of Communism.

Some of them may be recycled into the new team, but Mr. Gorbachev's first recruit for that team did not inspire hope among the campaigners for reform. Judging by his public record and the word of his colleagues, Mr. Yanayev, the new Vice President, is an honest, loyal, unimaginative man, an obedient lieutenant to tend the fortress but not a companion for new frontiers.

The appointment seemed to confirm that Mr. Gorbachev is more than ever dependent on the institutions of old power, and reinforced the impression that the period of reform has passed and that the period of law and order has arrived.

Mr. Gorbachev's isolation from the people in the insurgent opposition and his mistrust of their ambitions have grown steadily over the last year.

The self-styled democrats have long ago grown disenchanted with Mr. Gorbachev, and are in their own funk, frustrated by their inability to govern as the economy collapses and the old guard resists.

At the Congress, there was no sign left of any bond between Mr. Gorbachev and the intellectuals who made up his original cheerleading squad.

"I think he is a man with only one friend—Lukyanov," said Vitaly A. Korotich, editor of the popular weekly magazine *Ogonyok*. Anatoly I. Lukyanov is the Gorbachev protégé who was chairman of the Congress.

The new media stars of the Congress came from the far right—the two army colonels whose badgering helped drive Mr. Shevardnadze from the Government, and the striking blond party functionary who called for Mr. Gorbachev's impeachment.

The signals to the outside world were chilling: First the departure of Mr. Shevardnadze, a champion of partnership with the West even on such tricky issues as the Persian Gulf, then the platform given to the K.G.B. chief, Vladimir A. Kryuchkov, whose anti-Western tirade seemed intended to spook foreign investors.

SUMMER 1991

The processes unleashed by the collapse of Communism in Eastern Europe in 1989 were unfolding and compounding two years later. With Moscow's old Warsaw Pact allies seeking new ways of waging politics and business to replace the old ones, the focus of dramatic and violent upheaval shifted in the early part of the year to Albania and Yugoslavia, the two odd ducks of European Communism. In Albania, the idiosyncratic, at times pro-Chinese, Communist Party, finally lost its grip on the hermetic realm. There were demonstrations, and tens of thousands of young people began to flee in waves, jumping on freighters to cross the Adriatic to Italy, where authorities rounded them up and sent most of them back.

In Yugoslavia, which under Tito had bolted from Moscow's control while adhering to an idiosyncratic Communism, the once all-powerful League of Communists could no longer hold together the fractious country of six ethnically based republics and two autonomous regions. Old rivalries and enmities between Serbia, the largest republic, and Croatia, the next largest, flared into open warfare after Croatia had declared its independence. Serbian irregulars took up arms in those regions of Croatia where they were dominant and were backed up by units of the Yugoslav national army. The European Community, concerned that any change of borders through violence might serve as a dangerous precedent for the suddenly destabilized continent, sought to impose cease-fires, but the killings continued, and as summer ended, an all-out civil war loomed as a haunting prospect. The smaller alpine republic of Slovenia had also declared its independence like Croatia, but there, after a week of armed conflict, the national army pulled back. A cease-fire arranged by the European Economic Community seemed to be holding, and federal authorities in Belgrade appeared to be bowing to Slovenia's wish to strike out on its own.

But it was in the Soviet Union that the most momentous events took place. For much of the year, the situation in Moscow was one of slowly *but steadily dissolving institutions. Gorbachev, the man at the center, was pressed from one side by those who wanted to shed the burdens of the past quickly and those who feared that reform would only cost them their powers and perquisites. Abroad, Gorbachev was much praised; at home, he was more and more isolated. One by one, his old allies were becoming critics and rivals, bitter that Gorbachev was not turning out the Old Guard Communists who were using their waning powers to persistently block needed reforms. Some had warned Gorbachev that the hard-liners they believed he was coddling would turn violently against him. On August 16, Aleksandr Yakovlev, once Gorbachev's closest adviser in formulating the reforms of the perestroika period, quit the party in disgust and warned that a "coup d'état" was being planned. Yakovlev's warning came just as Gorbachev was preparing to return from a vacation in the Crimea to sign a treaty with nine Soviet republics on a new federal relationship that would further weaken the authority of the party bosses. On August 19 Yakovlev's warning came true.*

Gorbachev Is Ousted in an Apparent Coup by Soviet Armed Forces and Hard-Liners: Accused of Steering into a "Blind Alley"

By Francis X. Clines

MOSCOW, Monday, Aug. 19—Mikhail S. Gorbachev was apparently ousted from power today by military and K.G.B. authorities while he was on vacation in the distant Crimea.

The announcement by "the Soviet leadership" came as Mr. Gorbachev was about to proceed into a new era of power sharing with the nation's republics.

The sudden announcement this morning stunned the nation and left it groping for information as Kremlin officials declared a state of emergency. The apparent removal of Mr. Gorbachev, six years into his perestroika reform program, came three days after his former confidant and reform adviser, Aleksandr Yakovlev, left the Communist Party, warning of a coming coup d'état.

The Soviet news agency Tass cited Mr. Gorbachev's "inability for health reasons" to perform his duties as President. Vice President Gennady I. Yanayev was assuming presidential powers under a new entity called a State Committee for the State of Emergency. Its members include Vladimir A. Kryuchkov, chief of the K.G.B., and Dmitri T. Yazov, the Defense Minister.

The shocking announcement said that the committee, in assuming powers, had found that "a mortal danger had come to loom large" in the nation and that Mr. Gorbachev's reform program has gone into a "blind alley." The committee contended that the reforms had caused "extremist forces" to threaten the nation and leave it "just a step from mass manifestations of spontaneous discontent."

The scene on the streets of Moscow was calm at the hour of 6:00 A.M. when the announcement was made. Later in the morning, as the city approached a new work week, Muscovites heading downtown could see 10 armored personnel carriers moving a few miles north of Red Square toward the Kremlin. But there were no crowds or other signs of public reaction.

In fact, the public has been noticeably calm, even passive, in recent weeks as Mr. Gorbachev and the republic leaders prepared fresh plans to speed the nation to greater constitutional and democratic reforms.

The emergency committee's announcement contended that increasing domestic instability in the Soviet Union was "undercutting its position in the world." "We are a peace-loving nation and will unfailingly honor all assumed commitments," the Emergency Committee declared. "Any attempts at talking to our country in the language of diktat, no matter by whom, will be decisively cut short," the committee added, in language reminiscent of the cold war.

The Tass announcement insisted the state of emergency would be "temporary." It said that Mr. Yanayev stated that "all power in the country" had been transferred to the committee.

Kremlin announcements said that Mr. Yanayev issued a statement vowing that "in no way" did the removal of Mr. Gorbachev mean "renunciation of the course toward profound reform" in Soviet life.

However, the shift in power to central Kremlin authorities came after days of complaint from central Government authorities over what was to have been a new phase in Mr. Gorbachev's democratization program. On Tuesday, the leaders of the nation's 15 republics were scheduled to begin signing a new union treaty to shift considerable power away from the Kremlin and into the republics.

Kremlin authorities, including Anatoly Lukyanov, criticized the text of the union treaty, citing "how dangerous" the draft treaty could prove unless it was further amended.

Mr. Gorbachev was last seen two weeks ago, shortly after his meeting with President Bush at the start of his vacation.

Mr. Yakovlev, the former colleague and strategist, said in his announcement Friday that while the party was losing influence, it was still making "preparations for social revenge, a party and state coup."

Today's announcement, made through the traditional means of the Kremlin-controlled news media, stunned the Soviet public. It signaled that an attempt was being made to bring under heel Mr. Gorbachev's historic series of democratization reforms.

The occasion was eerie with the trappings of past Kremlin intrigues: classical music flooding the airwaves, interrupted by periodic readings by a monotoned announcer of the attempted change in power.

In the first hours following the emergency announcement, armed guards outside the state broadcasting studio here were denying entry to news professionals working at Radio Russia, one of the new glasnost-era independent news-gathering outlets. This indicated that the Kremlin committee that announced emergency powers might try to curtail independent information and open debate about their move. . . .

In the first day of the coup d'état, there were far more questions being raised than there were answers being provided. Where was Gorbachev? Was he alive? Who was really behind the coup?

K.G.B.-Military Rulers Tighten Grip; Gorbachev Absent, Yeltsin Defiant; West Voices Anger and Warns on Aid

By Francis X. Clines

MOSCOW, Aug. 19—The engineers of President Mikhail S. Gorbachev's ouster from power moved quickly today to reimpose hard-line control across the nation. The coup leaders, dominated by the military and the K.G.B., banned protest meetings, closed independent newspapers and flooded the capital with troops and tanks.

Boris N. Yeltsin, President of the Russian federated republic, who has often been at odds with Mr. Gorbachev, became one of his strongest supporters today, seeking to rally resistance to the Soviet leader's overthrow by climbing atop an armored truck and calling for a general strike on Tuesday to protest the move as an unconstitutional act, a coup d'état.

By nightfall, Mr. Yeltsin had some of his own Russian republic troops and armored combat vehicles moving to his headquarters, and some positive responses were heard to his call for a strike, notably from coal miners and auto workers in Siberia. The scene was set for a possible confrontation between troops loyal to Mr. Yeltsin and those under the command of the national authorities.

One death was reported, that of an unidentified driver said to have been killed in Riga, Latvia, one of the places under military control.

The nation was startled after Mr. Gorbachev, who had been on vacation in the southern Crimea since August 4, was ousted from power the day before he was due to return to Moscow to sign a new union treaty. The landmark accord would have begun a program for speeding constitutional reforms and limiting the Kremlin's ability to dictate the life of the country.

Mr. Gorbachev has been increasingly unpopular at home, in large part because of the country's profound economic troubles, and has been sharply criticized even by many of his former supporters.

Still, there was general disbelief here in Moscow at the coup plotters' assertion that Mr. Gorbachev was ill and therefore had to be relieved of power. Mr. Gorbachev's exact whereabouts were unknown. There was one report that he had been placed under house arrest in a naval hospital in Sevastopol in the Crimea.

The group now in charge is dominated by security and military leaders, and some top political figures, all of whom had strong disagreements with Mr. Gorbachev's democratization and economic-reform programs. This reform process had the further effect of doing away with the need for Communist Party supremacy.

The new ruling group calls itself the State Committee for the State of Emergency, or, in Russian, *Gosudarstvenny Komitet po Chrezvychainomu Polozheniyu.*

"Over the years, he has got very tired and needs some time to get his health back," contended Vice President Gennadi I. Yanayev, who said he had taken over as Acting President, and who directed a news conference at which he defended Mr. Gorbachev's overthrow and his assumption of presidential powers as necessary in the current state of economic and political crisis.

Mr. Yanayev also used the news conference, broadcast to the Soviet people, to announce a series of measures aimed at winning popular support. These included stronger anti-crime moves and improved housing.

The group also said it would continue basic reform programs, but its first decrees—imposing what amounted to martial law in Moscow, Leningrad and the Baltic republics, and closing the most independent press and television voices—contradicted the pledges to continue on the Gorbachev path.

Mr. Yanayev was asked what legal authority allowed the creation of the Emergency Committee, which is composed of eight Communist Party, military and intelligence figures noted for their hard-line inclinations. He responded that "sometimes there are critical situations that call for immediate action" and that, in any case, the Soviet Parliament would eventually approve the action in a special session on August 27.

Mr. Yeltsin, addressing a protest crowd of more than 20,000 Muscovites, decried the Gorbachev ouster as a lawless Kremlin putsch.

But the Yanayev committee, warning that it was prepared to "dismantle" agencies resisting its authority, cautioned him against carrying out his "irresponsible" resolve to lead a general strike.

Coal-mine leaders announced plans to begin closing pits in the major Ukrainian and Siberian coalfields.

In Moscow, all of the major independent newspapers, which had been in the vanguard of the more open press typical of recent years, were ordered shut pending "reregistration." But printers at the Government newspaper *Izvestia,* though free to publish, announced that they would not work.

Throughout the morning, tanks and armored personnel carriers lumbered to critical crossroads of the city, four of them spinning wildly in a circle outside the Bolshoi Theater in a roaring display of force that left passersby crying, "Shame!"

Several angry Muscovites ran into the road to retrieve chunks of the ripped-up macadam. "The final souvenirs of freedom," one man remarked.

Mr. Yanayev defended the necessity for the tanks, troops and a series of toughly worded orders aimed at overruling, where necessary, the centers of insurgent political power that might contradict the Kremlin's new special orders. The state of emergency would not be general throughout the nation, he said. The Emergency Committee spared such eastern republics as Uzbekistan and Kazakhstan, traditionally more obedient to Kremlin authority. But Leningrad and Moscow, centers of the opposition politics encouraged by six years of Gorbachev reforms, were among the first to receive state-of-emergency notices.

Reformist politicians in both cities, the Soviet Union's largest, sought to rally opposition. A large crowd began a night vigil outside Mr. Yeltsin's headquarters in the Russian republic headquarters building on the downtown bank of the Moscow River. Soviet tanks had been stationed there, with their crewmen leaning and watching casually through a long day, occasionally chatting with an angry civilian or joking with others.

Three of the tanks were suddenly turned around, as if in a nighttime lark, after Yeltsin loyalists said they had taken control of the vehicles. The Yeltsin supporters also claimed the defection of a score of Soviet paratroopers. But rumors abounded that the Kremlin forces might choose the time before dawn to make some confrontational move on the building.

Later, 30 more armored vehicles pulled up, and their crews turned out to be Russian troops loyal to Mr. Yeltsin. The crews, trailed by seven ammunition trucks, vowed to defend the building. The Soviets kept their distance.

Thus, ingredients of confrontation were gathering. A report from Leningrad said that Mayor Anatoly A. Sobchak told a crowd of about 2,000 outside city hall that the coup leaders first tried to press Mr. Gorbachev into signing his assent to his removal and, when he refused, placed him under house arrest in his dacha in the Crimea.

A close aide to Mr. Yeltsin reported that he sought to telephone Mr. Gorbachev at the dacha early Monday. The official said someone answered the phone and, when asked to summon Mr. Gorbachev for Mr. Yeltsin, responded: "We have been asked at this end not to disturb him."

In its first statements, the Kremlin special committee did not specifically comment on the strategic arms reduction treaty signed here earlier this month by Mr. Gorbachev and President Bush. But speaking in general terms, it declared that the Soviet Union was "a peace-loving nation and would unfailingly honor all assumed commitments." It added, however: "Any attempts at talking to our country in the languages of diktats, no matter by whom, will be decisively cut short."

522

It was difficult to immediately gauge the nationwide effectiveness of the plotters' seizing of power. Journalists faced fresh censorship, and the public at large seemed stunned or passive. Here in Moscow, most people steered clear of both the tanks and opposition protest rallies, which went on only a block or two from shopping lines and casual café scenes typical of the city.

The fate of the union treaty slipped deeper into doubt with each statement by the Kremlin committee criticizing its provisions, particularly those that would have shifted power from Moscow to the republics. Mr. Yanayev insisted that the treaty had not been put aside, although he said there should be no rush to sign it now, so that "every citizen can assess the document at his leisure."

He appeared at his news conference with several members of the committee, but not with the two people considered critical in the overthrow—Vladimir A. Kryuchkov, chairman of the K.G.B., and the Defense Minister, Marshal Dmitri T. Yazov.

The former Soviet Foreign Minister, Eduard A. Shevardnadze, dismissed the talk of Mr. Gorbachev's ill health as a pretext for a coup provoked by hard-line officials fearful over the pending shift of power from Moscow to the republics, a change Mr. Gorbachev had negotiated with republic leaders. The negotiations had produced a new treaty for a redesigned Soviet Union, and the first signatures were expected Tuesday at a Kremlin ceremony suddenly canceled in the wake of the coup.

"We were expecting it to happen," Mr. Shevardnadze said of the coup. "Unfortunately, Mikhail Sergeyevich did not draw the necessary conclusions," he said, adding that there was confusion to be cleared up, including whether Mr. Gorbachev might have known of the looming plot. "I'm not inclined to defend him," he said of his former mentor and friend.

The K.G.B. and defense chiefs stayed largely behind the scenes today, but the public did not doubt that they were the power behind the ouster. The other members of the Emergency Committee, besides the Vice President, are Oleg D. Baklanov, deputy chairman of the Soviet defense council; Prime Minister Valentin S. Pavlov; Interior Minister Boris K. Pugo, who commands the interior police; Vasily A. Starodubtsev, chairman of the Soviet farmers' union, and A. I. Tizyakov, president of an association of state enterprises.

At the news conference, Mr. Yanayev and other committee members insisted that they had an emergency program to deal with the nation's long-running crises. They spoke of attending immediately to the basic needs of food shortages and new housing, long the staples of traditional Soviet Communists' promises to do better. . . .

Moscow Fears It Awoke to a Nightmare
By Celestine Bohlen

MOSCOW, Aug. 19—As a dozen tanks rolled through Mayakovsky Square, kicking up a cloud of exhaust in the moist evening air, Alla Mikhailovna, in the capital for a visit with her seven-year-old son, stood on the sidewalk and cried.

"It is horrible, just horrible," said the 43-year-old geologist from Tashkent, who identified herself with her given name and patronymic, in the Russian fashion, but declined to give her last name. "I am so sad for my country. What will come of this? Where will it end? War? It is just so frightening."

Across this bedraggled city, people struggled through the day, trying to figure out what had happened to them overnight. They had awakened to find their President mysteriously gone, purportedly for "health reasons," a new State Committee for the State of Emergency in control and military vehicles roaming the city.

As the day wore on, doused by heavy rains, many Muscovites knew no more than they did when they listened to the first terse bulletins on the state-controlled television and radio. But what they knew was enough to make them stiffen with anxiety.

"We woke up to the noise of tanks on the streets," said Slava Ivanov, a 45-year-old driver. "Beyond that, I still don't know anything concretely. Where is Gorbachev? Where is Yeltsin? All I know is nothing good can come from tanks."

Several thousand people turned out to demonstrate against the putschists—as they were calling the new government that ousted Mikhail S. Gorbachev—to upbraid the young soldiers sitting in their tank turrets and to rally in defense of the Russian federated republic's Government.

As evening fell, barricades made of tree trunks, bathtubs and vehicles were erected around the Russian Government buildings on the banks of the Moscow River, as people prepared for an all-night vigil in anticipation of an army attack. But elsewhere, a strange silence seemed to fall on the population as people went about their business—

some with worried looks on their faces, others acting as if nothing more had happened than a change in administration.

"We can't figure it out," said Mikhail Argutinsky, a chauffeur. "It is a putsch, but somebody had to bring things back into order."

His wife, Anna, was not sorry to see Mr. Gorbachev gone. "Of course, he is not the only one to blame," she said, "but all I know is, before him, we lived better."

With no information except what was being released by the people in charge, the city seemed to split in two. At Manezh Square, near the Kremlin, and outside the Russian Government building where Boris N. Yeltsin had called demonstrators to come and protect the republic's elected leadership, the crowd swarmed with rumors, tips and some pieces of real news, hand-carried out of the building and read aloud over bullhorns.

But in other parts of the city, people had to make do with sources that seemed a throwback to an earlier era—leaflets glued to the walls of pedestrian tunnels, foreign radio stations and the old standby, word of mouth.

"They have closed the papers, but that's not so important," said Vladimir Sluzhekov, a reporter, as he stood by a surging crowd of demonstrators. "The radio—that's what hurts. Without the radio, no one knows what's going on except the people who are right here."

By evening, when about 25,000 people had already converged by the Russian Government building, long after pictures of protesters swarming over tanks had flashed on screens around the world, Margarita Selvova, a 63-year-old pensioner, emerged from her apartment off Moscow's main Ring Road to ask if and where people had gathered to protest the coup d'état.

"It is a terrible situation," she said. "It happened in 1917 when the Bolsheviks took over. In 1937, my uncle and my father were shot, and my mother was arrested. Now it is happening again, but people can't imagine it. We are a very unhappy nation." . . .

Driven by an instinct developed during countless pro-democracy meetings, several thousand people flocked to Manezh Square, outside the Kremlin walls, by late morning, arriving in time to block a column of armored personnel carriers that had pulled up alongside the Moskva Hotel.

Galina Viltsina, a 55-year-old primary-school teacher, came to the square as soon as she heard from a taxi driver that a "fascist coup" was under way. She tried to talk a young soldier into getting down and joining the people in the square, but to no avail. "He does not know anything; he does not understand anything," she said. "I did not argue with him. I talked with him like his mother, like a teacher."

Aleksandr N. Chikunov, a 42-year-old engineer, came as soon as he heard the news on the radio. He had switched channels looking for one of Moscow's alternative stations, only to find them broadcasting the same official bulletins.

Mr. Chikunov, a veteran of the invasion of Czechoslovakia, tried to share his own experience with the young soldiers. "I entered Prague in 1968 and I still have a bad conscience about it," he said. "I was a soldier then, like these guys. We were also sent like they are now, to defend the achievements of socialism. Twenty-three years have passed, and I still have a bad conscience." . . .

By midafternoon, as a thunderstorm began to darken the sky, the crowd from Manezh Square had moved toward the Russian republic building, leaving the square empty for tanks and armored personnel carriers to circle through.

Tanks had also appeared at the White House—as the hulking Russian republic building is nicknamed—lingering long enough for Mr. Yeltsin to urge reporters at a press conference to leave the building while they still could. The tanks drove on by.

Mr. Yeltsin came out briefly and spoke, unimpeded, from the top of an armored vehicle that was parked near the building. Later, Ruslan Khasbulatov, acting chairman of the Russian Parliament, took the bullhorn, telling the crowd, "Our only power is our people, our compatriots, you, our dear Muscovites.

"You have seen what shapes fascism may take," he said. "Only this word can be used to call an attempted coup d'état realized last night by our Soviet junta.

"We do not have radio or TV any longer; practically all communication channels are cut. Faxes do not work. But I do not think it will last long, provided there is mass support of Muscovites, Leningraders and other big cities. We shall wipe out this junta."

Confusion broke out at the back of the building when three military buses, with drawn curtains, pulled up in the parking lot. Word went out that the OMON, the "black beret" troops that had been used in the assault in Lithuania last January, were arriving. As people streamed toward the buses, a few women started yelling, "Bastards," until someone else said these troops had actually been summoned by Mr. Yeltsin to guard the building. "They are ours," a voice said in the crowd.

"But how do we know whether to trust them?" asked a young woman with doubt and fear in her voice.

Many people said they had awoken to events that caught them completely by surprise. Mr. Yeltsin, for example, was out of town, returning home from Kazakhstan.

But Sergei Grigoryants, editor of *Glasnost*, a newspaper that had been the first to test the limits of the new policy of free speech, came to the realization today that last night he had in fact been given a warning, whose significance he did not immediately grasp. "The windshield in my car was broken, so that I couldn't drive in," he said. "Nothing was stolen from the car, not even the cognac."

This morning, the newspaper's offices were blocked and the phone lines were out of order, Mr. Grigoryants said. . . .

With Yeltsin at large and active in Moscow, Western leaders, including President Bush, made it clear that they were not ready to consider the coup d'état as a **fait accompli.**

Bush Condemns Soviet Coup and Calls for Its Reversal
By Andrew Rosenthal

KENNEBUNKPORT, Maine, Aug. 19—In a sharp condemnation of the coup that overthrew President Mikhail S. Gorbachev, President Bush made a blunt demand today for Mr. Gorbachev's restoration to power and said the United States did not accept the legitimacy of the self-proclaimed new Soviet Government.

Back at the White House after rushing from his vacation home here, Mr. Bush issued a strongly worded statement that followed a day of consultations with other leaders of the Western alliance and a concerted effort to squeeze the new Soviet leadership by freezing economic aid programs. He decried the coup as a "misguided and illegitimate effort" that "bypasses both Soviet law and the will of the Soviet peoples."

The Bush statement, drafted after an afternoon of meetings with top aides at the White House, was much more forceful than the President's initial reaction this morning in Maine. It was in keeping with a unified Western effort to apply both diplomatic and economic pressure to the group of Soviet officials seeking to gain control of the Kremlin and the country.

In London, the British Government announced that it had frozen $80 million in economic aid to Moscow, and the European Community scheduled an emergency meeting for Tuesday in which it was expected to suspend a $1.5 billion aid program. . . .

Within a day after they announced their coup, the Communist conspirators were having an increasingly hard time implementing their decrees. In Moscow, Boris Yeltsin was rallying a stiffening opposition. There were reports that some Soviet army units were unwilling to follow the conspirators and thousands of ordinary people were turning out to support and defend Yeltsin as he was supporting and defending Gorbachev.

Resistance to Soviet Takeover Grows As Defiant Crowds Rally for Yeltsin
By Francis X. Clines

MOSCOW, Wednesday, Aug. 21—The leaders of the Kremlin coup, facing increased opposition, responded on Tuesday with a curfew and fresh armored movements in Moscow that provoked clashes with angry civilians.

The midnight violence, in which at least three people were killed defying the military curfew, occurred after a long, anxious day in which large crowds sought to protect the headquarters of Boris N. Yeltsin, President of the Russian republic.

As the Kremlin sought to press home freshly assumed powers, Mr. Yeltsin intensified his spirited holdout against the junta of military, K.G.B. and Communist Party figures who had deposed President Mikhail S. Gorbachev on Monday.

Mr. Yeltsin drew cheers from tens of thousands of Muscovites through the day and into the night with his calls for the resignation and criminal trial of the eight-member Kremlin group that staged the overthrow.

The coup leaders showed signs of disarray, with the announcement that Prime Minister Valentin S. Pavlov had been hospitalized and rumors that Defense Minister Dmitri T. Yazov had been replaced. The Yazov report could not be independently confirmed and was denied by a Kremlin official.

"Aggression will not go forward!" Mr. Yeltsin shouted to a throng of at least 30,000 gathered at midday outside the Russian federated republic's Parliament. "Only democracy will win."

The new Kremlin leaders demanded that Mr. Yeltsin cease his call for nationwide resistance and, in ordering an 11:00 P.M. curfew, dispatched scores of tanks and armored troop carriers moving about the city in an attempt to intimidate civilians.

Similar movements were reported in the Baltic republics, which first confronted Kremlin authority two years ago with independence demands. Republic officials there said they feared nighttime violence and attacks on their Government centers from union troops. But the Kremlin insisted that public order, not provocation, was the troops' mission.

Huge throngs of anti-coup crowds gathered in Leningrad to hear words of support for Mr. Gorbachev.

Throughout the day, the new leaders found their continuing series of executive orders and urgent announcements running up against a passive and increasingly resistant national audience.

Some of the leaders of the major republics began issuing statements of unequivocal opposition after their initial wariness on Monday. For example, President Nursultan Nazarbayev of Kazakhstan ended his watchfulness with a strong denunciation of the coup as illegitimate and a usurpation of power.

Aleksy II, Patriarch of the Russian Orthodox Church, also questioned the new leadership's legitimacy and called on Soviet soldiers to restrain themselves as they took up positions in civilian neighborhoods across the city.

"Bewilderment creeps in the conscience of millions of our fellow citizens who begin to question the legality of the newly formed State Committee for the State of Emergency," the Patriarch, a highly popular religious leader, said in a statement that called on the national Parliament, not the coup leaders, to restore stability.

While thousands protected Mr. Yeltsin's Parliament building Tuesday night and into this morning, an armored troop carrier stopped in a confrontation two blocks away on the city's main Ring Road and, witnesses said, three civilians were killed.

One man sought to climb atop the sealed vehicle and fell to his death under the wheels, according to witnesses. They said a second man was crushed against a barricade when the armored vehicle careered to escape, hitting a parked bus as a third man was crushed.

A crowd that had been watching soon responded angrily with

gasoline bombs and rocks, leaving the armored vehicle aflame, along with two other buses.

That was the first reported incident of violence and death in the first two days of the coup. A standoff marked by fright, uncertainty and growing popular resistance marked most of the day. . . .

"We're seeing the agony of the old regime," said Oleg D. Kalugin, a Soviet lawmaker and K.G.B. defector, in predicting the coup committee would be forced to retreat. "These are the old guys, simply crazy," he said.

The nation suffered a tense, unpredictable day under the new regime, with fresh rumors every hour. Russian republic officials reported the resignation of Defense Minister Yazov, leader of the armed forces and a critical figure in the coup committee.

That was quickly denied by the Kremlin, which was ringed with dozens of armored vehicles and hundreds of riot troops waiting near the Bolshoi Theater.

On Tuesday night, the roar of tanks on the move could be heard repeatedly and rumors intensified that the Kremlin might attempt a military attack on the Yeltsin headquarters. That was denied by Kremlin officials, but tension was high, with Muscovites watching from their windows as scores upon scores of armored vehicles swept through the main roads after the 11:00 P.M. curfew began.

Outside the Russian republic building, where the white marble walls were bathed in the glow of searchlights, crowds were ignoring the curfew and lugging tree limbs, railroad tracks and concrete chunks to strengthen their barricades in defense of Mr. Yeltsin.

Some of the tank troops seemed at least as anxious as the public.

"What do they know? They're not from Moscow," a city policeman said after one tank bumped into another in some late-night confusion on the city's main Ring Road, mostly deserted except for the passing armored vehicles.

The Kremlin coup committee made no appearance on Tuesday, restricting itself to fresh executive orders, broadcast on state-controlled television, demanding that all remaining news outlets in the print and electronic media operating in the republics submit to central authority.

But here in the capital, independent news outlets stayed open, using fax machines and at least one small-power radio station operating thus far beyond the Kremlin's notice.

The city's elaborate subway system, an ideal conduit for information, was papered with anti-coup pamphlets, and riders gathered in crowds to read President Yeltsin's exhortations to resist the coup committee.

"They will find themselves in the dock," he told the midday rally, sounding a theme repeated during the day that it would not be enough to see the coup leaders retreat from power, that criminal action was required. . . .

Bare-Fisted Russians Make Their Stand
By Celestine Bohlen

MOSCOW, Aug. 20—Inside the "war room" on the third floor of the Russian Parliament building, commanders of the republic's forces spent the afternoon poring over maps of Moscow and a floor plan of the 12-floor building, plotting how to stave off an anticipated attack by Soviet Army and Interior Ministry troops.

Their attire told the story of Russia's patchwork defense. Two men wore Soviet Army uniforms, another the World War I uniform of the Don Cossacks. Others, with pistols at their hips, were in camouflage suits, issued by a security firm called the Bells. The rest wore either suits and ties or beat-up jeans or baggy pants—just like the hundreds of volunteers who by early evening were ringing the building in a human chain.

The men in the war room were collecting whatever help was being offered. The phones rang with calls from citizens, one reporting an airlift of 35 light tanks at an airfield off Leningrad Prospekt, another advising of a construction battalion moving through the Solntsevo Region southwest of Moscow.

Workers at a joint-venture concern called offering to bring a truckload of food, while someone in Krasnoyarsk wanted to know what was going on.

Vladimir Nezhinsky, deputy administrative officer of the Russian Defense Committee, got a tip from a contact at Moscow City Hall that a curfew would be declared in the city this evening, and that the Soviet Army troops would be pulled out. Mr. Nezhinsky worried that if the rumor was true, this would leave a vacuum for the Spetsnaz, or special forces, to move in for the kill.

Boris N. Yeltsin, the President of the Russian republic, was in the building most of the day, issuing orders to tighten the republic's defense. In a speech to the crowd outside, he said his government was taking precautions "because the junta that seized power will not stop short of any steps to hold it."

"These actions are not aimed against Kazakhstan or Uzbekistan, but against democratic Russia," he said. "The state of emergency has been imposed only where the leadership is democratic, mainly in those regions. This makes it clear against whom this putsch was made."

Mr. Yeltsin urged the crowd to stay calm. "Don't provoke the military," he warned. "The military has become a weapon in the hands of the putschists. Therefore we should also support the military and maintain order and discipline in contact with them."

As the day wore on, the building, known familiarly as the White House, battened down for the battle that everyone was sure was coming.

Guards on the barricades tried to stop women from entering the building. Witnesses said members of the Government of Mr. Yeltsin's Russian federated republic were issued pistols, while some but not all of the men guarding the building's entrances were given bulletproof vests, helmets, gas masks and bottles filled with gasoline.

One box filled with Molotov cocktails stood in a corner of the war room, just in case. "If the tanks come, we'll throw them out there," said Viktor Gurov, a 36-year-old member of the Bells security company. "If any one of them asks for it, I will toss him the whole box." . . .

As support for Mr. Yeltsin grew in Moscow, it also became firmer in Washington.

Bush Snubs Chiefs of "Illegal Coup"
By R. W. Apple, Jr.

WASHINGTON, Aug. 20—President Bush today told the leaders of Monday's coup in the Soviet Union that the United States would refuse to establish normal relations with them, and he telephoned Boris N. Yeltsin to offer support.

"We are not giving up on the restoration of constitutional government in the Soviet Union," the President declared as tanks maneuvered in the streets of Moscow, well before the first signs that the coup might have stalled. Moving to coordinate his strategy with European leaders, who voted today to hold up most of the European Community's planned economic aid to Moscow, Mr. Bush dispatched Secretary of State James A. Baker 3d to a meeting of NATO foreign ministers in Brussels on Wednesday.

After Robert S. Strauss was sworn in as the new United States Ambassador to Moscow, Mr. Bush appeared with him on the White House lawn. The President said Mr. Strauss would travel to the Soviet Union immediately as a special envoy.

But to symbolize Mr. Bush's determination to help Mikhail S. Gorbachev regain office, Mr. Strauss was instructed not to present his credentials to the coup leaders—indeed, not to meet with them at all except in a dire emergency. . . .

Three days after it was proclaimed, the coup collapsed. Gorbachev was brought home. Yeltsin had triumphed. And Communism, it seemed, was about to be uprooted in the country where it had been most deeply entrenched.

Gorbachev Back As Coup Fails, but Yeltsin Gains New Power
By Serge Schmemann

MOSCOW, Thursday, Aug. 22—A coup by hard-line Communists collapsed on Wednesday as abruptly as it began, and President Mikhail S. Gorbachev returned to Moscow early this morning to reassert control.

Mr. Gorbachev landed at Vnukovo Airport on his return from his summer retreat in the Crimea, where he had been placed under house arrest early Monday at the start of the short-lived putsch. In impromptu remarks to Soviet television that were aired later on a morning news program, Mr. Gorbachev appeared weary but clearly angered by the efforts of the conspirators to get him to surrender power.

"The whole world should know about this, what exactly was being plotted," he said upon arriving at the airport, "and what it is that they did not succeed in getting from me."

Mr. Gorbachev described the coup leaders as "a miserable group" that had tried to "break" him and "to influence his family" by surrounding them with troops and isolating them for 72 hours.

The Soviet President congratulated the Soviet people for having had the "responsibility and dignity" to resist the takeover.

He particularly thanked the President of the Russian federated republic, Boris N. Yeltsin, for standing up to the coup leaders. Mr.

Gorbachev was expected to meet with the Russian leader later today.

Mr. Gorbachev's wife, Raisa, was also shown on morning television disembarking from the plane at the airport while holding a small child wrapped in a blanket. The Gorbachevs left for their country house in a Moscow suburb.

The Soviet President had said in a statement reported Wednesday by the evening television news program "Vremya" that he was "in full control of the situation" and that he would resume his full duties within a day.

The evening program also reported that he had restored contact with the Cabinet and the Defense Ministry—both under acting chiefs now that their leaders were disgraced—and to have talked by telephone with Mr. Yeltsin and President Bush.

Only one of the coup leaders—the K.G.B. chairman, Vladimir A. Kryuchkov—was reported under arrest early today. It was the first time a K.G.B. leader had been arrested since Lavrenti P. Beria was detained, tried secretly and shot in 1953 in the power struggle that followed the death of Stalin.

Reuters reported from Moscow that two other coup leaders, the Defense Minister, Marshal Dmitri T. Yazov, and Nikolai I. Tizyakov, had been detained, according to Sergei Stankevich, a member of the Soviet Parliament and an adviser to Mr. Yeltsin. But this report could not be independently confirmed. There were also unconfirmed reports that the other members of the State Committee for the State of Emergency would be put on trial.

The coup crumbled Wednesday as abruptly as it began, without any formal announcement from its leaders, who sent tanks into Moscow on Monday and declared themselves in command. It seemed simply to fizzle under the disdain of masses rallying to the summons of Mr. Yeltsin, who rose to condemn the coup almost from the moment it became known, and the irresolution of plotters who failed to garner support or even to maintain the loyalty of their forces.

On Wednesday, Mr. Yeltsin declared that the Communist Party had been "the organizing and inspiring force" behind the coup, and the implication was that with its last, desperate rear-guard action the once-formidable force that had controlled the Soviet Union for more than 70 years might finally be exhausted.

It remains a question whether Mr. Gorbachev, after his ordeal, will bolt the party he heads, as have Mr. Yeltsin and other former Gorbachev aides.

The awareness that the coup had failed came with the first gray light of dawn, when it became evident that army tanks had not moved against the headquarters of the Russian republic's Government in the capital.

Relief spread among the thousands of Muscovites who had spent two drizzly nights at makeshift barricades around the building, called the White House, a wedding-cake-like building on the banks of the Moscow River, from which Mr. Yeltsin marshaled the anti-coup forces.

Within hours, reports swept through a jubilant Moscow that the members of the Emergency Committee were in flight, and long columns of tanks and armored personnel carriers began to leave the capital, some decorated with Russian flags, to the cheers of jubilant Muscovites.

Like the marchers in Leipzig or the demonstrators in Prague who had brought down Communist regimes through the sheer force of their determination, Muscovites—even those who had not directly taken part in public demonstrations—felt a personal satisfaction in facing down forces that had held them so long in thrall.

"Weren't we great?" exclaimed one woman, capturing a joyous sense that the nation had united to thwart the long-awaited counter-offensive by the forces of the former Communist dictatorship. "Leave, just please leave," another woman shouted at the tanks.

According to the spokesman for the Russian republic's Government, the Russian Vice President, Aleksandr Rutskoi, and its Prime Minister, Ivan S. Silayev, along with other members of the Russian Government, flew to the Crimea Wednesday evening and met with Mr. Gorbachev. While they were there, two members of the Emergency Committee—the Defense Minister, Marshal Yazov, and the K.G.B. chairman, Mr. Kryuchkov—flew there with the chairman of the Soviet Parliament, Anatoly I. Lukyanov, and the deputy chief of the Communist Party, Vladimir A. Ivashko.

The spokesman said that in the course of a long talk between Mr. Gorbachev and the Russian delegation, Mr. Gorbachev was informed about the siege and the attempt to seize the Russian republic's headquarters. Mr. Gorbachev received Mr. Ivashko and Mr. Lukyanov but refused to receive Marshal Yazov and Mr. Kryuchkov. Then Gorbachev, who was in good health, after a rest, flew back with the Russian delegation, thanking members of the Russian Government and condemning the members of the Emergency Committee.

Mr. Kryuchkov flew back with Mr. Gorbachev and the Russians, and was arrested at Vnukovo Airport by the Russian Interior Ministry. Mr. Ivashko, Mr. Lukyanov and General Yazov were reported to have returned on another plane.

There was no immediate information on other members of the committee, except for Prime Minister Valentin S. Pavlov, who was in the hospital with hypertension. The independent Interfax news agency quoted Mr. Rutskoi as saying that the other members of the coup leadership would be arrested later, and that they would all be tried.

"Vremya" said Mr. Gorbachev expected that the "adventurists" would carry "full responsibility" for their actions, and the Soviet Prosecutor General's office announced it had opened an investigation of the Emergency Committee on charges of committing a "state crime." It was not known if the investigation would extend to others. Wednesday, Mr. Tizyakov was stripped of his job by his organization because of his role in the coup.

But even as Moscow waited for Mr. Gorbachev to reappear, it was evident that the balance of power and the course of the Soviet Union's history had shifted, that the Communists who had fought a rearguard action against change had suffered a potentially fatal blow, that Mr. Gorbachev himself was now beholden to the anti-Communist forces that had rescued him and, above all, to Mr. Yeltsin.

Mr. Yeltsin was the indisputable man of the hour, and the advocates of economic and political reform were clearly ascendant.

It was Mr. Yeltsin's dramatic condemnation of the coup virtually at the same time as the rebellion first became known early Monday morning that roused resistance across the Soviet Union and made his headquarters on the Moscow River into a rallying point of the opposition.

The image of Mr. Yeltsin addressing supporters from atop one of the tanks that had come over to his side became the icon of resistance. His statements were published by liberal papers across the Soviet Union and read out at mass rallies from Kamchatka, on the Pacific Coast, to Leningrad, on the Baltic.

Thousands of Muscovites heeded his call and formed a cordon around the White House, sealing approaches with makeshift barricades of buses, trucks and building materials. All across the nation, liberal politicians and supporters of Mr. Yeltsin organized demonstrations and mass meeting.

He issued decrees declaring the actions of the junta unconstitutional and assuming temporary control over all Government and security forces on Russian territory.

Addressing the Russian Parliament on Wednesday, Mr. Yeltsin declared that it was the defection to his side of several military units that had prevented the junta from interning the Russian Government. Mr. Yeltsin said that instead of obeying the coup leaders' orders, the Tulskaya Division had protected the Russian Parliament from attack. He expressed gratitude to the troops and their commanders for their action.

The normally fractious Parliament repeatedly rose to unanimously cheer Mr. Yeltsin as he denounced the coup in ringing tones: "This is an impudent coup, unprecedented in the conditions of a genuinely developing democratic society." . . .

One immediate consequence of the curbing of the far-right forces was the virtual certainty that the union treaty, the radically new federal organization that the Communists had tried to block through their coup, would quickly come into effect. The treaty, negotiated between Mr. Gorbachev and nine of the 15 republics, would devolve many of the powers of the center to republican governments in a "Union of Soviet Sovereign Republics."

Flexing his new muscles, Mr. Yeltsin declared that since Mr. Gorbachev had intended to sign the union treaty on Tuesday, he would henceforth consider it in force and was immediately declaring the Russian federated republic economically sovereign and master of all its resources.

The developments also portended an end to efforts to bring the independence-minded Baltic states to heel. Reports from Lithuania, Latvia and Estonia said that Soviet forces had begun lifting their siege of radio, television and communications centers, including centers that had been held by Moscow-controlled forces since January. . . .

Elsewhere, the collapse of the coup precipitated frenzied efforts by officials, institutions and news organizations, many of which had lain low for two days, to demonstrate their disgust with the plotters in a day-long flurry of news conferences.

The Defense Ministry (now under Gen. Mikhail A. Moiseyev), the chief of staff, the Cabinet (now under Deputy Prime Minister Vladimir I. Shcherbakov) and the Soviet Parliament all issued statements declaring fealty to Mr. Gorbachev.

Leaders of the Communist Party declared that the coup had been "inadmissible" and that from the outset they had demanded a meeting with Mr. Gorbachev, without success. At the same time, a Central Committee secretary, Sergei Kalashnikov, warned journalists against using the term "junta," arguing that leaders of the plot were "people who made a blunder in the estimation of a difficult situation."

Foreign Minister Aleksandr A. Bessmertnykh and Mr. Ivashko, the deputy chief of the Communist Party, separately explained their silence over the past two days by saying they were sick.

Mr. Bessmertnykh told a news conference that Soviet foreign policy would remain unchanged. "It is the same as was formulated by the President of the Soviet Union," he told a press conference.

The tone of official news organs changed radically through the day. "Vremya," the main evening news program that had toed the junta's line, now portrayed the collapse of the coup as a great triumph for constitutional order and showed long portions of Mr. Yeltsin's speech to the Russian Parliament. The Russian republic's radio and television stations, silenced for two days, returned to the air.

The Presidium of the Soviet Parliament quickly issued a resolution declaring the removal of Mr. Gorbachev illegal.

The head of the Russian Orthodox Church, Patriarch Aleksy II, pronounced anathema against the leaders of the coup. . . .

With the coup reversed, there were some who thought and many who hoped that the pace of political developments in the Soviet Union would slow for a while, if only to let people catch their breath. It did not work out that way.

Gorbachev Says Coup Will Hasten Reform; Yeltsin Leads the Celebration in Moscow
By Bill Keller

MOSCOW, Aug. 22—President Mikhail S. Gorbachev, chastened and isolated by his betrayal at the hands of men he trusted, said today that his rescue from the failed coup had taught him that he must join more closely with "democratic forces" and speed the pace of reform.

While elated Muscovites streamed through the streets in celebration of their triumph over the conspiracy, one of the putsch leaders, Interior Minister Boris K. Pugo, killed himself. And the circle of high-level Gorbachev confidants implicated in the plot widened to include the leader of the Soviet Parliament, Anatoly I. Lukyanov, who was accused by a high Soviet official of being the coup's mastermind.

But at a news conference tonight, the weary but steely Soviet President refused to join President Boris N. Yeltsin of the Russian federated republic and hold the Communist Party responsible for the rebellion. He reasserted his determination to remain as party leader, declaring that the party could still be purged of "reactionary forces" and made into a vehicle of national unity and reform.

Mr. Gorbachev left little doubt, however, that his 72-hour ordeal had transformed the chemistry of Soviet politics, establishing the anti-Communists who rallied against the coup as the predominant engine of political and economic change.

The Soviet leader spoke with emotion of his strengthened partnership with Mr. Yeltsin, who, by galvanizing the resistance to the conspiracy carried out by Communist hard-liners, became the ascendant power in the new Soviet politics. Mr. Gorbachev credited Mr. Yeltsin with the leading role in rebuffing the coup, saying the conspirators finally panicked because of the "implacable position" of the Russian leaders and their followers, including defections in the army.

Today Mr. Yeltsin led the capital in a day of explicitly anti-Communist rejoicing and mapped a mopping-up campaign against the vestiges of Communist power in his own republic. Mr. Yeltsin, who had been Mr. Gorbachev's bitter rival since the Soviet leader threw him out of the Communist Party Politburo four years ago, has by standing up to the conspirators made himself the most indispensable ally in the Soviet leader's campaign to remake the country.

"So many lies are being told about these two individuals, that it's probably difficult to understand, but we have been bound together by the situation," Mr. Gorbachev said. "We know what the situation is. We know who is who."

One of the most striking impressions during the Soviet leader's 90-minute news conference was a sense of his sudden isolation.

While many of Mr. Gorbachev's original collaborators in reform have quit the Communist Party and remain estranged by his devotion to it, the hard-liners upon whom he relied to run his government, the military and the police agencies have proven treacherous.

Today the Premier of the Russian republic, Ivan Silayev, charged that Mr. Lukyanov, Mr. Gorbachev's friend since they attended law school together in the 1950's and one of his most trusted aides, was "the chief ideologist of this junta."

Mr. Lukyanov was suspended today as chairman of the Soviet Parliament pending an investigation.

Mr. Gorbachev said he had met with Mr. Lukyanov, who insisted he had done his best to negotiate an end to the coup, but the Soviet leader sounded as though he needed to be convinced.

The governing Presidium of the Soviet Parliament announced that Mr. Lukyanov would not preside over an emergency session of the legislature on Monday, which is to include an assessment of his role in the crisis.

Mr. Pugo, named Interior Minister by Mr. Gorbachev last year, fired two bullets into his wife and then shot himself in the head while the authorities were en route to arrest him, the Russian television news program "Vesti" reported.

The Interior Minister, one of eight members of the State Committee for the State of Emergency that ousted Mr. Gorbachev on Sunday, died in a hospital. His wife survived but was in grave condition.

All but one of the remaining committee leaders, including Mr. Gorbachev's Prime Minister, Defense Minister and K.G.B. chief, were reported under arrest tonight. Among the other prominent figures arrested for complicity were Gen. Valentin I. Varennikov, the Deputy Defense Minister and commander of Soviet ground forces, and Valery Boldin, chief of Mr. Gorbachev's administrative apparatus at the Communist Party.

Mr. Gorbachev admitted that he had badly misjudged some of the men he appointed, especially Defense Minister Dmitri T. Yazov and the K.G.B. chief, Vladimir A. Kryuchkov, who the Soviet leader said had held his special trust.

"I see now that it was a mistake, and I'll tell you perfectly straightforwardly because I do not have any problem with speaking the truth, I believed particularly Yazov and Kryuchkov," he said. "I believed in them." . . .

In a televised address to the public tonight, Mr. Gorbachev said the takeover failed because the conspirators "underestimated the main thing—that the people, in these very difficult years, have been transformed."

"They have breathed the air of freedom, and nobody can any longer take that away from them," he said.

"We should not only see the disaster that occurred, but also we have to see this as an enormous opportunity, namely, an opportunity in the sense that our people's true position has been made clear."

Although the Soviet leader spoke with calm resolve of the steps he is taking to set his reform program back in motion, he paused at times to compose himself as he recounted details of his 72-hour ordeal under house arrest at his vacation home in the Crimea.

He said his wife, Raisa, had been badly shaken by the experience. "She is not feeling well at all, but we think this will pass," he said. "Yesterday we thought, well—anyway, it was hard, and you can understand why."

Mr. Gorbachev said that when his longtime aide, Mr. Boldin, arrived as the emissary from the conspirators with a demand to turn over power voluntarily, he said, "To hell with you," and told him that the plot was doomed. In an earlier interview, upon his arrival back in Moscow early this morning, the Soviet leader said he would have killed himself rather than go along.

While Mr. Gorbachev fielded calls from world leaders and began replacing the arrested members of his Government, Mr. Yeltsin basked in the cheers of a roaring throng outside his Government building, then sent them on a triumphal march through the city to Red Square. . . .

The collapse of the coup left many organizations scrambling to dissociate themselves from charges of complicity.

The K.G.B. today issued a statement insisting that its agents "have nothing in common with the illegal actions by the group of adventurists" and were embarrassed that the agency's head was among the conspirators. The Communist Party's Secretariat announced plans to "discuss the responsibility" of party members who took part.

Moscow Crowds Vent Anger on Communists
By Celestine Bohlen

MOSCOW, Aug. 22—The statue of Feliks Dzerzhinsky, founder of the Soviet secret police, was lifted off its pedestal in front of the headquarters of the K.G.B. tonight, a victim of an anti-Communist fever that swept this city as thousands of jubilant Muscovites savored their triumph over the coup this week.

Starting with a mass demonstration in front of the Russian federated republic's government building, where they cheered their beaming President, Boris N. Yeltsin, a crowd of almost 50,000 people drifted through the center of the city, waving the republic's newly adopted white, blue and red flag, and enjoying the first sunlight of the week.

In the middle of the afternoon, a group spun off up Manezh Square, past the Bolshoi Theater, toward the Lubyanka, as the K.G.B. head-quarters is called, where several young men began to go to work on the Dzerzhinsky statue. Starting at the bottom, they painted the word "executioner" around the base. Then they worked their way around the statue's greatcoat and its face, attaching metal wires that they then connected to a small bus parked nearby.

To the cheers of the growing crowd, the amateur team made a first attempt to topple the giant figure, only to be stopped by representatives from the Russian Government and Moscow City Hall offering their own expert advice and an official sanction of the project.

After lengthy consultation on how to dismantle the statue without disturbing the electrical connections in the subway station below it, four cranes moved in shortly before midnight, lifting the statue up by one arm and laying it on a flatbed truck.

"It's the end of the Communists, of Communist power," said Sergei Kalugin, a 30-year-old Muscovite. "Next, it will be the mausoleum's turn, then Lenin's statue." . . .

Emboldened by the failure of the coup, Yevgeny Dubrovin handed in his party card today, joining 4 million other party members—or more than 20 percent of the party rolls—who have quit in the past year. Mr. Dubrovin, an employee of the Soviet Oil Ministry, said he, too, would have quit earlier but, he said, "to be honest, in my job, it would have been a little risky."

Not so today, he said. "Now I am sure it will be fine," he said.

There were people in his office who had openly supported the junta during its brief hold on power, he said, but this morning they stayed quiet and looked gloomy. "But now we know who is who," he said.

In front of the Lubyanka, people were determined to strike while the iron was hot. When a member of the Russian Parliament, speaking through a bullhorn, warned that a more orderly removal of the Dzerzhinsky statue would take time, the crowd roared back with a chant, "Today, today." . . .

A triumphant Yeltsin lost little time in pressing his advantage over the man he had rescued, challenging him to renounce not just the men who had held him captive but the party in whose name they acted.

Yeltsin Is Routing Communist Party from Key Roles Throughout Russia; He Forces Vast Gorbachev Shake-up; Soviet President Is Heckled by the Republic's Parliament

By Francis X. Clines

MOSCOW, Aug. 23—A political shock wave swept through the Soviet Union in the aftermath of the failed coup today as the Communist Party reeled in retreat across the nation and President Mikhail S. Gorbachev yielded to the ascendancy of the Russian President, Boris N. Yeltsin.

Mr. Gorbachev, struggling to regain his leadership role after three days as a hostage to the coup plotted by hard-line Communists, spoke before the Russian republic's Parliament. During his appearance, broadcast on national television, he found himself facing an openly skeptical, at times abusive, audience. He was scorned by the lawmakers for remaining loyal to the party after the harrowing national ordeal of the last five days.

Mr. Yeltsin, who at times seemed to mock Mr. Gorbachev, spent a dynamic day prodding the Soviet leader for more power sharing and initialing fresh writs to shut down the Communist Party's newspapers and limit its activities on Russian soil. Mr. Yeltsin and other leaders of the Russian republic forced Mr. Gorbachev to replace his whole Cabinet and name many replacements loyal to Mr. Yeltsin.

The Russian President's move against the party was reflected across the Soviet Union as a wave of indignation and demands for change swept from the Baltic republics to central Asia.

The common theme was that, in the wake of the coup, the initiative had shifted to those prepared to confront and erase virtually all the practices and institutions that have dominated the governing of this troubled nation under the Communist system.

The mood of rising anger against the Communist Party and the K.G.B. injected an entirely new energy and uncertainty into the Soviet political crisis. While President Gorbachev warned against a "witch hunt," many officials rushed to join the wave of insurgency and said a full reckoning with the party and the state police was long overdue.

The party's newspapers and offices were being put under lock and key and its political perquisites removed across the land, from Moscow to Kirghizia. Party cells were banned in some hamlets, while

Communism's traditional mass propaganda outlets were handed over to presumed reformers. Publication of *Pravda*, the once-dominant party newspaper, was suspended because of its cooperation with the coup leaders.

Though the anti-party drive appeared to be gaining momentum without arousing any discernible opposition, the general uncertainty over the nation's future was, if anything, heightened by the still-unsettled shape of power sharing between the Kremlin and the republics. It was dramatically reflected in the changing relationship between Mr. Yeltsin and Mr. Gorbachev.

The shift of executive power toward Mr. Yeltsin was palpable throughout the day as he moved to end what he described as "the malignant influence of ideological demons." The husky Russian leader headed off an angry crowd of several hundred demonstrators outside the K.G.B. headquarters by announcing changes in Mr. Gorbachev's Cabinet as a sign of resolve to finally begin reforming the infamous organization.

President Gorbachev, who argued that it was unfair to blame all Communists for the coup attempt, found himself on rapidly shifting political ground as crowds, backed by the local authorities, brought down Lenin statues in the provinces.

Local governments in several regions took action to close down party offices, nowhere more prominently than in Moscow, where the party's Central Committee building, once the repository of total Soviet power, was closed to prevent officials from destroying documents. Groups were formed to protect the building from being overrun by mobs.

Seeking a unity theme, Mr. Gorbachev called on the nation to pursue a power-sharing compact with the republics that Mr. Yeltsin already was executing de facto, acting on the strength of a personal popularity that only grew in his defeat of the Kremlin junta that had held Mr. Gorbachev.

Russian lawmakers made no secret to the watching nation of how clearly they sensed the Soviet leader's dwindling powers. They interrupted Mr. Gorbachev's address with heckling and demands that he join in the rising public clamor to dislodge the Communist Party from its privileged position and explain why he made himself so vulnerable to Communist hard-liners in the Cabinet who fought his promises of reform and plotted his ouster.

Firmly on the defensive, Mr. Gorbachev finally drew a positive, rousing response from the chamber by admitting the Cabinet's weaknesses and declaring flatly, "This whole Government has got to resign."

Mr. Yeltsin, who was in charge of the parliamentary session, repeatedly called attention to his role in saving Mr. Gorbachev from the Kremlin plotters. He even interrupted the Soviet President, demanding that Mr. Gorbachev read aloud some evidence of how most of his own Cabinet failed to object to the coup and his arrest in a private session on Monday.

"Here, read this out," the Russian republic's President boomed at Mr. Gorbachev's shoulder.

"I will do this," replied Mr. Gorbachev, seeking to hold his own in this nationally televised tableau of their long-running rivalry. "I'll read it. Let me finish."

Mr. Yeltsin further demonstrated his relative strength when he called on Mr. Gorbachev to acknowledge that they had agreed privately that the next Soviet Prime Minister should come from the Russian republic. The Soviet leader concurred.

The first of several appointees in a new national Cabinet announced by Mr. Yeltsin to the protesters at the K.G.B. building was Gen. Yevgeny I. Shaposhnikov as Defense Minister, replacing one of the junta members, Marshal Dmitri T. Yazov. General Shaposhnikov was hailed for refusing to obey orders from the junta.

Gen. Mikhail A. Moiseyev had been Acting Defense Minister for two days, but had come under suspicion for allegedly cooperating with the coup.

Tonight Marshal Yazov made some remarks on Soviet television, the first by any of the conspirators since the takeover failed. "I very much regret what happened," he said. "In the final analysis, it brings shame on the armed forces, and I, as the person responsible for the armed forces, am responsible for what occurred."

The new K.G.B. chief is Vadim V. Bakatin, replacing Vladimir A. Kryuchkov, a leader in the coup. Mr. Bakatin, a well-known liberal, had served as Interior Minister, in charge of the national militia, but Mr. Gorbachev removed him last year in an effort to appease hardline critics.

To fill the post of national Interior Minister left open by the suicide of Boris K. Pugo, one of the chief plotters, Mr. Yeltsin pushed through the appointment of Viktor P. Barannikov, who until now had held a similar office in the Government of the Russian federated republic. In that post he outlawed Communist Party activity within the ministry.

With Mr. Gorbachev's safe return from detention, increasing numbers of Government officials have come forward pleading they were not disloyal. Chief among these was Foreign Minister Aleksandr A. Bessmertnykh, who was removed from office today. He said he was genuinely sick during the uncertain days of the coup and denied that he had been hiding. He said in an interview with ABC's "Nightline," that early in the week he had rejected the coup conspirators' demand that he sign a "terrible document" that was critical of President Bush's response to the coup and United States involvement in internal issues in the Soviet Union.

"If it had been sent, that would have been the start of another cold war," Mr. Bessmertnykh said. . . .

In his performance before the Russian Parliament, Mr. Gorbachev was applauded at times but generally pressed hard by questioners and hecklers, particularly over his continuing defense of the 15-million-member Communist Party as a useful political organization that was hardly the haven for coup plotters and reactionaries that its critics describe.

In the face of pressure, he warned the lawmakers against "anti-Communist hysteria."

"We must show our maturity and what we have achieved," Mr. Gorbachev said. "You will say that they raised their hand against us, wanted to turn us into meat; they wanted to annihilate us. That is all entirely true.

"But it has to be done according to the law, and so that we all together will be balanced and responsible," he said. "No one should be able to reproach us for carrying out a witch hunt."

But Mr. Yeltsin was not to be denied, and even signed a fresh executive order while Mr. Gorbachev was before the Parliament.

"On a lighter note," Mr. Yeltsin said with a big grin, "shall we now sign a decree suspending the activities of the Russian Communist Party?"

And he did, and there was no objection from Mr. Gorbachev, who acknowledged that Mr. Yeltsin's decrees this week had proved potent in building resistance to the coup. . . .

The Icons Topple

By Henry Kamm

TALLINN, Estonia, Aug. 23—From late afternoon well into the evening, the people of this capital city did something they said they had never done—they flocked to Communist Party headquarters; then they stood there and laughed.

They stood in a large arc that constantly renewed itself as men, women and children came and went and stared and pointed at an empty marble pedestal. Until early today, a larger-than-life bronze statue of Lenin had stood there in the familiar rhetorical pose, opposite the entrance to the modern headquarters building.

A crew came this morning and carried out a Government decision to remove the statue in the aftermath of the failure of the coup by doctrinaire Communists against the Government of President Mikhail S. Gorbachev.

"It was done with respect," said Aino Siiak, a retired economist, her voice full of sarcasm. "A crane came; they put a chain around his neck and took the great philosopher away."

While in Lithuania and Latvia, the two other Baltic republics, the Communist Party was virtually outlawed today, Estonians expressed their sentiments through a symbolic act.

"Estonians do things slowly," Mrs. Siiak said. "We have no temperament." The way in which she and many others at the scene gave vent to long-suppressed emotions suggested otherwise. Voices trembled and faces quivered as Estonians recalled their sentiments through the tumultuous days that began with the ouster of Mr. Gorbachev on Monday. . . .

A day later, Gorbachev reconsidered his views on the party.

Gorbachev Quits as Party Head; Ends Communism's 74-Year Reign

By Serge Schmemann

MOSCOW, Aug. 24—President Mikhail S. Gorbachev resigned today as the head of the Communist Party, disbanded its leadership and in effect banned the once-monolithic party from any role in ruling the vast country over which it had held iron control for more than seven decades.

With Communism under brutal assault across the Soviet Union and his own leadership in shambles in the aftermath of a coup attempt, Mr. Gorbachev abandoned his efforts to defend party leaders who had obviously collaborated in the putsch and finally dealt the party a fatal blow.

By doing so, Mr. Gorbachev seemed to be seeking some way of remaining a credible political force, something that would have been impossible if he had not repudiated the party.

In a series of terse statements and decrees read on the evening television program "Vremya," the President also ordered the Cabinet of Ministers, the inner Government council, to resign. He then created a committee headed by the Premier of the Russian federated republic, Ivan Silayev, a close aide of the republic's President, Boris N. Yeltsin, to take charge of the national economy.

This was part of an arrangement worked out by Mr. Yeltsin, who has emerged as the country's leading political figure since the coup attempt.

The committee includes Grigory V. Yavlinsky, a leading advocate of radical economic change in the country, auguring the long-awaited introduction of a sharp turn to a free-market economy. Other members of the committee are Arkady Volsky, head of an association of private and state-owned enterprises, and Yuri Luzhkov, a supporter of fundamental change who is head of the Moscow City Council.

The moves, announced at the end of another day filled with emotional and fast-paced developments arising from the coup, signaled a virtually complete surrender by Mr. Gorbachev to the liberal and democratic forces who had defied the coup and rescued him.

The actions were accompanied by continued turmoil in the Soviet republics, as Mr. Yeltsin accorded formal recognition to the independence of two more Baltic republics and the Parliament of the Ukraine, the nation's second-largest republic, declared its independence and set a referendum for December 1 to endorse it.

Mr. Gorbachev also ordered the Soviet Parliament to take all Communist Party property into custody until its future was decided "in strict compliance with Soviet and republican law."

Mr. Gorbachev did not disband the Communist Party, nor did he say he was resigning from the party himself. But in sweeping out its leadership, handing its vast properties to the mercies of democratically elected Parliaments and thrusting it out of all federal Government and security organs, he in effect decapitated the 15-million-member organization and left it to find its own place in the new order.

The dramatic gesture followed a broad campaign against the party that had already seen its headquarters sealed in Moscow and across the entire country, its major newspapers closed and its organization banned entirely in Moldavia and the Baltic republics. Leningrad had sealed off the party headquarters at the Smolny Institute, a site charged with symbolism as the place where Lenin had his first head-quarters.

In Moscow, Mr. Yeltsin, the acknowledged leader of the liberal and democratic forces now in ascendance, issued a decree sealing the archives of the K.G.B., the Interior Ministry and the military.

Mr. Gorbachev's actions came after an emotion-charged day in which tens of thousands of Muscovites turned out to bury three men killed in the coup. The nationally televised ceremonies seemed almost a funeral for the old order.

Against this background, Mr. Gorbachev's announcement, read by a newsreader on the evening television news, had the quality of a full surrender by the old order.

In the statement read over television after he reportedly met with the party leadership for several hours in an undisclosed location, since the Central Committee building was now not in his hands, Mr. Gor-bachev based his actions on the party leadership's complicity or si-lence during the coup.

"The Secretariat, the Politburo and the Communist Party's Central Committee did not take a stand against the coup d'état," the state-ment began. "The Central Committee did not manage to take a firm position of condemnation and opposition. It did not inspire Commu-nists to fight against the trampling of constitutional law.

"Among the conspirators were members of the party leadership," it said. "A number of party committees and the mass media supported the action of the state criminals. This placed millions of Communists in a false position."

But the President also defended the rank-and-file membership, as he had done twice since his return from house arrest in the Crimea, in effect appealing to the nation not to carry out a witch hunt against all party members.

"Many members of the party refused to collaborate with the con-spirators, condemned the coup and joined in the fight against it," he said. "No one has the right to blame all Communists, and I, as

President, consider it my duty to defend them as citizens against unfounded accusations."

In this situation, Mr. Gorbachev continued, the Central Committee, whose 300 members make up the inner circle of the party, "must take the difficult but honest decision to disband itself." The fate of republican and local organizations, he continued, "should be decided by themselves."

He then declared: "I consider it no longer possible to continue to carry out my duties as General Secretary of the Central Committee of the Communist Party, and I relinquish corresponding authority."

Mr. Gorbachev concluded with the hope that "democratically minded Communists" would work toward the creation of a new party "capable, together with all progressive forces, of actively joining in the continuation of fundamental democratic reforms for the sake of working people."

In a pair of decrees read after the announcement, Mr. Gorbachev dealt what was in effect the death blow to the party. He ordered an end to all actions by political parties and movements in the military, the security forces, the K.G.B. and the apparatus of government. All members of political parties and political movements, he decreed, could continue their political activities only outside these organs and on their own time.

In a second decree, Mr. Gorbachev ordered parliamentary deputies to take custody of all property of the Communist Party. Its ultimate fate, he said, would be decided according to the laws of the Soviet Union and the republics.

That in effect opened the way for the nationalization of all the party's vast holdings, since Russia and many other republics have already signaled their intention to seize party property. These include innumerable office buildings, luxury hotels, printing plants, residences and vacation homes, many of which have been put to commercial use in recent years to compensate for falling membership and to earn hard currency for party coffers.

The wealth of a party that argued so fervently at the same time against privatization or private property was a major source of growing public wrath with the Communists.

The death knell of the party as the dominant force in the Soviet Union sounded after a long and tortuous decline during the six years of Mr. Gorbachev's perestroika, during which it steadily lost authority but remained entrenched in virtually every branch of the central Government. . . .

Finally forced to disband the party leadership and to purge his Government, Mr. Gorbachev in effect left himself with no source of power, unless he can find some in the Soviet Parliament when it meets next week. But in the rout of Kremlin forces after the coup, it was unlikely that many deputies could be mustered to oppose the steamroller of the Yeltsin supporters. . . .

In the Ukraine, the Parliament decided by an overwhelming vote of 321 to 2, with six abstentions, to declare independence, calling a referendum for December 1 to give the measure its certain public support. Even before the referendum, the resolution declared only Ukrainian law valid on Ukrainian territory and the Ukraine sovereign over its resources, in effect stripping a republic of 51 million away from the Kremlin's control.

At the same time, Mr. Yeltsin recognized the independence proclaimed by Estonia and Latvia, as he had before with Lithuania.

The weakening of party control was sending the component parts of the federation spinning off on their own. Just hours after Boris Yeltsin gave his nod of approval to the independence drives of the Baltic republics, Estonia, Latvia and Lithuania were being recognized as sovereign equals by the first of what would soon become a diplomatic quorum. Meanwhile the leaders of other republics were rushing to declare their jurisdictions to be free of control from Moscow, though what such professions of independence meant was not always easy to grasp.

Rush Toward Disunion Spreads; Europe Embracing Baltic Independence; Purge of Military
By Bill Keller

MOSCOW, Aug. 25—Following quickly on the rout of the Communist Party, the unraveling of the Soviet Union itself gained speed today, with one republic after another joining the rush to independence or laying claim to powers of the central Government.

One day after the vital Ukraine declared its independence, Byelorussia unexpectedly followed suit, Moldavia announced it would vote on a similar declaration Monday, and Western governments began recognizing the secession of the three Baltic republics.

President Boris N. Yeltsin of the Russian republic, who has emerged in the aftermath of the failed coup by hard-liners as the predominant political figure in the country, said in a television interview that he hoped the mainstay republics would sign a treaty next month reorganizing the country into a looser federation.

But with 8 of the 15 republics now asserting or contemplating claims of full independence, there were growing doubts that even Mr. Yeltsin could find a formula to halt the dismembering of this nuclear superpower.

Aftershocks from the abortive coup against President Mikhail S. Gorbachev and the Soviet leader's subsequent abandonment of the Communist Party rolled across the country today.

A presidential spokesman announced that Mr. Gorbachev's military adviser, Marshal Sergei F. Akhromeyev, had killed himself on Saturday night. No evidence has surfaced implicating Marshal Akhromeyev, the former chief of staff of the armed forces, in the attempted coup, but he was instrumental in promoting the military commanders who participated, and he had publicly belittled the danger of a putsch.

The new Soviet Defense Minister announced plans for a wholesale purge that he said would replace "about 80 percent" of the top command structure with younger officers. "The people must be younger than we have had, more loyal, and not capable of unconstitutional gambits," said the minister, Gen. Yevgeny Shaposhnikov, who as commander of the air force defied the conspirators and supported Mr. Yeltsin.

Shake-ups were also anticipated in the K.G.B. and Interior Ministry, following the collaboration of top national security officials in the three-day coup.

Local governments across the country seized Communist Party buildings following Mr. Gorbachev's decree on Saturday effectively nationalizing the party's wealth. Citizens toppled monuments to Bolshevik heroes, prompting Mr. Yeltsin and other officials to plead for calm.

"There should be no euphoria of revenge," Mr. Yeltsin told a television interviewer tonight. "Otherwise we will lose our self-respect as democrats."

Mr. Gorbachev, who appears to have become essentially a junior partner in a coalition government with Mr. Yeltsin, was reported to be at work on a speech for an emergency session of the Soviet Parliament on Monday, which will seek to clarify the murky issue of just who is running the country.

Although the Soviet leader remains Commander in Chief of the armed forces, and is still formally in charge of the central Government, since his return from captivity he has ceded to the Russian President remarkable sway in dictating the shape of a future government. . . .

The Yeltsin team, which once called for Mr. Gorbachev's resignation, now plans to retain Mr. Gorbachev in a scaled-back role, presiding over military and foreign policy and such centralized economic structures as the electric power grid.

"Mikhail Sergeyevich has not yet exhausted his potential," said Ruslan Khasbulatov, chairman of the Russian Parliament, in an interview with the independent news agency Interfax. "I don't think that he needs to resign. We, the Russian Government, will help him a great deal."

Mr. Yeltsin said today that he believed the republics should be represented in the National Security Council as a check on the Soviet President's handling of defense policy, and Mr. Khasbulatov suggested that in the new federation, the President would be chosen by the republics rather than in a general election.

But aides involved in negotiations between the two leaders say that Mr. Gorbachev has not yet entirely resigned himself to the role of a figurehead. In the appointment of a new chief of the security agencies, Mr. Gorbachev successfully insisted on putting his own man in charge of the K.G.B., for example. The parliamentary session gives Mr. Gorbachev a chance—perhaps his last chance—to describe how he sees his future role.

But the redistribution of powers is complicated by the eruption of secessionist sentiment, which is worrisome to both leaders.

In the Ukraine, the independence declaration calls for the republic to assume control of Soviet military assets on its territory and create its own army. The declaration, which requires popular ratification in a referendum in December, leaves unanswered the question of the nuclear weapons deployed there.

Mr. Yeltsin faces the additional predicament that the disintegration of the union could spread to his own domain. The Russian federation includes dozens of ethnic homelands, many of them itching for greater sovereignty.

A Yeltsin aide said today the Russian President would support the wishes of the Ukrainian people, but expressed concern about the loss of such a key republic. In addition to the question of the military and the Ukraine's importance as a farming and industrial stronghold, the aide said, the loss of its 51 million Slavs would tilt the ethnic balance of the remaining union toward the Muslims of Central Asia.

That concern grew today with news that the Parliament in Byelorussia, the third Slavic republic, had approved an independence declaration. Byelorussia, with a population of 10 million the fifth-largest republic, has long been regarded as the most conservative of the republics in the European portion of the Soviet Union and has seemed relatively immune from the secessionist passions of its Baltic and Ukrainian neighbors.

The declaration was apparently designed by Byelorussian Communists, who still hold a majority in the Parliament, as a way of insulating themselves from Mr. Gorbachev's decree ordering confiscation of party property. A smaller nationalist faction in the Parliament also supported the move.

In another move to protect the party from the wave of anti-Communist sentiment, the hard-line Communist President of the republic, Nikolai Dementei, resigned under pressure.

The republic of Moldavia announced today that its Parliament would vote on secession on Tuesday, a measure that is expected to pass.

"Moldavia will no longer be part of an empire that is falling to pieces," the speaker of its Parliament, Alexandru Mosanu, told Reuters in Kishinev, the capital. "We shall become independent, and this is part of a chain reaction that no force in the world could stop now."

The Baltic states of Lithuania, Latvia and Estonia, whose claim to independence has been endorsed by Mr. Yeltsin but not by Mr. Gorbachev, today began to win international recognition. Denmark and Norway announced that they would establish diplomatic relations with the breakaway republics, which were forcibly annexed in 1940. . . .

It was only eight days since the coup was launched and five days since it was reversed, but developments in the Soviet Union were whirling so fast that both those events began to feel like ancient history. The old issues that had been raised by the seizure of Mr. Gorbachev—the fate of the party, the prospects of reform—had either been answered or were now irrelevant. The overriding questions related to the preservation of the Soviet state.

Gorbachev Pleads, but Breakaway Areas Defy Him, Putting Fate of Union in Doubt

By Francis X. Clines

MOSCOW, Aug. 26—President Mikhail S. Gorbachev appealed to the nation today to keep the Soviet Union together, but was all but drowned out by spiraling calls for independence by most of the nation's republics.

The Soviet leader, trying to rebound from the foiled coup of a week ago that has left the country in turmoil, acknowledged at an emergency session of the all-union Parliament that the old tightly organized Soviet Union, with power emanating from the Kremlin, could not be sustained. But he urged that the republics seek greater autonomy through a proposed new union treaty with the Kremlin.

But the majority of the nation's 15 republics seemed intent on pursuing independence drives that have exploded in the few days since the failure of the coup and the rise of the public's anger against the central Government and its Communist-dominated bureaucracies.

Typical of the reaction at the session of Parliament today was a statement by President Levon Ter-Petrosyan of Armenia. "The center is dead," he told the nation watching on television. "The center has committed suicide."

Around the Soviet Union, icons of the past like statues of Lenin continued to be destroyed. Rallies were held in Azerbaijan and other republics calling for an end to ties with Moscow, and moves accelerated for independence in Estonia, Latvia and Lithuania, the three Baltic republics. . . .

Addressing Parliament, Mr. Gorbachev promised new elections for national offices, including the presidency, six months after the signing of the union treaty. He said any republics that did not want to stay in the Soviet Union could then negotiate their secession. . . .

The surge for independence was complicated by emerging rivalries between Russia, the largest and most powerful of the 15 union republics, and other republics that did not want to be under Russian domination, even in a new, more loosely constructed nation.

Kazakhstan—the nation's second-largest republic in area, which has considerable natural resources but has long been considered a backwater in the Soviet Union—announced its withdrawal from the proposed union treaty.

In immediate reaction to that, the Russian Federation, the dominant republic, served notice that it would review its borders with any secessionist republics other than the Baltics. An aide to Boris N. Yeltsin, the President of Russia, said this referred mostly to parts of Kazakhstan and the Ukraine that have heavy concentrations of residents of Russian heritage.

The Ukraine, another major neighbor of Russia, already has an independence drive under way.

The Russian move appeared to be protective in the light of the centrifugal struggle taking over the nation, with dozens of long-postponed border grievances threatening to revive now that the republics will be setting more of their own agenda.

The three Baltic republics, the most European of the Soviet lands, were suddenly gaining official recognition from several nations in their demand to restore prewar independence lost to forced Soviet occupation.

In Uzbekistan, a predominantly Muslim region known primarily for its cotton harvests and long used by Moscow as a showplace of third world development, republic officials began drafting an independence campaign and claimed sovereignty over Soviet military units in the republic.

Kirghizia's President, Askar Akayev, delivered a blistering denunciation of the state of the union, called on Parliament to dissolve itself and "resolutely rejected" the union treaty as needing radical overhaul in the republics' favor. Kirghizia, a largely agricultural area, is also part of Central Asia, which has long been regarded as relatively quiescent in nationalist terms.

Some national and republic leaders professed to be hoping to patch together a rescue plan for the union amid a chorus of contrary demands for a loose federation, a looser commonwealth or an outright concession to dissolution. The prognosis was not immediately encouraging, as four months of negotiations over the union treaty appeared to be coming to naught.

A critical blow for union partisans came today when President Nursultan A. Nazarbayev of Kazakhstan rose to speak amid the confusion and tension of the debate in the Grand Kremlin Palace and announced he no longer could support a new union treaty he had been crucial in negotiating.

Signaling the republic's refusal to be under Russian influence now that the central Government was collapsing, Mr. Nazarbayev told the nation, "Kazakhstan will never be anyone's younger brother."

The reference was to the mammoth Russian republic, led by Mr. Yeltsin, which contains more than half the nation's population and much of its economic wealth and natural resources. The Kazakh leader rebuffed Mr. Yeltsin's appeal for a renewed union, one whose Government the ascendant Russian leader wants to see heavily staffed by ministers from Russia.

Mr. Yeltsin, a national hero a week ago as he stood up to the Kremlin coup, thus found himself tonight intent on reviving Russia's sovereignty but facing independence drives across both of Russia's major borders. To the southeast was Kazakhstan, suddenly on the move after decades of Kremlin loyalty, and to the southwest, the Ukraine, the second most populous republic, where an even bolder independence drive continued to gain momentum.

Parliament echoed with harsh and desperate speeches in which politicians railed at one another and pronounced the union a "cadaver" and "a political Chernobyl."

The shocking reversal of fervor for retailoring the union could be seen in the fact that, little more than a week ago, Mr. Yeltsin and Mr. Nazarbayev were close colleagues pushing the union treaty. They were preparing to sign the compromise pact in which Mr. Gorbachev vowed to begin a new era of power for the republics last Tuesday, two days after the coup was launched. The pact's promised goal was decentralized democracy, market economics, fresh elections and a binding constitution and judiciary. . . .

While the search continued for a new formula that might hold together a renewed and perhaps pared-down Soviet Union, a suddenly reinvigorated Mikhail Gorbachev threatened to resign if the political meltdown continued. Meanwhile, the attack on one of the old binding institutions of union was continuing with a vengeance.

K.G.B., Once a Pervasive Power, Is Quickly Being Brought to Heel
By Serge Schmemann

MOSCOW, Aug. 27—Mikhail S. Gorbachev disclosed today that a full-scale pruning of the K.G.B. had taken place, telling the Soviet Parliament that the governing board of the once pervasively powerful security and intelligence agency had been virtually disbanded and its military units reassigned to the army.

The newspaper *Moskovsky Komsomolets* also reported that the entire leadership of the Ninth Directorate of the K.G.B., the division that had been charged with security for top officials and included the men who confronted President Gorbachev at the outset of the coup, had been arrested.

The failure of the attempt to topple Mr. Gorbachev and reverse his policies has inspired and propelled a new campaign finally to bring to heel the K.G.B., the organization probably most closely identified with the horrors of the Stalinist dictatorship.

With revelations that the K.G.B. chief, Vladimir A. Kryuchkov, had been a principal plotter in the aborted putsch and that the agency's elite anti-terrorist "Group Alpha" had refused to move against the headquarters of Boris N. Yeltsin, President of the Russian republic, the forces that triumphed over the coup finally moved against the organization whose very initials were once only whispered.

When Mr. Kryuchkov was arrested at Mr. Gorbachev's Crimean retreat after the collapse of the coup, he was flown back separately from other prisoners in the President's plane as an especially dangerous culprit, a testament to the awesome might his organization commanded.

In addition to its armies of agents, the K.G.B. also commanded military units of armor, paratroopers, assault helicopters and motorized riflemen and border guards, who in the past led such major operations as the combat against Chinese forces in the dispute over borders. According to Mr. Gorbachev's announcement, all these forces have now been placed under military command and control.

Soon after his rescue, Mr. Gorbachev announced that he had named Vadim V. Bakatin, who had previously served as a relatively progressive chief of the Interior Ministry, to take charge of the K.G.B., with orders to purge its leadership, sharply reduce its cadres, break up its powers and place the agency under political control.

What had made these official moves against the agency possible was the demonstration from the outset of the brief coup that many people no longer quaked before the monolithic organization that had intimidated and repressed them for so long. Already in the aftermath of the coup, the darkened windows of the sprawling K.G.B. headquarters on Dzerzhinsky Square indicated that the agency was finally in retreat.

The K.G.B. combined the foreign-intelligence functions of the Central Intelligence Agency, the domestic policing of the Federal Bureau of Intelligence, responsibilities for controlling the borders and the role of a "Big Brother" political police. Since Mr. Gorbachev introduced perestroika to Soviet life in 1985, several laws had been passed and repeated assertions had been made that the agency's enormous apparatus had been reformed, brought under political control, made more friendly.

Indeed, American intelligence officials reported that the organization had been beset with defections, and both foreigners and Soviets sensed a distinct lessening of surveillance and pressures. K.G.B. officials gave interviews and opened a public relations office; Mr. Kryuchkov even invited the American Ambassador to his office for a chat.

The appointment of Mr. Kryuchkov in October 1988 was initially seen by Western intelligence analysts as an attempt to strengthen party control over the agency and to emphasize its foreign functions over its domestic controls. As a K.G.B. general, Mr. Kryuchkov had headed foreign espionage for 10 years.

But foreign diplomats and many Soviets never ceased suspecting that under the new clothing, the K.G.B. still maintained at least the potential for vast surveillance and control.

There was no indication that its staff, estimated at 700,000, plus at least as many informers, had been substantially reduced, or that the reported budget of 4.9 million rubles was anywhere near the truth. The agency also retained its enormous arsenal of special border forces and anti-terrorist commandos, and army units under its command.

A former K.G.B. general, Oleg Kalugin, who joined the ranks of the insurgent movement 18 months ago, confirmed many of the suspicions. He described Mr. Kryuchkov as an unreformed party apparatchik and said that the agency continued to infiltrate new democratic organizations, that it continued to have enormous privileges and that parliamentary controls were ineffective. He also said the organization was riddled with defections.

Despite his efforts at public relations, Mr. Kryuchkov himself began issuing statements and making speeches that reeked of cold war phrases about Western threats and attempts to undermine the Soviet Union. As recently as June, he gave a speech to a closed session of the Supreme Soviet warning of Western intrigues.

Finally, the bungled coup confirmed that Mr. Kryuchkov and the senior leadership had never really embraced perestroika, but that the junior ranks had become infused with the new liberties that had spread through society.

In an interview on Saturday, Mr. Yeltsin revealed that Group Alpha had refused to move on his headquarters even after direct threats from K.G.B. officers. And in an interview with Tass, leaders of the commando group said they could have taken the headquarters in half an hour but refused when they concluded that the order was illegal.

Group leaders said that when they were given the order to storm the headquarters, the Russian Parliament building, they began asking where it originated. As soon as they realized what it entailed, all subordinate commanders refused to obey. The decision to disobey "was without precedent for the servicemen, especially for our unit," said Mikhail Golovatov, a former deputy who has since taken over the leadership of the group. "There has never been a case of refusal to carry out orders since the group's formation in 1974."

Mr. Golovatov acknowledged there would have been bloodshed. But the resisters were no match for professionals, he said, adding, "Frankly speaking, we could have fulfilled our tasks in 20 to 30 minutes." . . .

Mr. Kalugin, now a member of the Soviet Parliament, said "friends still on the inside" of the agency told him that the burning of files had already begun, despite Mr. Yeltsin's efforts to seal its archives.

"Right after the coup d'état was over—at least when it seemed it was a failure—they started burning papers at K.G.B. headquarters," he said. "So we'll find considerably less than we would have found a year ago, or five years ago." . . .

In its heyday, the "Committee" had agents in virtually every workplace. Foreigners were watched with special care, their phones tapped and their cars often followed. Only the senior party leadership was exempted from the ubiquitous scrutiny.

As its initials changed from Cheka to G.P.U., O.G.P.U., N.K.V.D., N.K.G.B., M.G.B. and finally K.G.B., which stands for Committee for State Security, the organization spread to every corner of the Soviet empire, exercising control through intimidation, repression and murder. . . .

The centrifuge was spinning wildly. The Ukraine, it appeared, was on the verge of breaking away. For the Soviet state such an event would be calamitous, for unlike the Baltics, the Ukraine constituted a vital part of the Slavic heartland of the Soviet state. If it ever did achieve full independence it would, with its population of 51 million, become the fifth most populous country in Europe.

560

Soviet Leaders Press a Rebellious Ukraine to Remain in the Union

By Serge Schmemann

MOSCOW, Thursday, Aug. 29—With the future of the Soviet Union possibly hanging in the balance, delegates from the Russian republic and Soviet Parliament flew to the Ukraine on Wednesday to search for common ground with the nation's second most populous republic, which like many others is seized with secessionist fervor in the wake of the failed coup.

President Mikhail S. Gorbachev and a number of other prominent figures, notably Mayor Anatoly A. Sobchak of Leningrad and Eduard A. Shevardnadze, the former Foreign Minister, issued ever more urgent warnings that the Soviet Union must survive, even if in a new and yet undecided form.

Boris N. Yeltsin, the President of the Russian republic, whose power was enhanced because of his stand against the coup, has also come out strongly for preserving some form of union, and that is why his republic sent a delegation to the Ukraine on Wednesday to mollify the Ukrainians.

After several hours of talks, the Russian and Ukrainian officials pledged early today in a statement to take joint action against "uncontrolled disintegration" of the union.

It is hard to imagine the Soviet Union surviving as more than just a shell if it lacks the Ukraine, which is a principal supplier of food and has highly developed heavy and light industries. The three Slavic republics—the Ukraine, Byelorussia and Russia—are the core of the Soviet Union.

Mr. Yeltsin, according to Mr. Gorbachev, expressed support on Tuesday for an early signing of a new treaty to define relationships between the republics and the central Government in a new union. But despite his expressions of support, Mr. Yeltsin, by his actions in the past week in trying to enhance the powers of his republic, has tended to antagonize leaders of other republics as well as Mr. Gorbachev.

Speaking to the Soviet Parliament on Wednesday, Mr. Gorbachev displayed his irritation with Mr. Yeltsin's actions by issuing his first public criticism since the coup of Mr. Yeltsin's decrees imposing Russian control over central institutions, most recently the central bank, the Ministry of Finance and the Bank for Foreign Economic Relations.

Mr. Yeltsin's decrees assuming central powers during the coup were legitimate, Mr. Gorbachev said, but now "I have to say that it is unacceptable for anyone, including the Russian Supreme Soviet, the Russian Government and the President of Russia. Everything must be based on the Constitution, and now on cooperation."

For now, only the independence declared by the three Baltic republics—Lithuania, Latvia and Estonia—has won international recognition. A parade of foreign nations, including the European Community, have issued formal recognitions of the Baltic republics' independence, but it was unlikely that any would move quickly to recognize the independence of other republics. . . .

Ukraine and Russia Trying to Heal Their Injured Ties

By Francis X. Clines

KIEV, U.S.S.R., Aug. 28—Officials of the Russian republic and the Ukraine, meeting for emergency negotiations, sought to heal their damaged relations today and to search for some sort of "transitional" path to future association past the collapsing Soviet Union system.

In a message that ended a long day of anxious talks, the union's two most populous republics vowed joint action to prevent the "uncontrolled disintegration" of the national state.

They also sought to put a new focus on the Soviet political trauma by emphasizing the need for fresh economic agreements as a possible way to spark some future redesign of the political relationship among the Soviet republics.

As street crowds demanded independence, the Ukraine government joined other republics in speaking for some sort of loose confederation rather than a renewed federal union.

Participants said the emphasis in the talks in the Parliament building was on the need for an orderly dismantling of the failed Soviet system as the prelude to creating a healthier association among the republics.

"There's no use debating who is older, bigger or mightier," Leonid M. Kravchuk, the republic leader, declared after a meeting with Soviet and Russian officials who arrived in fear that the Ukraine's rapidly accelerating independence drive would seal the political demise of the Soviet Union in some chaotic fashion.

"Let's start like equals," said Mr. Kravchuk, the Parliament chairman and recently resigned Ukrainian Communist leader, who now has cast his lot solely with the Ukrainian nationalist cause. . . .

Gathered under a sign that proclaimed "No to Russian Imperialists," thousands of Ukrainians loudly rebuffed the pleas to national unity made by one of the visiting observers sent here from Moscow by the Soviet Parliament, the Mayor of Leningrad, Anatoly Sobchak.

"Independence!" the crowd shouted in reply as Mr. Sobchak sought vainly to argue for the advantages for holding to the union at such a critical moment.

"Whoever said being independent and being together are contradictory?" Mr. Sobchak asked in return, warning, "We don't want any Balkanization."

"The Soviet Union is falling apart," Mr. Sobchak conceded to reporters earlier in the day before facing the fervor of the Ukrainian crowds. "If disintegration proves uncontrollable, we are on the verge of collapse." . . .

While, the pace of developments was dizzying for many, some were viewing things with stolid wariness.

View from a City of Skeptics: A Coup? It Hardly Matters
By Bill Keller

KLIN, U.S.S.R., Aug. 28—Lenin stood untoppled and undefiled today on his pedestal in First of May Square, as serene as this provincial city after Russia's 10 days of panic, deliverance and recrimination.

Just 50 miles from the Moscow epicenter of the quake that shook down the Communist temple, this city of 95,000 weathered the tremors with an outward calm bordering on indifference and a conviction that nothing as important as the price of sausage will change as a result.

"It was interesting, but my thoughts were elsewhere," said Yuliya Gladyshev, 21 years old, who spent last week preparing for her wedding on Saturday to the driver of a bread truck.

"We've gotten used to it," she said. "They're always springing some surprise on the people—a price increase, a monetary reform. We all feel like laboratory rabbits.

"We've been through so much, and now a coup. Well, it was just more of the same drama. One thing we've learned from our history: we can endure anything."

If the coup makers had prevailed, ventured Roman Barkhatov, 24, the best man, "things would have been worse."

The bride retorted: "How do you know? Maybe it would have been better. What do we know? We're just subjects in an experiment."

For all the Moscow partisans who stood on the barricades last week, the view from this region of chemical and glass works, dairy farms and potato fields is probably more typical of how the country as a whole weathered the August upheavals.

It was not exactly apathy. It was more a numbing fatigue after six years of noise and disappointment since Mikhail S. Gorbachev came to power early in 1985—mixed with a stiffening of anxiety among those old enough to remember past repression. That, plus an abiding Russian sense that the intrigues in Moscow were beyond the ken of mere citizens.

"Everyone suffered through it in his soul," said Viktor A. Gladyshev, the bride's new brother-in-law and editor of the local newspaper, *Serp i Molot* (Hammer and Sickle). "But the first thought was that, come what may, we have to keep feeding our families."

The editor, who is 34, arrived at his office Monday, the first full day of the coup, and waited for the phone to ring with urgent questions and opinions from his 20,000 readers.

The phone remained silent, he said, "as if everyone had died."

Since then, only one reader, a frequent correspondent, has written to register her reaction to the coup—indignation and dismay.

On Coup Tuesday the editor dropped in at the Termo-Pribor instrument factory, which makes equipment for hospitals and the Defense Ministry, to canvass opinions of the workers. He found confusion and agitation, but no alarm.

"Among the younger workers, the main concern was how to avoid the draft," he said. "Everyone assumed they would start drafting people to enforce the military curfew."

Gennadi P. Lushnikov, a local anti-Communist, and his son Dmitri traveled the 50 miles southeast to Moscow to join the defiant crowd outside Boris N. Yeltsin's fortified headquarters, but this was regarded as so extraordinary that it merited an article in the newspaper.

"Nobody saw any sense in throwing down our work and going to Moscow," recalled Vasily D. Kuzmin, a young brigade leader at the Termo-Pribor plant. "Coup or no coup, people would be worse off if everyone stopped work." . . .

Raisa G. Smirnova, the party secretary at a state dairy farm in nearby Nudol, had been working the phones, mobilizing factory workers, soldiers and students for the annual potato crop, when she got word that the party could no longer guarantee the salaries of its farm and factory ward heelers.

She has signed up to return to her job as a schoolteacher.

"My heart is aching," she said. "I am a committed Communist, and no amount of moral terror will make me give up my views."

But even the death rattle of Communism stirred little excitement in the city, because the party's authority had already been in steady remission. Membership dwindled by a third, to 8,000, during three years of democratic ferment and economic disappointment. . . .

Today, in a tenement courtyard on the outskirts of Klin, where a Greek chorus of bench-sitting babushkas reviewed last week's events with durable equanimity, Mr. Yeltsin was a figure of near-mythic proportions.

"Everything was up in the air until we saw Yeltsin on television," a 70-year-old pensioner named Polina said. "Then he stepped out on the balcony with his jacket unbuttoned and his fist raised in the air—oy, just like Lenin," she marveled.

A neighbor interjected: "Right, dear. Only let's not speak of Lenin."

After Gorbachev quit the party after party property had been ordered seized by the individual republics, the decision of the Soviet Parliament to do the same things on a nationwide basis was essentially a symbolic act. But what a staggering symbol it was. Seventy-four years after the party was conceived as the chief engine of state and a vanguard to point the way to universal deliverance, it was ruled inoperative.

Soviets Bar Communist Party Activities; Republics Press Search for a New Order
By Serge Schmemann

MOSCOW, Aug. 29—After three hours of anguished debate, the Soviet Parliament voted today to suspend all activities of the Communist Party pending an investigation of its role in the coup. It was an action that confirmed the demise of the old regime even as the search quickened for new forms of association and order.

The fate of the party was already sealed before Parliament's vote. Individual republics had closed its offices and seized its vast properties and funds, and President Mikhail S. Gorbachev had quit as its General Secretary and had called on the leadership to step down.

But Parliament was the only national institution with the formal powers to act against the entire organization, and its decision served to confirm the indictment already passed by the people. While Parliament settled scores with the past, newly unfettered leaders of the republics searched for interim arrangements to prevent chaotic disintegration.

A Russian-Ukrainian agreement reached in Kiev in the early morning, after hurriedly arranged negotiations, declared it imperative to prevent the "uncontrolled disintegration" of the Soviet Union and to ensure its economic survival and security. The communiqué seemed to establish a model for interim agreements among the republics to safeguard the fundamental ties forged over decades as the tight central controls and Communist-dominated institutions of rule crumbled in the aftermath of the failed coup. . . .

Born of the utopian Marxism of the last century, the Bolshevik Party formed by Lenin was never meant for a democratic role in a multiparty system. Rather, it was meant to be the vanguard of the working class in the struggle against "class oppressors" and to be the chosen elite in the shaping of a new order.

It evolved under Stalin and his successors into a vast and privileged network of institutions that controlled all facets of Soviet life and numbered 19 million members. Even with its powers trimmed by Mr. Gorbachev's perestroika, the party continued to exert a powerful brake on any efforts to change the system, and Mr. Gorbachev himself continued to merge the powers of the presidency and party leadership until after the coup, when he finally resigned as General Secretary.

"We are talking about the liquidation, not of a party, because the Communist Party has long ceased to be a party, but about a superstate structure, parallel to the structures of power that it illegally usurped," one deputy argued. . . .

For all of its 74-year history, the Soviet state had been defined by the Communist Party. Now that the party had so abruptly withered, the shape, fate and very existence of that state was being called into question.

After the Breakup: E Pluribus . . . What?

By Bill Keller

MOSCOW, Aug. 29—The Soviet Union, born of the 1917 Revolution, was pronounced dead this week after a lingering illness. The cause of death was diagnosed as a congenital defect called Communism.

But even as the politicians delivered their funeral orations over the decomposing superpower, a process of reincarnation was under way.

No one could say with any certainty what the Soviet afterlife would look like, what territories would choose to take part in it, what powers it would be given, who would preside over it or how stable it would be.

Or, for that matter, what it might be called. Suggestions in the parlor of Parliament, where members today debated the liquidation and reanimation of their state, ranged from the earnest (the Commonwealth of Sovereign States of Europe and Asia, the Euroasian Economic Community) to the facetious (the Club of Crippled Nations, Russia and the 14 Dwarfs).

But even those dry-eyed at the demise of the forced and feeble union agreed that most, perhaps all, of the 15 scattering republics would be reunited in some altogether new configuration by economic necessity, military coexistence and cultural expediency.

"We are doomed to cooperate," said Aleksandr M. Yakovlev, a prominent lawyer and member of Parliament.

The first tendrils of the new collaboration were visible today in President Mikhail S. Gorbachev's decrees creating a National Security Council to coordinate law enforcement and oversee the military "during a period of transition" and establishing a committee to maintain the integrity of communications.

These committees, and others that are sure to come in fields like transportation and energy, do not represent the preservation of the union but the creation of something new and fragile. Both committees are to be composed of representatives from the republics, and their power will be limited by their ability to win the republics' consent.

There is a tentative quality to this delicate birth of a new community, since it is taking place in a Parliament that has lost its power, under the direction of a President, Mr. Gorbachev, whose only convincing authority is persuasion, under a Constitution that six republics have formally declared they do not recognize and that most of the others feel free to ignore.

The only cohesion is consensus. To keep the process from breaking down altogether, Mr. Gorbachev and the leaders of the Russian republic have twice sent delegations to soothe the feelings of republics—on Wednesday the Ukraine, today Kazakhstan—made restive by the ascendancy of Boris N. Yeltsin's Russia.

What keeps the tenuous undertaking in motion is a tacit understanding that none of the 15 scattering republics is sturdy enough to live completely on its own, at least not yet. For all the heady talk of sovereignty and all the bristle of old suspicions, most citizens recognize that they are bound by common interests that cannot be declared out of existence. Not one of the republics is ready to join the world economic community on its own, except as a charity case.

Visitors to almost any republic will hear the myth that if only they were freed from the thievery and exploitation of the center they would soon be robust nation-states.

Azerbaijanis speak of themselves as incipient oil sheiks. Tiny Moldavia points to its vineyards and imagines itself the next Bordeaux. Proud residents of impoverished Uzbekistan boast of self-sufficiency, although their main export crop is cotton, and even that colonial industry is threatened by the poisoning of the republic's rivers.

Even the biggest republics are rich, so far, only in potential.

The Ukraine, which claimed its independence last week, has wheat, but lacks the means to harvest it; coal, but the mines are near depletion; the lovely Black Sea coastline, but it is polluted and inadequately developed for world-class tourism.

Russia is a Klondike of natural resources, but the republic staggers under the burden of rusting industry and deteriorating infrastructure.

Most important, there is scarcely a factory in any republic that does not depend on its neighbors for cheap energy, raw materials or components, not to mention customers. The Soviet Union, Mr. Yakovlev observed, has been "one huge factory."

Thus a feature of the new community will surely be a web of agreements governing trade, currency exchange rates, banking practices and other rules of the market. At first these may be bilateral treaties, but most experts assume that some functions will be ceded to new superagencies, like those that oversee the economy of Western Europe.

"I think that after a very short time, union republics that are tied up by the unified economy will inevitably ask for the center to have some powers," Mr. Yakovlev said. "Because without it we will not be able to cooperate, to exchange, to survive economically."

Most republics also favor maintaining the integrity of the Soviet military, though they want a greater voice in running it.

The new mini-states founded on the ruins of the Soviet Union are likely to have small-scale national guards to defend their territory, a concept Mr. Gorbachev said today was fine with him.

But some kind of collective security is also likely, whether it consists of a broad, NATO-style alliance, as some politicians predict, or bilateral pacts with mighty Russia, as favored by the leaders of Armenia.

The Ukraine, which on Saturday claimed all Soviet military installations on its territory, has already begun backing down. Aside from the alarm at the prospect of a breakaway Ukraine armed with nuclear weapons, the republic was confronted with the cost of being a military power.

"When they calculated how much money would be needed to maintain the 650,000 soldiers based on the territory of the Ukraine, it turned out to be nearly equal to the entire republican budget," said Lieut. Col. Vasily A. Yerokhin, a member of the Soviet Parliament. "And that does not count the Black Sea fleet or the strategic nuclear forces."

Politicians in the republics also expect pacts or new superstructures to govern territorial claims, to protect the shared environment and to apportion the cost of the catastrophes, like the Chernobyl nuclear accident, that have been the Soviet Union's fate.

Another priority for the new community is to protect the human rights gains of the last few years.

Mr. Gorbachev made the Soviet Union a member in the club of civilized nations by freeing political prisoners, allowing a free press, lifting most political limits on foreign travel and legalizing opposition parties.

Whether the leaders of the new mini-states will share his enthusiasm for law and world opinion is a painfully open question. The President of breakaway Georgia, Zviad Gamsakhurdia, has silenced the independent press in his republic and, according to dissidents living in Moscow, has locked up scores of his political opponents.

Moldavian leaders used the attempted Soviet coup last week as a pretext to arrest ethnic minority leaders in that republic, charging them with collaboration.

"Many of the nations of Europe went through their periods of dictatorial power," said Yuri Shcherbak, the Deputy Prime Minister of the Ukraine. "Of course, it's entirely possible that we will have some very undemocratic national republics created here."

In a community where almost every republic has substantial minority enclaves of Russians and other ethnic groups, no republic can be indifferent to the internal policies of its neighbors.

As the republics feel their way to a new accommodation, only the most sensitive diplomacy will be able to keep in check old grievances that have festered under artificial union.

"A lot depends on words," said Dmitri S. Likhachev, a revered historian of old Russia, who stressed that such questions as the name of the new entity should not be taken lightly. He favors calling it a "commonwealth" or "community."

"I don't like the word "union," because it reminds me of the Soviet Union, which is no longer."

In the days and weeks that followed, the major components of the old Soviet Union struggled to redefine themselves and their relationship. Moscow accepted the independence of Estonia, Latvia and Lithuania. Gorbachev, showing renewed vitality, muscled the Congress of the People's Deputies into endorsing a vague plan meant to lead to a new constitution. Meanwhile power was to reside largely with a council composed of Gorbachev and the republican leaders. Nationalistic skirmishing was erupting in several parts of the shuddering empire. Old statues were being torn down. Once-cherished pins and medals of party affiliation were being sold as kitsch. The debate began on whether to remove Lenin's body from the the mausoleum in Red Square to the graveyard where his mother lay buried in Leningrad. And as the recently unthinkable became commonplace, the government of the Russian republic officially changed the name of Leningrad back to St. Petersburg. Revolutionary changes were continuing. The only certainty was that more surprises lay ahead.

EPILOGUE
Michael T. Kaufman

That 1989 was a remarkable and even politically miraculous year comparable with 1848 seems obvious enough. Two years later the chain reaction set off by the crash of the old order in Eastern Europe had even reached the Soviet Union, undermining Communism where it was first institutionalized and where it was most powerfully entrenched.

As the ground kept shifting and the political horizon tilted sharply, it was extremely difficult to establish political bearings on a daily basis, let alone to predict where the course was leading. In this vein, it is both useful and humbling to recall that just a few years ago no one—not the greatest of political scientists, not the most powerful of politicians or intelligence agencies—had envisioned even a fraction of what had taken place as Soviet-style totalitarianism started to give way in Eastern Europe. Similarly, there were certainly not many experts who as late as July of 1991 had envisioned or imagined that what now appears to have been the mortal agony of the Soviet Communist party and the system it managed would take less than two weeks.

As this book shows, the period has been better for journalists than for political scientists, because journalists deal with change in daily increments. Over the last two years these daily doses have been huge and often staggering.

Still, daunting as the dismal record of dud predictions may have been, any postscript has an obligation to look forward.

It seems a fairly safe bet that as the harness of Communism disintegrates further and the postwar division of Europe it helped to spawn dissolves, nationalistic differences and ethnic rivalries once thought to have vanished will move to the surface and grow in importance. Conflicts between Croats and Serbs, Czechs and Slovaks, Azerbaijanis and Armenians are the most strident but hardly the only clashes in the offing. Within the fraying Soviet Union the tapestry of nations and nationalities will certainly keep on unraveling, perhaps violently, and it is hard to imagine that a general peace can prevail.

Two revolutions are seemingly underway in the lands where Communism held sway, one essentially democratic and the other primarily nationalistic. The two drives necessarily converge and diverge. For example, as Ukrainians continue to gain a greater voice in shaping their destiny, they will quite understandably use their rising powers to express and assert their long-repressed identities to their neighbors, differentiating themselves from people who live close by or in their midst. So will the Moldavians, the Kirghiz, the Uzbeks and scores of other peoples.

Indeed, it seems that as the specter of a rekindled and presumably nuclear World War III of Superpowers grows ever less likely, the prospects of conflicts more like those that erupted in World War I loom into view. Instead of superpower rivalry and ideological competition, the current inflammatory issues are again those of self-determination, separatism, secession and the filling of power vacuums left by crumbling empires.

As such cold war institutions like the Warsaw Pact and Comecon evaporate, older, long-lapsed categories are likely to gain relevance. In some places the line that separated the defunct Ottoman empire from the holdings of the equally extinct Austro-Hungarian dynasty is growing sharper. Religious tensions, notably between the Eastern Orthodox and Roman Catholics, are mounting where the faiths abut.

With the East-West division of the planet no longer so dominant, countries are defining themselves and being defined by their neighbors according to other criteria. Within the former East bloc, for example, the northernmost countries—Poland, Czechoslovakia and Hungary—are widely considered to be probationary members of an integrated European community, while those nations of the southern tier—Rumania, Bulgaria, Albania and at least parts of a disintegrating Yugoslavia—are being held at arm's distance, like poor relations who are too impoverished, too rural, too politically unsophisticated to join what can only be described as the West. As for what parts of the Soviet Union can be brought into a Europe now emerging as an economic and cultural amalgam, this is a question certain to be debated for the rest of the century.

One aspect of this debate relates to the physical limits of the continent. Where, in fact, should Europe end? Should it stretch eastward to Lvov, to Kharkov, to Moscow? or further on to Siberia's oil? What were to be the confines of the "common European home" that Gorbachev has postulated? The western extremities of that new Europe were also not quite so certain. Should it include the United States and Canada? Certainly it would cost to bring some nations and peoples into this continental condominium, just as it would cost to keep some peoples and nations out. With expectations of better life rising sharply as liberated economies stagger and lurch into the unknown, it is not hard to imagine that the kind of migratory waves that have already taken place in Albania may continue, swamping the richer parts of Europe with economic refugees.

One thing that could smooth the transition from Communist systems that no longer function to unfathomable futures would be money. But there is not much money available, and the list of claimants is growing. Just how expensive the process of economic restructuring can be has been shown in the experience of a united Germany. It turned out that the Germans, the richest people in Europe, if not the world, lacked the resources to underwrite a trouble-free passage to free-market capitalism for former East Germans, who, after all, were probably the most industrially and materially advanced people of the East bloc. And if the Germans were finding it difficult to pay for the transformation of their own kith and kin, how was this to be done in Poland, Czechoslovakia and Hungary, not to mention Russia, Ukraine, the Baltic states and perhaps Kazakhstan?

September 5, 1991

INDEX

Berlin, West:
Bismarck exhibition in, 477–78
celebrations in, 183–84, 188
East German visitors to, 187–93,
198
emigration from Eastern Europe to,
496
Berliner Zeitung, 209–10, 243–44, 303,
309
Berlin Press Club, 318
Berlin wall, 260–61
building of, xiii, 168, 288
confrontations at, 189–90
opening of, viii, x, xiii, 175–78,
180–81, 183–84, 189–96, 200, 212,
215, 217, 222, 227, 235, 265, 272,
278, 288
Beryiozka, 259
Bessmertnykh, Aleksandr A., 538, 546
Bialystok, voter turnout in, 120
Biermann, Wolf, 484
Bilak, Vasil, 205, 305
Bild, 177, 359
Binder, David, 208–10, 216, 243–45,
260–62, 412–13
Bismarck, Otto von, German unity
under, 475, 477–78, 482
Bisztyga, Jan, 120
Blake, George, 153
Bloch, Wilhelm, 249
Bludov, Vladimir, 443
Bobu, Emil, 251
Bogdan, Eugenia, 340
Bohlen, Celestine, 332–34, 419–24,
428–29, 432–34, 462, 476–77,
488–91, 524–27, 531–32, 541–42
Bohley, Barbel, 167, 169
Bohme, Ibrahim, 388
Boldin, Valery, 540–41
Boldyrev, Vladimir A., 138–42
Boldyrev, Yuri, 451
Bolling, Klaus, 277–78
Bonner, Yelena G., 324–25
Botez, Sorin, 433–34
Brakov, Yevgeny A., 25, 28
Brandenburg Gate:
on eve of reunification, 478
reopening of, 330
Brandt, Willy, 177, 211, 331, 358
campaigning of, 372
fall of, 248
German reunification and, 180–81,
215

Bratislava:
demonstrations in, 230, 233, 239
general strikes in, 257, 259
Brazauskas, Algirdas, 22–24, 314, 379,
381, 392
Brezhnev, Leonid I., xv, 19, 54
Brezhnev doctrine, 163–64, 204, 302
British Broadcasting Corporation
(BBC), 96, 277, 341
Brno:
demonstrations in, 230, 239
general strikes in, 257
Bucauanu, Mikhail, 342–43
Bucharest:
fighting between security forces and
army of, 332, 335–38, 340–43
rioting by miners in, 432–34
Budapest:
disappointment and disillusionment
in, 494, 496
taxi blockade of, 496
Budapest Workers' Council, 134
Bulgaria, 300
Communist Party successes in,
428–29
demonstrations in, 186
ethnic rivalries in, 349–50
institutionalizing democracy in, 119
on invasion of Czechoslovakia, 302
parliamentary elections in, 428–29
and restoring links with Western
Europe, 234
rise of dissent in, xiv
Soviet relations with, 186–87
westward migration from, 496
Zhivkov's arrest and, 505
Zhivkov's resignation and, 184–87
Bulow, Andreas von, 214
Bunich, Pavel G., 419–20
Burlatsky, Fyodor M., 271, 274–76
Bush, George, 125, 248, 484
on aid to Soviet Union, 445–47
arms control and, 294–96, 298–99,
366, 413, 416–18, 426, 522
and changes in Germany, 182
China visited by, 49
end of cold war proclaimed by,
445–47
European policy of, 282–87, 318
German reunification and, 277,
284–86, 294–95, 299, 366, 399,
408, 424, 430–32
Gorbachev's relationship with, 300

578

590

Soviet Union (*cont'd*)
recruitment and prestige problems of Communist Party of, 137–38
reformation of, 567–70
regional intervention rights disavowed by, 163–66, 204, 271–72
religious freedom in, 290–91
revival of Marxism in, 262–64
Rumanian relations with, 229
Russian legal primacy over, 427–28, 537
Sakharov's death mourned in, 323–26
Stalinist brutality in, 7–8, 12–14
tumult of Eastern Europe as lesson and threat to, 361–63
Ukrainian sovereignty and, 457–58, 548, 551, 554, 556–57, 560–63, 566, 568
union treaty of, 518, 520, 523, 537, 552, 555–57, 561–62
unraveling of, 551–52, 554–55, 561–63, 566–67, 571–72
U.S. relations with, 51, 293, 295, 297–99, 316, 425, 438, 445–47, 463–64, 470, 528, 546
Vatican relations with, 292
what it means to be Communist in, 5–8
Yugoslav borders closed to citizens of, 495–96
Der Spiegel, 214, 268, 480
Spira, Steffie, 174
Sputnik, 316
Staasi, 250
Stahmer, Ingrid, 171
Stalin, Joseph, 3, 5–7, 319, 534
Baltic republics annexed by, 379, 392
brutality of, 7–8, 12–14
on Communist Party structure, 138
disdain for Pope expressed by, 291
and evolution of Communist Party, 566
Polish economy and, 208
secret agreements between Hitler and, 142–43, 228, 392
Stanculescu, Ion, 339
Stankevich, Sergei, 534
Starodubtsev, Vasily A., 523
Start (Strategic Arms Reduction Talks), 416–17, 522

State Department, U.S.:
on aid to Eastern European nations, 288
German reunification and, 286–87
on Mazowiecki's nomination for prime minister, 131
State Security Ministry, East German, 248–49, 467
dissolution of, 327
ransacking offices of, 353–54
Stefan, Tomas, 385
Stepan, Miroslav, 499
Stepanakert, anti-Azerbaijani activities in, 147, 150
Stephan, Annette, 191–93
Stephan, Gregor, 190–91, 193
Stephan, Joachim, 190–92
Stephan, Robert, 191
Stihl, Hans Peter, 203
Stoklosa, Henryk, 122
Stolz, Andreas, 157
Stoph, Willi, 197, 209, 220–21
Strauss, Robert S., 533
Strida, Pavel, 265–66
Sudetic, Chuck, 394, 505
Sumgait, anti-Armenian riots in, 146–47, 353
Suskine, Patrick, 480
Swiss Central Bank, 209
Szabo, Stephen F., 286
Szilagyi, Jozsef, 135
Szostkiewicz, Adam, 120
Szrajner, Ireneusz, 111–12
Szuros, Matyas, 133

Tadjikistan, ix
Tagliabue, John, 16–18, 20–21, 33–40, 110–23, 126–32, 184, 229–34, 309–10
Tass, 19, 319, 324, 352–53, 364, 380, 398, 407, 414, 490, 517–18, 560
Te Deum (Dvorak), 344
Termez, withdrawal from Afghanistan celebrated in, 14–16, 19
Ter-Petrosyan, Levon, 555
Thatcher, Margaret:
and changes in Germany, 182
European Community and, 215, 279–80
on future of NATO, 278
German reunification and, 277, 285
Tiananmen Square, xiii